THE PRESIDENCY

THE

A PICTORIAL HISTORY

FROM

★ ★ ★ ★ ★ ★ ★ ★ ★ ★ ★ ★ ★

PRESIDENCY

OF PRESIDENTIAL ELECTIONS

WASHINGTON TO TRUMAN

By STEFAN LORANT

THE MACMILLAN COMPANY

NEW YORK 1951

★ ★ ★ ★ ★ ★ ★ ★ ★ ★ ★ ★

In memory of my friend

DR. KURT M. GRASSHEIM

"*I know the job. It was conceived of the devil who in one of his large, jocular moments, wishing to get even with humanity, squeezed the old bean and thought up the ballot box and then laughed for a hundred years. After which the devil invented the Presidency by combining all the futile despair of Sisyphus with the agony of Tantalus and shaking in a jigger of the nervous irritation of a man with ants in his pants.*"

WILLIAM ALLEN WHITE

ACKNOWLEDGMENTS

During the seven years this work was in preparation, I received help, advice, and encouragement from many quarters. The list of those whom I have consulted, whose opinion I sought, who helped me in my research, is so long that the sheer mentioning of their names would run into many pages, so I hope they will forgive me if I thank them in this general way.

However, I should like to say a special word to a few of the assistants who helped me assiduously during the long years. First to my secretary, Mrs. Irene F. Weston, who worked with infinite patience, typing and revising the manuscript many times, offering advice and catching mistakes, a most wonderful and intelligent collaborator. Thanks are due to Miss Constance A. Foulk, who typed the second half of the book and was responsible for the minutious job of "caption fitting"—making all lines under the illustrations come out equal. Her poignant criticism and suggestions improved the book no end. I am extremely grateful to Miss Liljan Espenak, who helped me with the picture research; to Miss Fayette Smith and Mrs. Lucille Grigorieff, who assisted me in the early stages; to Roger Linscott for pulling together the research for the Coolidge and Hoover chapters.

I am also indebted to Henry R. Luce and the Editors of *Life* Magazine for permission to use *Life*'s magnificent photographs of the 1948 election; to Sylvester L. Vigilante and F. Ivor D. Avellino of the New York Public Library, who were always ready with advice; to Clarence S. Brigham, Director of the American Antiquarian Society, for assistance in finding some of the early cartoons; to members of the Library of Congress, the New York Historical Society, the National Archives, the Frick Art Reference Library, and my home-town library in Lenox.

I am deeply grateful to Merle Armitage, who designed the title page and the flyleaf; to Miss Ida M. Lynn, who prepared the index; to Franklin P. Adams for allowing me to quote a few stanzas of his verse "T. R. to W. H. T."; to the artists and cartoonists who let me reproduce their work (their names are printed in the List of Illustrations); and to all others who gave me a helping hand.

It would be thoughtless not to remember here my beloved grandmother, who, more decades ago than I care to remember, read to me the lines of Lewis Caroll

"Alice was beginning to get very tired of sitting by her sister on the bank, and of having nothing to do: once or twice she had peeped into the book her sister was reading, but it had no pictures or conversations in it, 'and what is the use of a book,' thought Alice, 'without pictures or conversations?'"

She had a lot to do that this book came into being.

STEFAN LORANT

"Farview"
Lenox, Massachusetts
July 1, 1951

CONTENTS

or cause, the court shall nevertheless proceed to pronounce judgment. The judgment shall be final and conclusive. The proceedings shall be transmitted to the President of the Senate, and shall be lodged among the public records for the security of the parties concerned. Every commissioner shall, before he sit in judgment, take an oath, to be administered by one of the judges of the supreme or superior court of the State where the cause shall be tried, " well " and truly to hear and determine the matter in question, according to the " best of his judgment, without favour, affection, or hope of reward."

Sect. 3. All controversies concerning lands claimed under different grants of two or more States, whose jurisdictions, as they respect such lands, shall have been decided or adjusted subsequent to such grants, or any of them, shall, on application to the Senate, be finally determined, as near as may be, in the same manner as is before prescribed for deciding controversies between different States.

X.

Sect. 1. The Executive Power of the United States shall be vested in a single person. His stile shall be, " The President of the United States of America;" and his title shall be, " His Excellency." He shall be elected by ballot by the Legislature. He shall hold his office during the term of seven years; but shall not be elected a second time.

Sect. 2. He shall, from time to time, give information to the Legislature of the State of the Union: and recommend to their consideration such measures as he shall judge necessary, and expedient: he may convene them on extraordinary occasions. In case of disagreement between the two Houses, with regard to the time of adjournment, he may adjourn them to such time as he think proper: he shall take care that the laws of the United States be duly and faithfully executed: he shall commission all the officers of the United States; and shall appoint to offices in all cases not otherwise provided for by this constitution. He shall receive Ambassadors, ~~and may correspond with the supreme Executives of the several States~~. He shall have power to grant reprieves and pardons, ~~but his pardon shall not be pleadable in bar of an impeachment~~. He shall be Commander in Chief of the Army and Navy of the United States, and of the Militia of the several States. He shall, at stated times, receive for his services, a compensation, which shall neither be encreased nor diminished during his continuance in office. Before he shall enter on the duties of his department, he shall take the following Oath or Affirmation, " I ———— so-" lemnly swear (or affirm) that I will faithfully execute the Office of Presi-" dent of the United States of America." He shall be removed from his office on impeachment by the House of Representatives, and conviction in the Supreme Court, of treason, bribery, or corruption. In case of his removal as aforesaid, death, resignation, or disability to discharge the powers and duties of his office, the President of the Senate shall exercise those powers and duties until another President of the United States be chosen, or until the disability of the President be removed.

XI

Sect. 1. The Judicial Power of the United States shall be vested in one Supreme Court, and in such Inferior Courts as shall, when necessary, from time to time, be constituted by the Legislature of the United States.

Sect. 2. The Judges of the Supreme Court, and of the Inferior courts, shall hold their offices during good behaviour. They shall, at stated times, receive for their services, a compensation, which shall not be diminished during their continuance in office.

Sect. 3. The Jurisdiction of the Supreme Court shall extend to all cases arising under laws ~~passed by the Legislature~~ of the United States; to all cases affecting Ambassadors, other Public Ministers and Consuls; to the trial of impeachment

THE STATE HOUSE IN PHILADELPHIA

THE CREATION OF THE OFFICE

"On Monday the 14th of May. A.D. 1787. and in the eleventh year of the independence of the United States of America, at the State-House in the city of Philadelphia—in virtue of appointments from their respective States, sundry Deputies to the foederal-Convention appeared." So begins the *Journal* of the Federal Convention. But on that day, as Madison noted, there were not enough deputies assembled "for revising the federal system of Government." The meeting was therefore postponed until Friday, May 25th, when George Washington was elected unanimously to preside over the Convention. He declared, when conducted to the chair, "that as he never had been in such a situation, he felt himself embarrassed; that he hoped his errors, as they would be unintentional, would be excused."

After a few days passed in discussing rules, on May 29th the Convention was ready to begin in earnest. Forty delegates from ten states were present. Thirty-four-year-old Edmund Randolph, Governor of Virginia and chairman of the Virginia delegation, "opened the main business," submitting a set of resolutions, drafted by Madison and carefully discussed by the seven Virginia delegates. These resolutions—which during the debates became known as the Virginia Plan—advocated a strong national government composed of three independent departments: the executive, the judiciary, and the legislative. The legislature was to have two branches, the lower House to be elected by the people, the upper House by members of the lower House. The seventh resolution of the Virginia Plan called for a national executive to be elected by the national legislature. It was the first time in the Convention that the office of the President was mentioned.

Charles Pinckney, a twenty-nine-year-old planter from South Carolina and a soldier of the Revolutionary War, submitted a counter-proposal regarding the Chief of State. He pleaded "that the executive power be vested in a President of the United States of America which shall be his style; and his title shall be 'His Excellency.'" With this the debates on the presidential office had begun.

The delegates to the Convention had to establish a number of principles regarding the executive. First, in how many persons should the power be vested; second, by what method should the President be chosen; third, how long should he hold office; fourth, what should be his duties.

The first question was left unanswered by

A DRAFT OF THE CONSTITUTION DEFINING THE PRESIDENT'S DUTIES, WITH WASHINGTON'S ANNOTATIONS

the Virginians, as the opinions of their members differed. The other delegates to the Convention could not make up their minds either. Some advocated a single individual for the office. Randolph feared "one-man power" and suggested a committee: one executive from the North, one from the South, and one from the Middle states. Heaven was on the side of the young republic when this idea was discarded.

When, on the first day of June, James Wilson of Pennsylvania, "one of the deepest thinkers and most exact reasoners in the Convention," made the motion, and Charles Pinckney seconded it, that the national executive should "consist of a single person," there was a "considerable pause" in the Convention Hall. This seemed to the delegates a revolutionary proposal. Washington broke the pregnant silence and asked the assembly if he should put the question.

The senior member of the Convention, eighty-one-year-old Benjamin Franklin, rose to his feet. No, it was a point of great importance, Franklin said, and he "wished that the gentlemen would deliver their sentiments on it" before "the question was put." One by one the delegates got up. For three long days nothing else was discussed. John Rutledge of South Carolina "animadverted on the shyness of gentlemen on this and other subjects" and declared that in his opinion the power should be vested in a single person, because a "single man would feel the greatest responsibility and administer the public affairs best." Roger Sherman, once a shoemaker, now a judge from Connecticut, of whom Jefferson wrote, "He never said a foolish thing in his life," suggested "that the legislature should be at liberty to appoint one or more [executives] as experience might dictate."

James Wilson "preferred a single magistrate, as giving most energy, dispatch and responsibility to the office." This was not Edmund Randolph's opinion, who "strenuously opposed a unity in the Executive magistracy," and regarded it as the "foetus of monarchy." Randolph argued that "the Executive ought to be independent. It ought therefore (in order to support its independence) to consist of more than one." Wilson was against this. He attested "that Unity in the Executive instead of being the foetus of Monarchy would be the

CONSTITUTIONAL CONVENTION IN PHILADELPHI

best safeguard against tyranny." His motion for a single magistrate was postponed by common consent, the committee "seeming unprepared for any decision on it."

When the poll was taken, seven states cast their votes for a single executive and only

HERE BETWEEN MAY 14 AND SEPTEMBER 17, 1787, THE OFFICE OF THE PRESIDENT WAS CREATED

three, Delaware, Maryland and New Jersey, against it. Thus the United States was to have only *one* President.

The next question was how to elect him. There were two practical ways of selecting the President: one, by popular vote; the other, by the national legislature. It soon became apparent that the majority of the delegates were against a popular election. Their objections were manifold: some said that it would benefit the large states (their greater population would be decisive in the election); others held the view that the people of the country would not know the comparative merits of the candidates and would therefore always vote for someone from their own state, someone whom they knew; and there were a few delegates who argued that the common people were neither competent nor could be trusted to make the right selection.

Roger Sherman opposed election by the people. He demanded that the Chief Executive be "accountable to the Legislature only."

George Mason of Virginia supported him. He said: "It would be as unnatural to refer the choice of a proper character for Chief Magistrate to the people, as it would to refer a trial of colors to a blind man. The extent of the country renders it impossible that the people can have the requisite capacity to judge of the respective pretentions of the candidates."

Gouverneur Morris's arguments sounded a different tune. "If the people should elect," he said, "they will never fail to prefer some man of distinguished character, or services; but if the Legislature elect, it will be the work of intrigue, of cabal and of faction." But no words could change the minds of the delegates. The poll showed that nine states were against popular election and only one, Pennsylvania, for it. And when the question of a choice by the national legislature was put, every state voted in the affirmative.

However, this was not the end of the argument. The delegates who had pleaded for popular election felt so strongly about the issue that they brought it before the Convention in different forms again and again. From their opposition emerged a compromise solution, embodying the idea of an electoral college.

James Wilson had already suggested an electoral plan as early as June 2, but his motion was voted down. So was Elbridge Gerry's proposal that the President should be elected by the governors of the states. Alexander Hamilton, in his five-hour speech on June 18, advocated the election of the executive by electors chosen by the people from election districts, but his plan did not receive serious consideration. On July 17th the motion that the executive should be chosen by electors appointed by the legislatures of the several states

was rejected. Then, only two days later, July 19th, the proposal of Oliver Ellsworth was adopted: that the Chief Magistrate should "be chosen by electors appointed by the Legislatures of the states in the following ratio; to-wit—one for each state not exceeding 200,000 inhabits. two for each above yt. number & not exceeding 300,000. and, three for each State exceeding 300,000."

The next day the Convention agreed upon the number of electors. Massachusetts, Pennsylvania and Virginia were each to have three; Connecticut, New York, New Jersey, Maryland, North Carolina and South Carolina two each; Rhode Island, New Hampshire, Delaware and Georgia one each.

The tenure of the presidential office was hotly debated, and the delegates could not come to an agreement upon this question until the very last. The original Virginia Plan left the term of office blank. Later the blank was filled in "for the term of seven years." Others suggested a shorter-term, advocating more frequent elections.

On July 19th, when it was decided that the election should be made through independent electors, Oliver Ellsworth moved that the term should be not less than six years. For, "if the elections be too frequent, the Executive will not be firm eno. There must be duties which will make him unpopular for the moment. There will be *outs* as well as *ins*. His administration therefore will be attacked and misrepresented." Ellsworth's motion was carried. The Chief Magistrate was to serve for only six years, but he could be re-elected and hold office for twelve consecutive years.

On July 24th Elbridge Gerry argued that "the longer the duration of his [the executive's] appointment the more will his dependence be diminished—it will be better then for him to continue 10, 15, or even 20 years and be ineligible afterwards."

Luther Martin, representing Maryland, was for an eleven-year term, Elbridge Gerry for fifteen years, William Davie for eight years. And Rufus King, who spoke for Massachusetts, suggested somewhat ironically that the executive should rule for twenty years, as "this is the medium life of princes."

The next day Gouverneur Morris spoke

New Hampshire	Massachusetts	Rhode Island	Connecticut	New York	New Jersey	Pennsylvania	Delaware	Maryland	Virginia	North Carolina	South Carolina	Georgia	Questions	ayes	noes	divided
	ay		ay	no		ay	no	no	ay	ay	ay	ay	Single Executive.	7	3	-
	no		ay	no	ay	no	no	no	no	no	no	ay	To strike out the words "People" in the first clause of the 4th resolution, and to insert the word "Legislatures"	3	8	-
	no		ay	ay	no	no	no	no	ay	no	no	no	To add a convenient number of the national Judiciary to the Executive in the exercise of the negative	3	8	-
	ay		ay	ay	ay	ay	ay	ay	ay	ay	ay	ay	That the second Branch of the national Legislature be elected by the individual Legislatures	11	-	-
	ay		no	no	no	ay	d.	no	ay	no	no	no	To vest the national legislature with a negative on all state laws which shall appear to them improper	3	7	1
	ay		no	ay	ay	ay	ay	ay	ay	no	ay	ay	To reconsider the mode of appointing the Executive	9	2	-
	no		no	no	no	no	d.	no	no	no	no	no	To appoint the national Executive by the Executives of the several States	-	10	1
	ay		ay	no	no	ay	no	d.	ay	ay	ay	ay	That the right of suffrage in the first branch of the national Legislature ought not to be according to the rule established in the confederation but according to an equitable rule	7	3	1
	ay		ay	ay	no	ay	no	ay	ay	ay	ay	ay	That the right of suffrage in the first branch be according to the whole number of white and three fifths of the other inhabitants	9	2	-
	no		ay	ay	ay	no	ay	ay	no	no	no	no	That in the second branch of the national Legislature each State have one vote	5	6	-
	ay		no	no	no	ay	no	no	ay	ay	ay	ay	That the right of suffrage in the second branch ought to be according to the rule established for the first, i.e. an equitable rule of representation	6	5	-

THIS ORIGINAL RECORD WAS KEPT BY THE SECRETARY OF THE CONSTITUTIONAL CONVENTION

against the second term, because "a change of men is ever followed by a change of measures. The self-sufficiency of a victorious party scorns to tread in the paths of their predecessors."

When the Committee of Five submitted its draft on August 6th the passage read: "The Executive Power of the United States shall be vested in a single person. His style shall be 'The

President of the United States of America'; and his title shall be, 'His Excellency.' He shall be elected by ballot by the legislature. He shall hold his office during the term of seven years; but shall not be elected a second time."

But this was not the final word. "Upon reconsidering that article," explained Charles Cotesworth Pinckney in his speech on January 18, 1788, in the South Carolina House of Representatives, when he fought for the ratification of the Constitution, "it was thought that to cut off all hopes from a man of serving again in that elevated station, might render him dangerous, or perhaps indifferent to the faithful discharge of his duty. His term of service might expire during the raging of war, when he might, perhaps, be the most capable man in America to conduct it; and would it be wise and prudent to declare in our Constitution that such a man should not again direct our military operations, though our success might be owing to his abilities?"

So when the Committee of Eleven, who had to act on "such parts of the Constitution as have been postponed, and such parts of reports as have not been acted on," reported on September 4 that the last sentence of the former resolution should be changed to read, "He shall hold his office during the term of four years," the delegates concurred. There it was: not six years or seven years, not fifteen or twenty, but a short term of four. And re-eligibility was not even mentioned.

The committee's change of mind came after the decision was reached that the Chief Magistrate should be chosen through independent electors and not through the legislature.

The independent electors contributed a guarantee for the future. The members of the committee had no longer to fear that the President, selected by the votes of the legislature, would become a servile tool of that body, kept in office for twelve years as a reward for his service or turned out after his first term because he resisted the will of the legislature.

They have agreed that the number of electors should equal the whole number of Senators and members of the House of Representatives; in other words each state should have as many presidential electors as the number of their Senators and Representatives together. So the Convention decided for a short term of four years. The matter of eligibility for a second, third, fourth term, was left to the people. It was for them to decide how many times they chose to vote for their President.

On the 17th of September, thirty-eight delegates signed the Constitution. George Mason refused his signature (so did Edmund Randolph and Elbridge Gerry), objecting that there was no "Declaration of Rights" in it and because "dangerous power and structure of the government . . . will set out a moderate aristocracy; it is at present impossible to foresee whether it will, in its operation, produce a monarchy, or a corrupt, tyrannical aristocracy; it will most probably vibrate some years between the two, and then terminate in the one or the other."

But the Sage of the Convention had better words for the document: "I confess that there are several parts of this constitution which I do not at present approve," Benjamin Franklin wrote in the speech which his friend, James Wilson, read to the delegates, "but I am not sure I shall never approve them. For having lived long, I have experienced many instances of being obliged by better information or fuller consideration, to change opinions even on important subjects, which I once thought right, but found to be otherwise. It is therefore that the older I grow, the more apt I am to doubt my own judgment, and to pay more respect to the judgment of others. Most men indeed as well as most sects in Religion, think themselves in possession of all truth, and that wherever others differ from them it is so far error . . . But though many private persons think almost as highly of their own infallibility as of that of their sect, few express it so naturally as a certain french lady, who in dispute with her sister, said 'I don't know how it happens, Sister, but I meet with no body but myself, that's always in the right.'

"In these sentiments, Sir, I agree to this Constitution with all its faults, if they are such. . . ."

Thus the debates ended and the Constitution, outlining the duties of the President of the United States, was submitted to the states for ratification.

By the United States in Congress assembled,

WHEREAS the Convention assembled in Philadelphia, pursuant to the Resolution of Congress of the 21st February, 1787, did, on the 17th of September in the same year, report to the United States in Congress assembled, a Constitution for the People of the United States; whereupon Congress, on the 28th of the same September, did resolve unanimously, " That the said report, with the Resolutions and Letter accompanying the same, be transmitted to the several Legislatures, in order to be submitted to a Convention of Delegates chosen in each State by the people thereof, in conformity to the Resolves of the Convention made and provided in that case:" And whereas the Constitution so reported by the Convention, and by Congress transmitted to the several Legislatures, has been ratified in the manner therein declared to be sufficient for the establishment of the same, and such Ratifications duly authenticated have been received by Congress, and are filed in the Office of the Secretary---therefore,

RESOLVED, That the first Wednesday in January next, be the day for appointing Electors in the several States, which before the said day shall have ratified the said Constitution; that the first Wednesday in February next, be the day for the Electors to assemble in their respective States, and vote for a President; and that the first Wednesday in March next, be the time, and the present Seat of Congress the place for commencing Proceedings under the said Constitution.

Cha Thomson secy

BROADSIDE ANNOUNCES THE DAY WHEN ELECTORS WERE TO VOTE FOR THE FIRST PRESIDENT

APRIL 30, 1789: THE FIRST INAUGURATION

THE FIRST ELECTION—1789

GEORGE WASHINGTON

George Washington had no rival for the Presidency. Even before the Constitution was adopted, the people of the country were unanimous that if they should select a President, Washington would be their choice.

By the summer of 1788 the Constitution was ratified. By autumn Congress had decided that the temporary seat of government would be New York. And on September 13, 1788, the lawmakers passed a resolution "that the first Wednesday in January next, be the day for appointing Electors in the several States, which before the said day shall have ratified the said Constitution; that the first Wednesday in February next, be the day for the Electors to assemble in their respective States, and vote for a President; and that the first Wednesday in March next, be the time, and the present seat of Congress the place, for commencing Proceedings under the said Constitution."

It was a tight schedule. In not quite four months—from September 13 to January 7—state legislatures had to be summoned, laws about the methods of election passed, and candidates for the presidential electors chosen and voted for.

While time was short, distances were great. Many legislators had to travel days by horseback or by coach to reach the seat of their government.

Before the news of the election reached some parts of the country, two weeks had gone by. The state governments had to seek solutions to a number of problems—and this in a great hurry. Should the states hold popular elections to choose the electors, or should the legislatures appoint them? And if they were to be elected by the people, what should be the methods of the election? On these questions the Constitution was silent.

The limited time was an indication that the Fathers of the Constitution intended to leave the appointment of the electors to the legislatures. A Philadelphia newspaperman reasoned that "if the people, as hath been asserted, are to choose the electors, is it possible that in the large States of Massachusetts, Virginia, etc., the returns can be made for the choice, notice given to the persons chosen, and the persons thus chosen have time to meet together in the short space of one month? No, it is impossible, and can only be remedied by the legislature, who, in fact, are 'the States' making the choice."

Five states adopted this method. In Connecticut, Delaware, Georgia, New Jersey, and

GEORGE WASHINGTON (1732-1799), the most prominent and trusted person in the country, was the obvious and un-animous choice of the 69 electors for the first U.S. presidential office.

JOHN ADAMS (1735-1826), hesitantly chosen by the Federal-ists for second place with Washington's and Hamilton's rather cau-tious approval, receiv-ed 34 electoral votes.

JOHN JAY (1745-1829), a lawyer, diplomat and first Chief Justice of the United States, received five votes of New Jer-sey, three of Delaware, and one of Virginia.

ROBERT H. HARRISON (1745-1790), served in the Revolutionary War, later became Chief Jus-tice of the General Court of Maryland. He received the six elec-toral votes of that state.

JOHN RUTLEDGE (1739-1800), "favorite son" of South Carolina and one of the men who wrote the South Carolina Constitution, received the six elec-toral votes of his state.

JOHN HANCOCK (1736/7-1793), an ar-dent patriot who signed the Declaration of In-dependence and be-came first Governor of Massachusetts, won four electoral votes.

THE ENTRY in the Senate Journal on Washington's and Adams's election to the Presidency and Vice-Presi-dency. Of the original thirteen states, only ten voted.

South Carolina the legislatures appointed the electors, while three states—Maryland, Penn-sylvania, and Virginia—held popular elections.

Massachusetts, always individualistic, in-vented a complicated system, merging the idea of popular election with that of legislative appointment. The people in each district were to vote for two candidates, both residents of the same district, and after the votes of all dis-tricts reached the General Court, the assembly was to choose one person from the two who received the highest number of votes. To com-plicate the matter further the General Court was to select two additional electors.

In the remaining two states (North Caro-lina and Rhode Island had not yet ratified the Constitution) a great battle was fought over the mode of election. In New Hampshire the two Houses were involved in a constitutional argument. In that state the electors were named by popular vote. However, a proviso in the electoral act ruled that in case no candidate should receive a clear majority, the General Court was to appoint the electors. As it turned out, none of the electors had the majority; so the choice of who should represent New Hampshire was left to the General Court. With this the trouble started. The two Houses disagreed on the procedure. The House of Representatives asked for a joint ballot, suggesting that each Representative and Senator should have one vote, while members of the Senate, who were in the minority, insisted on equal powers with the lower House. The arguments continued until the deadline for the appointments was reached. As the midnight hour approached, the House of Representatives gave up under protest and accepted the list of electors chosen by the Senate, otherwise Washington would have been elected without the electoral votes of New Hampshire.

In New York State a similar argument was in process. There the two Houses could not reach an agreement. Thus the votes of the state were lost, and New York did not participate in the first presidential election.

In the states where popular elections were held, the voting for the electors did not cause much excitement. As great political issues were not at stake, only a few people went to the polls.

The opponents of the Federalists—party lines were not defined yet—were so small in numbers that they did not put up candidates. They showed their disagreement with the Federalists simply by not voting.

On the first Wednesday in February, 1789, ten states presented sixty-nine electors in New York City. Two electors from Maryland did not appear: one stayed at home with the gout, the other was held up because of ice in the rivers. Two Virginia electors remained at home as well.

Each of the sixty-nine electors was ready to cast his vote for George Washington. But they had to choose two persons. The first had to have the majority of all votes to become President; the second had to have the next highest number of votes to become Vice-President.

For the second place there were a number of candidates. Jefferson was ruled out because he was from the same state as Washington. The Federalists searched for some Northern man from the New England states. They thought of nominating General Henry Knox, but he, like Washington, was a soldier; they canvassed Samuel Adams, but he had many enemies because of his early critical attitude toward the Constitution; they talked of putting

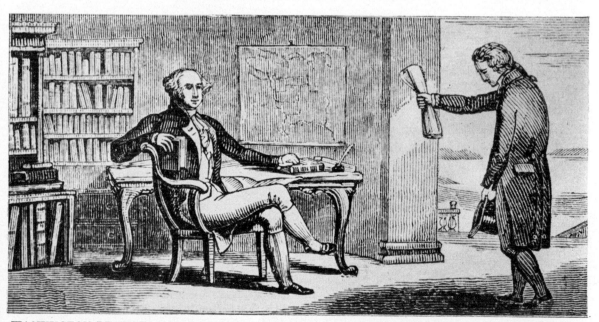

WASHINGTON RECEIVES NOTIFICATION OF HIS ELECTION AT HIS RESIDENCE IN MOUNT VERNON

GEORGE WASHINGTON'S ACCEPTANCE LETTER WHICH HE WROTE TO CONGRESS ON APRIL 14, 1789

forward Governor John Hancock's name, but Massachusetts needed his services. Alexander Hamilton, the best-known Federalist, could not run; he was still under thirty-five. Finally they turned to John Adams.

Hamilton had misgivings. He was disturbed about the "defect of the Constitution" concerning the choice of President and Vice-President. He feared that if some electors were to hold back "a few votes insidiously" from Washington but cast all their votes for John Adams, Washington would be defeated and Adams would become President. Therefore, he asked his Federalist friends to "waste" some votes for the second choice. There was never really any danger that Adams would receive the unanimous vote. Still, Hamilton—who strongly disliked him—urged the Federalists not to vote for the "Duke of Braintree," and the results show that a number of electors followed his advice. For Washington received the unanimous vote of all the sixty-nine electors, while

CONTEMPORARY WOODCUTS OF WASHINGTON'S JOURNEY TO NEW YORK

WASHINGTON ARRIVING AT GRAY'S FERRY ENROUTE FROM MOUNT VERNON TO NEW YORK CITY

TRIUMPHAL ARCH AND RECEPTION COMMITTEE GREET THE PRESIDENT-ELECT AT TRENTON, N. J.

only thirty-four were cast for Adams, the remaining thirty-five being scattered.

On the first Wednesday in March the new Congress of the United States was to meet to count the votes and announce the result of the election. On that day only a few Senators as-

NEW-YORK, April 24.

Yesterday arrived the illustrious GEORGE WASHINGTON, President of the United States, amidst the joyful acclamations of every party and every description of citizens.

On this great occasion, the hand of industry was suspended, and the various pleasures of the capital, were concentered to a single enjoyment.—Every mind was filled with one idea, and every heart swelled with one emotion. Absorbed and agitated by the sentiment which our adored leader and ruler inspired, the printer apprehends, that he cannot with perfect precision describe the various scene of splendour which this event exhibited. The eye could not rove with freedom through the various parts of this scene. One great object engaged it, and WASHINGTON arrested and fixed its gaze.

The President was received at Elizabeth-Town, by a deputation of three Senators, five Representatives of the Congress of the United States, and three officers of the State and Corporation; with whom he embarked in the barge, built for the purpose of wafting his excellency across the bay, and rowed by thirteen pilots of this harbour, dressed in white uniform; Thomas Randall, Esq. acting as cockswain.

No language can paint the beautiful display made on his excellency's approach to the city. The shores were crouded with a vast concourse of citizens, waiting with exulting anxiety his arrival.—His Catholic Majesty's sloop of war the Galvifton, (Mr. Dohrman's) ship North-Carolina, and the other vessels in port, were dressed and decorated in the most superb manner.—His excellency's barge was accompanied by the barge of the Hon. Gen. Knox, and a great number of vessels and boats from Jersey and New-York, in his train.——As he passed the Galvifton, he received a salute of thirteen guns, and was welcomed by an equal number from the battery.

The whole water scene was animated and moving beyond description. The grand gala formed an object the most interesting imaginable.

On his excellency's arrival at the stairs, prepared and ornamented, at Murray's wharf, for his landing; he was received and congratulated by his excellency, the Governor of this State, and the officers of the State and Corporation, and the following procession was formed. First. Col. Lewis, accompanied by two officers, and followed by the troop of dragoons, commanded by Capt. Stakes.—The German grenadiers, headed by Capt. Scriba—music.—Infantry of the brigade, under the command of captains Swartwout and Steddiford—Grenadiers, under Capt. Harfin.—Col. Bauman, at the head of the regiment of artillery—music.—Gen Malcom and aid—Officers of the militia.—Committee of Congress—The PRESIDENT, supported by Governor Clinton.—— The President's suite.—Officers of the State.—Mayor and Aldermen of New-York.—The French and Spanish Ambassadors, in their carriages.—The whole order followed by an amazing concourse of citizens.

The procession advanced through Queen street to the house fitted up for the reception of his Excellency, where it terminated. After which, he was conducted without form to the house of Governor Clinton, with whom his Excellency dined.—In the evening the houses of the citizens were brilliantly illuminated.

FROM THE NEW YORK *DAILY ADVERTISER*

WASHINGTON ARRIVES AT NEW YORK HARBOI

sembled in New York. Six weeks passed before a quorum could be formed. On April 6th, the honorable Senators elected John Langdon as "president for the sole purpose of opening and counting the votes for President of the United States." Members of the lower House proceeded to the Senate Chamber to witness the ceremony.

16

THE FOOT OF WALL STREET HE WAS GREETED BY HIGH DIGNITARIES OF THE STATE AND CITY

After "it appeared that George Washington Esq was elected President," the Senate named the former secretary of the Continental Congress, Charles Thomson, to take the formal notification of his election to the President-elect. Thomson left New York on horseback the following day, Tuesday, April 7th; two days later he was in Philadelphia; by Sunday he

had reached Baltimore; and half an hour past noon on Tuesday, a week after he had set out from New York, he arrived in Mount Vernon.

Washington asked for two days to prepare for the journey. He was mindful of the future. In a letter to his friend General Knox he wrote:

"In confidence I tell you (with the *world* it

17

would obtain little credit) that my movements to the chair of government will be accompanied by feelings not unlike those of a culprit, who is going to the place of his execution; so unwilling am I, in the evening of a life nearly consumed in public cares, to quit a peaceful abode for an ocean of difficulties, without that competency of political skill, abilities, and inclination which are necessary to manage the helm. I am sensible that I am embarking by the voice of the people, and a good name of my own, on this voyage; but what returns will be made for them, Heaven alone can foretell. Integrity and firmness are all I can promise."

On Thursday, the sixteenth of April, he left Mount Vernon to travel to New York. The journey turned into an ovation from the beginning to the end. In Alexandria, in Georgetown, in Baltimore, in Havre de Grace, in Wilmington, in Chester, in Philadelphia—in all these places, wildly cheering people lined the route. Speechmaking, military parades, banquets and choruses caused Washington to halt his coach every few miles. Trenton built triumphal arches to greet the President-elect. Thirteen young girls, representing the thirteen states, sang:

> "Welcome mighty Chief, once more
> Welcome to this grateful shore;
> Now no mercenary foe
> Aims again the fatal blow."

According to contemporary reports, this scene was so touching that many people wept. As Washington's carriage passed through Brunswick and Woodbridge there were more

ovations, more people, more cheering. At Elizabethtown, in the stately mansion of Elias Boudinot, the committee from Congress greeted him and accompanied him to Elizabethtown Point, where Washington boarded a boat manned by thirteen pilots of the harbor. The last part of the journey to Manhattan was made on water. Before Bedloe's Island a large sloop carrying about twenty gentlemen and ladies approached the presidential craft, singing an ode of welcome to the tune of "God Save the King." By this time the shores of New York were crowded with a great multitude; vessels in the harbor displayed their colors; salutes were fired.

When the barge landed at Murray's Wharf, at the foot of Wall Street, Washington was welcomed by Governor George Clinton and the Mayor of New York, James Duane. Then, in a great procession, he was led to the Franklin House in Cherry Street, his temporary residence. Bells were rung; banners were displayed from the fort and from every building.

At night the city was brilliantly illuminated. New York was in high spirits. Thousands had come to see Washington and the city was overcrowded. It was difficult to find sleeping quarters. One woman wrote home: "We shall remain here if we have to sleep in tents as many will have to do. Mr. Williamson promised to engage us rooms at Francis's but that was jammed long ago, as was every other decent public house; and now, while we are waiting at Mrs. Vanderwort's in Maiden Lane till after dinner, two of our beaux are running about town determined to obtain the best places for us to stay which can be opened for love, money or most persuasive speeches."

Inauguration day was Thursday, April 30, 1789. At half an hour past noon the President-elect left his house in Cherry Street. He took a seat in his cream-colored coach, drawn by four horses, with a man on the box and a lackey on one of the horses. At the head of the great parade were dragoons, artillery, grenadiers in brilliant uniforms. They were followed by carriages with members of the Senate committee. Then came the coach of Washington, and behind it a long line of carriages with chargés d'affaires, diplomats, and distinguished guests.

When the President-elect arrived at Federal

THE FIRST "WHITE HOUSE," Washington's residence in New York on the corner of Pearl and Cherry Streets.

THE Committees of both Houses of Congress, appointed to take order for conducting the ceremonial of the formal reception, &c. of the President of the United States, on Thursday next, have agreed to the following order thereon, viz.

That General Webb, Colonel Smith, Lieutenant-Colonel Fish, Lieut. Col. Franks, Major L'Enfant, Major Bleecker, and Mr. John R. Livingston, or requested to serve as Assistants on the occasion.

That a chair be placed in the Senate-Chamber for the President of the United States. That a chair be placed in the Senate-Chamber for the Vice-President, to the right of the President's chair; and that the Senators take their seats on that side of the chamber on which the Vice-President's chair shall be placed, That a chair be placed in the Senate-Chamber for the Speaker of the House of Representatives, to the left of the President's chair—and that the Representatives take their seats on that side of the chamber on which the Speaker's chair shall be placed.

That seats be provided in the Senate-Chamber sufficient to accommodate the late President of Congress, the Governor of the Western territory, the five persons being the heads of the three great departments, the Minister Plenipotentiary of France, the Encargado de negocios of Spain, the Chaplains of Congress, the persons in the suite of the President; and also to accommodate the following Public Officers of the State, viz. The Governor, the Lieutenant-Governor, the Chancellor, the Chief Justice, and other Judges of the Supreme Court, and the Mayor of the city. That one of the Assistants wait on these gentlemen, and inform them that seats are provided for their accommodation, and also to signify to them that no precedence of seats is intended, and that no salutation is expected from them on their entrance into, or their departure from the Senate-Chamber.

That the members of both Houses assemble in their respective Chambers precisely at twelve o'clock, and that the Representatives preceded by the Speaker, and attended by their Clerk, and other Officers, proceed to the Senate-Chamber, there to be received by the Vice-President and Senators rising.

That the Committee attend the President from his residence to the Senate-Chamber, and that he be there received by the Vice-President, the Senators and Representatives rising, and be by the Vice-President conducted to his chair.

That after the President shall be seated in his Chair, and the Vice-President, Senators and Representatives shall be again seated, the Vice-President shall announce to the President, that the members of both Houses will attend him to be present at his taking the Oath of Office required by the Constitution. To the end that the Oath of Office may be administered to the President in the most public manner, and that the greatest number of the people of the United States, and without distinction, may be witnesses to the solemnity, that therefore the Oath be administered in the outer Gallery adjoining to the Senate Chamber.

That when the President shall proceed to the gallery to take the Oath, he be attended by the Vice-President, and be followed by the Chancellor of the State, and pass through the middle door, that the Senators pass through the door on the right, and the Representatives, preceded by the Speaker, pass through the door on the left, and such of the persons who shall have been admitted into the Senate-Chamber, and may be desirous to go into the gallery, are then also to pass through the door on the right. That when the President shall have taken the Oath, and returned into the Senate-Chamber, attended by the Vice-President, and shall be seated in his chair, that the Senators and the Representatives also return into the Senate-Chamber, and that the Vice-President and they resume their respective seats.

Both Houses having resolved to accompany the President after he shall have taken the Oath, to St. Paul's Chapel, to hear divine service, to be performed by the Chaplain of Congress, that the following order of procession be observed, viz. The door-keeper and messenger of the House of Representatives. The Clerk of the House. The Representatives. The Speaker. The President, with the Vice-President at his left hand. The Senators. The Secretary of the Senate. The door-keeper, and messenger of the Senate.

That a Pew be reserved for the President—Vice-President—Speaker of the House of Representatives, and the Committees; and that pews be also reserved sufficient for the reception of the Senators and Representatives.

That after divine service shall be performed, the President be received at the door of the Church, by the Committees, and by them attended in carriages to his residence.

That it be intrusted to the Assistants to take proper precautions for keeping the avenues to the Hall open, and that for that purpose, they wait on his Excellency the Governor of this State, and in the name of the Committees request his aid, by an order or recommendation to the Civil Officers, or militia of the city, to attend and serve on the occasion, as he shall judge most proper.

April 29th, 1789.

OFFICIAL PROGRAM FOR THE FIRST INAUGURATION, ISSUED ONE DAY BEFORE THE CEREMONY

Hall, Vice-President John Adams greeted him and declared that the members of Congress were ready to witness his oath of fealty to the Constitution and to the duties of his office as President of the United States of America.

The sergeant at arms of the Senate led the President-elect to the balcony. Here, witnessed by thousands, Chancellor Robert R. Livingston read the oath: "I do solemnly swear that I will faithfully execute the office of President of the United States, and will, to the best of my ability, preserve, protect, and defend the Constitution of the United States." Washington, his right hand upon the Bible, repeated the oath. His firm voice was heard by the multitude as he said solemnly, "I swear, so help me God." Livingston stepped to the railing and exclaimed: "Long live George Washington, President of the United States."

The cheering of the people drowned his voice. The flag of the new republic went up over Federal Hall. Cannon roared; church bells pealed. Washington bowed to the cheering people, then walked back into the building to deliver his inaugural address.

"As the company returned into the Senate Chamber," wrote Senator Maclay, who witnessed the ceremonies, "the President took the chair and the Senators and Representatives their seats. He rose and all rose also and addressed them. This great man was agitated and embarrassed more than ever he was by the levelled cannon or pointed musket. He trembled and several times could scarce make out to read, though it must be supposed he had often read it before. He put the fingers of the left hand into the side of what I think the tailors call the fall of the breeches, changing the papers into his left hand. After some time he then did the same thing with some fingers of his right hand. When he came to the words *all the world*, he made a flourish with his right hand, which left rather an ungainly impression. I sincerely, for my part, wished all set ceremony in the hands of the dancing-masters, and that this first of men had read off his address in the plainest manner, without ever taking his eyes from the paper, for I felt hurt that he was not first in everything. He was dressed in deep brown, with metal buttons, with an eagle on

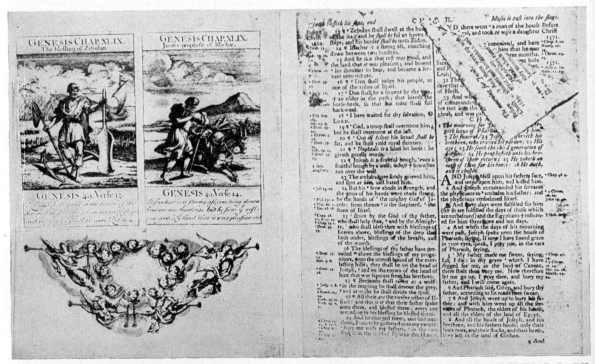

TWO PAGES OF THE BIBLE UPON WHICH GEORGE WASHINGTON TOOK THE PRESIDENTIAL OATH

"SO HELP ME GOD!" George Washington takes the oath administered by Chancellor Robert Livingston on the balcony of the Federal Hall in New York City. A contemporary engraving by Amos Doolittle after a drawing by Lecour.

them, white stockings, a bag, and sword."

But Fisher Ames, another eyewitness, noted that it was "a very touching scene and quite of the solemn kind. His aspect grave, almost to sadness; his modesty, actually shaking; his voice deep, a little tremulous, and so low as to call for close attention; added to the series of objects presented to the mind, and overwhelm-

A FANCIFUL REPRESENTATION OF WASHINGTON'S FIRST INAUGURAL ADDRESS. AN ENGRAVING BY

ing it, produced emotion of the most affecting kind upon the members."

That evening every one in New York was on the streets. Fireworks rocketed; cascades, serpents, fire trees and fountains of fire lit the skies. It was a memorable, unforgettable night.

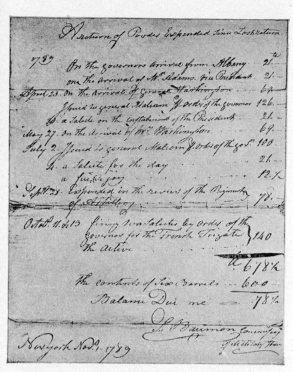

A BILL FOR FIREWORKS. Part of the sum was for powder used when Washington arrived in New York.

DD AFTER TOMPKINS H. MATTESON'S PAINTING

The United States had a President, the first to take office under the Federal Constitution— an event worthy of celebration.

WASHINGTON'S CABINET. From left to right: Knox, Jefferson, Randolph, Hamilton and the President.

23

WASHINGTON'S HOUSE IN PHILADELPHIA

THE SECOND ELECTION—1792

GEORGE WASHINGTON

The Constitution was a short document—a little over four thousand words. Out of these, less than four hundred were devoted to the presidential duties. They said that "The President shall be commander-in-chief of the army and navy of the United States, and of the militia of the several States"; that "he shall have power to grant reprieves and pardons for offences against the United States, except in cases of impeachment"; that "he shall have power, by and with the advice and consent of the Senate, to make treaties, provided two-thirds of the senators present concur; and he shall nominate, and by and with the advice and consent of the Senate, shall appoint ambassadors, other public ministers and consuls, judges of the Supreme Court, and all other officers of the United States, whose appointments are not herein otherwise provided for . . ." and that "he shall from time to time give to the Congress information on the state of the Union, and recommend to their consideration such measures as he shall judge necessary and expedient; he may, on extraordinary occasions, convene both Houses, or either of them, and in case of disagreement between them, with respect to the time of adjournment, he may adjourn them to such time as he shall think proper; he shall receive ambassadors and

other public ministers; he shall take care that the laws be faithfully executed, and shall commission all the officers of the United States." That was all.

The Founding Fathers had no desire to define in minute detail the duties of the President. They expected him to be a leader in political matters, and they knew that they could not prescribe rules for leadership. Thus they sketched only the outlines of his office. The President's relationship with Congress and with the future executive departments was purposely left vague.

At first nothing seemed to be very definite about the Presidency—not even the title. While Washington was on his journey to New York for his inauguration, both Houses of Congress argued how to address him. Should he be called in State papers "His Highness"? Should he be "His Excellency"? Or should one style him as "High Mightiness"?

The Senate thought "His Excellency" was not distinguished enough, and so the title was rejected and replaced by "His Highness, the President of the United States of America, and Protector of Her Liberties." However, when this recommendation reached the House, James Madison reminded his fellow legislators that the Constitution had already named the Chief Mag-

GEORGE WASHINGTON (1732–1799)
PAINTING BY GILBERT STUART

GEORGE WASHINGTON
(1732-1799) did not seek the presidential office for a second term. However, when Jefferson, Madison and Hamilton strongly urged him to remain at the helm of the government, he reconsidered his decision and received the unanimous vote of the 132 electors.

JOHN ADAMS
(1735-1826) was the Federalist choice for the Vice-Presidency. Although he was bitterly attacked and ridiculed by the opposition as a proponent of monarchy, he commanded enough electoral votes to defeat Clinton, candidate of the Virginia-New York alliance.

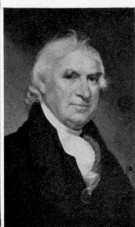

GEORGE CLINTON
(1739-1812), Revolutionary soldier, statesman, Governor of New York and one of the most vigorous opponents of the Federal Constitution, became the candidate of the New York malcontents and the followers of Jefferson for the vice-presidential office.

THOMAS JEFFERSON
(1743-1826), who opposed Hamilton on the Bank issue, organized the opposition against the Federalists, rallying behind him the farmers, mechanics and small shopkeepers of the country. Though not a candidate in this election, four votes were cast for Jefferson.

THE ELECTORAL VOTES FOR GEORGE WASHINGTO[N]

istrate as President of the United States. Why not keep that address? The title stuck, much to the dismay of John Adams, who loved the court language of the Old World. To call him President, fumed he indignantly, would be much too undignified, when there are "presidents of fire companies and clubs." And he predicted that if George Washington's title were to be so commonplace, the people "would despise him to all eternity," which shows that one cannot rely even on the prophecy of the first Vice-President.

Washington faced a formidable task. He had to organize a government, choose his chief advisers, appoint judges, set a pattern in dealing with Congress. He was aware of his great responsibilities. "I walk on untrodden ground," he

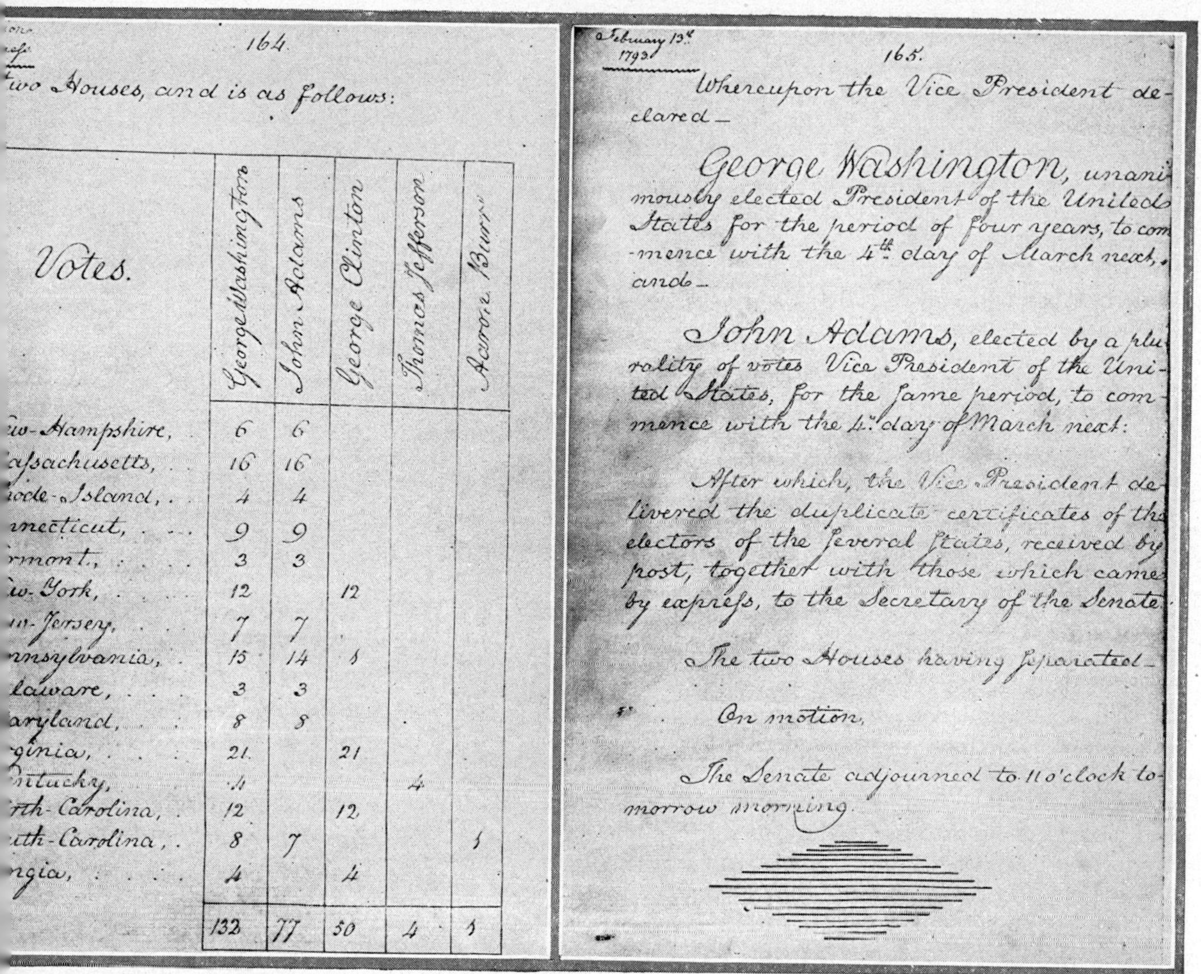

Votes.	George Washington Esq	John Adams	George Clinton	Thomas Jefferson	Aaron Burr
New-Hampshire,	6	6			
Massachusetts,	16	16			
Rhode-Island,	4	4			
Connecticut,	9	9			
Vermont,	3	3			
New-York,	12		12		
New-Jersey,	7	7			
Pennsylvania,	15	14	1		
Delaware,	3	3			
Maryland,	8	8			
Virginia,	21		21		
Kentucky,	4			4	
North-Carolina,	12		12		
South-Carolina,	8	7			1
Georgia,	4		4		
	132	77	50	4	1

two Houses, and is as follows:

February 13^d 1793

Whereupon the Vice President declared —

George Washington, unanimously elected President of the United States for the period of four years, to commence with the 4th day of March next, and —

John Adams, elected by a plurality of votes Vice President of the United States, for the same period, to commence with the 4th day of March next:

After which, the Vice President delivered the duplicate certificates of the electors of the several States, received by post, together with those which came by express, to the Secretary of the Senate.

The two Houses having separated —

On motion,

The Senate adjourned to 11 o'clock tomorrow morning.

) THE OTHER CANDIDATES, AS RECORDED IN THE ORIGINAL *SENATE JOURNAL* FOR FEB. 13, 1793

confessed. "There is scarcely any part of my conduct that may not hereafter be drawn into precedent." Puzzled over etiquette, he sent a number of questions to Adams and to Hamilton. He wanted to know whether he should meet people freely or see none, whether he should keep open house or have receptions only on national holidays, whether he should accept invitations to private tea parties or should receive visitors only one day a week.

To set the wheels of government in motion, much legislation was necessary. Congress created the "great departments" of State, Treasury, and War. Washington made his first appointments. For Secretary of State he chose Thomas Jefferson, who had returned from France; for the Treasury, Alexander Hamilton; for Secretary of War, his old friend General Henry Knox, while Edmund Randolph was to be his Attorney General. The three Secretaries and the Attorney General were already known collectively as the President's Cabinet, but not until Theodore Roosevelt's administration in 1907 was the Cabinet recognized as such by law.

Gradually the machinery of government began to grind. Congress established courts and post offices, sent a number of constitutional amendments to the states (ten of them were ratified—the Bill of Rights), decided about the census, fixed salaries, voted appropriations.

However, the most important and urgent business was to put the country's finances in order. The young and brilliant Secretary of the Treasury—Hamilton was thirty-two when he was appointed to office—submitted to Congress a report "for the adequate support of public credit," one of the greatest American State Papers. In Hamilton's opinion the debt of the United States, both foreign and domestic, "was the price of liberty," for which "the faith of America has been repeatedly pledged," therefore all obligations must be met. He suggested that the foreign and domestic debt should be funded at par and the war debts of the states should be assumed by the Federal Government.

These two proposals, funding and assumption, were ardently debated in Congress and throughout the country, touching on the nerve of the people and causing a tremendous excitement. One can well understand the reason for it. The majority of the government securities which Hamilton proposed to exchange at full value were now in the hands of the well-to-do, but originally they had been held by farmers, soldiers, small shopkeepers, who had received them for their services or for supplies furnished in the Revolutionary War. These people were not rich; they needed money, and they sold the certificates—sometimes for a song. If now the government should pay the full amount, who would benefit? The bankers and merchants and the speculators. So the question was posed: Why should they receive the full amount when they had not paid the full value for the certificates? Madison proposed a plan whereby the original holder would receive a part of the purchase sum, but his proposal was rejected. After a lengthy debate Congress voted for the funding of the debt at par, much to the joy of the merchants, bankers, and speculating Congressmen.

The question of funding out of the way, the battle for assumption began. Hamilton believed that by taking over the state debts, the individual states would have an increased interest in the new national government. It was fair to assume this—if only all the states had been equally in debt. But some of the Southern states had only small obligations, while others owed large sums. Quite naturally Virginians and Georgians were violently opposed to being taxed for the debts of Massachusetts. Thus during the struggle over assumption, the cleavage between the states deepened until it nearly wrecked the foundation of the nation.

The House of Representatives at first voted

PENNSYLVANIA SENATOR ROBERT MORRIS LEAD

against the assumption plan, defeating Hamilton by two votes, but the Secretary of the Treasury refused to give up the fight. He turned instead to Thomas Jefferson and made with him the most famous deal in American history. Jefferson and his friends desired the seat of the government for the South, while Hamilton and his Federalist followers were anxious to have the assumption measure passed. They traded votes, Jefferson supporting assumption, Hamilton and his friends helping with their votes to move the capital to the South. (To please Senator Robert Morris and his state, Pennsylvania, it was decided

28

that for the next ten years—until the Federal city on the Potomac could be laid out—Congress would meet in Philadelphia.)

After funding and assumption became law, Hamilton proposed establishment of a national bank. This roused the ire of Jefferson, who questioned the right of the government to create such an institution. Jefferson argued for a strict interpretation of the Constitution. Hamilton answered that as the Constitution gave the national government power to collect taxes, it therefore implied that a national bank could be founded to collect these dues.

The conflict of these two great Americans was not only a clash of two different characters and personalities; they represented two basic antagonistic American interests. Jefferson personified the slaveholding South, Hamilton the mercantile and financial North. Jefferson was for a free agrarian democracy, Hamilton for a strong national government. Jefferson disliked cities and dreamt of America as a nation of farmers; Hamilton desired legislative encouragement for the shipping and manufacturing interests. Jefferson spoke against the large banking and trading organizations as they fostered inequal-

29

PRESIDENT WASHINGTON'S FORMAL RECEPTIONS AND HIS "REPUBLICAN COURT" WERE STRONGI

ity; he put his trust in the people, to whom Hamilton reputedly referred in a moment of anger as "a great beast." Hamilton said: "All communities divide themselves into the few and the many. The first are the rich and well-born, the other the mass of the people. Turbulent and changing, they seldom judge or determine right." He wanted to "give therefore to the first class a distinct, permanent share in government."

In short, Hamilton was for the rule of the well-educated statesmen, supported by the propertied class; Jefferson for a government for and by the people.

The conflict over Hamilton's financial plans led to a political division in the nation. Gradually the opposition party emerged.

The Federalists, under the guidance of Hamilton, enjoyed the support of the mer-

30

ITICIZED BY THE ANTI-ADMINISTRATION FORCES

chants, shipowners, bankers and other city folk, while the opposition, led by Jefferson and Madison, drew their partisans mostly from the farming and planting communities.

To bring all anti-Federalists under the same political roof, Jefferson needed allies. In the summer of 1791, he left Philadelphia with his friend James Madison. The two men went north on a fishing and botanizing expedition, but be-

fore they even wet a line, they had a long talk with Aaron Burr, the influential New York politician who knew how to make good use of the benevolent society of the city, the Sons of St. Tammany. What the two Virginians discussed with Hamilton's enemy is not on record, but we can fairly assume it was not fishing. During their journey Jefferson and Madison also visited Governor Clinton, a leader of the New York malcontents. These conversations led to the political alliance between Virginia and New York. (Its pattern—the South and Tammany supporting the Democrats—is familiar this very day.)

When election year approached, Washington declared that he did not seek a second term. He asked Madison to think about "the best mode of announcing the intention" of his retirement and to work on a "valedictory address." Madison urged him to stay; so did Hamilton and Jefferson. "Your being at the helm will be more than an answer to every argument which can be used to alarm and lead the people in any quarter into violence or secession. North and South will hang together if they have you to hang on," wrote Jefferson to him.

Listening to the admonitions of his advisers, Washington reconsidered his decision. There was no doubt that he would be re-elected. He had no opponent; he was trusted and admired; the nation held him sacred. The enemies of the administration, the opponents of Hamilton's fiscal policies, singled out the Vice-President for their attacks. John Adams was an excellent target. He felt slighted in the vice-presidential chair, complaining that the office was not equal to his abilities. "My country," he said, "has in its wisdom contrived for me the most insignificant office that ever the invention of man contrived or his imagination conceived. And as I can do neither good nor evil, I must be borne away by others and meet the common fate."

The opposition accused Adams of being an adherent of monarchy, abused him for the supposed luxury with which he surrounded himself, ridiculed him for his utterance about "the rich, the well-born and the able," and for his unhappy remark that the Constitution was "a promising essay toward a well-regulated government." And in Virginia much was made of his decisive vote as president of the Senate

31

SECOND CONGRESS

OF THE

UNITED STATES:

At the Second Seſſion, begun and held at the City of Philadelphia, in the State of Pennſylvania, on Monday, the fifth of November, one thouſand ſeven hundred and ninety-two.

———————

An ACT providing compenſation to the Preſident and Vice-Preſident of the United States.

BE it enacted by the Senate and Houſe of Repreſentatives of the United States of America, in Congreſs aſſembled. That from and after the third day of March in the preſent year, the compenſation of the Preſident of the United States ſhall be at the rate of twenty five thouſand dollars per annum, with the uſe of the furniture and other effects belonging to the United States, and now in poſſeſſion of the Preſident : And that of the Vice-Preſident, at the rate of five thouſand dollars per annum, in full for their reſpective ſervices, to be paid quarter-yearly, at the Treaſury.

JONATHAN TRUMBULL, *Speaker of the House of Repreſentatives.*

JOHN ADAMS, *Vice-Preſident of the United States, and Preſident of the Senate.*

Approved, eighteenth of February, 1793

Gº: WASHINGTON, *Preſident of the United States.*

A CONTEMPORARY BROADSIDE ANNOUNCES THE SALARIES OF PRESIDENT AND VICE-PRESIDENT

against the ratio of one Representative for every 30,000 inhabitants, thus reducing that state's representation.

But all the accusations did not seem to impress the placid electorate. On election day only one tenth of the people who had formerly cast their votes for members of Congress went to the polls in states where popular elections were held.

Since the first election, Rhode Island and North Carolina had ratified the Constitution, and Vermont and Kentucky had been admitted to the Union, so fifteen states took part in the voting. Electors were appointed by the legislatures in Vermont, Rhode Island, Connecticut, New York, New Jersey, Delaware, South Carolina, Georgia, and Kentucky; by a combination of the legislature and the people in New Hampshire and Massachusetts; by popular vote in Maryland, North Carolina, Pennsylvania, and Virginia.

The electors had not pledged their votes, yet it was well known that each of the 132 would cast his for Washington. But who would be their second choice? The men from New York, Virginia, North Carolina, and Georgia preferred George Clinton and voted for him; altogether Clinton won fifty votes. But John Adams had seventy-seven, and so he remained Vice-President. The political alliance of New York and Virginia was not yet strong enough to challenge the supremacy of the ruling party. The Federalists remained in power, but the rapid growth of the opposition made their more thoughtful leaders apprehensive of the future.

CHARLESTON, Feb. 15

Extract of a letter from St. Eustatia, Jan. 20.

"Yesterday an express schooner, a tender, arrived, having been through the Windward Islands, to stop the sailing of all the ships. We learn that there was a hot press at Antigua, and with the combined powers against France. It is certain, the French navy were never on a better footing, having now 63 ships of the line ready for sea, who are anxious to signalize themselves, as their brave army have been."

Extract of a letter from Gibraltar, to a gentleman in this town, dated January 29th.

"We have still great appearance of an immediate war with France, and that all the powers of Europe will join therein against that unfortunate country, which continues in very great confusion."

NEW-YORK, March 2.

It is whispered, says a Boston paper, that the admirality have put the God, Mars, into actual service. Jupiter himself was commissioned yesterday. These gods are to be attended by their consorts, Juno and Venus, in the quality of smacks or busses. Cerberus, keeper of hell, Charon, the old Stygian boat-man, and Pluto, monarch of the infernals, are ordered to join them at the rendezvous in Portsmouth.

Hector, that trusty old Trojan, is summoned from his grave; Ajax, the gallant Grecian, Romulus, the founder of Rome, and Alexander the Great, are expected to sail in the course of next week.

The Prince of Wales has been have down, and the hold of the Princess Royal has been peeped into by the commissioners...

PITTSBURGH, March 2.

We hear that Col. Ebenezer Sproat, of Marietta, is appointed Adjutant General in the army of the United States. And that Brigadier General Putnam has resigned.

PHILADELPHIA, March 4.

Senate of the United States,
Monday, March 4.

A number of the members of the Senate, being convened, in pursuance of notices sent them from the President of the United States, in the Senate Chamber, the Speaker and Members of the House of Representatives, the secretary of the treasury, the secretary of state, the secretary of war, the attorney-general, the judges of the supreme court, and other officers of government, the foreign ministers, and a number of private citizens, ladies and gentlemen, were also present on the occasion. At twelve o'clock precisely, the President entered the hall. Mr. Langdon, President pro tempore, then rose and said, Sir, one of the judges of the supreme court of the United States is now present, and ready to administer to you the oath required by the constitution, to be taken by the President of the United States. The President on this addressed his "Fellow-citizens" in a short, but comprehensive speech, as follows:—

Fellow-Citizens,

I AM again called upon by the voice of my country, to execute the functions of its chief magistrate. When the occasion proper for it shall arrive, I shall endeavour to express the high sense I entertain of this distinguished honour, and of the confidence which has been reposed in me, by the people of united America. Previous to the execution of any official act of the President, the constitution requires an oath of office. This oath I am now about to take; and in your presence—that if it shall be found, during my administration of the government, I have in any instance violated willingly, or knowingly, the injunction thereof, I may (besides incurring constitutional punishment) be subject to the upbraidings of all, who are now witnesses of the present solemn ceremony.

Judge Cushing read the oath, which the President repeated after him, sentence by sentence, as follows:

I, George Washington, do solemnly swear, that I will faithfully execute the office of President of the United States; and will, to the best of my ability, preserve, protect, and defend the constitution of the United States.

The President then retired, and was saluted by three cheers of the people.

March 5. Captain Carnagie, of the snow Alexander, arrived here last Sunday from Lisbon, in 32 days—as he came out of the Tagus, he met a British Packet going in, the captain of which informed him, that there would be a declaration of war proclaimed by England against France, before he, Capt. Carnagie, should arrive there.—The capt. of the Packet took the Alexander for an English vessel. The opinion however does not correspond with Capt. Carnagie's information, when he left Leeds in England, only 10 days before the day of speaking this Packet; for it was then generally believed, that there would not be any declaration of war, but rather that an accommodation was likely to take place. Captain Carnagie being a very intelligent man, we should presume his information at least as much to be depended on as the British Captain's; and it further corresponds with other accounts of Mr. Pitt carrying on a negociation with the executive council of France.

BALTIMORE, March 6.

Yesterday arrived here from Cadiz, Captain Albert Smith, of the brig Apollo, which place he left the 17th of January.

Captain Smith has favoured us with the following interesting and important advices, viz. That Spain was making great preparations for war against France, which was hourly expected to be declared...

PETERSBURG, March 15.

A gentleman arrived at Pittsburg, and who has been through different parts of the Indian country, gives the following information, which...

HALIFAX, March 27.

Samuel Treadwell, Esq. is appointed Collector of the port of Edenton, vice Thomas Benbury, Esq. dec.

NOT ON THE FRONT PAGE. Washington's inauguration was not considered a very important event in the United States of 1793. The North Carolina *Journal* (above) began its report of the ceremonies on an inside left-hand page.

PRESIDENT'S HOUSE IN WASHINGTON

THE THIRD ELECTION—1796

JOHN ADAMS

"Nothing short of self-respect, and that justice which is essential to a national character, ought to involve us in war," wrote Washington, "for sure I am, if this country is preserved in tranquility twenty years longer, it may bid defiance in a just cause to any power whatever; such in that time will be its population, wealth and resource."

The President and his administration struggled to maintain the peace. It was a hard, tedious, exhausting task. Europe was in a turmoil. In France the Revolution was in full swing; war had been declared on Britain and on Spain.

The United States faced a difficult problem. She had a treaty of alliance with France and a treaty of peace with Britain. How to keep friendship with both allies when they were fighting against each other? What should America do if the British navy interfered with the French trade in the West Indian islands, which the United States had acknowledged in the Treaty of 1778 as a French possession? Declare war on England if that country were to attack the French trade routes?

The repercussions of the French Revolution reached the New World and stirred its people. Many Americans—especially among the farmers, mechanics, and small shopkeepers—saw in the ferment a continuation of their own Revolution, and they wholeheartedly and enthusiastically supported it. Not so the merchants, the bankers, the traders; not so the devoutly religious members of the middle class. They abhorred the upheaval which, in their belief, created only disorder, poverty, and mob rule. And they looked to England as the protector of man's rights and the bulwark and defender of civil liberties.

Thus a further division was caused—another step toward the formation of an opposition party. Citizens who upheld the ideas of the French Revolution rallied behind Jefferson and filled the ranks of the Democratic-Republicans,* opposing the Federalists, most of whom admired England and its political system.

Washington was unfaltering in his efforts to preserve peace. A few weeks after his second inauguration he issued a neutrality proclamation declaring that the United States was "to pursue a conduct friendly and impartial toward the belligerent powers."

* The name of the opposition party has undergone many changes. At first the supporters of Jefferson were called Federal-Republicans, then Democratic-Republicans; later the word "Democratic" was dropped. When Andrew Jackson reorganized the party, his followers began to call themselves Democrats—a name which has remained in use until the present day.

JOHN ADAMS (1735–1826)
PAINTING BY WILLIAM WINSTANLEY

35

JOHN ADAMS (1735-1826) was the Federalists' choice for the presidential office. Because of Hamilton's meddling he almost lost the election, winning it only by three votes.

THOMAS JEFFERSON (1743-1826), the leader of the opposition, became Vice-President. This was the only time that the President and Vice-President were of opposing tickets.

THOMAS PINCKNEY (1750-1828), lawyer, soldier and diplomat, was the Federalist candidate for Vice-President. He received 59 electoral votes but lost the office to Jefferson.

AARON BURR (1756-1836), soldier in the Revolution, lawyer, Senator, and rival of Hamilton, was selected as Jefferson's running mate but won not more than 30 electoral votes.

SAMUEL ADAMS (1722-1803), of Boston Tea Party fame, Revolutionary agitator and Governor of Massachusetts, was given the 15 stray votes of Virginia for the second place.

OLIVER ELLSWORTH (1745-1807), delegate to the Constitutional Convention, first Senator from Connecticut, Chief Justice, won 11 votes from three New England states.

In the same month the neutrality proclamation was issued, Citizen Genêt arrived in America to represent his country. He was greeted with enthusiasm by the Republicans, was wined and dined and cheered, and soon was outfitting ships to prey on British commerce and hiring volunteers to send against Spain. He demanded from Hamilton an advance installment of the United States' debt to France to finance these activities; he issued manifestoes, held meetings at which he spoke against the government, and did his utmost to get America involved in a war. It was not long before Washington and his Cabinet, exasperated by Genêt's activities, asked the French government for his recall.

That America's neutrality policy had greatly displeased the French was easy to understand. The French people had helped the new nation when it had fought for its independence, and they expected some kind of help in return. They had a treaty of alliance with the United States, and now that America stood aloof they felt betrayed. Yet they tried to keep the peace.

Not so the British. Stubborn and arrogant, still smarting over their defeat in the Revolutionary War, with bitter contempt for the new nation, they followed a haughty diplomacy. They refused to evacuate the Northwestern posts, although they had agreed to do so in the Treaty of Paris. They issued an Order in Coun-

THE ELECTORAL VOTE IN THE 1796 ELECTION

STATES	John Adams, Mass.	Thomas Jefferson, Va.	Thomas Pinckney, S. C.	Aaron Burr, N. Y.	Samuel Adams, Mass.	Oliver Ellsworth, Conn.	George Clinton, N. Y.	John Jay, N. Y.	James Iredell, N. C.	George Washington, Va.	Samuel Johnson, N. C.	John Henry, Md.	C. C. Pinckney, S. C.
N. H.	6	—	—	—	—	6	—	—	—	—	—	—	—
Vt.	4	—	4	—	—	—	—	—	—	—	—	—	—
Mass.	16	—	13	—	—	1	—	—	—	—	2	—	—
R. I.	4	—	—	—	—	4	—	—	—	—	—	—	—
Conn.	9	—	4	—	—	—	—	5	—	—	—	—	—
N. Y.	12	—	12	—	—	—	—	—	—	—	—	—	—
N. J.	7	—	7	—	—	—	—	—	—	—	—	—	—
Pa.	1	14	2	13	—	—	—	—	—	—	—	—	—
Del.	3	—	3	—	—	—	—	—	—	—	—	—	—
Md.	7	4	4	3	—	—	—	—	—	—	—	2	—
Va.	1	20	1	1	15	—	3	—	—	1	—	—	—
N. C.	1	11	1	6	—	—	—	—	3	1	—	—	1
S. C.	—	8	8	—	—	—	—	—	—	—	—	—	—
Ga.	—	4	—	—	—	—	4	—	—	—	—	—	—
Ky.	—	4	—	4	—	—	—	—	—	—	—	—	—
Tenn.	—	3	—	3	—	—	—	—	—	—	—	—	—
Electoral vote	71	68	59	30	15	11	7	5	3	2	2	2	1

Sir

I was born Oct' 19. 1735 in Quincy then the North Parish in Braintree, my Father was John Adams born in the same Parish, My Grandfather was Joseph Adams Junior born in the same Parish, My Great Grandfather was Joseph Adams Senior, and my Great great Grandfather was Henry Adams who came from England. These all lived died and were buried in this Parish as their Gravestones in the Congregational Church yard distinctly then to this day My Mother was Suzanna Boylston a Daughter of Peter Boylston of Brokeline I was educated partly at the public Grammar School and partly at a private Accademy under Mr Joseph Marsh, both in this Parish. In 1751 I entered Harvard Colledge in Cambridge. In 1755 took my degree of Batchelor of Arts, and immediately undertook the Care of the Publick Grammar School in Worcester where I lived in the Family and Studied Law in the Office of James Putman, till 1758 when I took my Second Degree at Colledge and the Oath of an Attorney in Boston In 1761 I was admitted a Barrister at Law in Boston in the Superiour Court of Judecature of the Province of Massachusetts Bay. In 1764 I married Abigail Smith, of Weymouth, a Daughter of the Reverend William Smith In 1767 my Son John Quincy Adams was born in this Parish . . . .

In 1755 I took a decided part against France and Great Britain too; thoroughly disgusted with their Folly, the Ignorance, the Cowardice or Treachery of her Conduct of the War against Canada. This Indignation was much increased by her degrading Treatment of our Troops through the whole War.

In 1760 and 1761, upon the first Appearance of the Design of Great Britain to deprive Us of our Liberties by Asserting the Souveraign Athority of Parliament over Us. I took a decided Part against her, and have persevered for Fifty five Years in opposing and resisting to the utmost of my power every Instance of her Injustice, and arbitrary Power, towards Us. I am Sir with much respect

your humble Servant

John Adams

JOHN ADAMS OUTLINES THE STORY OF HIS LIFE IN A FEW TERSE SENTENCES

cil, forbidding ships to trade with France or to carry provisions to the French colonies. They prohibited the loading of French colonial produce, whether in French or in neutral ships. They boarded American boats, taking the vessels' stores and manhandling the sailors.

The new nation was not willing to take these humiliations. Even the most loving admirer of England now realized that war with that country could hardly be avoided. But then the British diplomats, not wanting to be embroiled in hostilities with America while they were fighting the French, revoked the Order in Council. As soon as Washington was advised officially of this move, he sent Chief Justice John Jay to London to negotiate a treaty of peace and commerce between the two countries.

Jay had an admiration for English society and was an easy prey for Lord Grenville. For months he bargained with the British diplomats, and when the treaty was finally signed on November 19, 1794, it seemed that Grenville kept the upper hand. By the terms of the treaty the British were to evacuate the Northwestern posts. All American and British financial claims and the boundary disputes in the Northwest and Northeast were referred to a joint commission; the free navigation of the Mississippi was granted with special privileges for British ships. But about the two main grievances, the impressment of American sailors and the seizures of American vessels, the treaty said nothing.

It was not the best agreement for America, but it achieved what the country needed most—peace, and with it the continuation of English imports, from which Hamilton's treasury received its main tariff revenue.

However, when the American people learned of the treaty's high and mighty tone and of its provisions, their indignation ran high. They looked for a scapegoat—it was Jay. And the word went round that an American negotiator was no match for a foreign diplomat. Since legends grow to tradition, one hears this assertion occasionally even today, some hundred and fifty years after Jay returned from England.

With some amendments the Senate accepted Jay's Treaty by an exact two-thirds majority and not one vote more. Washington signed it because the agreement guaranteed peace when another war with the mother country might have been the end of the young nation. But all over the country John Jay was abused, his effigy burned on a hundred bonfires.

As election was near, the treaty became the main campaign issue. But another domestic incident was not forgotten by the enemies of the administration. It was the so-called "Whisky Rebellion." In 1794 the backwoods farmers in western Pennsylvania refused to pay the excise tax on whisky. Tax collectors were mishandled; therefore, so the Federalists said, the farmers had challenged the authority of the Federal Government. Washington, on the advice of Hamilton, called for 15,000 militia from Virginia, Maryland, and Pennsylvania and sent them against the disobedient taxpayers. However, the "rebellion" collapsed before the troops arrived. But the farmers, appalled by the administration's firm show of power, abused the President and Hamilton and were eager to cast their votes in the next election against the Federalists.

Washington was no longer a demigod. Newspaper writers called him a "tyrant" and a "dictator," an "impostor" who should be "hurled from his throne." The *Aurora* in Philadelphia declared: "If ever a nation was debauched by a man, the American Nation was debauched by Washington." Suffering under such attacks, he refused to accept the nomination for the third time. History books say that he declined it because he was against establishing a precedent. It may be so. But his popularity was at such a low ebb during the concluding years of his second term that this might have influenced his decision.

When it became known that Washington would not serve, the Federalists looked for a successor. Many names were mentioned. At a meeting of Federalist Congressmen and Senators —the first congressional caucus—John Adams was selected for the Presidency and Thomas Pinckney for second place. They were not formally presented as candidates, for the Constitution was still construed right to the letter; it was for the electoral college to make the choice.

The opposition named Thomas Jefferson, with Aaron Burr, who in the meantime had succeeded Governor George Clinton in power and influence, as his running mate.

This was the first election to be contested by

George Washington President
of the United States of America

To all and singular, to whom these
Presents shall come,— Greeting

Whereas a certain Treaty of Amity, Commerce,
and Navigation between the United States of
America and his Britannick Majesty, was
concluded and signed between their Plenipotentiary
the honourable John Jay chief Justice of the United
States, and their Envoy Extraordinary to his said
Majesty, and the Plenipotentiary of his Britannick
Majesty, the Right honourable William Wyndham,
Baron Grenville of Wotton, one of his Majesty's
privy Council, and his Majesty's Secretary of State
for foreign Affairs, at London on the nineteenth
day of November, in the Year of our Lord one
thousand seven hundred and ninety four; which
Treaty is word for word as follows; to wit:
"Treaty

"Treaty of Amity Commerce
and Navigation, between His
Britannick Majesty; and The United
States of America, by their President,
with the advice and consent of their
Senate.

"His Britannick Majesty

"and the United States of America, being desirous
"by a Treaty of Amity, Commerce and Navigation
"to terminate their Differences in such a manner, as
"without reference to the Merits of Their respective
"Complaints and Pretensions, may be the best calculated
"to produce mutual Satisfaction and good understanding;
"And also to regulate the Commerce and Navigation
"between Their respective Countries, Territories and
"People, in such a manner as to render the same
"reciprocally beneficial and satisfactory; They have
"respectively named their Plenipotentiaries, and given
"them full powers to treat of, and conclude the said
"Treaty, that is to say, His Britannick Majesty has
"named for His Plenipotentiary, The Right Honourable
"William Wyndham Baron Grenville of Wotton, One of
"His Majesty's Privy Council, and His Majesty's Principal
"Secretary of State for foreign Affairs; and The
"President of the said United States, by and with
"the advice and consent of the Senate thereof, hath
"appointed

MAIN CAMPAIGN ISSUE was the treaty between the United States and His Britannick Majesty, known as the Jay Treaty. While some of its terms were unfavorable to America, it achieved what the young country needed most—peace.

party candidates. The small farmers and mechanics, the discontented patriots, the antagonists of Hamilton's policies, the sympathizers with the ideas of the French Revolution, and those who protested against the Jay Treaty—all these men voted for Jefferson. The friends of England, the "rich and well-born," the followers of a strong-handed Federal Government—all these were behind the Federalist candidates.

The campaign started late—not beginning until the publication in September of Washington's Farewell Address, which the Republicans branded as a "campaign document." Soon the contest became bitter, newspapers, handbills, stump speakers on both sides violently attacking the candidates.

Oliver Wolcott, who became Secretary of the Treasury after Hamilton's resignation, wrote to a friend: "The extreme scurrility and abuse with which the President has been treated, gives an additional proof of human baseness. Constant reiteration of this kind, suffered to pass with impunity, would lead to debase the character of an angel. As reluctant as I feel at the retirement of the President, I believe upon reflection, it is probable he has chosen the proper time, both for himself and the country. Matters will be brought to a test. If Jefferson shall supply his place, which I trust will not be the case, however plausible his conduct will be, he never will have the northern confidence. Literary abilities and practical knowledge are not frequently conjoined, and he never will be thought to act but under the veil of hypocricy."

Sixteen states took part in the election. Tennessee, having been admitted to the Union, appointed electors through the legislature. North Carolina changed its method and elected by popular vote. In other states the voting procedure remained the same. Thus six states held elections by popular vote, and in ten the appointment of the electors was made by the legislatures.

While the campaign was at its height, the new minister of France, Citizen Adet, created a sensation by trying to influence the voting in favor of the Republican candidates, abusing the Federalist administration in a manifesto, and reproaching the government for violating its treaty with France. Whether his action, widely publicized at the time, really helped Jefferson is doubtful.

After the presidential electors were chosen, Hamilton asked the Federalist electors to give equal support to Adams and Pinckney because "everything must give way to the great object of excluding Jefferson." But Hamilton would not have been disappointed if the electors had cast their votes in such a way that Pinckney received the majority, "since he to every essential qualification for the office added a temper far more discreet and conciliatory than that of Mr. Adams." He told friends that "if chance should decide in favor of Mr. Pinckney, it probably would not be a misfortune."

But Hamilton's plan backfired. It failed to rob Adams of the Presidency, and the split in the Federalist vote made Jefferson Vice-President instead of Pinckney. This was the first and only time in the history of presidential elections that President and Vice-President were chosen from opposing tickets. Adams was deeply hurt; he never forgave Hamilton, "the bastard brat of a Scotch peddler."

There is an interesting report in the *United States Gazette* about a Federalist elector who was sent to the electoral college to cast his vote for John Adams but decided to vote for Jefferson. This caused one worthy citizen to complain bitterly: "What! Do I chuse Samuel Miles to determine for me whether John Adams or Thomas Jefferson shall be President? No! I chuse him to *act*, not to *think*." But even with Samuel Miles's vote against him, John Adams won the election by a slight margin. Seventy-one electors voted for him, and sixty-eight for Jefferson.

As Adams was president of the Senate, when the votes were counted he himself announced that "the whole number of votes are 138; seventy therefore make a majority; so that the person who has seventy-one votes, which is the highest number, is elected President, and the person who has sixty-eight votes, which is the next highest number, is elected Vice-President." Whereupon he sat down for a moment, and silence ruled in the Senate Chamber. When he rose again he proclaimed: "In obedience to the Constitution and laws of the United States, and to the commands of both Houses of Congress, expressed in their resolutions passed in the present session, I declare that John Adams is elected President of the United States for four years, to commence with the fourth day of March next."

On the next morning the Philadelphia *Aurora* stated: "When a retrospect is taken of the Washingtonian Administration for eight years . . . this day ought to be a JUBILEE in the United States, for the man who is the source of all the misfortunes of our country, is this day reduced to a level with his fellow citizens."

And Washington remarked sadly: "I now compare myself to the wearied traveller who seeks a resting place, and is bending his body to lean thereon. But to be suffered to do *this* in peace is too much to be endured by *some*."

John Adams was happy; now President, he felt himself to be manifestly fitted for the office. The inaugural ceremonies impressed him deeply. He reported to his wife, who was not present at the inauguration, that it was "the most affecting and overpowering scene I ever acted in. I was very unwell, had no sleep the night before, and really did not know but I should have fainted in presence of all the world. I was in great doubt whether to say anything or not besides repeating the oath. And now the world is as silent as the grave. All the Federalists seem to be afraid to approve anybody but Washington. The Jacobin papers damn with faint praise, and undermine with misrepresentation and insinuation. If the Federalists go to playing pranks, I will resign the office, and let Jefferson lead them to peace, wealth, and power if he will."

However, it did not come to that.

Dear Sir   Monticello Dec. 28. 1796

The public & the public papers have been much occupied lately in placing us in a point of opposition to each other. I trust with confidence that less of it has been felt by ourselves personally. in the retired canton where I am, I learn little of what is passing: pamphlets I see never; papers but a few, and the fewer the happier. our latest intelligence from Philadelphia at present is of the 16th inst. but tho' at that date your election to the first magistracy seems not to have been known as a fact, yet with me it has never been doubted. I knew it impossible you should lose a vote North of the Delaware, & even if that of Pensylvania should be against you in the mass, yet that you would get enough South of that to place your succession out of danger. I have never one single moment expected a different issue; & tho' I know I shall not be believed, yet it is not the less true that I have never wished it. my neighbors, as my compurgators could aver that fact, because they see my occupations & my attachment to them. indeed it is possible that you may be cheated of your succession by the trick worthy the subtlety of your arch-friend of Newyork, who has been able to make of your real friends tools to defeat their & your just wishes. most probably he will be disappointed as to you, & my inclinations place me out of his reach. I leave to others the sublime delights of riding in the storm, better pleased with sound sleep & a warm birth below, with the society of neighbors, friends & fellow laborers of the earth, than of spies & sycophants. no one then will congratulate you with purer disinterestedness than myself. the share indeed which I may have had

JEFFERSON CONGRATULATES ADAMS AND MAKES SOME SNEERING REMARKS ABOUT HAMILTON

THOMAS JEFFERSON (1743–1826)
PAINTING BY GILBERT STUART

IT IS A LEGEND that Thomas Jefferson rode
to his inaugural and hitched his horse to a post.

THE FOURTH ELECTION—1800

THOMAS JEFFERSON

Stubborn, opinionated, egotistic, quarrelsome,
jealous, distrustful, obstinate—these are only
a few of the adjectives which contemporaries
used when they described John Adams. Jefferson was kinder to him. "He is vain, irritable,
and a bad calculator of the force and probable
effect of the motives which govern men," wrote
he, but "this is all the ill which can possibly be
said of him. He is as disinterested as the being
who made him; he is profound in his views and
accurate in his judgment, except where knowledge of the world is necessary to form a judgment. He is so amiable, that I pronounce you
will love him if ever you become acquainted
with him."

Yet many who became "acquainted" with
"His Rotundity" were far from loving him.
Hamilton disliked him intensely, and Adams
could look in vain for affection among the
members of the Federalist party or of his own
Cabinet. His Secretaries of State, Treasury, and
War—Pickering, Wolcott, and McHenry—
listened rather to Hamilton than to the man
under whom they served.

From the very beginning of his administration Adams had serious political difficulties
with France. During the four years he occupied
the presidential chair, peace with that country
hung by a thread, and the President had to use
all his resourcefulness to avoid war. The relationship between the two countries became
strained when the United States ratified Jay's
Treaty. France regarded this as a violation of
the American-French agreement of 1778 and refused to receive Charles Cotesworth Pinckney
as United States Minister to France. The envoy
was even threatened with arrest if he did not
leave the country. Adams told Congress that the
French government had "treated us neither as
allies, nor as friends, nor as a sovereign state,"
and he proposed to show that "we are not a
degraded people, humiliated under a colonial
spirit of fear."

The President failed to mention why France
was provoked. He did not say that the French
felt deeply hurt because America had accepted
the British view of neutral rights, closed American harbors to French shipping, and stood
aside when Britain captured ships bearing provisions for France. It was because of this that

At your will & pleasure,
We're robbd of our treasure,
Which honesty bids you restore;
But gallic afsurance,
Beyond all endurance,
Insults us by demanding of more.

Leave grinning & shrugging,
We hate your close hugging,
Despise both your smiles & menaces:
First pay what you owe,
Then to H–ll you may go,
Old Nick will return your embraces.

THE FIVE-HEADED DIRECTORY WHICH GOVERNED FRANCE ASKS THE THREE AMERICAN ENV

Talleyrand, the French Foreign Minister, sent three intermediaries (called Mr. X, Mr. Y, and Mr. Z in the dispatches) to negotiate with the American en-

voys. They asked for a bribe, to which Pinckney, one of the envoys, replied: "No, no; not a sixpence!" When negotiations broke off America prepared for

CIVIC FEAST

Americans never
from freedom will sever,
...s, the voice of their mind;
the Monster may roar,
And make his throat sore,
Devil & death stop his wind.

...RY, MARSHALL, AND PINCKNEY—FOR MONEY

...he worst. During John Adams's administration American
...men-of-war had several victorious encounters with
...rench vessels. It was war in everything but name.

France followed the British example and began to retaliate against American commerce. In a short time she took more than three hundred American vessels.

Though the provocations for war were great, Adams was eager to maintain peace. He sent a commission of three men to France to negotiate a settlement. One of them was Elbridge Gerry, a Massachusetts Republican and an ardent friend of France; the other two were C. C. Pinckney, the rejected minister, and John Marshall—both Federalists.

When the envoys arrived in Paris, they were astounded to hear that the French Directory "were exceedingly irritated at some passages of the President's speech" and that "a sum of money was required for the pocket of the Directory and ministers, which would be at the disposal of M. Talleyrand; and that a loan would also be insisted on." In short, the three French intermediaries (to whom the dispatches referred as Mr. X, Mr. Y, and Mr. Z) asked the Americans for a bribe and a loan and told them that if they "acceded to these measures," all differences between the two countries would be solved. Half-deaf Pinckney shouted, "No, no; not a sixpence!"

After the commissioners' dispatches became known, the indignation of the American people knew no bounds. Adams told Congress that the negotiations were a failure and that the country should prepare for the worst. He exclaimed angrily: "I will never send another minister to France without assurances that he will be received, respected, and honored as the representative of a great, free, powerful, and independent nation."

The mood of the country changed overnight. Americans usually rally behind their government in times of danger, without regard to party allegiance. Thousands of men who had fought Adams and the Federalist policies now supported him in a wave of patriotism. Public opinion rose to defiant anger. "Millions for defense, but not one cent for tribute" became the slogan. The nation prepared for war. Congress revoked the treaties with France, voted appropriations for warships, created a Navy Department, revived the Marine Corps, increased the size of the regular army, confirmed Washington's appointment as commander in chief.

(turn to page 48)

45

THE FEDERALISTS TRY TO SILENCE CRITICISM:

He in a trice struck upon his head, enrag'd

THE ALIEN ACT, passed by the Federalists in the summer of 1798, gave the President power to order a dangerous alien out of the country or imprison him.

THE SEDITION ACT was directed against the French and Irish Republican radicals. It made punishable any false or malicious criticism of the Government, President, or Congress. The Republicans, who fought bitterly against these harsh and undemocratic acts, made them the central issue of the campaign.

THE VERMONTER MATTHEW LYON, WHO ONCE I The Federalists hated Matthew Lyon more than any other Republican, as the fiery Irishman, a proud Representative from the state of Vermont, talked and wrote freely against the royal manners of President Adams's

Who seiz'd the tongs to ease his wrongs,
And Griswold thus engag'd, sir.

Congress Hall,
in Philad.ª Feb. 15. 1798.
S. E. Cor. 6.ᵗʰ & Chesnut S.

AWL IN CONGRESS, WAS AMONG THE FIRST TO BE IMPRISONED BECAUSE HE CRITICIZED ADAMS

court. Lyon was the center of excitement in the House of Representatives when, in January, 1798, he had a fracas with the Connecticut Congressman Griswold. The two enemies belabored each other with firetongs and a stick. After the Sedition Act was passed, Lyon was one of the first to be prosecuted under it. He was fined $1,000 and committed to jail for four months. "First martyr under Federal law the junto dared to try on."

47

AARON BURR (1756-1836)   **THOMAS JEFFERSON** (1743-1826)

The Republican candidates were Thomas Jefferson and Aaron Burr. As both received an equal number of electoral votes, the election was thrown into the House of Representatives. There the Federalists tried to make Burr President.

ADAMS (1735-1826)   **PINCKNEY** (1746-1825)

The defeated Federalist candidates: John Adams received 65 electoral votes, Charles Cotesworth Pinckney 64.

Jefferson and his supporters blamed the Federalists for this state of affairs. Had it not been for the Jay Treaty, they said, peace with France would not have been upset and there would not have been any spoliation of American shipping. Nor would there have been an undeclared war on the open seas. The Federalists retorted that it was not the action of the United States which created the struggle; it was the outcome of the French Revolution, which was not only a "disgusting spectacle," but "immorality and plunder," and they predicted the same upheaval in America if in the next election the people should elect a Republican. Timothy Dwight of Yale, carried away in a Fourth of July oration, went so far as to prophesy that if Jefferson and his Republican followers were to succeed, "our wives and daughters . . . would . . . become . . . the victims of legal prostitution, soberly dishonored, speciously polluted." The cleavage between the factions deepened.

With patriotic fervor and war hysteria at a high pitch, the Federalists—longing for revenge on the Republicans—passed the Alien and Sedition Acts. These harsh laws, manifestations of political intolerance and party arrogance, were a bold attempt to check democracy. Their object was not only to stop the radical French influence in America and silence the voice of

THIRTY-FIVE TIMES the House of Representatives balloted for President. Each time the result was the same.
Thomas Jefferson had the support of eight states, Aaron Burr of six states, and two were divided. Before the thirty-
sixth ballot was cast, the Federalists received some assurances from Jefferson's quarter and Jefferson was elected.

foreign-born Republicans, but to wipe out all
criticism of the government.

The Alien Act gave the President the right
to expel from the country or to imprison any
alien who was "dangerous" or "suspect" of "any
treasonable or secret machinations against the
government," while the Sedition Act provided
for fining and imprisoning everyone who wrote
or distributed "any false, scandalous, and malicious writings" against the government of the
United States, or either House of Congress, or
against the President with the intent to "defame
said government and to bring them or either of
them into contempt or disrepute."

The Republicans were outraged. Jefferson
wrote: "I consider those laws as merely an
experiment on the American mind to see how
far it will bear the avowed violation of the Constitution. If this goes down, we shall immediately see attempted another Act of Congress
declaring that the President shall continue in
office during life, reserving to another occasion
the transfer of the succession to his heirs, and
the establishment of the Senate for life."

He and Madison drafted two sets of resolutions condemning the Alien and Sedition laws as
unconstitutional. Jefferson's resolutions were
adopted by the Virginia and Madison's by the
Kentucky legislature. The main thesis of these
resolutions was that whenever Congress over-

stepped its powers, as in the Sedition Act, the individual states had a right to declare "these Acts void and of no force"—the "states'-rights" theory of the Constitution.

During this turmoil of excitement, Adams kept a cool head. He was for peace, even if it should cost him his re-election. When he learned that Talleyrand, the Directory's foreign minister, was willing to receive an American ambassador "with the respect due to the representative of a free and independent nation," he —without consulting his Cabinet—sent the name of William Vans Murray to the Senate for confirmation. Murray was to travel to France immediately.

With the appointment of an American envoy the war bubble burst. Neither Hamilton nor the Federalists in Congress could oppose Adams's move, however much they resented it. They demanded only that the negotiations be conducted by a mission instead of one man. Adams agreed to this and named Oliver Ellsworth and William Richardson Davie to assist Murray. The commissioners reached Paris early in 1800, and for many months they conferred. Not before the last day of September were they able to sign an agreement.

By then the congressional caucuses of the two parties had already met and selected their candidates. The Federalists, secretly convening in the Senate Chamber, nominated John Adams and General Charles Cotesworth Pinckney.

When the Republicans learned of the Federalist caucus, they shouted "Tyranny!"; they called it a "jacobinical conclave," but all their epithets did not restrain them from holding a similar secret caucus and nominating their candidates: Thomas Jefferson and Aaron Burr. The latter, smarting over the result in the last election, when he had received thirty votes against Jefferson's sixty-eight, asked for a written guarantee that this time the Republicans would not withhold their votes from him. "This condition was complied with," noted Oliver Wolcott; "at any rate, an equal vote for Mr. Jefferson and Col. Burr was obtained."

It was a badly split Federalist party which went into the contest. The President had dismissed Pickering, his Secretary of State, and McHenry, his Secretary of War, who were under Hamilton's influence and who had made plans to bar his re-election. In the campaign Pickering and his supporters, called the "Pickeronians," assailed the Federalist Adams just as hard as they fought the Republican Jefferson.

Hamilton, intriguing and maneuvering as always, asked the Governor of New York to call the old legislature, in which the Federalists had a majority, and pass a law by which the people were to choose the electors by district. Through this he hoped to assure victory for the Federalist electors. Governor Jay refused to listen to Hamilton's suggestion, as it would only "serve party purposes, which I think it would not become me to adopt."

Politicians of other states were not so particular in changing their electoral systems. Virginia amended its law and voted on a general ticket, securing the state's twenty-one electoral votes for Jefferson. Massachusetts, where in the latest elections the Republicans had made great gains, changed its system, too, thus securing the state for Adams and Pinckney. In Pennsylvania there was meddling also.

The campaign was violent and vituperative. While President Adams was charged with ruining the country, the Federalist newspapers made much of Jefferson's alleged atheism. The Republicans recounted Hamilton's remark: "If Mr. Pinckney is not elected President, a revolution will be the consequence, and within the next four years I will lose my head or be the leader of a triumphant army!"

THE ELECTORAL VOTE IN THE 1800 ELECTION

STATES	Thomas Jefferson. Va.	Aaron Burr. N.Y.	John Adams. Mass.	C. C. Pinckney. S.C.	John Jay. N.Y.
New Hampshire	—	—	6	6	—
Vermont	—	—	4	4	—
Massachusetts	—	—	16	16	—
Rhode Island	—	—	4	3	1
Connecticut	—	—	9	9	—
New York	12	12	—	—	—
New Jersey	—	—	7	7	—
Pennsylvania	8	8	7	7	—
Delaware	—	—	3	3	—
Maryland*	5	5	5	5	—
Virginia	21	21	—	—	—
North Carolina	8	8	4	4	—
South Carolina	8	8	—	—	—
Georgia	4	4	—	—	—
Kentucky	4	4	—	—	—
Tennessee	3	3	—	—	—
Electoral vote	73	73	65	64	1

* One Maryland elector did not vote.

50

she has a child of very uncertain health. — the election is understood to stand 73.73.65.64. the Federalists were confident at first they could debauch Col°. B. from his good faith by offering him their vote to be President, and have seriously proposed it to him. his conduct has been honorable & decisive, and greatly embarrasses them. time seems to familiarise them more & more to acquiescence, and to render it daily more probable they will yield to the known will of the people, and that some one state will join the eight already decided as to their vote. the victory of the republi-

"THE FEDERALISTS WERE CONFIDENT at first they could debauch Col. B. from his good faith," wrote Jefferson to his daughter in January, 1801. They offered Burr the Presidency, but "his conduct has been honorable and decisive, and greatly embarrasses them." This little-known letter of Jefferson, which he mistakenly dated 1800, is proof enough that Aaron Burr could have become President if he would have played the Federalist game.

Towards the end of the campaign Aaron Burr got hold of a pamphlet which Hamilton had penned against Adams, describing the President's public life from the beginning of the War of Independence to the day when, in a fury, he dismissed the Secretaries of State and War from his Cabinet. Hamilton planned to print this bitter denunciation privately and send copies of it to Federalist electors so that they should withhold their votes from Adams and cast them for Pinckney. But his intrigue backfired. No sooner were the pamphlets on the press than Burr obtained a copy and made its contents public to the newspapers, much to the delight of the Republicans.

Sixteen states took part in the election. In Massachusetts, New Hampshire, and Pennsylvania the popular vote was discarded for the method of appointment by the legislature, while Rhode Island instituted the popular vote.

The Republicans won. Adams was defeated, but Jefferson was not President—yet. As both he and Burr received the same number of votes, it remained for the House of Representatives to make the choice. The manifest defect of the Constitution became apparent.

But the Federalists still nursed hopes that some clever political scheme might turn defeat into victory. One of their plans was to prolong the balloting in the House of Representatives until the fourth of March, and if by that date there was still a deadlock, both the presidential and vice-presidential offices would become va-

cant and a new election would have to be held. What they expected to gain from this is not quite clear. After all, the country had voted Republican, and if a new election were to be held, it would certainly have voted Republican again. But the resentful Federalists were ready to create chaos rather than to see Jefferson President.

Another of their plans was to give their support to Aaron Burr, who was not "infected with all the cold-blooded vices" and seemed less dangerous to them. "Mr. Burr has never yet been charged with writing libelous letters against the government of his country to foreigners, and his politics always have been open and undisguised," wrote the Federalist *Columbian Centinel*. And Gouverneur Morris noted in his diary: "It seems to be the general opinion that Col. Burr will be chosen President."

Hamilton, for all his antagonism toward Jefferson, opposed Burr. He remonstrated with his friends; he used all his powers to persuade them to think *first* of their country and only *then* of the party. He wrote to Gouverneur Morris: "I trust the Federalists will not finally be so mad as to vote for Burr. I speak with an intimate and accurate knowledge of character. His elevation can only promote the purposes of the desperate and profligate. If there be a man in the world I ought to hate, it is Jefferson. With Burr I have always been personally well. But the public good must be paramount to every private consideration."

51

Friends & fellow citizens

Called upon to undertake the duties of the first Executive office of our country I avail myself of the presence of that portion of my fellow citizens which is here assembled to express my grateful thanks for the favor with which they have been pleased to look toward me, to declare a sincere consciousness that the task is above my talents, & that I approach it with those anxious & awful presentiments which the greatness of the charge & the weakness of my powers so justly inspire, a rising nation, spread over a wide & fruitful land, traversing all the seas with the rich productions of their industry, engaged in commerce with nations who feel power & forget right, advancing rapidly to destinies beyond the reach of mortal eye, when I contemplate these transcendent objects, & see the honour, the happiness, & the hopes of this beloved country committed to the issue & the auspices of this day I shrink from the contemplation, & humble myself before the magnitude of the undertaking. utterly indeed should I despair, did not the presence of many, whom I here see, remind me, that in the other high authorities provided by our constitution, I shall find resources of wisdom, of virtue, & of zeal, on which to rely under all difficulties. to you then, gentlemen, who are charged with the sovereign functions of legislation, & to those associated with you, I look with encouragement for that guidance & support which may enable us to steer with safety the vessel in which we are all embarked, amidst the conflicting elements of a troubled world.

During the contest of opinion —"— through which we have past, the animation of discussions & of exertions has sometimes worn an aspect which might impose on strangers unused to think freely, & to speak & to write what they think. but this being now decided by the voice of the nation enounced according to — the rules of the constitution, all will of course arrange themselves under the will of the law, & unite in common efforts for the common good. all too will bear in mind this sacred principle that tho the will of the majority is in all cases to prevail, that will, to be rightful, must be reasonable; that the minority possess their equal rights, which equal laws must protect & to violate would be oppression. let us then fellow citizens unite with one heart & one mind, let us restore to social intercourse that harmony & affection without which liberty, & even life itself, are but dreary things. and let us reflect that having banished from our land that religious intolerance under which mankind so long bled & suffered we have yet gained little if we countenance a political intolerance, as despotic, as wicked & capable

JEFFERSON'S FIRST INAUGURAL ADDRESS COVERED FOUR PAGES IN HIS OWN HANDWRITING

Despite Hamilton's advice, a number of Federalists went on supporting Burr. They reputedly promised him their vote if he would continue the Federalist policy. "The means have existed," wrote the Federalist wirepuller James Bayard, "of electing Burr, but this required his co-operation. By deceiving one man (a great blockhead) and tempting two (not incorrupti-

as bitter & bloody persecutions. during the throes & convulsions of the antient world, during the agonising spasms of infuriated man, seeking thro' blood & slaughter his long-lost liberty, it was not wonderful that the agitation of the billows should reach even this distant & peaceful shore; that this should be more felt & feared by some & less by others; & should divide opinions as to measures of safety. but every difference of opinion, is not a difference of principle. we have called by different names brethren of the same principle. we are all republicans: we are all federalists. if there be any among us who would wish to dissolve this Union or to change it's republican form, let them stand undisturbed as monuments of the safety with which error of opinion may be tolerated, where reason is left free to combat it: I know indeed that some honest men fear that a republican government cannot be strong that this government is not strong enough but would the honest patriot in the full tide of successful experiment abandon a government which has so far kept us free and firm, on the theoretic & visionary fear, that this government, the world's best hope, may, by possibility, want energy to preserve itself? I trust not. I believe this, on the contrary the strongest government on earth. I believe it the only one, where every man, at the call of the law, would fly to the standard of the law and would meet invasions of their public order as his own personal concern. some times it is said that man cannot be trusted with the government of himself. can he then be trusted with the government of others? or have we found angels in the form of kings, to govern him? let history answer this question.

Let us then, with courage & confidence, pursue our own federal & republican principles; our attachment to these monuments preserved. kindly separated by nature & a wide ocean from the exterminat -ing havoc of one quarter of the globe; too high-minded to endure the degradations of the others possessing a chosen country, with room enough for our descendants to the thousandth & thou - -sandth generation, enjoying the most favourable temperatures of climate, entertaining a due sense of our equal right to the use of our own faculties, to the acquisitions of our own indus try, to honour & confidence from our fellow citizens, resulting not from birth, but from our action & their sense of them, enlightened by a benign religion, professed indeed & practised in various forms, yet all of them inculcating honesty, truth, temperance, gratitude & the love of man, acknoleges and adoring an overruling providence, which by all it's dispensations proves that it delights in the happiness of man here, & his greater happiness hereafter; with all these blessings, what more is

"WE ARE ALL REPUBLICANS; WE ARE ALL FEDERALISTS," SAID JEFFERSON IN HIS INAUGURAL

ble), he might have secured a majority of the States." But Aaron Burr, the "trickster," the "charlatan," and the "impostor" of history books, would not be a party to this. Had he agreed, he would have become the country's next President instead of Jefferson.

On the day the House of Representatives assembled in the nation's new capital, the whole

necessary to make us a happy & a prosperous people? still one thing more fellow citizens.
a wise & frugal government which shall restrain men from injuring one another, shall leave
them otherwise free to regulate their own pursuits of industry & improvement, & shall not take from
the mouth of labor, the bread it has earnd. this is the sum of good government, & this is
necessary to close the circle of our felicities.

About to enter, fellow citizens, on the exercise of duties which comprehend every
thing dear & valuable to you, it is proper you should understand what I deem the essential
principles of our government, & consequently those which ought to shape it's administration.
I will compress them within the narrowest compass they will bear, stating the general principle,
but not all it's limitations. — Equal & exact justice to all men, of whatever state or persuasion
religious or political: — Peace, commerce & honest friendship with all nations, entangling alliances
with none: — the support of the state governments in all their rights, as the
most competent administrations for our domestic concerns & the surest bulwarks against
anti-republican tendencies: — the preservation of the General government in it's whole constitutional vigour as the sheet anchor of our peace at home, & safety abroad: — free & frequent elections by the people, a mild and safe corrective of abuses which are
lopped by the sword of revolution where peaceable remedies are unprovided: —
— absolute acquiescence in the decisions of the majority, the vital principle of republics, from
which is no appeal but to force the vital principle & immediate parent of despotism: — a well
disciplined militia our best reliance in peace & for the first moments of war till regulars may
relieve them; — the supremacy of the civil over the military authority. — economy in the public expence that labor may be lightly burthend
and sacred preservation of the public faith.
the honest paiment of our debts; — encouragement of agriculture: and of Commerce as
it's handmaid. — the diffusion of information, & arraignment of all abuses at the bar of the
public reason: — freedom of religion; freedom of the press; & freedom of person, under the
protection of the Habeas corpus: — and trial by juries, impartially selected.
these principles form the bright constellation, which has gone before us & guided our steps through
an age of revolution & reformation. the wisdom of our sages & blood of our heroes have been
devoted to their attainment: they should be the creed of our political faith; the text of civic
instruction the touchstone by which to try the services of those we trust and should we wander
from them in moments of error or of alarm, let us hasten to retrace our steps & to regain the road which
alone leads to Peace, liberty & safety.

THE THIRD PAGE OF JEFFERSON'S INAUGURAL. There he wrote: "Equal and exact justice to all men,
whatever state or persuasion, religious or political; peace, commerce, and honest friendship with all nations,
entangling alliances with none . . . the preservation of the General Government in its whole constitutional vigor,
as the sheet anchor of our peace at home and safety abroad; a jealous care of the right of election by the people

54

I repair then, fellow citizens, to the post you have assigned me. with experience enough in subordinate offices to have seen the difficulties of this the greatest of all, I have learnt to expect that it will rarely fall to the lot of imperfect man to retire from this station with the reputation, & the favor which bring him into it. without pretensions to that high confidence you reposed in our first, and greatest revolutionary character ~~whose~~ ~~~~ whose preeminent services had entitled him to the first place in his country's love, ____ and destined for him the fairest page in the volume of faithful history, I ask so much confidence only as may give firmness & effect to the legal administration of your affairs. I shall often go wrong through defect of judgment. when right, I shall often be thought wrong by those whose positions will not command a view of the whole ground. I ask your indulgence for my own errors, which will never be intentional; and your support against the errors of others who may condemn what they would not, if seen in all it's parts. the approbation im -plied by your suffrage is a great consolation to me for the past; and my future solici- -tude will be to retain the good opinion of those who have bestowed it in advance, to conciliate that of others by doing them all the good in my power, and to be instrumental to the happiness & freedom of all.

Relying then on the patronage of your good will, I advance with obedience to the work ready to retire from it whenever you become sensible how much better choices it is in your power to make. and may that infinite power which rules the destinies of the universe, lead our councils to what is best, & give them a favorable issue for your peace and prosperity.

THE CONCLUDING FOURTH PAGE OF JEFFERSON'S MEMORABLE FIRST INAUGURAL ADDRESS

country looked anxiously to Washington. Men by the hundreds journeyed there, filling the boardinghouses and hotels. In one hostelry fifty people slept upon the floor with no beds but blankets and no coverings but their coats.

The counting of the electoral votes took place on February 11th. Jefferson, the presiding officer of the Senate, announced to the assembled Representatives and Senators that "no election had taken place" and it was therefore for the House of Representatives to choose the next President. After this the Representatives returned to their own hall. The galleries were cleared, the doors closed, and the voting began.

The House voted by states, each state ballot being determined by the majority of its delegates. In case of an evenly divided vote, the state was recorded blank. On the first ballot eight states were for Jefferson (New York, New Jersey, Pennsylvania, Virginia, North Carolina, Georgia, Kentucky, and Tennessee), six for Burr (New Hampshire, Massachusetts, Rhode Island, Connecticut, Delaware, and South Carolina), and two were divided (Vermont and Maryland). However, nine were necessary for a choice and so the voting had to proceed. A second ballot was taken with the same result. Every hour the Representatives had to cast their votes until "it shall appear that a President is duely chosen." At midnight the nineteenth ballot was taken. No change. Tired Congressmen sent out for their nightcaps; some of them slept in their seats, propped up with pillows, others snored on the floor; a sick man lay on his bed in the adjacent committee room. At two in the morning it was decided not to vote until four. At eight in the morning a motion was made to hold the next ballot at noon. When the ballot was taken the result was the same. Now the House adjourned till the next day. The Representatives voted—no change. Another adjournment till next day, when three ballots were taken. Again the same result.

The Federalist Bayard did his utmost to break the deadlock and tried to make a bargain with the Republicans. He intimated that "if certain points of the future administration could be understood and arranged with Mr. Jefferson . . . three States would withdraw from any opposition to his election." The "certain points" the Federalists referred to were the public credit, the maintenance of the navy, and an assurance that the small Federalist officeholders would not be turned out. It seemed that Jefferson made some kind of promise about these, whereupon Bayard, shortly before the thirty-sixth ballot, "came out with the most explicit and determined declaration of voting for Jefferson." The Federalist electors of Vermont, Delaware, and Maryland withheld their votes; thus Vermont and Maryland, where the votes were evenly divided before, went to Jefferson and in Delaware there was no vote at all. Jefferson now had the majority and was elected.

The inauguration ceremonies were simple. It is a legend that Jefferson rode on horseback to the inaugural and that he hitched his horse to a fence post. But it is true that he walked to the Capitol from his boardinghouse dressed in his everyday suit, surrounded by his followers and a group of drum-beating and flag-bearing militia. Aaron Burr, who earlier in the morning had taken the oath of office to preside over the Senate, received him and led him to the chamber where John Marshall, the recently appointed Federalist Chief Justice, administered the oath.

John Adams was not present at the inaugural ceremonies. He had sat up late the previous night, signing the commission papers of the newly named judges. He did not have much sleep. Early in the morning he left the muddy, swampy village of Washington and drove back to his home in Massachusetts.

With him passed the Federalist regime.

Monumental Inscription.

" That life is long which answers Life's great end."

YESTERDAY EXPIRED,
Deeply regretted by MILLIONS of grateful Americans
And by all GOOD MEN,
The FEDERAL ADMINISTRATION
Of the
GOVERNMENT of the United States :
Animated by
A WASHINGTON, an ADAMS ;—a
HAMILTON, KNOX, PICKERING, WOLCOTT, M'HENRY, MARSHALL,
STODDERT and DEXTER.
Æt. 12 years.

Its death was occasioned by the
Secret Arts, and Open Violence,
Of Foreign and Domestic Demagogues:
Notwithstanding its whole Life
Was devoted to the Performance of every Duty
to promote
The UNION, CREDIT, PEACE, PROSPERITY, HONOR, and
FELICITY OF ITS COUNTRY.

At its birth it found
The Union of the States dissolving like a Rope of sand
It hath left it
Stronger than the Threefold cord.

It found the United States
Bankrupts in Estate and Reputation ;
It hath left them
Unbounded in Credit ; and respected through
the World.
It found the Treasuries of the United States and
Individual States empty ;
It hath left them full and overflowing.
It found
All the Evidences of Public Debts worthless as rags
It hath left them
More valuable than Gold and Silver.

It found
The United States at war with the
Indian Nations ;—
It hath concluded Peace with them all.
It found
The Aboriginals of the soil inveterate
enemies of the whites ;
It hath exercised towards them justice and generosity
And hath left them fast friends.

THE DAY THOMAS JEFFERSON WAS INAUGURATED

It found
Great-Britain in possession of all
the *Frontier Posts* ;
hath demanded their surrender, and
it leaves them in the possession
of the United States.
It found
American sea-coast utterly *defenseless* ;
It hath left it *fortified.*
nd our *Arsenals* empty ; and *Magazines*
decaying ;
It hath left them full of *ammunition*
and *warlike Implements.*
d our country dependent on Foreign Nations
for *engines of defense* ;
It hath left
Manufactories of *Cannon* and *Musquets*
in full work.
It found
The American Nation at *War* with
Algiers, Tunis, and *Tripoli* ;
It hath
Made *Peace* with them all.
It found
rican Freemen in Turkish slavery, where
they had languished in chains for years ;
It hath
Ransomed them, and set them free.

———

found the war-worn, invalid *Soldier*
starving from want ;
, like BELISARIUS, *begging his refuse*
meat from door to door ;
It hath left
Ample provision for the regular
payment of his *pension.*

———

It found
he *Commerce* of our country confined
almost to *Coasting Craft* ;
It hath left it
ening every sea with its canvass, and
cheering every clime with its *stars.*

———

It found our
Mechanics and *Manufacturers* idle in
the streets for want of employ ;
It hath left them
of business, prosperous, contented
and happy.
It found
eomanry of *the country* oppressed with
qual taxes ;—their farms, houses and barns
decaying ; their cattle selling at the
sign-posts ; and they driven to
desperation and *Rebellion* ;
It hath left

Their coffers in cash ; their houses in repair ;
their barns full ; their farms overstocked ; and
their produce commanding ready money,
and a high price.
In short—
It found them *poor, indigent Malcontents* ;
It hath left them
Wealthy Friends to Order and good Government.

It found
The United States *deeply in debt to*
France and *Holland* ;
It hath *paid* ALL *the demands* of the former, and
the principal part of the latter.
It found the Country in a ruinous
Alliance with *France* ;
It hath honorably dissolved the connexion,
and set us free.

It found
The United States without a swivel
on float *for their defense* ;
It hath left
A NAVY—composed of Thirty-four ships of
war ; mounting 918 guns ; and manned
by 7350 gallant tars.

It found
The EXPORTS of our country, a mere song, in
value ;
It hath left them worth
Above SEVENTY MILLIONS of Dollars per annum.
In one word,
It found AMERICA *disunited, poor, insolvent,*
weak, discontented, and *wretched.*
It hath left HER
United, wealthy, respectable, strong,
happy and *prosperous.*
Let the faithful Historian, in after times,
say these things of its Successor, if it can.
And yet—notwithstanding all these services a d
blessings there are found
Many, very many, weak, degenerate Sons,
who lost to virtue, to gratitude,
and patriotism,
Open exult, that this Administration
is no more.
And that
The " Sun of Federalism is set for ever."
" *Oh shame where is thy blush ?*"

As one Tribute of Gratitude in these Times,
This MONUMENT
Of the Talents and Services of the deceased ;
is raised by

March 4th, 1801. ——— **The Centinel.**

EDERALIST *CENTINEL* PRAISED THE ACHIEVEMENTS OF THE OUTGOING ADMINISTRATION

A CRUDE POLITICAL CARTOON OF 1803

THE FIFTH ELECTION—1804

THOMAS JEFFERSON

Jefferson liked to think of his election as the "Revolution of 1800." With him in power, the people had no longer to fear monarchy and militarism; they could return to republican simplicity. This was a somewhat exaggerated notion. There was never any real danger of monarchy and very little of militarism in America. And the Revolution of 1800 was not so much a revolution as a realization of the masses that the well-to-do were not born to rule them. The Federalists, failing to recognize that the foundation of American life was democracy, were voted out of office.

The new President was an outstanding organizer and he was mindful of public opinion. Under his administration most of the Federalist legislation disappeared from the statute books. When the term of the hated Alien and Sedition Acts expired, they were not renewed. The judiciary and taxing systems were revised. Agriculture was encouraged, land settlement and Western migration furthered, a liberal naturalization law introduced, and a successful attempt was made to reduce governmental expenses and pay off the national debt. But the outstanding feat of his administration, an event which made Jefferson's re-election a certainty, was the Louisiana Purchase.

As the time approached, many proposals were put forth for altering the mode of election. The stalemate in 1800, when Jefferson and Burr received the same number of votes, and subsequent intrigues behind the scenes and in the House of Representatives made a change of the election system a necessity.

The method suggested for changing the mode of election was the obvious one. Instead of voting for two men, as the Constitution decreed—the one with the majority of all electoral votes becoming President, and the one with the next highest number Vice-President—the electoral college was to vote separately henceforth for President and Vice-President.

The law which Congress finally passed became the Twelfth Amendment to the Constitution. It said that in the future "The electors shall meet in their respective States and vote by ballot for President and Vice-President, one of whom, at least, shall not be an inhabitant of the same States with themselves; they shall name in their ballots the persons voted for as President, and, in distinct ballots, the persons voted for as Vice-President, and they shall make distinct lists of all persons voted for as President, and of all persons voted for as Vice-President, and of the number of votes for each; which lists

THOMAS JEFFERSON (1743-1826)
PAINTING BY REMBRANDT PEALE

59

THE CANDIDATES

THOMAS JEFFERSON
(1743-1826) was very popular in his first term. The U.S. was prosperous, taxes were repealed, the Territory of Louisiana acquired. His re-election was sure, and he received the votes of all states except Connecticut and Delaware, and 2 votes from Maryland.

GEORGE CLINTON
(1739-1812) was Jefferson's running mate. Burr, Vice-President in the first administration, had already fought his fatal duel with Hamilton. Clinton, whose alliance with Jefferson was the beginning of the Democratic party, received 162 electoral votes.

C. C. PINCKNEY
(1746-1825), Federalist general, a negotiator in France during Adams's administration who told the French that America would not give them a "sixpence," was the Federalists' choice for the Presidency. He had little chance of winning the election and received only 14 electoral votes.

RUFUS KING
(1755-1827) was the Federalist candidate for Vice-President. As Senator from New York, he supported Hamilton's financial measures, became director of the Bank of the United States. In 1796 he succeeded Thomas Pinckney as Minister to Great Britain, came home in 1803.

they shall sign and certify, and transmit sealed to the seat of government of the United States, directed to the President of the Senate. The President of the Senate shall, in the presence of the Senate and House of Representatives, open all the certificates, and the votes shall then be counted; the person having the greatest number of votes for President shall be the President, if such number be a majority of the whole number of electors appointed; and if no person have such majority, then from the persons having the highest numbers, not exceeding three on the list of those voted for as President, the House of Representatives shall choose immediately, by ballot, the President. But in choosing the President the vote shall be taken by States, the representation from each State having one vote. A quorum for this purpose shall consist of a member or members from two thirds of the States, and a majority of all the States shall be necessary to a choice. And if the House of Representatives shall not choose a President, whenever the right of choice shall devolve upon them, before the fourth day of March next following, then the Vice-President shall act as President, as in the case of the death or other constitutional disability of the President.

"The person having the greatest number of votes as Vice-President shall be Vice-President, if such number be a majority of the whole number of electors appointed; and if no person

THE ELECTORAL VOTE IN THE 1804 ELECTION

STATES	PRESIDENT		VICE-PRESIDENT	
	T. Jefferson. Va.	C. C. Pinckney. S. C.	George Clinton. N. Y.	Rufus King. N. Y.
New Hampshire	7	—	7	—
Vermont	6	—	6	—
Massachusetts	19	—	19	—
Rhode Island	4	—	4	—
Connecticut	—	9	—	9
New York	19	—	19	—
New Jersey	8	—	8	—
Pennsylvania	20	—	20	—
Delaware	—	3	—	3
Maryland	9	2	9	2
Virginia	24	—	24	—
North Carolina	14	—	14	—
South Carolina	10	—	10	—
Georgia	6	—	6	—
Kentucky	8	—	8	—
Tennessee	5	—	5	—
Ohio	3	—	3	—
Electoral vote	162	14	162	14

LOOK ON THIS PICTURE,   AND ON THIS.

See what a grace was seated on this brow:
An eye like Mars to threaten and command,
A combination, and a form, indeed,
Where every God did seem to set his seal,
To give the world assurance of a man.

THIS WAS____   New-York, June, 1807.

HERE IS____

_____ like a mildewd ear.
Blasting his wholesome brother.____

Vide Hamlet.

IN A POLITICAL CARTOON against Jefferson, Washington represents Order, Law and Religion, while Jefferson stands for Sophism, Tom Paine, Condorcet and Voltaire. He is "like a mildewed ear, blasting his wholesome brother."

have a majority, then from the two highest numbers on the list the Senate shall choose the Vice-President; a quorum for the purpose shall consist of two thirds of the whole number of Senators, and a majority of the whole number shall be necessary to a choice. But no person constitutionally ineligible to the office of President shall be eligible to that of Vice-President of the United States."

As there was very little time for the states to ratify the amendment before the next election—Congress did not pass it until December 8, 1803—a special act was introduced, prescribing that the voting for President and Vice-President should be held separately in 1804. As

it happened, the special act was not needed, for the amendment was ratified quickly, with thirteen states voting for it and only three (Massachusetts, Connecticut, and Delaware) against it.

With the Twelfth Amendment before the states, the Republicans prepared for the election. The congressional caucus for the selection of the candidates was no longer a matter of secrecy. It was held openly, properly discussed and advertised. There was little feeling about it at the time, and whether the caucus was constitutional or not evoked hardly any discussion. On February 25, 1804, one hundred and eight members of the two Houses assembled in a meet-

61

Sir.

The late President, mr Adams, having not long before his retirement from office, made several appointments to civil offices holden during the will of the President, when so restricted in time as not to admit sufficient enquiry & consideration; the present President deems it proper that those appointments should be a subject of reconsideration & further enquiry. he considers it as of palpable justice that the officers who are to begin their course as agents of his administration should be persons on whom he has personal reliance for a faithful execution of his views. you will therefore be pleased to consider the appointment you have received as if never made, of which this early notice is given to prevent any derangements which that appointment might produce.

DRAFT BY JEFFERSON NULLIFYING APPOINTMENTS OF THE OUTGOING ADAMS ADMINISTRATION

ing and nominated Thomas Jefferson for the Presidency and George Clinton of New York for the Vice-Presidency.

The Federalists, with little hope for success, did not make formal nominations, but recommended Charles Cotesworth Pinckney for President and Rufus King for Vice-President. They hardly put up a fight; they were resigned that Jefferson would carry the election. Business was good, the President extremely popular, his measures approved in all sections of the country. As John Randolph recorded: "Never was there an administration more brilliant than that of Mr. Jefferson up to this period. Taxes repealed; the public debt amply provided for . . . sinecures abolished; Louisiana acquired; public confidence unbounded."

Only in the New England states did the Federalists conduct a spirited campaign. In Massachusetts, where clergy and press were strongly for Federalist principles, the fight was especially bitter. In the newspapers Jefferson was assailed as being more interested in the achieve-

ments of the French Revolution than in the welfare of the United States, and accused of ruining the army and navy, corrupting the judiciary and squandering the nation's money—allegations which have recurred with great regularity every four years since then.

The leading Federalist newspaper of Jefferson's day stated that "The President has openly declared that honor, integrity, and a love of the Constitution are not yet qualifications for office. During his administration justice has been amended in favor of wicked and abundant violators of the laws of their country; men, destitute of principle and marked only for violence, have consequently obtained the first offices of government . . . The doors of Congress have been shut, or silence adopted for arguments to conceal from the people a knowledge of the transactions of their most important concerns. The internal taxes, imposed on luxuries, have been repealed, that the southern nabobs and whiskey patriots may enjoy their pleasures without contributing to the support

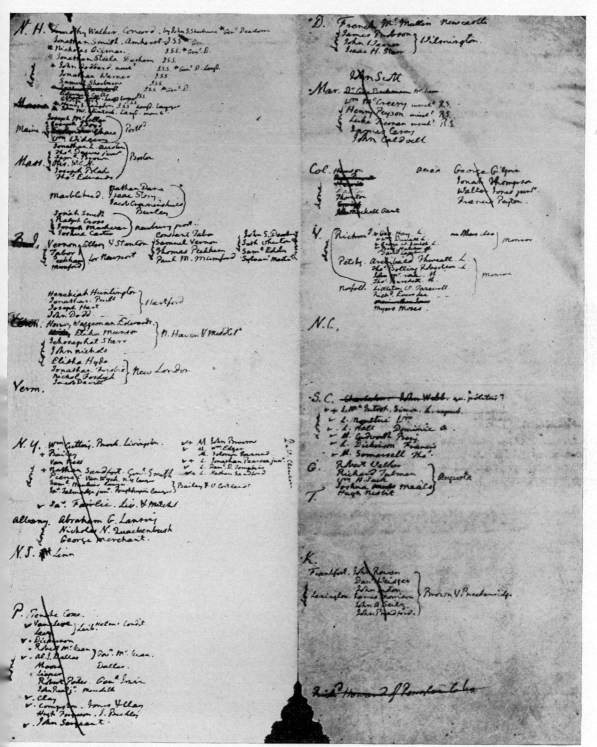

JEFFERSON'S APPOINTMENT LISTS, noting names of persons from every state who were helpful in the election. These trustworthy Republicans were given jobs, replacing Federalist officeholders. This hitherto unpublished manuscript shows that the spoils system was in operation in a limited sense long before Andrew Jackson.

Dec. 8. 1801.

Sir.

The circumstances under which we find ourselves at this place rendering inconvenient the mode heretofore practised, of making, by personal address the first communications between the legislative and Executive branches, I have adopted that by Message, as used on all subsequent occasions through the session. in doing this I have had principal regard to the convenience of the legislature, to the economy of their time, to their relief from the embarrassment of immediate answers, on subjects not yet fully before them, and to the benefits thence resulting to the public affairs. trusting that a procedure, founded in these motives, will meet their approbation, I beg leave through you, Sir, to communicate the inclosed message, with the documents accompanying it, to the honorable the Senate, and pray you to accept, for yourself and them the homage of my high respect and consideration. —

Th: Jefferson

THE BEGINNING OF A TRADITION. Jefferson sent this letter to the president of the Senate with his first message, saying that he found "inconvenient the mode heretofore practiced" of addressing the Legislature in person. Following his example, no President ever appeared before Congress until Wilson broke the tradition in 1913.

of government . . . Foreigners have been allured to ill-fated America in expectation of carrying on their nefarious projects with impunity."

According to this article in the *Columbian Centinel*, signed by "Hume," there was nothing worthy in Jefferson's administration. But its worst measure was "the purchase of a wilderness [of Louisiana] for fifteen millions of dollars which probably might have been acquired much more cheaply. Over this territory has Mr. Jefferson been constituted absolute monarch, clothed with a patronage, which may ultimately be death to national liberty."

Boston's other partisan newspaper, the *Independent Chronicle*, upheld Jefferson: "We know what Jefferson has done, but what a new administration may do under the guidance of a faction is uncertain. Never leave a certainty for an uncertainty." It would seem that this sentiment, too, has been borrowed and used in some of the later American presidential campaigns.

In the election seventeen states voted, Ohio having been admitted to the Union on February 19, 1803. According to a new apportionment, made after the census of 1800, the number of Representatives had increased from 106 to 142, of presidential electors from 138 to 176.

As was expected, Jefferson and Clinton won by a large majority. Backed by all states but two, they received 162 electoral votes, while the Federalists Pinckney and King got only fourteen. It was a clear endorsement of the Jeffersonian policies.

A FEDERALIST CARTOON against Jefferson, who is shown attempting to pull down the Federal Government of Washington and Adams. He is helped by the devil and fortified by a bottle of brandy.

PRESIDENT'S HOUSE IN WASHINGTON

THE SIXTH ELECTION—1808

JAMES MADISON

Under Jefferson's administration diplomatic relations with England went from bad to worse. The commercial agreements of the Jay Treaty remained valid only until 1807; the protection of American interests after that date was one of the main worries of the President and his Cabinet. The British, now at the height of their war with France, were not very particular about neutral rights. They searched American ships, impressed the seamen into their service, and seized the cargoes.

Congress, trying to safeguard American commerce, voted for the Nicholson Nonimportation Act in 1806, forbidding the import of all goods from Britain which the United States could manufacture at home or buy elsewhere. William Pinkney of Maryland journeyed to London with the act to assist James Monroe in his negotiations. The two envoys told the British diplomats that if Britain would sign a treaty, the Nonimportation Act would never be enforced against them.

While these talks were in progress, Napoleon issued his Berlin Decree, forbidding ships to carry goods to Britain. It was first-rate propaganda. The "blockade" seemed frightening on paper, though the French navy would never have been in a position to enforce it on the seas.

The British negotiators, willing to come to some agreement but bargaining till the end, told Monroe and Pinkney that the United States must disobey the decree, otherwise Great Britain would not sign the proposed pact.

As an answer to Napoleon's decree, Britain issued a series of Orders in Council forbidding world trade with France and blockading that country from the Elbe westward to Brest.

Now American vessels became the prey of both the British and the French, who seized and searched the ships, confiscated the goods, and impressed the seamen. When the British man-of-war *Leopard* attacked the American frigate *Chesapeake* in June, 1807, killing three sailors, wounding eighteen, and impressing four, the temper of America reached the boiling point. The country cried for retaliation.

Jefferson, struggling to keep the peace, issued a proclamation barring British warships from American ports and forbidding all British vessels to sail in American waters. He demanded reparations for damage and punishment of the English commander. "We have borne patiently a great deal of wrong," the President wrote, "on the consideration that if nations go to war for every degree of injury, there would never be peace on earth."

JAMES MADISON (1751-1836)
PAINTING BY GILBERT STUART

THE CANDIDATES

JAMES MADISON
(1751-1836) was chosen by Jefferson to succeed him. The caucus of Republican Congressmen made a "recommendation" to the electors to vote for Madison, whose candidacy was opposed by a section of his own party. However, he was elected with 122 electoral votes.

GEORGE CLINTON
(1739-1812), who failed to win support of the Federalists for the presidential nomination, became the candidate of the Republicans for the Vice-Presidency. Clinton, who died in office near the end of his term, showed hostility for Madison, whom he much disliked.

C. C. PINCKNEY
(1746-1825) was again the Federalist candidate for President. He had not much chance of winning the election, but did better than four years before, when as candidate against Thomas Jefferson, he received only 14 votes. In this election 47 electoral votes were cast for him.

RUFUS KING
(1755-1827) was Charles C. Pinckney's running mate, just as he had been in the previous election. This time the whole of New England, except for the state of Vermont, voted for the two Federalist candidates, who made it known that they were strongly opposed to a war with Great Britain.

Congress now voted the Embargo Act, closing American ports to foreign ships and barring the departure of all vessels from the United States. It was hoped that this measure might induce France and Britain to rescind their decrees.

But the decrees were not revoked, and trade with Europe came to a standstill. American shipowners and merchants had to endure great losses; shipbuilders closed down their yards; sailors loafed on land; the country's economy was disrupted. Smuggling flourished, regardless of the embargo. Jefferson was under constant attacks. An anonymous letter writer told him: "We are the shipping interest and we will take care that it shall not be destroyed by your attachment to France, your implacable enmity to G[reat] B[ritain], and in short, by your madness & folly." Another wrote: "You Infernal Villain. How much longer are you going to keep this damned Embargo on to starve us poor people?" Songs like this were popular:

"Oh, dear, what can the matter be?
Dear, dear, what can the matter be?
Oh, dear, what can the matter be?
The Embargo's so long coming off.
It promised to make great Bonaparte humble,
It promised John Bull from his woolsack to tumble,
And not to leave either a mouthful to mumble
At our nod to make their caps doff."

THE ELECTORAL VOTE IN THE 1808 ELECTION

STATES	PRESIDENT			VICE-PRESIDENT				
	James Madison, Va.	George Clinton, N.Y.	C. C. Pinckney, S.C.	G. Clinton, N.Y.	J. Madison, Va.	J. Langdon, N.H.	J. Monroe, Va.	Rufus King, N.Y.
New Hampshire	—	—	7	—	—	—	—	7
Vermont	6	—	—	—	—	6	—	—
Massachusetts	—	—	19	—	—	—	—	19
Rhode Island	—	—	4	—	—	—	—	4
Connecticut	—	—	9	—	—	—	—	9
New York	13	6	—	13	3	—	3	—
New Jersey	8	—	—	8	—	—	—	—
Pennsylvania	20	—	—	20	—	—	—	—
Delaware	—	—	3	—	—	—	—	3
Maryland	9	—	2	9	—	—	—	2
Virginia	24	—	—	24	—	—	—	—
North Carolina	11	—	3	11	—	—	—	3
South Carolina	10	—	—	10	—	—	—	—
Georgia	6	—	—	6	—	—	—	—
Kentucky*	7	—	—	7	—	—	—	—
Tennessee	5	—	—	5	—	—	—	—
Ohio	3	—	—	—	—	3	—	—
Electoral vote	122	6	47	113	3	9	3	47

* One Kentucky elector did not vote.

SMUGGLING WAS RAMPANT along the seacoast while the embargo was in force. The snapping turtle, or terrapin, was the artist's symbol of oppression. The smuggler's exclamation "Ograbme" is the word "embargo" read backward.

And after the poet had again asked what the matter could be, he came to the conclusion:

"The Embargo don't answer its end.
The PEOPLE are left in the dark yet to stumble
Their patience worn out, no wonder they grumble,
While daily they see their prosperity crumble,
And no hope their condition to mend."

The Federalists were quick to realize that by attacking the embargo policy of the Jefferson administration, they had a ready-made campaign issue on hand.

The question was whether Jefferson would run for a third term. To James Turner, a Senator from North Carolina who tried to influence him, he replied that "Genl Washington had established a precedent of standing only for two elections . . . that it was a precedent which he thot was obligatory upon himself—and from

which he could not depart, and to prove the sincerity of his profession of rotation in office, will be, now that he has the power, to imitate the great Washington and not suffer himself to be a third term candidate."

But these seemed not the only reasons for his refusal. Jefferson was tired of criticism and personal abuse. In the New England states the Federalist newspapers had conducted a relentless campaign against him. As early as January 13, 1807, when he was only halfway through his second term, the President exclaimed: "I am tired of an office where I can do no more good than many others, who would be glad to be employed in it. To myself, personally, it brings nothing but increasing drudgery and daily loss of friends." He had never been more unpopular than toward the end of his second term, but his influence was still strong enough to desig-

I tell you Johnny, you must learn to read Respect—Free trade—Seamans rights &c—As for you Mounseer Beau Napperty, When John gets his lesson by heart I'll teach you Respect—Retribution &c. &c.

Columbia TEACHING *John &...*

THE U. S. HAD GREAT DIFFICULTY KEEPING THE PEACE WITH FRANCE AND ENGLAND, AS TH...

nate his successor—James Madison, Secretary of State and another of the "Virginia Dynasty."

On January 21, 1808, the Virginia legislature held two caucuses. In the first the 119 members unanimously cast their votes for Madison; in the second some of the malcontents, dissatisfi[ed] with the administration policies, put Monro[e's] name forward and cast fifty votes for him a[nd] only ten for Madison. This boom for Monr[oe] was, however, of short duration.

I don't like that lesson. I'll read this pretty lesson.

S. Kennedy del — Wm Charles Sculp

ESSON

RDED AMERICAN RIGHTS ON THE HIGH SEAS

In the same week Senator Stephen Roe Brad-
ey of Vermont called a congressional caucus
Washington "in pursuance of the powers
ested in me" to deliberate on the nomination
f the next President. The phrase "in pursuance

of the powers vested in me" caused vigorous
protest among the members. Edwin Gray, a
Representative from Virginia, wrote an open
letter to the press, denouncing Bradley's "usurpation of power," and declaring that his call for
a meeting was "an invasion upon the most important and sacred right which belongs only
to the people."

Bradley and his friends fought back. They
were determined to make the nomination in a
caucus. The 139 Republican Representatives and
Senators were cajoled, intimidated, persuaded to
attend. But even so—only eighty-nine came.
They chose Madison for the Presidency and
Clinton for the Vice-Presidency.

The caucus announced the candidates in carefully selected words. "In making the foregoing
recommendation," the statement said, "the
members of this meeting have acted only in
their individual characters as citizens; that they
have been induced to adopt this measure from
the necessity of the case; from a deep conviction of the importance of Union to the Republicans throughout all parts of the United States
in the present crisis of both our external and
internal affairs; and as being the most practicable mode of consulting and respecting the
interests and wishes of all upon a subject so
truly interesting to the whole people of the
United States."

A number of dissidents in the Republican
ranks questioned the right of the caucus to
select the candidates. They issued an address to
the people in which they said that to make the
nominations in a congressional caucus was
hostile to the spirit and plain intent of the
Constitution, for that document made it the
express duty of the states to choose electors,
and of the electors to choose the President and
Vice-President.

The opponents of the caucus turned against
Madison's candidacy, for they doubted whether
he was able enough to steer the nation in such
perilous times. "We ask for energy, and we are
told of his moderation; we ask for talent and
are told of his unassuming modesty." Still,
Madison remained the candidate of the party.

The Federalists' ticket was not announced
until late in October, some five weeks before
the election. Only then did the Federalists declare that they were recommending their pre-

71

vious candidates—General Charles Cotesworth Pinckney of South Carolina for President and Rufus King of New York for Vice-President. They ran their campaign entirely on the embargo issue. The *Columbian Centinel* wrote on July 30, 1808: "The great foreign object of the Embargo makers was avowedly the destruction of England and her colonies. But after seven months' experience, and bringing thousands of Americans to beggary, these Virginia Embargoroons find that old England does not essentially feel any misery from the massacre; and that the British Colonies are growing vastly rich on the ruins of American commerce; and some of the late sticklers for the Embargo Laws are calling aloud for their repeal; and for going to *war with England!*"

In the New York *Herald* Jefferson was assailed because under him the country had seen "a political intolerance as despotic as wicked, and capable of bitter persecution," and "an adherence to an insidious policy, which has at length brought the nation into the most unexampled state of distress and debasement. . . . We have seen a ruinous embargo, the call of one hundred thousand militia, the equipment of numerous gunboats, and the raising of a standing army, recommended by the President, adopted."

William Cullen Bryant, still a youngster, wrote:

"Go, wretch! Resign the Presidential chair,
Disclose thy secret measures, foul or fair;
Go, search with curious eye for horned frogs
'Mid the wild wastes of Louisiana bogs:
Or where Ohio rolls his turbid stream
Dig for huge bones, thy glory and thy theme."

When election day came, seventeen states cast votes, the same number as in the previous election. Electors were chosen by legislatures in Vermont, Massachusetts, Connecticut, New York, Delaware, South Carolina, and Georgia; by the people on a general ticket in New Hampshire, Rhode Island, Pennsylvania, Virginia, and Ohio; by popular vote in Maryland, New Jersey, North Carolina, Kentucky, and Tennessee.

That Madison would be chosen was never in doubt; he received 122 electoral votes against the Federalist Pinckney's forty-seven.

72

THREE AMERICAN SAILORS DISCUSS THE EMBA

A short time before the inauguration ceremonies, Jefferson signed a bill repealing the embargo, acknowledging that this policy wa

...H A FEDERALIST EDITOR WHO URGES THEM NOT TO GO TO WAR WITH THE MOTHER COUNTRY

a failure. "Within a few days I retire to my family, my books and farms," he wrote to a friend, "and having gained the harbor myself, shall look on my friends still buffeting the storm, with anxiety indeed, but not with envy. Never did a prisoner, released from his chains, feel such relief as I shall on shaking off the shackles of power."

MADISON'S OFFICE IN WASHINGTON

THE SEVENTH ELECTION—1812

JAMES MADISON

Relations with Great Britain deteriorated. The Embargo Act was supplanted by Nonintercourse. This policy allowed American commerce with the world except with Great Britain and France, and even with those two countries trade could be renewed the instant they renounced their Decrees and Orders in Council against neutral shipping.

Great Britain was keen to ease the strained situation. Canning, the Foreign Secretary, sent David Erskine, a young man with an American wife, as British Minister to the States, hoping that Erskine might be able to negotiate a satisfactory agreement. It was not long before the English envoy came to terms with Madison, promising him the withdrawal of the Orders in Council, whereupon Madison hurriedly issued a proclamation restoring trade with Great Britain. Yet, when Canning heard of Erskine's "treaty," he recalled the envoy who supposedly had disregarded his instructions. The British Orders in Council remained in force, and Madison issued another proclamation restoring Nonintercouse with that country.

To safeguard American merchants under the Nonintercourse Act, Nathaniel Macon of North Carolina introduced a bill which allowed the importation of French and British goods to America if they were carried in American ships. The Senate had hardly defeated this bill when the House Committee on Foreign Affairs, of which Macon was chairman, came forth with another suggestion. Macon's Bill Number Two, as the proposal became known, repealed the Nonintercourse Act, leaving the door open for further bargaining with Great Britain and France.

It was not a bad plan. If Great Britain would repeal the Orders in Council, the United States would trade with her but not with France; and if France would withdraw her Decrees, the provisions of the Nonintercourse Act would be reapplied against Great Britain.

Napoleon, recognizing a good opportunity when he saw one, announced quickly "that the Decrees of Berlin and Milan are revoked, and that after 1 November they will cease to have effect—it being understood that the English are to revoke the Orders in Council." Madison, falling into the trap, issued a proclamation whereby Nonintercourse would be revived against Britain if she did not withdraw her Orders in Council within three months. But the ink on Madison's proclamation was hardly dry when Napoleon issued new regulations against American shipping—no less severe than those which had been repealed.

The situation with Great Britain reached a

JAMES MADISON (1751-1836)
PAINTING BY ASHER B. DURAND

JAMES MADISON
(1751-1836) was Republican candidate for re-election. There is a story that a group of Republican Congressmen demanded that he declare himself for war or lose the support of the party. About this time Madison shifted his policies. In the ensuing election 128 votes were cast for him.

ELBRIDGE GERRY
(1744-1814) was chosen by the Republican caucus for Vice-President. Gerry, the former Governor of Massachusetts, of "Gerrymander" fame, was strongly for war since in his opinion the U.S. was "degenerating into a nation of traders." In the election he received 131 votes, 3 more than Madison.

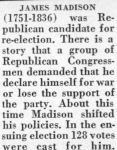

DE WITT CLINTON
(1769-1828), long-time Mayor of New York, was among the foremost politicians of his state. Candidate of the discontented New York Republicans who opposed Madison, he received Federalist support as well. Had Pennsylvania voted with the North, Clinton would have won.

JARED INGERSOLL
(1749-1822) graduated from Yale, studied law in England, and practiced in Philadelphia. A member of the Continental Congress and the Constitutional Convention, he was chosen by the Federalists of Pennsylvania for the vice-presidential office, winning eighty-nine electoral votes.

critical stage. The temporary renewal of trade with France had brought an English fleet to the American coast; the British navy fired at American vessels, searched them and impressed their seamen. The American minister returned from England.

War imminent, responsible statesmen in both countries worked for peace. A new English minister arrived in the States to make amends. He was to convince the American diplomats that as Napoleon had not really revoked the French Decrees, trade with Britain should be continued. And he was to make a satisfactory agreement about the *Chesapeake* affair. If he had come some time earlier, he might have been successful, but now an incident had changed the mood of the country. The *President*, an American ship, in an encounter with the *Little Belt*, a British man-of-war, had badly mauled her, with "all her rigging and sails cut to pieces." The *Chesapeake* was revenged. This victory was hailed with an outburst of enthusiasm. The people became aware that they were not without defense and that the American navy was not so inferior after all. Britain was asked sternly to repeal the Orders in Council. At first this was refused, but then the English reconsidered. The reason for it: Britain needed American

THE ELECTORAL VOTE IN THE 1812 ELECTION

STATES	PRESIDENT		VICE-PRESIDENT	
	James Madison, Va.	De Witt Clinton, N. Y.	Elbridge Gerry, Mass.	Jared Ingersoll, Pa.
New Hampshire	—	8	1	7
Vermont	8	—	8	—
Massachusetts	—	22	2	20
Rhode Island	—	4	—	4
Connecticut	—	9	—	9
New York	—	29	—	29
New Jersey	—	8	—	8
Pennsylvania	25	—	25	—
Delaware	—	4	—	4
Maryland	6	5	6	5
Virginia	25	—	25	—
North Carolina	15	—	15	—
South Carolina	11	—	11	—
Georgia	8	—	8	—
Kentucky	12	—	12	—
Tennessee	8	—	8	—
Louisiana	3	—	3	—
Ohio	7	—	7	—
Electoral vote	128	89	131	86

THE FEDERALISTS WERE AGAINST WAR, THE REPUBLICANS FOR IT. In this contemporary cartoon, drawn by William Charles, the ghost of Washington says: "I left with you a precious casket of choicest Blessings supported by three Pillars—Desist my sons from pulling at them. Should you remove one you destroy the whole." The three pillars are marked: Federalism, Republicanism, Democracy; the casket above: Liberty and Independence.

food and she needed the American market for her products—now that Napoleon had closed almost all Western Europe to British goods. On June 16, 1812, the Orders in Council were withdrawn. But by that time in Washington the lower House of Congress had already voted for war, and two days after the British repeal—a decision still unknown in America—the Senate concurred with the House.

Why did the American people suddenly become war-minded? The refusal of the British to revoke the Orders in Council was one reason. But a more valid one could be ascribed to the frontier situation. The settlers in the West cried for free land, and free land could be had only if the Indians and Britain were ready to surrender it. After Harrison fought the battle of Tippecanoe in November, 1811, a showdown with the Indians in the Northwest was inevitable. It was known that Tecumseh, the head of

the Indian Confederacy, had been supplied with British war material and was in constant communication with the English. Moreover, the Western pioneers felt hampered in their expansion by the British military posts which protected the fur trade south of the Great Lakes. Since it was to the common interest of the Canadian fur traders and the Indians to retard any further American advance in the West, the Northwest was strongly for settling the Indian and Canadian problems at the same time. In a war against Great Britain the United States would annex Canada, and such occupation would end the English-Indian alliance.

In the Southwest a somewhat similar situation was present. There the allies of the Indians were the Spaniards. In 1810 Madison had ordered the peaceful acquisition of West Florida, but for the Southern expansionists that was not enough; they clamored for the whole seacoast. They reasoned that if America should fight Great Britain, Spain would become that country's ally. Therefore it would be a farsighted policy to help the Northwest to occupy Canada; for this service the Northwest might later assist them in their campaign for the whole of Florida. Thus, both the Northwest and the Southwest clamored for war.

In the congressional elections of 1810 and 1811 the country had elected a number of young, vigorous Representatives, among them John C. Calhoun and Henry Clay. These young "War Hawks," as they were nicknamed, represented the war spirit of the West and they cried for "Canada, Canada, Canada!"

Madison held with the traditional American policy of keeping the peace, but suddenly his views changed. There is a story that this change took place because a congressional deputation visited him and asked Madison to declare himself for a war policy, otherwise they would not support him for re-election. Whether this was true—there is no authentic proof of the story— we do not know, but we do know that Madison sent his war message to Congress on June 1.

The congressional caucus renominated him, with John Langdon of New Hampshire as his running mate. When Langdon declined

THE BRITISH IMPRESSED AMERICAN SEAMEN

the nomination because of his age, a later caucus nominated Elbridge Gerry in his stead.

The New York Republicans were not content with Madison's candidacy. Influenced by the strong antiwar feeling in every part of the North and East and by the growing demand

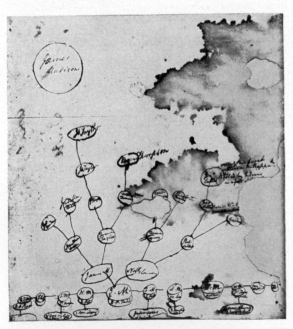

MADISON'S DRAWING OF HIS FAMILY TREE

IR SERVICE. THIS WAS ONE OF THE CAUSES WHICH LED TO WAR BETWEEN THE TWO COUNTRIES

that the country should abandon the Virginia rule and elect a Northern President, they held a separate caucus at Albany and nominated De Witt Clinton for the Presidency.

The issue of the campaign was simply this: Should America prosecute the war vigorously or should the difficulties with England he settled by peaceful means? A vote for Madison was a vote for war; a vote for Clinton for peace.

Eighteen states participated in the election, Louisiana having been admitted to the Union on April 8, 1812.

By the Virtue, Firmness and Patriotism of

JEFFERSON & MADISON,

Our Difficulties with England are settled—our Ships have been preserved, and our Seamen will, hereafter, be respected while sailing under our National Flag.

NEW-YORK, SATURDAY MORNING, APRIL 22, 1809.

IMPORTANT.

By the President of the United States.—A Proclamation.

WHEREAS it is provided by the 11th section of the act of Congress, entitled " An " act to interdict the commercial intercourse between the United States and Great Bri- " tain and France, and their dependencies ; and for other purposes,"—and that " in " case either France or Great Britain shall so revoke or modify her edicts as that they " shall cease to violate the neutral commerce of the United States," the President is authorised to declare the same by proclamation, after which the trade suspended by the said act and by an act laying an Embargo, on all ships and vessels in the ports and harbours of the United States and the several acts supplementary thereto may be renewed with the nation so doing. And whereas the Honourable David Montague Erskine, his Britannic Majesty's Envoy Extraordinary and Minister Plenipotentiary, has by the order and in the name of his sovereign declared to this Government, that the British Orders in Council of January and November, 1807, will have been withdrawn, as respects the United States on the 10th day of June next. Now therefore I James Madison, President of the United States, do hereby proclaim that the orders in council aforesaid will have been withdrawn on the tenth day of June next; after which day the trade of the United States with Great Britain, as suspended by the act of Congress above mentioned, and an act laying an embargo on all ships and vessels in the ports and harbors of the United States, and the several acts supplementary thereto, may be renewed.

Given under my hand and the seal of the United States, at Washington, the nineteenth day of April, in the year of our Lord, one (L. s) thousand eight hundred and nine, and of the Independence of the United States, the thirty-third.

JAMES MADISON.

By the President,
RT. SMITH, *Secretary of State.*

MADISON REVOKED THE EMBARGO when Erskine promised him that the British Orders in Council would be withdrawn. However, "Erskine's Treaty" was repudiated by the Foreign Office and the envoy was recalled.

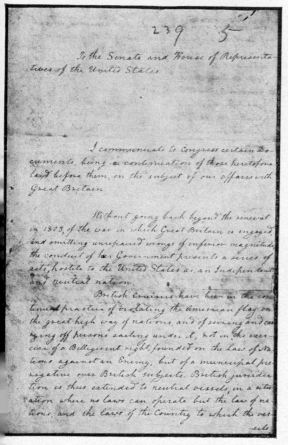

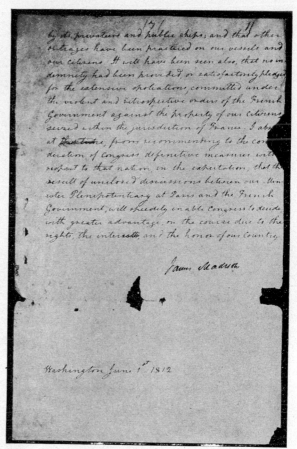

THE FIRST AND LAST PAGES OF PRESIDENT MADISON'S WAR MESSAGE TO CONGRESS IN JUNE

In the appointment of electors Massachusetts introduced a new note. Elbridge Gerry had been governor of that state for two years; he had been defeated for re-election shortly before the congressional caucus named him for the Vice-Presidency. Under him Massachusetts had been divided into senatorial districts so cleverly conceived that the Republicans received a majority in the Senate, although the House of Representatives was Federalist. One rearranged district had the peculiar shape of a salamander, whereupon a wit remarked that it rather looked like a "Gerrymander." When it came to the appointment of the presidential electors, the two Houses of the Massachusetts legislature had great difficulty in reaching an agreement.

The result of the election showed a sectional division: New England (except for Vermont) and the Middle states (except for Pennsylvania and part of Maryland) cast their votes for Clinton. But every state south and west of the Delaware had been carried by Madison, who received 128 electoral votes against De Witt Clinton's 89.

The opponents of Madison were eager to point out that the election figures proved that the Southern states ruled the Union. They said that the returns revealed how the Northern freemen were at the mercy of the Southern slaves. In the seven states that had voted for Madison and war, there were almost a million slaves without any share in government. Yet, as each 45,000 of them were entitled to one elector, they had given Madison and his war twenty-one electoral votes. And this boded ill for the future. Then, either the Southern states would drag the Northern states further into the war or the North must drag them out—and if neither could impose its will, the two sections would have to go their separate ways.

CEREMONY BEFORE THE CAPITOL RUINS

THE EIGHTH ELECTION—1816

JAMES MONROE

The war which the country had at first so enthusiastically welcomed was not a sinecure. Canada was not taken in two months as the War Hawks had predicted, and the British were not overcome in easy victories.

To prosecute a war one has to make sacrifices. But many Americans thought it was "unrepublican" of their government to tax them, and Gallatin—who recommended internal taxation—was severely criticized.

Including the revenue from the excise tax and stamp duty, all the taxes the government received did not amount to more than a third of the war expense; the rest had to be raised through loans. This proved to be a difficult undertaking. The bankers and merchants were against the war, and they were not too keen to lend their money to the government. In the whole of New England only three million dollars' worth of war bonds were sold.

The moral support of the people was not much better. Of a population of eight million, there were never more than thirty-five thousand volunteers in service at any one time. The war had to be fought by the state militias, and their number was small.

It was a sad situation with old, frightened officers in command, a green army ready to leave the battlefield at the slightest provocation. Detroit was lost; the attacks on Canada at Niagara were driven back. The advance on Montreal stopped before the troops reached Canada, since the militia was not willing to battle outside the boundaries of the United States.

After the first setbacks a renewed attempt was made to invade Canada. A fleet on Lake Erie was built to fight for control of the Great Lakes. And Captain Oliver Hazard Perry could soon report: "We have met the enemy and they are ours: two ships, two brigs, one schooner, and one sloop." William Henry Harrison, whose troops against Detroit had been thrown back in 1812, made another attack in the following summer, and this time he was successful. However, the other two campaigns—at Niagara and before Montreal—were failures.

The English army was in no better shape than the American army. They needed men and equipment, which came only after Napoleon's defeat in Spain. But the supplies were too little and they came too late. When they arrived the Americans were already prepared: most of the

JAMES MONROE (1758-1831)
PAINTING BY JOHN VANDERLYN

JAMES MONROE (1758-1831), Madison's choice for the Presidency, another of the "Virginia Dynasty." Although there was some opposition among the New York Republicans, the congressional caucus chose him rather than William H. Crawford, the brilliant candidate of the New York malcontents.

DANIEL D. TOMPKINS (1774-1825), Governor of New York, was first the candidate of the New York Republicans for President. But as he had not been in national politics, they put in place of his name that of Crawford. And when Crawford's candidacy came to nothing, Tompkins ran for the Vice-Presidency.

RUFUS KING (1755-1827), who twice before was the Federalist choice for Vice-President, was now the candidate for President, receiving all the 34 Federalist votes from Massachusetts, Connecticut and Delaware. First he opposed war, but when it came he supported the administration's measures.

JOHN E. HOWARD (1752-1827), soldier of Maryland who fought in the Revolutionary War and, when it ended, became delegate to the Continental Congress, Governor of Maryland and U.S. Senator. He was the Federalist choice for Vice-President, but was able to rally only the 22 votes from Massachusetts.

old and incompetent officers had been removed, and the regulars had been trained. Before the British army was ready to attack, Americans had crossed the Niagara River, taken Fort Erie, won the important battle at Lundy's Lane on Canadian soil, and outfought the enemy on Lake Champlain, sinking or capturing all its ships.

It was part of the British strategy to invade the United States at some southern spot in order to relieve the pressure on the Canadian frontier and divert the American fighting forces. In August 1814 fifty British ships with four thousand soldiers anchored at the Potomac. Soon the troops were marching toward Washington, the defenseless capital. Before the city a battle was fought, but the fight was over before it really began. The untrained American militia ran away and the way to Washington was open to the invaders. On August 24, the British took the capital; the President and his Dolly escaped only at the last moment. They missed seeing the burning of the official buildings, which was ordered by the British in retaliation for General Dearborn's raid on York (later known as Toronto), where American soldiers destroyed the two houses of the provincial Parliament.

Entrenched safely in Washington, the British troops marched to Baltimore, their next objec-

THE ELECTORAL VOTE IN THE 1816 ELECTION

STATES	PRESIDENT		VICE-PRESIDENT				
	James Monroe, Va.	Rufus King, N. Y.	D. D. Tompkins, N. Y.	John E. Howard, Md.	James Ross, Pa.	John Marshall, Va.	Robert G. Harper, Md.
New Hampshire	8	—	8	—	—	—	—
Vermont	8	—	8	—	—	—	—
Massachusetts	—	22	—	22	—	—	—
Rhode Island	4	—	4	—	—	—	—
Connecticut	—	9	—	—	5	4	—
New York	29	—	29	—	—	—	—
New Jersey	8	—	8	—	—	—	—
Pennsylvania	25	—	25	—	—	—	—
Delaware	—	3	—	—	—	—	3
Maryland	8	—	8	—	—	—	—
Virginia	25	—	25	—	—	—	—
North Carolina	15	—	15	—	—	—	—
South Carolina	11	—	11	—	—	—	—
Georgia	8	—	8	—	—	—	—
Kentucky	12	—	12	—	—	—	—
Tennessee	8	—	8	—	—	—	—
Louisiana	3	—	3	—	—	—	—
Ohio	8	—	8	—	—	—	—
Indiana	3	—	3	—	—	—	—
Electoral vote	183	34	183	22	5	4	

ELECTION DAY AT THE STATE HOUSE IN PHILADELPHIA. PAINTING BY JOHN LOUIS KRIMMEL

tive. But at Fort McHenry "the flag was still there," and the invaders were thrown back with heavy losses.

The final battles of the war were fought in the Southwest, where Andrew Jackson held command and led the fight against the Indians and the British. When the enemy tried to use Pensacola—in Spanish territory—as a base of operations, Jackson, disregarding neutral rights, raided and burned the town. Now the British troops marched against New Orleans, where a spectacular engagement was fought on January 8, 1815, in which almost two thousand British soldiers were killed, while on the American side the loss was only thirteen. At the time of Jackson's New Orleans victory, the peace treaty between America and England had already been signed at Ghent (December 24, 1814), but this was not generally known in the United States.

Meanwhile, the war which they so abhorred had turned the Federalist New England merchants against the Union. Dissatisfied with the government's war policy, they called a convention at Hartford, Connecticut, to discuss some amendments to the Constitution. There was a lot of talk of secession, of leaving the Union, but the counsel of the more conservative elements prevailed. In the convention seven resolutions were passed.

The first suggested that "representatives and direct taxes shall be apportioned among the several states which may be included within this Union"; the second asked that "no new state shall be admitted into the Union by Congress . . . without the concurrence of two thirds of both houses"; the third demanded that "Congress shall not have power to lay any embargo on the ships . . . of the citizens of the United States in the ports or harbors thereof for more than sixty days"; the fourth, that "Congress shall not have power, without the concurrence of two thirds of both houses, to interdict the commercial intercourse between the United States and any foreign nation"; the fifth said:

"Congress shall not make or declare war or authorize acts of hostility against any foreign nation, without the concurrence of two thirds of both houses. . . ."; the sixth, that "no person who shall hereafter be naturalized shall be eligible as a member of the Senate or House of Representatives. . . ."; the seventh, that "the same person shall not be elected President of the United States a second time; nor shall the President be elected from the same state two terms in succession."

The Hartford Resolutions were sent to Washington by commissioners who were to inform Congressmen what course the New England states had decided upon. But the commissioners came at the wrong time, for when they arrived at the capital, the city was in jubilant spirits, the news of Jackson's victory at New Orleans had just reached Washington. And when it became known that the peace treaty had been signed in Ghent, they could do nothing but pack up their satchels and return home. There could be no more talk of secession—the war was over, the resolutions were dead, and the Federalist party was facing ruin.

With peace restored, a Republican victory in the next presidential election was assured. Madison wanted his Secretary of State, James Monroe, to be his successor. Monroe had supposedly withdrawn from the contest in 1808 when an understanding was reached that he would become the next President. There was strong opposition to his candidacy, mainly among the New York Republicans, who asserted that the Virginia Dynasty had been in power long enough and that the time had come to elect a Northern President. But as the New England states were Federalist, they suggested choosing someone from the Middle states. At first the candidacy of Daniel D. Tompkins, Governor of New York, was proposed, but as Tompkins had not been in national politics, the opponents of Monroe agreed on William H. Crawford, though he, too, was a Virginian.

When the caucus met with fifty-eight Republican Congressmen present "to take into consideration the propriety of nominating persons or candidates for President and Vice-President of the United States," they had a choice between Monroe and Crawford. But since the meeting had such small attendance, no action

THE BRITISH BURN THE CITY OF WASHINGT

was taken, and a new caucus was called. Th next time 119 Congressmen came, only twenty nine less than the total number in Congress.

At the meeting Henry Clay moved a resolu tion that it was not expedient to present can

A CONTEMPORARY ENGLISH CARTOON, PRINTED IN LONDON IN 1814, SATIRIZING MADISON'S FLIGHT

didates selected by the caucus. His motion was rejected. But in the coffeehouses and in the newspapers many voices were raised, objecting to a congressional caucus. The Aurora *General Advertiser* wrote:

"The Constitution of the United States, in order to prevent those corrupt practices, which produced the ruin of other republics, declares that members of Congress shall not be electors, but that a president and vice-president shall

IN THIS ANTI-FEDERALIST CARTOON OF 1814, KING GEORGE III URGES THREE NEW ENGLAND S...

be elected by persons chosen for this purpose —all meeting in their several states on the same day. But this sound provision of the Constitution has long been evaded—members of Congress actually exercise the power which elects a president, and the electors contemplated by the Constitution are no more than so many clerks in each state, writing down t... decision made in Washington."

After this, the newspaper continued:

"You see in 1816, another president about... retire, and you see another caucus sitting to... upon his successor: Mr. Monroe having wit... drawn his opposition to Mr. Madison in 180...

O'tis *my Yankey boys! jump in my fine fellows, plenty molasses and Codfish; plenty of goods to Smuggle; Honours, titles and Nobility into the bargain* —

RETURN TO THE FOLD OF THE MOTHER COUNTRY

receives a return in kindness in Mr. Madison's influence for Mr. Monroe in 1816 . . . The succession has hitherto been complete, and will continue so, if the people will not see the truth." Another editorial summarized the issue in this sentence: "The real question will be— *Caucus usurpation or free elections.*"

To these attacks the defenders of the caucus replied that political machinery such as a nominating caucus was necessary, otherwise too many candidates would be named and the election would result in chaos.

With the selection of Monroe by the caucus (he received only eleven more votes than Crawford), his election was assured. The Federalists did not choose official candidates. A day before the polling the Boston *Daily Advertiser* remarked: "We do not know, nor is it very material, for whom the Federal Electors will vote." As it happened, most of them supported Rufus King and John E. Howard.

With no political issues at stake and no real party division, the campaign was one of the calmest in the history of presidential elections. Nineteen states voted, Indiana having been admitted to the Union on December 11. During the counting of the votes, objections were raised against the Indiana votes since they had been cast before that state's admission. A resolution to legalize them bogged down in a fruitless debate. It was a hypothetical argument, for regardless of Indiana, James Monroe was elected by a great majority.

The inauguration ceremonies were so widely discussed in the country that the newspapers were compelled to write them up at length— something they had not done since Washington's first inauguration.

It was the first time in our history that the inaugural address was delivered in the open. There was a strange reason for this. Henry Clay, the Speaker of the House, had a disagreement with the Senate committee which was preparing the ceremonies. Clay was against using the chamber of the House for the ceremonies because, in his opinion, the floor of the hall was not strong enough to support a great crowd. Clay's enemies quickly spread the rumor that he was only making difficulties because Monroe had not appointed him as Secretary of State. However, it seemed that the main argument between the committee and Clay developed about the use of the House furniture. As neither party would yield, the committee erected "an elevated portico" in front of the Capitol where Monroe, watched by a crowd of many thousands, delivered his inaugural address, a precedent which later became a tradition.

THE MONROE DOCTRINE

THE NINTH ELECTION—1820

JAMES MONROE

The Treaty of Ghent brought to an end an era in American politics; foreign relations long uppermost, gave way to domestic problems. The debates on the new political issues—tariff, internal improvement, slavery—cut across party lines and revealed sectional differences.

The tariff allied most of the Southern politicians with the representatives of Pennsylvania and the manufacturing districts in their demand for a protective policy; it drew commercial Massachusetts into opposition. The right of the government to make internal improvements was supported in the Middle and Western states, opposed by the Northeast. And the controversy over slavery, which rose to a national political issue in Monroe's first term, set North and South against each other. Some of these problems were not altogether new; they had simmered under the surface of events since the founding of the Republic, and even earlier.

As the country expanded into the West, the conflicting ideas of the manufacturing North and the slaveholding South became more and more apparent. The North feared that the vast land beyond the Mississippi might become slaveholding territory, and when the House Committee on Territories reported favorably on a bill "enabling" Missouri to draw up a constitution and apply for statehood, Congressman James Tallmadge introduced an amendment which was to forbid further slavery in the Louisiana Territory. The proposal created a tremendous excitement, and was hotly argued all over the country.

At that time eleven slave and eleven free states constituted the Union, twenty-two Senators representing each side. But in the House of Representatives the balance of political representation had shifted. When the Constitution was ratified, the population of the Southern states was about equal to that of the North. Now, thirty years later, the population of the North had grown to 5,144,000, and that of the South to only 4,372,000. In the House the North had 123 Representatives against the slave states' eighty-nine. It was natural that the South

91

JAMES MONROE (1758-1831) was not only candidate of the congressional caucus but of the entire country as well. It was the "era of good feelings," when the political harmony in the land was without discord. Twenty-four states voted and Monroe received all except one electoral vote.

DANIEL D. TOMPKINS (1774-1825), again Monroe's running mate, received 218 electoral votes. His political opponents criticized the bookkeeping irregularities during the war, when Tompkins, as chief of the N. Y. militia, supplied troops and equipment for his state's defense.

JOHN QUINCY ADAMS (1767-1848) received the dissenting electoral vote for the Presidency. It was cast by William Plumer, New Hampshire's former governor, who voted for Adams, so rumor has it, because he felt that George Washington should remain the only President elected unanimously.

RICHARD STOCKTON (1764-1828) won eight votes from the Massachusetts Federalists for the Vice-Presidency. He opposed war with England as "political insanity." Stockton believed that Britain had the right to impress American mariners and he condemned "the idle doctrine of free trade and sailors's rights."

should fight against a further strengthening of the already politically superior North. Thus the Southern states were unanimous in their protest against the Tallmadge amendment.

In the House the amendment was adopted, but in the Senate it was defeated. When the next Congress met, the district of Maine, with the approval of Massachusetts, applied for statehood. This admitted the possibility of a compromise. Maine could be admitted as a free state, while Missouri could join the Union as a slave state without upsetting the balance in the Senate between North and South. The Missouri Enabling Act—popularly known as the Missouri Compromise—was signed by Monroe on March 6, 1820. One of its noteworthy provisions said: "In all territory ceded by France to the United States . . . which lies north of thirty-six degrees and thirty minutes latitude, not included within the limits of the state . . . slavery . . . shall be, and is hereby, forever prohibited."

During the controversies over slavery, tariff, and internal improvements, Monroe kept his opinions to himself. He was well liked, and

THE ELECTORAL VOTE IN THE 1820 ELECTION

STATES	PRESIDENT		VICE-PRESIDENT				
	James Monroe, Va.	J. Q. Adams, Mass.	D. D. Tompkins, N. Y.	R. Stockton, N. J.	R. G. Harper, Md.	R. Rush, Pa.	D. Rodney, Del.
Maine	9	—	9	—	—	—	—
New Hampshire	7	1	7	—	—	1	—
Vermont	8	—	8	—	—	—	—
Massachusetts	15	—	7	8	—	—	—
Rhode Island	4	—	4	—	—	—	—
Connecticut	9	—	9	—	—	—	—
New York	29	—	29	—	—	—	—
New Jersey	8	—	8	—	—	—	—
Pennsylvania*	24	—	24	—	—	—	—
Delaware	4	—	—	—	—	—	4
Maryland	11	—	10	—	1	—	—
Virginia	25	—	25	—	—	—	—
North Carolina	15	—	15	—	—	—	—
South Carolina	11	—	11	—	—	—	—
Georgia	8	—	8	—	—	—	—
Alabama	3	—	3	—	—	—	—
Mississippi*	2	—	2	—	—	—	—
Louisiana	3	—	3	—	—	—	—
Kentucky	12	—	12	—	—	—	—
Tennessee*	7	—	7	—	—	—	—
Ohio	8	—	8	—	—	—	—
Indiana	3	—	3	—	—	—	—
Illinois	3	—	3	—	—	—	—
Missouri	3	—	3	—	—	—	—
Electoral vote	231	1	218	8	1	1	

*In each of these states, one elector died before the meeting of the electoral college.

supported by the whole country. It was the "era of good feelings"; the war was over, business was flourishing, prosperity unbounded. The political harmony was such that when a congressional caucus met, the Republicans extended an invitation to all members of Congress who might care to attend. Less than fifty Congressmen appeared, and they resolved not to name the candidate but to allow the people a free choice without any recommendation, so certain were they of Monroe's re-election.

Five new states voted in the election: Mississippi (admitted December 10, 1817), Illinois (admitted December 3, 1818), Alabama (admitted December 14, 1819), Maine (admitted March 15, 1820), and Missouri (which adopted a constitution in July, 1820, but was not admitted until August 10, 1821).

Monroe received all the electoral votes but one. The single vote cast for John Quincy Adams testified to the world that Mr. William Plumer, New Hampshire's former governor, was not satisfied with Monroe's record. It was said that he dissented for a sentimental reason—so that George Washington should remain the only President to receive the unanimous electoral vote—but Plumer, personally hostile to Monroe, seemed to cast his negative vote more in disapproval of Monroe's policies than as a tribute to Washington.

With the admission of new states the question arose, as it had four years before, whether a state's vote should be counted if that state had not yet been admitted to the Union. The debate this time was on the Missouri vote. As that state had not been admitted on the day the electoral votes were counted, it seemed obvious that Missouri had no right to participate in the election. But since the state did vote, a decision had to be reached whether the votes should be considered valid. A joint congressional committee ruled that if objections were raised against it, the votes should not be counted; but if no one objected, the votes should be included in the final result.* The Senate adopted the

committee's resolution only after a lengthy debate and only after it was assured that a bill would be introduced to eliminate such arguments in the future.

About Monroe's second inaugural, which was held on March 5—as the fourth fell on a Sunday—John Quincy Adams wrote in his diary: "A quarter before twelve I went to the President's house, and the other members of the Administration immediately afterwards came there. The Marshal and one of his deputies was there, but no assemblage of people. The President, attired in a full suit of black broadcloth of somewhat antiquated fashion with shoe- and knee-buckles, rode in a plain carriage with four horses and a single colored footman. The Secretaries of State, the Treasury, War, and the Navy followed, each in a carriage and pair. There was no escort, nor any concourse of people on the way. But on alighting at the Capitol, a great crowd of people were assembled, and the avenues to the hall of the House were so choked up with people pressing for admission that it was with the utmost difficulty that the President made his way through them into the House."

The English minister, who attended the ceremony, described it in a letter to a friend: "In addition to the squeezing and shoving which the poor *Prezzy* experienced at the door, his speech, which was indeed rather long, was occasionally interrupted by queer sounds from the gallery."

Officials and friends flocked to the presidential mansion, restored and painted white since the British ravaged it, to shake hands with the President. An elated, happy crowd filled the rooms of the "White House." "All the world was there," wrote Justice Story to his wife. "Hackney coaches, private carriages, foreign ministers and their suites were immediately in motion, and the very ground seemed beaten into powder or paste under the trampling of horses and the rolling of wheels. The scene lasted until 3 o'clock, and then all things resumed their wonted tranquility."

* This was the ruling of the congressional committee: "Resolved, that if any objection be made to the votes of Missouri, and the counting or omitting to count which shall not essentially change the result of the election, in that case they shall be reported by the President of the Senate in the following manner:

"Were the votes of Missouri to be counted, the result would be, for A. B., for President of the United States, – votes; if not counted, for A. B., as President of the United States, – votes; but in either case A. B. is elected President of the United States, and in the same manner for Vice-President."

AN EARLY CARTOON AGAINST ADAMS

THE TENTH ELECTION—1824

JOHN QUINCY ADAMS

WHEN President Monroe took the oath for the second time, the party unity which gave him well-nigh unanimous support in 1820 had vanished. Two years later, in 1822, the names of seventeen candidates were mentioned as possible successors to him, and before the year was out, the field had narrowed to six leading contestants.

These men had been put up by different sections of the country, and were expected to represent each section's interests. The New England states were behind John Quincy Adams, Monroe's Secretary of State, son of the second President, and a man of wide learning with a Puritan soul. The South presented John C. Calhoun, Secretary of War and a fiery nationalist, and William H. Crawford, who as Secretary of the Treasury was dispenser of patronage. The West proposed Henry Clay, twelve times Speaker of the House of Representatives, a charming and magnetic personality with all the faults and virtues of the Western gentry—a gambler, drinker, poker player; Andrew Jackson, the hero of New Orleans, whose fame rested more on his military exploits than on his political acumen; and De Witt Clinton, a clever politician soon to be Governor of New York.

If it had been within the power of Congress to select a candidate, the choice would have been William H. Crawford, who was in control of the party machine (the Treasury Department was filled with his partisans) and was endorsed by Jefferson and Madison.

To keep Crawford from running away with the prize, all the other candidates united against the caucus system of nominations. It was rumored in Washington that "Calhoun, Clay, Jackson and Adams have a perfect understanding" and that they would "give the caucus a death blow."

In the country the excitement against the caucus was intense. Four fifths of the politicians and four fifths of the nation's newspapers were against it. As the democratic spirit expanded with the opening of the West, as the franchise was extended and property qualifications were swept away, the people demanded a direct voice in the nomination and election of their President. Demurring against the long succession of Virginia-born Chief Executives and the custom of Presidents handing down the scepter to their Secretaries of State, they were unwilling to accept another aristocrat chosen by a small coterie of Washington politicians.

The followers of Andrew Jackson were most active in this battle. Knowing well that their candidate could never win caucus support, they forcefully attacked the caucus system.

95

JOHN QUINCY ADAMS
A DAGUERREOTYPE TAKEN IN 1848
SHORTLY BEFORE HIS DEATH

ANDREW JACKSON
(1767-1845), hero of New Orleans, was the candidate of the people, receiving 152,901 votes against Adams's 114,023. But as neither he nor the other candidates received a plurality, the election went to the House of Representatives, where the states chose J.Q.Adams.

JOHN QUINCY ADAMS
(1767-1848), who had only 84 electoral votes to Andrew Jackson's 99, was chosen President by the House of Representatives with 13 states for him, 7 for Jackson, 4 for Crawford. Adams was first of three Presidents to take office with a minority of popular votes.

WILLIAM H. CRAWFORD
(1772-1834), Monroe's Secretary of the Treasury, was the candidate of the congressional caucus. In this election he won forty-one electoral votes, four more than Henry Clay, and thus he became one of three candidates among whom the House of Representatives had to choose.

HENRY CLAY
(1777-1852) wielded unusual power in this election. As his name was not put before the House of Representatives, he could become the President-maker by releasing his own votes to one or the other of the chief contestants. In the end he supported Adams, who made him his Secretary of State.

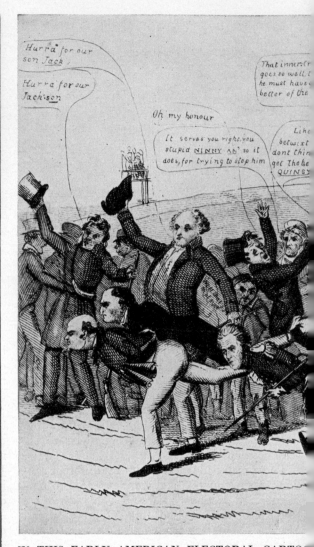

IN THIS EARLY AMERICAN ELECTORAL CARTO[

If—so the Jackson men thought—the states could be persuaded to direct their Senators and Representatives not to attend a caucus, there would be no caucus candidate. The legislature of Tennessee, Jackson's state, adopted a set of resolutions which were sent to other state legislatures for further discussion. In them Tennessee declared that the holding of a nominating caucus was unconstitutional and inexpedient. Unconstitutional because, though the caucus merely recommended a candidate to the electors and the recommendation was not obligatory, the members of the Congress actually went beyond their authority and attempted to

IDATES ADAMS, CRAWFORD AND JACKSON RACE FOR THE PRESIDENCY WHILE CLAY GIVES UP.

gain the election of two particular men—a prerogative not granted to them by the Constitution. Inexpedient because it violated the equality of the states by allowing the large delegations from the populous states to outvote the few members from the small states and name persons not necessarily acceptable to them; and because it might, by acquiring the force of precedent, become established and threaten the liberties of the American people. On these grounds, Tennessee asked its sister states to act upon the resolutions and prevent future caucus nominations.

Of all the states, only two—Maryland and Alabama—accepted the resolutions; the others either shelved them or came out against them.

Undeterred by opposition in Congress and out, a rump caucus of sixty-six men (two more sent proxies) met at Washington and proposed the nomination of William H. Crawford for the Presidency and Albert Gallatin for the Vice-Presidency.

The reaction against the caucus "recommendation" was immediate and violent. At Boston's Faneuil Hall a meeting chose John Quincy Adams as the candidate of Massachusetts, and he was soon endorsed by the other New England states. In the West and in a number of Southern states, a cry went up for Andrew Jackson, the "man of the people." In still other states, a compromise ticket was advocated, with "John Quincy Adams, who can write, and Andrew Jackson, who can fight." The supporters of Henry Clay in Ohio sent a list of names to the Columbus *Gazette*, saying that "We have thought proper to publish the following electoral ticket in favor of Clay," whereupon the Adams men named it the "We Ticket."

Of the four prominent candidates, Clay's political beliefs were the most clearly defined. He advocated Western expansion and internal improvement at Federal expense. He was for a tariff, for the United States Bank, and for the recognition of South American Republics. Crawford was an ardent states' righter and opponent of the tariff (though he hesitated to go on record about it lest he lose the votes of Pennsylvania and the Middle states), and on internal improvement he followed the con-

PAINTED BY COPLEY IN LONDON IN 1795

THE ELECTORAL VOTE IN THE 1824 ELECTION

STATES	POPULAR VOTE				ELECTORAL VOTE FOR PRESIDENT			
	Andrew Jackson.	John Quincy Adams.	William H. Crawford.	Henry Clay.	A. Jackson, Tenn.	J. Q. Adams, Mass.	W. H. Crawford, Ga.	H. Clay, Ky.
Me..............	—	10,289	2,336	—	—	9	—	—
N. H...........	—	9,389	643	—	—	8	—	—
Vt.†...........	—	—	—	—	—	7	—	—
Mass...........	—	30,687	6,616	—	—	15	—	—
R. I...........	—	2,145	200	—	—	4	—	—
Conn...........	—	7,587	1,978	—	—	8	—	—
N. Y.†.........	—	—	—	—	1	26	5	4
N. J...........	10,985	9,110	1,196	—	8	—	—	—
Pa.............	36,100	5,441	4,206	1,690	28	—	—	—
Del.†..........	—	—	—	—	—	1	2	—
Md.............	14,523	14,632	3,364	695	7	3	1	—
Va.............	2,861	3,189	8,489	416	—	—	24	—
N. C...........	20,415	—	15,621	—	15	—	—	—
S. C.†.........	—	—	—	—	11	—	—	—
Ga.†...........	—	—	—	—	—	—	9	—
Ala............	9,443	2,416	1,680	67	5	—	—	—
Miss...........	3,234	1,694	119	—	3	—	—	—
La.†...........	—	—	—	—	3	2	—	—
Ky.............	6,455	—	—	17,331	—	—	—	14
Tenn...........	20,197	216	312	—	11	—	—	—
Mo.............	987	311	—	1,401	—	—	—	3
Ohio...........	18,457	12,280	—	19,255	—	—	—	16
Ind............	7,343	3,095	—	5,315	5	—	—	—
Ill............	1,901	1,542	219	1,047	2	1	—	—
Total........	152,901	114,023	46,979	47,217	99	84	41	37

† In these six states electors were appointed by the legislature.

It is the first time in the history of presidential elections that the popular votes were preserved, though no great reliance can be given to these figures.

servative course of Madison and Monroe. Adams was for tariff and internal improvement, as was Jackson.

By the time the campaign reached its peak, John C. Calhoun was no longer considered a presidential possibility, but since he had the support for the second place of all the anti-caucus forces, his election to the Vice-Presidency was a certainty. The strength of Crawford was also on the wane, both politically and physically. In September, 1823, he had suffered a stroke, and thenceforth he lay in seclusion, incapacitated and almost blind. His followers tried to keep his illness a secret, but rumors that their leader was "sick—very sick," made the rounds, and Daniel Webster confided to his brother that he was anticipating Crawford's death.

Still the Crawford managers continued to fight his cause. Martin Van Buren, the clever New York politician, tried to persuade Clay to form a coalition with Crawford and take sec-

PAINTED BY ASHER B. DURAND IN 1834

DAGUERREOTYPE BY BRADY AROUND 1847

ond place on the ticket, for with the support of Ohio and Kentucky the election of Crawford was believed to be sure. Geneva-born Albert Gallatin, Crawford's running mate, who was under attack because of his foreign birth,* was asked to withdraw. The aged Gallatin gladly obliged, leaving the way open for a Crawford-Clay ticket. However, Clay refused to make the deal.

In the press and on the stump the personalities of the candidates were ardently debated. Fierce partisanship asserted itself. Clay bemoaned the fact that "the bitterness and violence of presidential electioneering increase as

* A candidate for President, and by implication for Vice-President as well, must be, according to the Constitution, "a natural-born citizen." But because the founding Fathers did not wish to bar from the Presidency such foreign-born men as Alexander Hamilton, James Wilson or Albert Gallatin, the Constitution outspokenly declared that a person would be eligible for the Presidency if he were "a citizen of the United States at the time of the adoption of this Constitution."

time advances. It seems as if every liar and calumniator in the country was at work day and night to destroy my character. . . ." But while he complained, he committed the same offense, assailing Jackson, the "military chieftain," in no uncertain terms.

The election began on October 29 and lasted until November 22. Each of the twenty-four states had its own election day, and because of this and the long distances to be traveled, the result did not become known until the middle of December. The figures showed that Andrew Jackson had ninety-nine electoral votes against John Quincy Adams's eighty-four, William Crawford's forty-one, and Henry Clay's thirty-seven. But since no candidate received a majority, the names of the three men with the largest number of votes were submitted to the House of Representatives, which was to choose the President.

Thus Henry Clay, the fourth candidate, wielded unusual power. By releasing his votes to one contender or another, he could become the "President-maker." Hence he was ardently courted by the supporters of Adams, Jackson and Crawford. "I am sometimes touched gently by a friend, for example, of General Jackson," noted Clay, "who will thus address me: 'My dear sir, all my dependence is upon you; don't disappoint us; you know our partiality was for you next to the hero, and how much we want a Western President!' Immediately after, a friend of Mr. Crawford will accost me: 'The hopes of our Republican party are concentrated on you; for God's sake preserve it. If you had been returned instead of Mr. Crawford, every man of us would have supported you to the last hour. We consider him and you as the only genuine Republican candidates.' Next a friend of Mr. Adams comes with tears in his eyes: 'Sir, Mr. Adams has always had the greatest respect for you, and admiration of your talents. There is no station to which you are not equal. Most undoubtedly, you are the second choice of New England and I pray you to consider seriously whether the public good and your own future interests do not point most distinctly to the choice which ought to be made?' How can one withstand all this disinterested homage and kindness?"

Clay kept silent as to his choice, and the nation could only guess. On January 9, 1825, he had a talk with Adams. An anonymous letter in the *Columbian Observer* of Philadelphia, printed on the 28th of that month, declared that "the friends of Clay have hinted that they, like the Swiss, would fight for those who would pay best. Overtures were said to have been made by the friends of Adams to the friends of Clay, offering him the appointment of Secretary of State for his aid to elect Adams. And the friends of Clay gave his information to the friends of Jackson, and hinted that if the friends of Jackson would offer the same price, they would close with them."

Clay was cut to the quick. He replied hotly, calling the anonymous letter writer "a base and infamous calumniator, a dastard and a liar." Yet three years later, Andrew Jackson himself asserted that one of Clay's men—James Buchanan —had approached him, offering a bargain.

On February 9, the House of Representatives assembled to choose the Chief Executive. Bal-

THE BALLOTING FOR PRESIDENT TOOK PLACE

loting proceeded by states, with one vote for each state. Thirteen states constituted the majority, and this was the exact number which rallied behind John Quincy Adams, giving him the Presidency (Maine, New Hampshire, Vermont, Massachusetts, Rhode Island, Connecticut, New York, Maryland, Louisiana, Kentucky, Missouri, Ohio, and Illinois). Seven states voted for Jackson (New Jersey, Pennsylvania, South Carolina, Alabama, Mississippi,

OLD HOUSE OF REPRESENTATIVES. HERE JOHN QUINCY ADAMS WAS CHOSEN FOR THE OFFICE

Tennessee and Indiana) and the remaining four for Crawford (Delaware, Virginia, North Carolina, and Georgia).

The Jackson men were enraged. Their candidate had received the majority of popular votes, and now he had been cheated out of the Presidency. All over the country rumors were abroad that a corrupt bargain had been made between Adams and Clay. Even before the House had assembled to make the choice, Jackson insinuated in a letter to William B. Lewis that "bargain and sale of the constitutional rights of the people" had been effected. And when it became officially known that the new President would appoint Henry Clay as his Secretary of State, Jackson wrote to Lewis: "So you see the *Judas* of the West has closed the contract and will receive the thirty pieces of silver. His end will be the same. Was there ever witnessed such a bare-faced corruption?"

THE ELEVENTH ELECTION—1828

ANDREW JACKSON

John Quincy Adams was a professional statesman of high order, a thorough scholar, but he was stern, stubborn, suspicious, and full of prejudices; he was tactless and lacked the gift of making friends. He characterized himself in his diary: "I am a man of reserve, cold, austere, and forbidding manners. My political adversaries say a gloomy misanthrope; my personal enemies an unsocial savage. With the knowledge of the actual defects of my character, I have not had the pliability to reform it."

The opposition harassed him like a pack of dogs. The charge that he had become President by making a deal with Henry Clay haunted him throughout his entire term. The "corrupt-bargain" story was repeated over and over again. Other men would have crumbled under such attacks, but not the dutiful Puritan.

"The life that I lead," he wrote in his diary, "is more regular than it has perhaps been at any other period. It is established by custom that the President of the United States goes not abroad into any private companies; and to this usage I conform. I am, therefore, compelled to take my exercise, if at all, in the morning before breakfast. I rise usually between five and six; that is, at this time of year, from an hour and a half to two hours before the sun. I walk by the light of moon or stars, or none, about four miles, usually returning here in time to see the sun rise from the eastern chamber of the White House. I then make my fire, and read three chapters of the Bible, with Scott's and Hewlett's Commentaries. Read papers till nine. Breakfast, and from nine till five P.M. receive a succession of visitors, sometimes without intermission—very seldom with an interval of half an hour—never such as to enable me to undertake any business requiring attention. From five to half-past six we dine; after which I pass about four hours in my chamber alone, writing in this diary, or reading papers upon some public business, excepting when occasionally interrupted by a visitor. Between eleven and twelve I retire to bed, to rise again at five or six the next morning."

The campaign for the next election began even before Adams was inaugurated, and it lasted during his entire term. To the "friends of General Jackson"—very soon to be called Democrats—it was not only a political but a personal contest. Their hero had been cheated out of the Presidency, and they were determined to right the wrong in the next election.

ANDREW JACKSON (1767-1845) was nominated by the legislature of Tennessee in 1825. Resigning from the Senate, he retired to the Hermitage, leaving the campaign to political managers who organized his following into a political party and gained the election for him.

JOHN C. CALHOUN (1782-1850), the Vice-President in the Adams administration, now joined Jackson, hoping to succeed Old Hickory as President. He was backed by his native South Carolina and a number of other Southern states which preferred Jackson to the nationalist Adams.

JOHN QUINCY ADAMS (1767-1848), the Puritan, could not match the colorful personality of Andrew Jackson. During one of the most scurrilous campaigns in American history, the opposition charged that Adams had won the Presidency four years before by a corrupt bargain with Clay.

RICHARD RUSH (1780-1859) was the administration vice-presidential candidate. He had been in public office since youth, but when Adams made him Secretary of the Treasury, John Randolph said that this was the worst appointment since Caligula made his horse consul.

One of the Jackson papers wrote: "It is the sovereign will of the people, the almighty voice of this great nation, that has been set at defiance."

As early as October, 1825, when the next election was still three years away, the Tennessee legislature put forward Andrew Jackson for the Presidency. This gave Old Hickory an opportunity to resign his seat in the Senate. He stayed at his home, the Hermitage, writing innumerable letters to his friends in Washington and in the various sections of the country, keeping his fingers on the pulse of the nation. And while his correspondence mounted, his followers were tightly knit into a political organization.

Nominally, the men who supported him were still within the fold of the Republican party, as were the supporters of Adams. But as the cleavage between the two factions deepened, new alignments became a necessity. The old party was certainly in need of some change. When, under Jefferson, the Democratic-Republicans had come into being, they had had

THE VOTES IN THE 1828 ELECTION

STATES	POPULAR VOTE FOR PRESIDENT		ELECTORAL VOTES FOR PRESIDENT		ELECTORAL VOTES FOR VICE-PRESIDENT		
	Andrew Jackson.	John Q. Adams.	A. Jackson, Tenn.	J. Q. Adams, Mass.	J. C. Calhoun, S. C.	Richard Rush, Pa.	William Smith, S. C.
Me.	13,927	20,733	1	8	1	8	—
N. H.	20,922	24,134	—	8	—	8	—
Vt.	8,350	25,363	—	7	—	7	—
Mass.	6,016	29,876	—	15	—	15	—
R. I.	821	2,754	—	4	—	4	—
Conn.	4,448	13,838	—	8	—	8	—
N. Y.	140,763	135,413	20	16	20	16	—
N. J.	21,951	23,764	—	8	—	8	—
Pa.	101,652	50,848	28	—	28	—	—
Del.*	—	—	—	3	—	3	—
Md.	24,565	25,527	5	6	5	6	—
Va.	26,752	12,101	24	—	24	—	—
N. C.	37,857	13,918	15	—	15	—	—
S. C.*	—	—	11	—	11	—	—
Ga.	19,363	No. opp.	9	—	2	—	7
Ala.	17,138	1,938	5	—	5	—	—
Miss.	6,772	1,581	3	—	3	—	—
La.	4,603	4,076	5	—	5	—	—
Ky.	39,397	31,460	14	—	14	—	—
Tenn.	44,293	2,240	11	—	11	—	—
Mo.	8,272	3,400	3	—	3	—	—
Ohio	67,597	63,396	16	—	16	—	—
Ind.	22,257	17,052	5	—	5	—	—
Ill.	9,560	4,662	3	—	3	—	—
	647,276	508,064	178	83	171	83	7

*In these two states electors were appointed by the legislature.

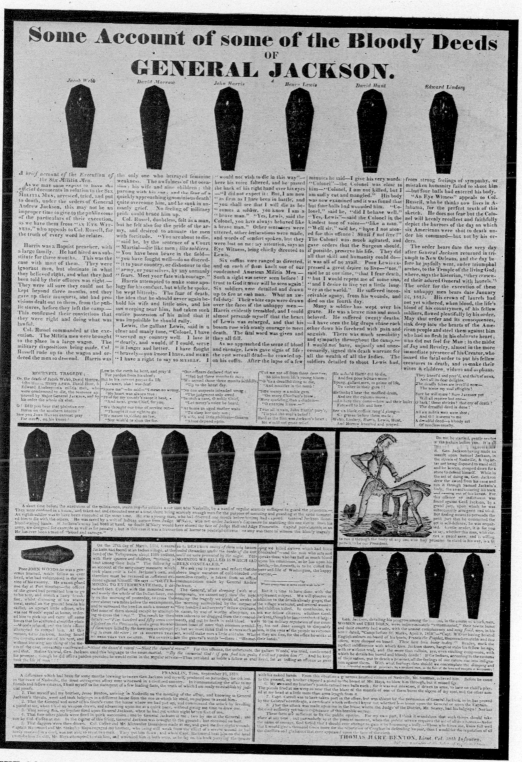

THE COFFIN HANDBILL was the best-known administration broadside against Jackson, recalling the death of six militiamen in the War of 1812, who were executed for desertion with Jackson's consent.

definite political principles, but since then a quarter of a century had passed, and during that time the party had become a political mixing pot. Strict constructionists and loose constructionists belonged to it, Jeffersonians and Hamiltonians alike. Conservative Federalists were in its ranks, asking protection for the manufacturing interests, and radical men of the frontier, demanding a wider application of democracy; New England bankers were side by side with Southern slaveholding plantation owners. As it was the only party in America, it was everybody's party.

But this superficial harmony, which dwindled with the years, vanished altogether when in the previous election four of the party's most prominent members fought for the Presidency. In the ensuing struggle the Democratic-Republicans split, and from the splinters two parties emerged. The Adams and Clay supporters became known as National Republicans, while the "friends of General Jackson" formed the nucleus of a revitalized Democratic party. To the General's "friends" belonged William H. Crawford and John C. Calhoun, now allied with Jackson, thanks to the organizing ability of Martin Van Buren, the former manager of Crawford, who cleverly welded the discordant elements into a solid opposition.

The campaign of 1828 began as a battle between two personalities—Andrew Jackson, the hero of New Orleans, and John Quincy Adams, the Puritan—but beneath the surface there were important political issues. The men who rallied behind Jackson were tired of the aristocratic Presidents from Virginia and Massachusetts and the principles of government which Adams represented. With the expansion of the democratic spirit, the people demanded a more equal distribution of wealth and burdens. The newly enfranchised masses believed that the government should be administered by people like themselves—not by a few holding power in the interests of a few. As one contemporary newspaper put it, the campaign "narrowed down between the people and the aristocracy."

Sectional differences regarding political questions of the day—the tariff, internal improvements and state sovereignty—further influenced the voters to line up behind one candidate or the other. New England and the Middle states,

EDITOR JOHN BINNS, WHO DEVISED THE COF

particularly New York and Pennsylvania, were for a tariff because it helped their expanding manufactures; the West, at first hesitant, gradually became a supporter of protection as well but the South, with its staple crop, was strongly opposed to it.

On internal improvement at Federal ex

BILL, STAGGERS UNDER THE WEIGHT OF THE COFFINS, PRESIDENT ADAMS, AND HENRY CLAY.

ense, the interest of the sections differed too. For the West, where farmers spent one half to two thirds of their profits for transporting their goods to the market, the building of roads and canals was a dire necessity. For the East, with plenty of roads, it was not a vital issue. For the South it was a sore point; the building

of roads would benefit the other sections while the South would be taxed for it.

How did the candidates stand on these issues? Jackson said: "My real friends want no information from me on the subject of internal improvement and manufactures, but what my public acts has afforded, and I never gratify my enemies. Was I now to come forward and reiterate my public opinions on these subjects, I would be charged with electioneering views for selfish purposes."

Of Adams it was known that he advocated internal improvement, and, because of his close association with Clay, it was believed that he would support Clay's "American System," which was for a high tariff and for improvements. Thus Adams consolidated behind him the New England and Midwestern manufacturers demanding tariff protection, the conservative remnants of the old Federalists, and some ardent Western groups crying for internal improvements. And naturally he had the votes of the Henry Clay followers.

Besides these he had the support of a new group, the Antimasons—the first organized third party in America. At first the Antimasons had no desire to be looked upon as a political party. Their movement started in 1826 out of a grievance, and the grievance was this: a man named William Morgan, a Freemason living in upper New York State, announced his intention of writing a book which would reveal the secrets of Freemasonry, whereupon the Master of the village Lodge sentenced him to prison for a small debt he owed. Some time later this same man was abducted by a group of Masons and taken to Fort Niagara, never to be seen again. Weeks passed, and eventually a body was found in the Niagara River, believed to be his. While there was no evidence to support this contention, still, in the opinion of the New York political boss Thurlow Weed, the body was "a good enough Morgan till after the election." As the excitement over Morgan's murder spread, the Antimasons' ranks swelled, and many meetings were held denouncing the Masons. Clever politicians recognized this golden opportunity and organized the discontented element into a political force, swinging its support to Adams.

And who was behind Jackson? Old Hickory was the "people's candidate." In Philadelphia the Workingman's party endorsed him. He was the man of the Western farmers and of the Eastern laborers, and he had the overwhelming support of the South. He was the champion of the "common people" (as John Adams called them), the hero of the "rabble" and the "mob." He personified democracy.

His campaign was managed by a new group of practical men, and their plans set a pattern for all later elections. They organized political meetings, which were held daily in every hamlet, village, and city of the nation. They formed committees which supplied the newspapers and the electorate with campaign material; in Washington a central correspondence committee came into being—the model for our present national committee. They collected funds, compiled lists of voters, and made arrangements for printing ballots. They founded newspapers, increasing in number as the campaign progressed; they issued pamphlets, broadsides and biographies.

They left nothing undone to defeat Adams. Their main cry was the "corrupt-bargain" story, reminding the electorate that Adams was a usurper in the presidential chair, and that he would never have become President had he not made a "corrupt bargain" with Clay. They assailed him because he distributed patronage, and they charged him with wasteful extravagance. One of Jackson's editors accused the prim Puritan of attempting, while he was in Russia, "to make use of a beautiful girl to seduce the passions of Emperor Alexander and sway him to political purposes." Others wrote columns about Adams's purchase of a billiard table and a set of ivory chessmen for the White House. In these stories these harmless articles became "gaming table and gambling furniture."

The Adams forces were no more reticent. In the administration papers Jackson was called an adulterer, a gambler, a cockfighter, a bigamist, a Negro trader, a drunkard, a murderer, a thief, a liar; he was described as ignorant, cruel, bloodthirsty, and even insane. A handbook said about him: "You know that he is no jurist, no statesman, no politician; that he is destitute of historical, political, or statistical knowledge; that he is unacquainted with the orthography, concord, and government of his language; you know that he is a man of no labor, no patience, no investigation; in short that his whole recommendation is animal fierceness and organic energy. He is wholly unqualified by education, habit, and temper for the station of President."

The Adams men did not stop at this. They dragged a most personal matter into the campaign: Jackson's marriage. It was asserted that

tion. The men who had voted for Jackson filled the city of Washington to capacity. "Where the multitude slumbered last night is unconceivable, unless it were on their Mother Earth, curtained by the unbroken sky," wrote one observer. And Daniel Webster related: "I have never seen such a crowd before. Persons have come five hundred miles to see General Jackson, and they really seem to think that the country has been rescued from some dreadful danger."

Jackson was staying at Gadsby's. The hostelry was crowded with his supporters, who roamed about the rooms, shook his hand, and waited for their rewards. The General cut a sad figure among this cheerful and tumultuous mass. Only a few weeks before, he had lost his beloved wife. "He was in deep mourning," wrote an Englishwoman who saw him on his way to Washington. "He wore his gray hair carelessly but not ungracefully arranged, and in spite of his harsh, gaunt features looked like a gentleman and a soldier."

Jackson felt a deep resentment against Adams, who had allowed Rachel's name to be dragged into the campaign. He firmly believed that the slanders of the administration papers had undermined the health of his wife, who had been desolate about the attacks. In one of her last letters Mrs. Jackson complained bitterly: "The enemys of the Genl have dipt their arrows in wormwood and gall and sped them at me . . . they have Disquieted one that haey had no rite to do." And she left this earth with the desire to be "rather a doorkepper in the house of God than to live in that palace at Washington."

At her funeral Jackson swore: "In the presence of this dear saint I can and do forgive all my enemies. But those vile wretches who have slandered her must look to God for mercy." He would not go near Clay, "the basest, meanest scoundrel that ever disgraced the image of his God"; he would not see Adams, would not make a courtesy call at the White House.

It was Adams who sent a messenger to Gadsby's, informing his successor that the White House would be ready for his occupancy on the 4th of March. "He brought me the answer," recorded the outgoing President in his ever-present diary, "that the General

cordially thanked him and hoped that I would put myself to no inconvenience to quit the house, but to remain in it as long as I pleased, even for a month." A few days later Adams informed Jackson that his packing might require two or three days beyond the 3rd. Jackson courteously replied, according to the messenger's report, that he did not wish to inconvenience the President, "but that Mr. Calhoun had suggested that there might be danger of the excessive crowds breaking down the rooms at Gadsby's . . ."; therefore, Jackson inquired whether he might go to the President's house "after the inauguration on Wednesday next." When Adams heard this, he "concluded at all events to leave the house on Tuesday"— which he did.

At half past eleven on inauguration day, the President-elect left Gadsby's and, accompanied by his friends, walked to the Capitol. Hundreds of cheering and shouting people crowded behind him, and more followed in carriages and wagons.

At noon he delivered his inaugural address on the eastern portico and was sworn into office by John Marshall. "The scene," wrote the *American Daily Advertiser*, "was a most beautiful and inspiring spectacle. The building, noble in its size, with its richly sculptured capitals and cornices, and the fine group in the pediment; the massy columns (one for each State in the Union); the far-spreading wings and terraces; the grounds and gates, with the crowd of carriages without; the line of soldiers in the park; the towering flight of steps, covered with members of Congress, officers of the army, foreign ministers, ladies dressed in all the varying hues of fashion; the President; the crowd of heads and the innumerable eyes bent on one spot, all taken together presented to the outward eye an assemblage of images never to be forgotten."

After the ceremonies the new President mounted his horse and rode down Pennsylvania Avenue. He was followed by a great many of his friends on horseback and by a shouting multitude. As he rode through the gates of the White House grounds, a mass of people surged after him. The presidential mansion had never seen such a sight before. Men from the country climbed with their muddy boots on damask

111

YOUNG AND OLD GREET ANDREW JACKSON, THE PEOPLE'S CHOICE, AS HE TRAVELS BY STAGE

chairs; they gobbled the drinks which the waiters brought in. "One hundred and fifty dollar official chairs [were] profaned by the feet of clodhoppers." Justice Story noted: "I never saw such a mixture. The reign of King Mob seemed triumphant." And Mrs. Bayar Smith related: "The noisy and disorderly rab ble . . . brought to my mind descriptions I hav

of the house. "High and low, old and young, black and white poured in one solid column into this spacious mansion. Here was the corpulent epicure grunting and sweating for breath—the dandy wishing he had no toes—the tight-laced miss, fearing her person might receive some permanently deforming impulse. Several thousands of dollars' worth of art glass and china were broken in the attempt to get at the refreshments; punch, lemonade, and other articles were carried out of the house in buckets and pails; women fainted; men were seen with bloody noses; and no police had been placed on duty."

Friends formed a cordon around the President, trying to protect him from the well-wishers. Jackson was "sinking into a listless state of exhaustion." After a while, he escaped through a back exit, hurried to his lodgings at Gadsby's, and went to bed, while on the lawn of the White House the punch-drinking celebration continued throughout the night.

John Quincy Adams did not hear the people's jubilant voices. Sad and resentful, like his father twenty-eight years before, he left the city, not wanting to take part in the inauguration of his successor. Before leaving the White House he made a note in his diary: "Three days more, and I shall be restored to private life and left to an old age of retirement, though certainly not of repose. I go into it with a combination of parties and of public men against my character and reputation such as I believe never before was exhibited against any man since this Union existed. Posterity will scarcely believe it, but so it is, that this combination against me has been formed, and is now exulting in triumph over me, for the devotion of my life and of all the faculties of my soul to the Union, and to the improvement, physical, moral, and intellectual, of my country. The North assails me for my fidelity to the Union; the South, for my ardent aspirations of improvement. Yet 'bate I not a jot of heart and hope.' Passion, prejudice, envy, and jealousy will pass. The cause of Union and of improvement will remain, and I have duties to it and to my country yet to discharge."

And so he did. The noblest part of John Quincy Adams's distinguished public career was still before him.

WASHINGTON FOR HIS FIRST INAUGURATION.

ad of the mobs in the Tuileries and at Versailles."

Men, women, children, farmers, laborers, ambassadors entangled and filled every corner

113

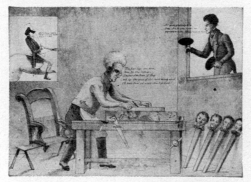

ANDREW JACKSON, CABINETMAKER

ANDREW JACKSON

Andrew Jackson was unlike any of his prede-cessors. He was not an aristocrat, nor had he been born in Virginia or Massachusetts. His parents migrated to America from the north of Ireland two years before his birth. They were without means; the father died before Andrew was born, and the family lived in abject pov-erty. Young Andrew Jackson was still a child when he joined the army together with his brother and fought in the Revolutionary War. The boys were captured by the British and thrown into prison, where they contracted smallpox. When Andrew was fourteen, his mother died. Left alone in the world, he edu-cated himself; later he studied law. As a young man he moved from South Carolina to Tennes-see, where he bought and sold many thousand acres of land, traded in horses and slaves, and owned a general store. A political, judicial, and military career was before him. Representative to Congress, Senator, superior judge of Ten-nessee, major general of his state's militia were some of the steps in this career. For a few years before the War of 1812, he lived the quiet life of a country gentleman on his comfortable estate, but with the coming of the war, his life

changed. Having earned a military reputation for his punitive expedition against the Creeks, Jack-son was made a major general in the army and called upon to defend New Orleans. The spec-tacular battle—fought after peace was agreed upon but not known in America—made the forty-eight-year-old general the hero of the war and his name a household word over the country.

In 1818 Jackson was sent against the Florida Indians, whom he chased and punished on Spanish territory. In 1823 his state chose him for the Senate; in 1824 he was a candidate for the Presidency, polling more votes than John Quincy Adams, whom the House of Repre-sentatives chose for the office, and in 1828 he was elected President. A meteoric rise indeed! From a small cabin to the White House—the first of such American careers.

Jackson, the people's President, shared the many virtues and faults of the Americans of his day. He was quick-tempered, roughhewn, half-educated and intolerant, but not quite as irascible as partisan historians would have us believe. Loyal to his friends, whom he trusted implicitly, he was oversuspicious of his en-emies. In politics stubborn, impetuous, un-

115

ANDREW JACKSON (1767-1845) was ready to run for re-election, although in his first message to Congress he advocated one term. The main campaign issue was his veto of the recharter of the Bank. Jackson won an overwhelming victory with 219 electoral votes against 49 for Clay.

MARTIN VAN BUREN (1782-1862) was Jackson's heir apparent. By astutely handling the Peggy Eaton affair, he endeared himself to Old Hickory, who made him Minister to Great Britain. Returning from there, he easily won the necessary two-thirds vote of the Democratic convention.

HENRY CLAY (1777-1852), National Republican candidate, could have become the candidate of the Antimasons—the first organized third party—by opposing Masonry. But he remained silent and so the Antimasons nominated William Wirt, further splitting the anti-Jackson votes.

JOHN SERGEANT (1779-1852), an outstanding Philadelphia lawyer and an intimate associate of Nicholas Biddle, director of the second U. S. Bank. Sergeant was chief legal and political adviser of the Bank. He was nominated for the Vice-Presidency by the National Republicans.

swerving; in private life chivalrous, charming, courteous. Old Hickory had not the political education of a John Quincy Adams, but what he lacked in knowledge he made up in intuition. He sensed what was right and what was wrong. And, strangely enough, most of his decisions have stood the test of time.

He started his administration with the ardent desire to free the civil service of corruption and incompetence. Of corruption he found little, of incompetence a great deal. The bulk of the post-office employees and other civil servants had held office for more than a quarter of a century, and they had come to believe that Federal jobs were lifetime appointments. As the new President began to "cleanse the Augean stables," fear spread through the government buildings. A clerk in the Auditor's office, worried about losing his job, cut his throat from ear to ear; another, in the Department of State, went raving mad. Jackson replaced the old officeholders with his faithful supporters, people who had voted for him. Whether they were

THE VOTES IN THE 1832 ELECTION

STATES	POPULAR VOTES FOR PRESIDENT		ELECTORAL VOTES FOR PRESIDENT				VICE-PRESIDENT			
	Andrew Jackson.	Henry Clay.*	A. Jackson, Tenn.	Henry Clay, Ky.	John Floyd, Va.	William Wirt, Md.	M. Van Buren, N. Y.	John Sergeant, Pa.	W. Wilkins, Pa.	Henry Lee, Mass.
Me.	33,291	27,204	10	—	—	—	10	—	—	—
N. H.	25,486	19,010	7	—	—	—	7	—	—	—
Vt.	7,870	11,152	—	—	—	7	—	—	—	—
Mass.	14,545	33,003	—	14	—	—	—	14	—	—
R. I.	2,126	2,810	—	4	—	—	—	4	—	—
Conn.	11,269	17,755	—	8	—	—	—	8	—	—
N. Y.	168,497	154,896	42	—	—	—	42	—	—	—
N. J.	23,856	23,393	8	—	—	—	8	—	—	—
Pa.	90,983	56,716	30	—	—	—	—	—	30	—
Del.	4,110	4,276	—	3	—	—	—	3	—	—
Md.	19,156	19,160	3	5	—	—	3	5	—	—
Va.	33,609	11,451	23	—	—	—	23	—	—	—
N. C.	24,862	4,563	15	—	—	—	15	—	—	—
S. C.†	—	—	—	—	11	—	—	—	—	11
Ga.	20,750	—	11	—	—	—	11	—	—	—
Ala.	—	—	7	—	—	—	7	—	—	—
Miss.	5,919	No can.	4	—	—	—	4	—	—	—
La.	4,049	2,528	5	—	—	—	5	—	—	—
Ky.	36,247	43,396	—	15	—	—	—	15	—	—
Tenn.	28,740	1,436	15	—	—	—	15	—	—	—
Ohio	81,246	76,539	21	—	—	—	21	—	—	—
Ind.	31,552	15,472	9	—	—	—	9	—	—	—
Ill.	14,147	5,429	5	—	—	—	5	—	—	—
Mo.	5,192	—	4	—	—	—	4	—	—	—
	687,502	530,189	219	49	11	7	189	49	30	11

† Electors were appointed by the legislature.
* The figures in the Henry Clay column include the votes for the Antimasonic candidate William Wirt.

The rejected Minister,
We never can make him President,
without first making him Vice-president

OLD HICKORY CARRIES MATTY on his back to the Capitol, the only way for Van Buren to "reach the throne." When the anti-Jackson forces in the Senate defeated Van Buren's nomination as United States Minister to Great Britain, the President was more determined than ever to make Van Buren "Vice-President and President afterwards."

suitable for the jobs was not examined too closely. "The duties of all public offices are so plain and simple," said he, "that men of intelligence may readily qualify themselves for their performance." Later in his administration William I. Marcy, justifying the dismissals of civil servants, coined the famous phrase: "To the victors belong the spoils."

But actually the spoils system was much less ruthless than Jackson's adversaries implied. The number of officeholders who were replaced was relatively small. Jackson was reluctant when it came to the removal of old soldiers. Thus he would not take away the job from the aged postmaster in Albany. "By the Eternal! I will not remove the old man," exclaimed Jack-

WHEN PEGGY EATON, bride of Jackson's Secretary of War, was snubbed by the wives of the other Cabinet members, Jackson declared war against Washington society and fought with iron determination for Peggy, whom he thought as "chaste as a virgin."

JACKSON REORGANIZED his cabinet, ousting Calhoun's friends and appointing stronger men in their places. Though he was ridiculed in cartoons showing the former Cabinet members as rats leaving the falling house, Jackson benefited by the change.

ANDREW JACKSON AND HIS NEW CABINET M
This cartoon, published in 1836, has nothing to d
with the Peggy Eaton affair, except as an indire
reference. From left to right are Mahlon Dicke
son, Secretary of the Navy who succeeded Woodbur

son. "He carries a pound of British lead in h
body." Neither would he dismiss the vetera
who had lost his leg on the battlefield, eve
though the man had not supported him in th
election. "If he lost a leg fighting for his cour
try, that is vote enough for me," said Ol
Hickory, endearing himself to all who hear
the story. Such was the make-up of Andre
Jackson. He took a great interest in people, h

...ther liked them or he hated them, they were ...ther good or bad; there was seldom a middle ...urse for him. His likes and dislikes, his sym-...thies and antagonisms came before his official ...ties, though quite naturally most of his battles ...r his friends and against his enemies were ...nnected with political issues.

...Soon after his inauguration the trouble ...arted—and what exciting trouble it was!

Major Eaton, Jackson's close friend and now his War Secretary, married Peggy O'Neale, the not-too-virtuous daughter of a Washington tavern-keeper. When the wives of the Cabinet members snubbed her, Jackson took up the cudgels and—remembering how his own wife had been maligned and slandered—became Peggy's champion, determined to force her on Washington's snob-ridden society. For him

119

Peggy was "chaste as a virgin!" and who was there to contradict the President's verdict? Unfortunately for Jackson there were quite a few. Aristocratic Mrs. Calhoun and the wives of other Cabinet members still would not talk to Peggy or invite her to their parties. Jackson fought back with iron determination. For the first few months of his administration, his energies were mainly concentrated on the private life of Peggy Eaton.

Martin Van Buren sided with Jackson in the battle. And he could do so easily. He was a widower, and there was no wife at home to carp at him and tell him how to behave toward the socially ostracized Peggy. He gave a party for her, he offered his arm and promenaded with her at official receptions, and thus endeared himself to Jackson. His behavior toward "Bellona, the Goddess of War," as Peggy was called in Washington, brought Van Buren nearer to the coveted presidential chair than anything else he had done. But the "Eaton Malaria" was not a purely social affair. The struggle to force ambitious Peggy on Washington was a symptom of the sectional and economic struggle that went on in the nation.

Jackson's support came mainly from the West and South. The Western frontiersmen rallied behind him because he fought privilege and corrupt rule, and because to them he was the champion of democracy. In the South the aristocrats, the well-educated, prominent men in national affairs upheld him because they believed that he would be more sympathetic to Southern demands than the nationalistic Adams. Calhoun, the leader of this latter group, threw in his lot with Jackson, hoping to succeed him in the Presidency. There was one obstacle in the path of this ambition: Van Buren. Thus the fight between the two began—for leadership in the party and for succession.

Their battle started with the Eaton affair. In the Cabinet, Van Buren, Eaton, and Barry were loyal Jackson men, while Ingham, Branch, and Berrien were behind Calhoun. The Jackson group acknowledged Peggy; the Calhoun men, influenced by their wives, rejected her. "Calhoun leads the moral party," wrote John Quincy Adams in his diary, "Van Buren that of the frail sisterhood."

THE THREE MAIN CANDIDATES FOR THE PR

On the left is Henry Clay, the candidate of the N
tional Republicans, laying his three cards marked U
Bank, Internal Improvement, and Domestic Manuf
tures on the table. In the center is William Wi
candidate of the Antimasons, first organized thi
party in America. Vice-President Calhoun hides

JOHN C. CALHOUN PLAY A POLITICAL GAME OF BRAG, AS POKER WAS CALLED THEN.

Nullification and Anti-Tariff cards under the table, while President Andrew Jackson's hand is marked Intrigue, Corruption, and Imbecility. This cartoon was intended to help the cause of Henry Clay, whose "American System" advocated continuation of the U.S. Bank, a protective tariff, and internal improvement at Federal expense. On Clay's insistence, recharter of the Bank became the big issue of the campaign. Jackson vetoed the measure, declaring that recharter would make "the rich richer, and the potent more powerful." In the election, however, the nation backed up the President, giving him 200,000 more popular votes than Clay.

At first Calhoun had a larger following than Van Buren, but in eight months the sly fox had become the President's friend and intimate. And while Jackson's heart opened to Van Buren, his feelings toward Calhoun cooled.

The estrangement between President and Vice-President grew by stages. The first rift was created by the Eaton affair. Jackson resented Mrs. Calhoun's attitude toward Peggy. Then came, in January 1830, the debate between Hayne and Webster, Robert Y. Hayne of South Carolina voicing nullification sentiments, obviously as a mouthpiece of Calhoun. The next step in their drifting apart occurred at the Jefferson birthday dinner. Jackson, addressing his words to the South Carolina nullifiers, offered the famous toast: "Our Federal Union, it must be preserved," to which Calhoun replied in a trembling voice: "The Union—next to our liberty the most dear." And then came the final break. Jackson wrote to Calhoun, asking him whether it was true that during the Seminole War in 1818, when Calhoun was Secretary of War in Monroe's Cabinet, he had suggested Jackson's arrest and proposed his trial for insubordination. Calhoun answered in a long and evasive epistle. The reply was to Jackson "full evidence of the duplicity and insincerity of the man," to whom he wrote brusquely that "understanding you now, no further communication with you on this subject is necessary." Calhoun was thrust into isolation. Daniel Webster observed shrewdly: "Calhoun is forming a party against Van Buren, and the President is supposed to be Van Buren's man. The Vice-President has great difficulty to separate his opposition to Van Buren from opposition to the President."

Duff Green, editor of the party's newspaper —the *Telegraph*—and a loyal supporter of Calhoun, devised an elaborate scheme for taking over the leading Democratic newspapers and

JACKSON FIGHTS the Bank, the many-headed monster. He hits with his veto the "four and twenty hideous satellites," the 24 branches of the powerful second Bank of the United States. The largest head of the monster is that of Nicholas Biddle, the aristocratic president of the Bank. Jackson is helped in his task by Major Jack Downing, a fictional character created by Seba Smith, whose letters on political subjects were a great vogue of the thirties. In the center of the cartoon is Martin Van Buren whom Jackson prods: "Matty, if thou art true, by the Eternal, come on; if thou art false, may the venomous monster turn his dire fang upon thee."

THE
HOUSE
THAT
JONATHAN BUILT,
Or Political Primer for 1832.

" A straw—thrown up to see which way the wind blows."

WITH TWELVE CUTS.

THE PEN OUTWEIGHS THEM ALL.

PHILADELPHIA:
PUBLISHED BY P. BANKS, AND SOLD BY JOHN M'KEWAN, Jr. No. 60, CHESNUT STREET,
AND THOMAS HOLDEN, No. 215, CHESNUT STREET.

1832

ADVERTISEMENT.

Buy a broom!! buy a broom!! buy a broom!!

In consequence of inability and old age, the advertiser is OBLIGED to *retire* from business, and would dispose of two efficient slaves, who have been accustomed to scrub in the "kitchen" and "back stairs," and are willing to do any dirty work to which they may be put.

Inquire at the sign of the "Globe," Washington.

Also for sale, if a good price can be obtained, the Astrologer of the nineteenth century, or Great Magician, with all the cups, balls, conjuring sticks, &c. &c. used by him, and which has brought to his late master and himself immense gain.

Inquire at the sign of the "Globe," as above.

" A distant age asks where the fabric stood."

THIS IS THE HOUSE THAT JONATH

" The seals of office glitter in his eyes,
He climbs, he pants, he grasps them—
To be a pest where he was useful once."

THIS IS

THE TRAITOR,

To glory unknown,
Who would barter his country
And fawn at a throne,
Who would put down the thing,
   That despite of attacks,
And attempts to restrain it
   By villanous acts,
Will poison the Vermin,
That plunder the Wealth,
That lay in the House
That Jonathan built.

" Ruffians are abroad—

THESE ARE

THE VICTIMS,

Of high-handed power,
Who groan in a prison
To this very hour—
Who despise the base Traitor,
To glory unknown,
Who would put down the Thing,
   That despite of attacks,
And attempts to restrain it
   By villanous acts,
Will poison the Vermin,
That plunder the Wealth,
That lay in the House
That Jonathan built.

" Great talents." Great offices will have

Great talents."

AND HERE IS

THE TYRANT,

Who, born to command,
Is the curse of the country—the *King* of
Against whom the People have taken the
The dotard of sixty—the play-thing of kr
Who would make us obey him, or render

A RARE CAMPAIGN BOOKLET OF THE 1832 ELECTION DENOUNCING JACKSON AS A TYRANT

placing them under Calhoun-supporting editors. But when Jackson and Van Buren heard of this plan, the *Telegraph* ceased to be the organ of the party. Francis P. Blair was summoned from Kentucky to start the *Globe*, which became th new mouthpiece of the President.

"— Not to understand a treasure's worth,
Till time has stolen away the slighted good,
Is cause of half the poverty we feel,
And makes the world the wilderness it is.

THIS IS

THE WEALTH

that lay
In the House that Jonathan built.

"A race obscene,
Spawn'd in the muddy beds of Nile, came forth
Polluting Egypt: gardens, fields, and plains,
Were cover'd with the pest;
The croaking noisance lurk'd in every nook;
No palaces, nor even chambers, scap'd;
And the land stank—so numerous was the fry."

THESE ARE

THE VERMIN

That plunder the Wealth
That lay in the House,
That Jonathan built.

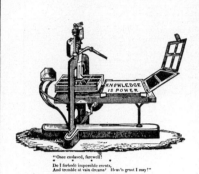

"Once enslaved, farewell!
Do I forbode impossible events,
And tremble at vain dreams? Heav'n grant I may!"

THIS IS

THE THING,

That despite of attacks,
And attempts to restrain it
By villanous acts,
Will poison the vermin
That plunder the wealth,
That lay in the House
That Jonathan built.

is the *Roman*,
Who *acts* as a *King*,
honours our country,
nd would put down the Thing,
          That despite of attacks,
nd attempts to restrain it,
          By villanous acts,
ill poison the Vermin,
hat plunder the Wealth,
hat lay in the House
hat Jonathan built.

But who now give him scorn:
They lament with the victims
          Of high-handed power,
Who groan in a prison
          To this very hour—
Who despise the base Traitor,
To glory unknown,
Who would barter his country
And fawn at a throne.
Yes, these are the men, who with high-handed power,
Hold our clergy in prison to this very hour:
The friends of the "Roman,"
Who acts as a king,
Who despises our country,
And would put down the Thing,
          That despite of attacks,
And attempts to restrain it
          By villanous acts,
Will poison the Vermin
That plunder the Wealth,
That lay in the House
That Jonathan built.

"Portentous, unexampled, unexplain'd!
          What man seeing this,
And having human feelings, does not blush,
And hang his head, to think himself a man?
I cannot rest
A silent witness of the headlong rage,
Or heedless folly, by which thousands die—
Bleed gold for Ministers to sport away."

AND THESE ARE
THE PEOPLE,

All tatter'd and torn,
Who lament the sad day
When the "Hero" was born;
Who once gave him praise,

THE GUILTY TRIO.
"Great skill have they in *palmistry*, and more
To conjure clean away the gold they touch,
Conveying worthless dross into its place;
Loud when they beg, dumb only when they steal.

          Dream after dream ensues!
And still they dream, that they shall still succeed,
And still are disappointed."

AND HERE ARE
THE TRIO

Of cabinet fame,
Amos Kendall and Lewis, and Blair of bad name,
The scullions who grovel and revel in shame:
Ay—these are the tyrants—the rulers of him,
Who, enfeebled by years, is in intellect dim,
The dotard of sixty—who, "born to command,"
Dishonours himself, and would ruin the land.
Ay—these are the minions the People oppose,
Apostates, and Tories, and Liberty's foes—
The friends of the Traitor, to glory unknown,
Who would barter his country, and fawn at a throne.

MMAND...KING OF THE LAND...WHO WOULD MAKE US OBEY HIM, OR RENDER US SLAVES."

Meanwhile Calhoun had published his correspondence with Jackson, infuriating Old Hickory, who regarded this as open defiance.

Jackson determined to reorganize his Cabinet and oust Calhoun's three friends from it. Van Buren proposed a sensible scheme. He was to

Yes, these are the men, who with high-handed power,
Hold our clergy in prison to this very hour:
The friends of the " Roman,"
Who acts as a king,
Who despises our country,
And would put down the thing,
                    That despite of attacks,
And attempts to restrain it,
                    By villanous acts,
Will poison the vermin,
That plunder the Wealth,
That lay in the House
That Jonathan built.

And this is Reform—the Reform of our Yeomen—
Who have slumbered too long with a Despot in Power—
Let them rouse for the contest, and show themselves Free-
men,

November, November—the second's the hour!
Let the blood of our sires, and the spirit that warmed it,
But impart a faint glow in the breast of each son,
And "the fight of good faith" will be fought as it should be,
And the battle for Right and for Liberty won.

" Burghers, men immaculate perhaps
In all their private functions, once combin'd,
Become a loathsome body, only fit
For dissolution.
                    —— Power usurp'd
Is weakness when oppos'd; conscious of wrong,
'Tis pusillanimous and prone to flight.
                    —— I could endure
Chains nowhere patiently; and chains at home,
Where I am free by birth-right, not at all."

THE LAST THREE PAGES OF THE ANTI-JACKSON CAMPAIGN BOOKLET ADVOCATING "REFORM"

resign as Secretary of State, hoping that Eaton would follow his course, thus finally ending the embarrassment over his wife. With their resignations, the President would have a free hand and could reshuffle his advisers. At first Jackson would not listen to such a plan—he was much too loyal to Van Buren—but he acquiesced when Van Buren promised to accept the post of United States Minister to Great Britain. Everything went as Van Buren had planned. Eaton offered his resignation; Calhoun's supporters were forced to go; the Cabinet was reorganized, and the President's prestige enhanced.

After this, Calhoun could hardly hope to succeed Jackson as President or to be his running mate if Jackson should seek renomination in 1832. But still he went on fighting, more determined than ever to eliminate Van Buren from the race. He joined forces with Webster and Clay, and the three worked in the Senate for the rejection of Van Buren's nomination as Minister to England. Churchill C. Cambreleng, one of Van Buren's trusted lieutenants, wrote to him: "Some of your best friends . . . wish most sincerely, and I am among the number, that the Senate would reject you! I know you will be annoyed at such a result—but it's the only thing that can remedy your error in going abroad—it's the only thing that can prevent the election in 1836 from going to the House. . . .

Something striking—something to unite the party on a successor is absolutely necessary. . . . If you could but be rejected—you would return in triumph—we should have . . . the King, commons, and people against the Lords —You would be identified with the party and without a competitor . . . but they are too cunning to do you such a service. . . . I say again I wish they would."

Calhoun, blinded by hatred, believed that the Senate's refusal would be a final blow to Van Buren's chances. "It will kill him dead!" he exclaimed. "He will never kick, sir, never kick." But Senator Thomas Hart Benton knew better. After the Senate had rejected Van Buren's nomination, he said: "You have broken a minister and elected a Vice-President."

Jackson took up Calhoun's challenge. He felt it a personal insult that the Senate would not accept a minister whom he had appointed. And he made immediate preparations to put Van Buren forward as a candidate for the Vice-Presidency.

It was during 1831 and 1832 that the first national conventions were held, replacing the old caucus system as a means of nominating candidates for the presidential and vice-presidential offices.

The first to hold such a convention were the Antimasons. Since the previous election they

126

Caption text within image:

DESPOTISM

a glorious prize, how bright it looks, keep steady my Friends you shall be exalted.

one step more and it will be within my grasp,

a little farther CAL" and we are safe.

Stop you have gone too far or by the Eternal, I'll h[...] you all.

must bear the Burthen, we are exalted or surrender.

Neighbour, [...]are[...]

DIS UNION
DECEPTION
CIVIL WAR
TREASON
S.C. ORDINANCE
NULLIFICATION

CONSTITUTION

E PLURIBUS UNUM

"DESPOTISM—ANARCHY—DISUNION" is the title of this cartoon issued at the height of the nullification crisis. When the South Carolina convention on November 19, 1832, declared the tariffs of 1828 ("the tariff of abominations") and 1832 null and void, and forbade Federal officers to collect the revenues, President Jackson made known that he would enforce the laws of the country with all the power at his command. "If a single drop of blood shall be shed there in opposition to the laws of the United States, I will hang the first man I can lay my hands on engaged in such conduct upon the first tree that I can reach," he said, and he issued an eloquent procla-mation to the people of South Carolina in which he branded nullification as "incompatible with the existence of the Union, contradicted expressly by the letter of the Constitution, unauthorized by its spirit, inconsistent with every principle on which it was founded, and destructive of the great objects for which it was formed." Jackson asked Congress for authority to deal with the situation and use force against South Carolina, but before any blood was shed, Henry Clay introduced a compromise measure for a gradual reduction of duties. Both warring antagonists—President Jackson and Calhoun—asserted that they had won their case.

Here John C. Calhoun walks up the steps toward the crown of Despotism. Hammond of South Carolina (left), who was active in the military preparations of that state, encourages him, and South Carolina's governor, Robert Y. Hayne (right), urges him to go on. But Jackson (far right) threatens that if they don't stop, he will hang them all.

had become a political party—the first organ-ized third party in American presidential elec-tions. In their meeting in Philadelphia on Sep-ember 11, 1830, they resolved to call a nominat-

ing convention at Baltimore a year later. In the meantime they looked around for an eligible can-didate. They turned to Henry Clay, but Clay—who was himself a Mason—was not willing to

127

PORTRAIT FROM LIFE. Jackson, the planter, at the Hermitage, as pictured by the painter Ralph Earl in 1835.

make a declaration against Masonry. They approached Richard Rush, but he declined; they talked to John Quincy Adams, who received their entreaties with little enthusiasm; finally they settled on Judge McLean, who was ready to resign from the Supreme Court. However, two weeks before their convention was to meet, McLean changed his mind and the Antimasons were without a candidate. John Marshall was sounded out but refused, then William Wirt, who reluctantly and halfheartedly accepted the nomination.

At the Antimasonic convention the committee on business recommended that the chosen candidates must receive "the votes of three-fourths of all the members present." It was the first time that more than a simple majority was asked for their election.

There were other innovations instituted by the Antimasons which became part of future convention proceedings: the formulation of a political platform, the naming of a rules committee, the close scrutiny of the delegates' credentials, the conducting of business by means of the committee system, and the unanimous acclamation of the candidates after they were nominated.

The next to meet were the National Republicans, who assembled in Baltimore on December 12, 1831. Because of bad weather and bad roads only 135 delegates appeared, who nominated Henry Clay for the Presidency with John Sergeant as his running mate. As the election was still a year away, the convention brought in a resolution recommending that another meeting be held by the young men of the party in May of the following year.

The last of the great conventions was that of the Democrats on May 21, 1832, to which every state but Missouri sent delegates. A committee reported the rules, among them "that each State be entitled in the nomination to be made of the candidate for the Vice-Presidency to a number of votes equal to the number to which they will be entitled in the Electoral Colleges . . . and that two-thirds of the whole number of the votes in the convention shall be necessary to constitute a choice." The rule was brought in on Jackson's insistence in order to make Van Buren's nomination a certainty, but it was re-adopted in all future Democratic conventions held during the next hundred years. Another of the committee's recommendations was the unit rule, whereby "the majority of the delegates from each State designate the person for whom the votes for that State shall be cast."

No one opposed Jackson's renomination. But the delegates had to choose a Vice-President as well. Old Hickory's desire was well known; he wanted Martin Van Buren for his running mate, whom he was to make "Vice-President first and President afterwards." The convention complied with his wishes; Van Buren received 208 votes on the first ballot against the forty-nine of Philip P. Barbour, who was Calhoun's man.

With the nomination of the candidates the campaign began. How different it was from the two previous campaigns in which Jackson had run for office! Neither in 1824 nor in 1828 were there great political issues at stake. In both elections the people had rallied behind Old Hickory or John of Braintree. In both elections personalities had played as great a part as issues. But now with three parties in the contest—the Democrats, the National Republicans and the

128

BORN TO COMMAND.

OF VETO MEMORY.

HAD I BEEN CONSULTED.

KING ANDREW THE FIRST.

THE CARTOONISTS OF THE OPPOSITION PICTURED JACKSON AS AN ABSOLUTE RULER.

Antimasons—the attention of the voters turned to an animated discussion of political principles.

For the past year the National Republicans had been in search of a suitable issue, and for a while it seemed that they might make Clay's American System the basis of their campaign. Daniel Webster had written to Clay: "Parties must now necessarily be started out anew; and the great ground of difference will be the tariff and internal improvements. You are necessarily at the head of one party, and General Jackson will be, if he is not already, identified with the other. The question will be put to the country. Let the country decide it."

But neither the tariff nor the internal improvement issue seemed to create great enthusiasm among the electorate. Henry Clay wrote to his Virginia manager that he hoped something "may turn up" which would "give a brighter aspect to our affairs."

And the something which did turn up was the recharter of the Bank of the United States. Jackson, who once wrote: "I hate ragg, tagg banks and empty pockets," was hostile to the monopolistic Bank. In his first message to Congress he had come out against a renewal of the institution's charter—which was to expire in 1836—as he believed that the Bank was unconstitutional and inexpedient, and because it had failed to establish a uniform and sound currency.

Nicholas Biddle, the Bank's aristocratic president, became uneasy about Jackson's attitude toward his institution and began to spend money on pamphlets against the President. Rumors were afloat that Jackson desired to make the destruction of the Bank his campaign issue. At first Clay told Biddle not to apply for the new charter until the election was over, but later on he reversed his opinion, thinking that the inevitable veto of Jackson would provide an excellent campaign issue.

As the National Republicans expected, Jackson vetoed the measure. The explanatory message—a joint work of the President and Chief Justice Taney—was indeed an excellent campaign document, but not for the National Republicans. Jackson pronounced the Bank un-American, undemocratic and unconstitutional. He said it was injurious to the country, as it would "make the rich richer and the potent more powerful"; he denounced the foreigners

CARTOON OF JACKSON'S RE-ELECTION SHOWS

who held one fourth of the Bank stock and spoke against the "advancement of the few at the expense of the many."

Ever since this veto message, the Democratic party has been associated with radicalism.

How well Jackson knew the people! He simplified the complex and impersonal Bank issue in a dramatic sentence: "Shall the rights of the common man be respected or shall the rich rule the country again?" There was never any doubt as to how the country would answer this question. The people were against the conservative

130

money policies of the Bank, its monopolistic position, its refusal to lend without ample security; they were against its fluctuating paper currency.

Biddle and the National Republicans, who became champions of the Bank, failed to comprehend the mood of the country. "Emperor Nick" spent a great amount of money for printing and distributing Jackson's veto message—hoping to influence the electorate against Old Hickory. It was a complete waste. Jackson knew better: "The veto works well. In-stead of crushing me as was expected & intended, it will crush the bank." He predicted: "Mr. Clay will not get one electoral vote west of the mountains or south of the Potomac in my opinion," and he was right.

Clay received only forty-nine electoral votes from six states; John Floyd, a friend of Calhoun, had the eleven votes of South Carolina; William Wirt won the seven votes of Vermont. The other 219 votes went to Jackson, indicating that an overwhelming majority favored the continuation of his policies.

Go it, ye Cripples!
Democratic Ticket.
FOR PRESIDENT,
Martin Van Buren.
FOR VICE PRESIDENT,
RICHARD M. JOHNSON.

AN ELECTORAL TICKET FROM OHIO

THE THIRTEENTH ELECTION—1836

MARTIN VAN BUREN

Jackson, receiving his mandate against the Bank, was ready for the kill. The "monster" had to die. Old Hickory made up his mind to withdraw the government funds from the Bank and deposit them in local institutions throughout the country. When Louis McLane, the Secretary of the Treasury, refused to sign the order, he was removed; so was William J. Duane, his unobliging successor. Not until Roger B. Taney, the Attorney General, replaced Duane in the Treasury did Jackson have his way.

The Senate fought back bitterly. Taney's appointment was not confirmed, and a resolution was passed against the President, who by his removal of the deposits had "assumed upon himself authority and power not conferred by the Constitution and laws, but in derogation of both." Thomas Hart Benton, Jackson's champion, made an eloquent appeal to have this censure removed from the *Journal*, but it took three full years before it was done.

While the Senators fought the "tyrant in the White House," the people of the country backed him up. They gave him credit for the good times, which they believed would not have come without his policies. In periods of prosperity life is full of hope, and during Jackson's second term America lived through such a boom as had never before been known. The President was acclaimed, admired, adored.

But opposition is democracy's lifeblood. In a democracy the President seldom carries the confidence of the whole country for any length of time and there are always some factions who will be against him. Andrew Jackson was disliked by the men of property, by the bankers, the merchants, the manufacturers, and these elements gathered together in the Whig party —a new designation under which the former National Republicans and their friends rallied.

The National Republicans, the Antimasons, the adherents of states' rights, the South Car-

MARTIN VAN BUREN
(1782-1862)

MARTIN VAN BUREN
(1782-1862) was Jackson's chosen successor and the Democratic convention nominated him on the first ballot. Though Van Buren was ridiculed in the campaign as a perfumed and corseted dandy, he won the election with 170 electoral votes to William Harrison's 73.

RICHARD M. JOHNSON
(1780-1850), soldier and Congressman, was Jackson's choice for the Vice-Presidency. In the campaign his followers sang: "Rumpsey, Dumpsey, Colonel Johnson killed Tecumseh." When he failed to win a majority, the election went to the Senate. He was chosen.

WILLIAM H. HARRISON
(1773-1841), Indian fighter, Governor of Indiana, General in the War of 1812 and Minister to Colombia, was one of the Whig candidates for President. The other candidates, favorite sons of their states, were John McLean, Daniel Webster, Hugh White.

FRANCIS GRANGER
(1792-1868), an ardent Antimason and political associate of Thurlow Weed, was chosen by the Antimasons and Massachusetts Whigs for the vice-presidential office. When the election was thrown into the Senate, Granger won only 16 votes to Richard Johnson's 33.

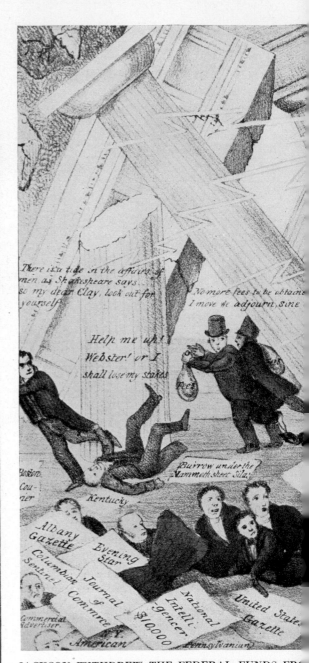

JACKSON WITHDREW THE FEDERAL FUNDS FR(

olina nullifiers, the supporters of Clay's American System, and the discontented Democrats who disagreed with Jackson's policies were now all Whigs. The different factions could not agree on political issues, but they were united in their hatred of Jackson. And they were determined to fight him and prevent him

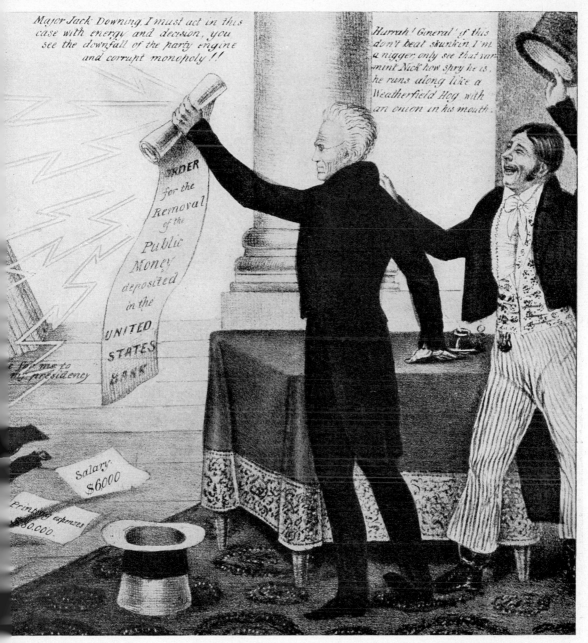

Major Jack Downing, I must act in this case with energy and decision, you see the downfall of the party engine and corrupt monopoly!!

Hurrah! General! if this don't beat skunkin I'm a nigger, only see that varmint Nick how spry he is, he runs along like a Weatherfield Hog with an onion in his mouth.

ORDER for the Removal of the Public Money deposited in the UNITED STATES BANK

...e me to ...presidency

Salary. $6000

Printing expenses $80.000.

...NK, BURYING POLITICIANS AND EDITORS SUBSIDIZED BY THE INSTITUTION UNDER ITS PILLARS.

...om naming a successor to be forced on the ...ectorate.

The President made no secret of his wish ...at Van Buren should follow him in the presi- ...ential chair. He knew that his protégé's nom- ...ation would not only be opposed by every ...Whig in the country, but by a great number of

his own party as well. And he knew that to achieve his aim he would have to act fast be- fore the opposition had time to organize its forces. Therefore, as early as February, 1835, Jackson proposed a national convention to consider the nomination of candidates for the Presidency and Vice-Presidency, to which del-

THE WITHDRAWAL OF THE FUNDS from the Bank of the United States, the resumption of specie payme~
other financial measures of the Jackson administration, added to a crop failure, created a severe depression in the ~

egates should be sent "fresh from the people."

When the Democratic convention met at Baltimore on May 20, 1835, twenty-two states and two territories (Arkansas and Michigan) were represented; only Alabama, Illinois, and South Carolina did not send delegates. At first there was no delegate from Jackson's own state, but it happened that a gentleman named Rucker was visiting in Baltimore at that time, and since he came from Tennessee and was willing to cast his vote for Van Buren, he was accepted as an official representative, his voice

counting for the whole fifteen votes allotted t~ that state.

But while Tennessee was thus "ruckerized,~ other states went to the opposite extreme. Lit~ tle Maryland, with ten electoral votes, sent n~ fewer than 181 delegates; and Virginia~ twenty-three electoral votes were represente~ by 108 men.

In the convention the two-thirds rule wa~ again accepted, making Van Buren's nominatio~ a certainty. However, there was considerabl~ opposition before the candidacy of R. W~

Resolved, That the resolution adopted by the Senate on the 28th day of March, in the year 1834, in the following words, " Resolved, That the President, in his late Executive proceedings in relation to the public revenue, has assumed upon himself authority and power not conferred by the constitution and laws, but in derogation of both," be, and the same hereby is ordered to be expunged from the journals of the Senate; because the said resolution is illegal and unjust, of evil example, indefinite and vague, expressing a criminal charge without specification; and was irregularly and unconstitutionally adopted by the Senate, in subversion of the rights of defence which belong to an accused and impeachable officer; and at a time, and under circumstances to ~~the public rights~~ the political rights and pecuniary interests of the people of the United States,

a serious injury

in serious injury and peculiar danger.]

It was determined in the affirmative – Yeas 33 Nays 13.

On motion by Mr Black,

The yeas & nays being desired by one fifth of the Senators present those who voted in the affirmative are Messrs Bell, Benton, Brown, Buchanan, Calhoun Clay, Clayton, Ewing, Frelinghuysen, Goldsborough Grundy, Hill, Kane, King of Ala. Knight, Leigh, Linn, McKean, Mangum, Moore, Morris, Naudain Prentiss, Robbins, Robinson, Ruggles, Shepley, Smith Swift, Tallmadge, ~~Tipton~~ Tomlinson, White, Wright,

Those who voted in the negative are Messrs Bibb, Black, Cuthbert, Hendricks Kent, King of Geo. Porter, Preston, Silsbee, Tipton, Tyler, Waggaman, Webster

On motion by Mr White,

To amend the same by striking out all after the word "is" where it first occurs and inserting in lieu thereof the words — rescinded, reversed, repealed and declared to be null and void

Mr King of Ala moved to amend the original motion of Mr Benton by striking out the words – "ordered to be expunded from the journal of the Senate;" and

IN THE JOURNAL OF THE SENATE, the censure of Jackson was not expunged until three years had passed. The conflict between Executive and Senate arose over Jackson's order to remove Federal deposits from the Bank. The President was violently assailed by Clay and Webster, and whether or not to enter his protest in the *Journal* was debated for three months. In the end Jackson won and the attempt to institute parliamentary government in America was defeated.

THE MOST POPULAR WHIG CANDIDATES were William Henry Harrison (on the left) and Daniel Webster (in center), while Henry Clay's star was falling. The Whigs, unable to agree on either of these candidates, fought Martin Van Buren with a number of favorite sons, hoping to throw the election into the House of Representatives.

Johnson for Vice-President was secured. Known as a friend of the workingmen and famed as the killer of the Indian chief, Tecumseh, Johnson was nonetheless frowned upon by the South, for he had lived with a mulatto woman who had borne him two daughters.

The legislature of Tennessee—Jackson's own state—would not consider Van Buren, the "Little Magician," and proposed Senator Hugh L. White for the Presidency. Jackson was enraged. On the day the legislature met, every Representative from Tennessee received three copies of the Washington *Globe* which contained vituperative attacks on White. They were sent under the President's frank and were addressed in Jackson's own handwriting. Still the Tennessee legislators would not yield.

The Whig newspapers vociferously attacked the "Van Buren convention"; they called it a substitute for the extinct caucus and ridiculed

it as a gathering of officeholders. Perhaps there was some envy behind these attacks; the Whigs, too, would have liked to hold a convention and nominate a candidate. But their group was uncohesive; it consisted of many different factions holding different political creeds, and the leaders of the party knew that the various factions could agree neither on political principles nor on the choice of a candidate.

Thus no Whig national convention was called. The party tried to fight Van Buren with a number of sectional candidates. The names of five "favorite sons" were put forward: William Henry Harrison seemed to be the most popular, with support from all parts of the country; from the Ohio legislature came the nomination of Judge John McLean, who was the candidate of the moribund Antimasons; the Whigs of Massachusetts were behind Daniel Webster; Tennessee was for Hugh Lawson

138

THE LOCOFOCOS, radical wing of the Democratic party in New York, fought monopoly, banks, vested interests. ...king equal rights for all, they were known as the Equal Rights party, but acquired their nickname when they ... matches — called locofocos — in order to continue a turbulent meeting at Tammany Hall after the regular ...emocrats turned out the gaslight to signify its end. Later, the term "Locofocos" came to mean all Democrats.

White; John Calhoun's supporters in the South upheld Senator Willie P. Mangum of North Carolina with John Tyler as his running mate.

The Whigs thought that the people in the various states would vote for the favorite sons rather than for Van Buren, and they hoped that through this scheme the election would be thrown into the House of Representatives, where anything might happen.

Undaunted, the Democratic rank and file refused to desert Van Buren, the party's official candidate. They were not won away from him when they read in the newspapers that the Little Magician's "mind beats round, like a tame bear tied to a stake, in a little circle, hardly bigger than the circumference of the head in which it is placed, seeking no other object than to convert the government into an instrument to serve himself or his office-holding friends." And they were ready to cast their vote for him even after they were told by Whig campaigners that "dandy" Van Buren was strutting and swaggering "like a crow in a gutter . . . laced up in corsets such as women in town wear, and if possible, tighter than the best of them" so that one found it "difficult to tell from his personal appearance whether he was a man or a woman."

The issues of the campaign were not as clearly defined as in 1832. This time there was no specific controversy, such as the fight over the United States Bank. The Democrats simply endorsed the policies of the Jackson administration, while the Whigs denounced the President and everything he stood for.

It had become fashionable to submit questions to the leading candidates, asking them for a declaration of their policies. To Van Buren, Harrison, and White five questions were submitted. "Will you if elected sign a bill to distribute the surplus revenue?" was the first. The second: "Will you if elected distribute pro-

THE POPULAR AND ELECTORAL VOTES IN THE 1836 ELECTION

| STATES | POPULAR VOTE | | | ELECTORAL VOTES FOR | | | | | | | | |
| | | | | PRESIDENT | | | | | VICE-PRESIDENT | | | |
	Martin Van Buren.	Whig Candidate.	Name of the Whig Candidate.	Martin Van Buren, N. Y.	William H. Harrison, O.	Hugh L. White, Tenn.	Daniel Webster, Mass.	Willie P. Mangum, N. C.	Richard M. Johnson, Ky.	Francis Granger, N. Y.	John Tyler, Va.	William Smith, Ala.
Maine	22,990	15,239	Harrison.	10	—	—	—	—	10	—	—	—
New Hampshire	18,722	6,228	Harrison.	7	—	—	—	—	7	—	—	—
Vermont	14,039	20,996	Harrison.	—	7	—	—	—	—	7	—	—
Massachusetts	33,542	41,287	Webster.	—	—	—	14	—	—	14	—	—
Rhode Island	2,964	2,710	Harrison.	4	—	—	—	—	4	—	—	—
Connecticut	19,291	18,749	Harrison.	8	—	—	—	—	8	—	—	—
New York	166,815	138,543	Harrison.	42	—	—	—	—	42	—	—	—
New Jersey	25,592	26,137	Harrison.	—	8	—	—	—	—	8	—	—
Pennsylvania	91,475	87,111	Harrison.	30	—	—	—	—	30	—	—	—
Delaware	4,153	4,733	Harrison.	—	3	—	—	—	—	3	—	—
Maryland	22,168	25,852	Harrison.	—	10	—	—	—	—	—	10	—
Virginia	30,261	23,468	White.	23	—	—	—	—	—	—	—	23
North Carolina	26,910	23,626	White.	15	—	—	—	—	15	—	—	—
South Carolina*	—	—		—	—	—	—	11	—	—	11	—
Georgia	22,104	24,876	White.	—	—	11	—	—	—	—	11	—
Alabama	20,506	15,612	White.	7	—	—	—	—	7	—	—	—
Mississippi	9,979	9,688	White.	4	—	—	—	—	4	—	—	—
Louisiana	3,653	3,383	White.	5	—	—	—	—	5	—	—	—
Arkansas	2,400	1,238	White.	3	—	—	—	—	3	—	—	—
Kentucky	33,435	36,955	Harrison.	—	15	—	—	—	—	15	—	—
Tennessee	26,129	36,168	White.	—	—	15	—	—	—	—	15	—
Missouri	10,995	7,337	White.	4	—	—	—	—	4	—	—	—
Ohio	96,948	105,404	Harrison.	—	21	—	—	—	—	21	—	—
Indiana	32,478	41,281	Harrison.	—	9	—	—	—	—	9	—	—
Illinois	18,097	14,983	Harrison.	5	—	—	—	—	5	—	—	—
Michigan	7,332	4,045	Harrison.	3	—	—	—	—	3	—	—	—
	762,978	736,250		170	73	26	14	11	147	77	47	23

* Electors were appointed by the legislature.

140

"GRAND MATCH between the Kinderhook Poney and the Ohio Ploughman" is the title of this cartoon. Harrison, the Whig candidate, is at left; Van Buren, candidate of the Democrats, and Jackson, the outgoing President, at right.

ceeds of sales of public lands?" The third: "Will you sign bills making appropriations to improve navigable streams above ports of entry?" The fourth: "Will you be willing to sign a bill chartering a national bank?" And the fifth asked the candidates' opinions as to whether the Houses of Congress had the constitutional right to expunge the records of a previous session (this, because the Senate had expunged the anti-Jackson resolution).

Harrison answered all questions in the affirmative except the last. Van Buren said that while he was for distribution of the surplus, he was not so certain that he would want to distribute the receipts from the sale of public lands—and of course he believed that Congress had the right to expunge any of its resolutions. White was noncommittal on three questions referring to his congressional record, but he advocated appropriations for the improvement of waterways and came out against the chartering of a national bank.

In this election a new group made its appearance. It was a radical section of the Democratic party—fighting monopoly, vested interests, and banking, and opposing paper money and

VAN BUREN, THE DANDY. The Little Magician's expensive habits were ridiculed maliciously by the Whigs.

labor-saving machines "by which drones are enabled to grow rich without honest industry." As the group asked equal rights for all men, it was called the Equal Rights party, or commonly known as the "Locofocos." They received this nickname after a turbulent meeting at Tammany Hall in which they opposed the nomination of some of the regular Democratic candidates. The exasperated regulars put out the lights in the hall, signifying the end of the meeting. However, the Equal Righters produced matches—called locofocos—from their pockets, lit candles and proceeded with the meeting; hence the name.

The actual contest was a dull affair with none of the excitement which marked the previous election. Twenty-six states voted, Arkansas and Michigan being the newcomers. The voting procedure was uniform now in twenty-five states out of the twenty-six. In every state save South Carolina—which held out until the Civil War—the choice of electors was made by popular vote. Martin Van Buren won with 170 votes against Harrison's seventy-three, White's twenty-six, Webster's fourteen, and Mangum's eleven.

As none of the four vice-presidential candidates received a clear-cut majority, the selection of the Vice-President went for the first and only time to the Senate, which chose Richard M. Johnson, giving him thirty-three votes against Francis Granger's sixteen.

During the counting of the electoral votes, Clay turned to Van Buren. "It is a cloudy day, sir," he observed. "The sun will shine," replied Van Buren confidently, "on the 4th of March, sir." A debate arose over the validity of Michigan's votes, since that state had not been admitted to the Union on the day of election. It was decided to announce the result in two ways: in one, Michigan's votes would be included; in the other, they would not.

On inauguration day Andrew Jackson, old, sick, and feeble but content, rode at the side

THE TWO PRESIDENTIAL CANDIDATES, VAN B

ATTEMPTED ASSASSINATION of a President, the first in American history. An insane man fired at President Jackson at the Capitol in 1835, but missed him.

of Van Buren in the phaeton made of woo from the frigate *Constitution*. Thousand cheered him along Pennsylvania Avenue. "F once," wrote Senator Benton, "the rising w eclipsed by the setting sun." It was a happy o casion for Old Hickory. Two days before th ceremonies he wrote to a friend that he w looking forward to seeing "the glorious scene Mr. Van Buren, once rejected by the Senat

142

...D HARRISON, ARE SHOWN AS BOXERS. AT LEFT, PRESIDENT JACKSON IS PRODDING HIS MAN.

...vorn into office by Chief Justice Taney, also ...ing rejected by the factious Senate." Now ...e day had come and with it his triumph.

...When the ceremonies were over, the outgo...g President walked slowly toward his car...ge. The crowd burst out in a tremendous ...out. The cry was such, noted Benton, "as ...ower never commanded, nor man in power ...ceived. It was affection, gratitude, and admi-

ration . . . the acclaim of posterity breaking from the bosoms of contemporaries."

A day later he visited Frank Blair in his home. There Jackson took his pipe and reminisced over his "reign." He talked of his achievements, he reviewed his failures. He said he had only two regrets. One was that he had not shot Clay, the other that he did not hang Calhoun.

OLD TIPPECANOE'S INAUGURATION

THE FOURTEENTH ELECTION—1840

WILLIAM HENRY HARRISON

AND JOHN TYLER

an Buren had scarcely warmed the presidential chair when the panic of 1837 broke
 over the country. A depression has many
causes, and bad times would have come even
if Jackson had not withdrawn the government's
funds from the Bank of the United States and
deposited them in "pet" banks throughout the
country. But this move and some of his other
measures accelerated the tempo of events.

These "pet" banks, many of them freshly
chartered, some of them without ample financial backing, threw themselves into the banking
business with the enthusiasm and optimism of
newcomers. They issued currency and gave
liberal loans. Their number increased from 329
in 1829—the year of Jackson's first inauguration—to 788 in 1837, when the panic broke.
Their capital grew from 110 million dollars to
290 millions, the circulation of their currency
from 48 million dollars to 149 millions, and
their loans jumped from 137 millions to 525
millions. The way to inflation was open.

Speculation was widespread throughout the
nation. The safest way of maintaining the
value of one's money during inflation is to get
rid of it. One buys things. One invests. One

speculates. In the Western part of the country
speculation in land was booming. Since transportation had become relatively easy and prices
for agricultural products were high, people
sought good Western land. However, before
the settlers arrived there, land speculators had
already bought up the choice sites, selling them
at good profits to others. Sometimes a parcel of
land changed hands as much as ten times before
it came into the possession of the real settler.
It was a "land-office business."

In 1834 the government sold four million
acres of land; the year after, it sold fifteen million acres, and in 1836, twenty million acres,
five times the acreage of two years before.
From such sales the Treasury received $4,857,-
000 in 1834, and in 1836 the receipts were $24,-
877,000.

The money from the land sales alone was
sufficient to pay for all government expenses.
And what happened to it? The Treasury deposited the receipts in the state banks; the
banks in turn loaned it out again—mostly to
land speculators, who immediately bought more
land from the government, paying for it with
the money they had borrowed from the banks.
(turn to page 148)

145

WILLIAM H. HARRISON (1773-1841), the aged "hero of Tippecanoe," was chosen as the Whig candidate in preference to Clay or Scott. In an exuberant campaign in which wealthy Harrison became the log-cabin, hard-cider candidate, he won with 234 electoral votes to Martin Van Buren's 60.

JOHN TYLER (1790-1862), received the vice-presidential nomination, supposedly because of a political deal in Virginia. Without this excellent bargain, Tyler would not have become President. Harrison died after a month in office, and Tyler became President without election.

MARTIN VAN BUREN (1782-1862), the outgoing President, was Democratic candidate for re-election. The ensuing campaign was highly emotional; political issues were stressed but lightly. Using old-fashioned tactics against the log-cabin brigades, the Democrats lost.

RICHARD M. JOHNSON (1780-1850), bitterly opposed as Van Buren's running mate in 1836, was not renominated by the Democratic convention in 1840. The choice of a Vice-President was left to the electorate. Nevertheless, Johnson went on the stump, campaigning for his re-election.

JACKSON'S LEGACY TO MARTIN VAN BUREN
The destruction of the U. S. Bank and distribution of the Treasury surplus in "pet" banks had far-reaching effects. The new banks issued "wildcat" currency; with this inflated money the people speculated in

CROUS COUNTRY WHICH SOON WAS IN THE THROES OF A SEVERE FINANCIAL DEPRESSION.

nd. To stop this process whereby the speculators ade fortunes and secured the most valuable public nds, Jackson issued the *Specie Circular*, demand- g payment in gold or silver for land sales after August 15, 1836. This government measure, aided by speculation and crop failures, led to a severe de- pression. Van Buren had hardly warmed the presiden- tial chair when the panic of 1837 engulfed the U.S.

The Treasury received the money, deposited it in the state banks, from which the speculators borrowed it again. Again they bought land, paying for it with borrowed money—and the cycle began anew, transferring "to speculators the most valuable public lands," as Jackson observed, and paying the government "by a credit on the books of the banks."

Such a situation could not last long. In July, 1836, Jackson decided to stop "the endless chain." In the *Specie Circular* he declared that the Treasury would not accept paper money for land sales after August 15. All the land purchased from the government after that date must be paid for in "specie"—in gold or silver. With this the speculative buying and selling came to a halt.

Another worry of the administration was the surplus. By 1835 every cent of the public debt had been paid off and the government had no outstanding obligations. It was therefore necessary to find a way to dispose of the surplus.

After much debate Congress ruled that the surplus should be loaned to the individual states. The states, upon coming into possession of this money, began to spend it, and they spent it quickly. They intensified their internal improvement programs, built roads and canals, gave loans to private business enterprise. By 1837 the debt of the individual states rose to 170 million dollars, a much larger sum than they could hope to repay from their tax resources.

The inflationary trend stimulated business, and the additional profit was spent on luxuries, mostly bought from abroad. The import of silk, for instance, rose from six million dollars in 1831 to almost twenty-three million dollars in 1836. With a great demand for goods, more was imported than exported. And the already unfavorable trade balance was increased by the crop failure of 1835, when European wheat had to be shipped to America.

Disaster was not far off. When American drafts and bills of exchange began to sell at a discount in London, the Bank of England raised its discount rates. And when English exporters refused to extend credit to their American customers but asked for hard money, the American businessmen, too, demanded gold or silver for

"THE TIMES" IS THE TITLE OF THIS BIT
Barefooted workers lean idly on a billboard advertising "money to loan at 7% per month" and a grand lottery scheme; in the background there is a run on the Mechanics Bank. In the center a widow and child

their merchandise. The bank vaults were soon empty—most of the gold and silver had already been shipped abroad.

LITHOGRAPH DRAWN BY EDWARD W. CLAY, ILLUSTRATING THE EFFECTS OF THE PANIC OF 1837.

...re begging; next to her lingers a sailor whose ...ip is tied up at the wharf. The factory is "closed ...r the present"; the Street Hotel is "for sale"; ...d in the Sheriff's office foreclosed property is auctioned off. The only thriving businesses are the Liquor Store and the Licensed Pawnbroker. Aloft in the sky, Jackson's hat and spectacles indicate that the country had him to thank for this unbounded misery.

The final blow came with the issuance of the ...Distribution Act, which required that the "pet" ...anks repay the borrowed government funds in specie, a heavy burden on the institutions. They met the first payment on January 1, 1837, but when they were to make the second on

149

HENRY CLAY CALLS ON PRESIDENT VAN BUREN AT SARATOGA AFTER MEETING THURLOW W

When Clay heard that in New York things were not well, he went to Saratoga in the summer of 1839 to confer with Thurlow Weed, the state's most in-fluential political boss, and also paid a courtesy on President Van Buren. But his conversations not bring any good results. The Whigs chose Ge

April 1, they were unable to do so. By May— two months after Van Buren's inauguration— every bank in the country had suspended specie payments; by summer the economic life of the nation was paralyzed. In England many firms, unable to collect their American debts, went into bankruptcy. This forced English co mills to close, which in turn brought d the price of cotton in America. With low p on cotton, the South suffered; the impoveri Southerners had to curtail their importatio farm produce from the West. The Wes

...tion
...upon
...sp...
...m...

...d that I will
...ain-I may
...hats fashi...

...ARED HIMSELF AGAINST CLAY'S CANDIDACY.
...rrison as their candidate (second from left). The
...arded gentlemen are Clay supporters who swore not
...shave till their hero should become President.

...rmers, losing an important part of their mar-
...t, cut down their purchases of goods from
...e Northeastern manufacturers, which re-
...ced production; thousands of factory work-
...s were dismissed. There was no escape from
...e depression which engulfed the nation.

Martin Van Buren, like all the other Presidents before and after him up to Theodore Roosevelt's time, believed that the Federal Government should not interfere with business. He adhered to the traditional American philosophy that it was not the duty of the President to help restore prosperity, but rather a task for private individuals. The President's responsibility was to keep the government's finances in order, and this Van Buren was determined to do. In a special session of Congress, the distribution of the surplus was repealed and the government was permitted to issue Treasury notes to meet expenses.

Van Buren also asked Congress for the establishment of an independent treasury where deposits would be safe in the future; he proposed strong vaults or subtreasuries in various parts of the country where government money could be kept. The opposition took up the issue at once. Whig politicians said that the Subtreasury Bill would be another measure against business; Henry Clay asserted that it would "reduce all property in value by two thirds."

The President fought stubbornly for the bill, which was not passed until 1840. By then the Whig National Convention had already met. It was a meeting of strangely heterogeneous ele-

THE LOG CABIN became a symbol for the Whig candidate. It all began with a harmless newspaper remark saying that if Harrison should be given a pension and a barrel of hard cider, he would be happy to sit out the rest of his days in a log cabin. Taking up the Democrats' challenge, the Whigs made Old Tippecanoe the "log-cabin and hard-cider candidate." Clay orated: "The battle is now between the log cabin and the palaces, between hard cider and champagne."

151

IN THE CAMPAIGN HARRISON, RICH OWNER OF 2000 ACRES, WAS REPRESENTED AS A SIMP[...]

This is an imaginary incident, picturing a visit of the leading Democratic politicians at Harrison's place in North Bend, Ohio. Francis P. Blair, editor of the *Globe*, Amos Kendall, the Postmaster General, and President Martin Van Buren, arriving in a [...] tuous coach with liveried lackeys, are discussin[...] to make Harrison unpopular with the electorate. [...] would portray him as a drunkard abolitionist [...]

ments. The cotton planters of South Carolina, fuming against protection, were Whigs. The manufacturers of Massachusetts, asking for protection, were Whigs. The bankers of Pennsylvania, who had despised Jackson's attitude toward the Bank of the United States, were Whigs. Southern conservatives, who had fought

Jackson and his "executive tyranny," [...] Whigs. Young Abraham Lincoln, adm[...] Henry Clay as his "beau ideal of a statesma[...] for whom I fought all my humble life," [...] Whig. Moneyed people who were afra[...] government interference were Whigs. [...] planters, crying for help against Cuba,

152

u seem fatigued, if you will accept
a log cabin with a Western farm—
u are welcome, I have no champagne
ou a mug of good cider, with some—
gs, and good clean beds. I am a
odsman. I have cleared some land
ndians, and made the Red Coats
e.

...ILE VAN BUREN WAS CALLED AN EPICURE.
...ison remarks that he has no champagne but he can
...ive the visitors "a mug of good cider and clean
...eds." Van Buren pities Harrison because he is poor,
"lives in a log cabin and ploughs his own ground."

Whigs. The former Antimasons were now
Whigs. Everyone who was against Van Buren
was a Whig.

How could all these factions agree on a common policy? The answer was: they could not.
n the convention Whig leaders did not even
ttempt to suggest a platform of principles;

they tried, instead, to unite in support of a
candidate who would be acceptable to all the
incongruous groups.

The outstanding figure in the Whig ranks
was Henry Clay. He was the favorite candidate
of many states, but it was feared that he could
not unite the various factions. He had been
in public life for three decades, and in thirty
years a politician collects many enemies. He
had definite political views—another great
handicap. As his American System favored a
policy of protection, he could not carry the
votes of the Southern anti-protectionists; as he
was a Mason, he could not rally the votes of
the anti-Masonic groups. When Clay saw that
he could not get the nomination, he declared:
"If my name creates any obstacle to Union and
Harmony, away with it, and concentrate upon
some individual more acceptable to all branches
of the opposition."

The Whig "Union-and-Harmony" convention had a choice between two military heroes
—General Winfield Scott and General William
Henry Harrison. Neither of them was an experienced statesman, neither a colorful personality.

When the balloting began, Henry Clay was
in the lead with 103 votes against General Harrison's ninety-four and General Scott's forty-
seven. For three full days the convention proceeded with the voting. At last Thurlow Weed,
the New York politician, tipped the scales, persuading his state to vote for "the hero of Tippecanoe." With New York's support sixty-
eight-year-old William Henry Harrison became the nominee, the oldest presidential candidate the United States ever had, receiving on
the final ballot 148 votes against Clay's ninety
and Scott's sixteen.

For the Vice-Presidency the convention
chose John Tyler of Virginia. It was said that
he secured the nomination through a deal made
a year before the convention met, when he had
agreed not to run in the senatorial contest
against the Whig Senator from Virginia. For
this kindness he was promised the vice-presidential office at the next convention. It was a
lucky deal for Tyler; without it he would never
have become President of the United States.

With Harrison's nomination the most exuberant, exciting and nonsensical campaign in

153

A NUMBER OF HARRISON ALMANACS EXTOLLED THE VIRTUES OF OLD TIPPECANOE AND WHIGS.

American presidential history began. A circus press agent could not have arranged for more ballyhoo than did Harrison's managers. The Whigs acclaimed their old candidate as the man of the young reformers, although Harrison himself was quiet about his policies. Before the last election Nicholas Biddle, director of the Bank, had advised him to "Say not one single word about his principles or his creed—let him say nothing—promise nothing. Let no committee, no convention, no town meeting ever extract from him a single word about what he thinks now and will do hereafter. Let the use of pen and ink be wholly forbidden."

And apparently "Old Tippecanoe" remembered Biddle's advice. He based his campaign on denunciation of the Democrats. Unemployment, closed factories, low cotton prices, di-

minishing land values—the depression with all its hardships—all these were blamed on Van Buren.

It was a strange contest, different from anything the country had seen before. In it Harrison, the wealthy son of a governor, became a simple backwoodsman. The Democratic press attacked this kind of truth-bending. The newspapers sneered at the "poverty" of Harrison, who lived on a luxurious estate of two thousand acres and employed an array of farmers. A correspondent to the Baltimore *Republican* reported that a friend of Clay told him after Harrison was nominated: "Give him a barrel of Hard Cider, and settle a pension of $2,000 a year on him, and my word for it, he will sit the remainder of his days in his Log Cabin, by the side of a 'sea-coal' fire and study moral philosophy."

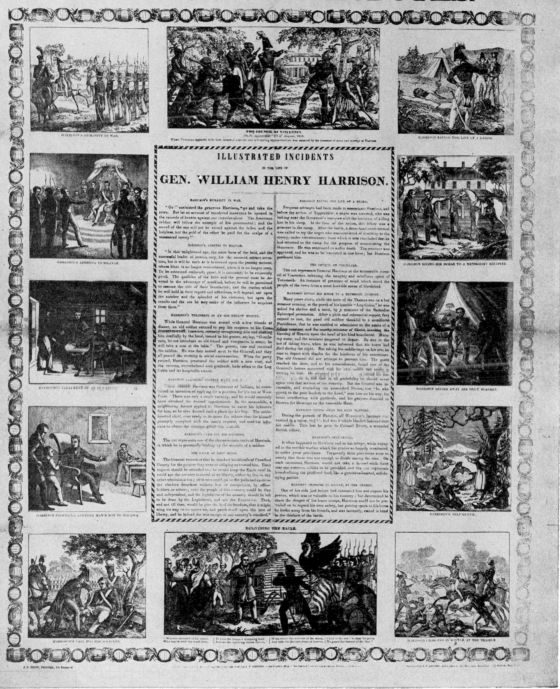

'LOG CABIN ANECDOTES.'

THOUSANDS OF BROADSIDES and printed handbills were distributed during the campaign in which the Whigs, unable to agree on a platform acceptable to all factions of the party, simply appealed to the emotions of the voters.

REFORM CANDIDATE HARRISON knocks out the Democrats. Democratic party managers Amos Kendall and Francis Blair are tumbling, bringing Van Buren down with them. From the log cabin Major Jack Downing, an imaginary figure representing public opinion, says: "I swan if the General haint knocked Amos into a cider barrel."

Clever Whig propagandists pounced upon this remark. This was the very thing they needed to bolster up their man. In no time Harrison became "the log-cabin and hard-cider candidate." Whig newspapers reiterated the story constantly, and the people were led to believe that Harrison was living in a log cabin, that he never drank strong liquor, and that he plowed and worked his own land like all the other humble frontiersmen.

The log-cabin sentiment caught the imagination of the masses, for the home of the pioneers was a symbol of the country—thousands had been born in log cabins, thousands were still living in log cabins. Log-cabin badges, log-cabin songs, log-cabin newspapers, Harrison almanacs, Tippecanoe handkerchiefs, Tippe-

canoe badges, Tippecanoe breastpins, cider barrels and coonskin caps were seen everywhere. All over the land log-cabin processions filled the streets of the cities, with real log cabins on floats, real smoke curling from the chimneys. Such a parade was held at Baltimore the night before the Democrats began their convention on May 4. It was said that 100,000 people attended it. Log cabins were drawn by six horses and adorned with foxskins and buckhorns—the latchstrings hung out and big barrels of hard cider were placed in the rear with gourds nearby. A delegation from Allegany rolled along a ball ten feet in diameter and covered with mottoes, inscriptions, quotations, and rhymes, while they sang to the tune of "The Little Pig's Tail":

THE 1840 CAMPAIGN ADDS NEW EXPRESSIONS TO THE LANGUAGE

THE ORIGIN OF O.K. was most probably "Old Kinderhook," Martin Van Buren's nickname and the name of his home. Here he is shown moving toward the White House with his Subtreasury Bill on his back, led by Jackson.

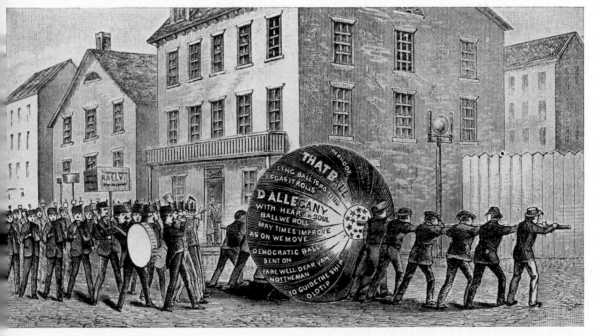

"IT IS THE BALL A-ROLLING on for Tippecanoe and Tyler too," sang the Whigs when a delegation from Allegany rolled a huge, inscribed ball through the streets of Baltimore. Thus the phrase "Keep the ball rolling."

"What caused this great commotion, motion, mo-
tion,
  Our country through?
  It is the ball a-rolling on
  For Tippecanoe and Tyler too, for Tippecanoe
    and Tyler too,
  And with them we'll beat little Van, Van
  Van is a used-up man;
  And with them we'll beat little Van."

Other Whigs, amid noise and acclamation,
carried banners with the verse:

"Farewell, dear Van,
  You are not our man;
  To guide the ship
  We'll try Old Tip."

The Democrats renominated Van Buren without opposition. However, as the states could
not agree on the vice-presidential candidate, the
convention resolved that it was "expedient at
the present time, not to choose between the
individuals in nomination," but to leave the decision to the electorate.

The Democratic platform was against internal improvement; for "no more revenue . . .
than is required to defray the necessary expenses of Government"; against the charter of
the U. S. Bank; against the abolitionists, who
tried "to induce Congress to interfere with
questions of slavery"; and for "separation of
the moneys of the Government from banking
institutions," which is "indispensable for the
safety of the funds of the Government and
the rights of the people."

TOWARD VICTORY. The Harrison hard-cider locomotive crashes into "Uncle Sam's Cab," unseating Van
Buren and forcing the horse down to its knees.

WILLIAM HENRY HARRISON WON THE ELEC

In the campaign, the Democratic voices were
too feeble to counteract the mass emotionalism
fostered by the Whigs. Directing their strategy

With a log cabin and barrel of hard Cider for a fulcrum public opinion for a lever, with old Tip, on the top end the ball of Locofocoism will be rolled into oblivion and a gallant soldier raised to the white house.
March 4th 1841.

WHITE HOUSE

CAPITOL

LOCO FOCO

Sub Treasury

TIP END

OBLIVION

NARROW MARGIN, POLLING 1,275,016 POPULAR VOTES AS OPPOSED TO VAN BUREN'S 1,129,102.

along old, proven lines, the Democrats tried to reason, to discuss and argue. They assailed Harrison because he was a member of the old Federal party of 1799—the party that established the National Bank, opposed the War of 1812, supported high tariff for protection and

159

internal improvements at government expense, and now called for a second assumption of state debts.

But this reasoning did not go over well with the masses, who sang:

"Make way for old Tip, turn out, turn out!
Make way for old Tip, turn out, turn out!
'Tis the people's decree,
Their choice he shall be,
So Martin Van Buren turn out, turn out!
So Martin Van Buren turn out, turn out!"

Farmers called their horses "Tip and Ty." It was said: "The hens in the West never lay an egg nowadays but they cackle: Tip-tip! Tip-tip! Tyler!"

(Van Buren was called "Old Kinderhook" after the place where he lived, and often by just the first letters of these two words. This seems to be the origin of "O.K." and not Jackson's supposedly faulty spelling of *Oll Korrect*.)

The Whigs attacked Van Buren with telling effect. They distributed a speech made by Charles Ogle in the House of Representatives on "The Royal Splendor of the President's Palace." Ogle described this palace "as splendid as that of the Caesars, and as richly adorned as the proudest Asiatic mansion"; and he said that the garden had rare plants, shrubs, and parterres in the style of the Royal Gardens in England and that men who looked after this were paid with the people's money to spend their time plucking up, by the roots, burdock and sheep sorrel. The country was astonished to read that the Blue Elliptical Saloon of the presidential mansion was garnished with gilt mirrors big as a barn door, and in it were chairs that cost $600 a set. And Whig newspaper writers declared that a democracy where the President sleeps on French bedsteads, walks on Royal Wilton carpets, and sits on French taborets, eats his *pâté de foie gras* and *dinde désossé* from silver plates with forks of gold, sips his *soupe à la Reine* with gold spoons from a silver tureen, and rides in a gilded maroon coach is no democracy at all.

The Democrats had little success with their defense of Van Buren—the people chose to believe Ogle's description.

In the midst of the campaign excitement, the assembly of a few men at Albany was hardly noticed. There a number of representatives

ONE MONTH AFTER HIS INAUGURATION HARR

from six states met and laid the foundation for a third party, which played an important part in future elections. They were the Abolitionists, who now for the first time named candidates for the presidential and vice-presidential offices.

The election began in Ohio and Pennsylvania on October 30 and ended in North Carolina on

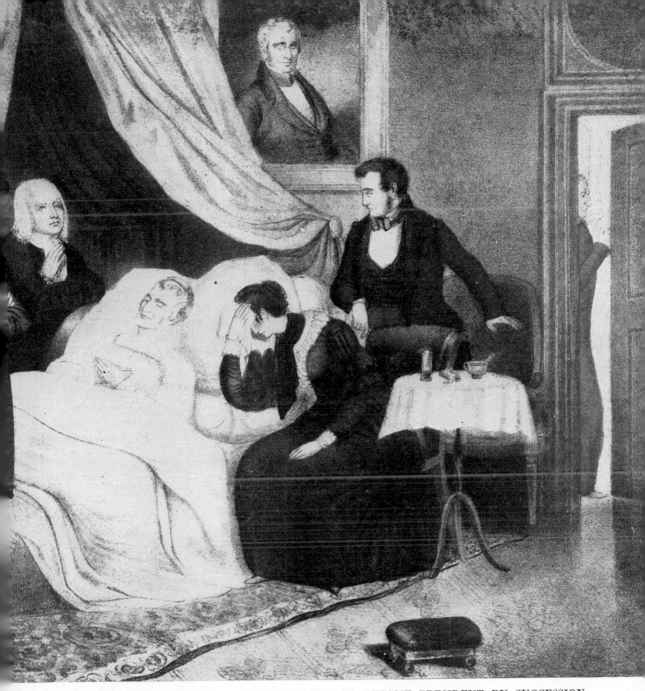

MAKING JOHN TYLER THE FIRST VICE-PRESIDENT TO BECOME PRESIDENT BY SUCCESSION.

November 12. The result was close. Harrison had 1,275,016 votes against Van Buren's 1,129,-102 and the Abolitionist James G. Birney's 7,069. In Maine, Old Tippecanoe won by only 411 votes, and in Pennsylvania by only 349 out of a total of 287,693. But the distribution of the votes was such that Harrison received 234 electoral votes against Van Buren's sixty.

The Democrats wailed: "The standard-bearer of the Federalist and Abolition party has been elected, if the process by which this has been brought about may be called an election. . . ."

But for the Whigs it was a day to celebrate. "The people are free again," their papers wrote.

"Our republican institutions are redeemed from the grasp of tyrants. Let the people . . . rejoice."

The neutral Philadelphia *Public Ledger* was more levelheaded in summing up the election: "For two years past, the most ordinary operations of business have been neglected and President-making has become every citizen's chief concern. The result being uncertain, some have been afraid to engage in new enterprises, others have retired from business, others have not dared to prosecute their business with the old vigor. Millions of dollars will now change hands on election bets; millions of days have been taken from useful labor to listen to stump orators, and millions more to build log cabins, erect hickory poles, and march in ridiculous, degrading, mob-creating processions; millions of dollars have been wasted in soul- and body-destroying intemperance, in paying demagogues for preaching treason and bribing knaves to commit perjury and cast fraudulent votes. However high the hopes inspired by the election of General Harrison, they will prove to be delusive. A national bank cannot be created; the sub-treasury cannot be repealed; the monetary expansion and speculation which the hopes of these measures will create will be quickly followed by contraction, by ruin, and the prostration of the speculators."

When inauguration day came, the President-elect rode to the Capitol on a white charger, escorted by many of his friends, and on the eastern portico he took the oath and delivered his address, which was full of allusions to Roman history and proconsuls. One month later he was dead. A cold developed into pneumonia, and that was the end of Old Tippecanoe. He was succeeded by John Tyler, the first Vice-President in our history to become President by succession.

THE POPULAR AND ELECTORAL VOTES IN THE 1840 ELECTION

STATES	POPULAR VOTE			ELECTORAL VOTES FOR					
				PRESIDENT		VICE-PRESIDENT			
	W. H. Harrison, Ohio. Whig	Martin Van Buren, N. Y. Democrat	James G. Birney, N. Y. Abolitionist	W. H. Harrison, Ohio.	Martin Van Buren, N. Y.	John Tyler, Va.	R. M. Johnson, Ky.	L. W. Tazewell, Va.	James K. Polk, Tenn.
Maine	46,612	46,201	194	10	—	10	—	—	—
New Hampshire	26,163	32,761	126	—	7	—	7	—	—
Vermont	32,440	18,018	319	7	—	7	—	—	—
Massachusetts	72,874	51,944	1,621	14	—	14	—	—	—
Rhode Island	5,278	3,301	42	4	—	4	—	—	—
Connecticut	31,601	25,296	174	8	—	8	—	—	—
New York	225,817	212,527	2,808	42	—	42	—	—	—
New Jersey	33,351	31,034	69	8	—	8	—	—	—
Pennsylvania	144,021	143,672	343	30	—	30	—	—	—
Delaware	5,967	4,874	—	3	—	3	—	—	—
Maryland	33,528	28,752	—	10	—	10	—	—	—
Virginia	42,501	43,893	—	—	23	—	22	—	1
North Carolina	46,376	33,782	—	15	—	15	—	—	—
South Carolina*	—	—	—	—	11	—	—	11	—
Georgia	40,261	31,921	—	11	—	11	—	—	—
Alabama	28,471	33,991	—	—	7	—	7	—	—
Mississippi	19,518	16,995	—	4	—	4	—	—	—
Louisiana	11,296	7,616	—	5	—	5	—	—	—
Kentucky	58,489	32,616	—	15	—	15	—	—	—
Tennessee	60,391	48,289	—	15	—	15	—	—	—
Missouri	22,972	29,760	—	—	4	—	4	—	—
Arkansas	5,160	6,766	—	—	3	—	3	—	—
Ohio	148,157	124,782	903	21	—	21	—	—	—
Indiana	65,302	51,604	—	9	—	9	—	—	—
Illinois	45,537	47,476	149	—	5	—	5	—	—
Michigan	22,933	21,131	321	3	—	3	—	—	—
	1,275,016	1,129,102	7,069	234	60	234	48	11	1

* Electors were appointed by the legislature.

162

JOHN TYLER (1790-1862)
PHOTOGRAPH BY
MATHEW B. BRADY

POLK DRIVES TO THE WHITE HOUSE

THE FIFTEENTH ELECTION—1844

JAMES K. POLK

That a campaign of slogans and of manufactured emotionalism could land a candidate in the Presidency was a new lesson for the Democrats. Now that it was over and log-cabin processions, hard-cider barrels, and Tippecanoe songs, badges, and emblems had become a matter of the past, they realized how effective it all had been. They did not laugh derisively any more about it; they felt outsmarted. They accused the Whigs of fraudulent practices and attacked them for using money to buy votes and for deceiving, cajoling, luring, seducing, enticing, intimidating, and bulldozing the electorate into giving its vote to Old Tippecanoe. But after all the abusive adjectives were spent, the Democrats began to work in earnest to regain the loss four years hence. Harrison had not even been inaugurated when they started preparations for the next election, boosting Van Buren as the party's candidate.

If the Democrats were bitter, the Whigs were no less so. They had elected a President, and now they had none. After one month in office, Tippecanoe passed away, and his place was taken by Vice-President John Tyler, a Southern aristocrat. The Northern Whigs were anxious to learn whether the new President would follow their faction's nationalistic policies. Before his nomination as Vice-President, Tyler had said that he was "a firm and decided Whig." But was he? He disagreed with Clay and the nationalistic wing of the party on every major political issue. He was against a protective tariff, opposed internal improvements at national expense, and resisted the distribution of receipts from the sales of public lands. Quite naturally, he upheld the political doctrine of the South. He was for states' rights, he did not believe that the Constitution gave the Federal Government authority to interfere with the institution of slavery, and he considered Jackson's nullification proclamation unconstitutional.

The new President had an independent mind. Tyler would not be used as a rubber stamp by the Cabinet he had inherited from Harrison. He vetoed the Whig bill for a national bank, which was to replace the subtreasury system. The Whigs were disturbed by this veto. Some Cabinet members—friends of Clay—consulted with the President, and then drafted a revised plan. Clay was confident that Tyler would be subservient to his wishes. "I'll drive him before

165

JAMES K. POLK (1795-1849)
DAGUERREOTYPE BY
MATHEW B. BRADY

JAMES K. POLK (1795-1849), the Democrats' compromise candidate and the first "dark horse" in presidential elections, won 170 electoral votes to Henry Clay's 105.

GEORGE M. DALLAS (1792-1864), Senator and Minister to Russia under Van Buren, received the Democratic nomination for Vice-President after Silas Wright had refused it.

HENRY CLAY (1777-1852), presidential candidate of 1824 and 1832, was again the Whig choice. Clay, who opposed the annexation of Texas, lost by less than 40,000 votes.

T. FRELINGHUYSEN (1787-1862), Mayor of Newark, Chancellor of the University of New York and a deeply religious man, was the Whigs' candidate for the Vice-Presidency.

JAMES G. BIRNEY (1792-1857) was once again the Abolitionist candidate. In New York, enough people voted for Birney to give this decisive state to the Democrats.

JOHN TYLER (1790-1862), outgoing President, was backed for the Presidency by a coalition of dissatisfied Whigs and Democrats, later withdrawing from the race.

me," he boasted. But when Congress passed the second bill on the bank, Tyler vetoed it again because, in his opinion, it did not safeguard the rights of the states.

Now the Whigs had had enough of the President's "turns and twists." The Cabinet, with the exception of Webster, resigned, and a caucus of Whig Congressmen declared that their political alliance with Tyler was terminated and in the future "those who brought the President into power can no longer, in any manner or degree be justly held responsible or blamed for the administration of the executive branch of the government."

As election year approached, a number of contestants vied with each other for the Democratic nomination. Martin Van Buren's, John C. Calhoun's, Richard M. Johnson's, James Buchanan's, and Lewis Cass's names were canvassed in the country.

Tyler—after he lost the Whig support—tried to shine as a Democrat, hoping that he might receive the nomination of the party. His supporters bought a number of Democratic newspapers, replaced the old editors with Tyler

THE VOTES IN THE 1844 ELECTION

STATES	POPULAR VOTE			ELECTORAL VOTE	
	James K. Polk, Tenn. Democrat	Henry Clay, Ky. Whig	James G. Birney, N.Y. Abolitionis	Polk and Dallas.	Clay and Frelinghuysen.
Maine................	45,719	34,378	4,836	9	—
New Hampshire.......	27,160	17,866	4,161	6	—
Vermont.............	18,041	26,770	3,954	—	6
Massachusetts........	52,846	67,418	10,860	—	12
Rhode Island........	4,867	7,322	107	—	4
Connecticut.........	29,841	32,832	1,943	—	6
New York...........	237,588	232,482	15,812	36	—
New Jersey..........	37,495	38,318	131	—	7
Pennsylvania........	167,535	161,203	3,138	26	—
Delaware...........	5,996	6,278	—	—	3
Maryland...........	32,676	35,984	—	—	8
Virginia............	49,570	43,677	—	17	—
North Carolina......	39,287	43,232	—	—	11
South Carolina*.....	—	—	—	9	—
Georgia............	44,177	42,100	—	10	—
Alabama...........	37,740	26,084	—	9	—
Mississippi.........	25,126	19,206	—	6	—
Louisiana..........	13,782	13,083	—	6	—
Kentucky..........	51,988	61,255	—	—	12
Tennessee..........	59,917	60,030	—	—	13
Missouri...........	41,369	31,251	—	7	—
Arkansas..........	9,546	5,504	—	3	—
Ohio..............	149,117	155,057	8,050	—	23
Michigan..........	27,759	24,337	3,632	5	—
Indiana...........	70,181	67,867	2,106	12	—
Illinois...........	57,920	45,528	3,570	9	—
	1,337,243	1,299,062	62,300	170	105

* Electors were appointed by the legislature.

The mountains labor and bring forth ridiculous mice! Here's the trap that will catch them!

Possession being nine points in the law I must head them both off!

Repudiation.

Dont be afeard it's only us!

VETO.

Volcano or Loco Focoism.

Free trade!

It's the old Kinderhook mouse and his nullifying crony!

National Faith

"THE MOUNTAIN IN LABOR" shows President Tyler sitting with his Veto sword before the Volcano of Loco Focoism, from which the Old Kinderhook mouse and his nullifying crony—Van Buren and Calhoun—emerge. On the left of the drawing Henry Clay utters the hope that the trap of National Faith will finally catch the two mice.

men, and worked hard to convince the readers that the President was a real and regular Democrat. Tyler, keen to be elected in his own right, sent a messenger to one of Van Buren's friends, offering Van Buren a place on the Supreme Court bench. The emissary argued that as Van Buren would not be able to get the Democratic nomination, it would be to his advantage to accept an appointment to the Supreme Court. Silas Wright, to whom the offer was made, replied: "Tell Mr. Tyler from me, that if he desires to give to the whole country a broader, deeper, heartier laugh than it ever had and at his own expense, he can effect it by making that nomination."

After this interview nothing more was heard of the proposal. Tyler's chances, like those of the other contenders, dwindled as spring came and, with it, the time for the two nominating conventions.

It seemed certain that the Whigs would nominate Henry Clay, and that Martin Van Buren would be the choice of the Democrats, having the support of twenty-four out of twenty-six states.

But all at once the political situation changed. John C. Calhoun, who had followed A. P. Upshur as Secretary of State, concluded a treaty with the Republic of Texas for its annexation to the United States, and shortly before the Whig nominating convention, President Tyler submitted the treaty to the Senate for ratification.

The two principal contestants were forced to announce their views on annexation. Both wrote letters, and these letters were published in their partys' newspapers on the same day—April 27, 1844—two weeks after the treaty had reached the Senate. In them, both Clay and Van Buren expressed similar opinions; both were against annexation. Clay said that "annexation and war with Mexico are identical" and that "Texas ought not to be received into the Union, as an integral part of it, in decided

167

opposition to the wishes of a considerable and respectable portion of the Confederacy."

But a far greater sensation was created by Van Buren's letter. The Democrats were bewildered. Van Buren, opposing the policies of his own party, explained in a lengthy argument why he had chosen this course. He was against annexation, so he said, because it would lead to war with Mexico and in such a contest the United States would be the wrongdoer in the eyes of the world. This he would not support. America had a character to maintain among the nations of the earth; lust of power had never in the past led us to aggression and conquest, and it should not so lead us in the future. It was an honest and courageous document, costing Van Buren the nomination.

The letters of the two prospective candidates President Tyler answered in his message to the Senate. He argued that if Texas were not annexed now, it would be lost forever, quoting Andrew Jackson, who warned that the "golden moment to obtain Texas must not be lost, or Texas must, from necessity, be thrown into the arms of England and be lost to the United States."

Thus the annexation issue was thrust on the two political parties shortly before their nominating conventions were to assemble.

As the Whig convention met only four days after Clay's opinions were published in the *National Intelligencer*, there was no time to organize an opposition to his candidacy on that account, and he was nominated by acclamation. The Whigs were united as never before— Tyler's alleged treachery gave them unity. Their convention was so harmonious that all business could be concluded in a single sitting. In their platform they were silent on the annexation issue. Using only general terms upholding the party's principles, they came out for "a well-regulated currency; a tariff for revenue to defray the necessary expenses of the government, and discriminating with special reference to the protection of the domestic labor of the country; the distribution of the proceeds from the sales of the public lands; a single term for the Presidency; a reform of executive usurpations; and generally such an administration of the affairs of the country as shall impart to every branch of the public service the greatest

A CAMPAIGN CARTOON SUPPORTING CANDI
This was a cartoonist's fantasy, not to be borne ou
by reality. Henry Clay, the candidate of the Whigs

practical efficiency, controlled by a well-regulated and wise economy."

The Democratic convention did not meet until a month later. After Van Buren made hi

ENRY CLAY. AS PRESIDENT TYLER LEAVES THE PRESIDENTIAL CHAIR, CLAY STEPS INTO IT.

ost the election to the nose-thumbing James Polk, running mate, George M. Dallas, and former Presi-
he Democratic nominee. At Polk's right are his dent Andrew Jackson, the beloved leader of the party.

ttitude known on annexation, many of his the cotton-growing and slaveholding territory.
most ardent supporters turned against him. But as the delegates to the nominating conven-
No longer was he acceptable to the Southern tion had already been chosen before the publi-
ving of the party, who demanded expansion of cation of his letter, the majority of them were

THE OPPOSING CANDIDATES, CLAY AND POLK, "POLITICAL COCK FIGHTERS" WHOSE STRUGG

instructed to vote for him. This posed a dilemma for the delegates. They knew that Van Buren's attitude on Texas had, in the meantime, changed the minds of their constituents, but as they were sent to the convention to support Van Buren, they were bound by their instruc-

tions. In this quandary a number of those from the South resigned; others were determined t disobey their instructions.

The Democratic Washington *Globe* asserte that Van Buren had not lost a single supporte because of his Texas letter. The anti-Van Bure

170

movement was the work of Calhoun, said the newspaper. "It is the last card of this desperate competitor who has been playing for twenty-five years for the Presidency with the frenzy of a gamester. It cannot win."

However, the opposition to Van Buren's can-didacy seemed more than the work of Calhoun. The enemies of the Little Magician played their cards shrewdly. At the beginning of the Democratic convention, General Saunders of North Carolina, who had championed the two-thirds rule in Van Buren's behalf four years before, proposed it again. This time the adoption of the rule was to work against Van Buren's interests. While he could win the nomination with a simple majority, he could not—since the Southerners were for annexation—gain the support of two thirds of the delegates.

The voting on the two-thirds rule showed an interesting division: 148 delegates were for its adoption, 116 against it. If the Northern delegates would have given their undivided support to Van Buren, they could easily have defeated it, for they commanded a majority. But the North realized that the candidate of the party must be acceptable not only to their section but to the West and South as well, otherwise he could not win against Clay.

As the balloting for the candidates began, the excitement became intense. Amidst scenes of confusion and disorder the delegates cast their votes. Van Buren needed 178 votes to be nominated. On the first trial 146 delegates supported him; eighty-three cast their votes for Lewis Cass, who was preferred by some Western and Southern delegates, and twenty-four for Richard M. Johnson. At each new trial Van Buren lost a few votes, until at the seventh his followers had dwindled to ninety-nine while those of Lewis Cass had increased to 123. After this the convention adjourned till the next morning.

"POLK AND CO. going up Salt River" is the title of this cartoon showing the Democrats Van Buren, Benton, Dallas, Jackson and the cock, James K. Polk.

171

A CANNON BALL called Texas is shot by Clay and Frelinghuysen against Van Buren, who is losing his balance on Jackson's shoulders and upsetting Benton, Polk and Dallas.

THE WHIGS CLEAN the Augean stable. Clay and Frelinghuysen throw their Democratic rivals out the window, while Congressman Wise refuses to let Lady Texas enter the room.

TEXAS AND TARIFF were the campaign issues. Clay rides on a seashell to the White House; Polk, Dallas and Benton float on the Texas bladders, leaving Van Buren to sink or swim.

THE HARRY-CANE hits James K. Polk, who is attacked by a woolly ram, while the tools of industries which favor high protective tariff shower heavily down upon his head.

It was apparent that North and South could not agree on either Van Buren or on Cass—and so a compromise candidate was sought. George Bancroft, of the Massachusetts delegation, pleaded for James K. Polk's candidacy, and during the evening he visited the New York and Tennessee delegates and received some kind of assurance from them.

The next morning, on the eighth ballot, Polk received forty-four votes. When it came to the ninth trial, Benjamin F. Butler of the New York delegation produced a letter from Van Buren authorizing the withdrawal of his name from the contest if that would produce harmony. Butler thought the time had come, and he withdrew Van Buren's candidacy, shifting the votes of his state to James K. Polk of Tennessee.

With this the stampede began. One by one the states climbed on the Polk bandwagon, making unanimous the nomination of the first "dark horse" in the history of American presidential elections.

The news of Polk's victory traveled fast; it was flashed by the newly installed telegraph to Washington. Senator Silas Wright was also informed by telegram that the convention had chosen him for the Vice-Presidency. But Wright, a friend and admirer of Van Buren, declined the honor with the terse sentence: "I am not and cannot under any circumstances be a candidate before your convention for that office." It was the first and only time that an elected candidate for the vice-presidential office refused the honor. The new choice of the con-

FOX IS BURIED. Van Buren, who failed to win the [Dem]ocratic nomination because he opposed annexation of [Texa]s, is borne to his grave by the decrepit Jackson horse.

CLAY DRIVES the Constitution Carriage, ramming the vehicles of President Tyler and Van Buren. However, the Democrats nominated neither of them, but turned instead to James K. Polk.

[CON]FLICTING STATEMENTS of Polk on the tariff are the [them]e of this cartoon. Most of the posters printed in this [electi]on came out for the Whigs and attacked the Democrats.

CLAY, THE CHAMPION, knocks out Van Buren. In reality it was Van Buren himself who, with his honest and courageous stand on Texas, made himself unavailable as Democratic candidate.

[con]vention was George M. Dallas of Pennsylvania.

To their platform of 1840 the Democrats [a]dded three planks. They declared that any law [for] the distribution of the proceeds of the pub[l]ic lands among the states would be inexpedient [a]nd unconstitutional; that the party was op[p]osed to taking from the President the limited [veto] which had "thrice saved the American [p]eople from the corrupt and tyrannical domina[t]ion of the Bank of the United States"; and ["]that our title to the whole of the Territory of [O]regon is clear and unquestionable, that no [p]ortion of the same ought to be ceded to Eng[l]and or any other power, and that the reoccu[p]ation of Oregon and the reannexation of Texas [a]t the earliest practicable period are great [A]merican measures, which the Convention

recommends to the cordial support of the Democracy of the Union."

The Democrats made the Texas treaty the main issue of their campaign. Their platform diplomatically linked the "reannexation of Texas" with the "reoccupation of Oregon." (The "re" referred to the alleged fact that Oregon had originally belonged to the United States by settlement and treaty and that Texas had originally been acquired through the Louisiana Purchase but was later surrendered to Spain.) "All of Texas, all of Oregon" was their effective and vote-getting slogan. Oregon would add "free" land to the United States and would thus help to win the Northern vote, while Texas was to enlarge the slave territory and carry the Southern vote. The Democratic plat-

173

JACKSON EXECUTES THE COON, WHIG PARTY SYMBOL. VAN BUREN AND BENTON LOOK ON.

form expressed the hope that in the next campaign the American democracy would place its trust "not in fictitious symbols, not in displays and appeals insulting to the judgment and subversive of the intellect of the people, but in a clear reliance upon the intelligence, patriotism, and the discriminating justice of the American people." This was a belated attack on the "Tippecanoe-and-Tyler-Too" campaign.

On the very day the Democrats met at Baltimore, another convention assembled in the same city. In this meeting some dissatisfied Whigs and disgruntled Democrats, many of them office-holders, put in nomination the name of John Tyler. However, the movement petered out. When the President realized that his chances were slim, he withdrew his name.

There was another candidate in the field: James G. Birney of New York. He was nominated by the Abolitionists, who had met in convention at Buffalo a year before, and his candidacy played an important part in this election.

The Abolitionist platform declared that "human brotherhood is a cardinal principle of true democracy, as well as of pure Christianity, which spurns all inconsistent limitations; and neither the political party which repudiates it, nor the political system which is not based upon it, can be truly democratic or permanent," therefore "the Liberty Party . . . will demand the absolute and unqualified divorce of the general government from slavery, and also the restoration of equality of rights among men."

When the campaign began, it became evident that the Democrats had learned their lesson in 1840. Observing how the Whigs had boosted Harrison, the log-cabin, hard-cider candidate, into the Presidency, they adopted the techniques of their adversaries. They were apt pupils in creating slogans. Now it was "Fifty-four forty or fight," meaning that the boundaries of the United States should extend to the fifty-four forty parallel, and "All Oregon or none," against which the Whigs' slogans were the feeble

"AN ELECTION SCENE" is the title of this satirical lithograph by Edward W. Clay which is "Respectfully inscribed the independent and vigilant Police of New York." From the window on the right the ballot box is emptied.

175

A GREAT WHIG POLITICAL PARADE ALONG BROADWAY. FROM THE *ILLUSTRATED LONDON NEWS.*

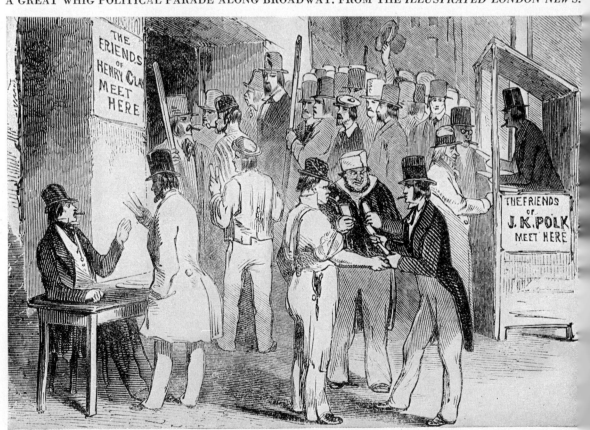

A NEWSPAPER ILLUSTRATION WHICH SHOWS THE SCENE OUTSIDE A NEW YORK POLLING BOOTH

"Redeem the country, restore prosperity," or simply "Hooray for Clay."

Clay was a far more popular candidate than James Polk, but in this election the personal popularity of the candidates was much less important than the annexation of Texas. Clay, trying to steer clear of the controversy, made conflicting statements. Polk, on the other hand, declared himself unequivocally for annexation.

When the ballots of the twenty-six states were counted, it was found that James K. Polk had been elected President with 1,337,243 votes against Henry Clay's 1,299,062—a very close vote. In four states Polk's plurality reached ten thousand; three states gave less than a thousand plurality. Polk won New York with 5,106 votes; in that state the Abolitionists polled 15,812. If the Abolitionists had not had a separate candidate, polling 62,300 votes in all, Henry Clay would have won the election, but James Birney as a third candidate took away enough votes from Clay to make Polk the President. Young Abraham Lincoln in Illinois, then an ardent Clay supporter, said: "If the Whig Abolitionists of New York had voted with us

. . . Mr. Clay would now be President, Whig principles in the ascendant and Texas not annexed; whereas, by the division, all that either had at stake in the contest was lost."

In no other previous election was fraud so openly practiced as in this one. Thousands of aliens were naturalized—often illegally—so that they could cast their votes for the Democrats. In New York State twenty thousand aliens became citizens before the election. In Louisiana a boatload of Democrats steamed from New Orleans up the Mississippi and stopped at three different places to allow the passengers to vote as many times. A political boss of Plaquemines, a parish below New Orleans, had fathered and financed the idea.

President Tyler interpreted the election as an endorsement for immediate annexation, and he suggested that Congress pass a joint resolution to that effect. The resolution was passed in February, 1845; Tyler signed it and sent it by a special representative to Texas for ratification. Four days later James K. Polk was inaugurated in a pouring rain—the road to America's "manifest destiny" was open.

...LK WON THE ELECTION. The states are represented by balloons. Jackson (in the sky) exclaims: "My country ...aved! I am now ready for my last resting place." A dead coon, symbol of the Whig party, is carried to his burial ...ce—the U.S. Bank. Above, an eagle flies with the banner: "The country is safe. Democracy is triumphant."

ZACHARY TAYLOR'S INAUGURAL SPEECH

THE SIXTEENTH ELECTION—1848

ZACHARY TAYLOR
AND MILLARD FILLMORE

Shortly after his inauguration President Polk confided his political objectives to George Bancroft. They were: (1) the revision of the protective tariff of 1842; (2) the reestablishment of an independent treasury; (3) the settlement of the Oregon boundary dispute with Great Britain; (4) the acquisition of California. Before Polk's term ended, he had achieved them all.

The dark horse of the 1844 convention—under whose Presidency the country's borders expanded to the Pacific—was one of America's most able administrators, yet his name is hardly known today.

Polk was a Democratic partisan through and through. For him only a Democrat was a real American, only a Democrat could be honorable and well-bred; for him the Whigs were inferior human beings, and if he found an exception among them, he noted in his diary: "Although a Whig, he seems a gentleman." He was pompous, suspicious, vindictive, without personal magnetism, and he seemed to have little humor. But he had an independent mind; he was serious, conscientious, fearless, hard-working; he had character and would not be swayed by

pressure groups. He knew how to transform his beliefs into realities, though sometimes he got lost in details. Stubbornly he stuck to his ideas, resting his hands heavily on the governmental wheel, supervising "the whole operations of the government." He was the only strong President between Jackson and Lincoln.

Under his administration events moved fast. In July, 1845, Texas accepted the terms of the joint resolution and was ready to become the twenty-eighth state in the Union. By then Mexico had already severed diplomatic relations with the United States. General Zachary Taylor stood on the Texan border with an army detachment, ready to "protect what, in event of annexation, will be our western frontier." In November President Polk sent John Slidell as emissary to Mexico to negotiate the Texas boundaries and to buy New Mexico and California from the Mexicans. The American envoy had this to offer: for the recognition of the Rio Grande as the southern and western frontier of Texas, the United States would assume Mexico's debt to American citizens; for the territory of New Mexico the United States was willing to pay five million dollars, and

ZACHARY TAYLOR
(1784-1850), hero of the Mexican War, was the Whig candidate for President. Seven free and eight slave states favored him. He won 163 electoral votes.

MILLARD FILLMORE
(1800-1874), a lawyer, Congressman, former Antimason, ran for the Vice-Presidency on the Whig ticket. On July 9, 1850, Taylor died and Fillmore followed him.

LEWIS CASS
(1782-1866) opposed the Wilmot Proviso and expansion in Mexico. Had it not been for Van Buren and his Free-Soil supporters, Cass would have won.

WILLIAM O. BUTLER
(1791-1880), a soldier and Congressman, was the Democratic candidate for the Vice-Presidency. A Southern slaveholder, he added strength to the ticket.

MARTIN VAN BUREN
(1782-1862), supported by N.Y. "Barnburners" and antislavery Free-Soilers, took enough Democratic votes from Cass to give the election to his opponent.

HENRY A. S. DEARBORN
(1783-1851), Massachusetts politician and vice-presidential candidate of the Native Americans, was an unsuccessful minority contender for office.

"money would be no object" for the purchase of California.

But Slidell was not received by President Herrera nor could he talk to General Paredes who in the meantime had overthrown the Herrera regime. On March 20, 1846, the American envoy was officially informed that Mexico refused to negotiate. On May 8 he was back in Washington and reported to the President, who had already composed a war message. The following day Polk decided to ask Congress for a declaration of war against Mexico. The President's reasons for war were the unpaid claims of American citizens and Slidell's treatment. Polk informed his advisers that he would send his war message to Congress on May 12. All the Cabinet members were in full agreement except George Bancroft, his Secretary of the Navy, who counseled restraint and impressed upon Polk that he should not act until Mexico committed some definite act of

THE VOTES IN THE 1848 ELECTION

STATES	POPULAR VOTE			ELECTORAL VOTE	
	Zachary Taylor Louisiana. Whig.	Lewis Cass, Michigan. Democrat.	Martin Van Buren, New York. Free-Soiler.	Taylor and Fillmore.	Cass and Butler.
Alabama	30,482	31,363	—	—	9
Arkansas	7,588	9,300	—	—	3
Connecticut	30,314	27,046	5,005	6	—
Delaware	6,421	5,898	80	3	—
Florida	3,116	1,847	—	3	—
Georgia	47,544	44,802	—	10	—
Illinois	53,047	56,300	15,774	—	9
Indiana	69,907	74,745	8,100	—	12
Iowa	11,084	12,093	1,126	—	4
Kentucky	67,141	49,720	—	12	—
Louisiana	18,217	15,370	—	6	—
Maine	35,125	39,880	12,096	—	9
Maryland	37,702	34,528	125	8	—
Massachusetts	61,070	35,281	38,058	12	—
Michigan	23,940	30,687	10,389	—	5
Mississippi	25,922	26,537	—	—	6
Missouri	32,671	40,077	—	—	7
New Hampshire	14,781	27,763	7,560	—	6
New Jersey	40,015	36,901	829	7	—
New York	218,603	114,318	120,510	36	—
North Carolina	43,550	34,869	—	11	—
Ohio	138,360	154,775	35,354	—	23
Pennsylvania	185,513	171,176	11,263	26	—
Rhode Island	6,779	3,646	730	4	—
South Carolina*	—	—	—	—	—
Tennessee	64,705	58,419	—	13	—
Texas	4,509	10,668	—	—	4
Vermont	23,122	10,948	13,837	6	—
Virginia	45,124	46,586	9	—	17
Wisconsin	13,747	15,001	10,418	—	4
	1,360,099	1,220,544	291,263	163	127

*Electors were appointed by the legislature.

PRESIDENTIAL BANNERS OF THE WHIG AND DEMOCRATIC CANDIDATES IN THE 1848 ELECTION.

hostility. That same evening news reached Washington that Mexican forces had crossed the Rio Grande and ambushed an American force.

The President quickly redrafted his war message. "The cup of forbearance has been exhausted," he wrote. "After reiterated menaces, Mexico has passed the boundary of the United States, has invaded our territory and shed American blood upon American soil." On May 13 Congress declared that "by the act of the Republic of Mexico, a state of war exists between that government and the United States."

Most of the Whigs opposed war. They asked some pertinent questions: Was the war made by the President or by Congress? Was it a war of conquest or for the boundaries? Did Mexico begin it or had American troops invaded her soil? The Whigs held that it was Polk who started the war in order to establish slavery in territories where it had not existed before. Congressman Abraham Lincoln, the lonely Whig from Illinois, introduced his "spot resolutions," asking the President on which particular spot

American blood had been shed and asserting that not Mexican but American troops had begun the hostilities.

Still the nation, unimpressed by the Whigs' arguments, cried for expansion. John C. Frémont, camping with his exploring party near the Klamath Lakes, moved into the lower Sacramento Valley. On June 14 American squatters hoisted a flag with a bear and a star on it and proclaimed the "California Republic." On July 2 Commodore Sloat, in command of the Pacific Squadron, took Monterey; a few days later he announced California a part of the United States. On August 1 Colonel Stephen W. Kearny marched into New Mexico with his troops, taking Santa Fe and proceeding with a small detachment to invade San Diego. Thus, only a few weeks after the declaration of war, the territories of Texas, California, and New Mexico were occupied by the United States.

On March 27, 1847, General Winfield Scott took Vera Cruz, and in April he began to move into the interior of Mexico. In the meantime

181

THE WHIGS ABANDONED HENRY CLAY, THEIR MOST PROMINENT SON, AND CHOSE GENERAL TAY

Zachary Taylor had been victorious in the Battle of Buena Vista (February 22-23) and was squeezing the Mexican troops from the north. On September 14 Mexico City was taken, marking the end of hostilities

In the peace treaty Mexico ceded Texas with the Rio Grande as boundary, to the Unite States; for New Mexico, Arizona, and Cali

e necessity of my Nature, Your Enemy,

F THE MEXICAN WAR, AS THEIR CANDIDATE.

nia she was to receive the sum of $15,000,000
l the United States was to assume the dam-
claims of Americans against the Mexican
vernment.

With election time near, the Whigs were in search of a candidate. Henry Clay was still the most outstanding figure in their ranks. But his insistence that the party should renounce "any wish or desire on our part to acquire any foreign territory whatever, for the purpose of propagating slavery, or of introducing slaves from the United States" was strongly opposed by the Southern faction—the "Cotton" Whigs— while his former proslavery pronouncements had turned the New England abolitionists—the "Conscience" Whigs—against him. The party's other giant, Daniel Webster, was hardly more available than Clay; he had no support in the South and he could not win the West.

All over the country meetings were held proposing General Taylor's candidacy. Whigs and Democrats alike rallied behind "Old Rough and Ready" and the public clamor for his nomination grew. The Whig politicians, who had shown some reservations at first, fell into line.

General Taylor's victories in Mexico, his Southern birth, his ownership of three hundred slaves, and his clean political record (it was so clean that in his whole life he had never cast a vote for anyone) made him the most desirable candidate. The trouble was that nobody seemed to know what his political convictions were.

Taylor was silent at first. On Washington's birthday, 1848—the first anniversary of the Battle of Buena Vista—the Louisiana state convention formally announced the General's nomination. The Whigs sang:

"Zachary Taylor was a brave old feller,
Brigadier General A No. 1.
He fought twenty thousand Mexicanos;
Four thousand he killed, the rest they "cut and
    run."
In the thickest of the fight Old Zachary appear-ed,
The shot flew about him as thick as any hail,
And the only injury he there receiv-ed
Was a compound fracture of his brown coattail."

A few weeks later the hard-pressed Taylor declared that he was "a Whig but not an ultra Whig" and "If elected, I would not be the mere President of a party. I would endeavor to act independent of party domination. I should feel bound to administer the government untrammeled by party schemes."

Cognizant of the fact that Taylor was a candidate with whom the party could win the elec-

183

THE CANDIDATE OF THE WHIGS. General Zachary Taylor, hero of Buena Vista, was the Whig choice for Presidency, though he declared that he was "a Whig but not an ultra Whig" and if elected "would not be the m President of a party" but "would endeavor to act independent of party domination, untrammeled by party scheme

Manifest Destiny.

New Mexico,
California Chihuahua,
Zacatecas. MEXICO, Peru,
Yucatan, Cuba.

A WAR
PRESIDENT.

GAS

PROGRESSIVE DEMOCRACY.

THE CANDIDATE OF THE DEMOCRATS. Lewis Cass, who had acquired the "General" title in the War of 1812 and had retained it for thirty-five years, is caricatured as an inciter of war because of his imperialistic policy toward Mexico. In hostile political cartoons like this, the artists stressed the unfortunate similarity of his name to *gas*.

ion, the Whig nominating convention in Phila-delphia chose him as their standard-bearer in preference to Winfield Scott, Henry Clay, and Daniel Webster, and selected Millard Fillmore of New York as his running mate.

On political principles the convention ob-served a deep silence. No committee of resolu-ions was appointed, no platform was issued, for greement on common principles was impos-ble. There were too many opposing factions n the party and they held too many different iews.

Nor were the forces of the Democratic party ny more cohesive. The controversy over slav-ry raged regardless of party lines, and the

quarrel between the two opposing Democratic factions of New York State—the "Hunkers" and the "Barnburners"—reached serious propor-tions. The Hunkers (so called because they hunkered for office) were the conservatives; the Barnburners (a name taken from the story of a Dutch farmer who thought the best way to get rid of the rats in his barn was to burn the barn down) were the more radical wing of the party, holding strong antislavery views.

To the Democratic nominating convention at Baltimore both the Hunkers and Barnburners sent a full delegation, thirty-six strong, and each faction claimed to represent the Democrats of New York. After much debate a Solomonic

THE SLAVERY QUESTION BECAME THE MOST VITAL ISSUE OF THE 1848 CAMPAIGN T Free-Soil candidate Martin Van Buren is pushed by Horace Greeley, editor of the New York *Tribune*, into the arms of a colored woman representing the radical, abolitionist Liberty Party. The title of this cartoon is "Marriage of the Free-Soil and Liberty Partie In the election, the Free-Soilers polled alm 300,000 votes in all, and in New York alone ab six thousand more than Lewis Cass, the regular De

solution was found: both delegations were admitted, but each delegate was allowed only half a vote. As this compromise did not satisfy either of the groups, the Barnburners left the convention in anger, and the Hunkers refused to vote.

For their candidate the Democrats cho General Lewis Cass of Michigan, an arde expansionist, who won the nomination agai Levi Woodbury and James Buchanan. Pre dent Polk, realizing that he had no hope

I nebber hab berry good pinion ob the gemman; but if he ax pardon for all he hab done and said agin us, I will shake hands wid de gemman.

Mercy on me! How bashful he is!

TWO MAJOR PARTIES TRIED TO IGNORE IT.

cratic candidate. Since both major contestants had, ithout New York, the same number of electoral votes, e 36 votes of that state decided the election and gave e Presidency to the Whig candidate, Zachary Taylor.

inning a renomination, had withdrawn his ame some time before.

The Democratic platform declared that the owers of government should be construed rictly; that Congress had no authority to carry on internal improvements, or establish a protective tariff; that the proceeds of the public lands should not be distributed; that the President should have the qualified veto; that government money should not be deposited in the banks, and that Congress had no power to meddle with the domestic institutions of the states. All efforts of the abolitionists and others to induce Congress to interfere with slavery were dangerous to the stability of the Union and ought not to be encouraged.

The Barnburners, opposing the nomination of Cass, reassembled again in a convention at Utica and proposed Van Buren for the Presidency and Henry Dodge of Wisconsin for the Vice-Presidency.

There were other minor candidates in the field. The Native Americans nominated General Henry A. S. Dearborn of Massachusetts for the Vice-Presidency; for the President they were satisfied with the Whigs' choice of General Taylor. The Liberty, or Abolition party chose John P. Hale of New Hampshire for President and Leicester King of Ohio for Vice-President. The Liberty League, a group which had broken away from the Liberty party, nominated Gerrit Smith for President and the Reverend Charles E. Foote for Vice-President. The Industrial Congress, asking for free land for settlers and exemption of the homestead from seizure for debts, came out for Gerrit Smith for the Presidency but nominated William S. Waitt for the second place.

Now that the Barnburners had selected Van Buren as their candidate on an antislavery platform, the interest of the country turned to another convention which was to meet in Buffalo in August. There the antislavery Whigs of New England, with the support of the Barnburners of New York and adherents of the Liberty party, chose Van Buren and Charles Francis Adams.

This ticket had strong appeal. It was to split the Democratic vote in the crucial state of New York, bringing defeat to the Democratic nominee. Most of the antislavery men united behind it and Hale, the candidate of the Liberty party, withdrew from the contest and came out in open support of Van Buren.

In the Buffalo meeting a strongly worded antislavery platform was adopted, declaring

(turn to page 191)

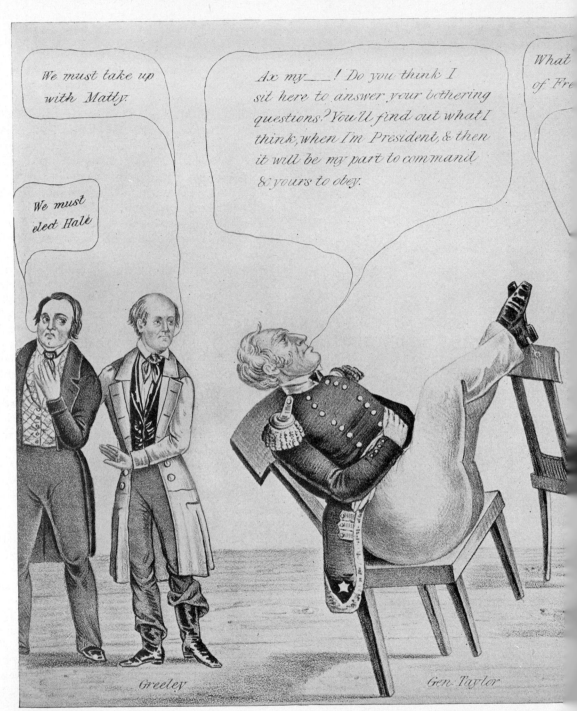

QUESTIONING A PRESIDENTIAL CANDIDATE ABOUT HIS BELIEFS WAS THE CUSTOM OF

General Taylor was asked by the newspapers and the voters to give an opinion on protective tariffs and whether Congress had the right to create such a system of revenue. He was also questioned about his position on free trade. The Whig candidate replied that he could not answer such questions until he had i gated them. But in a letter, on which his nomi was based, he explained that in such matters iff, currency, and internal improvement he would out the people's will as expressed through Co

We can't find out anything by him.

That's because he's got it in him.—A still tongue makes a wise head. Didn't he lick Santa Anna at Buena Vista

Office Seekers

CRAL TAYLOR EVADES HIS INTERROGATORS.
At left, Horace Greeley, who opposed Taylor's nomination because the General was not an open and decided Whig, says he will take up with Democrat "Matty" Van Buren, while the other voter exclaims that the people ought to elect John Hale, the Liberty party candidate.

TAYLOR IS EXAMINED by a phrenologist who is attempting to find out what the Whig candidate's political principles are. An assistant carefully takes down the findings about the "candidate of many parties."

FREE-SOILER VAN BUREN tries to bridge the chasm between the Democratic and Whig abolitionist platforms while Butler, Calhoun and Cass watch. The Salt River between the two platforms indicates defeat.

THE THREE CANDIDATES. Lewis Cass, the Democratic nominee, and Zachary Taylor, the Whig candidate, are tumbling into the Salt River while Van Buren, the man of the Free-Soilers, wins the "Buffalo Hunt."

SONG FOR TAYLOR who, according to the song-
ster, is the man "to fill the chair of Washington."

DEMOCRATIC CANDIDATE Lewis Cass, a "doughface," which was the popular term in the 1848 election fo
Northern man who was in agreement with Southern principles on slavery, is put into presidential oven to be bak

"KNOCKED INTO A COCK'D HAT" DEPICTS CANDIDATE CASS'S UPSET BY CANNONBALL TAYLOR.

that the participants in the convention assembled "as a union of freemen for the sake of freedom, forgetting all past political differences, in common resolve to maintain the rights of free labor against the aggression of slave power, and to secure free soil for a free people." It should be "the settled policy of the nation," said the platform, "not to extend, nationalize or encourage slavery but to limit, localize and discourage it." The new party inscribed on its banner "Free Soil, Free Speech, Free Labor, and Free Men," and because of this plank its adherents became known as the "Free-Soilers."

And so the slavery issue, which both the Democrats and Whigs had tried to evade, was injected into the campaign. The two major par-

ties had valid reasons to be silent on it. How could the Democrats advocate the extension of slaveholding territory without antagonizing their Northern, antislavery faction? And how could the Conscience Whigs, who were against slavery, come to terms with the Cotton Whigs, who advocated slavery, supported the Mexican War, and cried for expansion?

Matters came to a head when Polk asked Congress to appropriate two million dollars for the obvious purpose of making an advance payment to Mexico, and when David Wilmot, a Democratic Congressman from Pennsylvania, introduced his famous proviso that "neither slavery nor involuntary servitude shall ever exist" in the territory so acquired. The President angrily exclaimed that Wilmot's sugges-

191

tion was "a mischievous and foolish amendment," and he was determined to veto it. There was no real need for the proviso; the arid wastes of New Mexico and the cattle ranches of California were unsuitable for slave labor—they would not have become slaveholding territory. But after the proviso was introduced, it was upheld by the North, not only as a matter of principle but as a matter of sectional strategy, intensifying the struggle between North and South.

In the election the Democratic vote was split between Cass and Van Buren, thus the Whigs won. Not counting New York State, both major candidates, General Taylor and General Cass, had the same number of electoral votes—127. But as Van Buren, the candidate of the Free-Soilers, polled over 120,000 votes in that state which otherwise would have been cast for the regular Democratic candidate, New York's thirty-six electoral votes went to Zachary Taylor and gave him the Presidency. He received the majority of popular votes in seven free and eight slave states, while behind Lewis Cass were eight free and seven slave states.

This was the first time that presidential electors of the various states were appointed on the same day, in accordance with an act passed by Congress in 1845 designating "the Tuesday next after the first Monday in the month of November" as election day. Thirty states took part in the voting as four had been added to the Union since the previous election. The newcomers were Florida (admitted March 3, 1845), Texas (admitted December 28, 1846), Iowa (admitted December 28, 1846), and Wisconsin (admitted May 29, 1848).

Zachary Taylor's victory had three memorable results: (1) the large vote for Martin Van Buren, the Free-Soil candidate, indicated that in future elections the slavery issue could not be avoided; (2) the clean sweep that followed in the civil service caused Nathaniel Hawthorne to lose his job in the Salem Custom House, whereupon he began to write *The Scarlet Letter*; (3) an unsuccessful Democratic newspaper dismissed Walt Whitman, giving him time to create *Leaves of Grass*.

"THE DEMOCRATIC FUNERAL OF 1848." Martin Van Buren, the candidate of the Free-Soilers, pictured as a fox, and Lewis Cass, candidate of the Democrats, caricatured as a gas bag, are carried to their burial by Democratic Senators Houston, Benton and Calhoun. Behind them is borne the body of James K. Polk, the outgoing President.

192

MILLARD FILLMORE (1800-1874) FOLLOWED TAYLOR IN THE PRESIDENCY ON JULY 9, 1850

THE PRESIDENT-ELECT LEAVES CONCORD

THE SEVENTEENTH ELECTION—1852

FRANKLIN PIERCE

With every passing day the fight of the sections over slavery grew more and more bitter. Slavery was the main topic of discussion; argued up and down the country, it weighed heavily on the national mind, overshadowing—nay, eliminating all other political issues.

Congress had great difficulty deciding how the newly acquired territories should be organized—with or without slavery. And while the lawmakers talked, the settlers in the West lacked law and government. James K. Polk went out of office and still nothing had been done about California, New Mexico, or Utah, though Oregon was organized as a territory without slavery in 1848. The new President, Zachary Taylor, encouraged the inhabitants of California and New Mexico to draw up constitutions and apply for admission to the Union. The Californians, in urgent need of authorized civil government, lost little time in taking Taylor's advice. The gold rush had brought a multitude of "Forty-niners" to the country, and the temporary military government was not adequate for handling this rough and violent crowd; drunken brawls, robberies, murders, lynchings were the order of the day.

In September, 1849, in a convention held at Monterey, Californians drew up a constitution, ratified it, elected a governor and other officers, and these officials took over the government of the new "state" without even waiting for formal admission. The next year New Mexico followed the lead of California and adopted a constitution, as did the Utah Mormons.

The reaction in the South to the growth of free territory was bitter. Keenly aware of the shifting political equilibrium at its expense, the South was determined to resist the further strengthening of Northern power. If California were to be admitted as a free state, half the land from the Mexican conquest would be lost to slavery, and the political supremacy of the thirteen million in the North over the eight million people in the South would be further enhanced.

The fundamental political difference between North and South was this: the North was not willing to establish slavery where it did not exist before, while the South held that slaves were property and, as such, were protected by the Constitution; therefore, slavery should be allowed wherever the flag flew.

To bridge the two views, a number of compromise proposals were suggested. One was to

195

FRANKLIN PIERCE (1804-1869)
PHOTOGRAPH BY MATHEW B. BRADY

FRANKLIN PIERCE
(1804-1869), son of a Governor of N. H., lawyer and Senator, was the compromise candidate of the Democrats. He won 254 electoral votes to Scott's 42.

WILLIAM R. D. KING
(1786-1853), Senator from Alabama, Minister to France and president of the Senate after Fillmore, was the Democrats' choice for the Vice-Presidency.

WINFIELD SCOTT
(1786-1866), the 66-year-old, six-foot-five hero of the Mexican War, won the Whig candidacy against Webster and Fillmore after 53 ballots had been taken.

WILLIAM A. GRAHAM
(1804-1875), Secretary of the Navy under Fillmore and moving spirit of Perry's expedition to Japan, was the Whig choice for the Vice-Presidency.

JOHN PARKER HALE
(1806-1873), lawyer, Senator and ardent opponent of slavery, became the presidential candidate of the Free-Soil party, polling over 150,000 popular votes.

GEORGE W. JULIAN
(1817-1899), leading abolitionist, one of the antislavery men in Congress opposing the Compromise, became Free-Soil candidate for second place.

extend the 36° 30′ line of the Missouri Compromise to the Pacific Ocean, thus dividing the country into a free and a slaveholding territory; another advocated popular sovereignty, whereby the territories themselves should decide the slavery issue within their borders.

When Congress assembled in December, 1849 —for the first time since Taylor's inauguration— the President urged it to admit California as a free state, while New Mexico and Utah should join the Union without reference to slavery.

This was oil on the fire of the Southern hotheads. Robert Toombs threatened: "I do not hesitate to avow before this House and the country, and in the presence of the living God, that if by your legislation you seek to drive us from the territories of California and New Mexico, purchased by the common blood and treasure of the whole people, and to abolish slavery in this District, thereby attempting to fix a national degradation upon half the states of this Confederacy, I am for disunion."

THE VOTES IN THE 1852 ELECTION

STATES	POPULAR VOTE			ELECTORAL VOTE	
	Franklin Pierce, New Hampshire. Democrat.	Winfield Scott, New Jersey. Whig.	John P. Hale, New Hampshire. Free-Soiler.	Pierce and King.	Scott and Graham.
Alabama............	26,881	15,038	—	9	—
Arkansas...........	12,173	7,404	—	4	—
California..........	40,626	35,407	100	4	—
Connecticut........	33,249	30,359	3,160	6	—
Delaware..........	6,318	6,293	62	3	—
Florida............	4,318	2,875	—	3	—
Georgia............	34,705	16,660	—	10	—
Illinois............	80,597	64,934	9,966	11	—
Indiana............	95,340	80,901	6,929	13	—
Iowa..............	17,763	15,856	1,604	4	—
Kentucky..........	53,806	57,068	265	—	12
Louisiana..........	18,647	17,255	—	6	—
Maine.............	41,609	32,543	8,030	8	—
Maryland..........	40,020	35,066	281	8	—
Massachusetts......	44,569	52,683	28,023	—	13
Michigan..........	41,842	33,859	7,237	6	—
Mississippi........	26,876	17,548	—	7	—
Missouri...........	38,353	29,984	—	9	—
New Hampshire.....	29,997	16,147	6,695	5	—
New Jersey........	44,305	38,556	350	7	—
New York.........	262,083	234,882	25,329	35	—
North Carolina.....	39,744	39,058	59	10	—
Ohio..............	169,220	152,526	31,682	23	—
Pennsylvania.......	198,568	179,174	8,525	27	—
Rhode Island.......	8,735	7,626	644	4	—
South Carolina*....				8	—
Tennessee..........	57,018	58,898	—	—	12
Texas.............	13,552	4,995	—	4	—
Vermont...........	13,044	22,173	8,621	—	5
Virginia...........	73,858	58,572	291	15	—
Wisconsin..........	33,658	22,240	8,814	5	—
	1,601,474	1,386,580	156,667	254	42

* Electors were appointed by the legislature.

STUMP SPEAKING FOR A CANDIDATE IN THE COUNTRY. PAINTING BY GEORGE C. BINGHAM.

These were hard words; they boded ill for the future. Politicians, patriots, men of good will worked unceasingly to save the Union. On January 29, 1850, Henry Clay, emerging from a political retirement, submitted a number of resolutions to the Senate. In the hope that his resolutions would secure "the peace, concord and harmony of the Union," Clay proposed:

1. Admission of California as a free state;
2. Establishment of territorial governments without any restriction as to slavery in the rest of the territory acquired from Mexico;
3. Determination of the disputed boundary between Texas and New Mexico;
4. Assumption of the bona fide public debt of Texas contracted prior to annexation, upon the condition that Texas relinquish her claim to any part of New Mexico;

5. Agreement that slavery in the District of Columbia might not be abolished without the consent of Maryland, and of the people of the District, and without just compensation to the owners of slaves;
6. Prohibition of slave trade in the District of Columbia;
7. Enactment of a more stringent fugitive slave law;
8. Assertion that Congress had no power to interfere with the slave trade between the states.

These suggestions gave rise to one of the greatest and most distinguished debates in Congress. The old giants, Henry Clay, John C. Calhoun, and Daniel Webster, held the country spellbound with their oratory. The three men had begun public life four decades before and all three were to die within the next two

197

years, but with the last flickers of the fires that had burned so brightly in their souls, they once more spoke out.

Seventy-three-year-old Clay argued for the adoption of the resolutions. Consumption racked his lungs, still he held the floor of the Senate for the better part of two days, asking the North for concessions, appealing to the South for peace.

After Clay came Calhoun. Infirm, weak and emaciated—to die within a month—he could not deliver his speech himself; Senator Mason of Virginia read it for him. "I have, Senators," said he, "believed from the first that the agitation of the subject of slavery would, if not prevented by some timely and effective measure, end in disunion." Calhoun admitted that the South was discontented because "the equilibrium between the two sections has been destroyed," and that the only way to save the Union was to allow the South "an equal right in the acquired territory" (this meaning the admission of slavery in California and New Mexico). He asked for the restoration of the power the South had once possessed in the Federal Government and demanded that the North "cease the agitation of the slave question." But if the disputed issues could not be settled, he said, then "let the states we represent agree to separate and part in peace. If you are unwilling we should part in peace, tell us so, and we shall know what to do when you reduce the question to submission or resistance."

Daniel Webster answered him on March 7th. His words, pleading for the preservation of the Union and supporting the compromise, rang through the country. "Peaceable secession is an utter impossibility," said Webster. "I see that disruption must produce such a war as I will not describe in its twofold characters."

For nine months—from January to September—the compromise was discussed in and out of Congress. Jefferson Davis declared that he would "agree to the drawing of the line of 36° 30' through the territories acquired from Mexico, with the condition that in the same degree as slavery is prohibited north of that line, it shall be permitted to enter south of the line; and that the states which may be admitted into the Union shall come in under such constitutions as they think proper to form."

CONVENTION ALLEY

PRESIDENT FILLMORE LOOKS SMUGLY OUT OF

On July 9, 1850, while the debates were raging, President Taylor—an acid opponent of the compromise—passed away. Three days be-

... OF THE WHITE HOUSE WHILE WEBSTER, SCOTT, CASS, DOUGLAS CHASE THE NOMINATION.

...ore, during the Fourth of July ceremonies, to ...till his thirst he had consumed too many cher-...ies and wild fruits, drunk too much iced water and cold milk. Even a constitution such as Old Rough and Ready's could not take it.

With Vice-President Millard Fillmore in

(*turn to page 202*)

199

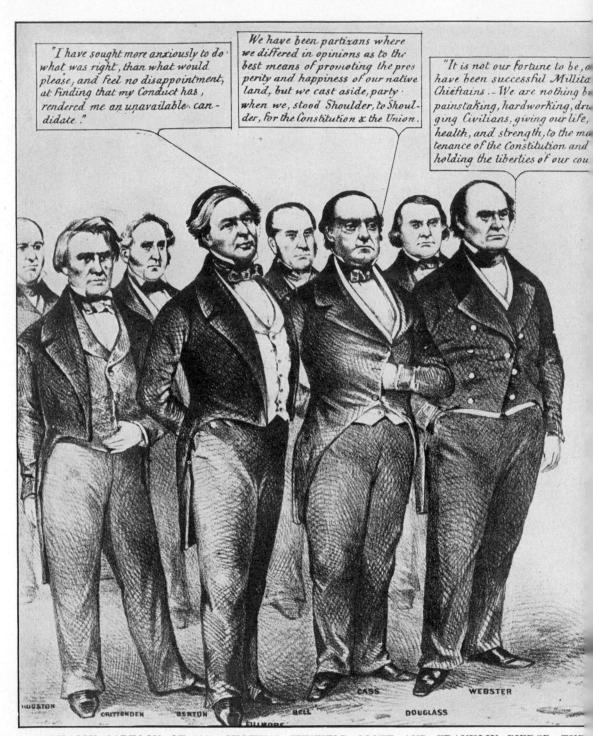

A CAMPAIGN CARTOON OF 1852, SHOWING WINFIELD SCOTT AND FRANKLIN PIERCE, THE

When the factions of the Democratic convention were unable to unite behind James Buchanan, Lewis Cass, or Stephen A. Douglas, they compromised on a dark horse candidate — pleasant, harmless, smiling Franklin Pierce of New Hampshire, who received the nomination on the 49th ballot. The Whigs had no eas

DEMOCRATIC CANDIDATES, WITH A NUMBER OF POLITICIANS WHO DESIRED THE NOMINATION.

e than the Democrats—their party too was split
the slavery issue. The Southern wing dictated
platform, favoring the Compromise; the Northern

wing named the candidate—General Winfield Scott, the
hero of the Mexican War. By this maneuver, the Whigs
hoped to bring together both sections of their party.

office, the administration's policy changed. Daniel Webster, who now became Secretary of State, supported the compromise, and the new President without much ado signed five different bills. The first admitted California as a free state. The second created the Territory of New Mexico without the Wilmot Proviso and provided for the payment of ten million dollars to Texas as an indemnity for the surrender of the New Mexican land. The third bill created the Territory of Utah. The fourth contained drastic measures against fugitive slaves and against persons who helped them to escape. And the fifth abolished slave trade in the District of Columbia.

The overwhelming majority of the American people acquiesced in the adoption of the compromise measures, believing that the solution which Clay offered the nation would keep the peace and would perpetuate prosperous times. Thus the country turned its attention toward the next presidential election.

THE TWO CANDIDATES IN THE PRESIDENTIAL

GENERAL SCOTT, the Whig candidate, crows: "Cock a doodle doo! I'm Bill Seward's cock!", an allusion to Senator Seward, the leader of the Northern Whigs, who was supposed to have great influence on Scott.

In the Democratic ranks three elderly men and a younger one vied for the nomination. Lewis Cass, James Buchanan, and William L. Marcy had been in public life for more than thirty years. They were challenged by the candidate of "Young America," thirty-nine-year-old Stephen A. Douglas.

At their nominating convention the Democrats fought each other bitterly and partisan feeling ran high. None of the four candidates was able to muster enough votes to win the nomination. Ballot after ballot was taken, with no significant change in the result.

ELD SCOTT IS REFERRING TO FRANKLIN PIERCE'S FAINTING SPELL IN THE MEXICAN WAR.

On the twenty-second trial Buchanan's vote ose to 104. Had Marcy come to his support, he Pennsylvanian might have received the nomination, but Marcy would not release his votes. After this the Douglas vote swelled to ninety-three; however, the old guard was on the alert; votes were switched to Cass, whose strength increased to 133 votes. When the thirty-third trial was over, the Buchanan forces, fearing Cass's nomination, asked for adjournment. This was on Friday.

That same evening the followers of Buchanan met in a conference to discuss further strategy. In their meeting they concocted an ingenious scheme, designed to prove that none of the other candidates would have the strength to secure the nomination. They decided to release the votes of the Buchanan states—except Pennsylvania, Georgia, and Alabama—to the other candidates, thus showing them that even with this support they could not succeed. And after they had proved the futility of further fighting, they hoped that the candidates would rally behind Buchanan.

The next morning Virginia voted for Dickinson, the manager of Cass; North Carolina and

Mississippi swung behind Marcy, who on the forty-sixth ballot received ninety-eight votes.

Behind the scenes efforts were made to break the deadlock. Edmund Burke, who had quietly prepared the way for a compromise candidate, wrote to his friend Franklin Pierce: "The thing is about ripe. We have intimations from Pennsylvania and Virginia that they will soon lead off for you. The South will come in, so will Maine, Connecticut, and I think, all New England. Michigan will also. The prospects are more encouraging than ever."

Burke was right. On the forty-seventh and forty-eighth ballots a number of delegates voted for Franklin Pierce. The Buchanan managers thought the time had come to try him out and show that he could not receive the nomination either. But then the situation got out of hand. On the forty-ninth ballot North Carolina swung behind Pierce, and with this a stampede began, all states changing their votes to the dark horse from New Hampshire. When the trial was over, all but six of the 286 delegates had voted for Pierce, the smiling, well-mannered politician with a winning personality and a blameless record.

The Democrats were relieved. Franklin Pierce seemed to them the proper candidate for the hour. He had not been long enough in public life to make many enemies, and about his political principles not much was known. The North supported him, and he had many friends in the South. "Young America" was delighted—Pierce was only forty-eight.

In their platform the Democrats repeated most of their 1848 resolutions; however, on the main political issues of the day they were explicit. They pledged themselves to the faithful execution of the compromise measures, including the Fugitive Slave Law, and promised resistance to "all attempts at renewing, in Congress or out of it, the agitation of the slavery question, under whatever shape or color the attempt may be made."

When the Whig convention assembled, its delegates had no less difficulty than the Democrats in choosing a candidate. Here, too, sectional differences seemed to present insurmountable obstacles.

Daniel Webster tried hard to win the nomination, expecting support from the South because of his Seventh of March speech. But the South thought President Fillmore a safer candidate, while the majority of the Northern Whigs supported General Winfield Scott, a military hero of the Mexican War.

Three hundred and ninety-six delegates formed the convention. On the first ballot President Fillmore received 133 votes against Scott's 131 and Webster's twenty-nine. Fifty times the convention balloted—without material change. Scott's vote was always between 131 and 139, Fillmore's between 122 and 133, and Webster's between twenty-eight and thirty-two.

As neither Fillmore nor Scott seemed to be making any headway, a compromise was sought. The Webster forces made a provisional deal with Fillmore's managers, whereby the Fillmore votes would be released to Webster if Webster could rally forty-one votes from the North. The bargain could not be consummated, for however hard the Webster men tried, they were unable to secure the support of so many Northern delegates.

With Webster out of the way, finally, on the fifty-third ballot, Winfield Scott was nominated.

The platform declared that the Whigs acquiesced in the compromise laws "as a settlement in principle and substance of the dangerous and exciting questions which they embrace, and so far as they are concerned, we will maintain them and insist upon their strict enforcement until time and experience shall demonstrate the necessity of further legislation."

Henry J. Raymond, editor of the New York Times, charged that the party managers had made a bargain with the Southern delegates allowing the South to dictate the platform while the North put up the candidate. The Southern delegates shouted: "It is a lie!", but Raymond's accusation was not so far-fetched as his enemies implied.

Scott's candidacy was received with mixed feelings in the Whig ranks. Northern Whigs exclaimed: "We accept the candidate, but spit upon the platform!" Many newspapers attacked the General, accusing him of being nothing but a puppet in the hands of Senator William Seward, a leader of the party whose radical antislavery views were feared by the Southern Whigs. Seward countered with

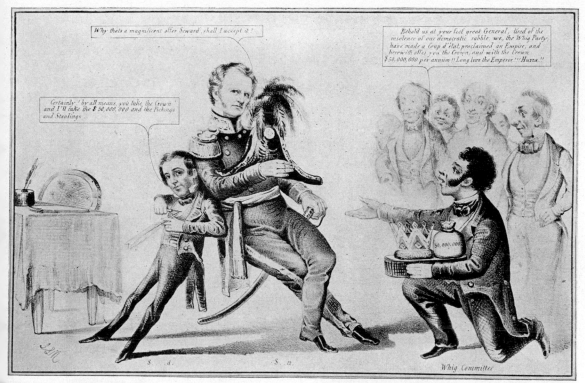

THE WHIG COMMITTEE offers its candidate, who leans on Seward, the crown of America and $50,000,000 a year. "Why that's a magnificent offer Seward. Shall I accept it?" And Seward, the power behind Scott, says "Certainly."

statement in which he declined "any public station or preferment whatever at the hands of the President of the United States, whether that President were Winfield Scott or any other man."

Other adverse voices were heard. Scott was a vulnerable candidate. Vain and pompous, he lent himself to easy ridicule. He was known to be sympathetic with the anti-foreign principles of the Native Americans and therefore he could not count upon the important Irish and German vote. Southern Congressmen assailed him because he never came out explicitly for the compromise measures.

The Northern, antislavery faction of the Whigs broke away, refusing to support Scott. They joined the group which assembled in a convention in Pittsburgh and called themselves the party of Free Democracy, nominating John P. Hale for the Presidency and George W. Julian for the Vice-Presidency. In their platform the Free Democrats declared that "slavery is a sin against God, and a crime against man,

which no human enactment or usage can make right; and that Christianity, humanity, and patriotism alike demand its abolition." They asked for the repeal of the Fugitive Slave Law, for free farms, cheap postage, recognition of Haiti, arbitration of international disputes, internal improvements at Federal expense, and a liberal policy toward the foreign-born, and accepted the slogan "Free soil, free speech, free labor and free men."

In addition to Pierce, Scott, and Hale there were a number of minor candidates. The Liberty Party nominated Gerrit Smith and Charles Durkee, and when both of them declined the honor, a second convention was called in which one section named William Goodell and Charles C. Foot, the other promised support for John P. Hale and George W. Julian. In the South the Democratic Southern Rights Convention in Montgomery rallied behind George M. Troup of Georgia and General John A. Quitman of Mississippi. In the North some discontented New England Whigs and Union

(turn to page 208)

"PAP, SOUP AND CHOWDER" is the title of this cartoon. Franklin Pierce, the Democratic candidate, rides to the White House on a horse, while the Whigs plod along, eating their favorite food. President Fi more, carried on the shoulders of the editor of t New York *Mirror*, eats Government Pap (a slang ter

r patronage); General Scott, the Whig candidate, tot-
rs on the shoulders of *Tribune* editor Horace Greeley,
illing his "hasty plate of soup"—a phrase he once
used and never lived down. Daniel Webster, enjoying
the chowder, is carried along on the back of James W.
Webb, editor of the New York *Courier and Enquirer*.

Democrats resolved to vote for Webster.

But even with so many contestants, the canvass offered very little excitement. Neither the Democrats nor the Whigs had a definite political program; both of them depended on the personalities of their candidates. It was known that Pierce supported the compromise measures, but what General Scott's policies were seemed to be a deeply hidden secret.

The Democrats were more confident of victory than the Whigs. They were satisfied with their platform and pleased with their candidate. The quarrel within their ranks over slavery was more or less patched up, and the party went into the election fairly united. All the defeated contestants for the nomination, Cass, Buchanan, Douglas, and Marcy, were ready to stump the country for Pierce.

> "We're bound to give the Whigs defeat
> With gallant Pierce and King."

ran one of their campaign songs.

The fashion of mudslinging was now a firmly established campaign feature. The Whig newspapers called Pierce a drunkard, "a hero of many a well-fought bottle," and named him a coward because of an incident in the Mexican War, when he had a fainting spell and had to be carried from the battlefield. The Whig editors omitted to mention that Pierce was exhausted by excruciating pain in his knee, which had been injured the previous day when his horse stumbled. However, in a presidential campaign truthful reporting is never a virtue of the opposing newspapers. The Whigs sang:

> "Two generals are in the field
> Frank Pierce and Winfield Scott,
> Some think that Frank's a fighting man,
> And some think he is not.
>
> 'Tis said that when in Mexico,
> While leading on his force,
> He took a sudden fainting fit,
> And tumbled off his horse.
>
> But gallant Scott has made his mark
> On many a bloody plain,
> And patriot hearts beat high to greet
> The Chief of Lundy's Lane.
>
> And Chippewa is classic ground,
> Our British neighbors know,
> And if you'd hear of later deeds,
> Go ask in Mexico."

Besides being a drunkard and a coward, the Episcopalian Pierce was accused of taking a stand against Catholicism, and Protestant audiences were told that one of his daughters had become a nun.

The Democratic newspapers retaliated. They hammered on Scott's nickname, "Old Fuss and Feathers," given to him by his army officers, and they ridiculed him because of two phrases he had once used. One was "a hasty plate of soup," the other "a fire upon the rear." These seemed to Democratic editors to be the acme of hilarity. Scott used the first phrase when, during the Mexican War, the Secretary of War had called at his office and he was out; on his return he had apologized that he had left the office only to take "a hasty plate of soup." The other he had written when he was going to the Rio Grande and, fearing the jealousy of the Democrats, had said that he must have the support of the administration, "for soldiers had a far greater dread of a fire upon the rear than of the most formidable enemy in front."

Thus the campaign proceeded, accusations being hurled from one camp to the other.

Scott's managers proposed that the General should travel through the country, address German and Irish audiences, and refute the Democratic charge that he was hostile to foreigners. The excuse for the tour was a visit to Blue Lick Springs in Kentucky, where Scott was to inspect a site for a military hospital. In reality the journey was a campaign for votes —familiar enough today for presidential candidates, but a novelty at that time.

Leaving Washington, Old Fuss and Feathers stopped at Pittsburgh, telling his audience that he had not come to the city to campaign but that official duties compelled him to travel West. In Cleveland he began his speech: "Fellow citizens. When I say fellow citizens I mean native and adopted as well as those who intend to become citizens." An Irishman interrupted: "You're welcome here," to which Scott replied with the clumsy compliment: "I hear that rich brogue. I love to hear it. It makes me remember the noble deeds of Irishmen, many of whom I have led to battle and victory." From Cleveland he traveled to Columbus, and from there to Blue Lick Springs, making frequent stops on the route to announce

SEWARD RIDES SCOTT TO VICTORY, prodding the candidate to take a long stride over the Whig platform plank about the acceptance of the Fugitive Slave Law. Then if he gets over it, he can "get over anything." Greeley of the *Tribune* follows them with Free-Soil soup while Henry Raymond of the *Times* watches with mild approval.

ow much he liked the foreign-born. After isiting the hospital site, Scott traveled through Kentucky, made a number of speeches in the doubtful state of Ohio, then swung through New York State, always repeating that he was ot on a political trip and that he loved that rich Irish brogue" and that "sweet German accent."

Pierce remained at home and was silent— even so, he won the election by a comfortable majority. Of the thirty-one states taking part in the election (the thirty-first state was California, admitted on September 9, 1850), Pierce carried every state but four, receiving 1,601,474 votes against Scott's 1,386,580 and John P. Hale's 156,667.

The result was a deathblow to the Whigs. Unable to agree over the slavery issue, shattered into fighting local groups, each jealously opposing the others, they disintegrated. Their two great leaders had passed away during the campaign—Clay in June, Webster in October— presaging the death of the party.

As usual, many explanations were made about the outcome of the election. The New York *Herald* asserted that Pierce had won because the people feared that if Scott should become President, he would parrot the radical anti-slavery views of Seward—thereby breaking the union of the country. But the explanation of the *National Intelligencer* seems more convincing. That paper said that the people had voted for Pierce not only because they looked upon the compromise measures as a final settlement on slavery, but because they were tired of the feeble, amicable neutrality of the administration and were ready for something positive, something that would uphold and advance the honor, dignity, and power of this great country among the nations of the earth.

On inauguration day there were snow flurries and a biting raw wind in Washington. The outgoing President called for Franklin Pierce at the Willard Hotel, and together they rode down to the Capitol. For Pierce the waving and cheering multitude did not lighten the gloom of a deep sorrow. A few weeks before, he had had the great misfortune to lose his eleven-

209

CAMPAIGN CARTOONS OF 1852

IN THIS PRE-CONVENTION cartoon, Webster leads the presidential footrace for the $100,000 purse—four years' presidential salary—ahead of Generals Scott and Pierce. But Webster lost, and in a few months he died.

THE TWO BIRDS not described by Audubon are the *Turkey Cockeyus Cum Fuss and Fetheribus* and the *Gamecockius Granitestater*, commonly known as Winfield Scott and Franklin Pierce. They stand opposing each other at the Mason-Dixon line. Scott says: "Get out of the way fellow! I want the whole of the road." Pierce replies: "Cock a doodle doo—ooo! Don't you wish you may get it! But you can't get over this line."

"A CONTESTED SEAT" is the title of this cartoon. Winfield Scott, holding fast to the presidential chair, remarks: "Sorry to disappoint you Pierce; but the people wish me to take this chair," and Pierce says: "Look out there! What you bout General? Do you want to knock a feller's brains out?" However, it was the other way round. Pierce was elected instead of Scott.

AN UNPUBLISHED ANTISLAVERY CARTOON SHO

year-old son in a railroad wreck, seeing hi die before his very eyes.

From the ceremonies the Vice-Presiden elect, William R. King of Alabama—the pri old bachelor—was absent. He was in Cuba,

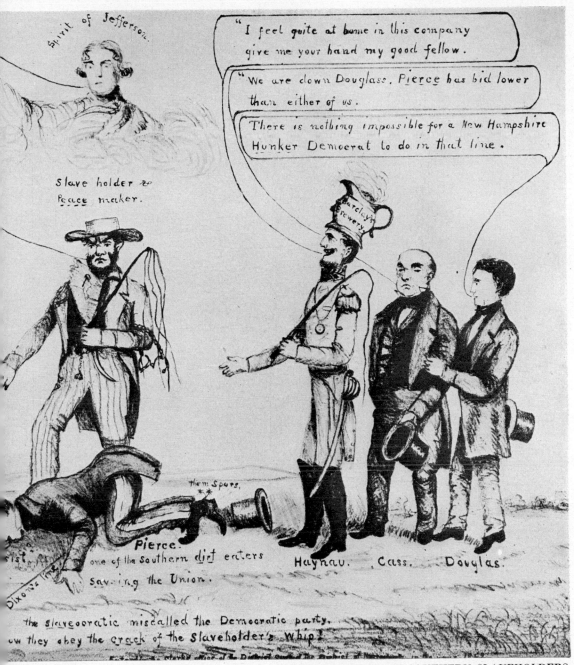

DEMOCRATIC CANDIDATE, FRANKLIN PIERCE, BOWING BEFORE THE SOUTHERN SLAVEHOLDERS.

ith tuberculosis. Congress passed a special act ermitting him to take the oath of office from consul on a plantation near Matanzas. A onth later he was dead.

Pierce took the oath from Chief Justice Taney and before a multitude of fifteen thousand onlookers delivered the inaugural address. He spoke freely without notes—the first and only time that the inaugural address was not read from a prepared manuscript.

JAMES BUCHANAN TAKES THE OATH

THE EIGHTEENTH ELECTION—1856

JAMES BUCHANAN

"I fervently hope that the question is at rest," said President Pierce in his inaugural address—speaking of slavery—"and that no sectional or ambitious or fanatical excitement may again threaten the durability of our institutions or obscure the light of our prosperity." It was wishful thinking. Scarcely two years passed before "fanatical excitement" shook the country to its foundations.

As the Compromise of 1850 offered only a temporary solution, the controversy over slavery was bound to recur sooner or later. That it had come so soon was chiefly due to the presidential aspirations of Stephen A. Douglas, the five-foot-four "Little Giant."

Pierce was a weak Executive. Under him the Democratic party disintegrated. Douglas, fearful that the party would suffer defeat in the next election, tried to stem the adverse tide. That he wanted to be a candidate in 1856 was beyond question. He outlined a three-point program which suggested how to dispose of the surplus revenue, how to improve rivers and harbors, and how to build a railroad to the Pacific. In the latter project the Little Giant

had a personal interest, as he represented Illinois in the Senate and he speculated in Chicago real estate and in Northwestern land. Douglas pleaded for a central and northern railway to the Pacific and asked that the eastern terminus of the railroad should be in Chicago, but St. Paul, Memphis, and New Orleans vied for the same privilege.

Congress was to investigate which of the proposed routes to the Pacific should be built. A $150,000 appropriation was voted for surveying the several possibilities. The survey was made under the direction of the War Department, and as the Secretary of War was Jefferson Davis, it was not so surprising that the engineers recommended the southern route. Besides, this route had great advantages. It was shorter than the others, it led through the already organized territories of Texas and New Mexico, and it would be not only cheaper but easier to build. Its disadvantage—that it had to pass through Mexican territory—was overcome when a piece of land over which the railway was to run was bought from Mexico for ten million dollars—the Gadsden Purchase.

213

JAMES BUCHANAN (1791-1868)
PHOTOGRAPH BY MATHEW B. BRADY

JAMES BUCHANAN (1791-1868) from Pennsylvania was the most available candidate of the Democrats because he had been in England all during the Kansas-Nebraska controversy.

JOHN C. BRECKINRIDGE (1821-1875), was Democratic candidate for Vice-President. He was very active in the campaign, his ticket receiving 174 electoral votes to Frémont's 114.

JOHN C. FRÉMONT (1813-1890), the first presidential candidate of the new Republican party, was also supported by the Northern wing of the antislavery "Know-Nothings."

WILLIAM L. DAYTON (1807-1864), former Senator of New Jersey, was Frémont's running mate. Once an independent Whig, Dayton later became Lincoln's Minister to France.

MILLARD FILLMORE (1800-1874), was chosen by the bigoted, intolerant, Catholic- and foreigner-hating Native Americans, or "Know-Nothings," and accepted by the Whigs.

A. J. DONELSON (1799-1871), Andrew Jackson's nephew and secretary, editor of the Washington *Union*, ran on Fillmore's ticket, receiving only the 8 votes of Maryland.

Douglas, who at first pleaded for the construction of not one but four different lines, was well aware that his cherished central route had to pass through unorganized territories, and as these territories were populated by Indians, it was feared that the red men would be a menace to the builders and a constant threat to the railroad. Therefore he proposed to move them to some other place, reasoning that if the land of the Missouri bend could be opened to settlers and the Indian country organized into a territory, the railway would have no interference.

As early as 1853 the Commissioner of Indian Affairs had drawn up plans for the removal of the Indians, and the House of Representatives had passed a bill to organize the land into the Territory of Nebraska. The territorial question was an urgent one; settlers were eager to enter the region. The bill had Douglas's whole-hearted support, though the Little Giant must

THE VOTES IN THE 1856 ELECTION

STATES	POPULAR VOTE			ELECTORAL VOTE		
	James Buchanan, Pennsylvania. Democrat.	John C. Frémont, California. Republican.	Millard Fillmore, New York. Whig.	Buchanan and Breckinridge.	Frémont and Dayton.	Fillmore and Donelson.
Ala.	46,739	—	28,552	9	—	—
Ark.	21,910	—	10,787	4	—	—
Calif.	53,365	20,691	36,165	4	—	—
Conn.	34,995	42,715	2,615	—	6	—
Del.	8,004	308	6,175	3	—	—
Fla.	6,358	—	4,833	3	—	—
Ga.	56,578	—	42,228	10	—	—
Ill.	105,348	96,189	37,444	11	—	—
Ind.	118,670	94,375	22,386	13	—	—
Iowa	36,170	43,954	9,180	—	4	—
Ky.	74,642	314	67,416	12	—	—
La.	22,164	—	20,709	6	—	—
Me.	39,080	67,379	3,325	—	8	—
Md.	39,115	281	47,460	—	—	8
Mass.	39,240	108,190	19,626	—	13	—
Mich.	52,136	71,762	1,660	—	6	—
Miss.	35,446	—	24,195	7	—	—
Mo.	58,164	—	48,524	9	—	—
N. H.	32,789	38,345	422	—	5	—
N. J.	46,943	28,338	24,115	7	—	—
N. Y.	195,878	276,007	124,604	—	35	—
N. C.	48,246	—	36,886	10	—	—
Ohio	170,874	187,497	28,126	—	23	—
Pa.	230,710	147,510	82,175	27	—	—
R. I.	6,680	11,467	1,675	—	4	—
S. C.*	—	—	—	8	—	—
Tenn.	73,638	—	66,178	12	—	—
Tex.	31,169	—	15,639	4	—	—
Vt.	10,569	39,561	545	—	5	—
Va.	89,706	291	60,310	15	—	—
Wis.	52,843	66,090	579	—	5	—
	1,838,169	1,341,264	874,534	174	114	8

* Electors were appointed by the legislature.

THE THREE CANDIDATES: John C. Frémont, the first presidential candidate of the newly formed Republican Party; Millard Fillmore, candidate of the Native Americans and Whigs; James Buchanan, the Democratic nominee.

have realized that the Senate would never pass it as proposed. He knew that the Southern Senators would never vote for the organization of a new territory in which slavery was forbidden, that they would never vote for a bill which would further strengthen the political supremacy of the North. Therefore he argued —with an eye on the South—that as the compromise measures of 1850 had left the territories of New Mexico and Utah free to choose whether they should be organized with or without slavery, these measures superseded the Missouri Compromise, which allowed slavery only south of 36° 30'; thus slavery could *now* be supported even north of the prescribed latitude. He proposed popular sovereignty for the unorganized territories, giving the territories

the right to decide about the slavery issue within their borders as they saw fit. Many Western and Southern Senators backed Douglas, yet during the debate—and because of Southern pressure—the bill was changed and amended, making the final measure much more radical than the Little Giant had intended at the beginning. One of the bill's provisions outspokenly repealed the Missouri Compromise; another called for the institution of two territories instead of one: Nebraska (with a presumably free constitution) and Kansas (with slavery).

Why Douglas introduced the Kansas-Nebraska Bill, one can only guess. Politicians and historians offer different explanations. Edward Bates, the Whig leader of Missouri, asserted

215

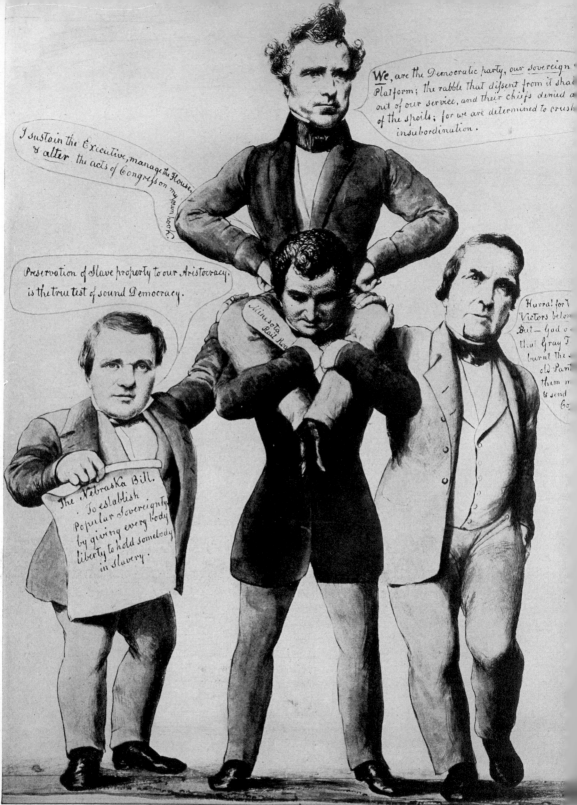

THE DEMOCRATS UNDER FRANKLIN PIERCE. The President sits on the shoulder of Lynn Boyd, Speaker of the House. At the left is Stephen A. Douglas, holding his Nebraska Bill; on the right, Senator Thomas Benton.

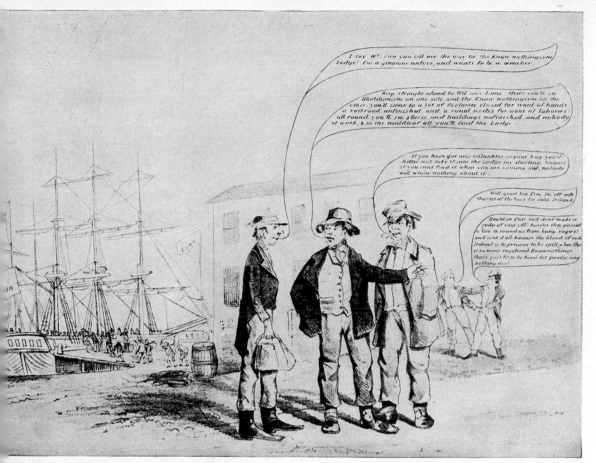

THE KNOW-NOTHINGS or as they were officially called, the Native Americans, exerted some influence in this election. They kept secret their political creed, violently opposed to foreigners and Roman Catholics. If they were asked about their beliefs, they answered, "I know nothing,"—hence the name. In the election Millard Fillmore was their official candidate, though he had no connection with the party and did not endorse the Know-Nothing policies.

that Atchinson, the president of the Senate, told Douglas: "Introduce this bill; you are strong at the North; this will give you the South, and you will be President." Another explanation was that through the measure the Little Giant hoped to save the disunited Democratic party. But a number of other factors added to the complexity of the issue. One was that the Missourians, afraid to be surrounded on three sides by free-soil territory, agitated against the organization of Nebraska without slavery.

During the debate of the bill, excitement ran high all over the country. And when it became law, the antislavery states were in a turmoil. Abolitionist lecturers fomented the temper of the people and Harriet Beecher Stowe's *Uncle Tom's Cabin* worked on their emotions. Douglas was denounced, attacked, abused in every city and village of the North. He could have traveled all the way from Boston to Chicago

by the light of his own burning effigies.

The fight over the bill deepened the rift between the opposing factions in both parties. As both the Democrats and the Whigs were split into pro- and antislavery groups, the time seemed to be ripe for the formation of a new organization in which the antislavery Whigs, Free-Soilers, and all Democrats opposed to the Kansas-Nebraska Act could unite.

The first step toward it was taken in the West. At a meeting in Ripon, Wisconsin, in the early months of 1854, a new association was recommended, to be based on a strong antislavery program. A few weeks later in Jackson, Michigan, an assembly of men met in an oak grove outside the village and laid the foundations of a new party—the Republican party.

For the future status of Kansas (that Nebraska would become a free territory was never in doubt), a big fight was in progress. Northern societies financed and sent emigrants to Kansas who were to keep the state "free," and settlers flocked from Missouri, believing in all honesty that Kansas was to become a slave state. At the voting for the territorial legislature, 6,307 votes were cast—although the total number of legal voters in Kansas was only about 1,500. "Border ruffians" from the South flocked into the territory on election day, "an unkempt, sun-dried, blatant, picturesque mob . . . with guns upon their shoulders, revolvers stuffing their belts, bowie-knives protruding from their boot-tops, and generous rations of whiskey in their wagons." They chased away election judges and they saw to it that the election results should be pleasing to the slaveholding interests. Popular sovereignty became a farce in the hands of the mob, and when the newly elected legislature met, it introduced drastic slave laws.

The antislavery settlers were not willing to take the decision lying down. Reinforced by Sharpe's rifles—"Beecher's Bibles"—sent to them by New England abolitionists, they called a convention at Topeka, drew up a constitution and submitted it to a vote. And when the constitution was adopted, they chose a governor and other state officers and asked Congress to admit Kansas to the Union as a free state. Thus two hostile governments—one pro- and one antislavery—waited for acknowledgment. President Pierce advised Congress that, in his opinion, the "free" government of Kansas was not the legal representative of that territory.

The discussion over slavery proceeded in Congress with renewed vigor. And while the lawmakers argued, the situation in Kansas went from bad to worse. The Federal marshal for the territory, with the help of armed Missouri gangs, served writs upon members of the antislavery government. A mob burned buildings in Lawrence and wrecked the offices of newspapers. Three days after the Lawrence outrage, fifty-six-year-old John Brown, a stern Calvinist and Puritan, "a man that had always been from his childhood impressed with the idea that God had raised him up on purpose to break the jaws of the wicked," set out with four of his sons, a son-in-law, and two neighbors, made a raid on a proslavery settlement near Pottawatomie Creek, and murdered five unarmed, innocent settlers.

THE DEMOCRATIC PLATFORM: BENTON, PIERCE

For John Brown held that "without the shedding of blood, there is no remission of sins."

The political temper of the country reached a boiling point. In the Senate, Southern Congressman Preston Brooks beat Senator Charles Sumner with a heavy cane after Sumner had made a speech about "the crime against Kansas." The South approved Brooks's cowardly deed; the North fumed with indignation.

It was at the height of this excitement—a few days after Brooks's assault on Sumner and only

VAN BUREN ARE UNDER CANDIDATE BUCHANAN; OVER HIM IS THE SOUTHERN SLAVEHOLDER.

week after John Brown's "massacre"—that the Democratic convention met at Cincinnati. Its proceedings began with violence. The Missouri "Regulars," opposing Senator Thomas Hart Benton, knocked down a doorkeeper of the convention who tried to prevent their entrance. But even so, the committee on credentials refused to acknowledge them as the representative delegation of Missouri.

New York again sent two sets of delegates. The convention ruled—as eight years before—

that the competing factions should be admitted with half a vote for each delegate.

For the presidential nomination there were four prominent candidates: Franklin Pierce, James Buchanan, Stephen A. Douglas, and Lewis Cass. Both Pierce and Douglas were acceptable to the South and also to the West; both of them upheld popular sovereignty; Douglas had introduced, President Pierce had signed the Kansas-Nebraska Act. But for this very reason they had to face strong opposition

CAMPAIGN CARTOONS OF 1856

"BUCK TAKING THE POT." James Buchanan holds the bucket of Union Soup, while Frémont stumbles over the Rock of Disunion with his Abolition spoon, and the blindfolded Millard Fillmore tries vainly to find the pot.

"THE MUSTANG TEAM." Frémont's cart, carrying the New York editors Greeley, Bennett, Raymond, and Webb, is stopped at the Union Tollgate. Frémont's cross signifies that he is a Catholic (but actually he was not).

EXPLORER FRÉMONT on the Greeley Abolition Nag is led by Senator Seward toward Salt River—defeat. Behind him are Henry Ward Beecher, carrying rifles ("Beecher's Bibles") to Kansas, and Kit Carson.

AN EARLY CARTOON AGAINST THE NE
In this lithograph by Currier & Ives, the Republica
candidate receives representatives of the different ra
cal and antislavery elements which made up the ne

from the Northern, antislavery wing. It soc
became apparent that the most available cand
date was James Buchanan from Pennsylvani
who had been Minister to Great Britain durir
the Kansas-Nebraska debates and therefore w
not involved on either side of the controvers

220

ORGANIZED REPUBLICAN PARTY AND ITS FIRST PRESIDENTIAL CANDIDATE, JOHN C. FRÉMONT.

party. First in line is a Negro, behind him is a Catholic priest, then comes an old woman preaching free love, followed by a drunken laborer insisting on equal division of property, then an advocate of women's rights, and finally a puritan prohibitionist who wants to abolish "the use of Tobacco, Animal food and Lagerbeer."

Buchanan led on the first ballot with 135½ votes, against Franklin Pierce's 122½, Stephen A. Douglas's thirty-three and Lewis Cass's five. As the balloting continued, Buchanan's strength increased until on the sixteenth trial he led with 168½ votes against Douglas's 121 and Cass's six. He needed only thirty more to reach the necessary two-thirds vote. This he received at the next trial, when Douglas released his supporters "to give effect to the voice of the majority." So Buchanan became the Democratic nominee.

The platform declared that the "party will resist all attempts at renewing, in Congress or out of it, the agitation of the slavery question, under whatever shape or color the attempt may be made." It took issue with the "adverse political and religious test which has been secretly organized by a party claiming to be exclusively American." The Democratic party resolved "that the foundation of this Union of States having been laid in, and its prosperity, expansion, and preeminent example of free government built upon, entire freedom in matters of religious concernment, and no respect of persons in regard to rank or place of birth, no party can be justly deemed national, constitutional, or in accordance with American principles which bases its exclusive organization upon religious opinions and accidental birthplace. And hence a political crusade in the nineteenth century, and in the United States of America, against Catholics and foreign-born, is neither justified by the past history or future prospects of the country, nor in unison with the spirit of toleration and enlightened freedom which peculiarly distinguishes the American system of popular government."

This plank was directed against the Native Americans or, as they were commonly called, the "Know-Nothings," a radical and nationalistic secret society combating the foreign-born and the Roman Catholics. The Know-Nothings fought against increased immigration for obvious reasons. Between the years 1845 and 1855 more than 300,000 immigrants had come to America yearly, driven to the New World by the Industrial Revolution and the German upheaval in 1848. The newcomers—Irish Catholics and German radicals—tended toward the Democratic party, which was then the poor man's party. As the Whigs were not willing to fight the foreign issue, so the Native Americans with their intolerant hatred, vigorous bigotry, and determined nationalism came to the fore. The party's deliberations were secret, its members answering questions about their political beliefs with "I know nothing"; hence the name "Know-Nothings."

At first the organization was successful. In the state elections of 1854 the Know-Nothings carried Massachusetts and nearly won New York. Their strength came from the cities of the Atlantic seaboard, where the hatred against immigrants was on the increase as they competed with American workers and undercut wages; and they had support in the South, which resented the foreigners because they increased the antislavery population and strengthened the political supremacy of the North.

In their first national nominating convention the Know-Nothings split into Northern and Southern factions. The battle over principles which had flamed in the meeting of their national council was fully ablaze, and it seemed that the views of the opposing groups were irreconcilable. A great number of Northern delegates withdrew when, after tumultuous scenes, a platform was accepted declaring that "Americans must rule America; and to this end native-born citizens should be selected for all state, federal, and municipal offices of government employment, in preference to all others," advocating "a change in the laws of naturalization, making a continued residence of twenty-one years . . . an indispensable requisite for citizenship," and demanding "opposition to any union between Church and State."

For their presidential candidate the Know-Nothings chose Millard Fillmore, who was not a member of the party, nor was he known to be in sympathy with its principles.

The Northern delegates, dissatisfied with the platform and the candidate, called a separate convention and prepared to name Supreme Court Judge John McLean as their candidate. The "North Americans"—as they became known—hoped that the Republicans, who were to hold their first nominating convention a few days later, would also support McLean. But this did not materialize. The majority of Republicans were behind John C. Frémont, explorer, soldier, and dashing pathfinder of the West, well aware that if the North Americans should nominate John McLean, the free-soil vote would be split and Frémont's chances would be impaired.

In this predicament the Frémont managers asked the North Americans to name Nathaniel P. Banks instead of McLean, with the understanding that Banks would withdraw after the convention and release his votes to Frémont.

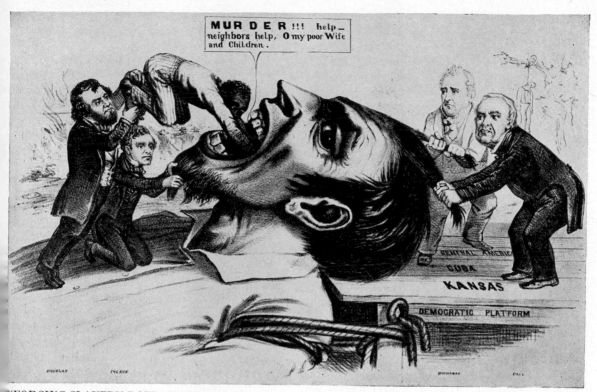

"FORCING SLAVERY DOWN THE THROAT OF A FREE-SOILER," as done by the four leading Democratic contenders for the presidential nomination. Douglas and Pierce are on the left, Buchanan and Cass are on the right.

This scheme was put in effect with the help of some $30,000—if one can believe the report of one observer—which the Republican managers freely distributed among the delegates of the North Americans. Thus when their convention assembled, everything went according to plan—Banks was nominated and waited to withdraw.

The Republicans met in Philadelphia on the anniversary of the Battle of Bunker Hill. It was their first nominating convention. Their chairman declared: "You are here today to give direction to a movement which is to decide whether the people of the United States are to be hereafter and forever chained to the present national policy of the extension of human slavery." The delegates and spectators cheered enthusiastically. There was a crusading fervor over the meeting. Its short platform advocated the saving of Cuba for the United States," and construction of a railroad to the Pacific by "the most central and practical route." Its most important plank declared that it was the duty of Congress to prohibit in the territories "those

twin relics of barbarism—polygamy and slavery."

The delegates—as planned—chose John C. Frémont for the Presidency and William L. Dayton for his running mate, the latter winning the nomination against the nationally unknown Illinois lawyer, Abraham Lincoln (who in an informal ballot received 110 votes), and thirteen other candidates. Frémont was selected because he seemed to be the most available man for the office. Seward was much too radical on the slavery issue and he had the enmity of the Know-Nothings; Salmon P. Chase was no less radical than Seward, besides being too much of a Whig. But Frémont was safe; he was sound on the territorial question, he had excellent Southern connections, had never uttered any statements which could harm the South, and "had no political antecedents." He had been a Democrat once, had the confidence of the German groups, and was well liked by the North Americans, who rallied behind him when Banks withdrew from the race.

The campaign was well under way when the

223

remnants of the Whigs held their convention, promising their support to Fillmore and Donelson, the original Know-Nothing candidates, but without endorsing the political principles of that party. The Whigs held that both the Democratic and Republican nominees were fostering sectional strife, and they pleaded for Fillmore, whose election would guarantee peace and the preservation of the Union. The Whigs had "no new principles to announce, no new platform to establish, but are content to broadly rest—where their fathers rested—upon the Constitution of the United States, wishing no safer guide, no higher law."

Thus three candidates were in the field: the Democrat Buchanan, the Republican Frémont, and Fillmore, representing the Know-Nothings.

As Frémont could not expect much support from the South, he had to carry almost the entire North to win the Presidency. There were 176 electoral votes from the free states against 120 from the slave states, so he needed 149 votes to win. A loss of only twenty-eight votes in the North meant defeat.

The issue of the campaign was "Bleeding Kansas" and the Republican slogan, "Free soil, free speech, and Frémont," was carried on banners, shouted in torchlight processions and at innumerable mass meetings.

The educated class—professors, clergymen, writers, scientists, and teachers—canvassed with great energy for the new party. Any one of them who knew how to make a speech made one—even the reserved Ralph Waldo Emerson addressed meetings, and so did shy William Cullen Bryant and Henry Wadsworth Longfellow. They fought the campaign with crusading fervor against the great moral wrong, slavery. Republican "Wide-Awake" companies marched through the streets carrying banners and transparencies, Republican fife-and-drum corps played tunes; there was an excitement similar to that in 1840, only this time the emotionalism stemmed from important political differences.

Influenced by the civil strife in Kansas, more and more converts from the ranks of the Whigs and the Democrats joined the Republicans. One of them was Hamilton Fish, whose conversion was "worth ten thousand votes." And the once-so-ardent Democrat George Bancroft declared that as the Democratic party had

BUCHANAN ON THE SLAVERY MONSTER is pulled into Kansas over the Mason-Dixon line. The three Doughfaces—proslavery Democrats from the North—drawing the chariot are Cass, Douglas and Pierce. The Republican candidate, Frémont, orders the monster back, and Fillmore sits on the fence.

HE MORNING AFTER THE ELECTION. The four editors on the left (Greeley of the New York *Tribune*, Bennett of the *Herald*, Webb of the *Courier and Enquirer*, and an unnamed German) acclaim Buchanan. The Republican candidate, Frémont, whom they had abandoned, now rides away on his horse with the parting words: "Like a foolish fellow you editors made me believe papers could do all things." On the right Fillmore is thrust down into "the dark and gloomy caverns of 'Know-Nothingism'" by Editor Raymond of the N. Y. *Times*, whom he blames for his defeat.

allen into a hopeless condition under "this bastard race that controls the organization, this unproductive hybrid got by southern arrogance upon northern subserviency," he would not vote for Buchanan.

During the canvass there was hardly any other issue discussed but slavery (except the homestead question, "a most gigantic scheme of confiscation and agrarianism" and a first step toward introducing communism and socialism"). Little personal invective was used, though the Democrats charged that Frémont was an illegitimate child, that he favored the Catholics, and that he had some shady deals with a San Francisco banking house. Still, the main argument against him was political—the Democrats told the electorate that if Frémont were elected, the South would secede and the Union would be dissolved.

In the Southern states, where Buchanan was certain of victory, the campaign was sluggish. There the Republicans had no organization at all; in eleven Southern states the names of their candidates did not even appear on the ballot. There the Whigs were already absorbed by the Know-Nothings. But in the Northern states, especially in Pennsylvania and Indiana, where state elections were held in October, the campaign was spirited and both parties worked hard to influence the result.

The Democrats made especially strenuous efforts to secure the votes of Pennsylvania. As their candidate was certain to receive the 112 Southern electoral votes, all Buchanan needed for his election were the twenty-seven from Pennsylvania and ten more votes (either Indiana or Illinois). Thus the struggle for votes in the Keystone State was keen. It was said that the Democrats spent half a million dollars to influence the election. Bankers and brokers from Wall Street, fearing a Republican victory which would lead to disruption of the Union and an upset money market, contributed freely to the campaign fund. August Belmont alone

INAUGURATION PROCESSION in honor of President Buchanan, passing through Pennsylvania Avenue.

BUCHANAN'S CABINET. Clockwise from bottom left: Thompson, Floyd, Cass, Cobb, Holt, Toucey, Black.

CABINET COUNCIL as shown in *Harper's Weekly*, the illustrated magazine which was founded in 1857.

JAMES BUCHANAN HELD THE FIRST PRESIDE

gave $50,000. Against this the Republicans we powerless; the new organization had not y learned how to tap the coffers of their rich su porters.

The ballots showed that the new party ha

TION IN THE EAST ROOM OF THE WHITE HOUSE TWO DAYS AFTER HE WAS INAUGURATED.

ost not only Pennsylvania and Indiana, but New Jersey, California, and Illinois as well. Buchanan won the election with 1,838,169 popular votes against Frémont's 1,341,264 and Fillmore's 874,534.

The Republicans went down in a "victorious defeat." The poet Whittier rhymed hopefully:

> "If months have well-nigh won the field,
> What may not four years do?"

Four years did a lot.

LINCOLN TAKES THE OATH

THE NINETEENTH ELECTION—1860

ABRAHAM LINCOLN

With the timid and ineffective Buchanan in the White House, the country drifted rapidly toward disunion. "The victory of Buchanan is the victory of Southern bullyism, the acknowledgment of Northern men that 'right or wrong' they yield because the South threatens to secede," said one political observer after Buchanan's election, and his words seemed to be borne out by subsequent events. The new President used complacent words in his inaugural: "The whole territorial question being thus settled upon the principle of popular sovereignty—a principle as ancient as free government itself—everything of a practical nature has been decided. May we not, then, hope that the long agitation on this subject of slavery is approaching its end, and that the geographical parties to which it has given birth, so much dreaded by the Father of his country, will speedily become extinct?"

Extinct? Only two days passed after Buchanan's inauguration when the Dred Scott decision roused the passions of the country. Chief Justice Roger B. Taney, speaking in the name of seven Democratic justices—five of them from the South—handed down the majority opinion that the Negro Dred Scott, who had brought suit for his liberty, was a slave even though he had resided in free territory during part of his life. Once a slave, always a slave!

And as Dred Scott's case raised the question whether the Missouri Compromise had been constitutional, the Supreme Court decided that it had not and that Congress had never had the right to exclude slavery from the Louisiana territory north of 36° 30′. Slaves were property and, as such, protected under the Constitution.

The South rejoiced. From now on, the new territories would not have the right to exclude slavery within their borders; from now on, popular sovereignty had no meaning at all. But in the North the reaction was equally violent—the abolitionists demanded strong measures against the spreading of slavery.

The animosity between North and South grew, the fire of antagonism kept alive by the events in Kansas. President Buchanan sent a new proslavery governor to the territory, and an election of delegates to a constitutional convention was called. The Free-State party de-

229

ABRAHAM LINCOLN (1809-1865)
PHOTOGRAPH BY MATHEW BRADY
TAKEN FEB. 23, 1861, IN WASHINGTON

ABRAHAM LINCOLN
(1809-1865), became the candidate of the Republican party. As the Democrats were split, Lincoln won the election against Douglas, Breckinridge and Bell.

HANNIBAL HAMLIN
(1809-1891), Senator from Maine, was Lincoln's running mate. Dissatisfied with the Democratic policy on slavery, he became a Republican in 1856.

STEPHEN A. DOUGLAS
(1813-1861), candidate of the Northern and Western Democrats after the Southern delegates withdrew in protest, received only twelve electoral votes.

JOHN C. BRECKINRIDGE
(1821-1875), candidate of the Southern Democrats, represented the slaveholding interests. Supported by President Buchanan, he received 72 electoral votes.

JOHN BELL
(1797-1869), candidate of the Constitutional Union party, made up of former Whigs and other conservatives working for the preservation of the Union.

EDWARD EVERETT
(1794-1865), the great orator, was Bell's running mate. Their ticket won 588,879 votes to Lincoln's 1,866,452, Douglas's 1,376,957, Breckinridge's 849,781.

THIS SHORT AUTOBIOGRAPHICAL SKETCH WH

clined to participate, and so the proslavery men carried the day. In October, 1857, the notorious Lecompton Convention met, framing proslavery constitution and submitting it to vote of the residents of the territory. The people were asked to vote for a "constitution with no slavery" or a "constitution with slavery. But there was a catch to this. One section declared that if the decision of the people should be for a constitution without slavery then slavery "should no longer exist in the State of Kansas, except that the right of property in slaves now in this territory shall in n

WROTE IN DECEMBER, 1859, WAS THE BASIS FOR SOME OF HIS CAMPAIGN BIOGRAPHIES.

...asure be interfered with." Whichever way ... people voted, slavery was there to stay. ...erefore, on election day most Free-State men ...ed away from the polls, and a proslavery ...stitution was adopted.

...n Congress Stephen A. Douglas castigated ... Lecompton fraud. "If Kansas wants a slave-...e constitution, she has a right to do it. It is ...e of my business which way the slavery ...se is decided, and I care not whether it is ...d down or voted up." But Douglas held that ... Lecompton scheme was a "trick, a fraud ...n the rights of the people." And he broke with the vacillating Buchanan, who, in fear of a Southern secession, upheld the Lecompton Constitution.

In the midterm election of 1858, the Buchanan administration suffered defeat in the North. The panic of 1857 and the President's proslavery stand turned many voters against the Democrats. Industrialists who desired a high protective tariff, bankers and financiers demanding a better banking system, settlers in the West hoping for free homesteads—they all turned Republican.

A most notable contest took place in Illinois.

231

THE PROMINENT REPUBLICAN CANDIDATES of 1860 as pictured in *Harper's Weekly*. In the cent William H. Seward, the favorite. Top left: Edward Bates, conservative jurist from Missouri. Top right: Nathan P. Banks, the favorite son of Massachusetts. Middle row: Wm. Pennington of New Jersey; Salmon P. Chase, Ohi Governor; John McLean, Supreme Court Judge from Ohio; Simon Cameron, Pennsylvania political boss. Botto row: John C. Frémont; Lincoln; John Bell, the candidate of the Constitutional Union Party, and Cassius M. Cl

THE WIGWAM, a temporary structure in Chicago, where on May 16 the Republican convention assembled.

TEN THOUSAND PEOPLE filled the huge hall, whe amidst great excitement the nominations were ma

There Stephen A. Douglas, fighting for his Senate seat, was opposed by the Springfield lawyer, Abraham Lincoln. In a series of joint debates the two men discussed the slavery issue. Lincoln sounded the keynote:

"We are now far into the fifth year since policy was initiated with the avowed object a confident promise of putting an end to slave agitation. Under the operation of that polic that agitation has not only ceased but has co

(turn to page 2

232

CANDIDATE OF THE REPUBLICANS. As Lincoln did not have a proper picture of himself, a Chicago photographer traveled to Springfield and took this "dressed up" photograph, which was used extensively in the campaign.

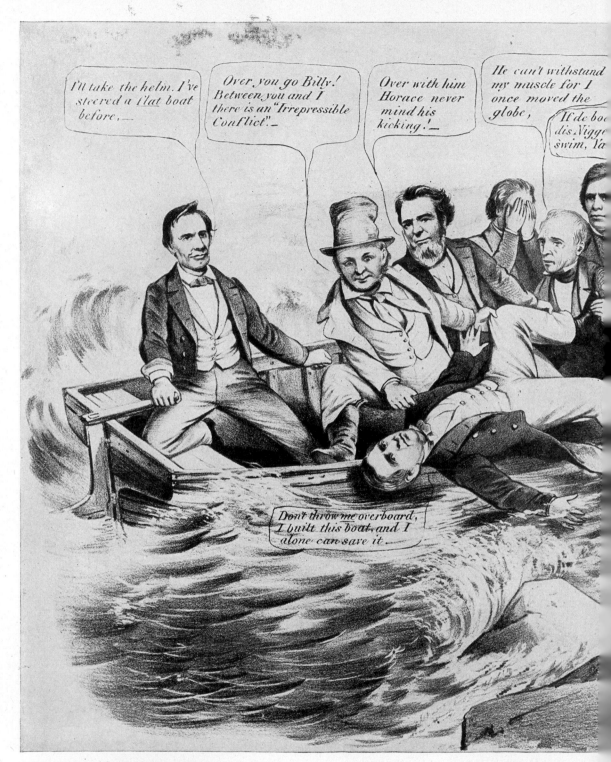

REPUBLICAN CANDIDATE William Seward, defeated in the convention, is thrown overboard while Lincoln takes the helm. Horace Greeley (next to Lincoln), the influential editor of the New York *Tribune*, by then unfriendly to his

...ormer political friend, gives the New York Senator the final push, helped by Ed. Bates and Francis P. Blair, editor of the Washington *Globe*. In the bow of the boat is James W. Webb, editor of the New York *Courier and Inquirer*.

THE DEMOCRATIC CONVENTIONS

THE DEMOCRATS met in Charleston, South Carolina, but after fifty-seven fruitless ballots they adjourned.

THE SOUTHERN DEMOCRATS withdrew in protest and maintained a separate convention in the same city.

THE DEMOCRATIC CONVENTION reassembled at Baltimore and finally nominated Stephen A. Douglas.

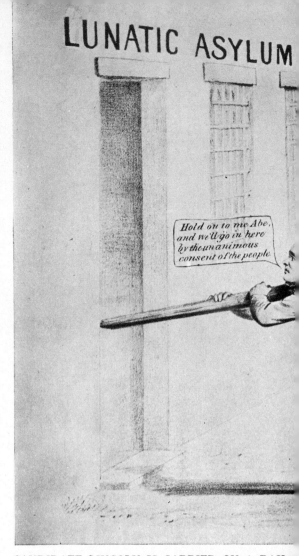

CANDIDATE LINCOLN IS CARRIED ON A RAIL

stantly augmented. In my opinion, it will not cease until a crisis shall have been reached and passed. 'A house divided against itself cannot stand.' I believe this government cannot endure permanently half slave and half free. I do not expect the Union to be dissolved—I do not expect the house to fall—but I do expect it will cease to be divided. It will become all one thing, or all the other. Either the opponents of slavery will arrest the further spread of it, and place it where the public mind shall rest in the belief that it is in the course of ultimate extinction; or its advocates will push it forward til it shall become alike lawful in all the States old as well as new, North as well as South."

Douglas, hard pressed by his opponent, de-

...ACE GREELEY TO A LUNATIC ASYLUM, PROMISING HIS SUPPORTERS EVERYTHING THEY WANT.

clared in Freeport that popular sovereignty was not entirely incompatible with the Dred Scott decision. The inhabitants of the territory could, so Douglas held, by "unfriendly legislation" jeopardize and make insecure property in slaves and in this way destroy slavery itself.

When the "Buchaneers," led by Jefferson Davis and John Slidell in the South, learned of Douglas's "Freeport Doctrine," they demanded a clear repudiation of the popular-sovereignty idea, and asked for congressional protection of slavery in all the territories. The great sectional dispute was rapidly nearing its climax.

Southern Congressmen voted against measures which would benefit the North. The Pacific railroad project and the Homestead Bill were killed. The North retaliated with "per-

sonal liberty laws," which made the Fugitive Slave Law a dead letter.

Sparks were flying to ignite the fire which soon was to engulf the nation. The righteous John Brown of Pottawatomie fame raided the United States Arsenal at Harper's Ferry in Virginia with eighteen men in a mad attempt to seize firearms and free the slaves. In the South indignation knew no bounds; newspapers and orators blamed the abolitionists and the Republican party for the dastardly attack; they held that Brown's raid was an organized attempt to invoke armed slave insurrection in the South.

This was the political picture when the Democratic convention assembled on April 23 in Charleston, the very center of proslavery agitation. The Southern Democrats presented

237

LINCOLN STORMS the White House, while the other three presidential candidates, John Bell, Stephen A. Douglas, and John C. Breckinridge—the last one helped actively by President Buchanan—try to get in by other means.

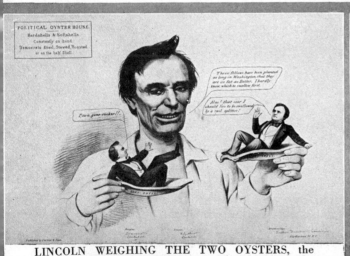

LINCOLN WEIGHING THE TWO OYSTERS, the "Softshell" Democrat Stephen A. Douglas, and the "Hardshell" proslavery Democrat, John C. Breckinridge.

DOUGLAS IS SPANKED by Mother Columbia with cattail called "News from Maine" because "he ha been a bad boy," and Uncle Sam expresses approva

an ultimatum to their Northern and Western brethren: "You must not apologize for slavery; you must declare it right; you must advocate its extension." To this Senator Pugh, delegate from Ohio, replied: "Gentlemen of the South you mistake us; we will not do it." The South was ready to withdraw if the convention faile to uphold Southern rights in the territories.

THE HELP-WANTED SIGN IS TAKEN DOWN by Uncle Sam, who is advising the three other presidential candidates—Douglas, Breckinridge, and the Unionist Bell—that he has concluded to "let Old Abe Lincoln have the place."

THE RAIL CANDIDATE. A Negro and Editor Greeley carry Abraham Lincoln on a rail marked "Republican Platform" — "the hardest stick I ever straddled."

THE FOUR CANDIDATES — Bell, Douglas, Breckinridge, and Lincoln — at an early version of baseball. Lincoln is on the plate, scoring a home run.

The fight in the convention raged around the personality of Douglas. He was "the pivot individual," as one observer remarked. "Every delegate was for or against him." Jefferson Davis told him that if he desired the nomination, he had to abandon the popular-sovereignty doctrine. Moreover, he must agree to the passing of a territorial slave code by Congress and

THE REPUBLICAN RAILROAD SMASHES THE DEMOCRATIC CARRIAGE in which the Democrats drive in opposite directions—cartoon drawn before the Baltimore convention. On the left Stephen A. Douglas (with a beard).

to the protection of slavery in all the territories, whether the people were for or against it. Douglas replied that he would accept the nomination only if the Democratic platform would adopt the principles of the Compromise of 1850; but if the delegates should vote for

"such new issues as the revival of the African slave trade or a Congressional slave code for the territories—it is due to candor to say that in such an event, I cannot accept the nomination if tendered to me."

The eloquent William Yancey of Georgia,

...nd Andrew Johnson, whose name was mentioned as a candidate, pull the cart; on the other end are Breckinridge and ...ane, representatives of the slavery interests and candidates of the Southern Democrats, driven by President Buchanan.

...the prince of fire-eaters"—"ready to precipi-ate the cotton states into a revolution, dis-olve the Union, and build up a Southern ...mpire"—demanded that the convention should ...dopt a platform before balloting for President ...nd Vice-President. The Douglas men were

willing to support this plea. They "had discov-ered, that whereas they had just about a ma-jority, it would be impossible for them to obtain a two-thirds vote in a full Convention. They were willing, therefore, that a few ultra-South-ern states might go out, and allow them to

BEFORE HIS SPRINGFIELD HOME CANDIDATE LINCOLN WATCHES A DEMONSTRATION BY HIS SUPPOR...

A POLLING BOOTH in New York City on November 6, 1860—as voters deposit their ballots for the next President.

A VOTER in New York City who was overcome by hi... inks" on election day is taken bodily to the police s...

nominate their man. All at once they became very cheerful on the subject of a disruption of the Convention. They could go North and get two votes (electoral) for their nominee, for every Southern vote that would leave the Con-

vention. Their game then was, to have three o... four states, at most, go out. They wanted a littl... eruption, but not a great one."

For many days the convention fought ove... the principles. There were two platforms unde...

242

"WIDE-AWAKES," A REPUBLICAN ORGANIZATION, PARADE FOR LINCOLN IN THE STREETS OF NEW YORK.

ELECTION RETURNS are watched by a throng of people before the New York *Herald* in the newspaper district.

DOUGLAS CAMPAIGNED till the very last. This unfriendly cartoon of him appeared in a Republican campaign paper.

discussion: the majority report upholding the views of the Southern slaveholders and calling for the protection of slavery in the territories, and a minority report which was more conciliatory toward the demands of the North.

After a fierce debate the convention adopted the minority report, save for the passage "the Democratic party will abide by the decisions of the Supreme Court of the United States on the questions of Constitutional law." The accept-

STATES	POPULAR VOTE				ELECTORAL VOTE			
	Abraham Lincoln, Illinois. Republican	Stephen A. Douglas, Illinois. Democrat	John C. Breckinridge, Kentucky. Democrat	John Bell, Tennessee. Constitutional Union	Lincoln and Hamlin.	Douglas and Johnson.	Breckinridge and Lane.	Bell and Everett.
Alabama.........................	—	13,651	48,831	27,875	—	—	9	—
Arkansas........................	—	5,227	28,732	20,094	—	—	4	—
California.......................	39,173	38,516	34,334	6,817	4	—	—	—
Connecticut.....................	43,792	15,522	14,641	3,291	6	—	—	—
Delaware........................	3,815	1,023	7,337	3,864	—	—	3	—
Florida.........................	—	367	8,543	5,437	—	—	3	—
Georgia.........................	—	11,590	51,889	42,886	—	—	10	—
Illinois.........................	172,161	160,215	2,404	4,913	11	—	—	—
Indiana.........................	139,033	115,509	12,295	5,306	13	—	—	—
Iowa...........................	70,409	55,111	1,048	1,763	4	—	—	—
Kentucky.......................	1,364	25,651	53,143	66,058	—	—	—	12
Louisiana.......................	—	7,625	22,861	20,204	—	—	6	—
Maine..........................	62,811	26,693	6,368	2,046	8	—	—	—
Maryland.......................	2,294	5,966	42,482	41,760	—	—	8	—
Massachusetts...................	106,533	34,372	5,939	22,331	13	—	—	—
Michigan.......................	88,480	65,057	805	405	6	—	—	—
Minnesota......................	22,069	11,920	748	62	4	—	—	—
Mississippi......................	—	3,283	40,797	25,040	—	—	7	—
Missouri........................	17,028	58,801	31,317	58,372	—	9	—	—
New Hampshire..................	37,519	25,881	2,112	441	5	—	—	—
New Jersey......................	58,324	62,801	—	—	4	3	—	—
New York.......................	362,646	312,510	—	—	35	—	—	—
North Carolina..................	—	2,701	48,539	44,990	—	—	10	—
Ohio...........................	231,610	187,232	11,405	12,194	23	—	—	—
Oregon.........................	5,270	3,951	5,006	183	3	—	—	—
Pennsylvania....................	268,030	16,765	178,871	12,776	27	—	—	—
Rhode Island....................	12,244	7,707	—	—	4	—	—	—
South Carolina*.................	—	—	—	—	—	—	8	—
Tennessee.......................	—	11,350	64,709	69,274	—	—	—	12
Texas..........................	—	—	47,548	15,438	—	—	4	—
Vermont........................	33,808	8,649	1,866	217	5	—	—	—
Virginia........................	1,929	16,290	74,323	74,681	—	—	—	15
Wisconsin......................	86,110	65,021	888	161	5	—	—	—
	1,866,452	1,376,957	849,781	588,879	180	12	72	39

* Electors were appointed by the legislature.

ance of the platform constituted a victory for Douglas and his supporters. One hundred and sixty-five delegates voted for the minority report and 138 against it—the division of the votes being practically on the Mason-Dixon line. But after the platform was adopted, a large number of Southern delegates walked out of the convention in protest. Alabama led the way, followed by Mississippi, Florida, Texas, then by the greater part of the delegations from Louisiana, South Carolina, Arkansas, Delaware, and Georgia—forty-five delegates in all. The speaker for the Mississippi delegation spoke with great emotion: "We say, go your way and we will go ours. But the South leaves not like Hagar, driven into the wilderness, friendless and alone, for in sixty days you will find a united South standing shoulder to shoulder."

The debates over the platform showed that North and South could not come to an agree-

> Springfield, Ill. Oct 19. 1860
> Miss Grace Bedell
> My dear little Miss.
> Your very agreeable letter of the 15th is received—
> I regret the necessity of saying I have no daughter—I have three sons—one seventeen, one nine, and one seven, years of age—They, with their mother, constitute my whole family—
> As to the whiskers, having never worn any, do you not think people would call it a piece of silly affectation if I were to begin it now?
> Your very sincere well-wisher
> A. Lincoln

LINCOLN'S ANSWER to an eleven-year-old girl who wrote to him suggesting that he should grow a beard

THE BEARDED PRESIDENT-ELECT. Lincoln began to grow a beard shortly after his election. This picture taken February 9, 1861, shortly before he left Springfield for Washington, was one of the first showing him with "whiskers."

ment. Neither of them would budge. For the Douglas supporters, candidate and platform were inseparable. They held that—regardless of the platform—neither an ultraslavery man nor a Northern man with Southern principles could carry a single Northern state.

With the seats of the Southern delegates empty, the rump Democratic convention proceeded with the nominations for President and Vice-President. Douglas needed 202 votes to receive the candidacy. But on the first trial he had only 145½ votes. In the next two days fifty-seven ballots were taken, during which his support did not increase materially. As his followers would not compromise on any other candidate, the convention adjourned, to meet again in Baltimore on June 18.

In the meantime the Constitutional Union party met in convention. Its members were the remnants of the Whigs and the Know-Nothings, mostly conservative old men disturbed by the disruptive forces which were tearing the Union apart. In their platform they recognized "no political principle other than the Constitution of the country, the union of the States,

THE DAY HE ARRIVED in Washington, February 23, 1861, Lincoln posed for the photographer, Mathew Brady.

246

and the enforcement of the laws." And they nominated John Bell of Tennessee for the Presidency and Edward Everett of Massachusetts for his running mate.

But the convention to which the whole country looked with intense interest was that of the Republicans. The new party attracted former Whigs, Free-Soil Democrats, abolitionists, political reformers, and protective-tariff devotees, and thousands of them came to Chicago when the convention met there on May 16.

A number of contenders vied for the Republican nominations, the favorite among them being William H. Seward, former Governor of New York. His affairs were in the hands of the astute political manager Thurlow Weed, who arrived with a battery of helpers and with pockets full of money. So certain were Seward's friends of his nomination that they set up a cannon upon the lawn of his home at Auburn to be fired as soon as the wire brought the news from Chicago.

Feverish work went on behind the scenes by the managers of the other candidates. Edward Bates, a conservative, respectable jurist and a former Whig from Missouri, had strong support from his home state as well as Indiana, Maryland, and Delaware, and it was rumored that he was the second choice of other states. Salmon P. Chase, the first Republican Governor of Ohio, had some strength, though he had in his own state the rivalry of Benjamin Wade. Thaddeus Stevens argued for Supreme Court Judge McLean's candidacy. But the most active were the managers of Abraham Lincoln from Illinois.

Judge David Davis, with whom Lincoln had ridden circuit in earlier days, established headquarters at his own expense at the Tremont House to work for his friend. He was helped by the able politician Norman B. Judd. Others of the party were Leonard Swett, who knew how to pull ropes, and Joseph Medill and Charles H. Ray from the Chicago Press & Tribune. The strategy of this group was to unite all anti-Seward forces and prove to them that Lincoln, who was neither a radical like Seward nor a conservative like Bates, and who "excited no hates anywhere" and "has made no records to be defended or explained," was the most "available" candidate.

BEFORE THE UNFINISHED CAPITOL PEOPLE ARE WAITING FOR LINCOLN'S FIRST INAUGURATION.

The tactics of Lincoln's managers were unsurpassed. They came to Chicago certain only of the Illinois votes. And they undertook the task of convincing the other delegates that their candidate was the one who would be able to carry the strategic states of Illinois, Indiana,

247

New Jersey, and Pennsylvania. Thus they went after the votes of the dubious states; they bargained, cajoled, courted, flattered, promised.

Lincoln wired from Springfield: "I authorize no bargains, and will be bound by none."

"Damn Lincoln!" cursed Dubois, one of his men. And they went on bargaining, trading, promising. Indiana was won over by the promise to make Caleb B. Smith (the chairman of the Hoosier delegation) Secretary of the Interior and William P. Dole Commissioner of Indian Affairs. Lincoln's managers pleaded so effectively with the New Jersey delegates, who were lined up behind the state's favorite son, Judge William L. Dayton, that they were confident New Jersey's second choice would be Lincoln and not Seward.

That Pennsylvania would vote on the first ballot for its favorite son, Simon Cameron, a rich machine politician, was certain. Would Lincoln's managers be able to gain the fifty-six votes of that state on the second or third trial?

Seward's strength lay in the East. His weakness was that the Eastern states would vote Republican in any case, thus the personality of the candidate was not of such paramount importance. So it was pure common sense when John A. Andrew, chairman of the Massachusetts delegation, consulted with his colleagues from the few doubtful states and told them: "You delegates all say that William H. Seward cannot carry the doubtful states. When we ask you who can, you from New Jersey give us the name of William L. Dayton, a most excellent and worthy man in every way, and entirely satisfactory to us; but when we go to Pennsylvania they name Simon Cameron; and Indiana and Illinois, Abraham Lincoln. Now it is impossible to have all these three candidates, and unless you delegates from the four doubtful states can agree upon some one candidate, who you think can carry these states, we from New England will vote for our choice, William H. Seward of New York; but if you will unite upon some one candidate and present his name, we will give him enough votes to place him in nomination."

On the day the convention met, William Seward was certain of the New York, Michigan, Wisconsin, and Minnesota votes and of some support in Maine. However, the dele-

gates of Rhode Island, Connecticut, and New Hampshire had met separately the previous evening and resolved not to support him as his long antislavery record would make him a poor candidate. Senator Jacob Collamer was Vermont's favorite son; Cameron, Pennsylvania's; Dayton, New Jersey's; Bates, Missouri's; Ohio was divided between Chase and Wade; and there were a number of minor contestants.

Ten thousand people filled the "Wigwam," the seat of the convention. First the platform was presented. As Horace Greeley, one of its drafters, was convinced that "An Anti-slavery man *per se* cannot be elected; but a tariff, River and Harbor, Pacific Railroad, Free Homestead man may succeed," the platform comprised all these good things.

After its adoption the convention adjourned without taking a ballot for President. At this point, the able journalist Murat Halstead reported, "So confident were the Seward men . . . of their ability to nominate their great leader, that they urged an immediate ballot and would have had it if the clerks had not reported that they were unprovided with tally-sheets."

But during the evening Lincoln's managers worked like beavers. They were after the fifty-six votes of the Pennsylvania delegation. It was at midnight that Joseph Medill met David Davis in the hotel lobby just as the judge was leaving the room where he had been conferring with the Pennsylvanians. "How will the vote?" Medill wanted to know.

"Damned if we haven't got them."

"How did you get them?"

"By paying their price." (The price was that Pennsylvania's favorite son, Simon Cameron, was to become Secretary of the Treasury.)

"Good heavens! Give Cameron the Treasury Department? What will be left?" worried Medill.

"Oh, what's the difference?" replied Davis. "We are after a bigger thing than that; we want the Presidency, and the Treasury is not a great stake to pay for it."

According to the deal, the Pennsylvania delegates would switch their votes on the second ballot to Judge McLean and on the third to Lincoln.

The next morning the confident Seward men

248

PRESIDENT-ELECT LINCOLN AND PRESIDENT BUCHANAN ON THEIR WAY TO THE INAUGURAL.

marched cockily through the streets of Chicago. They were positive that their man would be nominated. Their band played and they cheered and marched, and marched a little bit too far. When they returned to the Wigwam, there was no place for them—every seat was occupied—the structure was filled to capacity.

In the meantime the astute Lincoln managers had packed the convention hall with their supporters. Trainloads of them had been brought to Chicago without charge (Judd was the lawyer for the Illinois Railroad), and during the night the Lincoln men had printed tickets of admission, duplicating the regular ones. And while the Seward men marched through the streets, the Lincoln enthusiasts streamed into the Wigwam, ready to strain their vocal cords for "Honest Abe, the rail-splitting candidate."

First the names of the different candidates were put in nomination; then the voting began. The first ballot brought no great surprises. Calling the New England states first, Maine gave ten votes to Seward and six to Lincoln; Vermont was solidly behind its favorite son, Senator Collamer; Massachusetts cast twenty-one for Seward, four for Lincoln; Rhode Island's majority went to Judge McLean, Connecticut's to Bates. New York—as expected—cast all its seventy votes for Seward. New Jersey voted for Dayton, Pennsylvania's majority voted for Cameron, Maryland and Delaware for Bates. Virginia gave only eight to Seward and fourteen to Lincoln. Kentucky's vote was divided (between Seward, Lincoln, Chase, McLean, and Charles Sumner); Ohio's majority went to Chase. Then came Indiana. A tumultuous shout broke loose when all of the Hoosier State votes—twenty-six of them—were given to Lincoln. Missouri cast its votes for Bates, Michigan for Seward—as did Wisconsin and the majority of Texas. Iowa was divided. California and Minnesota were behind Seward, and Oregon went for Bates. The territories of Kansas and Nebraska and the District of Columbia gave Seward ten out of a total of fourteen.

The final result was 173½ for Seward, 102 for Lincoln, 50½ for Cameron, forty-nine for Chase, forty-eight for Bates, the other votes being divided among the lesser candidates.

The convention hall was bursting with excitement. Voices called impatiently: "Call the roll, call the roll."

249

PRESIDENT-ELECT, ARM-IN-ARM WITH PRESIDENT BUCHANAN, ENTERS THE SENATE CHAMBER

On the second ballot Lincoln's support increased. New Hampshire gave him nine votes, Vermont ten, and he gained five in Rhode Island and Connecticut. The cheer was deafening when Pennsylvania changed over to Lincoln, giving him forty-eight votes. The final result of the second ballot was Seward 184½, Lincoln 181.

Now came the third, Lincoln picking up all the time. He gained four in Massachusetts, one in Rhode Island, eight in New Jersey, four in Pennsylvania, nine in Maryland. Here is Murat Halstead's eyewitness account of the critical third ballot which gave the nomination to Lincoln:

"The number of votes necessary to a choice were 233, and I saw under my pencil as the Lincoln column was completed the figures 231½ —one vote and a half to give him the nomination.

"There are always men anxious to distinguish themselves on such occasions. There is nothing that politicians like better than a crisis. I looked up to see who would be the man to give the decisive vote. In about ten ticks of a watch Carter of Ohio was up. I had imagined Ohio would be slippery enough for the crisis. And sure enough! Every eye was on Carter, and everybody who understood the matter at all knew what he was about to do. He said: 'I rise (eh), Mr. Chairman (eh), to announce the change of five votes of Ohio from Mr. Chase to Mr. Lincoln.'

"One of the secretaries, with a tally sheet in his hand, shouted: 'Fire the salute! Abe Lincoln is nominated.'"

The Wigwam was in an uproar. Delegation after delegation changed its votes, making Lincoln's nomination unanimous.

Knapp, whom Lincoln had paid to go to Chicago and report to him, wired to Springfield: "Abe, we did it. Glory to God!" And Lincoln, who was sitting at the *Journal* office in Springfield, waiting for the wire, said quietly:

reckon there's a little short woman down at our house that would like to hear the news."

The Seward men were desolate. They were "so overcome by their favorite's defeat that they cried like heartbroken children. Tears flowed like water among the vast throng." But the other Republicans were happy, for they believed that Lincoln was the right choice.

A few weeks later the Democratic convention met again at Baltimore. A number of contested delegates from the South presented themselves. For three full days nothing else was discussed but their admission. When finally the Douglas factions from Alabama and Louisiana were admitted, all other anti-Douglas delegates from the South walked out. The chasm between the two sections of the party was as deep as ever.

On the first ballot, Douglas received 173½ votes, Guthrie ten, and Breckinridge five, while three votes were divided among four other candidates. Sanford A. Church of New York moved a resolution that the convention should concede Douglas's nomination, as he had received two thirds of the votes. There were strong objections to Church's proposal because —as it was pointed out—Douglas had never received the two-thirds vote of *all* the Democratic delegates, but only of those present. Whereupon Church withdrew his resolution. On the next trial the Douglas vote increased to 187½; Breckenridge had 7½, Guthrie, 5½. Again the Church resolution was introduced, and as the convention accepted it this time, Douglas received the nomination.

The Southern Democratic delegates who withdrew from the Charleston convention had already held a meeting in Richmond; now they met again in Charleston, joined by the seceding delegates of the Baltimore convention. In their assembly they adopted the rejected majority platform of the Charleston convention, demanding the protection of slavery in all territories, and nominated John C. Breckinridge of Kentucky for the Presidency.

Thus the Democratic party had two sets of candidates. Douglas was the choice of the North, standing on a popular-sovereignty platform, while Breckinridge was the proslavery candidate of the South. Because of this split Lincoln was certain to win.

A colorful campaign followed. The Republican "Wide-Awakes" marched through the streets wearing black-enameled circular capes and glazed military fatigue caps, carrying a rail with an oil lamp and a flag with the names of Lincoln and Hamlin. In Boston a rail-splitters' battalion held a demonstration—every one of the rail splitters standing at least six feet four inches in his stocking feet. The rivals of the Republicans had squads too. The "Bell Ringers," supporters of Bell and Everett, imitated the "Wide-Awakes"; other groups were called "Union Sentinels" and "Minute Men." In Brooklyn some Douglas supporters named themselves "The Chloroformers," as they were planning to put the Republican "Wide-Awakes" to sleep.

Lincoln, who made a resolution not to "write or speak anything upon doctrinal points" during the canvass, remained at home in Springfield, received visitors by the hundreds, wrote letters, shook hands. But Douglas was out campaigning. He warned against his opponent and said that a Republican victory would mean the secession of the South. In Douglas's opinion, "this country is in more danger now than at any moment since I have known anything of public life."

When the election returns were in, they showed that Lincoln had carried all the Northern states but one. In New Jersey the vote was so close that for days neither the Republican nor the Democrats knew who had won the state. The final result gave Lincoln four votes and Douglas three. California's electoral vote went to Lincoln, though his popular majority in that state was only 657.

The South—eleven out of the fifteen slave states—voted for Breckinridge, who was supported by the Buchanan administration; three states voted for the Bell-Everett ticket, and only one—Missouri—for Douglas. Lincoln had not a single electoral vote from the South.

The popular vote of thirty-three states (two new states had been admitted since the previous election—Minnesota on May 11, 1858, and Oregon on February 12, 1859) stood: Lincoln 1,866,452; Breckenridge, 849,781; Douglas 1,376,957; John Bell, 588,879. These figures showed that the majority of the country was for union and peace. Breckenridge, the only

LINCOLN DELIVERS HIS FIRST INAUGURAL ADDRESS, HEARD BY A MULTITUDE OF CITIZENS.

secession candidate, received less than one fifth of the total vote.

Lincoln remained in Springfield till February. The afternoon before he left for Washington he visited his law office to say good-by to his partner of over sixteen years—Billy Herndon. Looking at the battered law shingle, the President-elect told Herndon: "Let it hang there undisturbed." Then he added: "Give our clients to understand that the election of a President makes no change in the firm of Lincoln and Herndon. If I live, I'm coming back some time, and then we'll go right on practicing law as if nothing had ever happened."

On March 4 the new President was inaugurated. He gave a solemn warning to the South: In your hands, my dissatisfied fellow countrymen, and not in mine, is the momentous issue of civil war. The government will not assail you. You can have no conflict without being yourselves the aggressors. You have no oath registered in heaven to destroy the government, while I shall have the most solemn one to 'preserve, protect, and defend' it."

He pleaded: "We are not enemies, but friends. We must not be enemies. Though passion may have strained, it must not break, our bonds of affection. The mystic chords of memory, stretching from every battlefield and patriot grave to every living heart and hearthstone all over this broad land, will yet swell the chorus of the Union when again touched, as surely they will be, by the better angels of our nature."

But it was of no avail. A month later Confederate batteries fired on Fort Sumter.

LINCOLN'S SECOND INAUGURAL

THE TWENTIETH ELECTION—1864

ABRAHAM LINCOLN
AND ANDREW JOHNSON

On Sunday afternoon, April 14, 1861, Major Anderson left Fort Sumter "with colors flying and drums beating," saluting his flag with fifty guns. The tragic controversy between the two sections could no longer be solved by peaceful means.

The outbreak of hostilities unified the Northern political parties. Many of the Democrats joined the Republicans, and those who remained faithful to their old allegiance were behind the administration's war measures. Douglas—after visiting Lincoln—said: "There can be no neutrals in this war; only patriots or traitors."

But as the war with its mounting casualties dragged on, the opposition against Lincoln grew. It was not long before Wendell Phillips spoke of him as "a more unlimited despot than the world knows this side of China," and Charles Sumner declared: "Our President is now dictator, *imperator*—whichever you like; but how vain to have the power of a god and not use it godlike."

The opponents of the administration charged the President with inefficiency. A joint committee on the conduct of the war was formed in 1862, asking that Congress should be allowed to have greater participation in its management. Lincoln refused to concede this. The Constitution designated the President as commander in chief of the army, and as the conduct of the war was not a legislative but an executive function, Lincoln would not relinquish it.

With the approach of election year, the Republicans pondered whether to renominate the President. The country blamed Lincoln for the disastrous defeats in the war during 1862 and the winter of the following year; but with the victories of Gettysburg and Vicksburg, his star shone bright again.

Still, a number of party men wanted to replace him with Salmon P. Chase, the Secretary of the Treasury. Chase was a good administrator with strong antislavery views, and it was thought that he could bring the war to a conclusion much faster than the cautious Lincoln.

In January, 1864, a committee of Congress-

255

ABRAHAM LINCOLN (1809-1865)
PHOTOGRAPH BY MATHEW B. BRADY
TAKEN ON FEBRUARY 9, 1864

THE CANDIDATES

ABRAHAM LINCOLN (1809-1865) was renominated by the Republicans. At first it seemed that he would lose to McClellan, but when Sherman took Atlanta and Farragut captured Mobile Bay, his election became more certain. He won 212 electoral votes to McClellan's 21 votes.

ANDREW JOHNSON (1808-1875), coming from the ranks of the "poor whites" in the South, and a former Democrat, was nominated by the Republicans to give strength to their ticket in the border states. After Lincoln died in 1865, Johnson followed in the presidential chair.

GEORGE B. MCCLELLAN (1826-1885), erstwhile commander in chief of the Union forces, was selected by the Democrats as their candidate on a "stop-the-war" platform. This McClellan repudiated. Had it not been for timely Union victories, McClellan might have won the election.

GEORGE H. PENDLETON (1825-1889), a Representative and Senator from Ohio, was called "Gentleman George" because of his dignity and manner. A Douglas supporter and a leader of the peace wing of the Democratic party during the Civil War, be became McClellan's teammate.

men and prominent citizens consulted with him, and Chase consented to accept the nomination—if offered to him. Whereupon a circular was mailed out, signed by the Kansas Senator, Pomeroy, advocating Chase's nomination instead of Lincoln's. Chase wrote to the President offering his resignation "if there is anything in my action or position which, in your judgment, will prejudice the public interest under my charge." But the magnanimous Lincoln answered: "Whether you shall remain at the head of the Treasury Department is a question which I will not allow myself to consider from any other standpoint other than my judgment of the public service, and, in that view, I do not perceive occasion for a change."

The impulsive Horace Greeley, editor of the New York *Tribune*, wrote that not only Chase, but Frémont, Butler or Grant would make as good a President as Lincoln, and that the selection of any of them would preserve "the salutary one-term principle." This was a reference

THE VOTES IN THE 1864 ELECTION

STATES	POPULAR VOTE		SOLDIERS' VOTE		ELECTORAL VOTE	
	Abraham Lincoln, Illinois.	George B. McClellan, New Jersey.	Abraham Lincoln.	George McClellan.	Lincoln and Johnson.	McClellan and Pendleton.
Calif.	62,134	43,841	2,600	237	5	—
Conn.	44,693	42,288	—	—	6	—
Del.	8,155	8,767	—	—	—	3
Ill.	189,487	158,349	—	—	16	—
Ind.	150,422	130,233	—	—	13	—
Iowa	87,331	49,260	15,178	1,364	8	—
Kan.†	14,228	3,871	—	—	3	—
Ky.	27,786	64,301	1,194	2,823	—	11
Me.	72,278	47,736	4,174	741	7	—
Md.	40,153	32,739	2,800	321	7	—
Mass.	126,742	48,745	—	—	12	—
Mich.	85,352	67,370	9,402	2,959	8	—
Minn.†	25,060	17,375	—	—	4	—
Mo.	72,991	31,026	—	—	11	—
Nev.	9,826	6,594	—	—	2*	—
N. H.	36,595	33,034	2,066	690	5	—
N. J.	60,723	68,014	—	—	—	7
N. Y.	368,726	361,986	—	—	33	—
Ohio	265,154	205,568	41,146	9,757	21	—
Ore.	9,888	8,457	—	—	3	—
Pa.	296,389	276,308	26,712	12,349	26	—
R. I.	14,343	8,718	—	—	4	—
Vt.	42,422	13,325	243	49	5	—
W. Va.	23,223	10,457	—	—	5	—
Wis.	79,564	63,875	11,372	2,458	8	—
	2,213,665	1,802,237	116,887	33,748	212	21

* One of the three Nevada electors died before the election.
† The army vote from Kansas and Minnesota arrived too late and could not be counted.

OLITICIANS MEASURING Lincoln's shoes. One of the most forthright cartoons in support of his renomination. Vhile Gulliver Lincoln calmly sleeps, the pygmies are hard at work figuring out the size of the giant's boots.

UNION AND LIBERTY!   AND   UNION AND SLAVERY!

CARTOON SUPPORTING LINCOLN. On the right, General George McClellan, the Democratic nominee, shakes nds with Jefferson Davis, President of the Southern Confederacy; in the background a slave is being auctioned off.

257

UNCLE SAM REVIEWS THE PRESIDENTIAL CANDIDATES. ON OUTSIDE LEFT IS McCLELLA

to the prevalent custom of the last three decades, during which none of the Presidents served more than one term. Since Andrew Jackson's re-election in 1832, none of them had been chosen for the second time—and with the exception of Van Buren in 1840, none was even put in nomination by the party convention.

The Radical Republicans, in determined o position to Lincoln, called a convention Cleveland "for consultation and concert of a tion in respect to the approaching president election." They adopted a platform demandi "that the rebellion must be suppressed by for of arms, and without compromise," and th

CRATIC NOMINEE; NEXT TO HIM IS LINCOLN.

did not influence the regular Republican nominating convention, in which Lincoln received the nomination on the first ballot by almost unanimous vote. Every state save Missouri selected him. For the Vice-Presidency the convention named Andrew Johnson, a Democrat from the border states, whose choice irked the leader of the Radical Republicans, grumbling Thaddeus Stevens. Couldn't the Republicans find a candidate "without going down into one of those d——d rebel provinces to pick one up?" he wanted to know.

After the convention, a delegation from the National Union League went to Lincoln to congratulate him. "I do not allow myself," the President said to them, "to suppose that either the convention or the League have concluded to decide that I am either the greatest or best man in America, but rather they have concluded it is not best to swap horses while crossing the river, and have further concluded that I am not so poor a horse that they might not make a botch of it in trying to swap." The phrase "swap horses while crossing the river" became a stand-by of some later political campaigns.

The weeks after the Republican convention were weeks of anxiety. The Army of the Potomac was exhausted. The country yearned for peace. "I know," wrote Greeley to Lincoln on August 9, "that nine-tenths of the whole American people, North and South, are anxious for peace—peace on almost any terms—and utterly sick of human slaughter and devastation. . . . I firmly believe that, were the election to take place tomorrow, the Democratic majority in this state and Pennsylvania would amount to 100,000 and that we should lose Connecticut also. Now if the Rebellion can be crushed before November, it will do to go on; if not, we are rushing on certain ruin. . . . I beg you, implore you, to inaugurate or invite proposals for peace forthwith. And in case peace cannot now be made, consent to an *armistice for one year*, each party to retain, unmolested, all it now holds, but the rebel ports to be opened. Meantime, let a national convention be held, and there will surely be no more war at all events."

Some dissatisfied New York citizens went so far as to issue a call for another convention in Cincinnati on September 28 to nominate, if necessary, a new candidate for President.

he one-term policy for the presidency adopted y the people is strengthened by the force of he existing crisis, and should be maintained by onstitutional amendments." They nominated ohn C. Frémont for the Presidency and General John Cochrane for the Vice-Presidency. However, the Radical Republicans' choice

HOW LINCOLN'S FACE CHANGED DURING THE FOUR YEARS HE HELD OFFICE. THE FIRS

"Mr. Lincoln is already beaten," wrote Greeley on August 18. "He cannot be elected. And we must have another ticket to save us from utter overthrow. If we had such a ticket as could be made by naming Grant, Butler, or Sherman for President, and Farragut for Vice, we could make a fight yet. And such a ticket we ought to have anyhow, with or without a convention."

Voices were heard demanding that both Frémont and Lincoln should withdraw their names. "The withdrawal of Lincoln and Frémont, and the nomination of a man that would inspire confidence and infuse a life into our ranks would be hailed with general delight," said the editor of the Cincinnati *Gazette*.

On August 22 the insistent Thurlow Weed wrote to Seward: "When, ten days since, I told

Mr. Lincoln that his re-election was an im possibility, I also told him that the informatior would soon come to him through other chan nels. It has doubtless ere this reached him. A any rate, nobody here doubts it, nor do I se anybody from other states who authorizes th slightest hope of success. Mr. Raymond, wh has just left me, says that unless some promp and bold step be now taken all is lost. Th people are wild for peace. They are told tha that President will only listen to terms of peac on condition that slavery be abandoned."

The Republican National Executive Com mittee, meeting in New York City for consul tation on the very day Thurlow Weed wrot his letter, was gloomy over Lincoln's prospects Raymond, the editor of the New York *Time* who was chairman of the committee, informe

260

HOTOGRAPH WAS TAKEN IN 1861, THE LAST ONE A WEEK BEFORE HIS ASSASSINATION IN 1865.

he President that "the tiding is getting strongly against us," and he reported that Lincoln's chances were bad in virtually every part of the country.

On August 23, the day on which Lincoln received Raymond's letter, he seemed to have accepted the fact that he would be defeated in the election. He wrote out a memorandum and asked his secretaries to endorse it on the reverse ide of the sheet—not knowing what they igned. Only after the election was over did hey learn the secret. The document read: 'This morning, as for some days past, it seems exceedingly probable that this Administration will not be re-elected. Then it will be my duty o so co-operate with the President-elect as to ave the Union between the election and the nauguration, as he will have secured his election

on such ground that he cannot possibly save it afterwards."

It was a week later—on August 29—that the Democratic convention assembled in Chicago. Under the influence of Clement Vallandigham, leader of the "Copperheads," * a platform was adopted, declaring that "after four years of failure to restore the Union by the experiment of war . . . during which . . . the Constitution itself has been disregarded in every part, and public liberty and private right alike trodden down . . . the public welfare demands that immediate efforts be made for a cessation of hostilities, with a view to an ultimate convention of the States, or other peaceable means,

* Democrats who strongly opposed the war measures of the administration and Congress, believing that it was not possible to subjugate the South by force.

(turn to page 264)

GENERAL HAMLET McCLELLAN EXCLAIMS: "I KNEW HIM, HORATIO—A FELLOW OF INFINITE JEST."

THE COMMANDER IN CHIEF CONCILIATING THE SOLDIER VOTES ON THE BATTLEFIELD.

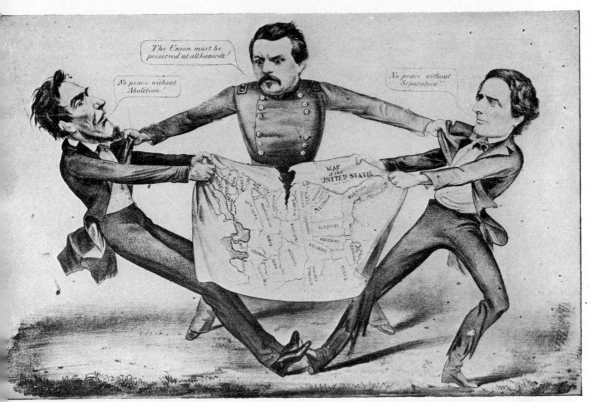

McCLELLAN TRIES TO HALT LINCOLN AND "JEFF" DAVIS AS THEY TEAR THE UNION APART.

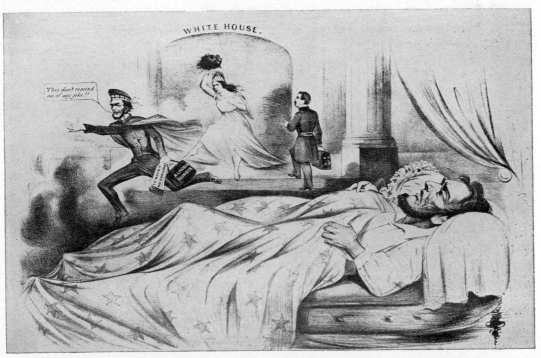

PRESIDENT LINCOLN DREAMS OF FLEEING THE WHITE HOUSE AS McCLELLAN ENTERS.

> Executive Mansion
> Washington, Aug. 23, 1864.
>
> This morning, as for some days past, it seems exceedingly probable that this Administration will not be re-elected. Then it will be my duty to so co-operate with the President elect, as to save the Union between the election and the inauguration; as he will have secured his election on such ground that he cannot possibly save it afterwards.
>
> A. Lincoln

WHEN LINCOLN THOUGHT THAT HE MIGHT LOSE THE ELECTION, HE ASKED HIS CABINET

to the end that, at the earliest practicable moment, peace may be restored on the basis of the Federal Union of the States."

For their presidential candidate the Democrats nominated George McClellan, the former commander in chief of the Union Army, and for his running mate, George Pendleton.

"Little Mac" accepted the nomination but re-fused the platform. "I could not look in t[he] face of my gallant comrades of the army a[nd] navy," wrote the General, "who have surviv[ed] so many bloody battles, and tell them that th[e] labors and the sacrifices of so many of our sla[in] and wounded brethren had been in vain; that v[e] had abandoned that Union for which we ha[ve] so often perilled our lives." In McClellan's op[in-]

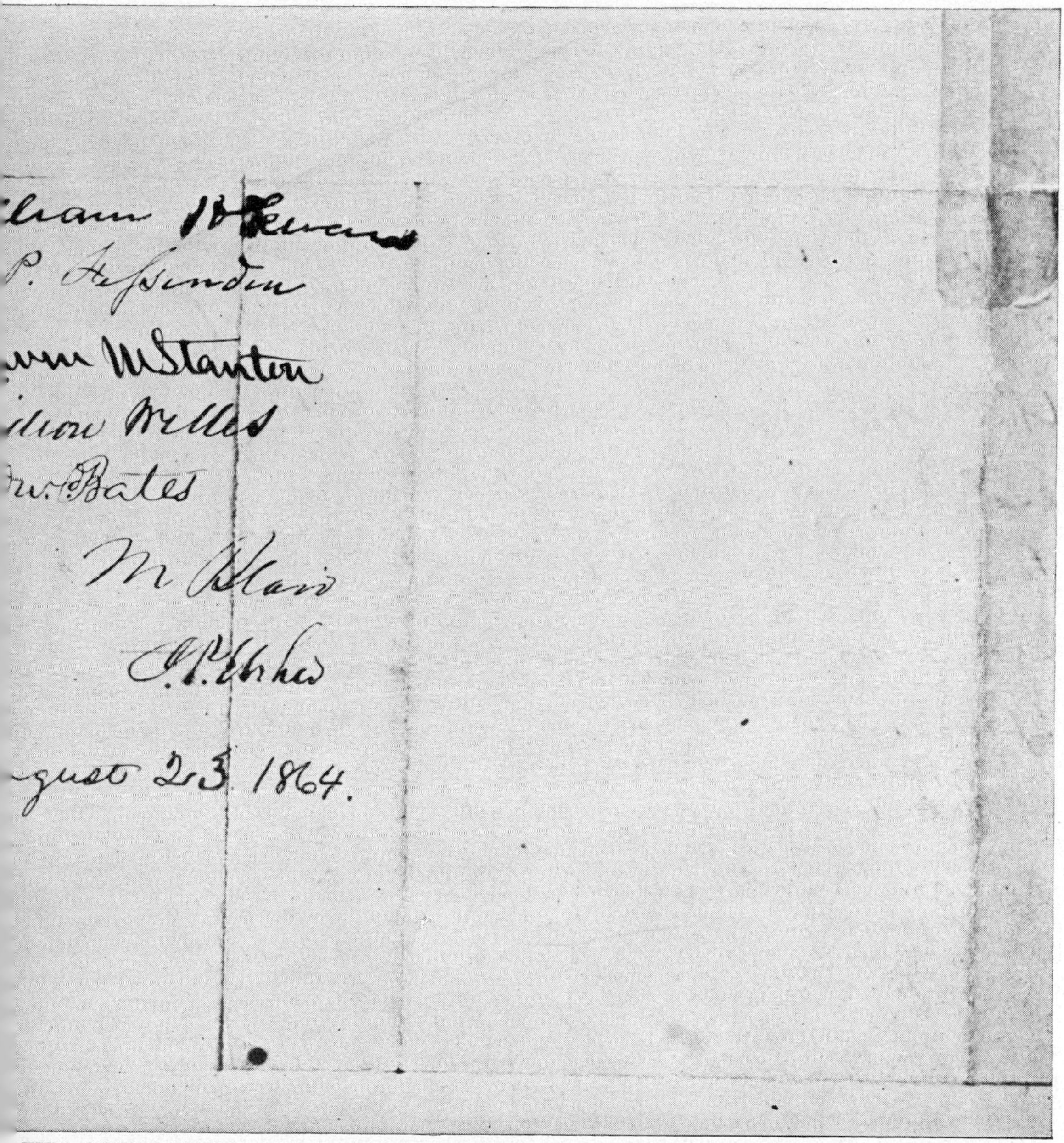

lham lᵗᵉ Sewan

P. Fefsenden

um M Stanton

idow Welles

mr Bates

M Blair

J. P. Usher

gust 23 1864.

THIS MEMORANDUM, BUT WITHOUT LETTING THE SECRETARIES SEE WHAT IT CONTAINED.

n, "No peace can be permanent without nion."

Within a few days the country learned how istaken the Democratic platform was in stat- g that the war was a failure. People could ad in their newspapers that General Sherman d taken Atlanta and that Admiral Farragut as the master of Mobile Bay.

This was good news for the North, wonderful, revitalizing news for the Republicans. Seward said confidently: "Sherman and Farragut have knocked the bottom out of the Chicago nominations." Frémont was persuaded to withdraw from the race. Chase, who in the meantime had resigned as Secretary of the Treasury, went on the stump for his former chief. "There

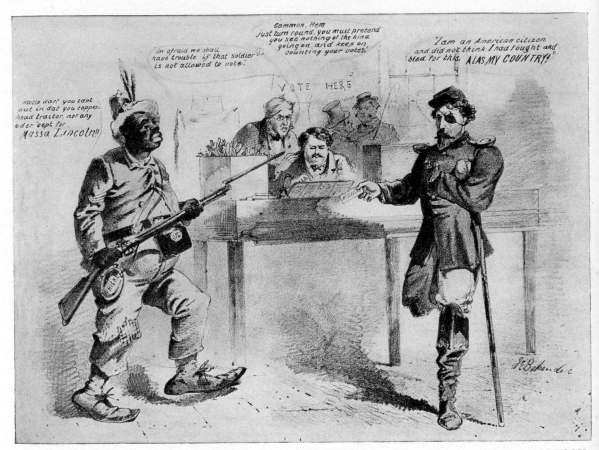

AN ARMED NEGRO SOLDIER PROTECTS THE "FREE BALLOT" IN THIS ANTI-LINCOLN CARTOON.

is not now, the slightest uncertainty about the re-election of Mr. Lincoln," wrote he on October 2. "The only question is, by what popular and what electoral majority. God grant that both may be so decisive as to turn every hope of rebellion to despair!"

The election bore out his prediction: Lincoln won with 2,213,665 popular votes against McClellan's 1,802,237. The ballots of the soldiers, which were counted separately, gave the President 116,877 votes, McClellan 33,748.

"I give you joy of the election," wrote Emerson to a friend. "Seldom in history was so much staked on a popular vote. I suppose never in history."

The result meant that in spite of all the misery which war brought to them, the people of the North were resolved "to finish the work they had begun." In the next Congress there would be enough Republican members to insure the passage of a constitutional amendment abolishing slavery.

A week before the electoral votes were counted, Congress passed a joint resolution declaring that as "the inhabitants and local authorities of the States of Virginia, North Carolina, South Carolina, Georgia, Florida, Alabama, Mississippi, Louisiana, Texas, Arkansas, and Tennessee rebelled against the government of the United States," they are therefore "not entitled to representation in the Electoral College for the choice of President and Vice-President."

Lincoln opposed this resolution as it would invalidate the votes of Louisiana and Tennessee, where the governments were recognized by him, with governors friendly and loyal to the Union at the helm. He pleaded for a magnanimous and mild reconstruction policy. But the lawmakers were of other opinion. Determined not to acknowledge the Louisiana and Tennessee votes

Office U. S. Military Telegraph,

WAR DEPARTMENT.

Washington, D. C. _October 13th 1864_

New York	33		New England States	39
Penn	26		Michigan	8
New Jersey	7		Wisconsin	8
Delaware	3		Minnesota	4
Maryland	7		Iowa	8
Missouri	11		Oregon	3
Kentucky	11		California	5
Illinois	16		Kansas	3
	114		Indiana	15
			Ohio	21
			W. Virginia	5
				117
			Nevada	3
				120

LINCOLN CAREFULLY CALCULATED how many electoral votes he might get, after he learned the outcome of the state elections in Pennsylvania, Ohio and Indiana. And as a prophet, the President was certainly not a bad one, for out of a total of 233 electoral votes (one Nevada elector died before the election), he received 212.

nd aware of the President's hostility toward heir joint resolution, they hastily concocted an ther measure. This—commonly known as the wenty-second Joint Rule—declared that it was for both Houses of Congress to decide whether questionable votes should be counted or not. As a result, the electoral votes of Louisiana and Tennessee were rejected.

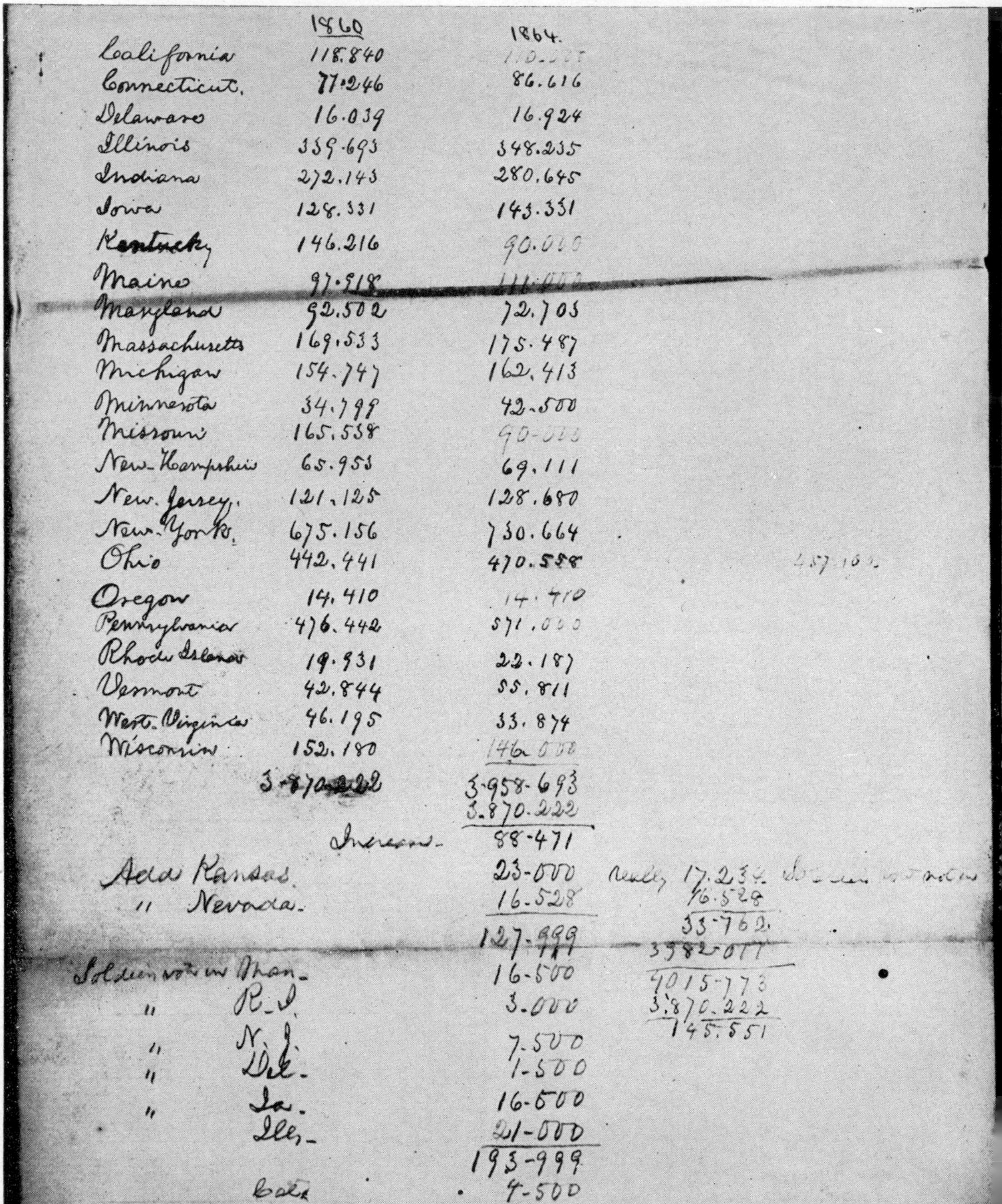

	1860	1864
California	118.840	110.000
Connecticut	77.246	86.616
Delaware	16.039	16.924
Illinois	339.693	348.235
Indiana	272.143	280.645
Iowa	128.331	143.331
Kentucky	146.216	90.000
Maine	97.918	111.000
Maryland	92.502	72.703
Massachusetts	169.533	175.487
Michigan	154.747	162.413
Minnesota	34.799	42.500
Missouri	165.538	90.000
New Hampshire	65.953	69.111
New Jersey	121.125	128.680
New York	675.156	730.664
Ohio	442.441	470.558
Oregon	14.410	14.410
Pennsylvania	476.442	571.000
Rhode Island	19.931	22.187
Vermont	42.844	55.811
West Virginia	46.195	33.874
Wisconsin	152.180	146.000
	3.870.222	3.958.693
		3.870.222

457.161

Increase — 88.471

Add Kansas — 23.000   Ready 17.234

" Nevada — 16.528   16.528

127.999   33.762.   3.582.077

Soldier vote in Mass. — 16.500   4015.773

" R.I. — 3.000   3.870.222

" N.J. — 7.500   145.551

" Del. — 1.500

" Ia. — 16.500

" Ill. — 21.000

193.999

Cal. — 4.500

LINCOLN MADE ON THIS SHEET A COMPARISON OF THE POPULAR VOTES IN 1860 AND 1864
The vote in 1864 turned out to be better than he expected. Lincoln won all the electoral votes except those of Delaware, Kentucky and New Jersey, and in two of these three states, McClellan led by only a small majority. In Delaware he had 612 votes more than Lincoln; in New Jersey his majority was a little over 7,000 in a total of 128,680

A SCENE ON ELECTION DAY BEFORE A POLLING PLACE IN NEW YORK'S "LOWER TWENTY."

A. LINCOLN,
Attorney and Counsellor at Law,
SPRINGFIELD, ILL.

TO WHOM IT MAY CONCERN

My old customers and others are no doubt aware of the terrible time I have had in *crossing the stream*, and will be glad to know that I will be back on the same side from which I started on or before the 4TH OF MARCH next, when I will be ready to *Swap Horses, Dispense Law, Make Jokes, Split Rails,* and perform other matters in a SMALL way.

AN ANTI-LINCOLN CAMPAIGN CARD, which the Democrats distributed to voters by the thousands.

TORCHLIGHT PROCESSION goes through streets of New York boosting General McClellan's candidacy.

When inauguration day came, the war was almost over. Lincoln spoke the immortal words: "With malice toward none, with charity for all, with firmness in the right as God gives us to see the right, let us strive on to finish the work we are in, to bind up the nation's wounds, to care for him who shall have borne the battle and for his widow and his orphan, to do all which may achieve and cherish a just and lasting peace among ourselves and with all nations."

It was not to be. Six days after Lee surrendered at Appomattox, John Wilkes Booth shot the President at Ford's Theater. At 7:22 in the morning of April 15 Abraham Lincoln died. A few hours later Andrew Johnson was sworn into office in the parlor of his hotel.

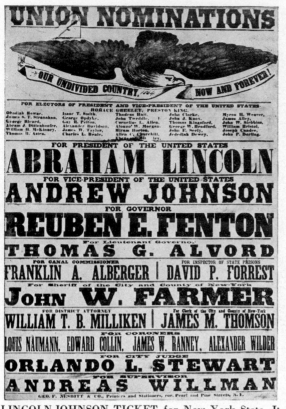

LINCOLN-JOHNSON TICKET for New York State. It
won with 368,726 votes to the McClellan ticket's 361,986.

Having served four years in the depths of a great
and yet unended national peril, I can view this
call to a second term, in nowise more flatteringly to
myself, than as an expression of the public judgment that I may better finish a difficult work,
in which I have labored from the first, than
could any one less severely schooled to the task.

In this view, and with assured reliance
on that Almighty Ruler who has so graciously
sustained us thus far, and with increased
gratitude to the generous people for their continued confidence, I accept the renewed trust,
with its yet onerous and perplexing duties and
responsibilities.

Please communicate this to the two Houses
of Congress.

The above is the original manuscript of Abraham Lincoln's
acceptance of his second presidential term in his own hand writing
delivered to the joint committee of Congress appointed to inform him officially
of his election.

ACCEPTING A SECOND TERM, Lincoln promises to finish "a difficult work in which I have labored from the first."

EXCITING SCENE IN THE LOWER HOUSE OF

The Radical Republicans were greatly relieved. They now had hope that under the new
President the "tender-hearted" policies toward
the South would cease. They believed that
Johnson would be a tool in their hands. An

... ON JANUARY 31, 1865, WHEN THE 13TH AMENDMENT, ABOLISHING SLAVERY, WAS ADOPTED.

...hey had good reasons for thinking so. John-
...son was himself a Southerner, a poor white, hat-
...ing the "slavocracy." He was supposed to have
...said: "Treason is a crime and crime must be
...punished. Treason must be made infamous and

traitors must be impoverished." For the Radical
Republicans such talk was sweet music. "By the
gods, there will be no trouble now in running
the Government," said Ben Wade of Ohio. But
Johnson also declared that his policy would be

LINCOLN DELIVERS HIS SECOND INAUGURAL ADDRESS

At this second appearing to take the oath of the presidential office, there is less occasion for an extended address than there was at the first. Then a statement, somewhat in detail, of a course to be pursued, seemed fitting and proper. Now, at the expiration of four years, during which public declarations have been constantly called forth on every point and phase of the great contest which still absorbs the attention, and engrosses the energies of the nation, little that is new could be presented. The progress of our arms, upon which all else chiefly depends, is as well known to the public as to myself; and it is, I trust, reasonably satisfactory and encouraging to all. With high hope for the future, no prediction in regard to it is ventured.

On the occasion corresponding to this four years ago, all thoughts were anxiously directed to an impending civil war. All dreaded it—all sought to avert it. While the inaugural address was being delivered from this place, devoted altogether to saving the Union without war, insurgent agents were in the city seeking to destroy it without war—seeking to dissolve the Union, and divide effects, by negotiation. Both parties deprecated war; but one of them would make war rather than let the nation survive; and the other would accept war rather than let it perish. And the war came.

One eighth of the whole population were colored slaves, not distributed generally over the Union, but localized in the Southern part of it. These slaves constituted a peculiar and powerful interest. All knew that this interest was, somehow, the cause of the war. To strengthen, perpetuate, and extend this interest was the object for which the insurgents would rend the Union, even by war; while the government claimed no right to do more than to restrict the territorial enlargement of it. Neither party expected for the war, the magnitude, or the duration, which it has already attained. Neither anticipated that

LINCOLN'S IMMORTAL SECOND INAUGURAL ADDRESS AS IT APPEARS IN HIS OWN HANDWRITING.

in all essentials . . . the same as that of the late President." Which of the two courses would he follow? The policy of vengeance advocated by the Radical Republicans, or the forgiving policy of Lincoln?

It did not take long for Andrew Johnson to realize that the Southern aristocrats were doomed and there was no necessity to fight them any longer. There were far greater tasks before the government than this. The Union had to be kept and it had to be made to function. The President accepted the loyal governments that Lincoln had recognized in Tennessee, Louisiana, Arkansas, and Virginia, and for the seven other states of the Confederacy he proposed a reconstruction program which was no less generous than Lincoln's. A provisional governor was appointed for each of these states, whose duty was to call constitutional conventions. These conventions had to invalidate their old ordinances of secession, abolish slavery, and repudiate all the Confederate war debts, but aside from these "musts," the people in each state were free to write their own constitution. As soon as this was ratified, officials could be elected and the state could again become a part of the Union.

During the "Presidential Reconstruction" pe-

THE CONCLUDING PAGES OF THE SECOND INAUGURAL ADDRESS AS LINCOLN PENNED IT

riod Congress was in recess. Johnson hoped to complete his reconstruction plans before December, when the new Congress was to meet. But seventy-three-year-old Thaddeus Stevens, with hate in his soul against the South, was exasperated by Johnson's course. "If something is not done," he said, "the President will be crowned King before Congress meets." He wrote to Johnson, asking him to "hold his hand and await the action of Congress," and in the meantime govern the South by "military rulers."

The fury of the Radicals was fanned when they learned of the laws which the new Southern governments had instituted to deal with the former slaves. They asserted that these "Black Codes"—like the Vagrancy Laws against wandering Negroes and Apprentice Laws assigning Negro youngsters to guardians for whom they had to work without wages—were nothing but brazen attempts to perpetuate slavery.

When Congress reconvened, Johnson's reconstruction program was almost completed. Newly elected Senators and Representatives from the Southern states were in Washington waiting to take their seats.

But the Radical Republicans, instead of admitting them, formed a joint committee on reconstruction which was to inquire whether the Confederate states were "entitled to be represented in either House of Congress." Thus the fateful struggle between Congress and President

(turn to page 277)

ON APRIL 14, 1865, the actor John Wilkes Booth entered the President's unguarded box in Ford's Theater at Washington and shot at Lincoln, mortally wounding him as he sat listening to the play, "Our American Cousin."

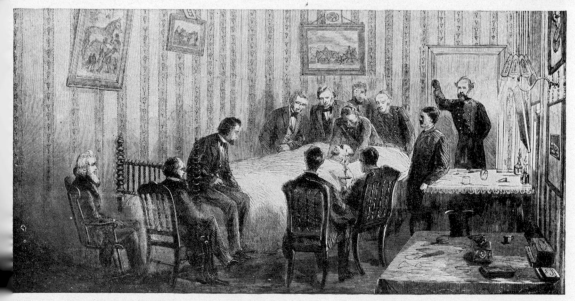

AT 7:22 THE NEXT MORNING, April 15, 1865, President Lincoln died without regaining consciousness in a small room of the Petersen house opposite the theater. This is how a *Harper's Weekly* artist recorded the scene.

THE NEW PRESIDENT TAKES THE OATH IN THE PARLOR OF THE KIRKWOOD HOUSE, WASHINGTON.

dent began. In the committee, consisting of fifteen members, unbending Thaddeus Stevens had the most influence. He looked upon the Southern states as "conquered provinces," and he was ready to treat them as such. Unfortunately, his revengeful plans—appealing to the base emotions of the people—had the support of a great number of Northern men.

Whatever legislation the Radicals proposed, the President vetoed it. Johnson refused to sign the Freedmen's Bureau Bill, because it would make the Negro the ward of the national government; he held that the bill was not necessary, as the former slaves had ample protection 'without resort to the dangerous expedient of military tribunals.'" The President's veto, which Congress was not able to overrule, was a further wedge between Johnson and the Radicals. The next one was the Civil Rights Bill, giving freedmen the same rights and privileges as the whites. Johnson vetoed it, but this time

he was overruled. Congress won. The Radical Republicans were determined that their ascendancy over the President should be permanent.

THE CABINET. Edwin Stanton, Secretary of War, is standing before President Johnson. Sitting: James Speed, Attorney General; Gideon Welles, Secretary of the Navy; John Palmer Usher, the Secretary of the Interior; William Dennison, the Postmaster General; and Hugh McCulloch, the Secretary of the Treasury.

277

ANDREW JOHNSON (1808-1875)
PHOTOGRAPH BY MATHEW B. BRADY

A BITTER CARICATURE AGAINST PRESIDENT JOHNSON AND SECRETARY SEWARD

The Joint Committee of Fifteen worked out a congressional reconstruction plan replacing Johnson's program. It proposed an amendment to the Constitution, guaranteeing all persons born or naturalized in the United States full protection in their civil rights. Ten Southern states (Tennessee in the meantime had been re-admitted to the Union) rejected ratification of the proposal, which later became the Fourteenth Amendment.

As midterm elections were near, Congress waited to hear from the people. The vote was to decide which of the two reconstruction plans was to be carried out—that of the President or that of Congress.

President Johnson traveled from Washington to Chicago in his "swing around the circle," campaigning for his policies. The Radicals organized demonstrations against him; hecklers roused his temper and goaded him into intemperate utterances; newspapers fought him relentlessly, charging him with drunkenness; cartoonists ridiculed him without mercy.

The nation upheld the Radicals, who carried both Houses of Congress by enormous majorities, giving them a mandate to pursue their policies.

When Congress reassembled, the Radical Republicans introduced an entirely new reconstruction plan, far more severe for the South than the proposals which were embodied in the Fourteenth Amendment. Johnson vetoed it, but Congress passed it over his veto.

The congressional reconstruction program divided the ten Southern states which refused to ratify the Fourteenth Amendment into five military districts—to be governed by generals of the Union Army. Instead of the "reconstructed" governments, new governments were installed. Negroes were given the vote; carpetbaggers—all their earthly belongings in their carpetbags—came down from the North and joined forces with Southern scalawags. Together with the naïve and uneducated Negroes they organized the legislatures. There was no end to corruption—money flowed like water; cupidity, ineptitude, and ignorance marked this era, although some good legislation for the underprivileged was enacted.

The Radicals imposed a firm rule on the South, and when a Republican told Thaddeus

PREPARING FOR THE HEATED TERM.

King Andy and his man Billy lay in a great stock of Russian ice in order to cool down the Congressional majority.

JOHNSON AND SEWARD were violently attacked by the newspapers because they made the Alaska Purchase.

"THE BIG THING."

OLD MOTHER SEWARD. "I'll rub some of this on his sore spot: it may soothe him a little."

SEVEN MILLION DOLLARS seemed fantastic for the "Russian Fairy Land" of ice, Eskimos, mountain peaks.

279

IMPEACHMENT CONTROVERSY. The Radical-sponsored Tenure of Office Act forbade the President to dismiss high [officials] without consulting Congress. When Johnson dismissed Stanton (right), he refused to give place to Gen. Thomas (l[eft])

IN THE ROTUNDA of the Capitol, spectators hold excited discussions during the impeachment trial of President Johnson.

THE LADIES' GALLERY of the Senate. Wives of Con[gress]men and famous guests follow the happenings on the

Stevens that he was conscience-stricken over the harsh measures against the South, Stevens replied: "Conscience! Tell your conscience to go to the devil, and follow the party line."

The "Crime of Reconstruction" fanned the hatred of the South against the North. By giving the vote to the Negro but denying it to the Southern whites, the Republicans were able to

"NFORTUNATE MAN," exclaimed Thaddeus Stevens in the House on March 2, 1868, addressing his words to President Johnson,
is surrounded, hampered, snared in the meshes of his own wickedness — unfortunate, unhappy man, behold your doom."

HOUSE COMMITTEE managing the impeachment of resident enters the Senate to present the indictment.

IMPEACHMENT committee preparing the indictment. From l.to r.: Ward, Stevens, Wilson, Logan, Boutwell, Julian, Bingham.

perpetuate their rule. For the next twenty years —until Cleveland was elected in 1884—Republican Presidents were to occupy the White House. But for the deeds of the carpetbag gov-

ernments, for the deeds of the bayonet rule, which kept the party in power, the Republicans had to pay dearly.

The Radical Republicans, firmly in the sad-

THE SERGEANT AT ARMS OF THE SENATE SERVES THE SUMMONS OF IMPEACHMENT ON JOHNSON

dle, passed the Tenure of Office Act. This law—directed against Andrew Johnson—forbade the President to issue military orders, to remove civil officeholders of the government, or dismiss high military officers without the consent of the Senate. It fixed the tenure of the Cabinet members for the duration of the President's term. Its prime purpose was to keep in office

THE PRESIDENT DISCUSSES WITH HIS COUNSEL THE ANSWER TO ARTICLES OF IMPEACHMENT.

Edwin Stanton, the Secretary of War and a close friend of the Radical Republicans.

The President, rightly convinced of the unconstitutionality of the Tenure of Office Act, resolved to fight it. He suspended Stanton and named General Grant as his *ad interim* successor. Johnson hoped to prove before the courts that Congress had no right to pass the act. However, the stubborn Stanton would not yield the office and the Senate would not confirm his successor, whereupon the bewildered Grant went back on his word to the President and turned the office back to Stanton. The exasperated Johnson named General Thomas in Stanton's stead, but the outcome of the struggle was the same. Again Stanton—backed by the Radicals—refused to give up the office.

The enraged Radicals were determined to break the President, who dared to challenge them. On February 24, 1868, the House of Representa-

tives voted to impeach him. The next day Thaddeus Stevens, trembling, infirm, but white with hate, appeared at the bar of the Senate and charged Andrew Johnson with "high crimes and

TAKING THE VOTE on the impeachment of President Johnson in the Senate Chamber on May 16, 1868.

REPORTERS ask information in Senate lobby during the secret session of the President's impeachment trial.

JOHNSON IS ACQUITTED. The newspaper reporters race to the telegraph office to file their dispatches.

PRESIDENT ANDREW JOHNSON, SURROUNDE

misdemeanors." A week later the seven managers appointed by the House laid before the Senate eleven articles of impeachment—nine of these concerned with the Tenure of Office Act.

On March 13—it was Friday too—Henry

Stanbery, the former Attorney General, appeared for President Johnson before the "Impeachment Court," assisted by a number of eminent lawyers. The defense had no difficulty pointing out that the only important charge

...MATS AND WASHINGTON SOCIETY, GIVES HIS LAST GALA RECEPTION IN THE WHITE HOUSE.

...e impeachment articles was that the President ...d violated the Tenure of Office Act.

The trial lasted till May 16, keeping the coun-...y in a high state of excitement. When the ...te on the eleventh article was taken, seven

Republican Senators sided with the Democrats. Thus the President was acquitted of the charges by the narrow margin of one vote. With this single vote, the presidential office as created under the Constitution escaped destruction.

THE INAUGURAL CEREMONIES

THE TWENTY-FIRST ELECTION—1868

ULYSSES S. GRANT

It was only four days after President Johnson was acquitted of the impeachment charges that the Republican nominating convention met in Crosby's Opera House at Chicago. The meeting was a cut and dried affair; all work was accomplished in two days.

There was only one name before the convention—that of Ulysses S. Grant; no other was even mentioned for the presidential nomination. General Grant had all the virtues of an ideal candidate. He was a successful war leader, well liked by his soldiers, he spoke little, his record was clean, his past was devoid of any scandal. He was folksy, more interested in horses and tobacco than in politics, a great advantage in times when people were tired of professional politicians.

Because of his previous political sympathies (the only time Ulysses Grant had ever cast a vote in a presidential election was in 1856, when he voted for the Democratic ticket), it would have been more natural for him to be the candidate of the Democrats instead of the Republicans. And were it not for the break with President Johnson, he might very well have been the Democratic nominee. But after the quarrel, Grant sounded the same tune as the Radical Republicans, asking for the impeachment of the President, and giving the impression that he, too, was a Radical Republican.

The Radicals were not so sure of this. Could Grant be trusted? Ben Wade, one of their leaders and since Lincoln's death president *pro tempore* of the Senate, journeyed to Covington to learn more about Grant's political beliefs. He met Dr. Cramer, Grant's brother-in-law, and was reassured that the General agreed with the policies of the Radical Republicans, which announcement made Wade so elated that he threw his hat into the air, breaking a globe of the chandelier.

Whether they liked it or not, the Republicans had no other choice but Grant. When the fall elections of 1867 showed a strong Democratic swing, they realized that they needed a strong and popular candidate with whom they would be sure to win. So it had to be him. The General was—according to the New York *World*—"at first shy; then he wavered; then enveloped himself in a thick mystery—and, at last, he has

ULYSSES S. GRANT
(1822-1885) became the
Republican candidate
by unanimous vote of
the 650 delegates. In
his letter of acceptance
Grant wrote, "Let us
have peace," a sentence
repeated over and over
in the campaign. He
won the election, but
his popular majority
was only 300,000 votes.

SCHUYLER COLFAX
(1823-1885), Speaker of
the House of Represen-
tatives, was selected by
the Republicans from
a long list of contend-
ers as General Grant's
running mate. In the
election, Republicans
won 3,012,833 popular
votes against which the
Democrats polled a mi-
nority vote of 2,703,249.

THE DEMOCRATIC CONVENTION met in New Yc
There the West chose the platform, the East the nomir

HORATIO SEYMOUR
(1810-1886), "The Great
Decliner," was nomin-
ated by the Democrats
when Western and East-
ern factions disagreed
on the other candidates.
He reluctantly accep-
ted the party's green-
back policy, whereby
repayment of govern-
ment bonds was to be
in paper and not gold.

FRANCIS P. BLAIR
(1821-1875), a general
and son of "Blair of the
Globe," received the
Democratic nomina-
tion for Vice-President.
He attacked the Recon-
struction Acts institu-
ted by the Radical
Republicans, demand-
ing that the President
should at once declare
them all null and void.

NEW YORK'S UNION SQUARE after announcer
of Seymour's and Blair's nomination by the Democ

changed his politics." During 1868 the popula
demand for him grew, and months before the
Republican convention met, it was obvious that
he would be chosen.

Thus, when in the Chicago convention Gen
eral John A. Logan proposed Grant's name, al
the 650 delegates, cheering and shouting, nom
inated him by acclamation. The band playe
"Hail to the Chief," and party workers carrie
a huge portrait of Grant onto the stage with th
inscription "Match Him." From eleven candi
dates competing for the second place, the con
vention selected Schuyler Colfax, the Speake

REPUBLICAN CONVENTION met in Chicago. [Pray]er by Bishop Simpson opened its proceedings.

THE PLATFORM was accepted without discussion. There was but one candidate for the Presidency: Ulysses Grant.

[LOG]A. LOGAN'S proposal of Grant as the candi-[date] [m]et with wild demonstrations by the 650 delegates.

THE CHEERING GALLERIES at Crosby's Opera House in Chicago enthusiastically acclaim Grant's nomination.

[o]f the House, "a good-tempered, chirping, [w]arbling, real canary bird."

The platform of the Republicans consisted of [f]ourteen planks. The first congratulated the [c]ountry "on the assured success of the recon-[s]truction policy of Congress"; the second asked [f]or "equal suffrage to all loyal men at the [S]outh," but declared that the solution of this [q]uestion "belongs to the people of those states." [T]he third called for "the payment of the public [in]debtedness in the uttermost good faith to all [c]reditors at home and abroad"; the fourth for [a]n "equalized and reduced" taxation; the fifth

was for a reduction of the national debt "over a fair period"; the sixth advocated diminishing the national debt "so to improve our credit that capitalists will seek to loan us money at lower rates of interest than we now pay"; the seventh, that "the government of the United States should be administered with the strictest econ-omy." The eighth plank was charged with emo-tion. "We profoundly deplore the untimely and tragic death of Abraham Lincoln," it said, "and regret the accession to the presidency of An-drew Johnson, who has acted treacherously to the people who elected him and the cause he was pledged to support; who has usurped high legislative and judicial functions; who has refused to execute the laws; who has used his high office to induce other officers to ignore and violate the laws; who has employed his executive powers to render insecure the property, the peace, the liberty and life of the citizen; who has abused the pardoning power; who has denounced the national legislature as unconstitutional; who has persistently and corruptly resisted, by every means in his power, every proper attempt at the reconstruction of the States lately in rebellion; who has perverted the public patronage into an engine of wholesale

corruption; and who has been justly impeached for high crimes and misdemeanors, and properly pronounced guilty thereof by the vote of thirty-five senators."

All this was sheer propaganda. Johnson was not "properly pronounced guilty" of the impeachment charges as the platform said, for even though thirty-five Senators voted against him they did not constitute the necessary two-thirds majority.

The ninth plank dealt with "naturalized citizens, who should be protected" in all their rights of citizenship, as though they were native-born; the tenth was for "bounties and pensions"

GENERAL GRANT AND HIS FAMILY ABOUT THE TIME HE RECEIVED THE REPUBLICAN NOMINATIO

CHIEF JUSTICE CHASE WAS A REPUBLICAN. BUT NOW HE COVETED THE DEMOCRATIC NOMINATION

for the "brave soldiers and seamen" and for their widows and orphans; the eleventh asked for encouragement and fostering of "foreign immigration, which in the past has added so much to the wealth, development, and resources, and increase of power to this republic." The twelfth—a significantly short plank—read: "This convention declares itself in sympathy with all oppressed peoples struggling for

their rights." The thirteenth asked for forbearance and magnanimity toward the people who are "reconstructing the southern state governments upon the basis of impartial justice and equal rights," and said that they should be "received back into the communion of the loyal people"; while the fourteenth upheld "the immortal Declaration of Independence."

The Republican press rejoiced over Grant's

291

candidacy. It was held that he was "stronger than his party," and that his choice "makes the nomination not partisan but national."

The Democrats began the mudslinging immediately. Their newspaper asserted that Grant was a thief who went off with a large part of a lady's family silver after he was entertained in her home during the war; they repeated the often-heard charge that Grant was an habitual drunkard, "a soaker behind the door and in the dark," and they even assailed him as a poor and inept soldier. His anti-Semitic "General Order No. 11" of December, 1862, was recounted, in which Grant forbade Jewish traders to do business with the troops.

Whom would the Democrats put up against him? The sentiment was divided among many candidates. Before their convention met, no less than forty-seven names were mentioned for the nomination. The favorites were Salmon P. Chase, George Pendleton, Thomas Hendricks and Francis Blair, but the followers of General Hancock and President Johnson had high hopes for their candidates as well.

Chief Justice Chase was originally a Republican. As presiding officer of the impeachment court, he conducted the trial with great impartiality, bringing upon his head the wrath of the furious Radicals. He had tried to win the Republican candidacy in 1860 and again in 1864, both times without success. Now, still bitten by the "deadly malady" of presidential fever, he was ready to accept the coveted honor from the hand of the Democrats. "Nothing would gratify me more than to see the Democracy turn away from past issues and take for its mottoes: 'Suffrage for all, amnesty for all; good money for all; security for all citizens at home and abroad against governmental invasion,'" he wrote in April, 1868, declaring the principles on which he would accept the Democratic call. His candidacy was strongly supported by Horatio Seymour, one of the pillars of the Democratic party, who believed that the nomination of the Chief Justice would successfully divide the Republicans. However, the rank and file of the party were not too enthusiastic about Chase, though it was admitted that he had "more qualifications for the Presidency than any other man in the country."

George H. Pendleton's popular support was far greater. He came from Ohio, had the backing of the Western states, and was a highly available candidate. But because of his advocacy of the "Ohio idea," which proposed the repayment of the bonds issued during the Civil War in greenbacks instead of gold, he was stoutly opposed in the Eastern states.

The third prominent candidate of the Democrats was General Francis P. Blair of Missouri. A few days before the convention met, Blair wrote the often-quoted letter to Colonel James O. Brodhead in which he said that "the real and only issue in this contest" was the overthrow of the Radical reconstruction in the South. This reconstruction would have been accomplished by November, insuring a Radical majority in the Senate, and making it impossible to undo the Radical plan by congressional action. "Must we submit to it? How can it be overthrown?" asked Blair. And he answered that the President should declare the Reconstruction Acts "null and void," compel the army "to undo its usurpations at the South," and "disperse the carpetbag State governments." He concluded: "It is idle to talk of bonds, greenbacks, gold, the public faith and the public credit. What can a Democratic President do in regard to any of these with a Congress in both branches controlled by carpetbaggers and their allies?" Blair asked for "a President who will execute the will of the people by trampling into dust the usurpations of Congress known as the Reconstruction Acts."

Of the other candidates, Thomas A. Hendricks was endorsed by his own state of Indiana, and backed by a number of delegates from other states as well; General Hancock was the favorite son of Pennsylvania; and many a delegate was still hoping that the tide would turn in favor of President Johnson.

The Democrats met in the newly completed Tammany Hall in New York at noon on July 4. The weather was "as hot as weather can well be. Too hot for the warm work on hand here," wrote the ambitious Kate Chase Sprague to her father. In the city's streets the "Pendleton escort" demonstrated, shouting and singing, with five-dollar-bill badges pinned on their coat lapels, cheering their throats hoarse for their "Young Greenback." They carried banners with the inscription: "The people demand pay-

THE TWO RIVAL CANDIDATES as Thomas Nast pictured them. When the Republican convention nominated Grant, a drawing of him erected on the platform was inscribed "Match Him." Nast called this cartoon "Matched." In it he contrasted the peace-loving general with the satanic Seymour, who addressed draft rioters as "my friends."

ment of the U.S. bonds in greenbacks and equal taxation. One currency for all. Pendleton the people's nominee. Convention ratify their choice."

On that hot Saturday the Democratic convention began its work. It appointed committees and read petitions and resolutions. One address came from the Woman's Suffrage Association, signed by Susan B. Anthony, asking the Democrats to acknowledge the principle of women's suffrage. The delegates roared with laughter. That was the funniest thing they had ever heard. Then they adjourned until Monday.

During the weekend, discussions took place in hotel rooms and over the dining tables about the platform and the candidate. The Eastern states—upholding the "hard-money" theory—

were against the inclusion of the greenback idea in the platform, and when they finally gave in, they were determined not to allow the West to name the candidate as well. When the platform was brought before the convention, the enthusiasm over the plank, "One currency for the government and the people, the laborer and the office-holder, the pensioner and the soldier, the producer and the landholder," was so great that it had to be read again.

The other planks asked for: "Immediate restoration of all States to their rights in the Union . . . amnesty for all past political offenses, and the regulation of the elective franchise in the States by their citizens . . . equal taxation of every species of property according to its real value, including government bonds and other

"THE BOYS IN BLUE AND THE BOYS IN GREY" IS THE TITLE OF THIS THOMAS NAST CARTOON SHO

public securities . . . equal rights and protection for naturalized and native-born citizens, at home and abroad."

"In demanding these measures and reforms," the Democrats declared, "we arraign the Radical party for its disregard of right, and the unparalleled oppression and tyranny which have marked its career." The congressional reconstruction policies of the Radical Republicans were castigated in strong words, culminating in

the resolution: "We regard the reconstruction acts (so called) of Congress, as such, as usurpations, and unconstitutional, revolutionary, and void." It was the same sentiment as expressed by Francis Blair in his letter to Colonel Brodhead

After the platform was adopted, the balloting for the presidential candidates began. On the first trial George H. Pendleton received 10 votes, President Johnson 65, Sanford E. Church favorite son of New York, 34, General Han

…PUBLICAN TICKET AND ITS SUPPORTERS AT THE LEFT, THE DEMOCRATS AT THE RIGHT.

…ck 33½, while the remaining votes were scat-
…ed among a number of lesser candidates. Six
…lots were taken on the first day. On the
…rth roll call North Carolina cast its nine votes
… Horatio Seymour, the permanent chairman
… the convention, but Seymour immediately
…clared: "I must not be nominated by this con-
…tion. I could not accept the nomination if
…dered, which I do not expect."

…The next day the supporters of three can-

didates struggled for supremacy. The fight
raged between George Pendleton, Thomas
Hendricks, and Winfield Hancock. "Gentleman George" led on the eighth ballot with
156½ votes, but after this trial his strength declined. On the eighteenth ballot the Hancock
vote rose to 144½, the Hendricks to 87. At this
trial Illinois gave up supporting Pendleton and
switched to Hendricks. Some of the Illinois delegates protested against the unit rule; a number

of them desired to remain loyal to Pendleton. A heated argument ensued. It seemed now that the Hancock group would win, for a strong movement for their candidate was under way. The chairman of the convention, sensing an impending stampede, speedily adjourned the meeting, much against the wishes of the majority. At this hour the Hancock forces were so certain of victory that a cannon in front of the convention hall was fired in their candidate's honor and newspapers announced the General's nomination.

However, during the night the situation changed. The opposing groups tried to reach a compromise. Hancock was unacceptable to New York and Ohio, the two decisive states. Ohio wanted Pendleton, but New York, while consenting to the Pendleton platform, was against his candidacy, which would have meant sacrificing all other political issues to the one question of finance.

When Ohio saw that Pendleton could not win, it switched to Hendricks on the next ballot. But Clement Vallandigham, one of Ohio's most prominent delegates and an ardent Chase supporter, rushed to Samuel J. Tilden, the chairman of the New York delegation, and besought him to cast the New York vote for Chase, in which case he and a number of his Ohio friends would do the same. Tilden refused to do so as long as the Hendricks vote did not fall off. Now Vallandigham realized that the only way to beat Hendricks was to swing the vote of the Ohio delegation to Horatio Seymour, chairman of the convention. Taking Seymour to an anteroom, Vallandigham asked him to withdraw from the rostrum and allow his name to be put in nomination. Seymour refused this. Vallandigham then told him that the Ohio delegation would vote for him whether he wanted it or not. Seymour, still adamant, replied that he would rise in the convention and refuse to accept the nomination. Nevertheless, on the next ballot Ohio presented Horatio Seymour's name, and cast the state's twenty-one votes for "a man whom the Presidency has sought and who has not sought the Presidency."

Seymour, greatly agitated, came to the rostrum and said: "Gentlemen, I thank you, and may God bless you for your kindness to me, but your candidate I cannot be." Vallandigham rose instantly, insisting that Seymour's name must stand. Seymour was again walking toward the platform to decline and to suggest Chase in his stead, for whom he had been working all the time, when friends stopped him, bustled him out a rear door, and drove him to the Manhattan Club. The reluctant candidate's cheek were wet with tears when he met a friend on the stairs of the club. He could only cry to him: "Pity me, Harvey! Pity me!"

In the convention hall the balloting went on. At the end of the twenty-second trial Hendricks had 145½, Hancock 103½, Seymour 2 votes, but then Wisconsin switched its vote to Seymour—the stampede began. Kentucky, Massachusetts, and North Carolina followed that state's example; others quickly climbed on the bandwagon. Then, amidst wild enthusiasm and great excitement, every state changed its vote until Seymour had them all.

All this happened with the speed of lightning. Seymour had no knowledge till twenty minutes previous to his nomination that he was seriously considered for the candidacy. He had hoped to put Chase's name before the convention at the right moment—but that moment did not come.

It was said that the moving spirit behind Seymour's nomination was Tilden, who had planned it long in advance. Gideon Welles wrote in his diary that it was effected by "duplicity, deceit, cunning management and sharp scheming."

For the second place the weary delegates selected Francis P. Blair, and then adjourned, happy to leave the hot city and the convention hall behind.

"The Great Decliner"—as Horatio Seymour became known—wept and hesitated, but finally accepted the nomination. The New York Tribune wrote:

"There's a queer sort of chap they call Seymour,
A strange composition called Seymour,
    Who stoutly declines,
    Then happiness finds
In accepting, does Horatio Seymour."

Now that the Democratic ticket was chosen, the Republicans were overjoyed, for Seymour and Blair seemed to them a weak combination, not hard to beat. Nevertheless, they le

"THIS IS A WHITE MAN'S GOVERNMENT"—an incendiary Nast cartoon against the Democrats. Francis Blair, Democratic vice-presidential candidate, joins an Irish Catholic and a Fifth Avenue capitalist in trampling on the Negro. Behind them a Southern school and a colored orphan asylum are burning.

nothing to chance and turned their heavy guns against Seymour, whom they assailed on every front page, stump, and pulpit because he had addressed a disorderly group of draft rioters in 1863 as "My friends." Newspaper writers invented a malicious tale that a hereditary insanity ran in his family. And Blair was called a "revolutionist" and an excessive drinker, which may well have been true. A bill for two days at

the Hartford Hotel showed that he spent $10 for board but $65 for whisky and lemons.

The Republican organization was faultless. The "well-to-do and the able," the Vanderbilts and the Astors were tapped, and from their pockets flowed generous contributions to the campaign chest. "At no time before in the history of presidential elections," writes the historian Oberholtzer, ". . . was a candidate put

THE MAN WHO WAS FOR THE REPUBLICANS

these "outrages," inflamed the minds of the people. Whatever the Democrats said in the South was used against them effectively in the North. The two parties refought the war from Sumter to Appomattox all over again.

In the Northern towns and villages "hundreds of thousands of meetings are held every evening," wrote Godkin, editor of *The Nation;* "thousands of bands of 'Boys in Blue' with oilskin capes and torches march in procession . . . and there is not a man of any note as a public speaker who has not an 'appointment' to speak somewhere every night until the 1st of November."

Three days before the state elections, Gideon Welles wrote: "The elections will, I think, be adverse to the Democrats next Tuesday and also in November. If so, a sad fate I fear awaits our country. Sectional hate will be established."

The Republicans won, and the Democrats made frantic efforts to improve their position. They warned the people that if they elected the "man on horseback," he would become a military dictator. Once in the White House, he would never leave it, remaining there as an uncrowned emperor. Seymour, aroused by the Democratic defeat, was at last goaded into action. He went on the stump, and prodded by

under so great a burden of obligation to rich men, which he would be asked to repay."

During July and the better part of August the campaign was slack, but it became more spirited as the state elections of September and October approached. Day after day the New York *Tribune* headed its political news with Miles O'Reilly's:

"So, boys! a final bumper
    While we all in chorus chant,
For next President we nominate
    Our own Ulysses Grant;
And if asked what state he hails from,
    This our sole reply shall be,
From near Appomattox Court House,
    With its famous apple tree."

There were daily reports of riots between whites and Negroes, reports of disorder and violence from the South. Both the Republicans and Democrats made frantic efforts to carry the reorganized states for their candidates. Republican orators in the North, greatly exaggerating

1864.   1868.
'TIS BUT A CHANGE OF BANNERS.

A CARTOON AGAINST THE DEMOCRATS

DEMONSTRATION IN NEW YORK CITY FOR THE DEMOCRATIC CANDIDATES SEYMOUR AND BLAIR

DURING THE CAMPAIGN GRANT REMAINED QUIETLY IN HIS HOME TOWN OF GALENA, ILLINOIS

THE NEGROES VOTE FOR THE FIRST TIME. The Radical Republicans brought in laws which gave Freedmen the franchise. In 1868 ten thousand former slaves went to the polls and voted as they were told to—for Ulysses Grant

President Johnson, campaigned energetically.

Yet all efforts seemed to be in vain. Reports from the land pointed to an overwhelming Republican victory in November. To stave off certain disaster, the New York *World* suggested on October 15 that Seymour and Blair should retire and other candidates should take their places—either President Johnson, who had done a lot for democracy, or Chief Justice Chase. This proposal caused a great stir, and politicians heatedly discussed its merits.

The conservative John Quincy Adams said: "It is now late to change the candidates. The election of General Grant is inevitable and such a movement would materially damage the interest of the democracy." Democratic Chairman August Belmont sounded more optimistic: "Our ranks are unbroken, our courage unabated. Once more to the breach and this time victory!"

The results of the election showed that Ulysses Grant had carried twenty-six states with 214 electoral votes. Seymour had won only eight states with eighty electoral votes. However, Grant's popular majority was not as large as these figures may indicate. He won by only 300,000 popular votes out of a total of nearly 5,750,000. Of the late Confederate states, North Carolina, South Carolina, Florida, Alabama, Arkansas, and Tennessee voted for Grant while Georgia and Louisiana were in the Seymour column. Virginia, Mississippi, and Texas were not accepted as reconstructed states and did not vote.

There were the usual charges of fraudulent voting—especially in New York. The Democrats carried that state by exactly 10,000 votes and it was rumored that Boss Tweed had manipulated the result because of Democratic bets on Seymour.

Grant won the election because of his personal popularity, because the Negroes in the South voted for him, and because the country agreed with the sentiment which he expressed in his acceptance letter: "Let us have peace."

During the counting of the electoral votes

THE VOTES IN THE 1868 ELECTION

STATES	POPULAR VOTE		ELECTORAL VOTE	
	U. S. Grant, Illinois, Republican	H. Seymour, New York, Democrat	Grant and Colfax.	Seymour and Blair.
Alabama...............	76,366	72,086	8	—
Arkansas..............	22,152	19,078	5	—
California............	54,592	54,078	5	—
Connecticut...........	50,641	47,600	6	—
Delaware..............	7,623	10,980	—	3
Florida*..............	—	—	3	—
Georgia...............	57,134	102,822	—	9
Illinois...............	250,293	199,143	16	—
Indiana...............	176,552	166,980	13	—
Iowa.................	120,399	74,040	8	—
Kansas...............	31,049	14,019	3	—
Kentucky.............	39,566	115,889	—	11
Louisiana.............	33,263	80,225	—	7
Maine................	70,426	42,396	7	—
Maryland.............	39,438	62,357	—	7
Massachusetts........	136,477	59,408	12	—
Michigan.............	128,550	97,069	8	—
Minnesota............	43,542	28,072	4	—
Mississippi†..........	—	—	—	—
Missouri.............	85,671	59,788	11	—
Nebraska.............	9,729	5,439	3	—
Nevada..............	6,480	5,218	3	—
New Hampshire......	38,191	31,224	5	—
New Jersey...........	80,121	83,001	—	7
New York............	419,883	429,883	—	33
North Carolina.......	96,226	84,090	9	—
Ohio................	280,128	238,700	21	—
Oregon..............	10,961	11,125	—	3
Pennsylvania.........	342,280	313,382	26	—
Rhode Island........	12,993	6,548	4	—
South Carolina.......	62,301	45,237	6	—
Tennessee...........	56,757	26,311	10	—
Texas†..............	—	—	—	—
Vermont.............	44,167	12,045	5	—
Virginia†............	—	—	—	—
West Virginia........	29,025	20,306	5	—
Wisconsin............	108,857	84,710	8	—
	3,012,833	2,703,249	214	80

* Electors were appointed by the legislature. † The "unreconstructed" states of Mississippi, Texas and Virginia did not vote in this election.

objections were voiced against the Louisiana and the Georgia vote. The objections to the Louisiana vote were overruled, but the two Houses could not agree over the vote of Georgia. The House of Representatives re-jected the Georgia vote because that state had not fully complied with the Reconstruction Acts and because elections in that state had not been free; the Senate decided that the objections were out of order. In the end the final count was declared in two ways, with and without the votes of Georgia.

There was only one more obstacle to the Presidency—the inauguration. Grant informed the committee on ceremonies that he would not ride in the same carriage with President Johnson, nor would he speak to him on inauguration day. The committee devised an elaborate scheme whereby Grant and Johnson were to ride in separate vehicles down Pennsylvania Avenue, the former on the left, the latter on the right side of the road.

But President Johnson had more sense than that. On inauguration day he remained in the White House, working at his desk until midday. When the Secretary of State came to fetch him for the ceremonies, Johnson told him: "I am inclined to think that we will finish up our work here by ourselves." And while Grant rode toward the Capitol, Johnson left the White House quietly.

Grant's inaugural address was a rigmarole of platitudes. He declared: "The responsibilities of the position I feel, but accept them without fear." To a Republican Senator this seemed to be blasphemy. "You know, Mr. McCulloch," said he to the Secretary of the Treasury, "I am not a religious man, but if I had been elected President, I should not have accepted the responsibilities without fear. I should on my knees have asked God to help me."

FRIENDS CONGRATULATE General Grant at his home in Galena, Ohio, after his election to the Presidency.

THE PRESIDENT OF THE SENATE, "Old Ben" Wade, reads the election results to both Houses of Congress.

301

GRANT TAKES THE OATH OF OFFICE

THE TWENTY-SECOND ELECTION—1872

ULYSSES S. GRANT

The few men who warned the country not to elect a general for the Presidency could now say, "I told you so!" Ulysses S. Grant turned out to be a poor President, perhaps the weakest the United States ever had. The qualities of a successful general do not seem to tally with those qualities which are needed to make a good Chief Executive. A general deals with soldiers. He gives orders, and the orders have to be executed. It is quite simple to find out which of the men are good soldiers. But a President deals with a different species of human beings— with politicians. How to choose the reliable from the shifty? It is much harder to ascertain which of the politicians are "good soldiers." More often than not Grant was attracted by the suave, easygoing, polished, wealthy, good-mannered person, and more often than not his choice was wrong. His judgment of men was deplorable. A great many of his associates were unscrupulous men intent only on enriching themselves, and a number of them were not only unethical, but downright dishonest.

Grant had a simple and naïve make-up. Once he made a friend, he stuck to him. When people sent expensive gifts, he accepted them and rejoiced over the generosity and thoughtfulness of the senders.

He was friendly toward Jay Gould, who persuaded him to forbid the Treasury Department the further sale of gold because that would help Western farm prices. The unsuspecting President was deceived by such talk and did what Gould asked, whereupon the elated speculator, with his accomplice Fisk, cornered the gold market. Between Monday, September 20, and "Black Friday," September 24, 1869, when Grant countermanded his order, the price of gold rose from 140 to 163½. It was a preposterous scandal; in a few days Gould made millions; in a few days businessmen, merchants, bankers lost a fortune. What a prelude to an administration!

Under Grant corruption spread through pub-

THE CANDIDATES

ULYSSES S. GRANT (1822-1885), renominated unanimously by the Republicans, received the votes of 31 states in the election while Greeley had the majority in six others.

HENRY WILSON (1812-1875), Massachusetts Senator, was Republican choice for Vice-President rather than Schuyler Colfax, whose presidential aspirations irked Grant.

HORACE GREELEY (1811-1872), brilliant editor of the New York *Tribune* and the Liberal Republicans' choice for President, was given somewhat unwilling support by Democrats.

B. GRATZ BROWN (1826-1885), Governor of Missouri, instrumental in founding the Liberal Republicans in opposition to Grant's policies, was selected for the Vice-Presidency.

CHARLES O'CONOR (1804-1884), candidate of the Straight Democrats who refused to support Greeley, also was the choice of the Labor Reformers after Judge Davis declined.

THOMAS A. HENDRICKS (1819-1885), Governor of Indiana, prominent Democratic candidate for the Presidency in 1868, got complimentary electoral votes after Greeley had died.

THE REPUBLICAN CONVENTION in Philadelphia renominated General Grant amidst great enthusiasm.

THE DEMOCRATIC CONVENTION in Baltimore endorsed the candidates of the Liberal Republicans

lic offices like wildfire. Patronage, graft, fraudulent practices brought the morale of the government to a new low. Friends and relatives of the President were rewarded with fat offices some of his Cabinet members were rich men whose only qualification was that they contributed heavily to the Republican party chest

The American people do not stand for such a state of affairs. It was not long before—as a protest against these malpractices—a reform movement started. The Liberal Republicans—as the adherents of reform within the Republican party were called—asked for a general house cleaning in the Federal administration and demanded a cessation of Federal military intervention in the Southern states.

Their movement began in the West when in Missouri some liberal-minded Republicans resolved to change a number of grossly vindictive

304

THE REVENGEFUL RECONSTRUCTION PROGRAM of the Radical Republicans, Grant's bayonet rule and the corruption of the carpetbag governments made the Southern states anti-Republican and created the "Solid South."

rovisions in their state constitutions against Southern sympathizers. They submitted amendments to remove these provisions. As the Radical Republicans—fearing the loss of their influence in the state—resisted the changes, the party split. In the election the Liberal Repub-

SENATOR CARL SCHURZ, at the Cooper Union in New York, attacks the great corruption under Grant.

THE NATIONAL COMMITTEE of Liberal Republicans meets at New York City to discuss their plans,

A HOTEL LOBBY in Cincinnati filled with excited debaters during the Liberal Republican convention.

THE LIBERAL REPUBLICANS—after much deliberation—named Horace Greeley as their candidate.

licans put up an independent ticket, campaigned for the adoption of the amendments, and won. From Missouri the revolt spread throughout the country. In 1870—two years before the presidential election—the Liberal Republicans organized themselves into an association and adopted a declaration of principles. And in January, 1872, they held a meeting asking for the "uprising of honest citizens," calling for a fight against the spoils system, and demanding an honest civil service.

The Liberal Republicans were determined to block the renomination of General Grant, determined to fight the "despot" who endorsed the "usurpations and corruptions" of his supporters.

They called a national convention to meet i Cincinnati on the first Wednesday in May "t take such action as their convictions of dut and the public exigencies may require."

On that day a strange assortment of delegate assembled in the Queen City. Believers in re form, believers in women's suffrage, crank fools, idealists, opportunists, regular part workers, intellectuals, curiosity seekers wer there; Germans came in swarms; politiciar from the South were seen. The Cincinnati E: position Hall, the scene of the convention, ha a capacity of eight thousand, but it proved t be small for such a crowd. The enthusiast delegates were eager to clean the Republica

LIBERAL REPUBLICANS WATCH THE MOUSE—B. GRATZ BROWN—EMERGE FROM THE MOUNTAIN

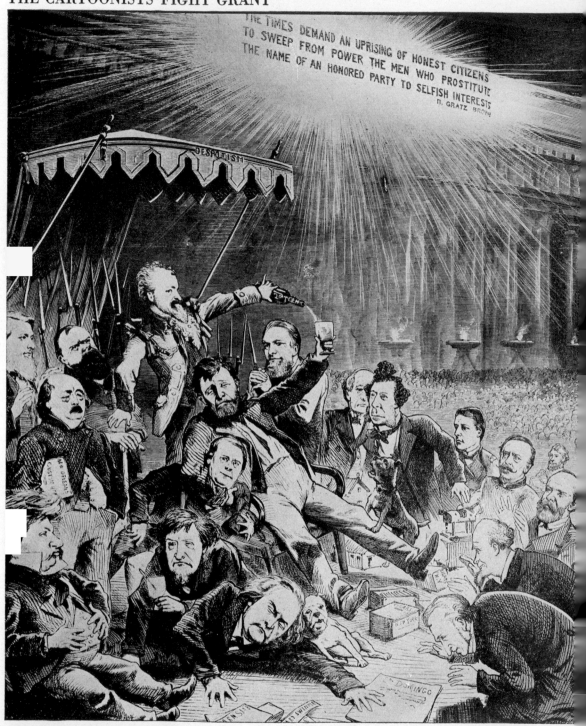

THE TIMES DEMAND AN UPRISING OF HONEST CITIZENS TO SWEEP FROM POWER THE MEN WHO PROSTITUTE THE NAME OF AN HONORED PARTY TO SELFISH INTERESTS

B. GRATZ BROWN

DESPOTISM

RADICAL REPUBLICANS, OFFICEHOLDERS, PATRONAGE SEEKERS, CABINET MEMBERS SURROUND

Matt Morgan, an English cartoonist, made savage drawings against Grant which appeared week after week in *Frank Leslie's Illustrated Newspaper.* In these cartoons the habits and morals of Grant—his drinking and gambling and his associations with unworthy men—were severely censured. Here Roscoe Conkling pour

party of corruption, to oust General Grant from the presidential chair, and to put in his place a man who would administer the government with honesty.

The real power behind the convention proceedings was a small group of newspaper editors. Four of them—Horace White of the Chicago *Tribune*, Samuel Bowles of the Springfield *Republican*, Murat Halstead of the Cincinnati *Commercial*, and Henry Watterson of the Louisville *Courier-Journal*—held regular meetings, forming policies and through their papers influencing public opinion. They were called the "Quadrilateral"—an allusion to the four fortified towns in Northern Italy supporting the Austrian occupation.

The platform of the Liberal Republicans, catering to the many different groups, began with a forceful statement, the work of Carl Schurz: "The administration now in power has rendered itself guilty of wanton disregard of the laws of the land, and of usurping powers not granted by the Constitution; it has acted as if the laws had binding force only for those who were governed, and not for those who govern. It has thus struck a blow at the fundamental principles of constitutional government and the liberties of the citizen.

KEN DESPOT: PRESIDENT ULYSSES S. GRANT
quor from the bottle marked "Second Term," while
e President's political associates worship him. At
ight, the Liberal Republicans watch disapprovingly.

HORSE-LOVER GRANT cries like a child. To the urging politicians he whines: "No! No! I don't want to go to the White House; I want to go to the races."

309

"The President of the United States has openly used the powers and opportunities of his high office for the promotion of personal ends.

"He has kept notoriously corrupt and unworthy men in places of power and responsibility, to the detriment of the public interest.

"He has used the public service of the government as a machinery of corruption and personal influence, and has interfered with tyrannical arrogance in the political affairs of States and municipalities.

"He has rewarded with influential and lucrative offices men who had acquired his favor by valuable presents, thus stimulating the demoralization of our political life by his conspicuous example.

"He has shown himself deplorably unequal to the task imposed upon him by the necessities of the country, and culpably careless of the responsibilities of his high office."

The platform proclaimed "the following principles as essential to just government. . . . Equality of all men before the law . . . equal and exact justice to all, of whatever nativity, race, color, or persuasion, religious or political"; the maintenance of the Union, with

EMPEROR GRANT, seated upon a pile of money-bags, replies to the pleas of the "Boys in Blue": "No! No! I make it a rule only to receive. I never give anything.

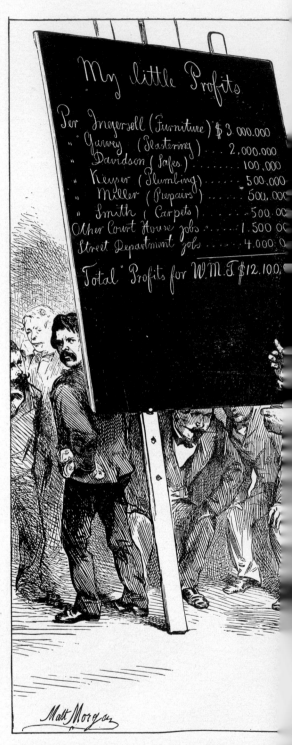

THE CARTOONIST MATT MORGAN IN *FRANK LE*
Grant says: "Now, Tweed, my boy, you see the troub
in your case is, that you did not pocket enough

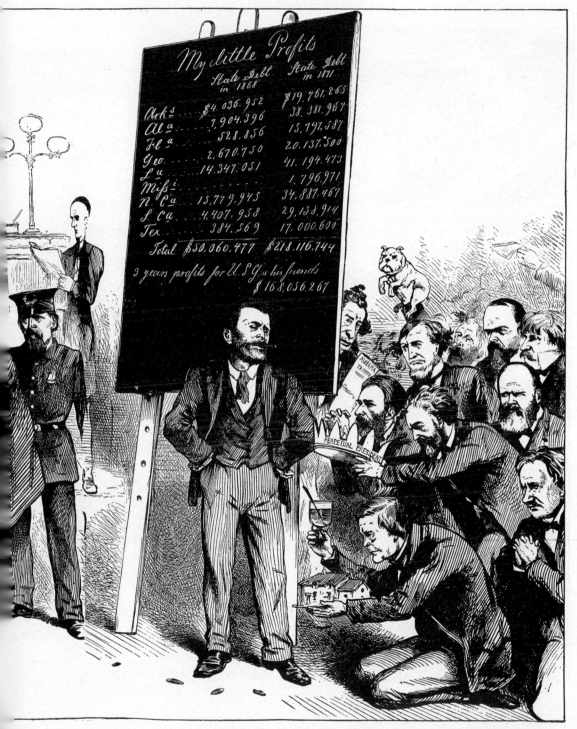

On the blackboard:

My little Profits

	State Debt in 1868	State Debt in 1871
Ark.ᵃ	$4.036.952	$19.761.265
Al.ᵃ	7.904.396	38.331.987
Fl.ᵃ	528.856	15.797.587
Geo.	2.670.750	20.137.500
L.ᵃ	14.347.051	41.194.473
Miss.ⁱ		1.796.971
N. Ca.	15.779.945	34.887.467
S. Ca.	4.407.958	29.158.914
Tex.	384.569	17.000.600
Total	$50.060.477	$218.116.744

3 years profits for U.S.G. & his friends
$168.056.267

ILLUSTRATED NEWSPAPER COMPARES BOSS TWEED'S PROFITS WITH THOSE OF PRESIDENT GRANT

up all your enemies. See what I have done. I have ... so much for myself and them fellows, that they want me to keep on doing it." The cartoonist's idea was not far afield; this is exactly what happened.

"LET US CLASP HANDS over the bloody chasm" wrote Horace Greeley when he accepted the nomination.

GREELEY IS REPRESENTED in this Nast cartoon as a man working hand-in-hand with the Ku-Klux Klan.

EDITOR GREELEY offering the nomination to farmer Greeley. Between the two stretches the "bloody chasm."

THE BLOODY HAND OF THE KU-KLUX KLANS

"emancipation and enfranchisement," and opposition to "any reopening of the questions settled by the Thirteenth, Fourteenth, and Fifteenth Amendments of the Constitution"; universal amnesty; supremacy of civil over military authority, and "state self-government" reformed civil service, for that service become "a mere instrument of partisan tyra and personal ambition, and an object of fish greed—a scandal and reproach u

ON THE RELUCTANT NEGRO BY CANDIDATE HORACE GREELEY AND SENATOR CHARLES SUMNER

free institutions"; a single term for the Presidency; maintenance of the public credit; a "speedy return to specie payments" in the interest of "commercial morality and honest government"; opposition to all further grants of public land to railroads and other private corporations.

On tariff the Liberal Republicans were vague. There were too many different groups whose views had to be taken into consideration. So the

313

compromise solution was to "demand a system of federal taxation which shall not excessively interfere with the industry of the people, and which shall provide the means necessary to pay the expenses of the government." But—as "there are in our midst honest but irreconcilable differences of opinion with regard to the respective systems of protection and free trade, we remit the discussion of the subject to the people in their congressional districts and the decision of Congress thereon, wholly free from executive interference, or dictation."

After the adoption of the platform, the convention turned to the choosing of the presidential candidate. It was commonly thought that Charles Francis Adams, the successful negotiator of the *Alabama* claims against Great Britain, the son of one President and grandson of another, would receive the nomination. He was favored by the Democrats, without whose support no Liberal Republican candidate could be elected. His weakness was his own frigid character.

The evening before the nominations began, B. Gratz Brown, Liberal Republican Governor of Missouri, and General Francis P. Blair, Senator from the same state, arrived in Cincinnati "fit for stratagems and spoils." Their arrival dumbfounded the Quadrilateral and made Schurz, the chairman of the convention, uneasy. What were the two up to?

When the balloting began, Charles Francis Adams was in the lead with 203 votes, followed by Horace Greeley—editor of the New York *Tribune*, who at this time was not considered too seriously for the nomination—with 147 votes; Lyman Trumbull had 100, Gratz Brown 95, David Davis 92½, and Andrew Curtin 62. After announcement of the result, Gratz Brown asked to be heard. He made a little speech, withdrawing himself as a candidate and asking the convention's support for Horace Greeley. His words created a great sensation. The delegates were in an uproar; cheering and shouting filled the hall.

With Gratz Brown's announcement the movement for Horace Greeley was under way. On the next ballot he received 239 votes. On the fifth ballot the Adams vote was 279, the Greeley vote 258. On the sixth, the Greeley vote increased to 332 as against Adams's 324.

Before the result of the ballot was announced, a number of states changed over to Greeley, giving him the majority. For the second place the convention chose Gratz Brown.

Many Liberal Republicans thought that Greeley's selection was a great blunder. A number of them met at Judge Stallo's house, where Carl Schurz pounded furiously on the piano while others cried. General Brinkerhoff exclaimed that the candidates were named by men "as clearly intruders" in the convention hall "as Satan was when he presented himself among the children of light."

From the newspapers came a deluge of criticism. "With such a head," said the New York *Evening Post*, "as is on Greeley's shoulders, the affairs of the nation would not, under his direction, be wisely administered; with such manners as his, they could not be administered with common decorum; with such associates as he has taken to his bosom, they could not be administered with common integrity." The New York *Times* wondered whether "so eminently shrewd a people as this would ever place such a man as Horace Greeley at the head of their government. If any one man could send a great nation to the dogs, that man is Mr. Greeley."

This prophecy seems to be a recurring one—ever since Jefferson ran for office in 1800. In every presidential election the country is going to the dogs—if one votes for the candidate whom the newspapers oppose. That the United States survives must be a constant surprise to the editors.

A month after the Liberal Republicans named Horace Greeley, the regular Republican convention met in Philadelphia. It was a "renomination" convention. It was known that all delegates would cast their vote for General Grant "whose modest patriotism . . . sound judgment . . . practical wisdom, incorruptible integrity . . . commended him to the heart of the American people." The Vice-President in the first administration, Schuyler Colfax, was replaced by Massachusetts Senator Henry Wilson, a former cobbler.

The last of the great conventions was that of the Democrats, who met in Baltimore's Ford Theater. The Democrats had learned from their defeat in the last election; they were chastened

(turn to page 318)

"SAVE ME FROM MY TOBACCO PARTNER!"

"Old Honesty." "Do, Somebody, arrest him, or I shall never get to the White House!"

NYTHING TO BEAT GREELEY. The eminent cartoonist, Thomas Nast, used every conceivable means to ridicule d discredit Horace Greeley. His brutal and unfair cartoons against "Old Honesty" did a great deal to undermine the beral Republican candidate's standing with the electorate. This drawing is an allusion to Greeley's acceptance the support of Tammany Hall, which was closely connected with the financial machinations of Boss Tweed.

WHAT H. G. KNOWS ABOUT HIS FRIENDS.

B. GRATZ BROWN.

"President GRANT has expressed precisely the opinion we should have expected from him concerning the GRATZ BROWN movement in Missouri. He considers it an effort to disorganize the Republican party without cause, which no good Republican who has the interests of the country and of the party at heart can fail zealously to combat. How any man professing Republicanism can fail to take the same view is one of the mysteries which only Revenue Reformers, Tammany Republicans, and other political nondescripts can be expected to understand."—*Tribune, September 21, 1870.*

THEODORE TILTON.

"If apples are wormy this year, and grapes mildew, and ducks' eggs addle, and bladed corn be lodged, it may all be ascribed to the unhallowed influence of Mr. TILTON'S 'Life of Victoria Woodhull.'"—*Tribune, September 11, 1871.*

HON. JAMES R. DOOLITTLE.

"The only corps of which Mr. DOOLITTLE can fairly be considered a leader is that represented by Thevardier in VICTOR HUGO'S 'Les Misérables,' who prowl about the battle-fields to plunder the dead and wounded, and march indifferently after one army or the other for the sake of the spoils."—*Tribune, July 18, 1868.*

HORATIO SEYMOUR.

"Sympathy with depravity amounts in him to a religious passion; meanness with him rises to the height of a holy fervor."—*Tribune, July 4, 1868.*

WHAT H. G. KNOWS ABOUT HIS PRESENT POSITION.

"I saw the other day a suggestion that I would probably be the best Democratic candidate to run against General GRANT for President. I thought that about the most absurd thing I ever heard or read......I am a decided enemy of that party, even in its most respectable aspects."—*HORACE GREELEY.*

"It seems to us unwise in an Editor ever to allow his name to go before the public as a candidate for any party nomination. It is such an appalling consideration, that running for a prominent office puts you under obligation to so many thousand people, who feel that your gratitude can never equal their deserts, that we think an Editor, who is already indebted to so many thousands for taking his paper and inducing others to take it, should never voluntarily incur a further obligation."—*Tribune, August 5, 1858.*

"I have no doubt that the policy you suggest is that which your party [the Democrats] ought to adopt......You only err as to the proper candidate. I am not the man you need. Your party is mostly Free Trade, and I am a ferocious Protectionist. I have no doubt that I might be nominated and elected by your help, but it would place us all in a false position."—*HORACE GREELEY, in Tribune, December 30, 1871.*

"The 'personal views of Mr. GREELEY' impel him to deprecate a Democratic national triumph as one of the gravest national calamities."—*Tribune, August 18, 1871.*

"May it be written on my grave that I was never its follower [the Democratic party], and lived and died in nothing its debtor."—*HORACE GREELEY.*

Gen. GRANT N
AND NEVER W

ANY

ON TO RICHM
1861.

SUPPORTERS OF CANDIDATE HORACE GREELEY—LIBERAL REPUBLICANS AND DEMOCRATS

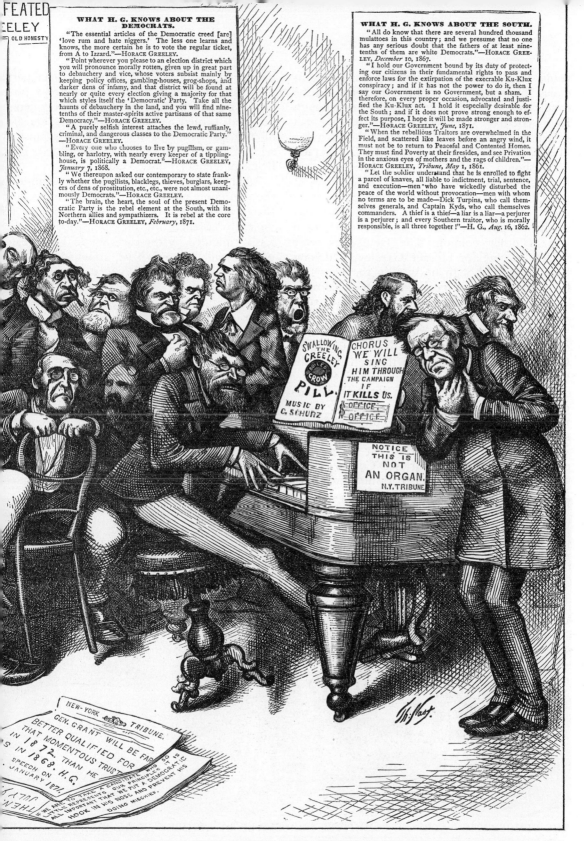

IN DISMAY TO THE CAMPAIGN TUNE WHICH CARL SCHURZ PLAYS FOR THEM ON THE PIANO

ready for "a new departure" from old principles. Thus they accepted the platform and the candidate of the Liberal Republicans, though Representative Voorhees of Indiana, "the tall sycamore of the Wabash," orated that it was a brazen audacity to expect that the Democratic party should support Horace Greeley. He said that it would be the same as if "the disciples of the Christian religion would turn away from their faith for one hour and worship Mahomet as the prophet of God." But the convention was of other opinion. The Democrats were willing to vote for Horace Greeley, a lifelong Republican, although he was, in the words of the Democratic National Committee chairman, "the most objectionable person"; in fact they would have voted for "anybody to beat Grant." "If the Baltimore Convention puts Greeley in our hymn book," said the Governor of North Carolina, "we will sing him through if it kills us."

There were bolters, "Straight-out" Democrats who would not vote for Greeley. They met in a separate convention, condemning the sale of the Democratic party to old Horace, who was nothing but a "white hat and a white coat," and nominated Charles O'Conor.

And there were other parties holding nominating conventions. The Labor Reform party, dominated by the trade unions, selected Judge David Davis for the Presidency, and when he declined, turned to Charles O'Conor. The Prohibition party, asking for legislation against the sale of intoxicating liquors, nominated James Black of Pennsylvania.

Again, as often in the past, the personalities of the two contenders were of greater importance than their political beliefs. Horace Greeley was violently assailed by the newspapers, mercilessly ridiculed by the cartoonists. The greatest of them all, Thomas Nast, attacked him week after week in *Harper's Weekly* with murderous cartoons. Greeley's appearance—his beard, his bearing, and sloppy clothes, his white hat and white coat—were all excellent targets; the sentence from his acceptance letter in which he said that both sides were "eager to clasp hands across the bloody chasm" was a recurring theme in the drawings. Poor Greeley confessed in bewilderment that he sometimes wondered whether he was running for the penitentiary or for the Presidency. He stumped the country, trying to reason with the voters, pleading for conciliatory policies toward the South, and denouncing the Republican speechmakers for "waving the bloody shirt."

THE DEMOCRATIC NATIONAL COMMITTEE IS RECEIVED BY GREELEY AT HIS CHAPPAQUA FARM

HORACE GREELEY ON HIS WESTERN TOUR ADDRESSES CITIZENS OF PITTSBURGH IN THE RAIN

James G. Blaine wrote in his memoirs: "His speeches, while chiefly devoted to his view of the duty and policy of pacification, discussed many questions and many phases of the chief question. They were varied, forcible, and well considered. They presented his case with an ability which could not be exceeded, and they added to the general estimate of his intellectual faculties and resources. He called out a larger proportion of those who intended to vote against him than any candidate had ever before succeeded in doing. His name had been honored for so many years in every Republican household, that the desire to see and hear him was universal, and secured to him the majesty of numbers at every meeting"

During the campaign Grant remained silent. There was nothing for him to say. His lieutenants did not rely on political issues—they relied on the magic of a full campaign chest.

THE REPUBLICAN NOMINEE KISSES BABIES

THE POPULAR AND ELECTORAL VOTES IN THE 1872 ELECTION

STATES	POPULAR VOTE — Ulysses S. Grant, Ill. Republican	Horace Greeley, N.Y. Lib. Republican and Democrat	Charles O'Conor, N.Y. Straight Democrat and Labor Reform	James Black, Pa. Prohibitionist	ELECTORAL VOTE FOR PRESIDENT — Ulysses S. Grant, Ill.	Thomas A. Hendricks, Ind.	B. Gratz Brown, Mo.	Horace Greeley, N.Y.	Charles J. Jenkins, Ga.	David Davis, Ill.	VICE-PRESIDENT — Henry Wilson, Mass.	B. Gratz Brown, Mo.	George W. Julian, Ind.	Alfred H. Colquitt, Ga.	John M. Palmer, Ill.	Thomas E. Bramlette, Ky.	Nathaniel P. Banks, Mass.	William S. Groesbeck, O.	Willis B. Machen, Ky.
Alabama	90,272	79,444	—	—	10						10								
Arkansas	41,373	37,927	—	—	6‡						6‡								
California	54,020	40,718	1,068	—	6						6								
Connecticut	50,638	45,880	204	206	6						6								
Delaware	11,115	10,206	487	—	3						3								
Florida	17,763	15,427	—	—	4						4								
Georgia	62,550	76,356	4,000	—			6	3‡	2			5		5			1		
Illinois	241,944	184,938	3,058	—	21						21								
Indiana	186,147	163,632	1,417	—	15						15								
Iowa	131,566	71,196	2,221	—	11						11								
Kansas	67,048	32,970	596	—	5						5								
Kentucky	88,766	99,995	2,374	—		8	4					8				3			1
Louisiana*	71,663	57,029	—	—	8‡						8‡								
Louisiana†	59,975	66,467	—	—		8‡						8‡							
Maine	61,422	29,087	—	—	7						7								
Maryland	66,760	67,687	19	—		8						8							
Massachusetts	133,472	59,260	—	—	13						13								
Michigan	138,455	78,355	2,861	1,271	11						11								
Minnesota	55,117	34,423	—	—	5						5								
Mississippi	82,175	47,288	—	—	8						8								
Missouri	119,196	151,434	2,439	—		6	8			1		6	5		3			1	
Nebraska	18,329	7,812	—	—	3						3								
Nevada	8,413	6,236	—	—	3						3								
New Hampshire	37,168	31,424	100	200	5						5								
New Jersey	91,656	76,456	630	—	9						9								
New York	440,736	387,281	1,454	201	35						35								
North Carolina	94,769	70,094	—	—	10						10								
Ohio	281,852	244,321	1,163	2,100	22						22								
Oregon	11,819	7,730	572	—	3						3								
Pennsylvania	349,589	212,041	—	1,630	29						29								
Rhode Island	13,665	5,329	—	—	4						4								
South Carolina	72,290	22,703	187	—	7						7								
Tennessee	85,655	94,391	—	—		12						12							
Texas	47,468	66,546	2,580	—		8						8							
Vermont	41,481	10,927	593	—	5						5								
Virginia	93,468	91,654	42	—	11						11								
West Virginia	32,315	29,451	600	—	5						5								
Wisconsin	104,997	86,477	834	—	10						10								
	3,597,132	2,834,125	29,489	5,608	286	42	18	—	2	1	286	47	5	5	3	3	1	1	1

During the counting of the electoral votes, a number of controversies arose. Objections were raised against the Arkansas and Louisiana votes, with the result that the returns of neither state were counted. The popular vote of Louisiana is given in two ways: * marks votes certified by the so-called "Custom-House" board; † marks votes certified by a returning board appointed by the Governor of Louisiana, Henry C. Warmoth, a Republican who joined the Greeley movement. The three Georgia votes for Greeley were rejected because Greeley was already dead when they were cast for him. The remaining five Greeley states cast their votes, as a complimentary gesture, for Thomas A. Hendricks.

They assessed and collected money by the hundred thousands of dollars.

"It was one of the strangest campaigns in history," writes Professor Randall. "Republicans excoriated a Republican President; Liberals labored without enthusiasm for a candidate whose choice was intolerable to them; Democrats supported a violent and abusive opponent; ex-Confederates in the South did battle for a foe who had denounced them as traitors and rebels."

That Grant would be re-elected was certain. Of the thirty-seven states (for the first time the election was held by popular vote in every state of the Union), thirty-one voted for him. Greeley carried Missouri, Texas, Georgia, Kentucky, Tennessee and Maryland, but not a single Northern state. Deeply hurt by his defeat, exhausted in mind and body, "the worst beaten man who ever ran for high office," smarting under the blow that the power of his newspaper had passed into the hands of Whitelaw Reid, he died insane three weeks after the election.

WITH GRANT RE-ELECTED
THE "BLOODY-CHASM"
CLOSES ON GREELEY

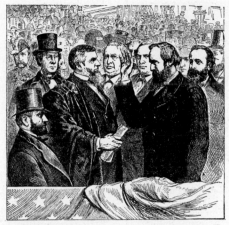

HAYES TAKES THE OATH OF OFFICE

THE TWENTY-THIRD ELECTION—1876

RUTHERFORD B. HAYES

Fraud and corruption only began to take root under Grant's first administration; during his second they came into full bloom, spreading from department to department. The Treasury had a contract with one John D. Sanborn, who collected some overdue taxes for the government out of which he pocketed $200,000. The Navy Department sold business to contractors. The Department of the Interior made a pretty penny from its dealings with land speculators. A "whisky ring," made up of a happy union of revenue officers and distillers, defrauded the government of millions of dollars; the Secretary of War received annual payments for the appointment of an Indian agent; the U. S. Minister to Brazil defrauded the Brazilian government of $100,000 and fled, leaving it to Uncle Sam to refund the money. Wherever one looked, one saw graft and corruption. Public morality was never lower than during this time. The President was manipulated by grafters, his naïveté incredible. Personally honest, he did not realize the evil-doing of the rogues who ran the government machinery. Scandal followed scan-

dal. And whenever one of the President's close associates was caught, Grant was the first to shield the scoundrel from his just desert.

The country was tired of such practices: tired of the Republican regime, tired of its Radical reconstruction policy, tired of the continuous "waving of the bloody shirt," tired of supporting further legislation against the South. The people desired peace; they wanted to forget the war.

Farmers in the Northwest complained of low farm prices and high rate charges. The panic of 1873 grew into a full-fledged depression. There were 5,183 business failures in 1873 alone —over 9,000 in 1876. Land and stock values diminished, vast numbers of workers were unemployed.

In the midterm election of 1874 the Republicans suffered a crushing defeat. Their more than two-thirds majority in the House of Representatives was wiped out. For the first time since the Civil War the Democrats were in control of the lower House, and though the Senate remained Republican, its majority was greatly

323

RUTHERFORD B. HAYES (1822-1893), of Ohio, three times governor of his state, was the candidate of the Republicans, defeating the favorite, Blaine, for the nomination.

WILLIAM A. WHEELER (1819-1887) was Hayes' running mate. Through trickery, the Republicans won an electoral majority even though Tilden had more popular votes than Hayes.

SAMUEL J. TILDEN (1814-1886), Governor of New York, prosecutor of the Tweed Ring, was Democratic candidate, although he faced the opposition of the Tammany organization.

THOMAS A. HENDRICKS (1819-1885), a "soft-money" man from Indiana, was Tilden's opponent for the nomination. Losing to Tilden, he reluctantly accepted second place.

PETER COOPER (1791-1883), New York philanthropist and inventor, was the candidate of the Greenback party which advocated paper money. Cooper received 81,737 votes.

GREEN CLAY SMITH (1832-1895), a former Governor of the Territory of Montana, and keen temperance man, was the candidate of the Prohibition party, receiving 9522 votes.

reduced. A Democratic victory in the next presidential election seemed inevitable.

A year before the election it was rumored that the President was not averse to accepting a third term. To the Liberal Republicans and Democrats these rumors were like a red rag to a bull. They would see to it that there should be no third term for Grant.

In Philadelphia a Republican state convention passed a resolution declaring "opposition to the election to the presidency of any person for a third term." President Grant, in a letter to General Harry White, the chairman of the convention, explained that he did not want a third term any more than he wanted the first. Still, he emphasized that the Constitution does not restrict the presidential tenure to only two

THE POPULAR VOTE IN THE 1876 ELECTION

STATES	S. J. Tilden, N. Y. Democrat	R. B. Hayes, Ohio. Republican	Peter Cooper, N. Y. Greenback	Green Clay Smith, Ky. Prohibitionist
Alabama	102,989	68,708	—	—
Arkansas	58,071	38,669	289	—
California	76,468	78,322	44	—
Colorado*	—	—	—	—
Connecticut	61,934	59,034	774	378
Delaware	13,381	10,752	—	—
Florida†	22,927	23,849	—	—
Florida‡	24,434	24,340	—	—
Georgia	130,088	50,446	—	—
Illinois	258,601	278,232	9,533	—
Indiana	213,526	208,011	17,233	141
Iowa	112,121	171,326	9,908	36
Kansas	37,902	78,322	7,776	110
Kentucky	159,696	97,156	1,944	813
Louisiana†	70,508	75,315	—	—
Louisiana‡	83,723	77,174	—	—
Maine	49,917	66,300	663	—
Maryland	91,780	71,981	33	10
Massachusetts	108,777	150,063	779	84
Michigan	141,095	166,534	9,060	766
Minnesota	48,799	72,962	2,311	72
Mississippi	112,173	52,605	—	—
Missouri	203,077	145,029	3,498	64
Nebraska	17,554	31,916	2,320	1,599
Nevada	9,308	10,383	—	—
New Hampshire	38,509	41,539	76	—
New Jersey	115,962	103,517	712	43
New York	521,949	489,207	1,987	2,359
North Carolina	125,427	108,417	—	—
Ohio	323,182	330,698	3,057	1,636
Oregon	14,149	15,206	510	—
Pennsylvania	366,204	384,184	7,187	1,319
Rhode Island	10,712	15,787	68	60
South Carolina	90,896	91,870	—	—
Tennessee	133,166	89,566	—	—
Texas	104,803	44,803	—	—
Vermont	20,350	44,428	—	—
Virginia	139,670	95,558	—	—
West Virginia	56,495	42,046	1,373	—
Wisconsin	123,926	130,070	1,509	27
Total Republican count	4,285,992	4,033,768	81,737	9,52
Total Democratic count	4,300,590	4,036,298	81,737	9,52

* Electors were appointed by the legislature to avoid another election. (Colorado was admitted to the Union in August 1876.)
† Republican count. ‡ Democratic count.

A GREAT NUMBER OF FRAUDULENT VOTERS WERE JAILED IN NEW YORK CITY ON ELECTION DAY.

terms and argued that the time might come when it would be inadvisable to change a President after eight years in office. Grant said that he would accept the nomination only "under such circumstances as to make it an imperative duty—circumstances not likely to arise."

This was anything but an outspoken repudiation. What if the Republican convention should declare that it was "an imperative duty" for Grant to serve again?

The Democrats were determined that "such circumstances" should not arise and that the country should not be drifted "upon the rock of Caesarism." In December, 1875, they introduced a resolution in Congress declaring that "the precedent established by Washington and other Presidents of the United States, in retiring from the presidential office after their second term, has become, by universal concurrence, a part of our republican system of government, and that any departure from this time-honored custom would be unwise, unpatriotic and fraught with peril to our free institutions." The resolution was carried not only by the votes of all Democratic Representatives, but seventy out of the eighty-eight Republicans supported it as well. Thus Grant's third-term dreams were ended.

With Grant disposed of, the Republican factions began to jockey their candidates into position. James G. Blaine of Maine, the charming, able, magnetic, and money-loving former Speaker of the House of Representatives, was the favorite; Roscoe Conkling, the New York Senator and political boss, had the support of the administration forces; the reformers were behind Benjamin H. Bristow of Kentucky, the Secretary of the Treasury and prosecutor of the Whisky Ring. The Pennsylvanians rallied

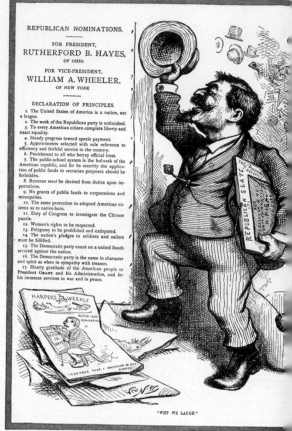

THOMAS NAST, whose political cartoons had great influence, rejoices over the Republican nominations.

THE DEMOCRATIC TICKET. Tilden and Hendricks are caricatured as an elastic two-headed Democratic tiger. Tilden supporting the "hard-money" idea of the East while Hendricks upheld the "soft-money" views of the West

326

REPUBLICAN ELEPHANT tramples over the wounded Democratic tiger — Tilden and Hendricks.

"MR. FACING-BOTH-WAYS." Samuel Tilden, the Democratic candidate, stands on the Reform platform.

hind their governor, General Hartranft; Indiana behind Senator Oliver P. Morton; Ohio behind Governor Rutherford B. Hayes. These were the most prominent names before the convention when it assembled at Cincinnati on June 14.

Robert G. Ingersoll from Illinois presented Blaine with all the flowery requisites of contemporary oratory. "Like an armed warrior, like a plumed knight, James G. Blaine marched down the halls of the American Congress," stated Ingersoll, "and threw his shining lance full and fair against the brazen forehead of every traitor to his country." The enthusiasm of the convention knew no bounds. "Blaine, Blaine, Blaine!" the delegates shouted, and cheered and sang. The tide in the "Plumed Knight's" favor ran so high that his opponents quickly asked for adjournment. They saw that

if the voting began, Blaine would be nominated on the first ballot. Still, the motion for adjournment would have been defeated by the Blaine forces, who commanded the majority, had not the lighting equipment of the hall given out. The main gas pipe was found to be cut through —the work of Blaine's opponents—and the meeting had to adjourn.

When the voting began the next morning, Blaine led the first four ballots, with Morton, Bristow, Conkling, and Hayes trailing him. But as responsible party leaders feared that his nomination would split the party, they were frantically searching for a compromise candidate. During the fifth ballot William A. Howard of Michigan, one of the founders of the Republican party, made an impassioned appeal for Governor Hayes. It did not make much of an impression. On the sixth and seventh ballots the

327

Blaine vote increased—it looked like victory for the Plumed Knight. But a nomination is not won until the last vote is cast. When Kentucky saw that Bristow could not win, it changed its support to Hayes, giving the signal for a stampede. Kentucky's lead was followed by all the other delegations who opposed Blaine, until Hayes had 384 votes and with them the nomination.

The platform was a weak document. It contained a mild and half-hearted resolution against the spoils system; declared itself in favor of protection and against polygamy; asked public aid to parochial schools. Although one plank advocated that all public officers should be held "to a rigid responsibility" and "that the prosecution and punishment of all who betray official trusts shall be swift, thorough, and unsparing," it did not come out frankly against the corrupt public service, and it did not promise any remedy of the existing conditions.

At their meeting the Republicans adopted a number of noteworthy resolutions which changed the procedure of all future conventions. One of them defined the order of business: first the report of the committee on credentials should be discussed, then the platform, and only after both had been dealt with should the nominations for candidates begin. Another resolution—directed against stampeding—ruled that the roll call had to be strictly adhered to and that after a state had announced its vote for a candidate, it could not change it on that same ballot, but had to wait until another ballot was cast. A further decision defeated the unit rule—in future conventions the delegates could record their votes individually and not as a unit.

Two weeks after the Republican convention the Democrats met at St. Louis. Only two serious contenders vied for the nomination. The wealthy Samuel J. Tilden, sixty-two-year-old

"The negroes of the South are free—free as air," says the parliamentary Watterson. This is what the *State*, a well-known Democratic organ of Tennessee, says, in huge capitals, on the subject: "Let it be known before the election that the farmers have agreed to spot every leading Radical negro in the county, and treat him as an enemy for all time to come. The rotten ring must and shall be broken at any and all costs. The Democrats have determined to withdraw all employment from their enemies. Let this fact be known."

GETTING THE NEGRO VOTE. "Of course he wants to vote the Democratic ticket!" says the Democratic vote solicitor. In this election, both parties committed frauds, both parties "influenced" the decision of the returning boards, both parties reverted to methods of intimidation, bribery and outright violence in order to gain a victory.

ON THE EVENING OF NOVEMBER TENTH it seemed that Tilden had won the election. His friends came to his house in Gramercy Park to celebrate the occasion and congratulate him on his victory. But the Republican managers fought the validity of some of the election returns and in the end secured the Presidency for Hayes.

bachelor Governor of New York, prosecutor of the Tweed Ring, representative of the reformers, faced Thomas A. Hendricks of Indiana, a "soft-money" man, the candidate of the West.

For the past few months a newspaper popularity bureau with a great number of editors, writers, and advertising copywriters had promoted Tilden's candidacy. The advertising firm of Goodsell Brothers made a survey of public sentiment throughout the country, distributed publicity releases and cartoons to local newspapers, sent Tilden literature to influential citizens. So when the day of the convention arrived, Tilden's name was uppermost in the minds of the Democratic delegates. But Tilden had enemies. The most formidable was John Kelly from his own state. Kelly, the leader of Tammany Hall, came with a strong delegation to St. Louis, ready to vote for Hendricks.

Over the headquarters of the Tammany delegation hung a banner: "New York, the largest Democratic city in the Union, is uncompromisingly opposed to the nomination of Samuel J. Tilden because he cannot carry the State of New York." It was Tammany's revenge on Tilden, who had investigated and prosecuted the grafts in the city administration, a deed Tammany was not soon to forget.

The platform, written by Manton Marble, the eminent editor of the New York *World*, stressed reform. "Reform is necessary to rebuild . . . the Union, eleven years ago happily rescued from the danger of a secession of States. Reform is necessary to establish a sound currency. Reform is necessary in the scale of public expenses. Reform is necessary even more in the higher grades of the public service." Reform, reform, reform was the main theme, reiterated again and again.

THE DISPUTED ELECTORAL RETURNS

PROTEST. Democratic Congressmen signing a protest against the counting of the Louisiana electoral votes in the House of Representatives on February 19, 1877.

APPROVAL. Conkling tells Chandler, after learning the decision of the electoral commission, to disband his "noble army of conspirators" as "there'll be no war."

THE ELECTORAL COMMISSION DELIBERATES O
The members of the commission—eight Republicans and seven Democrats — voted on the disputed returns from

When the balloting began, it became apparent that a "reform campaign without Tilden would be like the play of *Hamlet* with Hamlet left out"—thus, with hardly any opposition, Til-

den received the nomination. The next morning the chairman read a telegram from Missouri: "Fired one hundred guns for Tilden. Hope Hendricks will be Vice-President." The

NS FROM THE THREE CARPETBAG STATES — LOUISIANA, FLORIDA AND SOUTH CAROLINA.

ıisiana, South Carolina and Florida strictly along tisan lines. All the Hayes electors were accepted, all the Tilden electors rejected. Thus Hayes won the Presidency with 185 electoral votes to Tilden's 184.

vice was heeded, though it took some coaxing make Hendricks accept the second place. ome minor parties held nominating conven-ns. The Prohibition Reform party nominated

General Green Clay Smith of Kentucky; the Independent National convention, a successor to the Labor Reform and the Granger move-ments—opposing redemption of government bonds in gold and advocating paper money—named Peter Cooper for the Presidency.

What was to be the campaign issue? Would the present or the past be discussed? Would orators talk about the Civil War or would they campaign on the need for reform?

The cry for reform was almost as strong in the Republican ranks as it was among the Democrats. The only difference was that the Democrats openly advocated reform, while the Republican platform, for obvious reasons, was not so emphatic. On other issues the policies of the two parties were similar. Rutherford Hayes, the Republican candidate, was a hard-money man, so was Tilden; Tilden, like Hayes, was for civil service reform; Hayes was for withdrawal of the last Federal troops from the South, as was Tilden.

Rutherford Hayes accepted the nomination in a straightforward letter in which he denounced unredeemable paper money, deplored conditions in the Southern states, and held out hope for an early return to local self-government, free of Federal interference. He said that it was his "inflexible purpose" not to be a candidate for re-election. His letter was a more outspoken declaration of policies than was embodied in the Republican platform; it gained Hayes many friends; it won him many voters. One of them was Mark Twain, who said that the letter "corralled" his vote at once.

Tilden's acceptance letter took three weeks to compose; it turned out to be three times longer than the Democratic platform and said nothing that was new.

As the campaign got under way, the orators of the two parties talked more of the past than of present conditions; the Democrats criticized the Republicans for their reconstruction policy, and the Republicans denounced the Democrats for their stand during the years of the Civil War. The Republicans believed that "waving the bloody shirt" would be a good vote catcher. "A bloody-shirt campaign with money and Indiana is safe," wrote a party man from that state to Hayes; "a financial campaign and no money, and we are beaten." The Democrats campaigned on the "hard times," blamed the depression on the Republican administration, and dwelt on the scandals of the Grant regime, which they declared an "outrage."

As usual, there was a great amount of personal abuse. Against Hayes's private life not much could be said; he was a "goody-goody" with a blameless past. Tilden made an easier target for attacks; he was accused of being a "railroad shark" who was in the pay of the big corporations, and assailed as an income-tax evader.

For the first time in the history of presidential elections, professional publicity men managed the Democratic campaign. Newspapers received regular stories on Tilden; pamphlets and circular letters were sent out by the thousands. There was a literary bureau, a speakers' bureau, a bureau of correspondence, the latter under the personal supervision of Tilden, answering questions and accusations at once. Henry George stumped for Tilden, as did the Hungarian journalist Joseph Pulitzer. John Bigelow, Abram Hewitt, Manton Marble, Henry Watterson, Charles Dana, and other outstanding political organizers and publicists helped the cause of the man of whom the Democrats sang:

"Sam Tilden is a gentleman
  A true and honest man, sir;
And when we call for honest work
  He's just the chap to answer.
He represents the very truths
  That we have all been drilled in,
And we couldn't have to lead us on
  A better man than Tilden."

The first election returns seemed to favor the Democrats. By midnight of November 7—election day—the Tilden supporters were sure their man was to be the next President of the United States. Hayes went to bed in Ohio with the belief that he had lost the election.

Had it not been for four journalists, sitting up that night in the New York *Times* office, that would have been the official result. But these four men changed the course of history. As they watched the returns in the early morning hours, a dispatch came in from Democratic State Chairman Magone: "Please give your estimate of electoral votes secured for Tilden. Answer at once." The four Republican editors guessed that the Democrats were uncertain of the electoral result in the South.

One of the four—John C. Reid, the managing editor of the *Times*—rushed to the Fifth Av-

WHEN TILDEN REALIZED that resistance to the electoral commission's decision might cause civil war, he accepted the result. His manager declared: "I prefer four years of Hayes' administration to four years of civil war."

nue hotel where Zachariah Chandler, chairman of the Republican congressional committee, was sleeping in sweet exhaustion, partly as a result of the election, partly from the drinks he had consumed during the night. The two men, one dead sober and the other in not quite the same condition, evolved a plan. Telegrams were sent out to the Republican party heads in Louisiana, South Carolina, and Florida: "Hayes is elected if we have carried South Carolina, Florida and Louisiana. Can you hold your state? Answer at once."

The second edition of the *Times*—at six-thirty—gave Tilden 184 and Hayes 181 votes (assuming Louisiana and South Carolina for Hayes). Tilden needed one more vote for his election, as 185 constituted the majority. But the newspapers stated that Florida with its four votes was doubtful. Therefore, "if the Republicans have carried that state, as they claim, they will have 185 votes—a majority of one." Thus the struggle to secure the one-vote majority began, keeping the country in a state of wild excitement for weeks to come.

The next day the now-sober Chandler announced: "Hayes has 185 electoral votes and is elected." But Hayes was not so confident. He said in an interview in Cincinnati: "I think we are defeated in spite of recent good news. I am of the opinion that the Democrats have carried the country and elected Tilden."

The question was which of the two parties had actually won in the three Southern states with carpetbag governments. Who would receive the four electoral votes of Florida, the eight of Louisiana, and the seven of South Carolina? Would they be counted for Tilden or would they be counted for Hayes?

The Republicans sent "visiting statesmen" to these three states, where they had heart-to-

THE FINAL VOTE making the Republican Rutherford B. Hayes President, could not be announced until four o'clock the morning of March 2, when the president of the Senate revealed that Hayes had 185, Tilden 184 votes.

THE FINAL VOTE OF THE ELECTORAL COLLEGE.

STATES	Hayes and Wheeler.	Tilden and Hendricks.	STATES	Hayes and Wheeler.	Tilden and Hendricks.
Alabama	—	10	Missouri	—	15
Arkansas	—	6	Nebraska	3	—
California	6	—	Nevada	3	—
Colorado	3	—	New Hampshire	5	—
Connecticut	—	6	New Jersey	—	9
Delaware	—	3	New York	—	35
Florida	4	—	North Carolina	—	10
Georgia	—	11	Ohio	22	—
Illinois	21	—	Oregon	3	—
Indiana	—	15	Pennsylvania	29	—
Iowa	11	—	Rhode Island	4	—
Kansas	5	—	South Carolina	7	—
Kentucky	—	12	Tennessee	—	12
Louisiana	8	—	Texas	—	8
Maine	7	—	Vermont	5	—
Maryland	—	8	Virginia	—	11
Massachusetts	13	—	West Virginia	—	5
Michigan	11	—	Wisconsin	10	—
Minnesota	5	—			
Mississippi	—	8	Total	185	184

heart talks with members of the returning boards. In Louisiana the "talks" must have encountered some difficulties, for in that state the Democratic majority ran to over six thousand. But in the end the visiting statesmen from the North won their arguments. Their pocketbooks were probably quite a bit thinner than when they left home, but the Republican returning boards certified the state votes for Hayes; the "persuasions" were eminently successful. Rutherford Hayes could claim all nineteen votes from Louisiana, South Carolina, and Florida, providing him with that one-vote majority on which his election hung.

But the Democrats did not concede defeat. When the electoral college met in December, not only the certified Republican electors appeared from the three carpetbag states, but the Democratic electors were there as well, eager to cast their votes for Tilden and Hendricks. It was a highly confused situation. And to make it more complicated still, there was a conflict over the electoral vote of Oregon. In that state the Democratic governor declared one Republican elector ineligible and gave his place to the elector with the next highest number of votes. It was no coincidence that the member with the next highest vote belonged to the same party as the governor. Against this procedure the Republicans protested.

How were the votes to be counted? Which returns should be considered valid? The Senate had a Republican majority, the House a Democratic one. If the votes were certified by the Senate, the Republican majority would accept the Republican returns and vote against the Democratic ones. And if the House of Representatives had to decide, it would accept the Democratic votes and reject the Republican ones.

The makers of the Twenty-second Joint Rule, under which the count was to take place, had not foreseen such an emergency. The Republicans demanded that the count should be made by the president of the Senate, a Republican; the Democrats said the right to count the votes had been conferred on both Houses of Congress. There were three possibilities: one, that the Republican president of the Senate should count the votes, in which case Hayes would become President; two, that the two Houses should decide independently of each other which of the two returns should be accepted, in which case there would be no decision, since the Demo-

cratic House would uphold Tilden while the Republican Senate would support Hayes; three, that if members of both Houses voted jointly, each member casting one vote, Tilden would have a majority.

In January congressional leaders feared that the deadlock would continue into March and that the nation would be left without a President. Therefore, they suggested turning over the entire dispute to a special commission empowered to make a decision. This commission reported a bill, known as the Electoral Commission Law of 1877. It was a logical plan, worked out by common sense, suggesting that five Senators, five Representatives, and five Justices of the Supreme Court should form an electoral commission and decide about the disputed returns. Before the members of the electoral commission were chosen, it was understood that half of them should be members of the Democratic and half members of the Republican party. The fifteenth member was to be Judge Davis, who held independent views. Tilden accepted the electoral commission plan, which was virtually a Democratic victory. But, unexpectedly for the Democrats, five days before the commission was to meet, Judge Davis, who was thought to favor Tilden, retired from the Court and became Senator from Illinois. His place in the commission was taken by Justice Bradley—a Republican.

The count of votes began on the first day of February and lasted till the early morning hours of the second of March. On all disputed returns the commission voted strictly according to partisan lines, eight Republicans against seven Democrats. All Hayes electors from Florida, Louisiana, and South Carolina were accepted, all Tilden electors rejected.

The Democratic press protested vehemently. Democratic members of Congress talked of a filibuster which would go past March 4th, leaving the country without a President. Popular excitement was rising. Democratic forces were organized in a number of states. "Tilden or blood" was on many lips.

If Tilden had made an aggressive fight, he might have become President. But his make-up was not that of a fighter. He was a cautious, rather indecisive man, who pondered the issues and had difficulty making up his mind. Further-

MIDNIGHT, MARCH 3, 1877. President Grant and members of the Cabinet are patiently waiting at the Capitol to sign the last bills of the outgoing administration. Second from left is Hamilton Fish, the Secretary of State.

335

more, he was not in good health. Only the year before he had suffered a paralytic stroke, and since then he had been extremely worried about himself, carrying a small medicine chest with him wherever he went, watching his diet, and seeing to it that his frail body received a regular massage. At times he was so preoccupied with his health that nothing else mattered—not even the Presidency.

When he saw that resistance to the commission's decision might plunge the country into a civil war, he bowed to the inevitable. Abram Hewitt, managing Tilden's affairs, declared: "I prefer four years of Hayes' administration to four years of civil war."

Thus in the early hours of the morning of March 2, Senator Ferry could pronounce offi-

cially that "Rutherford B. Hayes, having received the majority of the whole number of electoral votes, is duly elected President of the United States for four years, commencing on the 4th of March, 1877."

It was said that the Democrats accepted Hayes's election only after they were promised that the Federal troops would be withdrawn from Louisiana and South Carolina, the last two carpetbag states. (Florida had meanwhile inaugurated a Democratic governor on January 2, 1877.)

Hayes denied that he had had any part in the bargain. Nevertheless, soon after his inauguration he gave orders for the withdrawal of the remaining troops from the South, thus ending the Radical reconstruction period.

THE BENEFICIAL RESULT of the disputed election. One of the new President's first orders was withdrawal of the troops from the last two carpetbag states. (Florida already had a Democratic Governor.) With this the sordid era of reconstruction came to an end. This drawing is a fantasy of the Republican cartoonist, C. S. Reinhart. In it the Old Democratic Party wails that President Hayes has stolen her child—the South—while Columbia says, "O! bless you, sir! You've brought us all together again!" In reality the situation was entirely different, for the withdrawal of Federal troops resulted in emergence of the Solid South, bulwark of the Democratic party ever since.

Here lies THE DEMOCRATIC TIGER GREATLY MOURNED BY THE BEREAVED FILIBUSTERS

FTER THE ELECTION result was announced, and Hayes became President by one electoral vote, the bandaged t laurel-crowned Republican elephant drawn by Nast moans: "Another such victory and I am undone."

JAMES GARFIELD TAKES THE OATH

THE TWENTY-FOURTH ELECTION—1880

JAMES A. GARFIELD
AND CHESTER A. ARTHUR

Rutherford Birchard Hayes could never make the people forget the circumstances of his election. Democratic cartoonists pictured him with "fraud" written over his brow, his enemies called him "Rutherfraud" B. Hayes. Yet he gave the country an honest administration.

He faced almost insurmountable obstacles. During the first half of his term he was opposed by a hostile Democratic House of Representatives; during the second half of his tenure both Houses of Congress were against him. Hayes attempted to introduce a "thorough, radical and complete" civil service reform, making a number of good appointments, but he was not able to gain the confidence of the civil service reformers. While he was successful in cleaning the government of corruption, he was not able to halt the malpractices of the railroads, and he kept his eyes closed against trusts and land frauds. During his administration labor unions rose to great importance; there were strikes all over the country. Hayes had little ability to deal with such a situation. He understood the past, but the present with its complex economic forces seemed a mystery to him.

When election year approached, the Republicans were uneasy about the future. They realized that the power which they had successfully retained since 1861 was nearing an end. Their party was divided into two hostile factions: the "Stalwarts" and the "Half-Breeds." The Stalwarts, led by New York Senator Roscoe Conkling, belonged to the conservative element resisting all demands for reform; the Half-Breeds, under James G. Blaine, professed more liberal views. By present standards there was no great fundamental difference between the policies of the two factions; they had come into being mainly because Conkling and Blaine disliked each other. Blaine once described Conkling in Congress as a "majestic, supereminent, overpowering, turkey-gobbler strut," and Conkling deeply resented the insult. The two men drifted apart.

339

JAMES A. GARFIELD (1831-1881)
WITH HIS DAUGHTER MOLLY

THE CANDIDATES

JAMES A. GARFIELD (1831-1881), Senator from Ohio, became Republican compromise choice when Grant and Blaine forces blocked each other at the nominating convention.

CHESTER A. ARTHUR (1830-1886), a friend of the spoilsman and opponent of reform, was chosen as Garfield's running mate to please the "Stalwarts," succeeding him in 1881.

WINFIELD S. HANCOCK (1824-1886) called "The Superb," a general in the Civil War, was chosen by the Democrats, but lost the election to James Garfield by less than ten thousand votes.

WILLIAM H. ENGLISH (1822-1896), a conservative Indiana banker who retired from politics before the Civil War, reemerged on the political scene as Hancock's running mate.

JAMES B. WEAVER (1833-1912) from Iowa was the candidate of the National Greenback Labor party. With B. J. Chambers of Texas as his running mate, he polled 308,578 votes.

NEAL DOW (1804-1897), a Quaker from Maine, was the Prohibition candidate. Though he polled only a little over 10,000 votes, the prohibition movement was growing.

Conkling and the Stalwarts supported the nomination of General Grant, who had recently returned from a triumphant world tour and was not averse to taking up residence in the White House again; the Half-Breeds desired the Presidency for James G. Blaine. But there were other contenders with strong support: John Sherman, the Secretary of the Treasury, George F. Edmunds, Senator from Vermont, Elihu B. Washburne of Illinois, and William Windom, Senator from Minnesota. The strategy to defeat Grant was clear—all the opposing candidates and their followers were to unite their forces and combat him collectively. However, this was no easy matter. When the Republican convention assembled in Chicago, the General's initial support was formidable; over three hundred Stalwart delegates had pledged their votes to him. If the unit rule—requiring that each state pass its votes as a solid block for the candidate favored by a majority of its delegates—could have been enforced, Grant would have had no difficulty in attaining the nomination on the first ballot. Therefore the first step of Grant's opponents was to defeat the acceptance of the unit rule. Organized by James Garfield of Ohio, they won this important victory.

After the unit rule was voted down, the platform was submitted to the convention—an agglomeration of commonplace phrases, a verbose, meaningless document. It extolled the achievements of the Republican administration and made such high sounding declarations as "that the peace regained should be cherished

A WHITE HOUSE EVENING. President Rutherford [B.] Hayes and his family are listening to Carl Schurz at th[e] piano, while in the background John Sherman, Secretar[y] of the Treasury, talks to one of the Hayes childre[n.]

"WE HAVE COME TO STAY" is the title of this prophetic cartoon by Thomas Nast. The South had had enough of harsh Republican rule, enough of the Radical reconstruction period, enough of the corrupt carpetbag governments. After the Federal troops were withdrawn from the South, political support of the Republicans waned very rapidly, and the Southern states swung solidly into the Democratic column where they have remained ever since.

THE STALWARTS

EX-PRESIDENT GRANT was the candidate of the "Stalwarts," anti-Hayes wing of the Republican party. He was managed by New York's Senator Roscoe Conkling (aloft), who hated Blaine, chief of the "Half-Breeds."

LEADER OF THE STALWARTS was Senator Roscoe Conkling, whom James G. Blaine described as a "majestic, supereminent, overpowering, turkey-gobbler strut."

"CINDERELLA OF THE REPUBLICAN PARTY
After Grant (center) returned from his triumphal world tour, Roscoe Conkling (at right) and the "Stal-

. . . that the liberties secured to this generation should be transmitted undiminished to future generations . . . that the commerce, already so great, should be steadily encouraged," that "the Constitution of the United States is a supreme law, and not a mere contract," and that "the intelligence of the nation is but the aggregate

"...UGHTY SISTERS"—A CARTOON BY JOSEPH KEPPLER FOR THE HUMOROUS MAGAZINE *PUCK*.

...rts" worked hard to win for him the Republican ...nination, overlooking President Hayes (sitting on the hearth), who was not able to gain the confidence of either the "Stalwart" or the "Half-Breed" factions.

...the intelligence in the several States, and the ...stiny of the nation must be guided, not by ...e genius of any one State, but by the average ...nius of all."

...On the more positive side the platform de-...red that the Federal Government should aid ...e work of popular education"; it asserted

that "slavery having perished in the States, its twin barbarity, polygamy, must die in the Territories," and it demanded "that everywhere the protection accorded to citizens of American birth must be secured to citizens of American adoption."

The platform was adopted without much discussion and the convention listened with great patience to the nominating speeches. Roscoe Conkling made an impassioned appeal for General Grant, beginning with the verse:

"And when asked what state he hails from,
Our sole reply shall be:
He hails from Appomattox
And its famous apple tree."

Conkling told the convention that the impending election would determine whether this country should be "republican or Cossack." He said that President Grant had shown that "communism, lawlessness and disorder, although it might stalk high-headed and dictate law to a whole city, would always find a foe in him," and he attacked the reformers as "charlatans, jayhawkers, tramps, and guerillas—the men who . . . forage now on one side and then on the other."

When Conkling submitted Grant's name, the convention cheered for fifteen minutes. I seemed that Grant would walk away with th nomination. But immediately after the "humar ocean in tempest" quieted, James Garfield o Ohio offered John Sherman's name in a mas terly speech. Garfield said that Sheman woul be a candidate who would create "party har mony," which is the main requisite to winnin an election. "In order to win victory now, w want the vote of every Republican—of ever Grant Republican and every anti-Grant Re publican in America—of every Blaine man an every anti-Blaine man."

When the speechmaking extolling the cand dates' virtues was over, the convention beg the balloting. On the first trial Grant led wit 304 votes, followed by Blaine with 284, She man 93, Edmunds 33, Washburne 31, and Wir dom 10. After twenty-eight ballots the conver tion adjourned. The decision seemed to be f away. Grant had the undiminishing support c

THE HALF-BREEDS

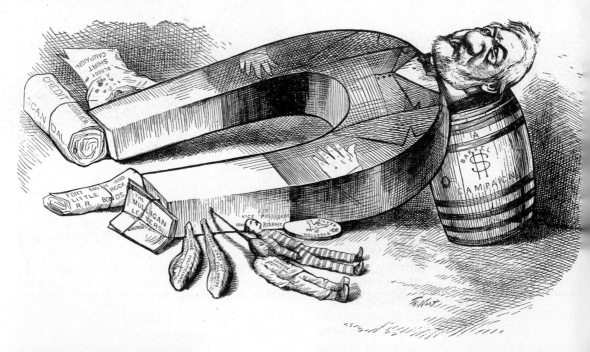

LEADER OF THE HALF-BREEDS, the men who followed Hayes, supporting his reform measures, was the "m netic" James G. Blaine, who desired the nomination for himself. But Blaine had been involved in a shady deal w the Little Rock and Fort Smith Railroad in Arkansas. For land grants from the government, the railroad g Blaine some bonds in return. This came to light when Blaine's letters about the transactions became kno

"THE PLUMED KNIGHT," James G. Blaine, was the chief rival of ex-President Grant for the Republican nomina-
ion. "Like an armed warrior, like a plumed knight, James G. Blaine marched down the halls of . . . Congress and
hrew his shining lance full and fair against the brazen forehead of every traitor to his country . . ." said Robert
ngersoll in the 1876 convention. From then on the famous cartoonist, Thomas Nast, drew Blaine with plumes.

THE REPUBLICAN CONVENTION IN CHICAGO

THE GALLERIES CHEER A NOMINATING SPEECH

THE NEW HAMPSHIRE DELEGATION ARRIV

TIRED DELEGATES IN SEARCH OF A HOTEL ROOM

DELEGATE FROM MICHIGAN HAS THE FLO

the Stalwarts, but his enemies held their ground and their forces remained unbroken.

Next day, when the voting continued, Massachusetts transferred 21 votes to John Sherman, whose strength gradually increased until on the thirtieth ballot he received 120 votes—but three ballots later the boom for him was over.

About this time Sherman telegraphed the convention: "Whenever the vote of Ohio will be likely to assure the nomination of Garfield, I appeal to every delegate to vote for him. Let Ohio be solid. Make the same appeal in my name to North Carolina and every delegate who has voted for me."

On the next ballot—the thirty-fourth—17

votes were given to James A. Garfield, who managed Sherman's affairs. Garfield protested: "I rise to a point of order. No man has a right without the consent of the person voted for to announce that person's name and vote for him in this convention. Such consent I have no given." The chairman of the convention inter rupted him, and Garfield had to sit down.

Now the delegates saw how the deadlock could be broken. On the thirty-fifth ballot 5 of the Blaine votes were transferred to Garfield At this trial Grant was still leading with 31 votes against Blaine's 257 and Sherman's 99. Bu the Garfield bandwagon was on the move. O the next ballot most of the Blaine votes wer

MONEY FLOWED FREELY in the campaign. Here Republican Chairman Marshall Jewell and Democratic Chairman William H. Barnum beg for funds. The Republican tells government employes to contribute so that they can "keep the places;" the Democrat woos them with the hope that their money will help them "to get the places."

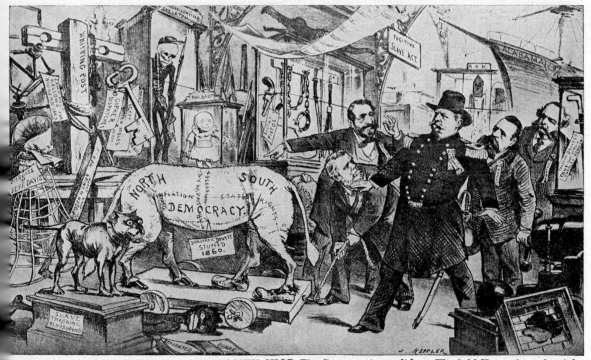

INSPECTING THE DEMOCRATIC CURIOSITY SHOP. The Democratic candidate, Winfield Hancock, at the sight of the old, two-ended Bourbon war-horse, exclaims in horror: "Great Scott! Am I to be the head of that?"

THE VOTES IN THE 1880 ELECTION

STATES	POPULAR VOTE				ELECTORAL VOTE	
	James A. Garfield, Ohio. Republican	Winfield S. Hancock, Pa. Democrat	James B. Weaver, Iowa. Greenbacker	Neal Dow, Maine. Prohibitionist	Garfield and Arthur.	Hancock and English.
Ala...........	56,221	91,185	4,642	—	—	10
Ark...........	42,436	60,775	4,079	—	—	6
Calif.........	80,348	80,426	3,392	—	1	5
Colo..........	27,450	24,647	1,435	—	3	—
Conn..........	67,071	64,415	868	409	6	—
Del...........	14,133	15,275	120	—	—	3
Fla...........	23,654	27,964	—	—	—	4
Ga............	54,086	102,470	969	—	—	11
Ill...........	318,037	277,321	26,358	443	21	—
Ind...........	232,164	225,522	12,986	—	15	—
Iowa..........	183,927	105,845	32,701	592	11	—
Kan...........	121,549	59,801	19,851	25	5	—
Ky............	106,306	149,068	11,499	258	—	12
La............	38,637	65,067	439	—	—	8
Me............	74,039	65,171	4,408	93	7	—
Md............	78,515	93,706	818	—	—	8
Mass..........	165,205	111,960	4,548	682	13	—
Mich.........	185,341	131,597	34,895	942	11	—
Minn.........	93,903	53,315	3,267	286	5	—
Miss.........	34,854	75,750	5,797	—	—	8
Mo...........	153,567	208,609	35,135	—	—	15
Neb..........	54,979	28,523	3,950	—	3	—
Nev..........	8,732	9,613	—	—	—	3
N. H.........	44,852	40,794	528	180	5	—
N. J.........	120,555	122,565	2,617	191	—	9
N. Y.........	555,544	534,511	12,373	1,517	35	—
N. C.........	115,874	124,208	1,126	—	—	10
Ohio........	375,048	340,821	6,456	2,616	22	—
Ore.........	20,619	19,948	249	—	3	—
Pa..........	444,704	407,428	20,668	1,939	29	—
R. I........	18,195	10,779	236	20	4	—
S. C........	58,071	112,312	566	—	—	7
Tenn........	107,677	128,191	5,917	43	—	12
Tex.........	57,893	156,428	27,405	—	—	8
Vt..........	45,567	18,316	1,215	—	5	—
Va..........	84,020	128,586	—	—	—	11
W. Va.......	46,243	57,391	9,079	—	—	5
Wis.........	144,400	114,649	7,986	69	10	—
	4,454,416	4,444,952	308,578	10,305	214	155

Louisiana voted for two Republican tickets. Maine voted for a fusion Democratic ticket, consisting of three Democrats and four Greenbackers; it also voted for a straight Greenback ticket. Virginia voted for two Democratic tickets. Total vote, 9,218,958

HANCOCK'S NOMINATION, according to W. A. Rog infuses the emaciated Democratic party with new bl

GARFIELD IS CONGRATULATED by friends and zens of Cleveland after his nomination by the Republic

GENERAL GRANT ACKNOWLEDGES a great Republican campaign demonstration in New York on October 11.

The Nation, "a singular document, and suggests the conclusion that all the conventions have now begun to treat the platform as a joke. It appears to have been the composition of Mr. Watterson, of the Louisville *Courier-Journal*, and reads like a highly inflammatory 'editorial' from that

DEMOCRATIC TROJAN HORSE. "Forewarned, de-fenders of the city will not be misled by a figurehead."

"WHO IS TARIFF?" asks Democratic Candidate Hancock in this cartoon by Nast, "and why is he for revenue only?"

CAMPAIGNING. Garfield gave numerous talks from back of his train. Here he speaks at Poughkeepsie.

REPUBLICAN CANDIDATES James Garfield and Chester Arthur meet at the railroad station in Albany, N. Y.

paper. It pledges the party to its constitutional doctrines and traditions; promises opposition to 'centralizationism,' the 'dangerous spirit of encroachment,' and the consolidation of the power of all departments in one; declares that there must be 'no sumptuary laws,' and insists on 'the separation of Church and state,' without defining it; and 'honest money,' but evades the silver question; and demands a tariff for revenue only. It insists on the subordination of the military to the civil power; on 'a general and thorough reform of the civil service,' without saying in

"FORBIDDING THE BANNS"—ONE OF KEPPLER'S BOLDEST CARTOONS AGAINST GARFIELD, W

James Garfield is shown as the bride of Uncle Sam. Behind him are his two prim bridesmaids—Carl Schurz and Whitelaw Reid—and Marshall Jewell, Republican com- mittee chairman. At the last minute William H. Barnum the Democratic chairman, appears with the Crédit Mobi ier baby. Garfield, who was supposed to have taken

what such a reform would consist; and on a 'free ballot.' It castigates the Republicans in the usual style for the exercise of 'corrupt and despotic power' at elections, for fraud in 1876-7, and 'execrates' the Administration for 'making places in the civil service a reward for political crime'; demands legislation prohibiting in future

the 'billeting of villains on the people'; glorifie Samuel J. Tilden, and bids him goodby; de nounces Chinese immigration except for 'trave education, and foreign commerce,' and suggest the use of public money for public purpose only; pronounces the Democratic party the pro tector of the laboring man from 'the cormorant

REW FOR THE POLITICAL WEEKLY, *PUCK*.

mall bribe from the Crédit Mobilier funds—$329 only—
ys bashfully: "But it was such a little one." In the cam-
aign, the figure 329 was used as a cabalistic symbol.

nd the Commune,' an alliteration which must
ave greatly tickled the author, but the meaning
f which is painfully uncertain; and finally, con-
ratulates the country on 'the honesty and thrift
f the Democratic Congress.' The reading of it,
xcept the plank about the *billeting of villains*
. . is said to have received but little attention."

TWO NAST CARTOONS AGAINST HANCOCK

353

THE INAUGURATION OF PRESIDENT GARFIELD WAS CELEBRATED BY AN ELABORATE BALL, H▌

There were smaller parties holding nominating conventions. The National Greenback Labor party met in Chicago and chose General James B. Weaver as their candidate for Presi-

dent. The Prohibitionists nominated Genera▌ Neal Dow, a militant Quaker from Main▌

Between the two major parties there wer▌ no clearly defined issues. "Both parties wer▌

NEW BUILDING OF THE NATIONAL MUSEUM.

THE CABINET. Clockwise: Windom, Secretary of the Treasury; Hunt, Secretary of the Navy; McVeagh, Attorney General; Kirkwood, Secretary of the Interior; James, Postmaster General; Lincoln, Secretary of War; Blaine, Secretary of State, and President James A. Garfield.

THE TWO NEW YORK SENATORS, Roscoe Conkling and Thomas Platt, resigned from their posts after a bitter quarrel with President Garfield over the questions of patronage and "senatorial courtesy." When Conkling submitted his resignation, Platt declared: "Me too."

ompletely bankrupt," writes the historian John). Hicks. "The issues that divided them were istorical merely. The Republican Party had ome into existence because of the stand it had taken on slavery, and it had lived on because of its determination to free the slaves, to save the Union, and to punish the South. Its program was now finished and its excuse for existence

355

THE ASSASSIN, Charles J. Guiteau, a disappointed office seeker, made his successful attempt on Garfield's life in order "to rid the country of a traitor" and elevate the Stalwart, Chester Arthur, to the Presidency.

WAITING FOR THE AMBULANCE, Garfield is supported by a Mrs. Smith. Secretary of State James G. Blaine, who was with Garfield, is overcome by horror.

CONTEMPORARY REPRESENTATION OF THE

had disappeared. The Democrats, likewise, ha so long centered their attention upon the issue of slavery, the Civil War, and reconstructio that they failed to observe that the era in whic

THE WASHINGTON RAILWAY STATION ON JULY 2, 1881. GARFIELD WAS SHOT IN THE BACK.

these issues meant anything had rolled by. The platforms of the two parties in 1880 revealed few real differences of opinion as to policies and no real awareness of the problems that con-

fronted the nation. Neither Democrats nor Republicans seemed to sense the significance of the vast transformation that was coming over business, nor the critical nature of the relationship

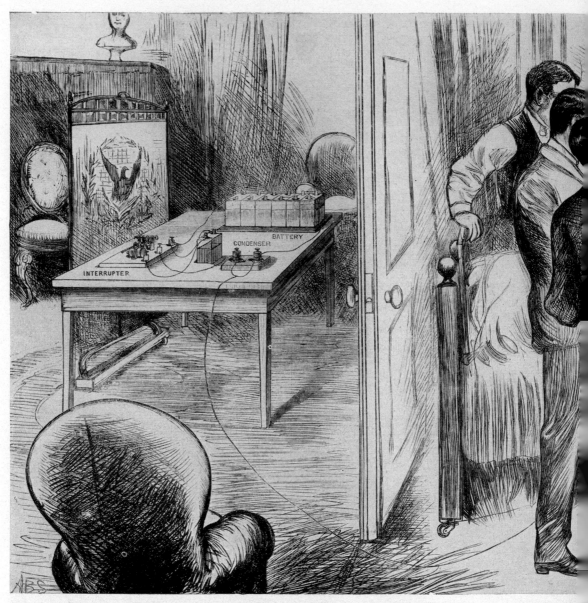

IN A BEDROOM OF THE WHITE HOUSE DOCTORS TRY TO DISCOVER THE EXACT LOCATION O

between labor and capital, nor even the necessity of doing something definite about civil service reform, the money problem, and the tariff. The Republican Party existed to oppose the Democratic Party. Real issues cut across both parties, and even when recognized, which was rare, had to be evaded or ignored. When the Republican Convention prepared to adopt the customary meaningless platitudes about civil service reform, a delegate from Texas named

Flanagan protested in plain language: 'Wh: are we here for?' What, indeed, if not for th offices?"

Without real political issues at stake—save th tariff question—the campaign turned to a livel and exhaustive discussion of the beliefs, behavic and private lives of Garfield and Hancock. Bot the Republicans and the Democrats exploite their candidates' war records. Each party did utmost to outdo the other in playing up th

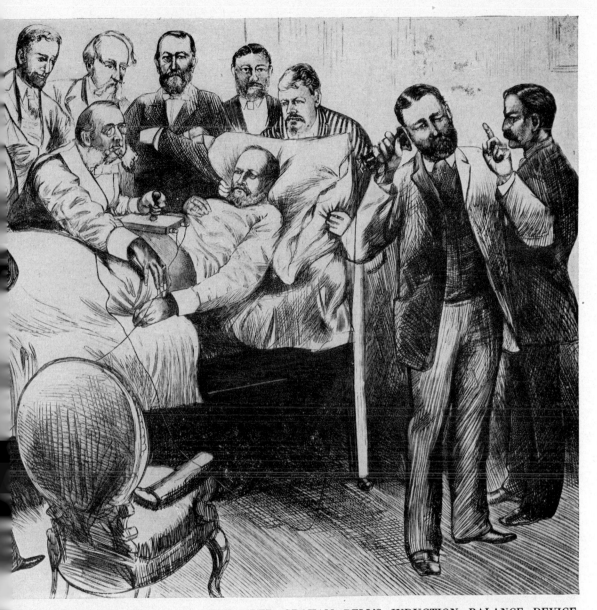

…IN'S BULLET BY MEANS OF ALEXANDER GRAHAM BELL'S INDUCTION BALANCE DEVICE.

…eroism of its man and minimizing the bravery …f the other.

Republican orators again attempted to "wave …e bloody shirt," but sectional hatred, sectional …ifferences failed to stir any more. Democratic …rators recalled the frauds of the last election …—that did not work either.

The "silver-tongued" Robert G. Ingersoll …implified the issues of the election: "I believe …1 a party that believes in good crops; that is glad when a fellow finds a gold mine; that rejoices when there are forty bushels of wheat to the acre. . . . The Democratic party is a party of famine; it is a good friend of an early frost, it believes in the Colorado beetle and the weevil."

Garfield was attacked by the Democrats because he was the alleged recipient of a $329 dividend from the ill-famed Crédit Mobilier, the holding company of the Union Pacific Rail-

CABINET MEMBERS listen gravely to Dr. Agnew's report. Secretary of State Blaine is seated at the table. Fourth from the left is Secretary of War Robert Lincoln.

THE PRESIDENT'S WIFE, who nursed her mortally wounded husband with great devotion, prepares special food for Garfield in the kitchen of the White House.

A *HARPER'S WEEKLY* ARTIST WAS ALLOWE

road. When the Union Pacific—in 1867—fear legislation adverse to its interests, the com pany distributed valuable stocks to membe of Congress, and Garfield was one of the The Garfield supporters daringly accepted t

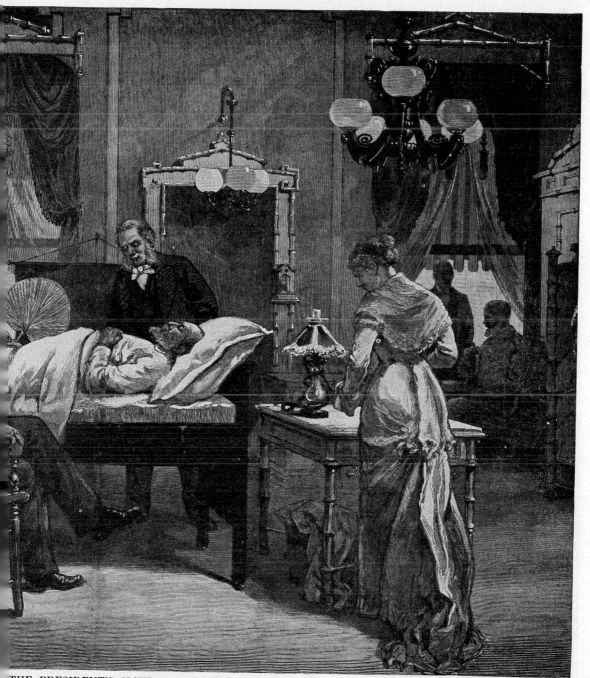

THE PRESIDENT'S SICKROOM IN THE WHITE HOUSE AND DRAW THIS AUTHENTIC PICTURE.

ue. They painted the number 329 on trans-
rencies, they shouted, "Three twenty-nine,"
ey chalked 329 on walls, scratched it on doors
til the number acquired the mysterious signi-
ance of a cabalistic symbol.

Another effective piece of Democratic campaign propaganda was the forging of Garfield's
name to a letter advocating the admission of
Chinese labor to California. During the final
days of the campaign this letter was reproduced

in thousands of copies and distributed along the West coast, where it influenced many voters.

There were cheaper slurs. It was said that Garfield had an unpaid tailor's bill at Troy, New York, and that during the war he had stolen furniture and bedding from a widow in the South.

General Hancock, "the Superb," was a less vulnerable target than Garfield. His past was blameless; he was a colorless man. The Chicago *Tribune* wrote that the General "does nothing but eat, drink, and enjoy himself sensually." Another newspaper asserted that Hancock's son had made a clandestine marriage with a young lady whose father was a rebel sympathizer.

And so the campaign continued, following the usual pattern of charge and countercharge, of personal invective, slurring, and mudslinging. Garfield, who did his utmost to please both the Stalwarts and the Half-Breeds, won by a small margin. His majority was not more than 9,464 out of a vote of over nine million. From the thirty-eight states taking part in the election, he received 4,454,416 votes against Hancock's 4,444,952. The smaller candidates held the balance. James B. Weaver polled 308,578 Greenback votes, Neal Dow 10,305 from the Prohibitionists. If either of them had thrown his support to Hancock, the Democrats would have won easily.

Garfield's presidential term had hardly begun when it was over. On July 2, 1881, four months after he took the oath, he was shot by Charles J. Guiteau, a disappointed office seeker, as he entered the railway station in Washington. Guiteau's motive was to rid the country of a "traitor" and elevate the "Stalwart" Arthur to the Presidency. For weeks Garfield battled for his life. On September 19 he died, and Chester Alan Arthur became President.

TO ESCAPE THE HEAT of Washington, President Garfield is removed from the White House at great risk and sent by special train to a cottage in Elberon, N. J. But his life could not be saved and he died a few weeks later.

362

ARTHUR TAKES THE OATH OF OFFICE. At half-past one in the morning of September 20, a few hours after resident Garfield died, Judge Brady administered the oath to Vice-President Chester Arthur at his private home.

CLEVELAND'S INAUGURAL ADDRESS

THE TWENTY-FIFTH ELECTION—1884

GROVER CLEVELAND

Before Chester A. Arthur stepped into high office he was known as a friend of the spoilsman and an enemy of the reformers, but as Chief Magistrate he suggested to Congress that "original appointments should be based upon a certain fitness"—the same demand as was voiced by the reformers.

To remedy existing conditions in the civil service, a bill was introduced by "Gentleman George" Pendleton and passed by the Democratic Congress in 1883. This law—the Pendleton Act—authorized the President to appoint three civil service commissioners, who were to provide "open competitive examinations for testing the fitness of applicants for the public service," leaving it to the President to expand the "classified service" as he saw fit. At first only the lowest officers were classified—about 12 per cent of the total appointees—but gradually the list increased, circumstances furthering its expansion. As it happened, Arthur—a Republican President—was succeeded by Cleveland—a Democrat, who was followed by Harri-

son—a Republican. Harrison gave way to Cleveland again, and after Cleveland came McKinley —a Republican. As each President—before leaving office—desired to protect his appointees, the classified list was extended. Thus the office-holders already "blanketed" into the civil service could remain in their jobs without taking the required examinations, but after their places were vacated through resignation or death, their successors could receive appointments only on recommendation of the commission. Thus the civil service grew. By 1900 the number of civil servants under the merit system was about a hundred thousand; by 1919 it almost topped the half-million mark.

The other major effort of the Arthur administration was the revision of the tariff. The high protection rates slowed down and hurt our overseas trade; foreign countries erected barriers in retaliation, and American raw products met with discrimination abroad. As the United States was in dire need of foreign markets, tariff revision became a necessity.

365

GROVER CLEVELAND (1837-1908), the very able Governor of New York, was chosen by the Democrats. He was supported by the Independent Republicans—known as "Mugwumps."

THOMAS A. HENDRICKS (1819-1885), quadrennial presidential candidate, a conservative "old-guard" Democrat from Indiana, was chosen for second place but died within a year.

JAME. G. BLAINE (1830-1893), again candidate for the Republican nomination, was chosen despite opposition from the party reform element, and almost won the election.

JOHN A. LOGAN (1826-1886), a general in the Civil War, was Blaine's running mate. The Republicans lost New York—and with it the election — by only 1,149 popular votes.

BENJAMIN F. BUTLER (1818-1893) of Massachusetts, who had the surreptitious support of Tammany Hall, was the official Greenback candidate, with Alanson West as running mate.

JOHN P. ST. JOHN (1833-1916) of Kansas was the candidate of the Prohibitionists. With William Daniel of Maryland as his running mate, he received over 150,000 votes.

OUTSIDE THE HALL good Republicans who could find seats within rejoice in cheering the candid[

Both issues—the tariff and civil service reform—cut across party lines. In general the Republicans favored high duties, while the Democrat advocated tariff for revenue only. But ther were many tariff reformers in the Republica ranks, and the Democrats had their share protectionists. Similarly, civil service reforme could be found in both parties. As party lin were indistinct, the outcome of the election d pended more upon the character and personal ties of the prospective candidates than on pol ical principles.

The Republicans met first as usual. Th chaplain who opened the proceedings in Ch cago on June 3 thanked God for the splend history of the party and expressed the hope th

366

DE THE HALL pandemonium broke loose when Blaine's name was put in nomination. The convention be- u "mass meeting of maniacs." Though the Independent wing of the party strongly opposed Blaine, he won.

he coming political campaign may be con- icted with that decency, intelligence, patriot- m and dignity of temper which become a free id intelligent people." If Reverend Griswold uld only have looked into the future, his ords would have been even more fervent.

The most prominent name before the dele- tes was James G. Blaine. The Plumed Knight d sought the nomination twice before—in 76 and in 1880; both times the Republicans ose someone else.

Since the last convention Blaine had been arfield's Secretary of State; his policies—to it a closer relationship between the South nerican republics and the United States, to ex- id United States trade in Latin America, and

to construct across the Isthmus of Panama a canal which would be controlled solely by this country—were policies of a statesman with vision. Unfortunately Blaine had had no oppor- tunity to carry them out. With Garfield's death he gave up his office, retired into private life, and wrote his memoirs, *Twenty Years in Con- gress*, with an eye on the next election.

From the very first day of the Republican convention, the delegates fought over his can- didacy. The national committee, in which his supporters had the upper hand, attempted to secure the convention's temporary chairman- ship for ex-Governor Powell Clayton of Ar- kansas, a Blaine man. Henry Cabot Lodge pro- tested against this and suggested John R.

(*turn to page 370*)

A FAMOUS POLITICAL CARTOON: GILLAM'S SATIRE ON JAMES G. BLAINE, THE TATTOO

ERSONAL HONESTY WAS STAINED BY HIS DEALS WITH THE LITTLE ROCK RAILROAD.

THE DELEGATES CHEER after Grover Cleveland—whose nomination for the Presidency was at first violent[ly] fought by the Tammany delegation—became the official choice of the convention without further oppositio[n]

TORCHLIGHT PROCESSION in Chicago for Cleveland, who was loved "for the enemies he has made."

INSIDE THE HALL of the convention after the u[nit] rule was upheld, ensuring Cleveland's nominati[on]

Lynch, a Negro delegate from Mississippi, for the post. Then twenty-five-year-old Theodore Roosevelt, delegate at large from New York, climbed the rostrum, removed his dapper straw hat, and making his first appearance on the national stage, urged the delegates to vote individually for the temporary chairman. "Let each man stand accountable to those whom he rep[re]sents for his vote," said Roosevelt sternly. "[Let] no man be able to shelter himself behind t[he] shield of his state. . . . One of the cardinal do[c]trines of American government is the accou[nt]ability of each man to his people; and let ea[ch] man stand up here and cast his vote a[s]

THE DEMOCRATIC CANDIDATE AND THE ASSASSIN. John Kelly, leader of Tammany, trying to rob Cleveland of the nomination, threw his support to the blundering, former Radical Republican, Gen. Benjamin Butler.

can go home and abide by what he has done."
With their proposal accepted and Lynch
safely installed in the chair, the anti-Blaine
forces were in happy expectation of things
to come. But the selection of the temporary
chairman turned out to be their only vic-

tory during the convention's proceedings.
The struggle for Blaine's nomination and his
acceptance by the whole party, if nominated,
continued. A resolution was offered whereby
no delegate was to be entitled to hold his seat
who would not pledge himself to support the

(turn to page 374)

THE PLUMED KNIGHT, as Thomas Nast pictured James G. Blaine, holds the fort behind a barricade of money-bags.

DONNING THE CLEAN SHIRT of Reform, unfamiliar with the garment, puts it on upside

ASKING FOR THE IRISH VOTE Blaine says that when he is President, he will take strong steps against Britain.

ASKING FOR LABOR VOTE he begs q "Does public plunder for private gain protect

PERSONALITY. One part of Blaine wanted
le the Mulligan scandal, the other to fight it.

BLAINE'S CARPETBAG refers to his memoirs, *Twenty
Years in Congress,* with which he bid for the nomination.

RISHMEN try to carry James G. Blaine into
ite House, but Uncle Sam blocks the door.

FINANCIER JAY GOULD offers Blaine a partnership.
He will accept it if ". . . I'm let in on the ground floor."

THE DEMOCRATS ATTACKED BLAINE by making public some of his recently discovered corresponden
which revealed that he probably had been guilty of accepting bribes from the Little Rock railroad of Arkan

nominee of the convention. "There are already
whispers in the air," said George Knight of
California, presenting the proposal, "of men
high in the Republican party, or that once
stood high in the party, openly and avowedly
declaring that they will not support one man
if he be nominated by this convention. . . .
That kind of men we want to know, and the
sooner they are out of the Republican party,
the better." As Knight referred to certain editors in his speech, George William Curtis, the
editor of *Harper's Weekly* and one of the tar-

gets of Knight's attack, rose and protested w
great emotion. "A Republican and a free n
I came into this convention. By the grace
God, a Republican and a free man I will
out of this convention. Twenty-four years a
I was here in Chicago and took part with
men who nominated the man who bears
most illustrious name in the Republican pa
The gentleman last upon the floor says that
dares any man on this floor to vote against
resolution. I say to him in reply that the pres
tation of such a resolution in a convention s

THE REPUBLICANS ATTACKED CLEVELAND because he once had an illicit relationship with a thirty-six-year-old woman, Maria Halpin. There was strong evidence that Cleveland was the father of her illegitimate son.

this is a stigma, is an insult to every honor-ble member who sits here." After Curtis's eech, which was strongly applauded, Knight ithdrew the resolution.

A vague and noncommittal platform was opted, and the delegates listened patiently to ng-winded nominating speeches. Judge West, eaking for Blaine, orated: "Nominate him and e campfires and beacon lights will illuminate e continent from the Golden Gate to Cleo-tra's Needle. Nominate him and the millions no are now waiting will rally to swell the column of victory that is sweeping on." As he mentioned Blaine's name, pandemonium broke loose in the hall. The delegates jumped on the chairs, the cheering deepened into a roar, "fully as deafening as the voice of Niagara." Flags, shields, and banners were stripped from the walls, people danced in excitement and paraded up and down the aisles, shouting, cheering, and repeating the magic name. It was a scene unre-hearsed and fresh, born of enthusiasm. Men tore off their coats and waved them wildly, others tossed hats and umbrellas into the air.

A helmet, decorated with a white plume, was carried on the platform.

Andrew D. White, president of Cornell University, who was present as a delegate at large from New York, described the scene as "absolutely unworthy of a convention of any party, a disgrace to decency, and a blot upon the reputation of our country."

The tide of eloquence following this outburst lasted long past midnight. Sixteen nominating speeches were made, taking five full hours to deliver. When the balloting began the next morning, Blaine was leading on the first roll call with 334½ votes. President Arthur—backed by all the Southern delegates—had 278 votes Senator Edmunds, the "presidential glazier" and candidate of the reformers, followed with 9: votes. General John A. Logan of Illinois had 63½ votes, Senator John Sherman of Ohio had 30, while the remaining votes were divided among a number of lesser candidates. Genera William Tecumseh Sherman, whose nomination was boosted by his friends, told inquirers that "in no event and under no circumstances" would he be a presidential candidate. He said in a letter to Blaine that he would account him

"GLORYING IN THEIR SHAME" is the name of this Nast cartoon showing Blaine, "the thick-skinned animal," in arena with W. W. Phelps and Whitelaw Reid on his back. It alludes to Godkin's widely-quoted remark that wh he was Secretary of State, the Plumed Knight had "wallowed in spoils like a rhinoceros in an African po

"HIS SIN." Henry Ward Beecher, who staunchly defended Grover Cleveland against vicious personal attacks, was himself assailed by the cartoonists. Here Beecher says to Cleveland: "Your burden is too heavy; let me carry it."

elf "a fool, a madman, an ass," to embark, at ixty-five years of age, on a political career.

If the Arthur and Edmunds forces could have een merged behind President Arthur, Blaine ould have been robbed of the nomination. ut the opposition to Arthur—notably from the Jew England states—would not compromise. hus Blaine became the candidate of the Reublicans on the fifth ballot.

The reaction to his nomination was immediate. The reform element of the party was in an uproar. They fought Blaine bitterly, for they desired a candidate who would not be dominated by special groups, party bosses and grafters. They were averse to a man whose past was tainted by corruption, who, as Godkin said, "had wallowed in spoils like a rhinoceros in an African pool."

CARTOONS AGAINST THE MUGWUMPS

THE INDEPENDENT REPUBLICANS are tempted by G. W. Curtis, the editor of *Harper's Weekly*, with an apple from the Garden of Eden—it is Cleveland's head.

THE MUGWUMPS WAIT with their cronies to get into the White House. Carl Schurz carries the Independent party, while George Curtis sits on the step

THE INDEPENDENTS were not very numerous, wrote *The Judge*. "This is the third time they have marched around. There are about nine of them, not ninety thousand."

The revolt against Blaine spread with the speed of lightning. Republican newspapers refused to support him; reform clubs and independent committees within the party were "united to rebuke corrupt men and corrupt methods in politics." The split within the party widened. Prominent Republicans fighting for reforms met with leading Democrats and told them that if the Democratic convention would name an honest and progressive candidate, acceptable to the Republican reformers, they would not only campaign for him, but would vote for him as well.

This augured well for the Democrats. With the votes of the Independent Republicans, their candidate was certain to win. They rallied behind Grover Cleveland, the reform Governor of New York, who was thoroughly acceptable to the bolting Republicans.

When the Democratic delegates arrived

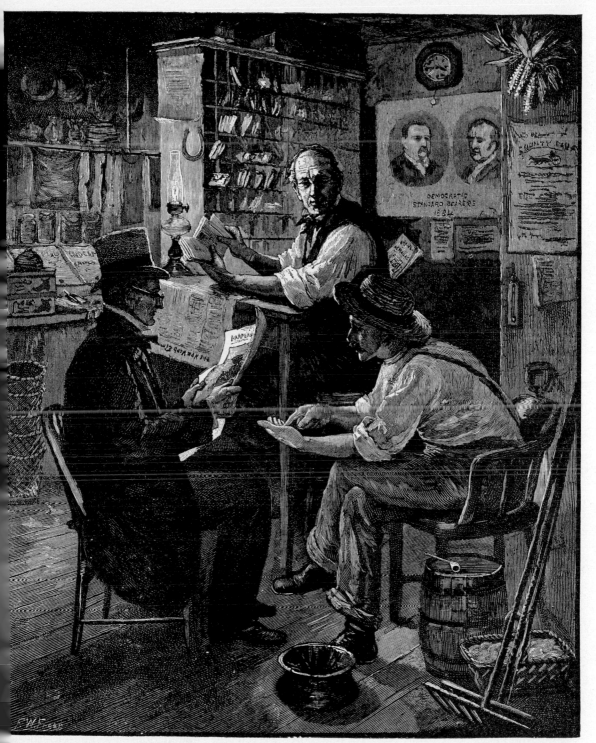

THE BIG QUESTION of the campaign: "Should Mr. Blaine be honored with the Presidency when his mere nomination has so shamefully lowered the moral tone of the Party?" Debated in every village and hamlet, in post offices and drugstores, it was the main point of controversy between conservative and progressive Republicans.

Chicago, Cleveland's name was on all lips. His not-too-dangerous rivals for the nomination were Thomas F. Bayard of Delaware and the old and infirm Allen G. Thurman of Ohio.

But far weightier than they was the opposition of Tammany Hall. John Kelly, the leader of the Tammany delegation, said pointedly to an interviewer when he was asked about Cleveland's chances: "Butler is a good man." He meant General Benjamin Butler, the former Radical Republican, now the Tammany candidate. And for a day or two it seemed that Tammany might muster enough strength to block Cleveland's nomination. But when the Brooklyn delegation declared itself for him, the vote of New York was secure for Cleveland. "Fire and smoke burst from the nostrils of Tammany," reported the New York *Sun;* "their henchmen paced the lobbies raging like lions."

Still, Tammany would not give up the fight. On the first day of the convention it opposed the acceptance of the unit rule, thus trying to split the electoral votes of New York. And when the convention upheld the unit rule and Cleveland's name was officially put before the delegates, Grady, one of Tammany's leaders, shouted: "Cleveland cannot carry the state of New York."

Over this a prolonged debate began. Some of the delegates extolled Cleveland's virtues, others spoke denouncing him. The feeling of the majority was best expressed by Edward S. Bragg of Wisconsin, who said that the convention was sick of Tammany; sick of its greed, its jealous spirit, its squabbles, its predictions of defeat. Bragg recalled that Tammany was always kicking and bolting; it had opposed Tilden and stabbed Hancock in the back; during the past years it was responsible for nothing but mischief. He concluded that the young men of Wisconsin, in whose name he spoke, "love Cleveland for his character, but they love him also for the enemies he has made."

Grady, red in the face, was on his feet in an instant. "On behalf of his enemies I reciprocate the sentiment." But it was rearguard action; Tammany had lost the fight. It could no longer take the nomination from Grover Cleveland, who on the first ballot received 392 votes against Bayard's 170, Thurman's 88, and Randall's 78. After this, the meeting adjourned.

GENERAL BUTLER, THE CANDIDATE OF TAM

During the night a bargain was made betwe the managers of Cleveland and Samuel J. Ra dall, Pennsylvania's favorite son, who was to lease his delegates to the New Yorker in retu for the control of the patronage in Penns vania. Thus on the second ballot Cleveland ceived the nomination. To console the guard, Thomas A. Hendricks of Indiana w chosen for the Vice-Presidency.

HE PRESIDENTIAL NOMINEE OF THE GREENBACK PARTY, GETS HIS SUPPORTERS INTO LINE.

What kind of a person was the man who was ble to rally the Democrats and Independent Republicans behind him? The Boston *Adver-iser* summed him up: "Cleveland is stout, has well-fed look, is indeed a good liver, has the ir of a man who has made up his mind just ow he ought to behave in any position where e may find himself. He is getting bald; he is etting gray—though his white hair does not show conspicuously, as his complexion is sandy. He dresses well, carries himself well, talks well on any subject with which he is familiar, and on any subject with which he is not familiar he does not venture to talk at all."

Besides the two major conventions, a number of smaller conventions were held. The Greenbackers named General Benjamin F. Butler for the Presidency, as did the Anti-Monopoly party, which declared in its platform that "labor and capital should be allies" and that "corporations, the creatures of law, should be controlled by law."

The Independent Republicans, meeting in New York City, rejected the motion to form a third party and agreed to support Grover Cleveland. In their address to the country, they declared that "the paramount issue this year is moral rather than political." They were given the nickname "Mugwumps," an Algonquin Indian term, meaning "chief." They asked for an honest government, conducted in an efficient and economical way, and not one which would serve the selfish interests of special groups. They wanted a President whose integrity was without blemish, and they demanded civil service reform.

As the campaign progressed, the number of Mugwumps grew. Carl Schurz, Henry Ward Beecher, President Eliot of Harvard were Mugwumps. Republican newspapers joined the crusade for good and honest government. The New York *Times*, the *Herald* and the *Evening Post* were against Blaine; *Harper's Weekly*, *The Nation* and *Puck* turned away from him. Their lead was followed by many others all over the country.

With no political issues to argue—both parties being in agreement over the national policy—the campaign became nothing more than an exposé of the personal lives of the two contestants.

The Independents unearthed and published further compromising letters of Blaine's relating to his business deals with the Little Rock and Fort Smith Railroad. The letters deepened the suspicion that Blaine, who had so indignantly asserted his innocence after the "Mulligan Letters" became known, was not so guiltless after all. The Plumed Knight had ended an incriminating note to Warren Fisher, a business associate, with the remarks: "Kind regards to Mrs. Fisher. Burn this letter." As soon as the letter was made public, these two sentences became one of the main slogans of the campaign. Democratic demonstrators chanted in unison:

"Burn this letter! Burn this letter!
Kind regards to Mrs. Fisher."

"THE ANGEL OF LIGHT" IS NO ONE ELS

and:

"Blaine! Blaine! James G. Blaine!
The con-ti-nen-tal liar from the
state of Maine."

The Mugwumps attacked Blaine with mercy. The English-born cartoonist Gill drew him as a tattooed man for *Puck*; Godl

ER CLEVELAND, AS PAINTED BY HENRY WARD BEECHER AND ADMIRED BY CURTIS AND SCHURZ.

n *The Nation*, printed a series of Blaine's con-
radictory statements in parallel columns. These
vere distributed in pamphlet form by the hun-
lreds of thousands.

Would the Republicans suffer these attacks
n their candidate without retaliation? No, they
vould not. On July 21st, the Buffalo *Evening
Telegram* printed an article headlined, "A Ter-

rible Tale," which revealed that some time before Cleveland had carried on illicit relations
with a thirty-six-year-old widow, Maria Halpin,
and that she had borne him an illegitimate child.
Now Cleveland's name was sullied no less
than Blaine's. Other newspapers took up the
attack, magnifying, falsifying, and embellishing
the facts.

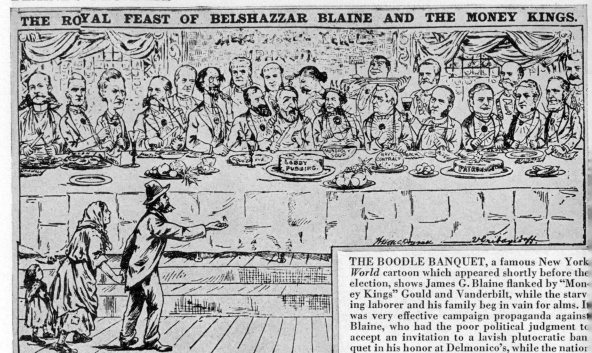

THE ROYAL FEAST OF BELSHAZZAR BLAINE AND THE MONEY KINGS.

THE BOODLE BANQUET, a famous New York *World* cartoon which appeared shortly before the election, shows James G. Blaine flanked by "Money Kings" Gould and Vanderbilt, while the starving laborer and his family beg in vain for alms. It was very effective campaign propaganda against Blaine, who had the poor political judgment to accept an invitation to a lavish plutocratic banquet in his honor at Delmonico's, while the nation was in the throes of a severe economic depression.

The dismayed Democrats asked Cleveland how to combat the accusations, and Cleveland replied with great common sense: "Tell the truth!" It was true that he had had illicit relations with Maria Halpin, but whether the child was his he did not know. Neither did the bibulous Mrs. Halpin seem to be certain about it.

Had the scandal been publicized before the Democratic convention, Cleveland would probably not have been nominated. And had it been published somewhat later—nearer to election day—he might have lost the contest. But as it happened, the Democrats had enough time to counteract the damage. They argued that the real issue of the election was not the private conduct of the candidates, but their public integrity. "We are told that Mr. Blaine has been delinquent in office but blameless in private life," a Mugwump said, "while Mr. Cleveland has been a model of official integrity but culpable in his personal relations. We should therefore elect Mr. Cleveland to the public office which he is so well qualified to fill and remand

THE REVEREND DR. BURCHARD near the end of the campaign made a speech referring to the Democratic party as one "whose antecedents have been rum, Romanism and rebellion." As Blaine, who was on the platform, failed to repudiate this attack on Catholicism, it was asserted that the remark turned enough of the Irish Catholic voters against him to lose the election.

A VOTER CASTS HIS BALLOT: WILL IT BE BLAINE, CLEVELAND OR THE BOTTLED-UP BUTLER?

Mr. Blaine to the private station which he is admirably fitted to adorn." Godkin, in *The Nation*, was even more to the point. Which was better for the Presidency, he asked, a man who like Cromwell, Franklin, Hamilton, and Webster had been unchaste, or a man who had sold his word in order to destroy documentary evidence of his corruption?

A CITIZEN GOES FORTH TO THE POLLS, GAILY DECORATED WITH EMBLEMS OF THE ELECTION

35 Precincts out of 112 in Hamilton Co Ohio Show met Rep. gain 2067

ELECTION NIGHT in Columbus, Ohio. A magic lantern projects returns on a screen, delighting the audience.

In the cities the Republican marchers measured their steps to the rhythm of a jingle, chanting in derision:

"Ma! Ma! Where's my pa?
Gone to the White House. *Ha! Ha! Ha!*"

At first some of the Republican leaders refused to stump for Blaine. Conkling, when asked why he was not speaking for him, gave the classic answer: "I do not engage in criminal practice." But as the campaign progressed, most of the recalcitrants fell in line and came out for the Plumed Knight—even rebellious Theodore Roosevelt spoke for him.

In the final weeks it became more and more evident that the election would be decided by a small margin. Tammany's opposition to Cleveland was fraught with danger. If enough votes could be withheld from him in New York City—Tammany's stronghold—Cleveland would lose the election.

Fate came to Cleveland's rescue. A delega

*CROWDS ARE WAITING FOR THE
RETURNS BEFORE NEW YORK
SUN AND TIMES BUILDINGS*

"STABBED IN THE BACK" was the title of this cartoon in the Blaine-supporting weekly, *The Judge*.

tion of clergymen met Blaine in New York and one of them, Dr. Burchard, made a speech in which he referred to the Democratic party as one "whose antecedents have been rum, Romanism and rebellion." The campaign-tired Blaine probably did not even hear the words. But the newspapers reported them in headlines. Blaine was accused of being an anti-Catholic because he did not repudiate the sentiments at once. When he denounced the statement, it was too late; election day was around the corner and the Democrats knew how to keep aflame the anger of the large Catholic voting population in New York. As Blaine lost that decisive state by only the slight margin of 1,149 votes out of a total of 1,167,214, it is probable that except for Burchard's speech he would have become President of the United States.

There were other incidents which may have influenced the final result. One was the humiliat-

ing treatment of Miss Frances E. Willard by the Republican platform committee in Chicago. Miss Willard came to the convention with a petition signed by 20,000 people asking the Republicans to support the temperance cause. The members of the committee took her petition, and when she left, asked a delegation of brewers and distillers what they should do with it. "Kick it under the table" was the advice—and that is where the petition was found. The Prohibitionists redoubled their efforts. In the election their candidate polled over 150,000 votes, most of them taken from the Republicans.

Another was a banquet at Delmonico's shortly before election day, attended by the wealthiest people in the country. Blaine, who was fond of the rich, believing them to be the

THE VOTES IN THE 1884 ELECTION

| STATES | POPULAR VOTE | | | | ELECTORAL VOTE | |
	Grover Cleveland, N.Y. Democrat	James G. Blaine, Me. Republican	Benjamin F. Butler, Mass. Greenbacker	John P. St. John, Kan. Prohibitionist	Cleveland and Hendricks	Blaine and Logan
Ala.	93,951	59,591	873	612	10	
Ark.	72,927	50,895	1,847	—	7	
Calif.	89,288	102,416	2,017	2,920	—	8
Colo.	27,723	36,290	1,953	761	—	3
Conn.	67,199	65,923	1,688	2,305	6	
Del.	16,964	12,951	6	55	3	
Fla.	31,766	28,031	—	72	4	
Ga.	94,667	48,603	145	195	12	
Ill.	312,355	337,474	10,910	12,074	—	22
Ind.	244,990	238,463	8,293	3,028	15	
Iowa	177,316	197,089	—	1,472	—	13
Kan.	90,132	154,406	16,341	4,495	—	9
Ky.	152,961	118,122	1,691	3,139	13	
La.	62,540	46,347	—	—	8	
Me.	52,140	72,209	3,953	2,160	—	6
Md.	96,932	85,699	531	2,794	8	
Mass.	122,481	146,724	24,433	10,026	—	14
Mich.	149,835	192,669	42,243	18,403	—	13
Minn.	70,144	111,923	3,583	4,684	—	7
Miss.	76,510	43,509	—	—	9	
Mo.	235,988	202,929	—	2,153	16	
Neb.	54,391	79,912	—	2,899	—	5
Nev.	5,578	7,193	26	—	—	3
N. H.	39,183	43,249	552	1,571	—	4
N. J.	127,798	123,440	3,496	6,159	9	
N. Y.	563,154	562,005	16,994	25,016	36	
N. C.	142,952	125,068	—	454	11	
Ohio	368,280	400,082	5,179	11,069	—	23
Ore.	24,604	26,860	726	492	—	3
Pa.	392,785	473,804	16,992	15,283	—	30
R. I.	12,391	19,030	422	928	—	4
S. C.	69,890	21,733	—	—	9	
Tenn.	133,258	124,078	957	1,131	12	
Tex.	225,309	93,141	3,321	3,534	13	
Vt.	17,331	39,514	785	1,752	—	4
Va.	185,497	139,356	—	138	12	
W. Va.	67,317	63,096	810	939	6	
Wis.	146,459	161,157	4,598	7,656	—	11
	4,874,986	4,851,981	175,370	150,369	219	182

Total vote, 10,052,706.

388

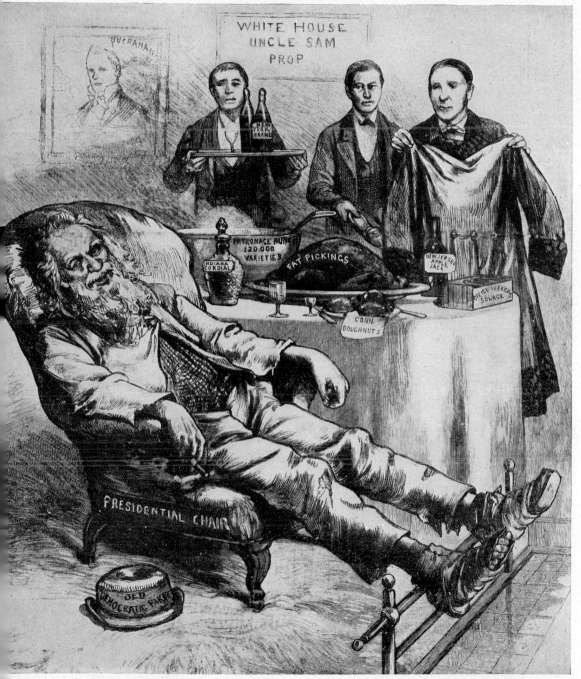

Labels within image: BUCHANAN · WHITE HOUSE UNCLE SAM PROP · NEW YORK BRAND · PATRONAGE PUNCH 120,000 VARIETIES · INDIANA CORDIAL · FAT PICKINGS · NEW JERSEY APPLE JACK · CONN. DOUGHNUTS · OFFICE SEEKERS SOLACE · PRESIDENTIAL CHAIR · OLD DEMOCRATIC PARTY

LAST! THE OLD DEMOCRAT IS BACK IN THE CHAIR AGAIN—AFTER TWENTY-FOUR YEARS.

lars of the nation, was the honored guest of the millionaires. The next day the New York World published a famous cartoon, "Belshazzar's Feast," showing the plutocrats at the dining table, eating choice food and drinking champagne while the starved figures of an unemployed laborer and his family beg them for crumbs. The "Boodle-Banquet" cartoon was

THE PRESIDENT-ELECT, with President Arthur, leaves the White House for the inaugural ceremony.

THE STUBS FAMILY at the inaugural ball. Says Mrs. Stubs to her spinster daughter: "Now then, Matilda Jane, look your prettiest; the President's a bachelder, you know. If your Pa gets the Post-Office, an' Seth gets into the Custom-heouse, an' Mary Susan into the Treasury, there's no tellin' but what you might fill the vacancy in the White Heouse. My! an' then wouldn't we just cut a figger in Stubsville."

THE INAUGURATION BALL, WITH DIPLOMAT

made into posters by the Democrats and put on billboards, turning many labor voters agai Blaine, who could take part in such a feast wl hundreds of thousands in the nation were s

ERS WHIRLING THE LADIES. A DRAWING BY T. De THULSTRUP FOR *HARPER'S WEEKLY.*

ering from bad times; hard hit by the depression. Cleveland won the election with a majority of only 23,000 votes. He received 4,874,986 popular votes to Blaine's 4,851,981. Outside the Solid South he carried Connecticut, New Jersey, Indiana, and New York. After twenty-four years of Republican rule, the country had a Democratic President again.

HARRISON'S INAUGURATION

THE TWENTY-SIXTH ELECTION—1888

BENJAMIN HARRISON

With a Democratic President in the White House, the long Democratic drought ended. Officeholders and job seekers descended upon Cleveland, who in his desire to please both the regular Democrats and the Independent Republicans—without whose votes he could not have been elected—brought the wrath of both groups upon his head.

The regular Democrats complained because the President "unreasonably" recognized the need for civil service reform. For these men "reform" simply meant chasing the Republican incumbents out of office and replacing them with Democrats. "Turn the rascals out," they advised Cleveland. And Cleveland had to acquiesce a great many times and give their henchmen jobs. Because of this the Mugwumps accused him of being the captive of the party bosses. In trying to serve both masters, the President pleased neither of them.

However, both his friends and his enemies had to acknowledge that Cleveland's accomplishments were great. He gave the country an honest administration; he appointed a competent Cabinet; he fought successfully against waste and corruption; he vetoed hundreds of pension bills introduced by overgenerous Congressmen for the veterans of the Grand Army of the Republic—a benevolent and patriotic order whose main business seemed to be to squeeze from the government more and larger pensions; he carefully checked appropriations for public buildings, rigorously cutting expenses which he did not deem to be necessary. For him public office was a public trust.

Cleveland saw that the high tariff rates were leading the country to disaster. In December, 1887, he dedicated his entire annual message to Congress to the tariff issue—a revolutionary departure from precedent—urging a general reduction of the duties and especially the removal of tariffs on raw materials. Arguing against the high rates, he said that high tariff increased the cost of living for the many in order to pile up fortunes for a few. Exorbitant duties gave the Treasury a yearly surplus of $100,000,000, an

THE CANDIDATES

BENJAMIN HARRISON (1833-1901), grandson of the ninth President and staunch supporter of Blaine, became the Republican candidate on Blaine's recommendation. Fought on the tariff issue, the election went to Harrison though Cleveland had a popular majority of over 100,000 votes.

LEVI P. MORTON (1824-1920), Congressman, former envoy to France, was the choice of the Republicans for Vice-President. They received 233 electoral votes to the Democrats' 168, but if the election had been honestly conducted in New York and Indiana, the Democrats would have won.

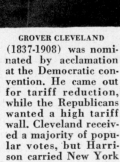

GROVER CLEVELAND (1837-1908) was nominated by acclamation at the Democratic convention. He came out for tariff reduction, while the Republicans wanted a high tariff wall. Cleveland received a majority of popular votes, but Harrison carried New York and won the election.

ALLEN G. THURMAN (1813-1895) from Ohio, 75 years old, known for his red bandanna, was the second choice of the Democrats. More a liability than an asset, his political beliefs were opposed to Cleveland's. Sick and infirm, he "would rather be at home with his dear old wife."

unhealthy symptom of impending business stagnation. "It is a condition which confronts us, not a theory," Cleveland told the country.

Aware that the Republican Senate would not repudiate the high rates, the President pleaded with his own party, which had a decisive majority in the House, to make a declaration in favor of a low tariff. The House of Representatives voted for the Mills Bill—a distinctly party measure—advocating a somewhat lower tariff, with wool, flax, hemp, salt, lumber, and tin plate on the free list. But when the bill reached the Republican Senate, it was killed and a substitute measure was offered which not only maintained the high rates, but in many cases substantially increased them.

THE VOTES IN THE 1888 ELECTION

STATES	POPULAR VOTE				ELECTORAL VOTE	
	Benjamin Harrison, Ind. Republican.	Grover Cleveland, N. Y. Democrat.	Clinton B. Fisk, N. J. Prohibitionist.	Alson J. Streeter, Ill. Union Labor.	Harrison and Morton.	Cleveland and Thurman.
Ala.........	56,197	117,320	583	—	—	10
Ark.........	58,752	85,962	641	10,613	—	7
Calif........	124,816	117,729	5,761	—	8	—
Colo........	50,774	37,567	2,191	1,266	3	—
Conn........	74,584	74,920	4,234	240	—	6
Del.........	12,973	16,414	400	—	—	3
Fla.........	26,657	39,561	423	—	—	4
Ga.........	40,496	100,499	1,808	136	—	12
Ill.........	370,473	348,278	21,695	7,090	22	—
Ind.........	263,361	261,013	9,881	2,694	15	—
Iowa........	211,598	179,887	3,550	9,105	13	—
Kan.........	182,934	103,744	6,768	37,726	9	—
Ky..........	155,134	183,800	5,225	622	—	13
La..........	30,484	85,032	160	39	—	8
Me..........	73,734	50,481	2,691	1,344	6	—
Md..........	99,986	106,168	4,767	—	—	8
Mass........	183,892	151,856	8,701	—	14	—
Mich........	236,370	213,459	20,942	4,541	13	—
Minn........	142,492	104,385	15,311	1,094	7	—
Miss........	30,096	85,471	218	22	—	9
Mo..........	236,257	261,974	4,539	18,632	—	16
Neb.........	108,425	80,552	9,429	4,226	5	—
Nev.........	7,229	5,362	41	—	3	—
N. H........	45,728	43,458	1,593	13	4	—
N. J........	144,344	151,493	7,904	—	—	9
N. Y........	648,759	635,757	30,231	626	36	—
N. C........	134,784	147,902	2,787	32	—	11
Ohio........	416,054	396,455	24,356	3,496	23	—
Ore.........	33,291	26,522	1,677	363	3	—
Pa..........	526,091	446,633	20,947	3,873	30	—
R. I........	21,968	17,530	1,250	18	4	—
S. C........	13,736	65,825	—	—	—	9
Tenn........	138,988	158,779	5,969	48	—	12
Tex.........	88,422	234,883	4,749	29,459	—	13
Vt..........	45,192	16,785	1,460	—	4	—
Va..........	150,438	151,977	1,678	—	—	12
W. Va......	77,791	79,664	669	1,064	—	6
Wis.........	176,553	155,232	14,277	8,552	11	—
	5,439,853	5,540,329	249,506	146,935	233	168

California cast 1591 votes for Curtis, American; Illinois 150 votes N. Y. 2668 votes for Cowdrey, United Labor. Total vote, 11,381,032.

HE COULD HAVE BEEN NOMINATED. James G. Blaine (right) had the strongest Republican following but declined to run. During the convention he was abroad with Carnegie (left), advising the delegates to "take Harrison."

Neither chamber pressed its proposal; both the Democratic House and the Republican Senate merely desired to go on record about it, for both parties wanted to let the voters know where they stood. The next election was near and it was expected that the campaign would be fought on the tariff issue. The debates in Congress made it clear that the Republicans were for high protection, the Democrats for revision downward.

By the time the Democratic nominating convention met in St. Louis, there was no doubt that Cleveland would again be the party's choice. He was favored not only by the rank and file of the party, he was supported not only by the workers and laborers, but by the bankers and financiers (who approved him because of his hard-money and anti-silver policy), and by the merchants and shopkeepers (who no longer feared that business would be adversely affected by the Democratic administration).

Thus, when it came to the nomination, Cleveland's name was not even submitted to a formal vote; he was chosen by acclamation. For the

THE REPUBLICAN PARTY TICKET OF 1888

395

second place the convention chose Allen G. Thurman of Ohio, the "noble old Roman." (Hendricks, the Vice-President under Cleveland, had died in office during the first year of his term.) The seventy-five-year-old Thurman was known and loved more for his appearance than for his political principles, which were entirely in opposition to Cleveland's. But his red bandanna, which he meticulously used after indulging in a pinch of snuff, became a symbol. Hundreds of red bandannas were waved enthusiastically in the convention hall when he received the nomination. A Virginia politician remarked disdainfully: "I think you have nominated a pocket handkerchief!"

The platform, over which a hard battle was fought between the radical and conservative wings of the party, reaffirmed the tariff plank adopted in 1884 and endorsed "the views expressed by President Cleveland in his last earnest message to Congress . . . upon the question of tariff reduction." It recommended "the early passage of the bill for the reduction of the revenue now pending in the House of Representatives."

Who would be the choice of the Republicans? A month before the convention met in Chicago, over four hundred delegates declared themselves in favor of:

"Blaine, Blaine, James G. Blaine,
We've had him once and we'll have him again."

At that time the Plumed Knight was in Europe. He had left the United States the year before without declaring whether he desired the candidacy or not. But in a letter written on January 25, 1888, from Italy, he told the Republican National Committee not to put forth his name as a candidate because of "considerations entirely personal to myself." Rumors were buzzing that he was ill, and others that his letter should not be taken seriously, that Blaine would accept if drafted.

"The Republican Party wants Blaine for the candidate and means to have him," wrote *The Nation*. The great majority of the delegates were lined up behind him; he was still "the greatest living Republican," supported by the big business and manufacturing interests. To the Republicans he was the most available candidate, a man who had almost won the elec-

THE REPUBLICAN CONVENTION in Chicago chos Harrison when Sen. Sherman failed to win enough vote

THE DEMOCRATIC CONVENTION in St. Louis, whe President Cleveland was renominated by acclamatic

tion four years before, losing it by a slight margin because of errors and unhappy accidents which were not likely to occur again.

When the movement on his behalf was under way, Blaine wrote another letter on May 17 from Paris—this time to Whitelaw Reid, the editor of the *Tribune*—in which he declared: "If I should now by speech or by silence, by omission or commission, permit my name in any event to come before the convention, I should incur the reproach of being incandid with those who have always been candid with me."

But even after the letter was published, the

EMONSTRATION before Harrison's home in Indianap-
s after he won the nomination on the eighth ballot.

NGRATULATIONS poured into Harrison's office,
ere he looked at letters and dispatches with his wife.

BOTH PARTIES WERE BIDDING for the votes of the
veterans of the Grand Army of the Republic by allowing
them more liberal pensions. This cartoon was drawn
by Joseph Keppler and appeared in the magazine, *Puck*.

Blaine supporters asserted emphatically—and
Blaine's enemies feared—that the Plumed
Knight was still in the race. Senator John Sherman, one of the leading Republican contestants
for the nomination, wrote to Mark Hanna on
he day the convention began: "My theory is
hat Blaine is a candidate, has been from the
eginning, and will be until defeated." It was
amazing how Blaine, who had been so dis-
redited in the previous campaign, maintained
is hold over the Republican party. Although
e was thousands of miles away, he dominated
he convention more effectively than any other
olitician present.

When the balloting began, John Sherman
was in the lead with 229 votes, followed by
Walter Q. Graham of Indiana with 111 votes,
Chauncey M. Depew of New York with 99,
ex-Governor Russell A. Alger of Michigan
with 84, Benjamin Harrison of Indiana with 80,
Senator William B. Allison of Iowa with 72, and
Blaine with 35. Altogether, there were votes for
fourteen different candidates.

After five ballots, when it had become evident that Sherman, the leading candidate, had
not the strength to consolidate his position, the
convention adjourned for the weekend. Sherman's managers sensed that a stampede for

397

Blaine was in the making. Some of the Senator's most ardent supporters asked him to withdraw in favor of someone on whom the factions could agree. Murat Halstead, the keen observer of many conventions, wired to Sherman the news that "the Ohio delegation is already broken" and that "the Governor goes next ballot for Blaine. He thinks you have no chance left." In Halstead's opinion, "Blaine will certainly be nominated, unless the movement can be checked by placing McKinley in nomination and concentrating the anti-Blaine forces."

Other Sherman supporters had the same notion. George F. Hoar told him in another wire: "Your nomination now seems impossible. If you promptly telegraph Ohio delegation, authorizing them to present McKinley, he will probably be nominated. Otherwise it looks like Blaine." Mark Hanna, the political boss from Cleveland, also asked Sherman to withdraw his name in favor of McKinley to "save the party from the Blaine lunatics." The Sherman forces lost their courage. D. M. Legett telegraphed the candidate: "Your case looks hopeless, made so by the Blaine tricksters. Blaine must be defeated or we are ruined. Believe a majority would unite on McKinley if he were free. Don't delay final action too long. I believe you have power to defeat Blaine."

But John Sherman, cool and unimpressed, sitting in Washington hundreds of miles away from the convention, would not listen to such advice. He wired to Mark Hanna, who quietly fostered McKinley: "Let my name stand. I prefer defeat to retreat . . . I like McKinley, but such a movement would be unjust to others . . . a breach of implicit faith."

The Blaine men, seeing that Sherman's defeat was imminent, were now "open and aggressive." They bombarded their hero with cables, urging him to reverse his stand and become an avowed candidate. Blaine answered from London: "Earnestly request my friends to respect my Paris letter," and advised the delegates to "refrain from voting for me." But even this was not taken for an answer. A cable went to Carnegie, Blaine's host in England, asking for his intervention. Carnegie remonstrated with the Plumed Knight, but Blaine was "immovable." So Carnegie cabled in a secret code, advising the convention in Blaine's name to "take Trump and Star," which meant Harrison and Phelps.

Thus, when the convention proceeded with the voting, Harrison's support increased from 231 on the sixth ballot to 544 on the eighth. The delegates had heeded Blaine's advice and taken as their candidate Benjamin Harrison, a Blaine supporter of long standing with a clean, almost empty political record. Harrison had been a general in the Civil War and was a descendant of illustrious forebears—a great-grandson of a signer of the Declaration of In-

(turn to page 401)

BALLOTING IN NEW YORK. A voter is pondering whether to choose Cleveland or Harrison for President.

PARADE IN INDIANA, where the Republicans use money in abundance to influence the election resul

HE TARIFF WAS THE MAIN ISSUE of the campaign. The Republicans clung to high tariff, the Democrats to vision downward. In this scene on New York's Broadway, supporters of Benjamin Harrison chant: "Trade, trade, free trade!" The Cleveland chorus answers: "Don't, don't, don't be afraid; only low tariff so don't be afraid!"

THE OUTGOING PRESIDENT, Grover Cleveland, happily says goodbye to his successor, Benjamin Harrison
who leans against the door to keep out storming hordes of office seekers hungrily descending upon the White House

THE NEW PRESIDENT, Benjamin Harrison, "a slave of many masters" at the administration patronage mill.
is working hard, driven by the party bosses, to produce offices for all party regulars who supported him at po

THE POWER BEHIND THE PRESIDENTIAL CHAIR FOR THE NEXT FOUR YEARS: JAMES G. BLAINE.

ependence, and a grandson of President Wil-
am Henry Harrison.

The Blaine supporters chanted sadly:

"We'll vote this year for Tippecanoe
And for James G. Blaine in '92."

The platform brazenly declared that the Republican party "favor the entire repeal of internal taxes, rather than the surrender of any
part of our protective system." *The Nation*
wrote of this plank:

"BENJAMIN HAS DONE PRETTY WELL FOR HIS TRIBE SO FAR, BUT THERE ARE LOTS MORE TO C[

"It is so at variance with all former deliverances of the party, with scores of resolutions of state legislatures under Republican control, with hundreds of speeches and votes of Republican statesmen now living, with the report of the Republican tariff commission only five years ago, and with the recommendation of success[Republican Presidents and Secretaries of Treasury, that the party can be likened only the man who made a monster of which he came the unhappy victim. Protection is Frankenstein of the Republican party."

402

ON SPOILSMEN DESCEND ON WASHINGTON.

he campaign issue was clear-cut. It was the
ff. Money poured into the Republican cam-
n chest, contributed by businessmen and
ufacturers who had grown rich because of
protection. "Put the manufacturers of
nsylvania under the fire and dry all the fat

out of them" was the advice of Matt Quay,
cheerfully followed by the Republican campaign managers. The American Iron and Steel
Association, one of the most influential industrial organizations wielding political power,
dug deep into its coffers. Its members could do
so without pain; Andrew Carnegie alone took
$1,500,000 out of his mill in a single year, and
this profit was largely due to the high tariff
rates. So money flowed freely from the industrialists' pockets to elect Harrison, the protectionist. More than $3,000,000 were collected—
an enormous sum for the times.

Blaine—after his return from Europe in
August—campaigned vigorously for Harrison.
He spoke in meeting after meeting, talking of
nothing else but the tariff, giving his listeners
the impression that tariff protection could never
be high enough.

The Republicans organized societies promoting tariff reforms but defending protection;
stump speakers toured the country explaining
to the farmers what tariff reduction would mean
to them. They pointed to the plight of the English farmers, blaming their misery on the free-
trade principles of that country. Protection was
invoked as a form of patriotism. McKinley—to
become President eight years later—orated:
"Let England take care of herself, let France
look after her interests, let Germany take care
of her own people, but in God's name let
Americans look after America."

In the big industrial plants Republican manufacturers told their workers that tariff reduction would bring disastrous results. There were
slips in the pay envelopes warning them that
they would be without employment if Cleveland were elected.

The Democrats urged Cleveland to go on
the stump. But the President felt that this was
not compatible with the dignity of the office,
and insisted that the members of his Cabinet
stay away from campaigning as well.

How different was this campaign from the
Cleveland and Blaine contest four years before.
Personal invective played very little part in it.
The Republican allegation that Cleveland beat
his young wife, whom he had married during
his term, drew a statement from Mrs. Cleveland
that it was "a foolish campaign story without a

shadow of foundation," and that she could "wish the women of our country no greater blessing than that their homes and their lives may be as happy, and that their husbands may be as kind, as attentive, considerate and affectionate as mine."

An incident probably harmful to Cleveland occurred when the British minister, Sir Lionel Sackville-West, lured into a trap by a communication from California, gave to an inquirer the foolish advice that he should vote for Cleveland because a Democratic administration would be more conciliatory and friendly to the mother country than a Republican one.

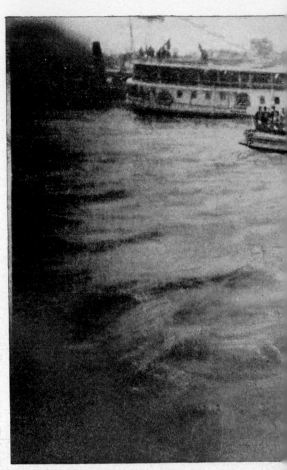

IN APRIL, 1889—ONE HUNDRED YEARS AFTER

PRESIDENT HARRISON addresses crowds in New York City, commemorating the day a hundred years before when Washington came there for his inauguration.

When Sackville-West's letter was published Cleveland was dubbed the "English candidate." The New York *Tribune* wrote that the President was ready to yield to "British interests at the sacrifice of American rights." The Irish, bitter about the failure of Home Rule, about Gladstone's resignation, and Balfour's severe measures against their country, were in the mood to withhold their votes from anyone who was friendly to Great Britain. Democratic leaders demanded that Sackville-West be handed his passport. A. K. McClure wrote Cleveland, "Now kick out Lord Sackville with your biggest boot of best leather, and you've got 'em Hesitation is death."

In the election thirty-eight states voted. Outside the Solid South the Democrats carried only two states—Connecticut and New

INAUGURATION — BENJAMIN HARRISON REENACTS WASHINGTON'S ARRIVAL IN NEW YORK.

rsey; all the others voted Republican. As
w York and Indiana, the two pivotal states,
re in Harrison's column, he won with 233
ctoral votes against Cleveland's 168, though
veland's popular majority was a hundred
usand larger.

The candidates of minor parties showed sur-
sing strength. Clinton B. Fisk, the Prohibi-
ist, received 249,506 votes, and Alson J.
eter, the choice of the Union Labor party,
led 146,935.

n New York—the decisive state in nearly all
tions—Harrison's majority was roughly
oo. This victory, giving him the election,
most probably the result of a political deal.
Republican support of the Tammany Dem-
t David B. Hill (a sworn enemy of Cleve-
) in the gubernatorial election, Hill ex-

erted his own influence on behalf of Harrison.

In the other crucial state—Indiana—money
was freely used to extract votes. Dudley, the
Republican manager, issued a circular directing
the party workers to divide the floaters (men
who sold their vote to the highest bidders) into
blocks of five, "and put a trusted man in charge
of these five with necessary funds, and make
him responsible that none get away, and that
all vote our ticket."

Thus through bribery, intrigue, and fraud,
Harrison became President. When he heard the
result he said with great elation: "Providence
has given us the victory," to which Matt Quay,
chairman of the Republican National Committee, retorted: "Think of the man! He ought to
know that Providence hadn't a damn thing to
do with it."

405

CLEVELAND TAKES THE OATH

THE TWENTY-SEVENTH ELECTION—1892

GROVER CLEVELAND

Benjamin Harrison was a tiny man in a big job. He said little, he did little, he was meek and somewhat bewildered, and he docilely signed the bills which the Republican Congress laid on his table. Harrison served his party well, but not the people; he was the tool of a small coterie of ruthless, money-grabbing individuals who looked more after their own good than the welfare of the country.

Harrison was the king of the spoilsmen. (His Postmaster General boasted that within a year he had changed 31,000 out of 55,000 postmasters.) He was the saint of the veterans. (Under his administration the number of pensions for the members of the Grand Army of the Republic was doubled.) He was the pet of the manufacturers and industrialists. (During his term Congress passed the McKinley Tariff Bill, increasing the duties on manufactured articles and helping the industrialists to enormous profits.)

The surplus which troubled the Cleveland administration very soon ceased to worry Harrison. "God help the surplus," said his Commissioner of Pensions, and James Tanner was as good as his word. The "Billion-Dollar" Congress spent the money of the taxpayers with great ease. After all, said Speaker Reed, who ruled the House with a strong hand, this was a "billion-dollar country." Appropriations for river improvements, for coastal defenses, for Federal buildings increased at such speed that within two years the government was in need of funds. Where were the days of surplus? Gone like the snows of yesterday.

To such doings the country reacted vigorously. In the midterm congressional election the Republicans were disastrously defeated and their majority in the House of Representatives was wiped out. The new House seated no less than 235 Democrats, and there were only 88 Republicans to oppose them. It was a decisive answer to the activities of the Fifty-first Congress.

Meanwhile, from the West and South rebellious winds were blowing. Farmers, suffering under high mortgages and brutal fore-

GROVER CLEVELAND (1837-1908) was chosen by the Democrats for the third consecutive time. He won decisively with 277 electoral votes to Harrison's 145 and Weaver's 22.

ADLAI E. STEVENSON (1835-1914) was picked by the Democrats for Vice-President to appease the Silverites, whose suggestion for free silver was vetoed in the convention.

BENJAMIN HARRISON (1833-1901) was again the Republican choice, but high tariff and lavish expenditures during his administration lost him the support of the voters.

WHITELAW REID (1837-1912), Harrison's running mate, feared rioting at Homestead would cut Republican votes. He vainly begged Carnegie to recognize workers' demands.

JAMES B. WEAVER (1833-1912), candidate of the radical People's party, fighting against the abuses of the railroad monopolists and for the farmers, won over 8% of the votes.

JOHN BIDWELL (1819-1900) from California, was the candidate of the Prohibitionist party. With J. B. Cranfill of Texas as his running mate, he won 250,000 votes.

closures, deeply resentful against monopolists and bankers who were—so they thought—deliberately robbing them, organized themselves in "Alliances," fighting bitterly against the abuses of the railroad companies and against the corruption and brutality of big business and its control of the government. They were in the mood to follow the advice of the articulate Mary Elizabeth Lease, one of the leaders of the movement, who told them to "raise less corn and more hell." Soon they formed a third party—the People's party.

When the time of the nominating conventions arrived, the major parties turned to their last candidates—the Republicans to President Harrison, the Democrats to ex-President Cleveland. Both Harrison and Cleveland had rivals in their parties, but none could seriously challenge their strong positions. Blaine's name was again mentioned by Republicans, one of them saying earnestly that "the ladies and the babies in the cradle want Blaine," while Republican marchers sang:

> "We are for the man from Maine,
> He will get there just the same."

But the Plumed Knight was a tired and sick man. Destined to die within a year, he refused to let his name be put in nomination.

Cleveland's candidacy was again challenged by Tammany Hall, which preferred David B. Hill, the former Governor and now Senator from New York. However, when the conventions balloted, the Democratic and Republican favorites were nominated on the first ballot, the Republicans choosing Harrison with 535½ votes to James G. Blaine's 182½ and William McKinley's 182, and the Democrats selecting Grover Cleveland with 617⅓ votes to David Hill's 114.

The platforms of both parties contained a great many words but very few ideas. The Republicans recited the blessings which they had conferred upon the country, commended the "able, patriotic, and thoroughly American administration of President Harrison," and reaffirmed their belief in "the American doctrine of protection."

And the Democrats denounced "the Republican protection as a fraud, a robbery of the great majority of the American people for the benefit of the few," demanded a tariff "for the

READY FOR ANOTHER BOUT in the political arena. This cartoon against Cleveland shows him in his corner seconded by John Bull, branding him as the "English Candidate" in the eyes of the Irish voters. His gloves are marked "Free Trade," a Republican slur against Democrats, and the eyepatch is a reminder of his defeat in 1888.

purposes of revenue only," and proclaimed that the McKinley Tariff Law enacted by the fifty-first Congress was "the culminating atrocity of class legislation."

More outspoken than the platform of the two major parties was the proclamation of principles of the new People's party—the Populists. "We meet in the midst of a nation brought to the verge of moral, political, and material ruin," began the preamble. "Corruption dominates the ballot-box, the legislature, the Congress, and touches even the ermine of the bench. The people are demoralized; most of the states have been compelled to isolate the voters at the polling-places to prevent universal intimidation or bribery. The newspapers are largely subsidized or muzzled; public opinion silenced; business prostrated; our homes covered with mortgages; labor impoverished; and the land concentrating in the hands of the capitalists. The urban workmen are denied the right of organization for self-protection; imported pauperized labor beats down their wages; a hireling standing army, unrecognized by our laws, is established to shoot them down, and they are rapidly degenerating into European conditions. The fruits of the toil of millions are boldly stolen to build up colossal fortunes for a few, unprecedented in the history of mankind; and the possessors of these, in turn, despise the republic and endanger liberty. From the same prolific womb of governmental injustice we breed the two great classes of tramps and millionaires."

They were the same words which Ignatius Donnelly had written and recited with great effect a few months before, when delegates from many states assembled in St. Louis to discuss the principles of the new party.

SMALL MAN IN A BIG CHAIR was the notion the people of the country had about President Harrison.

BLAINE, SECRETARY OF STATE UNDER HARR

The Populist platform was divided into three main parts, relating to three principal issues finance, transportation, land. On finance, i asked for "a national currency, safe, sound and flexible"; it demanded the "free and unlimited coinage of silver and gold at the present legal ratio of sixteen to one," and that "th amount of circulating medium be speedily in

DOMINATING PERSONALITY. RUMORS FLEW THAT HE WANTED THE NOMINATION HIMSELF.

reased to not less than fifty dollars per capita." pleaded for "a graduated income tax" and r the establishment of postal savings banks.

About the second important issue, transortation, it stated: "Transportation being a eans of exchange and a public necessity, the overnment should own and operate the railoads in the interest of the people."

And on the land question the platform declared: "The land, including all the natural sources of wealth, is the heritage of the people, and should not be monopolized for speculative purposes, and alien ownership of land should be prohibited. All land now held by railroads and other corporations in excess of their actual needs, and all lands now owned by

411

aliens, should be reclaimed by the government and held for actual settlers only."

A number of other principles were embodied in the platform, such as public ownership of the telegraph and telephone, a secret-ballot system, pensions for ex-Union soldiers and sailors, a rigid enforcement of the eight-hour law, a single presidential term, and direct popular voting for Senators.

It was a radical, progressive platform. It was not only an enumeration of political demands, but an enunciation of a creed. It was a declaration of war against monopolies, against greedy financiers, against railroad corporations. It contained phrases long to be remembered. "Wealth belongs to him who creates it, and every dollar taken from industry without an equivalent is robbery." "If any will not work, neither shall he eat."

For their candidates the 1,400 Populist delegates chose James B. Weaver of Iowa for the first place and James G. Field of Virginia for the second. Both men had fought in the Civil War, Weaver for the Union and Field on the Confederate side.

With the candidates of the three parties chosen, the campaign got under way. It was a

J. Keppler

THE FIFTY-FIRST, OR "BILLION-DOLLAR" CON

"GOD HELP THE SURPLUS," said James Tanner, Harrison's Pension Commissioner. He spent funds liberally — "nothing was too good for an old soldier."

clean, dull, listless affair, devoid of personal issues. The colorful exhibitionism of former contests had disappeared; streets were no longer jammed by torchlight parades and marching processions; no more "Boys in Blue," no more "Wide-Awakes" tramped through the cities

THE SURPLUS LAVISHLY. THE NATIONAL GRAB-BAG SEEMED OPEN TO EVERYONE.

he tunes of brass bands. No more "waving the bloody shirt," no more exploitation of sectional animosity. But there was still plenty of boasting and singing for the candidates. The versifiers in the newspapers produced much campaign poetry, and the Republicans chanted:

"Let every honest fellow from Maine to Oregon,
Let every honest fellow, unless he's a son-of-a-gun,
Let every honest fellow, unless he's a son-of-a-gun,
Let every honest fellow be sure and vote for
      Benjamin Harrison."

THE POPULISTS BELIEVED that the fat Republican monopolist, protected by Congress, grew richer because of the high tariff wall, while the farmer, with his house and tools heavily mortgaged and prices low, grew poorer. Their movement was the first great struggle of the masses in America against the privileged classes.

Cleveland and Harrison commanded the respect of the country. Both of them had served one term in the White House. Harrison was an uninspiring, Cleveland a forceful candidate. Of course Harrison was in a more difficult position than Cleveland. He had to defen the deeds of the Republican Congress—the high tariff, the lavish appropriations for pensions—and he had to find reasons for the extravagan way in which the nation's money was spent

THE PEOPLE'S PARTY, commonly called Populists, emerged in 1891 from the Farmers' Alliances, rallying in its ranks the impoverished farmers of the West and South. It blamed the malpractices of the railroads and ruthless methods of the plutocrats for economic evils, and for a cure suggested expansion of money—free coinage of silver.

Neither candidate campaigned in the usual sense. Cleveland remained at his home at Buzzard's Bay, suffering not only from the gout, but "from an excess of medicine rather than the lack of it." From his retreat he wrote letters,

keeping in touch with the party bosses. And Harrison kept away from the crowds, mourning his wife's death.

But General Weaver, the Populist candidate, was on his feet. He traveled through the West

(turn to page 418)

THE REPUBLICAN CAMPAIGN MANAGERS, MATT QUAY AND WADE DUDLEY, AUCTION OFF

Signs on door: SENATORIAL ELECTION ROOM. UP STAIRS TAKE ELEVATOR.

...DENTIAL CHAIR TO THE "MONEY KINGS," WHO ARE EAGER TO BUY THE NEXT ELECTION.

and South, accompanied by Mrs. Lease, an "orator of marvelous power and phenomenal psychological force," making speeches, talking to hundreds of well-attended meetings. He forcefully attacked the plutocracy which has "usurped the government and is using it as a policeman to enforce its insolent decrees." He said that "the corporation has been placed above the individual and an armed body of cruel mercenaries permitted, in times of public peril, to discharge police duties which clearly belong to the state," and protested strongly against such practices.

Weaver's argument proved itself dramatically when in July three hundred Pinkerton men hired by the Carnegie steel plant at Homestead, Pennsylvania, fought a pitched battle with the workers of that plant. The fight was the climax of an argument between the management of the steel mill and its employees.

THE DEMOCRATS assembled in Chicago and nominated former President Cleveland on the first ballot.

THE REPUBLICANS gathered at Minneapolis and nominated President Harrison on the first ballot.

418

THE NATION'S ILLS ARE SHOWN IN THIS CAR

The month before, the company had announced a reduction of wages. There was little valid reason for it. Business was good, the high tariff protected the steel mills, the owners' profits soared. The wage cut was an arrogant and highhanded challenge to the workers, a galling demonstration of the mastery of management over labor. When the union officials attempted

PARING THE ROBBER BARONS OF THE MIDDLE AGES WITH THE ROBBER BARONS OF THE DAY.

to negotiate, the company refused to recognize the union and without further ado closed the steelworks. Thousands of employees who had worked in the mills for years were locked out, deprived of their jobs because the management was determined to stamp out their union.

The company hired nonunion men and with them it attempted to reopen the plant. Fearing trouble, it engaged Pinkerton men to protect the mills against violence. When the heavily armed mercenaries approached Homestead in barges, five thousand workers were at the riverbanks waiting for them.

A battle began and lasted for two days. The workers fired from an entrenchment and

419

CLEVELAND WAS ASSAILED by his opponents because he ran for the Presidency three consecutive times.

SPENDING THE SURPLUS was the favorite hobby of little Benjamin Harrison, according to the Democrats.

pumped oil upon the water, trying to set it on fire; sticks of dynamite were thrown against the Pinkerton men, who fought back from the barges. Finally the state militia appeared, ending the fight, and under its protection the mills were opened with nonunion labor.

Public opinion denounced the arrogant behavior of Carnegie and Frick, the overlords of Homestead. Republican leaders, apprehensive of the political consequences, appealed to them to modify their stand, but neither Carnegie nor Frick would cooperate. Cleveland, in his acceptance speech, came out bluntly for the workers' rights. He referred to the crushing of the union as "the tender mercy the workingman receives from those made selfish and sordid by unjust governmental favoritism." Newspapers recalled that the same steel magnates who now reduced the wages of their workers had not so long ago pleaded for tariff protection as a means of keeping wages high. Why should wages be cut now in a time of great

industrial prosperity? Why should they be reduced, when at the same time the owners of the steel mills, protected by a high tariff, could amass a fortune? These were the questions the people asked—and election day was only four months away.

All signs pointed to a Republican defeat. In the September elections in Vermont and Maine the Republicans lost heavily. The November election proved the trend. The returns of forty-four states (North Dakota, South Dakota, Montana, and Washington were admitted in November, 1889; Idaho and Wyoming in July, 1890) showed a decisive victory for Cleveland. He won with 277 electoral votes to Harrison's 145, capturing not only the doubtful states of New York, New Jersey, Connecticut, and Indiana, but sweeping Illinois, Wisconsin, and California as well.

In the election the parties formed strange and confusing alliances. In five Western states —Colorado, Idaho, Kansas, North Dakota, and

Wyoming—the Democrats voted for the Populist ticket as the best means of defeating the Republicans. Farmers who formerly voted Republican were now in the Populist ranks. In the South the Republicans voted with the Populists to weaken the Democrats.

Of the minor candidates, Weaver, the Populist, received over a million votes and Bidwell, the Prohibitionists' choice, polled over 150,000. The impressive figure for the Populist ticket showed that the agrarian resentment could no longer be ignored by the two major parties.

Godkin summed up the result in *The Nation:* "Mr. Cleveland's triumph today has been largely due to the young voters who have come on the stage since the reign of passion and prejudice came to an end, and the era of discussion has opened. If the past canvass has consisted largely of appeals to reason, to facts, to the lessons of human experience, it is to Mr. Cleveland, let us tell them, that they owe it. But they are indebted to him for something far more valuable than this—for an example of Roman constancy under defeat, and of patient reliance on the power of deliberation and persuasion of the American people. Nothing is more important, in these days of boodle, of cheap bellicose patriotism, than that this confidence in the might of common sense and sound doctrine and free speech should be kept alive."

THE POPULAR AND ELECTORAL VOTES IN THE 1892 ELECTION

STATES	POPULAR VOTE					ELECTORAL VOTE		
	Grover Cleveland, New York. Democrat	Benjamin Harrison, Indiana. Republican	James B. Weaver, Iowa. Populist	John Bidwell, California. Prohibitionist	Simon Wing, Massachusetts. Socialist-Labor	Cleveland and Stevenson.	Harrison and Reid.	Weaver and Field.
Alabama	138,138	9,197	85,181	239	—	11	—	—
Arkansas	87,834	46,884	11,831	113	—	8	—	—
California	117,908	117,618	25,226	8,056	—	8	1	—
Colorado	—	38,620	53,584	1,638	—	—	—	4
Connecticut	82,395	77,025	806	4,025	329	6	—	—
Delaware	18,581	18,083	13	565	—	3	—	—
Florida	30,143	—	4,843	475	—	4	—	—
Georgia	129,361	48,305	42,937	988	—	13	—	—
Idaho	—	8,599	10,520	288	—	—	—	3
Illinois	426,281	399,288	22,207	25,870	—	24	—	—
Indiana	262,740	255,615	22,208	13,050	—	15	—	—
Iowa	196,367	219,795	20,595	6,402	—	—	13	—
Kansas	—	157,237	163,111	4,539	—	—	—	10
Kentucky	175,461	135,441	23,500	6,442	—	13	—	—
Louisiana	87,922	13,281	13,282	—	—	8	—	—
Maine	48,044	62,931	2,381	3,062	336	—	6	—
Maryland	113,866	92,736	796	5,877	27	8	—	—
Massachusetts	176,813	202,814	3,210	1,539	649	—	15	—
Michigan	202,296	222,708	19,892	14,069	—	5	9	—
Minnesota	100,920	122,823	29,313	12,182	—	—	9	—
Mississippi	40,237	1,406	10,256	910	—	9	—	—
Missouri	268,398	226,918	41,213	4,331	—	17	—	—
Montana	17,581	18,851	7,334	549	—	—	3	—
Nebraska	24,943	87,227	83,134	4,902	—	—	8	—
Nevada	714	2,811	7,264	89	—	—	—	3
New Hampshire	42,081	45,658	292	1,297	—	—	4	—
New Jersey	171,042	156,068	969	8,131	1,337	10	—	—
New York	654,868	609,350	16,429	38,190	17,956	36	—	—
North Carolina	132,951	100,342	44,736	2,636	—	11	—	—
North Dakota	—	17,519	17,700	899	—	1	1	1
Ohio	404,115	405,187	14,850	26,012	—	1	22	—
Oregon	14,243	35,002	26,965	2,281	—	—	3	1
Pennsylvania	452,264	516,011	8,714	25,123	898	—	32	—
Rhode Island	24,335	26,972	228	1,654	—	—	4	—
South Carolina	54,692	13,345	2,407	—	—	9	—	—
South Dakota	9,081	34,888	26,544	—	—	—	4	—
Tennessee	138,874	100,331	23,447	4,851	—	12	—	—
Texas	239,148	81,444	99,688	2,165	—	15	—	—
Vermont	16,325	37,992	43	1,415	—	—	4	—
Virginia	163,977	113,262	12,275	2,738	—	12	—	—
Washington	29,802	36,460	19,165	2,542	—	—	4	—
West Virginia	84,467	80,293	4,166	2,145	—	6	—	—
Wisconsin	177,335	170,791	9,909	13,132	—	12	—	—
Wyoming	—	8,454	7,722	530	—	—	3	—
	5,556,543	5,175,582	1,040,886	255,841	21,532	277	145	22

Total vote—12,050,384.

GROVER CLEVELAND DELIVERS THE INAUGURAL SPEECH TO A SHIVERING CROWD AT THE CAPI

IS RIGHT IS EX-PRESIDENT HARRISON.

INAUGURATION DAY

AFTER THE CEREMONIES, the new President and the ex-President return together to the White House.

PENNSYLVANIA AVENUE on inauguration day. Columns of troops are marching to the reviewing stand.

On election night Cleveland's friends assembled at his house, happily celebrating his victory. Among the exuberant crowd Cleveland was thoughtful and silent. Looking at the joyful throng, he said: "While we find in our triumph a result of popular intelligence which we have aroused, and a consequence of popular vigilance which we have stimulated, let us not for a moment forget that our accession to power will find neither this intelligence nor this vigilance dead or slumbering. We are thus brought face to face with the reflection that if we are not to be tormented by the spirits which we have ourselves called up, we must hear, above victorious shouts, the call of our fellow countrymen to public duty, and must put on a garb befitting public servants."

It was the sentiment of a noble soul.

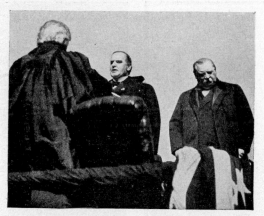

McKINLEY TAKES THE OATH OF OFFICE

THE TWENTY-EIGHTH ELECTION—1896

WILLIAM McKINLEY

Two months after Cleveland began his second term, a severe financial depression swept over the country. The abundance of crops and the low price for farm products reduced purchasing power; overinvestment in railways stopped further expansion; the economic distress in Europe left its mark on the American market. Within a year there were 5,000 business failures; 158 national banks went into liquidation; 4,000,000 workers were without employment. The gold reserve of the Treasury, tapped by withdrawals by England and other European countries, and by financiers and speculators, dwindled.

While gold was scarce, silver was abundant. Under the Sherman Silver Purchase Act the Treasury was committed to buy yearly a large amount of silver. But as the silver certificates were also redeemable in gold, the speculators exchanged them for the much sought after metal, shipping the gold bullion to Europe, where high premiums were paid for it. Thus the gold resources of the Treasury were drained until the reserve was under the crucial hundred-million mark.

President Cleveland realized that some measure had to be taken to ease the Treasury's burden. He called a special session of Congress and asked the lawmakers to repeal the Silver Purchase Act. But as a great number of Democrats were for the free coinage of silver, Cleveland had to employ the help of the gold-standard Republicans, and with their assistance the repeal was passed. The silver Democrats were enraged; they denounced the President as a tool of the Wall Street financiers. From then on, Cleveland faced hostile opposition from an influential segment of his own party.

The President believed in the "sound-money" policies of the conservative economists of the time—that the notes of the Treasury had to be backed by gold. But gold was scarce, and the scarcity created a steady brake on the country's economy. Under this the farmers suffered most. The prices for their products were low, their mortgages and loans heavy; more grain and more livestock were needed to buy one gold dollar. It was argued that if the government would allow the coinage of silver, the money situation could be eased; the resulting inflation would drive prices up, and mortgages and loans could be paid off in cheaper money.

425

WILLIAM McKINLEY (1843-1901), Governor of Ohio, was Hanna's choice for President. Hanna worked hard for McKinley's nomination and spent $100,000 before the campaign to promote his popularity. The plan succeeded. Nominated on the first ballot, McKinley carried the election.

GARRET A. HOBART (1844-1899), McKinley's running mate. The campaign was fought on the silver issue with the West and South for free coinage and North and East for the gold standard. Backed by a lavish campaign fund, supported by all the industrial states, McKinley and Hobart won.

WILLIAM J. BRYAN (1860-1925), one of the great orators of his time, became the Democratic candidate after he roused the enthusiasm of the delegates with his Cross of Gold speech. Also endorsed by the Populists, Bryan campaigned widely, demanding the coinage of free silver, but lost.

ARTHUR SEWALL (1835-1900), rich shipbuilder of Maine, was the Democratic choice for the second place. The Populists, who accepted Bryan for the Presidency, would not take the plutocratic Sewall for Vice-President. They nominated the out-and-out Populist Thomas E. Watson.

REPUBLICAN CONVENTION in St. Louis, where because of Mark Hanna's thorough preparation, his friend William McKinley was nominated on the first ballot.

THE GREAT MOMENT. J. B. Foraker presents McKinley's name for the presidential nomination. The Republican platform favored the existing gold standard.

A pamphlet, published in 1894, explained these theories in simple language understandable to everyone. Written by William H. Harvey *Coin's Financial School* greatly influenced the thinking of a large number of people. In the

DEMOCRATIC CONVENTION in Chicago, where William Jennings Bryan made his "Cross of Gold" speech and won the nomination on a free-silver platform.

THE COLISEUM, scene of the Democratic convention. After a fierce fight, the silver wing of the party won and the gold-standard men prepared to bolt.

booklet, "Coin," the young financial expert, reviewed the situation. He said: "Hard times are with us; the country is distracted; very few things are marketable at a price above the cost of production; tens of thousands are out of employment; the jails, penitentiaries, work-houses and insane asylums are full; the gold reserve at Washington is sinking . . . a huge debt hangs like an appalling cloud over the country . . . hungered and half-starved men are banding into armies and marching toward Washington; the cry of distress is heard on every hand . . . riots and strikes prevail throughout the land; schemes to remedy our ills when put into execution are smashed like box-cars in a railroad wreck, and Wall Street looks in vain for an excuse to account for the failure of prosperity to return since the repeal of the Silver Purchase Act."

In Coin's opinion, adherence to the gold standard only deepened the depression. He explained that the country's prosperity or want depended upon money abundance or money scarcity, and ever since silver money was abolished, the circulation of currency had not been sufficient for the economy. Property and commodity values had sunk, while gold rose to new heights. Yet all the gold in the world, if melted into blocks, could be placed behind the counter of one of Chicago's largest banks.

This was—so Coin continued—nothing but a conspiracy against the farmer. The Eastern capitalist came West, collected the money and left the countryside in great need. There was not enough money to make the rounds or to keep the economy going. To remedy this situation, Coin suggested that silver should be used as well as gold; thus credit would multiply, money would circulate, prices would rise, and the debtor would no longer be at a disadvantage.

The campaign for free coinage of silver at the old ratio of 16 to 1—one of the main Populist issues in the 1892 election—grew in importance. It was now taken up by more and more Democrats. During 1893 and 1894, in many parts of the country, the supporters of free silver among the Democrats fused with the Populists; in the majority of the Western and Southern states the silver Democrats won the upper hand in the party organizations; in state after state the Democratic conventions declared themselves for free silver and against Cleveland's monetary policies.

The other major political issue confronting Cleveland was the tariff. Reduction of the duties had been a pledge of the Democrats in

427

the last campaign and the President was determined to fulfill it. But when the Wilson Bill, proposing such reductions, reached the Senate, a great number of Eastern Democrats joined forces with the Republicans and changed the measure beyond recognition. No less than 634 changes were suggested, nearly all of them favoring and maintaining high protection. When the bill was finally passed, Cleveland, who held that "a tariff for any other purpose than public revenue is robbery," denounced it as a product of "party perfidy and party dishonor." He complained bitterly that "the livery of Democratic tariff reform has been stolen and worn in the service of Republican protection." However, as the new measure—bad as it was—offered some improvement over the McKinley Tariff, the President allowed it to become law without his signature.

One provision of the bill was fought with great determination by its opponents. It was the income tax provision, levying for the first time a 2 per cent tax on incomes above $4,000. When it was tested in the Supreme Court, the Court ruled by a five to four decision—one justice changing his mind at the last minute—that a tax on income was unconstitutional.

Professors Morison and Commager, in their book, *The Growth of the American Republic*, have given an excellent analysis of the economic situation: "This year, 1894, the year of the Wilson Tariff and the income tax decision, was the darkest that Americans had known for thirty years. Everything seemed to conspire to convince the people that democracy was a failure. Prices and wages hit rock-bottom and there seemed to be no market for anything. Half a million laborers struck against conditions which they thought intolerable, and most of the strikes were dismal failures. Ragged and hungry bands of unemployed swarmed over the countryside, the fires from the hobo camps flickering a message of warning and despair to affrighted townsfolk."

The Pullman workers in Chicago asked for restoration of a 20 per cent wage cut, and when the company refused, they went on strike. Their resistance spread, and soon all railway movement around Chicago was halted. Cleveland, in his desire to prevent interference with the flow of mail, dispatched Federal

"BLAME THE THING — I CAN'T MAKE IT WO

troops against the strikers over the protest o
Governor John Peter Altgeld.

Jacob Coxey, taking with him his wife an
small son, Legal Tender, marched to Wash
ington with his "army," suggesting the buildin
of roads as a means of giving jobs to the unem

428

CLEVELAND AS HE LABORS OVER THE KEYBOARD OF THE ADMINISTRATION TYPEWRITER.

loyed. Coxey was abused, his men arrested ecause they "trespassed" on the Capitol lawn. He was called a crackpot and a lunatic, yet a ew decades later another Democratic President nade use of a similar device to create work.

In the midterm congressional election the Democrats suffered defeat. The Republicans, with a majority in both Houses of Congress, were confident of the future, boasting that in the next presidential election any Republican— even a rag doll—could become the President.

Mark Hanna, the Ohio millionaire-business-

(turn to page 432)

AT DEMOCRATIC HEADQUARTERS in Chicago, Governor John P. Altgeld of Illinois has a conference wit
Senator James K. Jones, chairman of the national committee, and Bryan, the Democratic-Populist candidate

AT REPUBLICAN HEADQUARTERS in New York, Mark Hanna, whose management of the campaign was m
terly, confers with the influential New York boss, Thomas Platt. Matt Quay, political boss of Pennsylvania, liste

THE FRONT-PORCH CAMPAIGN of William McKinley, who on Mark Hanna's advice remained at his home in Canton, Ohio, but spoke from his front porch to hundreds of delegations which came from all over the country.

THE WHIRLWIND CAMPAIGN of William Jennings Bryan, who traveled 18,000 miles, speaking more than 600 times. His theme was "the free and unrestricted coinage of silver and gold at the present legal ratio of 16 to 1."

A CARTOON AGAINST THE POPULISTS saying somewhat incorrectly that "it is the big humbugs and not the goldbugs" that are bothering our farmers. One insect is marked Bryan, the other Watson—the Populist candidates

man and chief Republican wirepuller, made up his mind long before the Republican convention met that the party's candidate should be his friend William McKinley, the Governor of Ohio. And if Hanna made up his mind about anything, he did not rest until he had achieved his goal. His adoration of McKinley, whom he had rescued from bankruptcy, was a strange phenomenon. "I love McKinley!" he said. "He is the best man I ever knew." Just why he loved McKinley is not easy to comprehend. Mark Hanna was a materialist, a ruthless go-getter; moral considerations affected him little. He believed in the power of money and that the strong should rule over the weak. McKinley was a different kind of man—a politician and a parliamentarian; for him the will of the majority was law. But Hanna knew that this will could be swayed, could be manipulated.

So with great energy, money, and the resourcefulness of a publicity agent, he started a movement on McKinley's behalf. He hired a private railroad car and in it his prospective candidate traveled throughout the country,

showing himself to the people, shaking hands and making friendly little speeches. The billboards of the cities which he visited were covered with posters welcoming "the advance agent of prosperity." And while McKinley put himself on view, Hanna worked behind the scenes. He made contacts with the local managers of the party, argued, talked, gave promises, and handed out money. This campaign-costing Hanna more than $100,000—was s effective that when the Republican conven tion assembled in St. Louis, the "spontaneous demand for McKinley was almost unanimou

The Republicans had greater difficulty t agree on the platform than to choose a cand date. The disagreement arose over whether the should issue a vague or a firm declaration r garding the party's financial policies. McKinle and Hanna advised against a firm declaratio but the Eastern delegates were for it.

There is a story that on Monday, June 1 at a St. Louis hotel, a man walked into Hann room "and without any preliminary greetir he said: 'Mr. Hanna, I insist on a positi

432

FARMER GETS UP AT A COUNTY MEETING TO ASK A QUESTION OF A BRYAN STUMP-SPEAKER.

:claration for a gold-standard plank in the plat-
rm.' Hanna looked up and said: 'Who in hell
e you?' The man answered: 'Senator Henry
abot Lodge of Massachusetts.' 'Well, Senator
enry Cabot Lodge of Massachusetts, you can
) plumb to hell. You have nothing to say
out it,' replied Mr. Hanna. Lodge said: 'All
ght, sir; I will make my fight on the floor of
e convention.' 'I don't care a damn where
)u make your fight,' replied Hanna."

Lodge did not have to fight on the floor,
r the gold-standard men won their point
fore the platform reached the convention.
was realized that it would have been useless
avoid the issue, for it was known that the
:mocrats would make a declaration for free
ver. So the platform announced that "the
:publican party is unreservedly for sound
)ney . . . unalterably opposed to every mea-
:e calculated to debase our currency or im-
ir the credit of our country . . . therefore,
:posed to the free coinage of silver." On the
iff the platform emphasized the Republican
rty allegiance "to the policy of protection as

the bulwark of American industrial independence and the foundation of American development and prosperity."

Henry M. Teller of Colorado, the leader of
the silver forces among the Republicans, presented a minority report offering a substitute
financial plank. It stated that "the Republican
party favors the use of both gold and silver as
equal standard money, and pledges its power to
secure the free, unrestricted, and independent
coinage of gold and silver at our mints at the
ratio of sixteen parts of silver to one of gold."

When the motion was rejected, the irate Teller, overcome by emotion, left the hall with
some thirty delegates from the Rocky Mountain
states. It was a dramatic scene as the "Silverites"
took up their banners and marched down the
main aisle, waving their flags amid abuse from
the others. The chairman, John M. Thurston
of Nebraska, remarked wryly that as enough
delegates remained behind, the convention
should proceed with its business.

After this incident the nominating speeches
began. William B. Allison's, Thomas B. Reed's,

433

Levi P. Morton's names were put in nomination; then Joseph B. Foraker spoke for McKinley. His speech was interrupted by frequent cheering, sometimes for as long as twenty-five minutes. The convention chairman left his place to second McKinley. He orated: "On behalf of that dismantled chimney and the deserted factory at its base, that the furnaces may once more flame, the mighty wheels revolve, the whistles scream, the anvils ring, the spindles hum . . . that the firesides again may glow, the women sing, the children laugh, yes, and on behalf of that American flag and all it stands for and represents, for the honor of every stripe, for the glory of every star, that its power may fill the earth and its splendor fill the sky, I ask for the nomination of that loyal American, that Christian gentleman, soldier, statesman, patriot, William McKinley."

The last of the nominating speeches was made on behalf of Matthew Quay; then the convention was ready to begin with the voting. It took only a single ballot to nominate McKinley, who received 661½ votes—about eight times more than the candidate with the next highest vote. Of his opponents, Reed had 84½, Quay 61½, Morton 58, Allison 35½. For the Vice-Presidency the convention chose Garret A. Hobart of New Jersey, a friend of Mark Hanna.

It was three weeks after the Republican convention that the Democrats met in Chicago. As thirty states in the West and South had already passed resolutions approving the free coinage of silver at a ratio of 16 to 1, the delegates from these states were determined to write a "silver" platform. Richard ("Silver Dick") Bland told an interviewer that the Democrats of the West were convinced that "the gold standard meant bankruptcy" and that the convention would declare for "the free coinage of silver at 16 to 1 and d——n the consequences!"

Bland's prophecy was borne out by succeeding events, for the convention proceedings were dominated by the adherents of free silver. "The sceptre of political power has passed from the strong, certain hands of the East to the feverish, headstrong mob of the West and South," wrote the New York *World*. The Silverites won all their battles: they chose one of their men for the temporary chairmanship, upsetting the choice of the national committee;

they augmented the representation of each territory from two members to six; they unseated the gold-standard delegation from Nebraska and admitted the free-silver delegation headed by William Jennings Bryan; they rejected four gold delegates from Michigan and acknowledged in their stead four silver delegates, so that under the unit rule the solid vote of that state would be cast for the Silverites' principles.

In their platform the Democrats declared "that the act of 1873 demonetizing silver without the knowledge or approval of the American people has resulted in the appreciation of gold and a corresponding fall in the prices of commodities produced by the people; a heavy increase in the burden of taxation and of all debts public and private; the enrichment of the money-lending class at home and abroad; the prostration of industry and impoverishment of the people."

Because of this—the platform continued—the Democrats were "unalterably opposed to monometallism, which has locked fast the prosperity of an industrial people in the paralysis of hard times. Gold monometallism is a British policy, and its adoption has brought other nations into financial servitude to London. It is not only un-American, but anti-American, and it can be fastened on the United States only by the stifling of that spirit and love of liberty which proclaimed our political independence in 1776 and won in the war of the Revolution. We demand the free and unlimited coinage of both silver and gold at the present legal ratio of sixteen to one."

On the tariff the platform declared that the "duties should be levied for purposes of revenue, such duties to be so adjusted as to operate equally throughout the country," and "that taxation should be limited by the needs of the government, honestly and economically administered."

Sixteen delegates of the committee on resolutions submitted a minority report which declared "that the experiment on the part of the United States alone of free silver coinage and change in the existing standard of value independently of the action of other great nations would not only imperil our finances, but would retard or entirely prevent the establishment of international bimetallism, to which the effort

IE POPULISTS PREDICTED THAT THIS WOULD HAPPEN IF WILLIAM McKINLEY WERE ELECTED.

the government should be steadily directed. would place this country at once upon a ver basis, impair contracts, disturb business, ninish the purchasing power of the wages of oor, and inflict irreparable evils upon our na- n's commerce and industry."

Therefore, so the minority report continued, ntil international cooperation among leading tions for the coinage of silver can be secured,

we favor the rigid maintenance of the existing gold standard as essential to the preservation of our national credit, the redemption of our public pledges, and the keeping inviolate of our country's honor. We insist that all our paper and silver currency shall be kept absolutely at a parity with gold."

With both reports before the convention, the debate began. Senator Benjamin ("Pitchfork (turn to page 438)

BEFORE "THE CRIME OF '73."

THIS IS THE ONLY KIND OF MONEY LITTLE WILLIE BRYAN EVER SAW IN "THE GOOD OLD FREE-COINAGE DAYS."

"TO ASK THE MAJOR TO DEFINE HIS ATTITUDE ON THE FI
QUESTION AT THIS TIME IS BOTH CRUEL AND UNJUS

HOW THE TWO FOREMOST PICTORIAL WEEKLIES COMMENTED ON THE CAMPAIGN. THE ILLUST

A SURE WINNER IF BRYAN IS ELECTED.

TEMPTED.

IN 1861
[WILL]IAM MC KINLEY
[WAS] UPHOLDING HIS
[COUNT]RY'S HONOR,—

HE'S DOING
IT YET!

IN 1861
THIS IS WHAT
WILLIAM J. BRYAN
WAS DOING,—

AND HE'S DOING
IT YET!

THE DEADLY PARALLEL.

LEADER ALTGELD AND HIS MASK.

[THE ILLUSTRATI]ONS AT THE TOP ARE FROM *HARPER'S WEEKLY*, AT THE BOTTOM FROM *LESLIE'S WEEKLY.*

THOU SHALT NOT STEAL.

A HOPELESS CASE.

Ben") Tillman of South Carolina leaped upon the platform and raged against the gold standard. President Cleveland was "a tool of Wall Street," Tillman shouted, and he asked for Cleveland's impeachment. The main speaker for the minority report was David Hill, the former Governor of New York. "I am a Democrat," Hill began, "but I am not a revolutionist." But as his speech was little more than an academic discussion of the matter, he made scant impression on the excited delegates. Two more speakers in support of the minority report fared no better.

The air was filled with high tension when William Jennings Bryan mounted the rostrum. He was cheered, and the cheers rolled on and on. When they subsided and a hush came over the audience, he began to speak. His words could be heard in every corner of the hall. "We do not come as aggressors," Bryan said. "Our war is not a war of conquest; we are fighting in the defense of our homes, our families, and posterity. We have petitioned, and our petitions have been scorned. We have entreated, and our entreaties have been disregarded. We have begged, and they have mocked when our calamity came. We beg no longer, we entreat no more, we petition no more. We defy them."

And twenty thousand voices echoed, "We defy them." Bryan posed the question: "Upon which side will the Democratic party fight; upon the side of the 'idle holders of idle capital' or upon the side of the 'struggling masses'?" The delegates sat breathless as the man on the platform reached the climax of his oratory: "You come to us and tell us that the great cities are in favor of the gold standard. We reply that the great cities rest upon our broad and fertile prairies. Burn down your cities and leave our farms, and your cities will spring up again as if by magic; but destroy our farms and grass will grow in the streets of every city in the country. . . . Having behind us the producing masses of the nation and the world, supported by the commercial interests, the laboring interests and the toilers everywhere, we will answer their demand for a gold standard by saying to them: 'You shall not press down upon the brow of labor this crown of thorns, you shall not crucify mankind upon a cross of gold.' "

Thus he ended, and twenty thousand people shouted: "Bryan, Bryan, Bryan!" It was one of those great moments, to be remembered for a lifetime. The cheering masses felt they had found their leader. The words of "the boy orator of the Platte" (which river Senator Foraker described acidly as "only six inches deep but six miles wide at the mouth") stirred the audience to a passionate outburst.

With a free-silver platform adopted, the convention was ready to begin balloting. Overnight William Jennings Bryan had become a strong contender for the nomination, challenging the favorite Richard P. Bland. It is true that on the first ballot his votes were less than Bland's (119 to Bland's 235), but four ballots later he won the nomination, with a great number of delegates favoring the gold standard abstaining from voting. For the Vice-Presidency the convention chose Arthur Sewall, a rich shipbuilder from Maine.

The third of the great conventions was that of the People's party. The Populists had made great strides since the last election. In the midterm congressional election of 1894 they had polled nearly a million and a half votes—42 per cent increase over their vote two years before. Their political issue—free silver—was now in the platform of the Democrats, and the majority of the Populist delegates were ready to accept the candidate of the Democrats—William Jennings Bryan. But there were many who were against this. The "middle-of-the-road men," as the opponents were called, advocated separate nominations and no alliance with either the Democrats or the Republicans. And particularly they would not hear of accepting the Democratic choice for the Vice-Presidency—Arthur Sewall, the rich shipbuilder. To block acceptance of Sewall, the middle-of-the-road men carried a motion whereby the nomination of the vice-presidential candidate was to precede the selection of the presidential candidate. Because of this successful maneuver, the Populists were able to nominate their own man, Thomas E. Watson, for the Vice-Presidency. For the first place they took Bryan.

The Prohibitionists' convention was no more harmonious than the meetings of the other parties. Here, too, the split came over the silver issue. One faction—the "Narrow Gaugers"—opposed free coinage and advocated a narrow plat-

THE MAN WHO MADE THE PRESIDENT. Mark Hanna, the Cleveland millionaire (on the left), spent a vast amount of his own money to secure the presidential nomination for his good friend William McKinley (on the right).

rm, consisting of only one plank prohibiting e manufacture and sale of intoxicating liquors. e "Broad Gaugers" favored a platform con- ting of many planks—a declaration similar that of the Populists. The Narrow Gaugers on their battle, whereupon the Broad Gaugers thdrew from the convention. Meeting again the National party, they accepted a platform oring free silver and nominated Joshua vering of Maryland for the Presidency. The rrow Gaugers nominated Reverend Charles Bentley of Nebraska.

Those Democrats who favored the gold stand- , and who were determined not to support Democratic platform nor the official candi- e, met in Indianapolis. Calling themselves the ional Democratic party, they adopted a plat- m against the coinage of silver and nominated n M. Palmer for the Presidency. The Repub- n seceders, Teller and his group, advocating silver, supported Bryan.

What an exciting campaign it was; the coun- had not seen its like for a long time. The main argument centered upon the silver issue, but the controversy over silver versus gold was more than a fight over monetary policies. The "battle of the standards" was really the struggle of the agrarian South and West against the industrial East, a fight between debtor and creditor for the ultimate control of government and economy; men with money against men without money.

The big businessmen, in fear of losing their privileges, contributed heavily to the Republi- can campaign fund, spending millions to stave off "anarchy." The Republican slogan was "A full dinner pail," and McKinley promised pros- perity if the country would elect him. Factory workers found slips in their pay envelopes (a device used against Cleveland four years be- fore): "If Bryan is elected, do not come back to work. The plant will be closed."

The Democratic candidate traveled around the country, carrying on an exhausting, aggres- sive campaign. Bryan visited twenty-nine states, made some 600 speeches, simplifying and drama-

THE SILVER-TONGUED ventriloquist and his dummies. "If the show succeeds, he'll get all the profits"—an inference that the campaign was really conducted to further the interests of the big silver-mine owners.

"PROUD AS A PEACOCK with two tails." William Jennings Bryan ran on the Democratic ticket with Sewall as the candidate for the Vice-Presidency; and on the Populist ticket with Thomas Watson as his running mate.

tizing the causes of economic ills and offering the cure-all: free coinage of silver. In his opinion what the country needed was an abundance of silver money and good times would be back again. He spoke against the plutocrats, who should be held in check by the government, for if the government was not "greater than the banker of Wall Street," it was "no government at all." He said that for the financiers there was "not a law, human or divine, which they would respect," because they thought they were "bigger than the government and greater than the Almighty." It was only the "common people" who had "ever supported a reform that had for its object the benefit of the human race." In another speech he told his audience "Look at the people who are at the head of the gold-standard propaganda of the United States. Nineteen hundred years ago "the meek and lowly Saviour threw the same kind of people out of His temple because they had made His house a den of thieves." And Bryan, who liked to allude to the Bible, said: "The Creator has made men," He had not used "any superior kind of mud when He made financiers."

He strongly denied the accusations of the Republicans that he was a "revolutionary and an anarchist." No, he was none of these; he was only a crusader for humanity. He spoke for the distressed farmers of the West and South and against the forces which in his opinion caused the distress—the industrialists, the railroads, and the trusts. But whatever he said, the underlying factor of all his attacks was the fear that the government might come under the never-ending supremacy of the plutocrats.

For McKinley the astute Mark Hanna—who as "Dollar Mark" was more under attack than the candidate himself—devised a new kind of campaign. The Republican standard-bearer was to remain at his home in Canton and speak from the front porch of his house to delegations which came to see him, their fares paid by the Republican campaign management. Delegation after delegation came; on some days McKinley spoke twenty times to people on the lawn and shook hundreds of hands. His speeches were "so strong, so varied, so pertinent, so full of facts briefly set forth, of theories embodied a single phrase, that they formed the house text for the other speakers of the party," s

ILLIAM JENNINGS BRYAN AS HE LOOKED WHEN HE RECEIVED THE DEMOCRATIC NOMINATION.

McKINLEY ACCEPTS THE CONGRATULATIONS OF THE PEOPLE WHO CAME TO SHAKE HIS HAND

WILLIAM JENNINGS BRYAN AND HIS WIFE POSE FOR PHOTOGRAPHERS DURING THE CAMPAIGN

THE POPULAR AND ELECTORAL VOTES IN THE 1896 ELECTION

| STATES | POPULAR VOTE | | | | | | | ELECTORAL VOTE | | | | |
| | | | | | | | | PRESIDENT | | VICE-PRESIDENT | | |
	William McKinley, Ohio. Republican	William J. Bryan, Nebraska. Democrat	Bryan and Watson. Populist	John M. Palmer, Illinois. Nat. Democrat	Joshua Levering, Maryland. Prohibitionist	C. E. Bentley, Nebraska. National	C. H. Matchett, New York. Socialist Labor	McKinley.	Bryan.	Hobart.	Sewall.	Watson.
Alabama	54,737	131,226	24,089	6,462	2,147	—	—	—	11	—	11	—
Arkansas	37,512	110,103	—		839	893	—	—	8	—	5	3
California	146,688	144,766	21,730	2,006	2,573	1,047	1,611	8	1	8	1	—
Colorado	26,271	161,269	2,389	1	1,717	386	160	—	4	—	4	—
Connecticut	110,285	56,740	—	4,336	1,806	—	1,223	6	—	6	—	—
Delaware	20,452	16,615		966	602	—	—	3	—	3	—	—
Florida	11,257	31,958	1,977	1,772	644	—	—	—	4	—	4	—
Georgia	60,091	94,672	440	2,708	5,716	—	—	—	13	—	13	—
Idaho	6,324	23,192			181	—	—	—	3	—	3	—
Illinois	607,130	464,523	1,090	6,390	9,796	793	1,147	24	—	24	—	—
Indiana	323,754	305,573	—	2,145	3,056	2,267	324	15	—	15	—	—
Iowa	289,293	223,741	—	4,516	3,192	352	453	13	—	13	—	—
Kansas	159,541	171,810	46,194	1,209	1,921	630	—	—	10	—	10	—
Kentucky	218,171	217,890	—	5,114	4,781	—	—	12	1	12	1	—
Louisiana	22,037	77,175	—	1,015	—	—	—	—	8	—	4	4
Maine	80,461	34,587	2,387	1,866	1,589	—	—	6	—	6	—	—
Maryland	136,978	104,746	—	2,507	5,922	136	588	8	—	8	—	—
Massachusetts	278,976	105,711	15,181	11,749	2,998	—	2,114	15	—	15	—	—
Michigan	293,582	237,268	—	6,968	5,025	1,995	297	14	—	14	—	—
Minnesota	193,503	139,735	—	3,222	4,363	—	954	9	—	9	—	—
Mississippi	5,123	63,793	7,517	1,071	485	—	—	—	9	—	9	—
Missouri	304,940	363,652	—	2,355	2,169	293	599	—	17	—	13	4
Montana	10,494	42,537	—		186	—	—	—	3	—	2	1
Nebraska	103,064	115,999	—	2,797	1,243	797	186	—	8	—	4	4
Nevada	1,938	8,377	575					—	3	—	3	—
New Hampshire	57,444	21,650	379	3,520	779	49	228	4	—	4	—	—
New Jersey	221,367	133,675	—	6,373	5,614	—	3,085	10	—	10	—	—
New York	819,838	551,369	—	18,950	16,052	—	17,667	36	—	36	—	—
North Carolina	155,222	174,488	—	578	676	245	—	—	11	—	6	5
North Dakota	26,335	20,686	—	—	358	—	—	3	—	3	—	—
Ohio	525,991	477,497	2,615	1,858	5,068	2,716	1,167	23	—	23	—	—
Oregon	48,779	46,662	—	977	919	—	—	4	—	4	—	—
Pennsylvania	728,300	433,230	11,176	10,921	19,274	870	1,683	32	—	32	—	—
Rhode Island	37,437	14,459	—	1,166	1,160	5	558	4	—	4	—	—
South Carolina	9,313	58,801	—	824	—	—	—	—	9	—	9	—
South Dakota	41,042	41,225	—		683	—	—	—	4	—	2	2
Tennessee	148,773	166,268	4,525	1,951	3,008	—	—	—	12	—	12	—
Texas	167,520	370,434	79,572	5,046	1,786	—	—	—	15	—	15	—
Utah	13,491	64,607	—	21	—	—	—	—	3	—	2	1
Vermont	50,991	10,607	461	1,329	728	—	—	4	—	4	—	—
Virginia	135,388	154,985	—	2,127	2,350	—	115	—	12	—	12	—
Washington	39,153	51,646	—	1,668	968	148	—	—	4	—	2	2
West Virginia	104,414	92,927	—	677	1,203	—	—	6	—	6	—	—
Wisconsin	268,135	165,523	—	4,584	7,509	346	1,314	12	—	12	—	—
Wyoming	10,072	10,655	286	—	136	—	—	—	3	—	2	1
	7,111,607	6,509,052	222,583	134,645	131,312	13,968	36,373	271	176	271	149	27

he Populist vote—Bryan and Watson—is included in the Bryan column.   Total vote, 13,936,957.

is friend John Hay. They were flashed over the vires and printed in every Republican paper.

The foreign issues—the annexation of Hawaii nd the restoration of the queen to her throne; Britain's controversy with Venezuela, which rew such a strong declaration from Cleveland hat it was feared it might cause war between England and America; the insurrection in Cuba nd the threatening of the American sugar interests—were all widely discussed topics at that me but had little influence on the election.

Mark Hanna's campaign was eminently successful. McKinley won, receiving over seven million votes against Bryan's 6,500,000. Fourteen million people went to the polls, the greatest number on record. (In Pennsylvania 190,000 more voted than in 1892; in Ohio, 158,000 more; in Illinois, 217,000 more; in Indiana 83,000 more.)

Bryan was supported by the eleven states of the Solid South and the Western states of Colorado, Idaho, Kansas, Montana, Nebraska, Nevada, South Dakota, Utah, Washington, and Wyoming; he also won the border state of Missouri. But all the states of the industrial North and the Middle West, as well as California and Washington, were for McKinley. It

THE McKINLEY FAMILY leaving their home in Canton, Ohio, to take up residence in Washington.

THE INAUGURAL SPEECH. The outgoing President, Grover Cleveland, listens to his successor.

was clearly an Eastern victory against the West and South, the result being somewhat influenced by the rise in wheat prices during the summer. In both Houses of Congress the Republicans had a comfortable majority, though in the Senate the Silverites held the balance of power.

On the night of the election, and after the result was known, McKinley, his wife, and mother were kneeling in the bedroom. The old lady had her arm around her son and was praying fervently: "Oh God, keep him humble."

The financiers and businessmen were jubilant. Gold came out from its hoarding places; brokers' offices in New York and London were open all night, doing a thriving business. The defeat of Bryan and Populism gave the industrialists a respite. They could breathe freely; no one was to interfere with their monopolistic ambitions.

THE CLOSING FEATURE OF INAUGURATION

The most acute observation about the election was made by Tom Johnson, Mayor Cleveland, who called it "the first great prote

THE GRAND BALL IN THE LAVISHLY DECORATED PENSION OFFICE BUILDING IN WASHINGTON.

of the American people against monopoly—the first great struggle of the masses in our country against the privileged classes. It was not free silver that frightened the plutocrat leaders. What they feared then, what they fear now, is free men."

McKINLEY GOES TO HIS INAUGURATION

THE TWENTY-NINTH ELECTION—1900

WILLIAM McKINLEY
AND THEODORE ROOSEVELT

When President McKinley began his term, the worst of the depression was already over and the future looked bright. Prosperity would have come even if the country had elected Bryan, but as it was McKinley who occupied the presidential chair, the Republicans took credit for the return of good times.

In their last campaign the Republicans had promised to tackle two main issues on the domestic front: one was the tariff, the other was currency.

A revised tariff bill—introduced by Congressman Dingley—was soon enacted, raising the duties on many products and building a high protective wall around America.

Over the currency issue the furore had not died down. In the Senate a sizable group still advocated free silver, and the administration had to bide its time, hoping that in the midterm election the number of silver Senators would be reduced. But the silver issue found its solution in a way the Democrats and Populists least expected. The scarcity of gold vanished when new gold mines were discovered in Australia, South Africa, and the Klondike. In addition, methods of extracting gold from the ore were greatly improved—thus the gold production, which had been practically static through the years, was suddenly more than doubled. The Treasury, having more gold in reserve, issued more banknotes, and with more money the cry for the coinage of silver became subdued. There was no longer any need to revert to silver when there was sufficient gold.

In the second half of McKinley's administration (after the midterm election the number of silver Senators diminished), Congress enacted a currency bill declaring the gold dollar as the standard unit of value and making every other form of money in use redeemable in gold.

But more than on domestic issues, the interest of the country was focused on problems brought about by the Cuban insurrection. The revolution of 1895 had gained momentum and grown in violence. The insurgents on the island, fighting the political oppression and economic exploitation of their Spanish overlords, conducted a reckless guerrilla warfare. Trains were destroyed, properties wrecked, sugar plantations burned.

447

*PRESIDENT McKINLEY
AND HIS WIFE*

THE CANDIDATES

WILLIAM MCKINLEY
(1843-1901), the candidate of the Republicans for a second term. As prosperity had returned to the country, he was sure to win. Imperialism was the foremost campaign issue, and the Republicans won a decisive victory with 292 electoral votes to the Democrats' 155.

THEODORE ROOSEVELT
(1858-1919), Spanish War hero and Governor of New York, became vice-presidential candidate through efforts of Thomas Platt, who was determined to get rid of Roosevelt as Governor of New York. When McKinley died in September, 1901, Roosevelt became President.

WILLIAM J. BRYAN
(1860-1925), leader of the Democratic party, was again their candidate on a platform opposing imperialism and the trusts and endorsing free silver. American policy in the Philippines was the most widely discussed issue. Though he campaigned strenuously, Bryan lost.

ADLAI E. STEVENSON
(1835-1914) of Illinois, former Greenbacker who was for low tariff and sympathized with aims of the Silverites, was Vice-President during Cleveland's second administration. In this election he was again chosen for the second place, defeating David Hill for the nomination.

In the outcome of the Cuban fighting the United States had a vital interest. American investment in sugar plantations was estimated to be $50,000,000, while American trade with that island was more than twice that amount.

Besides the economic interests, there were political and moral considerations. The political one was the importance of an isthmian canal and its defense; the moral one was the brutal policy of Spain against the helpless Cubans—the concentration-camp methods of the Spanish general, "Butcher" Weyler, who herded thousands of the island's inhabitants behind barbed wire, caring little about providing adequate living quarters and food.

The temper of the Americans was kept at boiling point by the lurid atrocity stories of the "yellow press." As months went by, jingoism became rampant; intervention was urged, and the cry for the liberation of Cuba increased. America talked itself into a war.

McKinley, who had been elected on a platform calling for Cuban independence, offered his good services to Spain in September, 1897, but the offer was rejected. The President was at first against armed intervention and he said so in his annual message to Congress two months later.

And except for two events which occurred in the second week of February, 1898, a peaceful solution of the controversy might have been reached. But the publication of a private letter written by the Spanish Minister to the United States, in which the envoy called McKinley a vacillating and shifty politician, "yielding to the rabble," and a far more serious incident—the explosion of the battleship *Maine* in the port of Havana, in which 268 lives were lost—made a settlement without war a seeming impossibility.

Public sentiment demanded intervention; the Hearst papers, the warmongers, the jingoists had the upper hand. At the beginning of March the House of Representatives appropriated $50,000,000 for national defense. A fortnight later the American envoy in Spain delivered a dispatch to the Spanish government demanding the cessation of hostilities in Cuba.

McKinley, obsessed with the idea that if he did not yield to the popular demand he would lose his leadership in the party, sent his war

THE POPULAR AND ELECTORAL VOTES IN THE 1900 ELECTION

STATES	POPULAR VOTE								ELECTORAL VOTE	
	McKinley and Roosevelt, Republican.	Bryan and Stevenson, Democrat.	Wooley and Metcalf, Prohibition.	Debs and Harriman, Social-Democrat.	Malloney and Remmel, Socialist-Labor.	Barker and Donnelly, Mid-Road Populist.	Ellis and Nicholson, Union Reform.	Leonard and Martin, United Christian.	McKinley and Roosevelt.	Bryan and Stevenson.
Alabama	55,512	97,131	2,762	—	—	4,178	—	—	—	11
Arkansas	44,800	81,142	584	27	—	972	341	—	—	8
California	164,755	124,985	5,087	7,572	—	—	—	—	9	—
Colorado	93,072	122,733	3,790	714	684	389	—	—	—	4
Connecticut	102,572	74,014	1,617	1,029	908	—	—	—	6	—
Delaware	22,535	18,863	546	57	—	—	—	—	3	—
Florida	7,420	28,007	2,234	601	—	1,070	—	—	—	4
Georgia	35,056	81,700	1,396	—	—	4,584	—	—	—	13
Idaho	27,198	29,414	857	—	—	232	—	—	—	3
Illinois	597,985	503,061	17,626	9,687	1,373	1,141	572	352	24	—
Indiana	336,063	309,584	13,718	2,374	663	1,438	254	—	15	—
Iowa	307,808	209,265	9,502	2,742	259	613	—	707	13	—
Kansas	185,955	162,601	3,605	1,605	—	—	—	—	10	—
Kentucky	226,801	234,899	2,814	770	299	2,017	—	—	—	13
Louisiana	14,233	53,671	—	—	—	—	—	—	—	8
Maine	65,412	36,822	2,585	878	—	—	—	—	6	—
Maryland	136,185	122,238	4,574	904	388	—	147	—	8	—
Massachusetts	239,147	157,016	6,208	9,716	2,610	—	—	—	15	—
Michigan	316,269	211,685	11,859	2,826	903	837	—	—	14	—
Minnesota	190,461	112,901	8,555	3,065	1,329	—	—	—	9	—
Mississippi	5,753	51,706	—	—	—	1,644	—	—	—	9
Missouri	314,092	351,922	5,965	6,139	1,294	4,244	—	—	—	17
Montana	25,373	37,145	298	708	169	—	—	—	—	3
Nebraska	121,835	114,013	3,655	823	—	1,104	—	—	8	—
Nevada	3,849	6,347	—	—	—	—	—	—	—	3
New Hampshire	54,799	35,489	1,279	790	—	—	—	—	4	—
New Jersey	221,754	164,879	7,190	4,611	2,081	691	—	—	10	—
New York	822,013	678,462	22,077	12,869	12,621	—	—	—	36	—
North Carolina	132,997	157,733	1,006	—	—	830	—	—	—	11
North Dakota	35,898	20,531	731	520	—	111	—	—	3	—
Ohio	543,918	474,882	10,203	4,847	1,588	251	4,284	—	23	—
Oregon	46,526	33,385	2,536	1,494	—	275	—	—	4	—
Pennsylvania	712,665	424,232	27,908	4,831	2,936	638	—	—	32	—
Rhode Island	33,784	19,812	1,529	—	1,423	—	—	—	4	—
South Carolina	3,579	47,233	—	—	—	—	—	—	—	9
South Dakota	54,530	39,544	1,542	169	—	339	—	—	4	—
Tennessee	123,180	145,356	3,860	413	—	1,322	—	—	—	12
Texas	130,641	267,432	2,644	1,846	162	20,981	—	—	—	15
Utah	47,139	45,006	209	720	106	—	—	—	3	—
Vermont	42,569	12,849	383	39	—	367	—	—	4	—
Virginia	115,865	146,080	2,150	145	167	63	—	—	—	12
Washington	57,456	44,833	2,363	2,066	866	—	—	—	4	—
West Virginia	119,829	98,807	1,692	219	—	268	—	—	6	—
Wisconsin	265,760	159,163	10,027	7,048	503	—	—	—	12	—
Wyoming	14,482	10,164	—	—	—	—	—	—	3	—
	7,219,525	6,358,737	209,157	94,864	33,432	50,599	5,698	1,059	292	155

Total vote, 13,973,071.

message to Congress in the second week of April, declaring: "In the name of humanity, in the name of civilization, in behalf of endangered American interests which give us the right and the duty to speak and to act, the war in Cuba must stop." With the war message before Congress, the Committee on Foreign Affairs in both the House of Representatives and the Senate reported a preamble and resolutions on Cuba, authorizing the President "to intervene at once to stop the war in Cuba, to the end and with the purpose of securing permanent peace and order there."

After a fiery debate in both Houses, a significant amendment—the Teller Amendment—was added to the resolutions already adopted. In it the United States disclaimed "any disposition or intention to exercise sovereignty, jurisdiction, or control over said island, except for the pacification thereof," and promised that after the restoration of peace, the government and control of the island would be left to its people. On April 20 McKinley signed the joint resolution, and a few days later the United States was at war with Spain.

At the beginning of the war, the treaty for

WHO SHALL BE VICE-PRESIDENT? As Garret Hobart, McKinley's first Vice-President, died in office, a new candidate had to be found. Here McKinley ponders who shall get the job. It finally went to Theodore Roosevelt

THIS WAS THE REASON—so one cartoonist asserted—why Mark Hanna did not want Theodore Roosevelt to receive the Republican vice-presidential nomination.

the annexation of Hawaii still had not been ratified by the American Senate. But after Admiral Dewey was victorious in the Battle of Manila Bay, the hesitancy of the Senators to ratify the treaty ceased. Now it was thought of paramount importance to deny other countries—meaning chiefly Japan—the possibility of obtaining sovereignty over these islands. Thus on May 17 a joint resolution was reported declaring that as the government of Hawaii had consented to the cession of all rights of sovereignty over the islands to the United States, the cession was "accepted, ratified and confirmed."

The majority of the Democratic Senators opposed this resolution. They said that it was against the spirit of the Constitution to occupy a distant territory; America should never become an imperialist power. But as it was feared that if the United States did not accept the cession Japan might conquer the islands, the joint resolution was adopted, and the American flag was hoisted at Honolulu on August 12.

"THAT MAN CLAY WAS AN ASS" says Mark Hanna to McKinley. "It's better to be President than to be right." During the 1900 campaign, the supporters of William Jennings Bryan built up a legend that President McKinley was nothing but a tool in the hands of Hanna, whom the political cartoonists, following the example of Homer Davenport of the New York *Journal*, consistently pictured as a gross plutocrat covered with dollar signs. But "Dollar Mark" did well for his friend. McKinley was elected **for a** second term by a safe majority of 860,788 popular votes.

By this time the hostilities against Spain were already over. "It has been a splendid little war," wrote John Hay to his friend Theodore Roosevelt. It was most certainly an easy war, without much sacrifice or bloodshed.

On July 26 Jules Cambon, the French ambassador, asked the United States for peace terms on behalf of the Spanish government. McKinley dictated them four days later. These were the demands: Spain was to evacuate and relinquish Cuba, and to cede Puerto Rico and an island in the Ladrones. The United States was to occupy the city, harbor, and bay of Manila pending the final disposition of the Philippine Islands.

On the day the American flag was hoisted at Honolulu, a preliminary peace treaty was signed in Washington by the American Secretary of State and Jules Cambon for Spain. And in October five American commissioners met in Paris to negotiate the final peace.

When the treaty came before the Senate for ratification in the first week of January, 1899, the Democrats opposed it. They took great exception to the provisions which asked for the occupation of the Philippines. All over the country arguments were heard whether America should become imperialistic. From both Democratic and Republican ranks strong resistance was offered against McKinley's policies. The newly formed Anti-Imperialist League protested vociferously against the establishment of a colonial system by the United States.

It seemed that the administration would not be able to muster the necessary two-thirds majority to ratify the treaty. Half an hour before the final vote—at two-thirty in the afternoon of February 6, 1899—the Republicans were still one vote short. To their rescue came William Jennings Bryan, who—though decidedly against the treaty's imperialist provisions—used his influence on behalf of ratification. The reason for Bryan's intervention in this battle was an obvious one: he desired to fight the coming presidential election on this issue.

As the date of the nominating conventions arrived, there was little doubt that both the Republicans and Democrats would revert to the same candidates as four years before—McKinley and Bryan.

THEODORE ROOSEVELT, who as Governor of N. pleased Sen. Platt (right), became McKinley's running

THE REPUBLICAN CONVENTION in Philadelp tended by twenty thousand people, was a harmoniou

THE DEMOCRATIC CONVENTION in Kansas nominated the "peerless leader," William Jennings

RK HANNA, devoted friend of President William McKinley, whose campaign he managed in 1896 and whom he rescued from bankruptcy, speaks to the Republican convention, recommending McKinley's renomination.

N'S NOMINATION by the Democratic convention was d by outbursts of enthusiasm from the crowded floor.

WILLIAM JENNINGS BRYAN, the Democratic candidate, makes acceptance speech in Indianapolis.

THE NEW ISSUE: IMPERIALISM

BRYAN REPAINTS the old "Free-Silver" sign of the 1896 campaign with the new issue—"Imperialism."

"THE NEW HOOP." Democratic Chairman Jones says to Bryan: "That old Imperialism hoop is safer, William."

PRESIDENT McKINLEY MEASURES UNCLE SAM

The Republican convention in Philadelphia would have been remembered as one of the dullest in history had it not been for circumstances regarding the vice-presidential nomination. As Vice-President Garret A. Hobart had died in office, the Grand Old Party was in search of a substitute. President McKinley suggested Senator Allison; Mark Hanna's choice

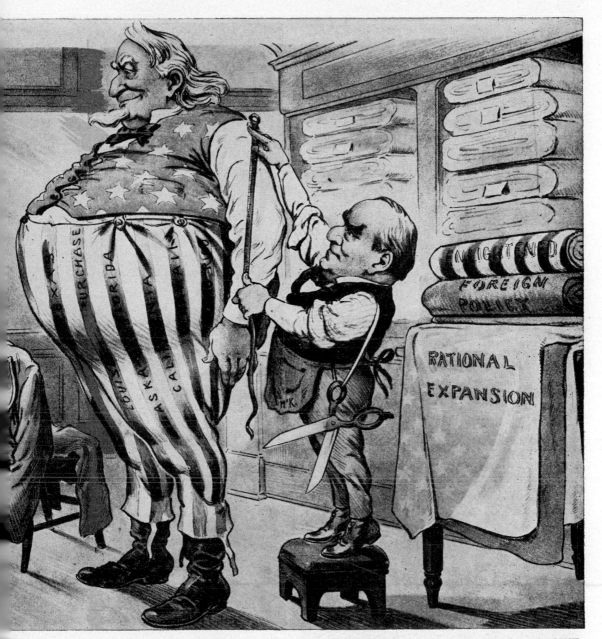

...W SUIT OF "EXPANSION" CLOTH WHILE THE ANTI-IMPERIALISTS OFFER HIM SOME MEDICINE.

...vas Cornelius N. Bliss, the Secretary of the ...nterior. But neither Allison nor Bliss desired ...he nomination.

Theodore Roosevelt, New York's young ...overnor, the hero of San Juan Hill in the ...panish-American War, was the favorite of the ...epublican rank and file. However, Mark ...Ianna, the Republican chairman, thought him

"unsafe." Ordinarily, this would have been sufficient to wipe out the contestant's name from the slate. But Thomas Platt, the boss of the New York machine, joined hands with Matt Quay, the boss of Pennsylvania, and the two forced Hanna to accept Theodore Roosevelt as the vice-presidential candidate. This was not because they admired Roosevelt's qual-

455

BRYAN'S NEW BALLOON HEADS FOR EXPLOSION

FOUR MORE YEARS OF "FULL DINNER PAILS"

THE DEMOCRATIC DONKEY IS SWALLOWED A

ities; it was not because they believed tha
Roosevelt would make a good Vice-Presiden
Platt sought the vice-presidential office for h
"protegé" in order to get rid of him as Gover
nor of New York, in which office Roosevel
was not as submissive to Platt's wishes nor s
manageable as the party bosses would hav
liked him to be.

THE BIG POPULIST BOA CONSTRICTOR, WHICH BEARS THE HEAD OF WILLIAM JENNINGS BRYAN.

Roosevelt, afraid that the Vice-Presidency would mean his political death, demurred against Platt's conspiracy. He went to Mark Hanna and told him that he was not a candidate. "What I want is to be Governor of New York," said Roosevelt. Hanna would have liked to see Roosevelt, whose "dangerous" ideas were upsetting to businessmen, re-

ceive another term as governor, and he was willing to support him in the impending gubernatorial campaign. He said to McKinley: "You know, a President sometimes dies and where would we be if Roosevelt should come to the White House?"

But in the convention, when Roosevelt made the seconding speech for President McKinley's

457

THE REPUBLICANS told the country that prosperity had returned because of their high protective tariffs and their sound-money policy. The country, thoroughly enjoying the good times, did not care very much what brought prosperity about — so long as it would stay.

HIS RUNNING MATE.

THE ROUGH RIDER Theodore Roosevelt, Republican vice-presidential candidate, campaigned vigorously while McKinley stayed in Washington. "Teddy" declared himself in favor of the foreign policy of the administration, which advocated the taking of Cuba and the Philippines.

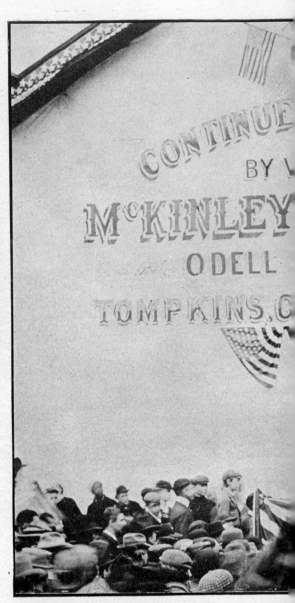

THEODORE ROOSEVELT MAKING A CAMP

nomination, there was such an ovation for him that he "stood flushed and almost dazed by the tremendous character of his greeting." The delegates, shaking off their lethargy, showed that their preference for the Vice-Presidency was the Rough Rider. Thus the Republican ticket became "William McKinley, a Western man with Eastern ideas; and Theodore Roosevelt, an Eastern man with Western characteristics." After seeing the great enthusiasm

PERITY
R
OSEVELT,
DRUFF,
TAYLOR.

...H IN NEW YORK, HIS HOME STATE, WHILE NEWSPAPER REPORTERS TAKE NOTES OF ADDRESS.

...oosevelt could do nothing but acquiesce. And ...Hanna said to McKinley: "Now it is up to ...ou to live."

The Republican platform boasted in exultant ...erms about the achievements of the McKinley ...dministration. It recalled that four years ago, ...when the people then assembled at the polls, ...fter a term of Democratic legislation and ad-...inistration, business was dead, industry para-...zed and the national credit disastrously

impaired. The country's capital was hidden away, and its labor distressed and unemployed. The Democrats had no other plan with which to improve the ruinous conditions which they had themselves produced than to coin silver at the ratio of 16 to 1." The Republicans proudly reminded the country that it was they who had restored prosperity "by means of two legislative measures—a protective tariff and a law making gold the standard of value"; they re-

459

ELECTION NIGHT IN NEW YORK

THE *TRIBUNE* NEWSROOM early in the evening. The editors were making the first election forecasts.

IN THE BILLIARD ROOM of the Waldorf-Astoria Hotel, a well-to-do crowd waits for election returns.

CROWDS GATHERED on the rooftops in the Madison Square district to watch the election night fireworks.

"I-TOLD-YOU-SO" HATS APPEARED IN H[...]

asserted their "steadfast opposition to the free and unlimited coinage of silver." Their platform spoke in ambiguous words of restraining the trusts—recognizing "the necessity and propriety of the honest cooperation of capital to meet new business conditions, and especially

our rapidly increasing foreign trade," but condemning "all conspiracies and combination[s] intended to restrict business, to create monopolies, to limit production or to control prices."

On foreign issues the Republican platform favored "the construction, ownership, contr[ol]

... WHEN THE ELECTION OF McKINLEY AND ROOSEVELT WAS CONCEDED BY THE DEMOCRATS.

...d protection of an isthmian canal," approved ...he annexation of the Hawaiian Islands," ac...pted the Treaty of Paris as the only way "to ...stroy Spain's sovereignty throughout the ...'est Indies and in the Philippine Islands," and ...edged "independence and self-government"

for Cuba. All this sounded good to the voters.

The Democratic convention, which assembled in Kansas City, was no more exciting than the Republican. As expected, the party nominated William Jennings Bryan by acclamation, while for the second place Adlai E.

Stevenson—the former Vice-President under Cleveland—was selected in a contest with David B. Hill of New York.

The platform of the Democrats was built around three main issues: imperialism, trusts, and free silver. "The burning issue of imperialism, growing out of the Spanish War," so the platform announced, "involves the very existence of the Republic and the destruction of our free institutions. We regard it as the paramount issue of the campaign." In a spirited passage the Democrats told the country: "We hold that the Constitution follows the flag and denounce the doctrine that an Executive or Congress . . . can exercise lawful authority . . . in violation of it. We assert that no nation can long endure half republic and half empire, and we warn the American people that imperialism abroad will lead quickly and inevitably to despotism at home." The Democrats demanded "a prompt and honest fulfillment of our pledge to the Cuban people and the world that the United States has no disposition nor intention to exercise sovereignty, jurisdiction or control over the island of Cuba, except for its pacification." They denounced the Philippines policy of the administration because "the Filipinos cannot be citizens without endangering our civilization," and spoke out against militarism, which "means conquest abroad and intimidation and oppression at home."

When this plank was read, the delegates burst out in a tumultuous ovation. Banners with the inscription, "Lincoln abolished slavery; McKinley has restored it," were carried through the hall. From the roof a seventy-foot-long flag was unfurled, bearing the words: "The Flag of the Republic forever; of an Empire never!"

On the trust issue the Democratic platform was clearer than the Republican. It declared that "private monopolies are indefensible and intolerable. They destroy competition, control the price of raw material and of the finished product, thus robbing both producer and consumer"; therefore stringent laws against corporations should be enforced, otherwise "all wealth will be aggregated in a few hands and the Republic destroyed."

On silver the old plank for "the free and unlimited coinage of silver and gold at the present legal ratio of 16 to 1" was adopted, but only after a sharp fight in the committee on resolutions.

The platform flatly condemned the Dingley Tariff Law "as a trust-breeding measure," denounced the currency bill, favored an amendment to the Constitution providing for the election of Senators by popular vote, asked for an "intelligent system of improving the arid lands of the West," and for statehood for the territories of Arizona, New Mexico, and Oklahoma. Other planks demanded home rule and a territorial form of government for Alaska and Puerto Rico, and favored the "immediate construction, ownership and control of the

CONTRASTING PERSONALITIES IN THE CAMPAIGN. McKinley dons a top hat and shows himself decorous to the people, but Theodore Roosevelt, second on the ticket, canvasses votes on horseback, wearing a wide sombrero

FOR THE SECOND TIME PRESIDENT McKINLEY TAKES THE OATH FROM CHIEF JUSTICE FULLER.

VICE-PRESIDENT-ELECT ROOSEVELT ARRIVES AT THE CAPITOL FOR THE INAUGURAL CEREMONY.

THE LAST PHOTOGRAPH OF McKINLEY. The President and his wife leaving the residence of their host, John G. Milburn, in Buffalo, at nine o'clock on the morning of September 6, 1901. He was shot that afternoon

THE TEMPLE OF MUSIC in Buffalo where McKinley was assassinated during the Pan-American Exposition.

Nicaraguan Canal by the United States."

Besides the Republicans and Democrats, a number of minor parties held nominating conventions and chose candidates.

The Social Democratic party, appearing for the first time in a national election, named Eugene V. Debs for the Presidency. In their platform they demanded: first, "revision of our Federal Constitution, in order to remove the obstacles to complete control of government by the people, irrespective of sex"; second, "the public ownership of all industries controlled by monopolies, trusts and combines"; third, "the public ownership of all railroads, telegraphs and telephones; all means of transportation; all waterworks, gas and electric plants, and other public utilities"; fourth, "the public ownership of all gold, silver, copper, lead, iron, coal and other mines, and all oil and gas wells"; fifth, "the reduction of the hours

KINLEY IS SHOT by anarchist Leon Czolgosz as he greets the guests at a public reception in his honor. The
assin advanced toward the President as if to shake his hand and discharged a revolver hidden in a handkerchief.

labor in proportion to the increasing facil-
es of production"; sixth, "the inauguration
a system of public works and improvements
for the employment of the unemployed, the
public credit to be utilized for that purpose";
seventh, "useful inventions to be free, the in-

MARK HANNA AND FRIENDS wait for the physicians' bulletins in front of the Milburn mansion where McKinley lay between life and death. At first there was hope for his recovery, but he grew worse and died a week later

THE ASSASSIN, Leon Czolgosz, desolate behind his prison bars, was executed for the crime he had committed.

ventors to be remunerated by the public eighth, "labor legislation to be national, instead of local, and international when possible ninth, "national insurance of working people against accidents, lack of employment, and want in old age"; tenth, "equal civil and political rights for men and women, and the abolition of all laws discriminating against women eleventh, "the adoption of the initiative and referendum, proportional representation, and the right of recall of representatives by the voters," and finally, "abolition of war and the introduction of international arbitration."

The Populists, no longer as important as at the last election, again endorsed Bryan, as did the silver Republicans and the Anti-Imperial League. But the middle-of-the-road faction of the Populists, which had disapproved of the

THE VICE-PRESIDENT ARRIVES. Theodore Roosevelt passes through the police lines on his way to the Milburn house. When it became apparent that McKinley would not recover, he was hastily summoned to Buffalo.

fusion with the Democrats in 1896, named its own candidates—Wharton Barker of Pennsylvania for the Presidency and Ignatius Donnelly for the Vice-Presidency. The United Christian party, the Socialist-Labor party, the Union Reform party, and the National Prohibition party also nominated standard-bearers.

The campaign's main issue was imperialism. The Democrats charged McKinley and the Republicans with the abandonment of America's traditional anti-empire policy and with the subjugation of millions of defenseless people. McKinley replied in his acceptance letter that "no blow has been struck except for liberty and humanity and none will be," and claimed that the Republican administration had not subdued but liberated ten million people from the yoke of imperialism." He added

A LARGE CROWD WAITS anxiously in the streets for the latest news about the President's condition.

467

THE FLOWER-BANKED COFFIN OF McKINLEY ARRIVES AT CANTON, OHIO, HIS OLD HOME TOWI

warningly: "There must be no scuttle policy."

As tradition forbade the President to go on the stump, the brunt of the Republican campaign was borne by the vice-presidential candidate. Teddy Roosevelt roused the enthusiasm of his audience wherever he went; people liked his direct approach and warm personality, and they found his Harvard accent fascinating.

Bryan repeated his performance of fot years before, making six hundred speeches twenty-four states, his sonorous baritone ring ing with indignation against imperialism an the trusts.

The outcome of the election was never que tioned, though Mark Hanna was apprehensi for weeks, fearing that the general politic

THE ROOM AT THE WILCOX HOUSE IN BUFFALO WHERE ROOSEVELT TOOK THE OATH OF OFFICE.

pathy and overconfidence of the Republicans might jeopardize McKinley's chances. From the forty-five states which voted in November, McKinley received 7,219,525 votes against Bryan's 6,358,737.

Senator Platt could rejoice. That "cowboy" Roosevelt was leaving the governor's house at Albany to become president of the Senate— an office which the sly New York Senator believed would mark the end of Roosevelt's political career. But fate intended otherwise. On September 6, 1901, McKinley was shot by the anarchist Leon F. Czolgosz as he attended a public reception in Buffalo. Eight days later he died and forty-three-year-old Theodore Roosevelt became President of the United States.

T.R. TAKES THE INAUGURAL OATH

THE THIRTIETH ELECTION—1904

THEODORE ROOSEVELT

After Theodore Roosevelt became President, an English weekly described him as:

A smack of Lord Cromer, Jeff Davis a touch of him;
little of Lincoln, but not very much of him; itchener, Bismarck and Germany's Will,
piter, Chamberlain, Buffalo Bill."

es, he was all this and a lot more.

Roosevelt came from a wealthy house, his ther being the son of one of the richest men New York; (his ancestor Claes Martenszen an Rosenvelt arrived in this country in 49); he was a graduate of Harvard and died law at Columbia. As a young man wrote an important work, *The Naval ar of 1812*, and he was a naturalist of merit. d while he loved books, he was also a man action. He led the horseless Rough Riders San Juan Hill, he enjoyed hunting big me, and he was a perfect cowboy. In addi-n, Roosevelt had a full and varied political reer. He began it as assemblyman in Albany 1882; seven years later President Harrison pointed him as civil service commissioner; in 5 he became police commissioner in New

York; after McKinley's election in 1896 he was made Assistant Secretary of the Navy. Leaving this office to volunteer in the Spanish-American War, he returned as a hero, and was elected Governor of New York. These, in a nutshell, were the milestones of his activities until he was named as the vice-presidential candidate.

Roosevelt was a reformer; he had progressive ideas, but he was more conservative than radical, believing in the existing economic system of the country as long as its abuses could be remedied and as long as its financial leaders could be kept in check.

When McKinley lay between life and death in his bed at Buffalo, the Wall Street bankers looked with despair into the future. With Roosevelt in the presidential chair they were prepared for the worst. They feared that the impetuous Rough Rider would attack the big business interests. The anxiety of the financiers revealed itself in a letter which Roosevelt's brother-in-law dispatched to Buffalo by special messenger a day before McKinley's death, and in which he told the future President that "there is a feeling in financial circles here that

THEODORE ROOSEVELT (1858-1919) was named by the Republicans. He won an overwhelming victory in the election, beating the Democrats with 7,628,785 votes to Alton Parker's 5,084,442

CHARLES W. FAIRBANKS (1852-1918), lawyer and Senator from Indiana, became the vice-presidential candidate, because as Roosevelt put it, "Who in the name of heaven else is there?"

ALTON B. PARKER (1852-1926) of N. Y., was chosen by the Democrats, hoping that he could rally the Republican businessmen who were dissatisfied with the Roosevelt policies.

HENRY G. DAVIS (1823-1916), 81-year-old millionaire from West Virginia, was selected for second place by the Democrats, who hoped he would contribute to their campaign fund.

EUGENE V. DEBS (1855-1926), editor and labor leader, was the candidate of the Socialists with Benjamin Hanford of New York as his running mate. The ticket got 402,895 votes.

SILAS C. SWALLOW (1839-1930) of Pennsylvania became the candidate of Prohibitionists after General Miles declined to run. At the polls, the Prohibitionists won 258,950 votes.

THE REPUBLICAN CONVENTION in Chicago, Roosevelt was nominated unanimously by the dele

THE DEMOCRATIC CONVENTION in St. Louis Alton B. Parker, who defeated William Randolph

in case you become President you may chan matters so as to upset the confidence . . . the business world, which would be an aw blow to everybody."

But Roosevelt did not need the warning. knew that he had to take it easy—for a wh anyhow. He reassured the country that would "continue, absolutely unbroken, policy of President McKinley."

CARTOON, "The Convention Has Arrived,"
s how solidly Republicans backed Roosevelt.

THE REPUBLICAN TICKET. Theodore Roosevelt and
Charles Fairbanks, a conservative politician from Indiana.

ER'S TELEGRAM to the convention, favor-
e gold standard, caused a great sensation.

THE DEMOCRATIC CANDIDATE, Alton B. Parker (right),
is formally notified of his nomination at Esopus, New York.

There were rumors of a break between
Mark Hanna and Roosevelt. The Republican
chairman, deeply moved by McKinley's death,
lamented that now "that damned cowboy is
president of the United States." Other reports
said that on the funeral train the disconsolate
Hanna and the new President had a long talk
and parted as friends. "He's a pretty good little
cuss after all," Hanna is supposed to have said.

In any case, a month after McKinley's death
he wrote a friendly letter to Roosevelt, advising him to "go slow."

The new President followed his advice. He
sent a very moderate first message to Congress.
The part against trusts was especially toned
down after consultation with Hanna. The in-
imitable Mr. Dooley thought that Mr. Roosevelt's attitude about the trusts could be

expressed in one sentence: "On wan hand I wud stamp thim under feet; on th' other hand not so fast."

But Roosevelt was not a man who could "go slow" for very long. A few more months and he was ready to fight the "malefactors of great wealth." His first attack against big business came when Philander Knox, his Attorney General, asked for the dissolution of the Northern Securities Company. This was a challenge to the mighty J. P. Morgan, who had made the merger a year previously, aiming at a railroad monopoly in the Northwest. The financier and his friends hurried to Washington. "If we have done anything wrong," he said to the President, "send your man (meaning Attorney General Knox) to my man (naming one of his lawyers) and they can fix it up." "That can't be done," said Roosevelt firmly. And Knox added: "We don't want to fix it up; we want to stop it." When Morgan saw he could not get any promise, he asked Roosevelt: "Are you going to attack my other interests?" The Presi-

dent answered: "Certainly not, unless we find out that in any case they have done something we regard as wrong."

The Northern Securities case before the courts was only the curtain-raiser in Roosevelt's battle against the trusts. To win it the President needed the country's support, so he went on a speaking tour, traveling through New England and the Western states, taking the people into his confidence. Roosevelt told his listeners that "the biggest corporation, like the humblest private citizen, must be held to strict compliance with the will of the people." He castigated the wealthy who "go into wild speculation and lose their heads"; he attacked the rich who get richer while the poor get poorer. The thousands who came to hear him cheered; they approved his action. Here at last was a man after their own hearts—a President who came to talk to them and told them what he was going to do. The country had not known anyone like him since Andrew Jackson.

The anxious millionaires saw the handwriting

MARK HANNA, HARD-PRESSED BY HIS ENEMY FORAKER, HANDS ROOSEVELT THE ENDORSEME

474

"HE'S GOOD ENOUGH FOR ME," HOMER DAVENPORT'S CARTOON FOR THEODORE ROOSEVELT.

ROOSEVELT'S NEW CAMPAIGN MANAGER SQUEEZES MONEY OUT OF THE BIG CORPORATION

on the wall. James J. Hill, the railroad king, in a letter to a friend, wrote despairingly of the injustice that he and other men like him "should be compelled to fight for our lives against the political adventurers who have never

done anything but pose and draw a salary

Roosevelt's popularity grew with the pass ing of every day; he won friends easily. H had the country's wholehearted support whe in 1902 he brought the coal operators and t representatives of the miners' union together in an effort to bring to an end a serious coal strike which was paralyzing the country. His trust-busting activities were applauded, and labor acknowledged that he was on their side when they fought for their legitimate rights.

But more than for his handling of domestic issues, Roosevelt was admired for his dealing with foreign affairs. "Speak softly and carry a big stick" was an African proverb which became his maxim. He interfered without hesitation when Britain, Italy, and Germany dispatched their warships into Venezuelan waters, blocking the coast in an effort to collect money which Venezuela owed them. The President's attitude in preventing the "spanking" of a small country, even if that country was ruled by "a villainous little monkey" (as Roosevelt referred to the Venezuelan President), was instrumental in settling the controversy.

In another South American incident Roose-velt showed equal firmness. When European governments, exasperated by Santo Domingo's evasion in paying its debts, threatened the forcible collection of the pledged customs receipts, Roosevelt made it clear that the United States still adhered to the Monroe Doctrine. To the doctrine he added his much-discussed corollary, in which he declared: "Brutal wrong-doing or an impotence which results in a general loosening of the ties of civilized society may finally require intervention by some civilized nation, and in the Western Hemisphere the United States cannot ignore this duty." These words created fear in South America. Would the United States chastise the small states if they misbehaved—if they didn't pay their debts? It seemed so.

In neither Venezuela nor Santo Domingo did the United States have a personal interest. But in Colombia it had. As American influence spread in the Pacific, an isthmian canal became

THEODORE ROOSEVELT VOTES ON NOVEMBER 8, 1904, AT A POLLING PLACE IN OYSTER BAY.

a necessity. The obvious place to dig such a canal was either Nicaragua or Colombia, but when a negotiated treaty was submitted to Colombia, that country refused to ratify it. Whereupon—and not without American help—a convenient revolution took place. Roosevelt recognized the new government in a hurry and signed a treaty with its new representatives. Years later Roosevelt said proudly, "I took Panama."

But however great Roosevelt's achievements were, he was disturbed that he was only President by accident, that he had not been voted into office by the people. "I'd rather be elected to that office than have anything tangible of which I know. But I shall never be elected to it. They don't want me," he said with self-pity (meaning by *They* the party bosses—Hanna, Platt, and the others).

Roosevelt exaggerated. Though there was some opposition to him, it was safe to assume that he would be the party's choice in 1904. That the party bosses and the leaders of big business were anxious to bring him under their influence was only natural. They felt that the President's suit against the Northern Securities Company, his intervention in the coal strike, his messages to Congress against the trusts, and his anti-trust speeches were ample proof that Roosevelt had decided to fight the big business interests. Some of the financiers thought that it would be wise to replace him with Mark Hanna. But the astute Hanna knew better; tired and sick, to die within a year, he realized that he could not become President. On the other hand, he was not averse to using the boom for his candidacy as a weapon by which Roosevelt could be put under obligation.

But before Hanna could fortify his position, Senator Foraker, who was jealous of Hanna and would have liked to supplant the old man as national chairman, precipitated a conflict and ruined the plan. In May, 1903, the senior Senator from Ohio invited the press into his office and gave out a statement that "Roosevelt had made a good President" and that he was "the most popular man in the United States." Therefore he suggested that the Ohio Republican state convention scheduled for the following month should come out for Roosevelt's nomination. "I do not know of any

reason why Ohio should not declare for him," he said. As Foraker let it be known that any opposition to Roosevelt's nomination was Hanna's work because Hanna himself desired the office, the old man was forced to issue a statement. Enraged over Foraker's challenge of his authority, he answered much too rashly. "I am not, and will not be a candidate for the presidential nomination," he told the press the same day, and then he enumerated the reasons why the Republicans in Ohio should not commit themselves on the presidential nomination a year ahead of the national convention.

But after Hanna released his statement, he must have had misgivings. Mindful of how Roosevelt—then traveling through the West—would react to it, Hanna sent a wire to the President: "The issue which has been forced upon me in the matter of our state convention this year endorsing you for the Republican nomination next year has come in a way which makes it necessary for me to oppose such a resolution. When you know all the facts, I am sure you will approve my course."

Upon receipt of Hanna's telegram, Roosevelt replied at once, giving his answer simultaneously to the press. "I have not asked any man for his support," he wired Hanna. "I have nothing whatever to do with raising this issue. Inasmuch as it has been raised, of course those who favor my administration and my nomination will favor endorsing both, and those who do not will oppose."

Poor Hanna, outmaneuvered on one side by Foraker, on the other by Roosevelt, had to acknowledge defeat. "In view of the sentiment expressed I shall not oppose the endorsement of your administration," he wired back.

Roosevelt was elated. To his friend Cabot Lodge he wrote: "Hanna was my only formidable opponent so far as this nomination is concerned. The whole incident has entirely revived me. . . . This last business gave me a new and vivid interest in life." And he went on speaking and working for his renomination.

As the date of the Republican convention approached, the President was busy making preparations. Elihu Root was to be temporary chairman, and as he was to make the keynote address, Roosevelt briefed him on what to emphasize. The winning of Panama, the

"THE MYSTERIOUS STRANGER." McCUTCHEON'S CARTOON ABOUT MISSOURI'S DEFECTION IN 1904.

Northern Securities suit, Cuban independence, the administration of the Philippines, the Alaska boundary, the Department of Commerce and Labor, the Open Door to China, the Venezuela affair, the administration's enforcement of the Monroe Doctrine—these were the main achievements of his administration, these were to be mentioned in the platform.

That the convention would choose Roosevelt was a certainty. All 994 delegates voted for him, and named Charles Warren Fairbanks for the Vice-Presidency by acclamation.

The Democrats, meeting in St. Louis, turned away from Bryan, the twice-defeated candidate. This time they nominated a conservative, "safe and sane" candidate—a New York judge—Alton B. Parker. The party's eastern wing regained control and the influence of the West diminished; Bryan and the populist doctrines were relegated to the background. The Democrats hoped to make a better showing by adhering to their traditional policies and choosing not only a "safe and sane" man but a "safe and sane" platform. They figured that the Republican businessmen might rather give their support to Parker than to Roosevelt. For the second place they named the eighty-one-year-old Henry G. Davis of West Virginia, a strange choice indeed. They expected that the millionaire Davis would contribute freely to the campaign chest—an idle hope.

Bryan, strongly opposing the nomination of Parker, whose opinions were unknown, asked the Democrats for a renewed declaration for free silver, but his move was defeated.

After Parker heard of his nomination, he sent a telegram to the convention declaring that he regarded the gold standard "as firmly and irrevocably established and shall act accordingly." And if the convention did not approve his views, he would decline the nomination. The excited delegates replied to Parker: "The platform adopted by this con-

479

THE POPULAR AND ELECTORAL VOTES IN THE 1904 ELECTION

STATES	POPULAR VOTE						ELECTORAL VOTE	
	Roosevelt and Fairbanks, Republican.	Parker and Davis, Democrat.	Swallow and Carroll, Prohibition.	Debs and Hanford, Socialist.	Corregan and Cox, Socialist-Labor.	Watson and Tibbles, Populist.	Roosevelt and Fairbanks.	Parker and Davis.
Alabama	22,472	79,857	612	853	—	5,051	—	11
Arkansas	46,860	64,434	993	1,816	—	2,318	—	9
California	205,226	89,404	7,380	29,535	—	—	10	—
Colorado	134,687	100,105	3,438	4,304	335	824	5	—
Connecticut	111,089	72,909	1,506	4,543	575	495	7	—
Delaware	23,712	19,359	607	146	—	51	3	—
Florida	8,314	27,040	5	2,337	—	1,605	—	5
Georgia	24,003	83,472	685	197	—	22,635	—	13
Idaho	47,783	18,480	1,013	4,949	—	353	3	—
Illinois	632,645	327,606	34,770	69,225	4,698	6,725	27	—
Indiana	368,289	274,335	23,496	12,013	1,598	2,444	15	—
Iowa	307,907	149,141	11,601	14,847	—	2,207	13	—
Kansas	212,955	86,174	7,306	15,869	—	6,253	10	—
Kentucky	205,277	217,170	6,609	3,602	596	2,511	—	13
Louisiana	5,205	47,708	—	995	—	—	—	9
Maine	64,438	27,649	1,510	2,103	—	—	6	—
Maryland	109,497	109,446	3,034	2,247	—	—	1	7
Massachusetts	257,822	165,772	4,286	13,604	2,365	1,290	16	—
Michigan	364,957	135,392	13,441	9,042	1,036	1,159	14	—
Minnesota	216,651	55,187	6,253	11,692	974	2,103	11	—
Mississippi	3,187	53,374	—	392	—	1,424	—	10
Missouri	321,449	296,312	7,191	13,009	1,674	4,226	18	—
Montana	34,932	21,773	335	5,676	208	1,520	3	—
Nebraska	138,558	52,921	6,323	7,412	—	20,518	8	—
Nevada	6,864	3,982	—	925	—	344	3	—
New Hampshire	54,163	34,074	750	1,090	—	83	4	—
New Jersey	245,164	164,516	6,845	9,587	2,680	3,705	12	—
New York	859,533	683,981	20,787	36,883	9,127	7,459	39	—
North Carolina	82,442	124,121	361	124	—	819	—	12
North Dakota	52,595	14,273	1,140	2,117	—	165	4	—
Ohio	600,095	344,674	19,339	36,260	2,633	1,392	23	—
Oregon	60,455	17,521	3,806	7,619	2,211	753	4	—
Pennsylvania	840,949	337,998	33,717	21,863	2,211	—	34	—
Rhode Island	41,605	24,839	768	956	488	—	4	—
South Carolina	2,554	52,563	—	22	—	1	—	9
South Dakota	72,083	21,969	2,965	3,138	—	1,240	4	—
Tennessee	105,369	131,653	1,891	1,354	—	2,506	—	12
Texas	51,242	167,200	3,995	2,791	421	8,062	—	18
Utah	62,446	33,413	—	5,767	—	—	3	—
Vermont	40,459	9,777	792	859	—	—	4	—
Virginia	47,880	80,650	1,382	218	56	359	—	12
Washington	101,540	28,098	3,329	10,023	1,592	669	5	—
West Virginia	132,628	100,881	4,600	1,572	—	339	7	—
Wisconsin	280,315	124,205	9,672	28,240	223	530	13	—
Wyoming	20,489	8,930	217	1,077	—	—	3	—
	7,628,785	5,084,442	258,950	402,895	33,490	114,546	336	140

Total vote, 13,523,108.

vention is silent upon the question of the monetary standard, because it is not regarded by us as a possible issue in this campaign, and only campaign issues are mentioned in the platform. Therefore, there is nothing in the views expressed by you in the telegram just received which would preclude a man entertaining them from accepting a nomination on said platform." And so the judge remained the Democratic candidate.

The ensuing campaign, devoid of any new issues, was as dull as Parker. The Wall Street bankers, who were not supposed to support Roosevelt, swung behind him. He was now even upheld by the *Sun*, the newspaper of big business. In a five-word editorial, probably the shortest ever written, the *Sun* declared "Theodore! With all thy faults."

But the campaign apathy disappeared when Joseph Pulitzer published an eight-column editorial in the New York *World*, in which he asked Roosevelt some pertinent questions. Pulitzer wanted to know why the Bureau of Corporations had done nothing so far. Was it because big businessmen, "pouring money into your campaign chests, assume they are buy

THE YOUNGEST PRESIDENT of the United States, Theodore Roosevelt, reads his inaugural address in which he dealt with the preparation of an adequate national defense and the establishment of social and industrial justice.

ng protection?" And why had the head of he Bureau become the national chairman? Roosevelt had chosen George Cortelyou as national chairman after Mark Hanna died earlier in the year.) Pulitzer wanted to know: (1) How much has the beef trust contributed to Mr. Cortelyou? (2) How much has the paper trust contributed to Mr. Cortelyou? (3) How much has the coal trust contributed to Mr. Cortelyou? (4) How much has the sugar trust contributed to Mr. Cortelyou?

At first Roosevelt remained silent. But when a month later Parker asserted that the corporations had paid blackmail money so that the Bureau of Corporations would not reveal damaging facts about them, he found his voice. "That

481

TEDDY COMES INTO HIS OWN

AFTER ROOSEVELT WON the election by an overwhelming majority, he issued a statement to the press
in which he declared that "the wise custom which limits
the President to two terms regards the substance and not
the form, and under no circumstances will I be a candidate for or accept another nomination." He regretted it.

"AVE THEODORE!", A CARTOON SHOWING

"ALL HIS OWN." Roosevelt, whose greatest desire
was to become President in his own right, was much
elated over his victory. On the night before his inauguration he said to his friends: "Tomorrow I shall come
into my office in my own right. Then watch out for me!"

contributions have been made is not the que-
tion at issue," Roosevelt announced, but "t
assertion that there has been any blackma
direct or indirect, by Mr. Cortelyou or
me is a falsehood."

The election was a great victory for Roo
velt, who won by the enormous majority
2,500,000 votes, while Alton B. Parker v

482

POLITICAL CAPTIVES AND RETAINERS IN A TRIUMPHAL PROCESSION TO THE WHITE HOUSE.

unable to carry a single state north of the Mason and Dixon line.

When the result became known, Roosevelt said with great satisfaction: "I am no longer a political accident." On that very day he told the country: "On the 4th of March next I shall have served three and a half years and this . . . constitutes my first term. The wise custom which limits the President to two terms regards the substance and not the form; and under no circumstances will I be a candidate for or accept another nomination."

He was to regret his rashness. Some time later he confided to a friend: "I would cut my hand off right there," putting his finger on his wrist, "if I could recall that written statement!"

TAFT DELIVERS HIS INAUGURAL SPEECH

THE THIRTY-FIRST ELECTION—1908

WILLIAM H. TAFT

"Tomorrow I shall come into my office in my own right," said Theodore Roosevelt to a friend a day before his inauguration. "Then watch out for me!"

Now that Roosevelt was President in his own right, the "Imperial Years" were under way. They were exciting, busy years. The President's fingers seemed to be in every pie.

He mediated between Russia and Japan, bringing the Russo-Japanese War to an end; he intervened in the Moroccan crisis and war between Germany and France was avoided. And while he took vigorous interest in foreign affairs, he did not neglect to show strong leadership in the battle over domestic issues. "Don't flinch, don't foul, hit the line hard" was one of his favorite aphorisms, and he lived by it. He hit out hard against the "malefactors of great wealth"; he kept on crusading against the trusts, dramatizing their evil influence.

Under his administration Congress enacted a great number of important laws. The most notable was directed toward the regulation of railroad rates. A meat inspection bill and a pure food law were passed; national forest reserves were established; soil conservation was furthered; the construction of the Panama Canal begun.

While Theodore Roosevelt sat in the presidential chair the American people had rarely a dull moment, for their President supplied them with a wonderful spectacle. If Roosevelt was not in the deep waters of political controversy, he was in the midst of a bitter personal quarrel. And the people loved him for it; they found him amusing and colorful; they watched him with awe. A prominent Englishman reported that the two most remarkable things he saw in the United States were "Niagara Falls and the President . . . both wonders of Nature." If he had wanted to remain President, he could have received the nomination again; the country was ready to elect him for what Roosevelt would have called a "third term."

But Roosevelt was not seeking another term. He reminded his followers of the statement which he had issued the day of the last election, declaring that he would "under no circumstances" be a candidate for renomination. But who would be? Who would be the man to succeed him and continue his policies?

The names of Elihu Root, the Secretary of

WILLIAM HOWARD TAFT
AND HIS PREDECESSOR
ON INAUGURATION DAY

THE CANDIDATES

WILLIAM H. TAFT (1857-1930), a jovial, 330-pound personality, with a most infectious chuckle, was the successor whom Roosevelt picked to carry on with policies begun by him.

JAMES S. SHERMAN (1855-1912) was Taft's running mate as a gesture to the conservatives. The Republican ticket was victorious with 7,677,788 votes to Democrats' 6,407,982.

WILLIAM J. BRYAN (1860-1925) who in the 1904 election had stepped aside for a "safe-and-sane" man, again was Democratic choice but suffered the third defeat of his career.

JOHN W. KERN (1849-1917) of Indiana, ardent Democrat from boyhood, was second on the Democratic ticket. He campaigned vigorously over the country on a reform platform.

EUGENE V. DEBS (1855-1926), Socialist candidate backed by a great many immigrants, now ran for the third time, his vote increasing to 420,890 over the 98,864 received in 1900.

EUGENE W. CHAFIN (1852-1920) of Illinois was the Prohibitionist candidate with Aaron Watkins of Ohio as his running mate. They received in this election 252,511 popular votes.

State, of Charles Hughes, the Supreme Court judge, of Warren Fairbanks, the Vice-President, of Robert La Follette, the Senator from Wisconsin, of "Uncle Joe" Cannon, the Speaker of the House, were mentioned with frequency. But when it came to the choice of a successor, Roosevelt selected the man whom he addressed in his letters as "Dear Old Fellow"—William Howard Taft.

The friendship between Roosevelt and Taft was an old one, dating back to 1890 when both were at the bottom of the political ladder. At that time they were both living in Washington, Roosevelt holding the job of civil service commissioner, Taft of Solicitor General.

After Roosevelt became President, he relied on Taft more than on any other man. He used him as his handy man. Wherever there were difficulties, he dispatched him to smooth the troubled waters. And the jovial, considerate, friendly Taft with the infectious chuckle, "grabbing a time-table and throwing a change of clothing into a traveling bag," journeyed to the scene of upset, soon "making two laughs echo where one groan was heard before." It was the same whether the place was Panama (to iron out construction obstacles), Tokyo (to smooth tempers when California barred Japanese from public schools and forbade them to own land), Rome (to discuss matters with the Vatican regarding the landholdings of Catholic friars in the Philippines), or China (to persuade the government to lift the boycott against American goods).

Taft's laugh became known as "one of our great American institutions"; his friendliness and humanity were fine diplomatic assets. He liked people and people liked him. "I think Taft has the most lovable personality I have ever come in contact with," said Roosevelt. It was only natural that the country began to think of him as a presidential possibility. Taft was not only a kindly soul, he was not only a good negotiator, but he was a good jurist and an outstanding administrator, which he proved when he served in the Philippines as America's first governor.

Ever since late in 1902, when Roosevelt first offered him an appointment on the Supreme Court bench, Taft had been pondering. He himself would rather have had a judicial career

HILARIOUS DRAWING by the English cartoonist, Bernard Partridge, for *Punch*. Roosevelt says to Taft, whom
e chose to succeed him, "There, there, sonny, I've fixed you up so they won't know the difference between us."

THE REPUBLICAN CONVENTION

TWELVE THOUSAND people were present in Chicago's coliseum where William H. Taft was nominated.

PARADE IN CHICAGO of supporters of Philander C. Knox, Roosevelt's trust-busting Attorney General.

CHARLES TAFT, brother of the Republican candidate, worked hard for William Taft's nomination and election.

"MILES STANDISH" ROOSEVELT SPEAKS FOR "

than anything else, and he was supported i this by his mother, who said: "I do not war my son to be President. A place on the Su preme bench, where my boy would administe justice, is my ambition for him. His is a judici mind and he loves the law." But his wife an his brother were of another opinion an thought he should try for the Presidency.

So when the first offer came from Roosev

" TAFT AND THE WISE PRISCILLA ASKS, "WHY DON'T YOU SPEAK FOR YOURSELF, JOHN?"

appoint Taft to the Supreme Court, the
overnor of the Philippines cabled: "Great
onor deeply appreciated but must decline. . . .
onditions here would make my withdrawal
iolation of duty. . . . Nothing would satisfy
dividual taste more than acceptance. I long
or a judicial career but if it must turn on my
resent decision I am willing to lose it."

Some months later the temptation returned.

Again a vacancy occurred in the Supreme
Court and again Roosevelt wrote: "Dear Will,
I am awfully sorry, old man, but . . . I shall
have to put you on the Supreme Court."

Taft winced. He hesitated to accept the appointment and played for time. He answered
the President: "I recognize a soldier's duty
to obey orders, but I presume on our personal
friendship to make one more appeal." And

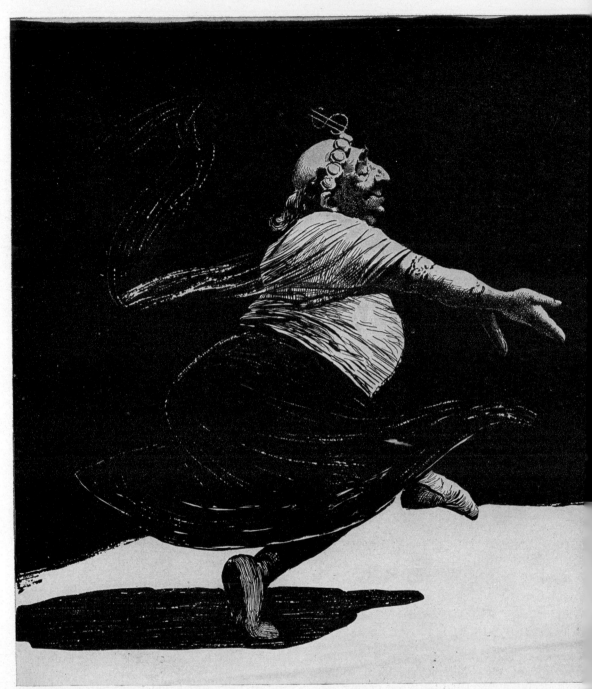

"SALOME" BRYAN MAKES HIS THIRD BID FOR THE NOMINATION BEFORE THE DEMOCRATIC

Roosevelt told the "Dear Old Fellow" to "stay where you are. I shall appoint someone else to the Court."

A year passed and Taft made great progress

with "the little brown brothers." In the fa of 1903 Roosevelt issued another call for hin this time it was the office of the Secretary War. And this time Taft was ready to lea

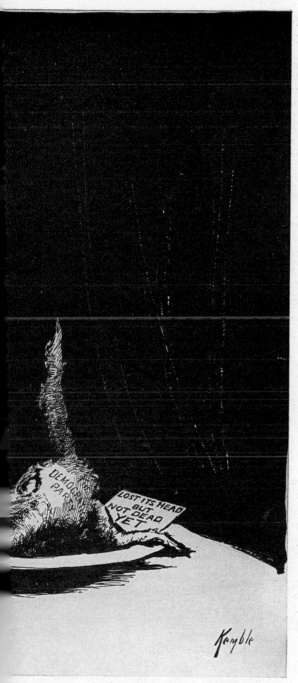

H HAS LOST ITS HEAD BUT IS "NOT DEAD YET."

he Philippines and come home. To Mrs. Taft
he new post "was much more pleasing than
he offer of the Supreme Court appointment
ecause it was in line with the kind of work I

wanted my husband to do, the kind of career
I wanted for him and expected him to have,
so I was glad there were few excuses for refusing to accept it open to him."

Taft returned to Washington and his popularity as Secretary of War in Roosevelt's Cabinet grew. Early in 1906 there was another vacancy in the Supreme Court, and now for the
third time Roosevelt offered him the office.
The President wrote Taft a letter on the 15th
of March, leaving the decision to him. "It
is a hard choice to make," wrote Roosevelt,
"and you yourself have to make it. You have
two alternatives before you, each with uncertain possibilities, and you cannot feel sure
that whichever you take, you will not afterwards feel that it would have been better if
you had taken the other."

For three and a half months Taft thought
it over. His political friends advised him to
accept. But his wife and his brother Charles
urged him to decline and make himself available for the presidential nomination.

Taft made a formal statement, somewhat
hesitantly, somewhat reluctantly. "I am not
seeking the presidential nomination," he said,
but added: "I am not foolish enough to say
that in the improbable event that the opportunity to run for the great office of President
were to come to me, I should decline it, for
this would not be true." This was an announcement that he was available.

As the convention year approached, it
seemed certain that the Democrats would turn
to Bryan again. Their "safe and sane" candidate, Judge Parker, and their "safe and sane"
platform in the last election had brought them
a greater defeat than ever before. So they were
ready to try again with Bryan and with a
progressive platform. No serious contender
was in the field to challenge the "peerless
leader's" candidacy, though William Randolph
Hearst's Independent League made preparations to battle against both the Democratic and
Republican choices.

That Taft would be the nominee of the Republicans was also virtually certain. Early one
morning in 1908 Roosevelt's secretary, William
Loeb Jr., told the President that "we must
have a candidate. If things continue to drift

(turn to page 494)

491

THE REPUBLICAN CANDIDATE, William Howard Taft, went on an extensive campaign tour which carried through the Middle Western and Western States. Here he delivers a speech from the back of his special t

TAFT CAMPAIGNING in an automobile. In the back seat of beflagged vehicle sits the venerable Gen. Keifer.

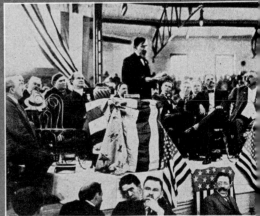

JOHN W. KERN, the Democratic vice-preside didate, accepts the nomination in a speech at Ind

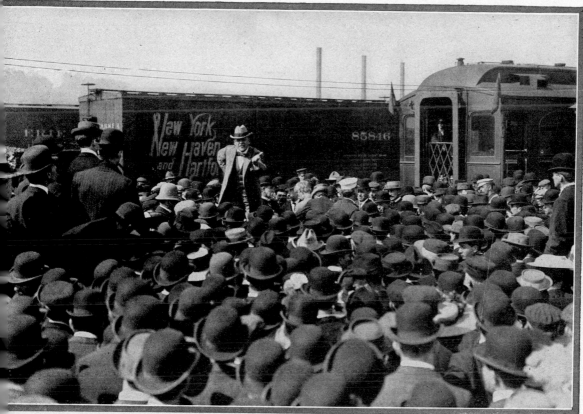

SOCIALIST CANDIDATE, Eugene V. Debs, campaigned extensively in his train, nicknamed "The Red
cial." He visited many parts of the country, making speeches to propagate the Socialist party program.

SHERMAN, the Republican vice-presidential
delivers his acceptance speech at Utica, N. Y.

WILLIAM J. BRYAN, the choice of the Democrats for
the Presidency, accepts the nomination at Lincoln, Neb.

493

"FORWARD MARCH!", a cartoon against Bryan, shows the Democratic candidate walking the road of Radicalism, while his party takes the path of Conservatism.

"THE TWICE-BELTED KNIGHT." William Jennings Bryan, who suffered defeat in 1896 and in 1900, starts out once more on the back of the Democratic donkey.

ONE OF THE FUNNIEST CARTOONS OF TH

along as now, our friends may lose contro
Roosevelt replied that the man whom
would like to have succeed him was Eli

494

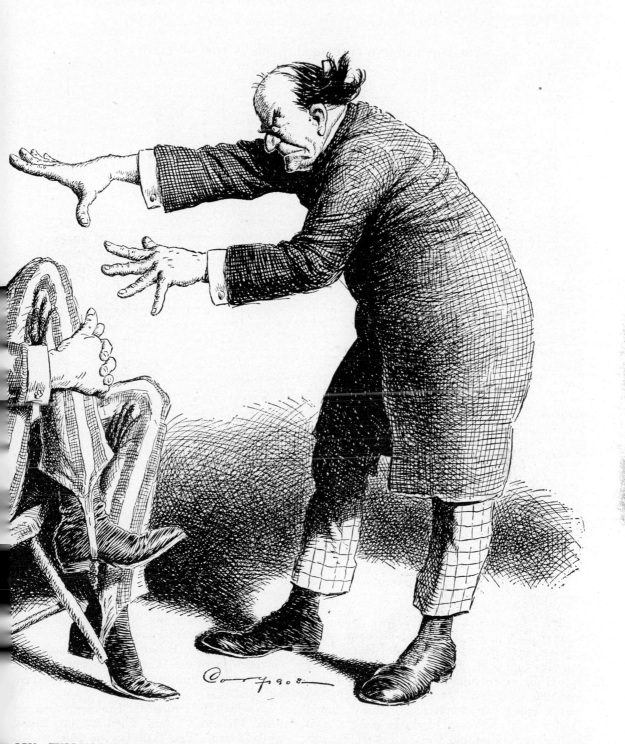

IGN: WILLIAM JENNINGS BRYAN IS TRYING WITHOUT SUCCESS TO HYPNOTIZE UNCLE SAM.

Root. He had once said to a friend that he would rather see Elihu Root in the White House than any other man now possible. I would walk on my hands and knees from the White House to the Capitol to see Root made President. But I know it cannot be done. He

THE POPULAR AND ELECTORAL VOTES IN THE 1908 ELECTION

STATES	Taft and Sherman, Republican.	Bryan and Kern, Democrat.	Chafin and Watkins, Prohibition.	Debs and Hanford, Socialist.	Gilhaus and Munro, Socialist-Labor.	Watson and Williams, Populist.	Hisgen and Graves, Independence.	Taft and Sherman.	Bryan and Kern.
	POPULAR VOTE							ELECTORAL VOTE	
Alabama	26,283	74,374	665	1,399	—	1,568	495	—	11
Arkansas	56,760	87,015	1,194	5,842	—	1,026	289	—	9
California	214,398	127,492	11,770	28,659	—	—	4,278	10	—
Colorado	123,700	126,644	5,559	7,974	—	—	—	—	5
Connecticut	112,815	68,255	2,380	5,113	608	—	728	7	—
Delaware	25,014	22,071	670	239	—	—	30	3	—
Florida	10,654	31,104	553	3,747	—	1,946	1,356	—	5
Georgia	41,692	72,413	1,059	584	—	16,969	77	—	13
Idaho	52,621	36,162	1,986	6,400	—	—	119	3	—
Illinois	629,932	450,810	29,364	34,711	1,680	633	7,724	27	—
Indiana	348,993	338,262	18,045	13,476	643	1,193	514	15	—
Iowa	275,210	200,771	9,837	8,287	—	261	404	13	—
Kansas	197,216	161,209	5,033	12,420	—	—	68	10	—
Kentucky	235,711	244,092	5,887	4,185	404	333	200	—	13
Louisiana	8,958	63,568	—	2,538	—	—	82	—	9
Maine	66,987	35,403	1,487	1,758	—	—	700	6	—
Maryland	116,513	115,908	3,302	2,323	—	—	485	2	6
Massachusetts	265,966	155,543	4,379	10,781	1,018	—	19,239	16	—
Michigan	333,313	174,619	16,795	11,527	1,086	—	734	14	—
Minnesota	195,843	109,401	11,107	14,527	—	1,276	426	11	—
Mississippi	4,363	60,287	—	978	—	—	—	—	10
Missouri	347,203	346,574	4,284	15,431	868	1,165	402	18	—
Montana	32,333	29,326	827	5,855	—	—	481	3	—
Nebraska	126,997	131,099	5,179	3,524	—	—	—	—	8
Nevada	10,775	11,212	—	2,103	—	—	436	—	3
New Hampshire	53,149	33,655	905	1,299	—	—	584	4	—
New Jersey	265,326	182,567	4,934	10,253	1,196	—	2,922	12	—
New York	870,070	667,468	22,667	38,451	3,877	—	35,817	39	—
North Carolina	114,887	136,928	—	345	—	—	—	—	12
North Dakota	57,680	32,885	1,496	2,421	—	162	43	4	—
Ohio	572,312	502,721	11,402	33,795	721	162	439	23	—
Oklahoma	110,558	122,406	—	21,779	—	434	244	—	7
Oregon	62,530	38,049	2,682	7,339	—	—	289	4	—
Pennsylvania	745,779	448,785	36,694	33,913	1,222	—	1,057	34	—
Rhode Island	43,942	24,706	1,016	1,365	183	—	1,105	4	—
South Carolina	3,965	62,290	—	100	—	—	43	—	9
South Dakota	67,536	40,266	4,039	2,846	—	—	88	4	—
Tennessee	118,324	135,608	300	1,870	—	1,081	332	—	12
Texas	65,666	217,302	1,034	7,870	176	994	115	—	18
Utah	61,165	42,601	—	4,890	—	—	92	3	—
Vermont	39,552	11,496	799	—	—	—	804	4	—
Virginia	52,573	82,946	1,111	255	25	105	51	—	12
Washington	106,062	58,691	4,700	14,177	—	—	249	5	—
West Virginia	137,869	111,418	5,139	3,679	—	—	46	7	—
Wisconsin	247,747	166,662	11,505	28,147	314	—	—	13	—
Wyoming	20,846	14,918	66	1,715	—	—	64	3	—
	7,677,788	6,407,982	252,511	420,890	14,021	29,146	83,651	321	162

Total vote, 14,885,989.

couldn't be elected. There is too much opposition to him on account of his corporation connections." Root knew this too. When Loeb came to him with the message that Roosevelt would like to see him in the White House, he told the secretary: "Please tell the President that I appreciate deeply every word, but I cannot be a candidate. It would mean a fight in the convention and I could not be elected. I've thought it all out. Thank the President, but tell him I am not in the running."

When Loeb returned with the message, Roosevelt said: "We had better turn to Taft. See Taft and tell of our talk today—tell him all of it so that he will know my mind."

Loeb left the White House immediately, walked over to the War Department, and told Taft that "the President has decided to declare for you."

To which Taft replied: "I must go over and thank Theodore." And when he did, Roosevelt told him: "Yes, Will. It's the thing to do." That was how Roosevelt chose his successor.

When the Republican convention met, the delegates had only to ratify their master' choice. Taft became the official candidate o

"LONE I DIDN'T DO IT," Bernard Partridge's classic cartoon which appeared in the English weekly, *Punch*. Roosevelt lifts his successor over the election hurdle, the breathless and elated Taft says, "Thank you, Teddy!"

the party on the first roll call, with 702 votes against Philander C. Knox's 68, Charles E. Hughes's 67, and a number of candidates with lesser votes.

The day before Taft's nomination there was a memorable scene in the convention. When Henry Cabot Lodge, the permanent chairman, referred in his speech to Theodore Roosevelt as "the best abused and the most popular man in the United States today," there was such an outburst of applause and cheering for Roosevelt that it could not be stilled for forty-nine minutes. The chant rose from the floor: "Four—four—four years more." It seemed that a stampede for Roosevelt's renomination was under way. Lodge cut the delegates short: "Anyone who attempts to use his name as a candidate for the Presidency impugns both his sincerity and his good faith." After this the cheering subsided and Lodge could proceed with his speech.

Mrs. Taft, who was waiting in Washington for the convention news, wished that the cheers for her husband would last longer than that "to get even for the scare that Roosevelt cheer of forty-nine minutes" had given her. But when Taft's name was put into nomination, the cheering lasted only twenty-nine minutes.

The Democrats met at Denver, and the choosing of the site was an indication that the Western faction of the party was back in the saddle and that Bryan, the mouthpiece for Western demands, would be the nominee again. When his name was put into nomination, the applause lasted for no less than eighty-seven minutes.

There were a number of minor conventions. The Populists nominated Thomas E. Watson, their old war-horse; the Socialist party selected Eugene V. Debs; the Socialist-Labor convention supported Martin B. Preston, who at that time was serving a term of twenty-five years' imprisonment in the Nevada State Prison, but after it became apparent that he was ineligible, August Gilhaus was placed at the head of the ticket. The Prohibitionists named Eugene W. Chafin, and the Independence party, the outgrowth of Hearst's Independent League, was behind Thomas L. Hisgen.

Originally, neither Taft nor Bryan desired to make an extensive political campaign. Bryan wanted to remain at home and make "front-porch" speeches, and Taft announced that he would not travel through the country and fight for his election. But before the campaign was over, both candidates changed their minds, and from the end of September until the day of the election, Taft was constantly traveling and addressing rallies of his supporters. Roosevelt admonished Taft: "Hit them hard, old man! Let the audience see you smile always, because I feel that your nature shines out so transparently when you do smile—you big, generous, high-minded fellow. Moreover let them realize the truth, which is that for all your gentleness and kindliness and generous good nature there never existed a man who was a better fighter when the need arose."

As the differences in the political principles of the two parties were slight, the campaign was unexciting. When it was over, Taft had won. He polled about 50,000 more votes than

Ha ha! you are making up your Cabinet. I in a light-hearted way have spent the morning testing the rifles for my African trip. Life has compensations!

Ever yours,

T. R.

A NOTE FROM THEODORE ROOSEVELT TO TAFT, WRITTEN ON THE LAST DAY OF THE YEAR 190

...AUGURATION DAY. There was a blizzard the night before and the streets of Washington were covered with ...w as President and Mrs. Taft returned to the White House in an open carriage flanked by Secret Service men.

...osevelt had received four years before, while ...yan gained 1,323,000 more votes than Parker. ...Inauguration day was beset by heavy snow, ...et, and rain. "Even the elements do pro- ...t," remarked Taft as he left the White House. ...d Roosevelt answered: "I knew there would ...a blizzard when I went out."

...Because of the bad weather, the inaugural ...remonies took place in the Senate Chamber ...d not on the portico of the Capitol. After ...y were over, Theodore Roosevelt, cheered ...every one present, left the hall dramatically, ...nt to the railroad station, and boarded a train ...his home at Oyster Bay. With this gesture ...wanted to emphasize that the stage from ...w on belonged to his successor. The new ...esident drove back to the White House ac- ...mpanied by his wife.

...The next day a Boston paper remarked: ..."e hope he will be President Taft in reality, ...simply an echo of President Roosevelt."

REPORTERS AND CARTOONISTS bewail the end of T. R.'s term. Who will provide interesting copy now?

WILSON'S FIRST INAUGURATION

THE THIRTY-SECOND ELECTION—1912

WOODROW WILSON

At the time Roosevelt left for Africa in his search for the "great adventure," his friendship for Taft was unimpaired. Rumors of a rift between President and ex-President were without foundation. "People have attempted to represent that you and I were in some way at odds during this last three months," wrote Taft to his predecessor a few weeks before his inauguration, "whereas you and I know that there has not been the slightest difference between us." Loose tongues in Washington gossiped that Taft was ungrateful to Roosevelt, that he had sent him a letter in which he named his brother Charley as the man who was mainly responsible that he became President. What Taft actually said was far from hurtful to Roosevelt's feelings. "You and my brother Charley," wrote he, "made my nomination and election possible."

No, there was no shadow over the friendship in 1909. Roosevelt left the country with confidence and trust in his successor, believing that the policies which he began would be followed by Taft.

But things turned out differently. It soon became evident that Taft was not the President the country needed in a time of political and social turmoil. With little gift for leadership, with no instinct for showmanship, always swaying and vacillating, he seemed a poor Executive if one compared him with Roosevelt.

The country felt let down. Gone were the dramatic quarrels of the Roosevelt days, gone were the excitement and the coining of amusing phrases—under Taft life had little glamor. Though under his administration a great number of excellent laws were passed, he was remembered more for his failures than for his achievements. And as his behavior antagonized the Progressive Republicans, a schism in the party ranks became inevitable.

The first rift between the Progressives and the President came over the tariff. Taft not only acquiesced to the Payne-Aldrich Bill, a highly protective measure, but blundered into its defense by exclaiming that it was "the best bill the Republican party ever passed." This was more than the Progressives could take. Their feelings toward the President grew more hostile when they learned that he had removed Chief Forester Gifford Pinchot, a close friend of Roosevelt's, from his post after Pinchot em-

501

THE CANDIDATES

WOODROW WILSON (1856-1924), ex-president of Princeton University and Governor of New Jersey, was chosen by the Democrats, defeating Champ Clark on the 46th ballot.

THOMAS R. MARSHALL (1854-1925), Governor of Indiana, the vice-presidential choice of the Democrats. His remark, "What this country needs is a good 5c cigar," won him fame.

WILLIAM HOWARD TAFT (1857-1930), the outgoing President, was the regular Republican candidate for re-election. Attacked by Roosevelt, his former close friend, Taft lost the contest.

JAMES S. SHERMAN (1855-1912), who was Vice-President during Taft's administration, was renominated by Republicans for second place, but died before the end of the campaign.

THEODORE ROOSEVELT (1858-1919) left the Republican party to campaign on the Progressive third-party ticket, winning 4,119,507 votes to Wilson's 6,293,019 and Taft's 3,484,956.

HIRAM JOHNSON (1866-1945) of California, Roosevelt's running mate on Progressive or "Bull Moose" ticket. The split in the Republican party ranks gave the election to Wilson.

broiled himself in a controversy over conserva-tion with Ballinger, the Secretary of the Inte-rior. And when Taft took the side of "Uncl Joe" Cannon, the ultraconservative Speaker the House, who was under heavy attacks b the Progressives, the final break between Pres dent and Progressives could no longer b avoided. The Progressives held that Taft was tool in the hands of the conservative wing an that he would never follow the policies c Roosevelt.

With the party badly split by these diffe ences, Republican prospects for the midter election looked dark indeed. Roosevelt was st abroad, visiting the capitals of Europe, givir lectures, receiving the Nobel Peace Prize, repr senting the United States at King Edward funeral. But though he "had a thoroughly go time," he felt homesick. In June, 1910, boarded a ship at Southampton which was take him back to the United States. Before sailed, a letter from Taft reached him. "It is no a year and three months since I assumed offi and I have had a hard time," wrote Taft Roosevelt. "I do not know that I have h harder luck than other Presidents, but I know that thus far I have succeeded far le than have others. I have been conscientious trying to carry out your policies but my meth of doing so has not worked smoothly."

In his letter Taft reviewed his administr tion's achievements. He sounded like a boy tr

(turn to page 50

THE DEMOCRATIC CONVENTION in Baltim where, after forty-six ballots Wilson defeated Cl

ROOSEVELT DESIRES A THIRD CUP OF COFFEE. In this cartoon by Boardman Robinson which appeared in the New York *Tribune* on February 27, 1912, lampooning Roosevelt's "third-term" candidacy, T. R. says: "Hey waiter! Bring that over here. When I said I wouldn't take the third cup a little while ago, I only meant I wouldn't take it right on top of the other two." This is a reference to a statement Roosevelt made after he was elected in his own right in 1904. Elated over his victory, he announced he would not accept a successive nomination.

UBLICAN CONVENTION in Chicago where amid ultuous scenes President Taft was renominated.

BULL MOOSE CONVENTION in Chicago, called by the bolting Progressives, nominated Theodore Roosevelt.

CAMPAIGN CARTOONS OF 1912

DARLING IN THE NEW YORK *GLOBE*, JANUARY 9

CARTER IN THE NEW YORK *WORLD*, F

MACAULEY IN THE NEW YORK *WORLD*, JAN. 18

KETTEN IN THE NEW YORK *WORLD*, F

OLITICAL CARTOON BY H. T. WEBSTER

MACAULEY IN THE NEW YORK *WORLD*, JUNE 7

MACAULEY IN THE NEW YORK *WORLD*

DONAHEY IN THE CLEVELAND *PLAIN DEALER*

THESE FOUR CARTOONS BY C. R. MACAULEY OF THE N. Y. *WORLD* REVEAL DRAMATICALLY THE

ing to impress the teacher that he *had* learned his lesson. He told Roosevelt that the tariff bill was "not as radical a change as I favored, but still a change for the better"; he asserted that the tax on corporations would provide "a useful means of discovering and supervising the affairs of our corporations"; he mentioned that Arizona and New Mexico—the last two of the forty-eight States—would be admitted to the Union; and he boasted that the chief conservation measures would soon become law. But Taft was full of complaints about the insurgent Senators from the Midwest, who "have done all in their power to defeat us."

Roosevelt felt "very uncomfortable," hearing of the struggle. He wrote to his friend Cabot Lodge that he was "anything but happy over the prospect of being at home," and added: "As for what you say about the American people looking to me for leadership, it is unfortunately preposterous, and makes me more uncomfortable than ever. That is why I got out of the country, and apparently I ought to have stayed out of the country even longer."

In other letters which he wrote to Senato Lodge during the months before he returned t America, Roosevelt made apologies for Ta and attempted to explain the actions of h successor. "I am sincere when I say that I a not yet sure whether Taft could with wisdo have followed any course save the one he did he wrote. "The qualities shown by a thorough able and trustworthy lieutenant are totally di ferent, or at least may be totally different, fro those needed by the leader, the commande Very possibly if Taft had tried to work in m spirit, and along my lines, he would have faile that he has conscientiously tried to work f the objects I had in view, so far as he cou approve them, I have no doubt."

Roosevelt believed that "there is at least good chance that a reaction will come in (President Taft's) favor. Everyone believes h to be honest, and most believe him to be doi the best he knows how. I have noticed ve little real personal abuse of him, or inde attack upon him." The former President tri hard to maintain confidence in Taft.

EVELT'S POLITICAL POSITION BETWEEN THE REPUBLICAN AND BULL MOOSE CONVENTIONS.

But however friendly Roosevelt felt toward Taft, he looked to the midterm election with great uneasiness. He knew that the party would be defeated. "The trouble is that the Cannon-Aldrich type of leadership down at bottom represents not more than, say, ten per cent of the rank and file of the party's voting strength," wrote Roosevelt to Lodge, "but if the great mass—the ninety per cent of the party—the men who stand for it as their fathers stood for it in the days of Lincoln, get convinced that the ten per cent are not leading them right, a revolt is sure to ensue."

Roosevelt still hoped "that Taft will retrieve himself yet," but even if he failed to do so, "I most emphatically desire that I shall not be put in the position of having to run for the Presidency, staggering under a load which I cannot carry, and which has been put on my shoulders through no fault of my own. Therefore my present feeling is that Taft should be the next nominee, because, if the people approve of what he has done, it is unfair to me to have to suffer for the distrust which others

have earned, and for which I am in no way responsible."

However, Roosevelt's ideas changed as soon as he reached home. A few days at Oyster Bay, a number of conversations with the insurgent Senators, convinced him that only a progressive leadership could avert defeat in the impending election, and so the impulsive Teddy threw himself headlong into the political whirlpool, forgetting his past pronouncements and promises.

From August until election day he traveled through the West and South, attempting to stem the tide against the party, but to no avail. The election results justified his worst fears. The House went Democratic (the country elected 289 Democrats against 161 Republicans), and while the Senate remained Republican, it did so by only a slight majority (51 Republicans against 41 Democrats).

After the midterm election the Republican insurgents redoubled their efforts to block Taft's renomination in 1912. Convinced that he could not be re-elected, they sought some-

"I AM AS STRONG AS A BULL MOOSE," said Theodore Roosevelt, and so the symbol of the new party became th bull moose. Cartoonists drew T. R. with a moose and photographers made montages of him on the animal's bacl

"THE MIRAGE." A cartoon of T.R. with the big stick and the bull moose, surveying his prospects for 1916.

one to replace him. The National Progressiv Republican League, formed at the beginning o 1911, proposed Robert La Follette as a presi dential candidate. La Follette attempted to se cure Roosevelt's blessing for his candidacy, bu Roosevelt, though friendly toward the Wiscor sin Senator, would not endorse him. And with out his approval the movement for La Follett was bound to collapse.

In his magazine articles Roosevelt becam increasingly critical of the administration, an in his speeches his former benevolence towar Taft was noticeably lacking. As the year 191 wore on, Roosevelt's feelings became openl hostile.

The jovial Taft was bewildered and gravel hurt. "If I only knew what the Presider wanted," he remarked to his aide, Archie Bu (he still thought of Roosevelt as "President" ar referred to him as such), "I would do it, b you know that he has held himself so aloof th I am absolutely in the dark. I am deep

ROLLIN KIRBY'S DRAWING AGAINST THEODORE ROOSEVELT APPEARED IN THE NEW YORK *SUN*.

ROOSEVELT, THE PROGRESSIVE CANDIDATE, WAS ASSAILED BY E. W. KEMBLE OF *HARPER'S W*

wounded, and he gives me no chance to explain my attitude or learn his." For Taft the motives of his former friend in his attacks against the administration were a complete puzzle. "I don't know what he is driving at except to make my way more difficult," he remarked, and added sadly that it was a very painful thing "to see a devoted friendship going to pieces like a rope of sand."

For this Taft was as much to blame as Roosevelt. He made mistake after mistake; under the thumb of the conservatives, he abandoned most of Roosevelt's policies. As months went by, Roosevelt reached the decision that he himself must become a candidate to save the party from defeat in the next presidential election.

The movement on his behalf was seriously under way when a number of governors signed a petition, reciting the history of the progressive movement and calling on him to take the lead of the progressive forces in their battle for the "New Nationalism."

Roosevelt declared: "My hat is in the ring," and he wrote to the governors that "I will accept the nomination for President if it is tendered to me, and I will adhere to this decision until the convention has expressed its preference."

As soon as the boom for Roosevelt began in earnest, Taft took the offensive. He made a violent speech in which he attacked the men who "are seeking to pull down the pillars of the temple of freedom and representative government," calling them "political emotionalists or neurotics, who have lost that sense of proportion . . . which made our people . . . the greatest self-governing people that the world ever knew."

Now it was open war between Taft and Roosevelt, war without mercy. The two for

DREW HIM AS MONARCH, DICTATOR AND ENEMY OF BIG BUSINESS AND THE CONSTITUTION.

ner friends assailed each other with increasing vituperation. Roosevelt blamed Taft for yielding to "the bosses and to the great privileged interests" and accused him of being "disloyal to very canon of ordinary decency." Answering Roosevelt's charges, Taft replied: "I deny all of them. I do not want to fight Theodore Roosevelt, but sometimes a man in a corner fights. I am going to fight." And in another speech he aid: "Condemn me if you will, but condemn e by other witnesses than Theodore Roosevelt. I was a man of straw; but I have been a an of straw long enough. Every man who has lood in his body, and who has been misrepreented as I have . . . is forced to fight."

Accusations flew back and forth from one amp to the other. Franklin P. Adams satirized e battle of the two former pals in the verse, T.R. to W.H.T.", which was gleefully read l over the country:

"Or ever the knightly fight was on,
The skirmish of smear and smudge,
I was a king in Washington
And you were a circuit judge.

"I saw, I took, I made you great,
Friendly, I called you 'Will.'
And back in Nineteen Hundred and Eight,
Out in Chicago, Ill.,
I made the convention nominate,
And now—the terrible chill.

"For many a sun has set and shone
On the path we used to trudge,
When I was a king in Washington
And you were a circuit judge.

"I passed the lie and you passed it back,
You said I was all untruth;
I said that honesty was your lack,
You said I'd nor reck nor ruth;
You called me a megalomaniac,
I called you a Serpent's Tooth. . . ."

THE LATEST ARRIVAL AT THE POLITICAL ZOO

DRAWN BY E W KEMBLE

HARPER'S *WEEKLY* ATTACKED ROOSEVELT

THEODORE ROOSEVELT WAS NEARLY DRAG

As the battle between Roosevelt and Taf
grew in bitterness, compromisers in the party
suggested that both men should withdraw in
favor of a candidate who would be acceptable

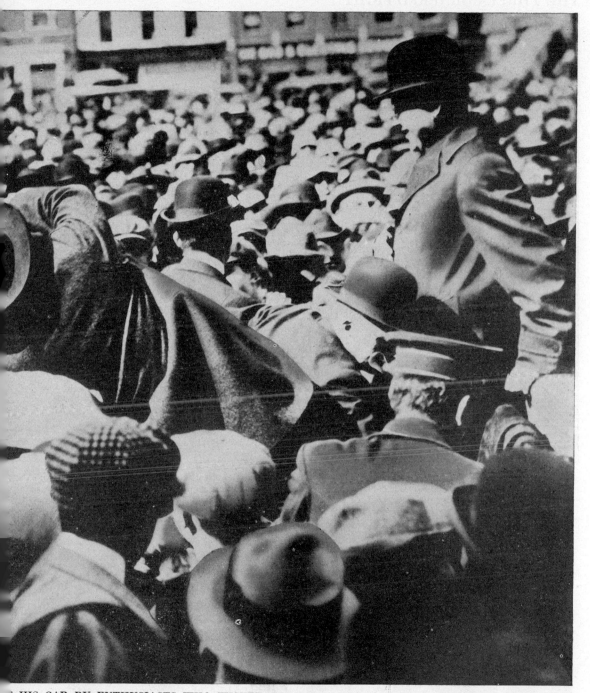

HIS CAR BY ENTHUSIASTS WHO WISHED TO SHAKE HIS HAND AT EASTON, PENNSYLVANIA.

both of them. The name of Charles Evans ughes was mentioned, but neither Taft nor oosevelt was in a mood to withdraw. "I'll me the compromise candidate," Roosevelt said defiantly. "He'll be me. I'll name the compromise platform. It will be our platform."

This was the situation when the Republican convention assembled in Chicago. Unbending

WILSON ACCEPTS the nomination at his home on August 7, promising tariff reform and regulation of the trust and demanding laws to protect labor, promote education and conserve national resources. "We desire to set up government that cannot be used for private purposes either in the field of business or in the field of politics.

THEODORE ROOSEVELT campaigns against Taft and his conservative policies on a Chicago street corner.

and hostile, the Taft and Roosevelt forces faile to realize that the party would be wrecke in the ensuing struggle. Roosevelt came to th convention to direct the strategy in person ar win the nomination from Taft. However, the was little hope for his success, for the part bosses and the machine were with the Presiden

The Roosevelt faction challenged the crede tials of more than two hundred delegat pledged to Taft, but as the Taft men had t upper hand in the convention, it was of avail. Most of the contested seats were giv to Taft supporters, thus ensuring victory f the President. Roosevelt issued a stateme when it became clear that he could not chosen. "The people have spoken, and the po ticians will be made to understand that they a the servants and not the masters of the ra

ILLIAM H. TAFT took little part in the campaign, but whenever he spoke, he attacked with great violence his rmer friend, Theodore Roosevelt, who had helped to secure the presidential office for him in 1908. Toward the d of July, sensing his impending defeat, he said: "There are so many people in the country who don't like me."

d file of the plain citizens of the Republican rty," he said, charging that "there is no form rascality which the Taft men have not re-rted to."

This made the indomitable Mr. Dooley say: wint to bed last night thinkin' th' counthry s safe, so I put out th' cat, locked th' dure . . . ' pulled into th' siding f'r th' night. Whin I t up I had a feelin' that somethin' was rnin'. . . . But I cudden't find annything rong till I opened up th' pa-apers an', much to e relief, found that it was not me pants but th' public that was on fire. Yes, sir; th' republic doomed to desthruction again."

The night before the convention began to llot, Roosevelt addressed a huge meeting in other hall in Chicago, making a memorable eech. He told the assembly that Taft had

AN ANXIOUS MOMENT. Confronting the three candidates, Uncle Sam says: "Eeny, Meeny, Miny, Mo. . . ."

THE VOTERS JUDGE THE THREE PUMPKINS WHO COMPETED FOR THE FIRST PRIZE IN 1912

surrendered to the machine and that a great number of delegates were seated in the convention who had no right to be there. "What happens to me is not of the slightest consequence; I am to be used, as in a doubtful battle any man is used, to his hurt or not, so long as he is useful and is then cast aside and left to die. I wish you to feel this. I mean it; and I shall need no sympathy when you are through with me . . . We fight in honorable fashion for the good of mankind, unheeding of our individual fates with unflinching hearts and undimmed eyes; we stand at Armageddon, and we battle for the Lord."

The following day the regular Republican convention chose Elihu Root as permanent

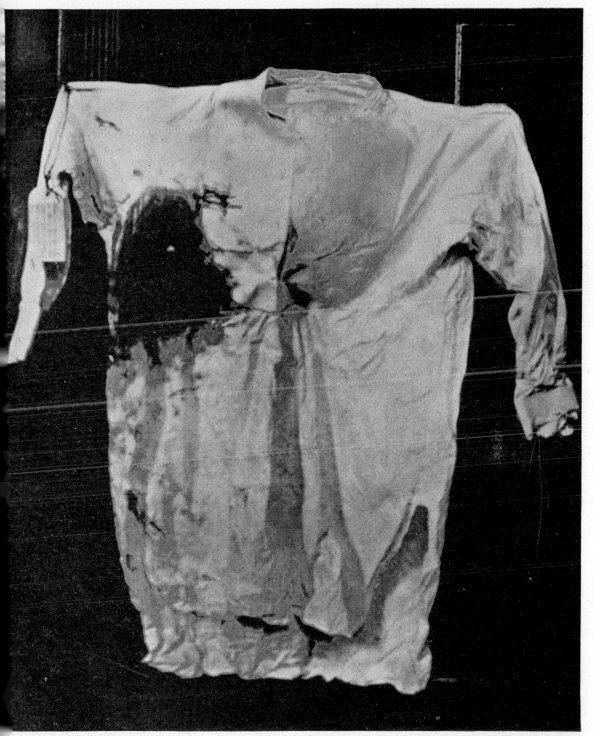

ROOSEVELT'S BLOODY SHIRT, after he was shot at Milwaukee by a madman. The assassin, John Schrank, decided to kill Roosevelt after the late President William McKinley appeared in his dreams and ordered him to do so. A note found on him read: "Let it be the right and duty of every citizen to forcibly remove a third-termer."

chairman, with 558 votes against 501 for McGovern, the candidate of the Roosevelt forces. Root's election was a clear indication that Taft would be renominated. During the voting the audience demonstrated for Roosevelt. For the people in the galleries the Taft political machine was nothing but a steamroller, and so every time the newly elected chairman rose— the driver of the machine—they shouted "Toot, toot!" and rubbed sandpaper sheets together, imitating the noise of the imaginary steamroller.

In the convention hall wild rumors made the rounds. The story went from mouth to mouth that Roosevelt, with a selected group of men, would come and take possession of the building at three o'clock in the morning, when everyone was asleep.

Roosevelt had no such plans. At two o'clock in the morning of June 20, after the credentials committee had endorsed the disputed Taft delegates, he said: "So far as I am concerned, I am through. I went before the people and I won. . . ." Then he uttered the challenge: "Let us find out whether the Republican party is the party of the plain people . . . or the party of the bosses and the professional radicals acting in the interests of special privilege." Did this mean that Roosevelt would not accept the convention's choice? That he would break away from the party and run on a separate ticket?

Two days later the convention renominated Taft with 561 votes to Roosevelt's 107. But Taft's victory was not as large as these figures seem to indicate. Most of the Roosevelt supporters, 344 delegates in all, refrained from voting.

Now that Taft had become the party's official nominee, the opposition to him gathered together in a separate meeting, pledging enthusiastic support to Roosevelt.

> "We will follow Roosevelt,
> Follow! Follow!
> Anywhere! Everywhere!
> We will follow on!"

And Roosevelt told his cheering followers: "If you wish me to make the fight, I will make it, even if only one state should support me."

This meant the splitting of the party. This meant a break away from the regular Republican organization. Whether it meant the formation of a new party was not certain at first. But a few weeks later, when financial support was obtained for the new organization, the delegates of the Progressive party (the official name of the third party) assembled in Chicago in a nominating convention. Roosevelt, who said to reporters that he was feeling "as strong as a bull moose," made a long address to the twenty thousand people who endorsed him as their candidate. Attacking the two old parties, he called them "husks, with no real soul within either, divided on artificial lines, boss-ridden and privilege-controlled, each a jumble of incongruous elements, and neither daring to speak out wisely and fearlessly what should be said on the vital issues of the day."

The Progressive platform demanded regulation of the trusts, urged development of agricultural credit, and endorsed all the current reforms, such as the direct primary, women's suffrage, an easier way to amend the Constitution, tariff revision downward, better working conditions in the factories, the prohibition of child labor, minimum-wage standards and an eight-hour day in industry.

With the split in the Republican ranks, there was no doubt that the Democrats would win the election. In the party's nominating convention at Baltimore, Woodrow Wilson, New Jersey's progressive governor, was chosen after a long and hard fight. When the balloting began Champ Clark, the Speaker of the House, was apparently the favorite, and after the tenth ballot his victory seemed sure; he had the majority, but as the two-thirds rule was still adhered to, the voting continued. During the fourteenth ballot William Jennings Bryan made the dramatic announcement that he would not vote for anyone who was supported by Tammany. Thus the chances of Woodrow Wilson rose. Yet it was not until the forty-sixth trial that he received the nomination.

The ensuing campaign was largely a contest of personalities, a three-cornered fight between the placid Taft, the crusading Roosevelt, and the rational Wilson, though there was a fourth candidate, Eugene V. Debs, the representative of the Socialists. The Wilson policies, known

(turn to page 521

THE END OF THE CAMPAIGN. The Republican elephant in this E. W. Kemble cartoon says to the Bull Moose: "Well, you've helped rip me apart and 'downed' yourself! Now I hope you're satisfied." On the tree hangs T. R.'s hat.

519

THE POPULAR AND ELECTORAL VOTES IN THE 1912 ELECTION

STATES	POPULAR VOTE						ELECTORAL VOTE		
	Wilson and Marshall, Democrat.	Roosevelt and Johnson, Progressive.	Taft and Sherman, Republican.	Chafin and Watkins, Prohibition.	Debs and Seidel, Socialist.	Reimer and Francis, Socialist-Labor.	Wilson and Marshall.	Roosevelt and Johnson.	Taft and Sherman.
Alabama	82,439	22,689	9,731	—	3,029	—	12	—	—
Arizona	10,324	6,949	3,021	265	3,163	—	3	—	—
Arkansas	68,838	21,673	24,297	898	8,153	—	9	—	—
California	283,436	283,610	3,914	23,366	79,201	—	2	11	—
Colorado	114,223	72,306	58,386	5,063	16,418	—	6	—	—
Connecticut	74,561	34,129	68,324	2,068	10,056	475	7	—	—
Delaware	22,631	8,886	15,998	623	556	1,260	3	—	—
Florida	36,417	4,535	4,279	1,854	4,806	—	6	—	—
Georgia	93,171	22,010	5,190	147	1,014	—	14	—	—
Idaho	33,921	25,527	32,810	1,537	11,960	—	4	—	—
Illinois	405,048	386,478	253,613	15,710	81,278	4,066	29	—	—
Indiana	281,890	162,007	151,267	19,249	36,931	3,130	15	—	—
Iowa	185,325	161,819	119,805	8,440	16,967	—	13	—	—
Kansas	143,670	120,123	74,844	—	26,807	—	10	—	—
Kentucky	219,584	102,766	115,512	3,233	11,647	956	13	—	—
Louisiana	60,966	9,323	3,834	—	5,249	—	10	—	—
Maine	51,113	48,493	26,545	945	2,541	—	6	—	—
Maryland	112,674	57,786	54,956	2,244	3,996	322	8	—	—
Massachusetts	173,408	142,228	155,948	2,754	12,616	1,102	18	—	—
Michigan	150,751	214,584	152,244	8,934	23,211	1,252	—	15	—
Minnesota	106,426	125,856	64,334	7,886	27,505	2,212	—	12	—
Mississippi	57,164	3,627	1,511	—	2,017	—	10	—	—
Missouri	330,746	124,371	207,821	5,380	28,466	1,778	18	—	—
Montana	27,941	22,456	18,512	32	10,885	—	4	—	—
Nebraska	109,008	72,689	54,216	3,383	10,885	—	8	—	—
Nevada	7,986	5,620	3,196	—	3,313	—	3	—	—
New Hampshire	34,724	17,794	32,927	535	1,981	—	4	—	—
New Jersey	78,289	145,410	88,835	2,878	15,801	1,321	14	—	—
New Mexico	20,437	8,347	17,733	—	2,859	—	3	—	—
New York	655,475	390,021	455,428	19,427	63,381	4,251	45	—	—
North Carolina	144,507	69,130	29,139	117	1,025	—	12	—	—
North Dakota	29,555	25,726	23,090	1,243	6,966	—	5	—	—
Ohio	423,152	229,327	277,066	11,459	89,930	2,623	24	—	—
Oklahoma	119,156	—	90,786	2,185	42,262	—	10	—	—
Oregon	47,064	37,600	34,673	4,360	13,343	—	5	—	—
Pennsylvania	395,619	447,426	273,305	19,533	83,164	704	—	38	—
Rhode Island	30,142	16,878	27,703	616	2,049	236	5	—	—
South Carolina	38,355	1,293	536	—	164	—	9	—	—
South Dakota	48,942	58,811	—	3,910	4,662	—	—	5	—
Tennessee	130,335	53,725	59,444	825	3,492	—	12	—	—
Texas	221,589	26,755	28,853	1,738	25,743	442	20	—	—
Utah	36,579	24,174	42,100	—	9,023	509	—	—	4
Vermont	15,350	22,070	23,305	1,154	928	—	—	—	4
Virginia	90,332	21,777	23,288	709	820	50	12	—	—
Washington	86,840	113,698	70,445	9,810	40,134	1,872	—	7	—
West Virginia	113,197	79,112	56,754	4,517	15,248	—	8	—	—
Wisconsin	164,409	58,661	130,878	8,467	34,168	698	13	—	—
Wyoming	15,310	9,232	14,560	434	2,760	—	3	—	—
	6,293,019	4,119,507	3,484,956	207,828	901,873	29,259	435	88	8

Total vote, 15,036,442.

THE SUPREME COURT AT THE INAUGURATION

TAFT AND WILSON LEAVE FOR THE CAPITOL

PRESIDENT-ELECT WILSON AND PRESIDENT TAFT LEAVING FOR THE INAUGURAL CEREMONIES.

collectively as the "New Freedom," did not differ very much from Theodore Roosevelt's New Nationalism. Overshadowed by these two progressive-minded candidates, Taft seemed like an arch-reactionary.

Wilson, aided by Josephus Daniels, the head of his publicity bureau, attacked Roosevelt's paternalistic trust and labor program. He proclaimed: "Every form of special privilege and private control must cease. . . . Private control of politics . . . bosses and the machines must go. . . . Private interests, special favors, must not be encouraged by the government." He asked the country to vote for a Democratic Congress so that the proposed progressive legislation could be enacted.

On October 14, as Roosevelt was leaving his Milwaukee hotel to address an audience, he was shot by an anti-third-term fanatic. With a great sense of the dramatic, he exclaimed: "I will make this speech or die. It is one thing or the other." The bullet was still in his body as he spoke to a hushed audience, and his followers sang "Onward, Christian Soldiers."

Both Taft and Wilson halted their campaigns until Roosevelt recovered. Fortunately a spectacle case in his pocket had deflected the bullet and his injury was not a serious one.

The election result was no surprise. Wilson won, carrying forty out of the forty-eight states with 6,293,019 votes to Roosevelt's 4,119,507 and Taft's 3,484,956. When the students of Princeton University came to congratulate the President-elect on the eve of the election, Wilson told them: "I myself have no feeling of triumph tonight. I have a feeling of solemn responsibility." And Roosevelt said: "The fight is over. We are beaten. There is only one thing to do and that is to go back to the Republican party. You can't hold a party like the Progressive party together . . . There are no loaves and fishes."

WILSON'S SECOND INAUGURATION

THE THIRTY-THIRD ELECTION—1916

WOODROW WILSON

In his first inaugural Woodrow Wilson spoke of "the things that ought to be altered." He mentioned the "tariff which cuts us off from our proper part in the commerce of the world . . . and makes the government a facile instrument in the hands of private interests"; he said that the banking and currency system of the country needed overhauling; he attacked the "industrial system which, take it on all sides, financial as well as administrative, holds capital in leading strings, restricts the liberties and limits the opportunities of labor, and exploits without renewing or conserving the natural resources of the country." Furthermore, he demanded reforms in agriculture and pleaded for more effective conservation and irrigation measures. It was an ambitious program, to be accomplished within the framework of the existing social system.

A month after his inauguration, Wilson appeared before Congress and delivered his message to the lawmakers in person. More than a century had passed since the Chief Magistrate had talked directly to the assembled body of both Houses. Ever since Jefferson, who preferred to send his messages in writing,

it had been customary for all Presidents to communicate with Congress in this way. Wilson's departure from this time-honored tradition signified a new era in politics. "We must abolish everything," said the President, "that bears even the semblance of privilege or any kind of artificial advantage." The message itself was short—it was so concise that the newspapers could print it in its entirety on their front pages.

Fresh winds blew on Capitol Hill. The President molded his followers into a united party. Impending legislation was discussed beforehand in party caucuses, where agreements were reached as to the party's position, the majority settling all matters in dispute. Sometimes the President himself came to the Capitol to confer on party strategy or to "persuade" a recalcitrant legislator and win his support. During these years the Democratic party gave up its states'-rights tradition and became the party of progressive nationalism.

The reforms which Wilson promised the country were enacted one by one. The Underwood-Simmons Tariff reduced the duties of the Payne-Aldrich Tariff. (One of the provi-

THE CANDIDATES

WOODROW WILSON (1856-1924) was renominated by the Democrats, whose campaign slogan was "He kept us out of war." He received 3,000,000 more votes than in 1912-

THOMAS R. MARSHALL (1854-1925) was renominated by acclamation for Vice-President. The Democratic ticket won by a slight margin of 277 electoral votes to 254 for Republicans.

CHARLES EVANS HUGHES (1862-1948), Justice of the Supreme Court, was Republican and Progressive candidate. Had he not lost California by 3,806 votes, he would have won the election.

CHARLES W. FAIRBANKS (1852-1918) from Indiana, Vice-President under Roosevelt, a conservative but not reactionary politician, was again Republican candidate for second place.

ALLAN L. BENSON (1871-1940) of N. Y., became the candidate of the Socialist party. With George R. Kilpatrick as running mate, he received more than half a million votes.

FRANK J. HANLY (1863-1920) from Indiana formed Prohibition party ticket with Ira Landrith of Massachusetts as running mate. In the election they received 220,506 votes.

SENATOR OLLIE JAMES, CHAIRMAN OF THE D

sions of the new tariff bill was the income tax—made constitutional through the adoption of the Sixteenth Amendment.) The Glass-Owen Federal Reserve Act set up a series of sectional banks, held together by a Federal Reserve Board. The Clayton Anti-Trust Act and the Fed-

CRATIC CONVENTION, HANDS WILSON THE NOTIFICATION AT SHADOW LAWN, N. J. ON SEPT. 2.

eral Trade Commission Act were directed against the formation of monopolies and against the unfair practices of the big corporations. A number of bills were passed to ease the plight of labor. The first Secretary of Labor was appointed (though the department had been created under Taft); the Keating-Owen Child Labor Bill prohibited children under fourteen years from working in factories, a measure later found unconstitutional by the Supreme Court. Agriculture was not neglected; the Smith-Lever Act provided that the Federal

Government should contribute the same amount of money—dollar for dollar—as the states were ready to invest for agricultural extension. This first "dollar-matching" bill was followed by the Federal Highways Act and many other measures carrying the dollar-matching principle into the field of road building and education.

All the laws which the Democrats enacted under Wilson's first administration dealt with domestic matters. Foreign policy was thought to be so inconsequential that Wilson, in his first message to Congress, did not even mention it. But before his first term was over, America's relations with foreign countries had become more important than domestic issues. When Wilson took the oath in 1913, a European war seemed a distant possibility; a year later it was a stark reality.

Before 1914, the United States' main foreign worry was Mexico. Ever since the 1910 revolution, America's billion-dollar investment in that country had been in jeopardy. President Díaz was supplanted by Madero in 1911, but two years later Madero—a friend of the United States—was murdered, and General Huerta took his place. Wilson refused to recognize the new President and declared a policy of "watchful waiting." In April, 1914, the watchful waiting came to an end. American marines and bluejackets landed in Mexico and took Vera Cruz, preventing the landing of German munitions. The controversy was finally settled through negotiations and war between the two neighboring countries was averted.

By then Europe was aflame. On July 28 Austria declared war on Serbia; on August 1 Germany was at war with Russia; and four days later, Germany began to fight France. On August 4 President Wilson issued the first of a series of neutrality proclamations stating that the United States would keep out of the European conflict; it would remain neutral.

The war created a great boom in American trade and industry. Supplies and food were badly needed in Europe, and American ships took their precious cargo to the warring nations. All the produce of the United States could be sold at good prices abroad. Thus factories worked overtime, the number of unemployed sank to an all-time low, the wages of the workers and the profits of the industrialists, businessmen, and farmers rose to a record high.

But it was unlikely that the United States could maintain an uninterrupted flow of goods to Europe. Both the British and the Germans were dissatisfied. The British, resentful that America was selling goods to Germany, intercepted and held our vessels for months. The Germans, smarting under the British blockade, retaliated by declaring a war zone about the British Isles, threatening to sink all vessels within the area and warning the United States not to send ships through the danger zone. Wilson protested to Germany in strong words, informing the German government that if their "sink-on-sight" rule resulted in the loss of American lives, Germany would be held to "strict accountability."

On May 7, 1915, the *Lusitania*, one of the greatest of the English passenger liners, was torpedoed by a German submarine. In the disaster 1,100 persons were lost, including 124 Americans. The mood in the United States was for an immediate declaration of war. But Wilson, refusing to stampede the country into war, said: "There is such a thing as a man being too proud to fight." He scored a diplomatic victory when the German ambassador promised that German submarines would not sink liners without warning nor disregard the safety of noncombatants.

Yet the German submarine warfare proceeded with unabated fury. On March 24, 1916, the *Sussex*, a French steamer, was sunk with the loss of three American lives. Wilson dispatched another protest, demanding that Germany "should now immediately declare and effect an abandonment of its present methods of submarine warfare against passenger and freight-carrying vessels," otherwise the United States "can have no choice but to sever diplomatic relations altogether."

The President realized by then that the European war could not be ended through negotiations but would be fought to the bitter end. Thus during 1916 he acquiesced to a program of military preparedness, not unmindful of the impending presidential campaign. A series of acts were driven through Congress, strengthening the military and naval forces of the nation.

PLAY BALL. The Democratic cabinet team chosen by President Wilson to help him in his new administration. Left to right, upper row, are Franklin K. Lane, Secretary of the Interior; William C. Redfield, Secretary of Commerce; David F. Houston, Secretary of Agriculture; Albert S. Burleson, Postmaster-General. Lower row, Josephus Daniels, Secretary of the Navy; William B. Wilson, Secretary of Labor; William Jennings Bryan, Secretary of State; James C. McReynolds, Attorney-General; William Gibbs McAdoo, Secretary of the Treasury. Seated in the front is Lindley M. Garrison, Secretary of War. This photomontage appeared in *Harper's Weekly* in March, 1913.

and winning the approval of the business and industrial interests of the country.

That Wilson would be the candidate to succeed himself was never in doubt. In him the Democratic party had found its new leader, and he had no rivals when the convention assembled at St. Louis. He was universally acclaimed as the man who kept the country out of war. Governor Martin Glynn of New York, in his keynote address, spoke eloquently of Wilson's pacifism. "This policy may not satisfy . . . the fire-eater or the swashbuckler but it does satisfy the mothers of the land at whose hearth and fireside no jingoistic war has placed an empty chair. It does satisfy the daughters of the land from whom bluster and brag have sent no lov-

ing brother to the dissolution of the grave." Carried away by his own oratory, the Governor went on: "It does satisfy the fathers of this land and the sons of this land who will fight for our flag and die for our flag when Reason primes the rifle, when Honor draws the sword, when Justice breathes a blessing on the standards they uphold."

Hearing these lofty sentences, the delegates' enthusiasm rose; the hurrahs for peace swelled to such magnitude that the party leaders became uneasy; the convention was getting out of hand. True, the party was for peace, but not peace at any price, as Governor Glynn's address might have implied. And Wilson desired that the issue of Americanism—not pacifism—

should be emphasized before the convention. He wished to repeat the ideas which he had stressed in his Flag Day speech—that the English-Americans and the German-Americans were wrong in thinking that they could indulge in a double loyalty, and that the first loyalty of every American, even the "hyphenated American," was to America.

But when the convention staged such a spontaneous demonstration for pacifism, it seemed that the Americanism issue would get lost. McCombs, one of the party leaders, quickly scrawled on a piece of paper the phrase, "But we are willing to fight if necessary," and sent it to Glynn, who incorporated it in his oratory.

On the second day Senator Ollie James of Kentucky, the permanent chairman of the convention, a shrewd orator with "the face of a prize-fighter, the body of an oak and the voice of a pipe organ," made an impressive speech. Sensing the mood of the delegates, James spoke of Wilson, who "without orphaning a single American child, without widowing a single American mother, without firing a single gun, without the shedding of a single drop of blood . . . wrung from the most militant spirit that ever brooded above a battlefield an acknowledgment of American rights and an agreement to American demands."

The delegates shouted themselves hoarse in approval of these sentiments. They wanted to hear more of such speeches. Insistently they called for their old leader, William Jennings Bryan, who was present as a newspaper reporter, and who finally rose and told the convention that "I agree with the American people in thanking God we have a President who has kept—*who will keep*—us out of war."

When the balloting began, Senator Hughes proposed a move to suspend the rules and make Wilson's nomination by acclamation, but one delegate from Illinois opposed this. Thus Wilson was chosen "by the vote of 1092 to 1."

The Democratic platform incorporated two significant planks: one was for "the extension of the franchise to the women of the country by the states upon the same terms as to men"; the other was a denunciation of the hyphenated Americans. "Whoever," this plank said, "is activated by the purpose to promote the interest of a foreign power, in disregard of our

own country's welfare . . . and whoever by arousing prejudices of a racial, religious or other nature creates discord and strife among our people so as to obstruct the wholesome process of unification, is faithless to the trust which the privileges of citizenship repose in him and disloyal to his country."

The Republicans had already selected their candidate to oppose Wilson. It was Charles Evans Hughes, Associate Justice of the Supreme Court. Hughes was indeed the most acceptable candidate to both factions of the party. His fine record as Governor of New York was approved by the Progressives and his decisions on the Supreme Court bench won the respect of the conservative element. It was thought that his nomination would bring the two factions together again and heal the wounds of the 1912 election.

The Progressives met in a convention the same day as the regular Republicans. They, too, chose a presidential candidate—Theodore Roosevelt.

Although great efforts were made to unite both conventions behind the same candidate, the Progressives refused to desert Roosevelt, while the Republican regulars were not willing to support him. Roosevelt himself said: "It

THE SMILE OF A MAN IN LOVE. Wilson and Mrs. Ga at the World Series in 1915. He married her—"the only wom an I know who can wear an orchid"—a few weeks late

528

ROLLIN KIRBY OFTEN PICTURED CHARLES EVANS HUGHES AS CANDIDATE OF THE GERMANS.

ould be a mistake to nominate me unless the untry has in its mood something of the eroic."

Roosevelt declined the Progressive nomina-on by telegraph, but reserved the right to ange his mind should the Republican plat-form be silent on the important issues of the war. "I'll support Hughes," said he, "but not unless he declares himself. We must know where he stands on national honor, national de-fense and all other great questions before we accept him." Later, as the campaign was in full swing, Roosevelt withdrew his name and endorsed Hughes, the party's official candidate. Thus the Battle of Armageddon ended—the Progressive party ceased to be.

The Progressives could easily return into the Republican fold; this time there was hardly any difference between the platforms and political objectives of the two groups. Both agreed that the country should be "ready for any emergency," both were for a "policy of tariff protection to American industries," both were for improvement of industrial conditions, conservation of natural resources and rural credit; both favored Federal regulation of business, both asked for child-labor and workmen's compensation laws, both came out for women's suffrage.

During the campaign the two factions regained their unity, and while here and there the former animosity remained, on the whole harmony was restored.

The Democrats were confident of victory. Wilson appointed Vance McCormick of Pennsylvania, the "steam engine in boots," to manage the campaign, and he turned out to be an excellent choice. In New York City he built up a strong campaign organization, the strongest the Democratic party ever had, and through clever methods he lured many independent voters and a great number of Progressive Republicans into supporting the Democrats. The Woodrow Wilson Independent League was a great success.

But however much he pressed Wilson, the President refused to take an active part in the campaign. "Don't worry, McCormick, this is exactly what people want. They want the President at a time like this to stay on his job. Let Hughes run about the country if he wishes to."

THE REPUBLICAN CANDIDATE, CHARLES E. HUGHES, ADDRESSES CROWDS AT PARKSBURG, OHIO

WILSON MADE VERY FEW SPEECHES, BUT HIS LUCID ARGUMENTS WON HIM FRIENDS AND VOTES.

Wilson believed that he could win the election without going on the stump. "I am inclined," he wrote to his friend Bernard Baruch, "to follow the course suggested by a friend of mine who says that he has always followed the rule never to murder a man who is committing suicide slowly but surely."

Hughes campaigned with great energy, but the issues which he discussed did not rouse the electorate. The Democratic campaign slogan that Wilson "kept us out of war" was effective. To this Hughes could only answer that we ought to end our shilly-shally relationship with Mexico and Germany.

While on the whole the voters were not too enthusiastic about Hughes, there was also a good deal of opposition to Wilson's liberal domestic policies. Yes, Hughes could have won the presidency if he had not blundered in California. There, taken in tow by the conservative

national committeeman William H. Crocker, who still nursed ill feelings toward the state's governor, Hiram W. Johnson, a candidate for the Vice-Presidency on the Bull Moose ticket four years before, Hughes was prevented from meeting Johnson. It was an irreparable mistake.

The astute New York Congressman, John W. Dwight, remarked that Hughes could have been elected for a dollar, if "a man of sense, with a dollar, would have invited Hughes and Johnson to his room when they were both in the same hotel in California. He would have ordered three Scotch whiskies, which would have been seventy-five cents, and that would have left a tip of twenty-five cents for the waiter. . . . That little Scotch would have brought those men together; there would have been mutual understanding and respect and Hughes would have carried California and been elected." But as no one spent the dollar on

in his attack on Wilson, kept up his barrage until the very end. "There should be shadows now at Shadow Lawn," (the name of Wilson's home) said he in his final speech of the campaign at New York's Cooper Union, "the shadows of the men, women and children who have risen from the ooze of the ocean bottom and from graves in foreign lands; the shadows of the helpless whom Mr. Wilson did

"THE NEW RINGMASTER," a cartoon on women voters by Herbert Johnson for the *Saturday Evening Post.*

drinks, Hughes lost California by less than 4,000 votes—and with it the election.

As the campaign entered the final weeks, Wilson's foreign policy was subjected to heavy criticism. Theodore Roosevelt attacked the man who "kept us out of war," distorting the phrase in his speeches until it sounded like a promise that under no circumstances would the U. S. go to war. The impetuous Roosevelt asserted that if he had been President when the *Lusitania* was sunk, he would have seized every German vessel interned in American waters. When the Democratic campaign chairman asked Hughes for an endorsement of Roosevelt's position, the Republican candidate answered: "I would have made it known . . . that we should not tolerate a continuance of friendly relations . . . if that action were taken, and the *Lusitania* would never have been sunk."

In his own speeches Hughes advocated "a flag that protects the American in his lawful rights wherever his legitimate business may take him." He attacked the Adamson Eight-Hour Law, calling it a "forced law" and "labor's gold brick," and stated that he was for "America first."

Toward the end of October, the Republicans realized that their attack on Wilson's foreign policy had failed; so they began to discuss the tariff, the old chestnut of presidential campaigns. Only Theodore Roosevelt, unwavering

THE ELECTORAL VOTE IN 1916

STATES	POPULAR VOTE				ELECTORAL VOTE	
	Wilson and Marshall, Democrat.	Hughes and Fairbanks, Republican.	Hanly and Landrith, Prohibition.	Benson and Kirkpatrick, Socialist.	Wilson and Marshall.	Hughes and Fairbanks.
Ala.........	99,409	22,809	1,034	1,925	12	—
Ariz.......	33,170	20,524	1,153	3,174	3	—
Ark........	112,148	47,148	2,015	6,999	9	—
Calif.......	466,200	462,394	27,698	43,259	13	—
Colo.......	178,816	102,308	2,793	10,049	6	—
Conn.......	99,786	106,514	1,789	5,179	—	7
Del........	24,753	26,011	566	480	—	3
Fla........	55,984	14,611	4,855	5,353	6	—
Ga.........	125,845	11,225	—	967	14	—
Idaho......	70,054	55,368	1,127	8,066	4	—
Ill.........	590,229	1,152,549	26,047	61,394	—	29
Ind........	334,063	341,005	16,368	21,855	—	15
Iowa.......	221,699	280,449	3,371	10,976	—	13
Kan........	314,588	277,658	12,882	24,685	10	—
Ky.........	260,990	241,854	3,036	4,734	13	—
La.........	79,875	6,466	—	292	10	—
Me.........	64,127	69,506	597	2,177	—	6
Md.........	138,359	117,347	2,903	2,674	8	—
Mass.......	247,885	268,784	2,993	11,058	—	18
Mich.......	285,151	339,097	8,139	16,120	—	15
Minn.......	179,152	179,544	7,793	20,117	—	12
Miss.......	80,422	4,253	—	1,484	10	—
Mo.........	398,025	369,339	3,884	14,612	18	—
Mont.......	101,063	66,750	—	9,564	4	—
Neb........	158,827	117,257	2,952	7,141	8	—
Nev........	17,776	12,127	348	3,065	3	—
N. H.......	43,779	43,723	303	1,318	4	—
N. J.......	211,645	269,352	3,187	10,462	—	14
N. M.......	33,663	31,163	112	1,999	3	—
N. Y.......	759,426	869,115	19,031	45,944	—	45
N. C.......	168,383	120,988	51	490	12	—
N. D.......	55,206	53,471	—	—	5	—
Ohio.......	604,161	514,753	8,080	38,092	24	—
Okla.......	148,113	97,233	1,646	45,190	10	—
Ore........	120,087	126,813	4,729	9,711	—	5
Pa.........	521,784	703,734	28,525	42,637	—	38
R. I.......	40,394	44,858	470	1,914	—	5
S. C.......	61,846	1,550	—	135	9	—
S. D.......	59,191	64,217	1,774	3,760	—	5
Tenn.......	153,282	116,223	147	2,542	12	—
Tex........	286,514	64,999	1,985	18,963	20	—
Utah.......	84,025	54,137	149	4,460	4	—
Vt.........	22,708	40,250	709	798	—	4
Va.........	102,824	49,356	783	1,060	12	—
Wash.......	183,388	167,244	6,868	22,800	7	—
W. Va......	140,403	143,124	175	6,140	1	—
Wis........	193,042	221,323	7,166	27,846	—	13
Wyo........	28,316	21,698	373	1,453	3	—
	9,129,606	8,538,221	220,506	585,113	277	254

J. M. Parker, Progressive for Vice-Presidency, received 41,894 votes.
Reimer, Socialist-Labor, 13,403.   Total vote, 18,528,743.

"THE EIGHT-HOUR GLASS," a cartoon against Wilson drawn by Herbert Johnson for the *Saturday Evening Post*.

"HIS HAPPY HOMECOMING," a cartoon for Wilson by Rollin Kirby which appeared in the New York *World*.

not dare protect lest he might have to face danger; the shadows of deeds that were never done; the shadows of lofty words that were followed by no action; the shadows of the tortured dead."

The Democrats—in a last minute appeal—distributed hundreds of thousands of leaflets: "You are working—not fighting!" said one. "Wilson and peace with honor. Hughes with Roosevelt and war." Posters appeared on city walls: "Alive and happy—not cannon fodder!"

When the votes were counted in the late evening of November 7, it was found that New York had gone for Hughes and every other Eastern state north of the Potomac except Maryland and New Hampshire. The Midwest, save Ohio, was for Hughes as well, and beyond the Mississippi, the states of Iowa, South Dakota, and Minnesota were for the Republican candidate. All indications pointed toward a Republican victory. Not counting the 13 electoral votes of California, Hughes had 254 electoral votes in his column. With California, his strength would have been 267 electoral votes—one more than the necessary majority.

During the night, extras came off the New York presses conceding the election to Hughes.

In the Hotel Astor, the Republican candidate went to bed, believing that he had been elected. On the roof a large electric sign spelled the victorious name: "Hughes." Times Square was filled with a cheering multitude. At eleven o'clock members of the Republican and Union League Clubs, with two bands, marched thousands strong to the hotel, cheering their next President.

But the next day, reports came from California which indicated that Hughes had not carried the state yet. And when all the votes were in, they showed that he had lost it by less than 4,000, while Governor Hiram Johnson, whose support he refused and who was running for the Senate, amassed a 300,000 majority over his opponent.

Wilson, backed by an almost solid South and West, won with a popular majority of almost 600,000 votes. Since his last election he had gained nearly three million votes. The New York *World* exclaimed: "A new era in American politics!" and added: "Nothing better has happened in a generation than this shifting of the political balance to a section which still maintains the old ideals of the Republic."

HARDING TAKES THE INAUGURAL OATH

THE THIRTY-FOURTH ELECTION—1920

WARREN G. HARDING
AND CALVIN COOLIDGE

Wilson began his second term in the White House with a determination to maintain the course of at least technical neutrality which the nation had steered precariously during the first two and a half years of the conflict in Europe. During the campaign of 1916 he had never made an out-and-out pledge to keep that neutrality intact. But he was fully conscious of the fact that his victory at the polls had been brought about largely by antiwar sentiment, and he knew that the success of the Democratic slogan "He kept us out of the war" represented, to some extent, a popular mandate.

As he attempted to implement this mandate, however, it soon became apparent that control of the situation rested more with the belligerents than with the American government. Scarcely a month after the election, Wilson issued an appeal to both sides, asking for a statement of terms on which hostilities might be ended. The German reply, though prompt, evasively stated that the Central Powers would make their terms known at the council chamber and indicated that they would be stringent. The Allies' reply, equally unsatisfactory, demanded the return of all territories conquered by the Central Powers and heavy reparations. Neither side, in short, would accept anything less than victors' terms.

In the face of this impasse, Wilson delivered to the Senate in January a speech calling for "peace without victory" and outlining terms which he still hoped might become the basis for a negotiated settlement. Within a week Germany, convinced that an economic blockade would bring England to her knees, announced a decision that dashed these hopes—and, ultimately, the hopes for American neutrality—to pieces. Effective immediately, said the German government, unrestricted submarine warfare would be resumed against merchant shipping in the war zones, whether Allied or neutral.

Wilson did not hesitate. He broke off diplomatic relations with Germany and asked Congress for authorization to arm merchantmen. When the latter measure was blocked by a

535

WARREN G. HARDING (1865-1923)
ON THE STEPS OF THE CAPITOL

THE CANDIDATES

WARREN G. HARDING
(1865-1923), Senator
from Ohio, was chosen
by Republicans in a
"smoke-filled" hotel
room in Chicago when
the two leading con-
testants deadlocked.

CALVIN COOLIDGE
(1872-1933), Governor
of Massachusetts, was
Republican choice for
second place. His main
achievement was break-
ing the Boston police
strike the year before.

JAMES M. COX
(1870-19—), Governor
of Ohio, was the Demo-
cratic nominee. He was
badly defeated, receiv-
ing only 127 electoral
votes to the Republi-
can candidate's 404.

FRANKLIN ROOSEVELT
(1882-1945), Assistant
Secretary of the Navy
under Wilson, was Cox'
running mate, cam-
paigning for ratifica-
tion of the peace treaty
and League of Nations.

EUGENE V. DEBS
(1855-1926), recurring
Socialist candidate for
the Presidency dur-
ing the previous two
decades, won in this
election a record So-
cialist vote of 919,799.

P. P. CHRISTENSEN
(1869-19——) of Utah,
was candidate of the
Farmer-Labor party
with Max S. Hayes of
Ohio his running mate.
Their ticket polled
over 260,000 votes.

THE COLISEUM in Chicago on the day when Warre[n]
Harding became standard-bearer of the Republican party

BOTH CANDIDATES were sons of Ohio. Cox was th[e]
state's Governor and Harding was the state's Senato[r]

Senate filibuster, the President said that "a littl[e]
group of willful men, representing no opinio[n]
but their own, have rendered the great gover[n]-
ment of the United States helpless and co[n]-
temptible"—and then obtained the authorizatio[n]
from an unrepealed statute of 1797. Althoug[h]
the President had not yet resigned himself [to]
the fact that America would enter the war, [it]
was obvious that neutrality was now in th[e]
balance.

Events soon tipped the scales. On March [1,]
American public opinion was inflamed by

536

FRANKLIN ROOSEVELT, DEMOCRATIC VICE-PRESIDENTIAL CANDIDATE, SPEAKS IN WASHINGTON.

HARDING AND COOLIDGE CONFER WITH WILL HAYS, WHO MANAGED REPUBLICAN CAMPAIGN.

State Department charge that Germany had suggested to Mexico an alliance by which the latter would gain Texas, New Mexico, and Arizona in the event of Allied-American defeat. And on March 27 came the news that three American ships had been sunk. Wilson summoned a special session of Congress and asked for a declaration of war against Germany. On April 6, 1917, the resolution was passed by overwhelming majorities.

During America's first months in the war, Wilson reached the height of his popularity. The same uncompromising idealism which was later to spell his political downfall made him a natural leader in what most Americans felt to be a righteous crusade. The war, as he saw it, was a people's war, and under his leadership the American people were welded into a firm na-

tional unity which enabled them to accept readily the sacrifices necessary to effective participation. Perhaps his greatest contribution lay in the formulation of war aims and in his conviction that only a just peace could be a lasting peace. This conviction he expressed in January, 1918, when he went before Congress with the famous Fourteen Points, which he offered as a basis for such a peace. Six of these points, general in nature, called for "open covenants, openly arrived at," freedom of the seas, removal of trade barriers, disarmament, impartial adjustment of colonial claims, and establishment of a League of Nations. The remaining eight points cited specific war aims which, though victors' terms, were not unduly harsh on Germany.

Reaction to the Fourteen Points, both at home and abroad, was outwardly enthusiastic.

but in actual fact they committed only America, as later became painfully apparent. Their significance lay in the fact that Germany, in defeat, seized upon them as basis for making peace. In October, 1918, Germany appealed to the President for an armistice; on November 11, after extensive negotiations, the fighting ended.

Meanwhile, in the November elections for Congress, Wilson had suffered a defeat which was to have a disastrous effect on his subsequent political fortunes. Several factors contributed principally to this setback: his own mistake in making a public plea for a Democratic Congress, the opposition from "bitter-enders" like Theodore Roosevelt who felt that Wilson's Fourteen Points were not sufficiently stringent, and (at the other extreme) the continuing opposition to his policies from antiwar groups. The election put the Republicans in control of both the Senate and the House. Their majority in the Senate amounted to only one vote, but it threw control of the all-important Foreign Relations Committee into the hands of the President's personal enemies.

Despite this defeat at home, Wilson deter-

A CHARGE AGAINST the Republicans. Privilege-seeking interests contributed heavily to the campaign.

"HERE D'YA WANT THIS?" asks the moving-man. x points toward the parlor, Harding toward the attic.

mined to go to Paris as head of the American commission for negotiating the peace—a great mistake. Another was that in choosing the members of his commission he took no one who represented the Republican party or the Senate, which would have to ratify any decisions made at the conference table.

At Paris he encountered further difficulties. Although he received huge popular ovations, the Allied prime ministers, greedy for the spoils of war, showed scant respect for the idealism contained in his Fourteen Points. Pitted against the combined strategy of England, France, and Italy, he ended by agreeing to compromise after compromise. In the end he was victorious on only one major point: the acceptance of his dream of a League of Nations as an integral part of the peace treaty.

Three months later, in February, 1919, Wilson returned to America for his last and greatest

OFF TO THE POLLS. A satirical comment by A. B. Frost on women's suffrage, granted on August 26, 1920.

the patrician and scholarly Senator from Massachusetts, who held the strategic post of Chairman of the Senate's Foreign Relations Committee. Although publicly on record for a League of Nations as early as 1915, Lodge shrewdly saw the situation as an opportunity to bring about a personal defeat for Wilson, whom he hated, and to push the Republican party back into power. His method, he said privately, would be to kill the League and the treaty, not by direct attack, but by "the indirect method of reservations." After keeping the treaty in committee for several months, he reported it back to the Senate with fourteen modifying recommendations, as though in answer to the President's Fourteen Points. Wilson's followers, combined with the irreconcilables, voted it down by a narrow margin.

The President, by this time, was a sick man. In the late summer, when the Foreign Relations Committee was hammering away at his hard won treaty, he decided to take the issue directly to the people. Against the advice of his phys-

battle—the fight to win ratification of the treaty (including the League Covenant) in the United States Senate. The debate soon divided the Senate, and the American people, into four main groups: the "ratificationists," who wanted Senate approval of the treaty immediately; the "mild reservationists," who wanted only minor changes in it; the "extreme reservationists," who demanded extensive alterations; and the "irreconcilables," who wanted no part of it. Broadly speaking, a majority of the American public, press, and even the Senate wanted to see approval of the treaty and the League; by making a few concessions to the reservationists the President could probably have obtained its acceptance in short order. This he refused to do. Convinced that the American people were behind him and aware that revising the treaty would impede world ratification by inducing other nations to do likewise, he refused to consider any modifications.

The President's unbending attitude played directly into the hands of Henry Cabot Lodge,

"IF I SHOULD DIE before I wake . . ." prays Republican elephant in this Webster cartoon from L

Life

October 28, 1920   Vol. 76. Copyright, 1920, Life Publishing Company   No. 1982   Price 15 Cents

THE WOMAN OF AMERICA is congratulated by Columbia on receiving the vote. The long and ardent fight for women's suffrage, led by Susan B. Anthony and Carrie Chapman Catt, ended in 1920 when the last state ratified the
19th Amendment. From then on American women took an increasingly active part in the political life of the nation.

THE THIRD PARTY—LA FOLLETTE'S INDEPENDENT PROGRESSIVES—IS LEFT IN THE CORNER WHEN

cians—for the strain of events had already weakened him severely—he set out on a speaking tour. On the evening of September 25, after a speech at Pueblo, Colorado, his strength ebbed dangerously and the remaining speaking dates were canceled.

From October until the end of his term, the President was confined to his bed most of the time, partially paralyzed, mentally exhausted, intellectually embittered. In effect, though not in fact, the nation carried on without a Chief Executive. He received no visitors, and his death

IS LURED AWAY BY THE TWO OTHER GIRLS.

ing down completely, he was summarily dismissed by the President. Even Colonel House, Wilson's longtime confidant and advisor, found that his letters to the President went unacknowledged.

As the time for the political conventions approached, it became evident that America was ready for a wave of reaction against the sacrifice and high-minded idealism of the war years. Business interests were anxious to kick off governmental traces and return to a policy of *laissez faire*. The public, eager to get things back to normal as soon as possible, turned cheerfully from the weighty problems of reconstruction to the more dramatic aspects of presidential campaigning. To add a fillip to the electioneering, the passage of the Nineteenth Amendment meant that 1920 would mark the first presidential year in which women would go to the polls along with the men.

In the Republican camp there was an abundance of would-be candidates. When the convention opened in Chicago early in June, the leading contenders were General Leonard Wood, a soldier in the Roosevelt tradition; Governor Frank O. Lowden of Illinois, a longtime champion of agricultural interests; and Senator Hiram Johnson of California, the Bull Moose vice-presidential candidate in 1912. Also among the aspirants were Herbert Hoover, who had built his reputation as Food Administrator during the war; Calvin Coolidge, the Massachusetts governor who had gained national prominence by breaking the Boston police strike of 1919; and Warren G. Harding, a personable but obscure Senator from Ohio. Behind the scenes, the influence of big business pervaded the atmosphere more heavily than it had at any convention since the days of Mark Hanna. From William Boyce Thompson, the copper baron, to Harry Sinclair, whose oil empire was to play a major part in the next administration's destiny, the representatives of special interests were both numerous and active.

Senator Lodge sounded the keynote of the convention: "We must be now and ever for Americanism and Nationalism, and against Internationalism!" The party platform, though less dogmatic, conformed to the tone of the Senator's address by castigating everything Wilsonian. It charged the Democrats with lack of

ings with the outside world were channeled through the small coterie, headed by Mrs. Wilson, who guarded his sickbed. When Robert Lansing, his faithful Secretary of State, began arranging for informal Cabinet meetings in order to keep the executive branch from break-

preparedness for both war and peace, it favored cutting the public debt and lowering taxes on the wealthy, it denounced the high cost of living but declared for a high protective tariff. In the field of foreign affairs it straddled the issue of the League of Nations by saying that "the Republican Party stands for agreement among nations to preserve the peace" but that this must be done "without compromising national independence."

As balloting got under way, it was soon apparent that the convention was faced with a deadlock. In the first few tests General Wood and Governor Lowden showed nearly equal strength, but neither was close to the necessary majority. The scene was now set for the famous decision "at two o'clock in the morning in a smoke-filled room," which Harry Daugherty, Senator Harding's campaign manager, had predicted many months before. Over the protests of a majority of the delegates, the party elders adjourned the convention for the day and assembled privately in a suite at the Blackstone Hotel to decide what dark horse could be trotted out to break the deadlock.

When the delegates reassembled the next morning, Warren Gamaliel Harding became the presidential candidate of the Republicans. For the second place the party leaders hoped to push through the nomination of Senator Irvine Lenroot of Wisconsin, but the delegates, in their only burst of rebellion, named Calvin Coolidge instead.

The nomination of Harding, certainly one of the darkest dark horses ever to reach the White House, came as a surprise even to the candidate himself. A small-city newspaper publisher with modest political ambitions, his career in the Senate had been unimaginative, unaggressive, and unpublicized. A few days before his nomination he had despondently told Nicholas Murray Butler that "the convention will never nominate me" and that he was quitting politics for good. His seemingly miraculous rescue from obscurity can be attributed in part to the shrewdness of Daugherty, his campaign manager, and to the accidental factor of the convention deadlock; but even more, it was a result of the peculiar temper of the times. The Republican leaders, sensing America's postwar mood, saw in Harding not only a man who would be pliable to their wishes, but also one whose character was almost diametrically opposite to that of the man in the White House. Where Wilson was cultivated, urbane, aloof, Harding was a jovial small-town personality, friendly to a fault and completely without intellectual ambitions. Where Wilson was a liberal who distrusted big business, Harding was a conservative who wanted to free businessmen from governmental regulation. Harding was an eminently "practical" man, with few convictions, and none that could not be compromised. Harding's philosophy was neatly summed up in a statement which he made a few weeks before his nomination: "America's present need is not heroics but healing; not nostrums but normalcy; not revolution but restoration." Normalcy was to be the keyword of his campaign.

The Democratic convention, meeting in San

CALVIN COOLIDGE, the Republican vice-presidential candidate, and his wife voting at Northampton, Mass.

WARREN HARDING, Republican presidential candidate, and his wife cast their ballots at Marion, Ohio.

THE POPULAR AND ELECTORAL VOTES IN THE 1920 ELECTION

STATES	POPULAR VOTE					ELECTORAL VOTE	
	Harding and Coolidge, Republican.	Cox and Roosevelt, Democrat.	Debs and Stedman, Socialist.	Christensen and Hayes, Farmer-Labor.	Watkins and Colvin, Prohibition.	Harding and Coolidge.	Cox and Roosevelt.
Alabama	74,690	163,254	2,369	—	757	—	12
Arizona	37,016	29,546	222	15	4	3	—
Arkansas	71,117	107,409	5,111	—	—	—	9
California	624,992	229,191	64,076	—	25,204	13	—
Colorado	173,248	104,936	8,046	3,016	2,807	6	—
Connecticut	229,238	120,721	10,350	1,947	1,771	7	—
Delaware	52,858	39,911	988	93	986	3	—
Florida	44,853	90,515	5,189	—	5,124	—	6
Georgia	43,720	109,856	465	—	8	—	14
Idaho	91,351	46,930	38	6	9	4	—
Illinois	1,420,480	534,395	74,747	49,630	11,216	29	—
Indiana	696,370	511,364	24,703	16,499	13,462	15	—
Iowa	634,674	227,921	16,981	10,321	4,197	13	—
Kansas	369,268	185,464	15,511	—	—	10	—
Kentucky	452,480	456,497	6,409	—	3,325	—	13
Louisiana	38,538	87,519	—	—	—	—	10
Maine	136,355	58,961	2,214	—	—	6	—
Maryland	236,117	180,626	8,876	1,645	—	8	—
Massachusetts	681,153	276,691	32,269	—	—	18	—
Michigan	762,865	233,450	28,947	10,480	9,646	15	—
Minnesota	519,421	142,994	56,106	—	11,489	12	—
Mississippi	11,576	69,277	1,639	—	—	—	10
Missouri	727,521	574,924	20,924	3,291	5,142	18	—
Montana	109,430	57,372	—	12,204	—	4	—
Nebraska	247,498	119,608	9,600	—	5,947	8	—
Nevada	15,479	9,851	1,864	—	—	3	—
New Hampshire	95,196	62,662	1,234	—	—	4	—
New Jersey	615,333	258,761	27,385	2,264	4,895	14	—
New Mexico	57,634	46,668	—	1,097	—	3	—
New York	1,871,167	781,238	203,201	18,413	19,653	45	—
North Carolina	232,848	305,447	446	—	17	—	12
North Dakota	160,072	37,422	8,282	—	—	5	—
Ohio	1,182,022	780,037	57,147	—	294	24	—
Oklahoma	243,831	217,053	25,726	—	—	10	—
Oregon	143,592	80,019	9,801	—	3,595	5	—
Pennsylvania	1,218,215	503,202	70,021	15,642	42,612	38	—
Rhode Island	107,463	55,062	4,351	—	510	5	—
South Carolina	2,244	64,170	28	—	—	—	9
South Dakota	109,874	35,938	—	34,707	900	5	—
Tennessee	219,829	206,558	2,268	—	—	12	—
Texas	114,538	288,767	8,121	—	—	—	20
Utah	81,555	56,639	3,159	4,475	—	4	—
Vermont	68,212	20,919	—	—	774	4	—
Virginia	87,456	141,670	807	240	824	—	12
Washington	223,137	84,298	8,913	77,246	3,800	7	—
West Virginia	282,007	220,789	5,618	—	1,528	8	—
Wisconsin	498,576	113,422	85,041	—	8,647	13	—
Wyoming	35,091	17,429	1,288	2,180	265	3	—
	16,152,200	9,147,353	919,799	265,411	189,408	404	127

Socialist-Labor, 31,175, Single Tax, 5,837. Total vote, 26,711,183.

Francisco three weeks after the Republicans, had little choice but to stand on Wilson's record. The platform urged immediate ratification of the treaty, tax reform, governmental economy, and reconstruction measures to combat the high cost of living. It opposed compulsory arbitration of labor disputes ("labor is not a commodity, it is a human") and pledged "adherence to the fundamental progressive principles of social, economic, and industrial justice."

When it came to choosing a candidate, the Democrats found that three contenders dominated the field: William Gibbs McAdoo, the President's son-in-law; A. Mitchell Palmer, the Attorney General; and Governor James M. Cox of Ohio. Like Harding, Cox was an Ohio newspaper publisher who had gone into politics, but there the resemblance ended. By temperament and conviction he was a progressive in the Wilsonian tradition.

William McAdoo, though he led on the first

THE REPUBLICAN PRESIDENT-ELECT rides with Wilson to Capitol to take the oath. In front are "Uncle Jo⟨ Cannon, once all-powerful Speaker of the House, and Philander C. Knox, Roosevelt's trust-busting Attorney Genera⟨

few ballots, made no strenuous attempt to win the nomination and suffered considerably from his vulnerable position as "crown prince" of the administration. Palmer, who ran second in the early balloting, was severely handicapped by liberal opposition to the notorious "Red-hunts" which he had conducted during the previous year. In the end—and it took forty-four ballots to bring about the necessary two-thirds majority—Governor Cox won the nomination, largely because he was satisfactory to the party leaders and because he had made few enemies.

For his running mate Cox recommended a handsome young New Yorker with a patrician background, a magnetic personality, and an impressive record as Assistant Secretary of the Navy during the war. His name was Franklin Delano Roosevelt. Knowing that young Roosevelt was not popular with New York machine

politicians, Cox consulted the Tammany bos⟨ Charles F. Murphy, before making his prefe⟨ ence known. "I don't like Roosevelt," Murph⟨ told Cox's emissary. "He is not well known ⟨ the country. But this is the first time a Dem⟨ cratic nominee for the Presidency has show⟨ me courtesy. That's why I would vote for th⟨ devil himself if Cox wanted me to. Tell him w⟨ will nominate Roosevelt on the first ballot ⟨ soon as we assemble." Murphy made good h⟨ promise the next morning.

As the campaign developed, neither candida⟨ seemed to stir the public's imagination. Havir⟨ delivered his acceptance speech from an in⟨ provised platform in his home town of Mario⟨ Harding proceeded to conduct a "front-por⟨ campaign" in the same homely manner. F⟨ received Republican leaders and rank and f⟨ at his house, delivering a series of speech⟨

546

which were emotionally reassuring, if intellectually inconsistent. He was in favor of deflation, the return of railroads to private ownership, restricted immigration, and a high tariff; on the subject of the League, he was as elusive as the Republican platform.

With only moderate success, Cox tried to inject some vigor into the campaign. In contrast to Harding, he stumped the country tirelessly. One of his campaign trips set a new record: he devoted twenty-nine days to a Western swing through eighteen states—from which, as it turned out, he received no electoral votes whatsoever. His first act on receiving the nomination had been to visit Wilson's sickbed at the White House, and throughout the campaign he stood steadfastly by the President's record and by the League of Nations.

It was a hopeless stand. When the ballots were counted in November, Harding emerged with 16,152,200 popular votes as against only 9,147,353 for Cox. The electoral vote was an overwhelming 404 to 127; even Tennessee, a traditional Democratic stronghold, threw its support to Harding.

The voting was unexpectedly light, with less than half of the eligible voters going to the polls. In many respects the most remarkable aspect of the election returns was the vote polled by Eugene V. Debs, the candidate of the Socialist party. Although in Federal prison for sedition during the entire campaign, he received a total of 919,799 votes.

Many times on his sickbed President Wilson said that the principles for which he had fought would be vindicated by the American people at the polls. Their overwhelming answer was the last great defeat of his career.

THE INAUGURAL ADDRESS, A CONGLOMERATION OF PLATITUDES, IS DELIVERED BY HARDING.

547

HARDING'S CABINET poses on the White House lawn. Front row, from left to right, are John Weeks, Secretary of War; Andrew Mellon, Secretary of the Treasury; Charles E. Hughes, Secretary of State; President Warren G. Harding; Vice-President Calvin Coolidge; Edwin Denby, Secretary of the Navy. In the back row, left to right, are Albert Fall, Secretary of the Interior; Will Hays, Postmaster General; Harry M. Daugherty, Attorney General; Henry C. Wallace, Secretary of Agriculture; Herbert C. Hoover, Secretary of Commerce; and James J. Davis, the Secretary of Labor.

PRESIDENT HARDING'S COFFIN lies in state in the Rotunda of the Capitol. Harding died in San Francisco and was deeply mourned by the nation. The shocking scandals of his administration were not yet common knowledge.

548

COOLIDGE TAKES THE OATH after President Harding died suddenly and mysteriously on August 2, 1923. This is a photomontage of the event showing the Vice-President as he was sworn in at the old family homestead in Plymouth, Vermont, by his father, a justice of the peace. The ceremony took place early in the morning of August 3.

CALVIN COOLIDGE TAKES THE OATH

THE THIRTY-FIFTH ELECTION—1924

CALVIN COOLIDGE

Harding—elected by a record-breaking majority—seemed to personify the public's eagerness to substitute a policy of "business as usual" for Wilsonian idealism. His easygoing cordiality was exemplified in his first official act: he threw open the long-shuttered White House gates to tourists and sight-seers. Mrs. Harding struck a popular and revealing note when she said that she and the President were "just folks."

A better indication of what was to come, however, was the list of the new President's Cabinet appointments. The men he picked were, in many cases, honest and able—and in many other cases, just the opposite. Among the former were Charles Evans Hughes, his Secretary of State, and Herbert Hoover, his Secretary of Commerce. Among the latter were Harry F. Daugherty, Harding's campaign manager, who became Attorney General, and former Senator Albert B. Fall, who was appointed Secretary of the Interior despite the fact that he was a vigorous anti-conservationist.

An unprincipled group of Harding's erstwhile political acquaintances, later to become known as "the Ohio Gang," followed the new President to Washington, aware that his naïve and trusting personality would create lucrative opportunities for skulduggery at the taxpayers' expense.

With "normalcy" as its goal, the new administration quickly embarked on the job of returning the country to a peacetime footing. Convoking a special session of Congress a month after his inaugural, Harding urged a broad program that included creation of a long-needed Federal budget system, establishment of higher tariff barriers, cutting down of war taxes, restriction of immigration, and extreme governmental economy. The program met relatively few obstacles at the start. Wartime powers, including governmental ownership of the railroads, were slowly liquidated; step by step, Federal regulation of the nation's business life was eliminated wherever possible. Although the Republicans took their victory at the polls as a rebuff for the Treaty of Versailles, they opened negotiations with Germany, and on August 25, 1921, a peace treaty was finally signed.

By far the greatest accomplishment of the Harding years, however, was the International Conference on Limitation of Armaments. On

551

THE CANDIDATES

CALVIN COOLIDGE
(1872-1933) was nominated by the Republicans. Enjoying great prosperity, the people gave him a popular majority of 7,400,000 votes over John Davis.

CHARLES G. DAWES
(1865-1951) of Illinois became Coolidge's running mate when Governor Frank Lowden, also of Illinois, refused to accept the nomination for second place.

JOHN W. DAVIS
(1873-19——) was selected by Democrats in the longest convention in history. He was nominated on the 103rd ballot after Smith and McAdoo deadlocked.

CHARLES W. BRYAN
(1867-1945), Governor of Nebraska and the brother of the "peerless leader," William Jennings Bryan, was chosen by the Democrats for Vice-President.

ROBERT LA FOLLETTE
(1855-1925) of Wisconsin was the candidate of a new third party, backed by progressives and labor. He received almost five million votes in the election.

BURTON K. WHEELER
(1882-19——), the Senator from Montana, was named as La Follette's running mate. In the election, only 51 per cent of the voting population went to polls.

STATES	POPULAR VOTE			ELECTORAL VOTE	
	Coolidge and Dawes, Republican.	Davis and Bryan, Democrat.	LaFollette and Wheeler, Progressive Socialist, and others.	Coolidge and Dawes.	Davis and Bryan.
Alabama	45,005	112,966	8,084	—	12
Arizona	30,516	26,235	17,210	3	—
Arkansas	40,564	84,795	13,173	—	9
California	733,250	105,514	424,649	13	—
Colorado	195,171	75,238	69,945	6	—
Connecticut	246,322	110,184	42,416	7	—
Delaware	52,441	33,445	4,979	3	—
Florida	30,633	62,083	8,625	—	6
Georgia	30,300	123,200	12,691	—	14
Idaho	69,879	24,256	54,160	4	—
Illinois	1,453,321	576,975	432,027	29	—
Indiana	703,042	492,245	71,700	15	—
Iowa	537,635	162,600	272,243	13	—
Kansas	407,671	156,319	98,461	10	—
Kentucky	398,966	374,855	38,465	13	—
Louisiana	24,670	93,218	—	—	10
Maine	138,440	41,964	11,382	6	—
Maryland	162,414	148,072	47,157	8	—
Massachusetts	703,476	280,831	141,284	18	—
Michigan	874,631	152,359	122,014	15	—
Minnesota	420,759	55,913	339,192	12	—
Mississippi	8,546	100,475	3,494	—	10
Missouri	648,486	572,753	84,160	18	—
Montana	74,138	33,805	65,876	4	—
Nebraska	218,585	137,289	106,701	8	—
Nevada	11,243	5,909	9,769	3	—
New Hampshire	98,575	57,201	8,993	4	—
New Jersey	676,277	298,043	109,028	14	—
New Mexico	54,745	48,542	9,543	3	—
New York	1,820,058	950,796	474,925	45	—
North Carolina	191,753	284,270	6,697	—	12
North Dakota	94,931	13,858	89,922	5	—
Ohio	1,176,130	477,888	357,948	24	—
Oklahoma	226,242	255,798	41,141	—	10
Oregon	142,579	67,589	68,403	5	—
Pennsylvania	1,401,481	409,192	307,567	38	—
Rhode Island	125,286	76,606	7,628	5	—
South Carolina	1,123	49,008	620	—	9
South Dakota	101,299	27,214	75,355	5	—
Tennessee	130,882	158,537	10,656	—	12
Texas	130,023	483,586	42,881	—	20
Utah	77,327	47,001	32,662	4	—
Vermont	80,498	16,124	5,964	4	—
Virginia	73,359	139,797	10,379	—	12
Washington	220,224	42,842	150,727	7	—
West Virginia	288,635	257,232	36,723	8	—
Wisconsin	311,614	68,096	453,678	—	—
Wyoming	41,858	12,868	25,174	3	—
	15,725,003	8,385,586	4,826,471	382	136

Wisconsin gave 13 electoral votes to La Follette and Wheeler. Faris a Brehm, Prohibitionists, received 57,551 votes. Worker's (Communis 36,386, Socialist-Labor, 27,650, American, 23,867, Commonwealth-La 2778. Total vote, 29,085,292.

Armistice Day, 1921, the administration dr matically called the conference to order und the able chairmanship of Charles Evans Hugh To the surprise of American liberals, who ha predicted that the conference would limit itse to the usual polite platitudes and vague resolv the Secretary of State promptly presented t delegates with a clear-cut and drastic progra calling for a ten-year holiday on naval co struction and setting up the famous "5-5-

THE AGING WILLIAM JENNINGS BRYAN, three times Democratic nominee, was present at the exhausting, sixteen-day convention in New York City. When the chief candidates—Alfred E. Smith of New York and William G. McAdoo of California—deadlocked, the compromise choice of the party became John W. Davis on the 103rd ballot.

ratio by which the signatory powers—United States, England, Japan, France, and Italy—agreed to limit their construction of capital ships. Eventually the agreement was abrogated by Japan, but for more than a decade it kept the danger of an out-and-out armaments race in check and, moreover, resulted in huge budgetary savings for every government concerned.

On the surface things seemed to be going well for the Harding administration, but behind the scenes the President's weakness of character and the carelessness of many of his appointments were bearing ugly fruit. Most of the inside story came out in piecemeal fashion during subsequent years, and it was not until the end of the decade that the whole truth was known, but there was already talk in political circles indicating that corruption in high places was rife. One key figure in the sordid proceedings was Daugherty, the President's principal advisor, whose influence, lobbyists learned, was often for sale. Another was Charles R. Forbes, a political adventurer and former army deserter who, as head of the Veterans' Administration, regularly accepted graft in awarding contracts for hospital buildings and supplies.

Most flagrant of all, however, were the notorious "Teapot Dome" scandals, traced to Secretary of the Interior Fall. Shortly after taking office, Fall had persuaded Secretary of the Navy Denby to turn over to the Department of the Interior control of naval oil reserves at Teapot Dome, Wyoming, and Elk Hills, California. On the pretext that wells adjacent to these reserves were draining off government oil, Fall proceeded to lease the lands to private oil interests in an arrangement whereby the Navy received a percentage of the oil thus extracted. Outwardly this seemed reasonable, and it was not until considerably later that Fall was found to have accepted substantial bribes from the oil men for his services.

GOOD FRIENDS. It was Franklin D. Roosevelt, Wilson's Assistant Secretary of the Navy, who for the second time made the nominating speech in the Democratic convention for Alfred E. Smith, New York's popular governor.

It is unlikely that Harding was a party to the evil-doing of his appointees. That he did know a good deal of the truth about them by the summer of 1923, however, seems certain. To add to his difficulties, the midterm elections of the previous fall had cut the Republican majorities in Congress substantially and had given the balance of power in the Senate to the radical Republicans of the "farm bloc," who proceeded to obstruct much of his legislative program. Seeking respite from these problems, the President set out on an Alaskan visit in July. On the return trip he received a long coded message from Washington that put him in a state of near collapse, and at San Francisco he was rushed to the Palace Hotel for a rest. On the night of July 28 his physicians described his condition as extremely grave, and five days later a grief-stricken nation learned that its President was dead.

The circumstances surrounding Harding's death have never been cleared of mystery. He was variously reported to have been suffering from ptomaine poisoning, bronchial pneumonia, and apoplexy, and in later years rumors of unnatural death were widely circulated. Whatever the specific cause, it is probable that he was greatly weakened by his knowledge of the impending disgrace that faced him, due to the double-dealing of his associates.

The public knew nothing about this at the time. When a special train carried his body back

FRANKLIN D. ROOSEVELT puts Al Smith's name in nomination. This marked his return to politics, three years after he had been stricken by infantile paralysis.

to Washington to lie in state before being taken to Marion for burial, the nation's display of grief was described by a New York *Times* reporter as "the most remarkable demonstration in American history of affection, respect and reverence for the dead." That the President's death was, in many respects, fortunate both for himself and his party came to light later as Senator Walsh of Montana and others investigated the administration's record. Eventually Denby and Daugherty both resigned their offices under fire, and a dozen others—including Fall, Forbes, and Colonel T. W. Miller, the Alien Property Custodian—were sent to prison.

EERS FOR AL SMITH in Madison Square Garden ed for 73 minutes, but when the balloting began neir Smith nor his strongest rival, William G. McAdoo, able to secure the necessary two-thirds majority.

Meanwhile, the nation was taking its first close look at the new President, Calvin Coolidge. Although a Vermonter by birth, Coolidge had begun his career as a lawyer in Massachusetts and had worked his way, step by step, to the governorship of the state by the time the Republicans nominated him as Vice-President. A man of simple manners and few words, he was conscientious, honest, and consistently conservative, both in personal habits and political convictions. His personality, reserved and aloof, contrasted severely with Harding's open friendliness. One observer remarked that he had probably been "weaned on a pickle."

The manner in which he assumed the highest office in the land was in itself almost symbolic of the Spartan simplicity to which he rigorously subscribed. The news of Harding's death had found him vacationing at his family's modest farmhouse in Vermont. Awakened by a messenger at two o'clock in the morning, he went down to the sparsely furnished parlor and there, by the light of a kerosene lamp, took the oath of office as President. It was administered by his father, the local justice of the peace.

With Coolidge in the White House, the Republican program went ahead with few perceptible deviations, although the dishonest elements were gradually weeded out of the administration. It soon became apparent that Coolidge, riding on the crest of a wave of economic prosperity, was becoming an extremely popular President, despite his lack of "political glamor." In December, 1923, he let it be known that he would seek the presidential nomination in 1924, and by January it was already evident that there would be little or no opposition. When Hiram Johnson of California was mentioned as a possible competitor for the nomination, a Republican national committeeman reflected the opinion of most political observers by saying: "I wish my chances of Heaven were as good as the chances of President Coolidge to carry California against Hiram Johnson."

When the Republican convention opened in

BARGAIN DAY IN WASHINGTON. A cartoon satirizing the effects of the Harding administration on the nation capital. National monuments are being trucked away and the essentials of good government are up for auction

COOLIDGE, THE SIMPLE FARMER, mows the hay in his Vermont fields, wearing a smock and a battered hat. Pictures such as this were of great propaganda value in promoting the Republican candidate's chances for re-election.

Cleveland on June 10, the senatorial clique that had dominated the 1920 convention was no longer in evidence. Senator Lodge, who had been the loudest voice four years before, received no committee appointments and was, according to one authority, assigned to such a poor hotel room that he repaired to the quarters of his former secretary, Louis A. Coolidge.

The party platform was a clear reflection of Coolidge's views on virtually all major points. It stressed governmental economy and debt reduction; it approved the World Court and arms limitation; it promised agricultural reforms, condemned compulsory arbitration of labor disputes, and advocated continued restriction of immigration.

The nomination of Coolidge, a foregone conclusion, took place on the first ballot, with only 44 out of 1209 delegates casting their votes for other candidates. Governor Lowden of Illinois declined a nomination for the Vice-Presidency, and the delegates finally chose as the President's running mate Charles G. Dawes, a former Chicago banker who had served under Harding as the first Director of the Budget. Several delegates had suggested the nomination of William E. Borah of Idaho, but the aging Senator indignantly squelched all overtures. It was reported, indeed, that Coolidge himself had once asked him to share the ticket—and that Borah had replied: "In what position?"

In contrast to the brevity and harmony of the Republican convention, the Democrats assembled in New York's Madison Square Garden two weeks later amid an atmosphere of wide-open dissension. At first glance it seemed as though they had a made-to-order issue in the Harding scandals. Senator Pat Harrison of Mississippi, the keynote speaker, capitalized on this point when he charged that "in the guarded orchards of this [Republican] administration the golden apples of special privilege have been

557

gathered by the favored few. . . . Show this administration an oil well and it will show you a foreign policy." But no amount of pointing at Republican shortcomings could conceal the fact that the Democratic party was violently split on a fundamental issue: the Ku-Klux Klan.

During the early 1920's, the Klan's program of racial and religious bigotry had been gaining hundreds of thousands of eager followers in the areas of the South and the West where the Democrats were strongest. At the convention the forces were almost evenly divided between the anti-Klan delegates, largely from the East and the large cities, and the delegates who either supported the Klan or felt that it should not be openly disavowed. The first skirmish in this battle took place in the platform committee, which—after four days of wrangling—refused to condemn the Klan by name. The fight was carried to the floor of the convention, where an amendment proposed by the anti-Klan forces was defeated by only one vote.

On other issues the platform was less explosive. It denounced "Republican corruption,"

attacked monopolies, advocated lower railroad rates and lower tariffs, defended the income tax, and came out for a government-owned merchant marine. On foreign affairs it promised international cooperation and endorsed disarmament.

When it came to nominations, the Democratic party was again rent asunder by the Klan issue. The champion of the anti-Klan forces was New York's able governor, Alfred Emanuel Smith, who received a seventy-three-minute ovation when Franklin Delano Roosevelt, crippled by infantile paralysis but undaunted in spirit, put his name in nomination. To the pro-Klan delegates Smith's urban liberalism and, above all, his Catholicism were anathema. Their own candidate, though he disavowed much of what they stood for, was William Gibbs McAdoo.

As ballot after ballot was taken, the favorite sons dropped out, but neither Smith nor McAdoo could command the two-thirds majority necessary for victory. Longevity records were broken as the fortieth, fiftieth, seventieth,

THE SCANDALS OF THE HARDING ADMINISTRATION were heatedly discussed in the campaign and cartoonists made corruption their theme. Here the Republican elephant sweeps out trash and Uncle Sam washes his linen

WHISTLING IN THE DARK, CALVIN COOLIDGE WONDERS, "B-B-BUT HOW DEAD ARE THEY?"

REPUBLICAN CANDIDATES CALVIN COOLIDGE AND CHARLES G. DAWES PRESENT THEMSELVES

THE COOLIDGES DOING CHORES IN VERMONT.

THE COOLIDGES LEAVING FOR THE CAMPAIGN.

intieth ballots were taken. Finally, when it became obvious that neither candidate could break the deadlock, the delegates wearily turned to other contenders. On the 103rd ballot the nomination went to John W. Davis, a brilliant and moderately liberal New York lawyer who had represented West Virginia in Congress before the war and had served under President Wilson as Solicitor General. For Vice-President the convention nominated Charles W. Bryan, Governor of Nebraska, whose main qualification was that he was the brother of William Jennings Bryan.

The year 1924 was to see the birth of still another party and another set of candidates. While the Republicans and the Democrats sat back to survey the work of their conventions, a third party, calling themselves the Progressives, were formulating a platform of their own in Cleveland. Their roots went back to the economic unrest of the period just after the war, and their aim was the merging of farmers and laborers into one great party which would break the power of the private monopoly sys-

tem over the economic and political life of the American people."

Nominated by acclamation, Robert M. La Follette, the fighting liberal from Wisconsin, was allowed to write his own platform. It advocated government ownership of transportation, extensive conservation measures, low tariffs, broad labor legislation, election of Federal judges, and a constitutional amendment providing that Congress might, by reenacting a statute, override a judicial veto. For his running mate La Follette selected Burton K. Wheeler, Democratic Senator from Montana.

As the campaigning moved into full swing, it became evident that the strongest weapon in the Republican arsenal was the abundant prosperity which the country was enjoying. Davis, in his acceptance speech, charged the Republicans with "corruption in administration and favoritism to privileged classes in legislation," but the nation was not in a mood for reform and his accusations stirred little fervor. To add to the Democrats' problems, it became obvious that, despite his widely recognized honesty and

PRESIDENT COOLIDGE FILLS OUT HIS ABSENTEE BALLOT ON THE LAWN OF THE WHITE HOU

PRESIDENT COOLIDGE AND HIS REORGANIZED CABINET. Left to right, seated: Harry S. New, Postmaster General; John W. Weeks, Secretary of War; Charles E. Hughes, Secretary of State; Coolidge; Andrew Mellon, Secretary of the Treasury; Harlan F. Stone, Attorney General; Curtis Silbur, Secretary of the Navy. Left to right, standing: James J. Davis, Secretary of Labor; Henry C. Wallace, Secretary of Agriculture (father of Henry A. Wallace, FDR's Vice-President); Herbert C. Hoover, Secretary of Commerce; Hubert Work, Secretary of the Interior.

competence, Davis himself was in several respects a political liability. As corporation counsel to many Wall Street interests, he was vulnerable to attack from labor and farm groups.

Coolidge remained quietly in Washington during most of the campaign. He avoided the limelight—even to the extent of refusing a degree of Doctor of Laws from Yale University—and seemed to feel that active campaigning was somehow undignified. In his first speech after the Republican convention, he stated his strongest conviction: "I am for economy. After that I am for more economy. At this time and under present conditions, that is my conception of serving the people." His subsequent speeches were few, and he responded to Democratic attacks with complete silence. In reply to the Democratic slogan, "A Vote for Coolidge Is a Vote for Chaos," the Republicans struck a more popular chord with "Keep Cool and Keep Coolidge." Their strategy of identifying Coolidge with prosperity, "standpatism," and plain speaking was well illustrated by a three-line editorial which appeared in the Republican

New York *Herald Tribune* under the headline, "The 1924 Choice":

A vote for La Follette is a vote for Bryan.
A vote for Davis is a vote for Bryan.
A vote for Coolidge is a vote for Coolidge.

The election was a Republican landslide: Coolidge received 15,725,003 popular votes; Davis, 8,385,586; and La Follette, 4,826,471. The Democrats suffered badly from the inroads of the Progressives. Although La Follette won only 13 electoral votes (all from Wisconsin), he polled four times as many popular votes as Davis in California and twice as many in seventeen states west of the Mississippi.

Shortly after the elections, Coolidge's father died in Vermont. The President, who had been unable to leave his duties in Washington to be at the bedside, was deep in sorrow. With characteristic understatement he later wrote:

"During his last month I had to resort to the poor substitute of a telephone. When I reached home, he was gone. It costs a great deal to be President."

563

DELIVERING THE INAUGURAL ADDRESS

THE THIRTY-SIXTH ELECTION—1928

HERBERT HOOVER

In his inaugural address, the first ever broadcast by radio, President Coolidge tersely repeated his pledge to enforce economy, reduce taxes, and avoid governmental interference with business. "We are not without problems," he declared. "But our most important problem is not to secure new advantages but to maintain those we already possess." On this characteristic note, the era of Coolidge prosperity entered its full bloom.

It was, essentially, a negative era from the point of view of governmental activity. In the eyes of Coolidge and the men around him, the best government was the least government. The President made no attempt to work closely with Congress, to take issues to the people, or to use his executive powers forcefully. It was a period of economic prosperity, and the President's job, as he saw it, was to encourage private enterprise to the utmost and keep the government from "rocking the boat."

This did not mean, however, that there was complete harmony between the President and the Congress. Within a few weeks of his inaugural, Coolidge found himself faced with a Senate rebellion when he nominated Charles B. Warren, a corporation lawyer and Republican leader from Michigan, for the vacant post of Attorney General. Suspicious of Warren's associations with the "sugar trust," Senate insurgents joined forces with the Democrats and, by a one-vote margin, refused to confirm the appointment.

This marked the first time in half a century that a Cabinet appointment had failed to win confirmation, but what hurt the President even more was the fact that Vice-President Dawes, who could have saved the nomination by casting a vote for confirmation in his role as president of the Senate, was napping in his hotel room when the crucial roll was called. Insiders suggested that his absence from the Senate Chamber could be explained by the fact that Warren had been the only delegate from Michigan who voted against Dawes's nomination at the 1924 convention; but whatever the explanation, his action earned him undying enmity from the President and destroyed Warren's hopes for the office. When the President obstinately submitted the Warren nomination to the Senate a second time, the vote was 46 to 39 against confirmation.

(turn to page 568)

*HERBERT HOOVER
WITH HIS WIFE*

ON WASHINGTON'S 195th BIRTHDAY, COOLIDGE SPOKE TO A JOINT SESSION OF THE SENATE

ALSO PRESENT WERE MEMBERS OF THE SUPREME COURT, CABINET AND DIPLOMATIC CORPS.

HERBERT C. HOOVER
(1874-19——),Secretary
of Commerce, was the
choice of the Republi-
cans for President. In
this election, the Re-
publicans carried five
states in the Solid South.

CHARLES CURTIS
(1860-1936) from Kan-
sas, lawyer, ardent ad-
vocate of prohibition
and majority leader of
the Senate, was selected
by the Republicans as
Hoover's running mate

ALFRED E. SMITH
(1873-1944) was nom-
inated by the Demo-
crats on the first ballot.
He campaigned vigor-
ously but was badly de-
feated with 87 electoral
votes to Hoover's 444.

J. TAYLOR ROBINSON
(1872-1937), Senator
and former Governor
of Arkansas, chairman
of the Democratic con-
vention, received the
nomination for the
vice-presidential post.

NORMAN THOMAS
(1884-19——), former
clergyman, pacifist and
editor of *The Nation*,
was the Socialist can-
didate for the Presi-
dency. In the election
he polled 267,420 votes.

J. HUDSON MAURER
(1864-1944),64-year-old
President of the Penn-
sylvania Federation of
Labor and veteran So-
cialist, was nominated
by his party for the of-
fice of Vice-President.

THE FACE OF THE HAPPY WARRIOR.

In the realm of domestic affairs, the ma
issue of the Coolidge years was the McNa
Haugen bills for farm aid, a storm center
Congress from 1924 to 1928. Rooted in
depressed agricultural prices which had k
the nation's farmers far behind the rest of
nation in its march toward economic ple
the various bills presented by Senator Cha
McNary of Oregon and Representative Gil
N. Haugen of Iowa during those years sou
to separate farm produce for export from f
produce for domestic consumption, and in
way keep the domestic price level from b

UEL SMITH, GOVERNOR OF NEW YORK, WAS THE CHOICE OF THE DEMOCRATS IN THIS ELECTION.

epressed by the world price. After being voted own twice by successively narrower margins, the bill was submitted again at the end of 1926, and passed by both Houses. The President, whose objections to the bill were primarily used on claims that it represented governmental interference in the nation's economic life, vetoed it and was sustained. Undaunted, the backers of the bill brought it in again, and again were defeated by a presidential veto. It was not until the following decade that the principles of the McNary-Haugen Bill were enacted into law, but during Coolidge's stay in

GOVERNOR ALFRED E. SMITH accepts the nomination of his party in the Assembly chamber at Albany.

569

SMITH'S BROWN DERBY became a symbol; his warm personality won him many friends—but not the election.

the Senate defeat and the issue died without further debate.

The most notable accomplishment of the Coolidge administration in the field of foreign affairs was the initiative provided by the United States in bringing about the Kellogg-Briand Treaty, which was signed in Paris on August 27, 1928. The fifteen signatory powers, including Germany, Italy, and Japan, solemnly renounced war "as an instrument of national policy"—but failed to explain how such a renunciation was to be enforced.

Despite his lack of aggressiveness as Chief Executive, the identification of Coolidge with American prosperity made him a popular President. People liked his dry wit, his frugal habits, his innate conservatism, and the "good conscience" which enabled him to sleep eleven hours a day on the average. It was taken for granted that he could win renomination in 1928 if he desired it. The whole nation waited eagerly for an expression of his intentions, but

the White House this was the most bitterly contested question before the administration.

In foreign affairs the President again found himself at odds with Congress on a major issue. Although a man of primarily isolationist sentiments, he had long been on record for American participation in the World Court, and in early 1925 a resolution endorsing such a move was submitted to Congress. The measure won an overwhelming victory in the House, but in the Senate it encountered vigorous opposition from Senator Borah of Idaho, an isolationist who had inherited from Senator Lodge the strategic office of Chairman of the Foreign Relations Committee. In a move reminiscent of his predecessor's machinations against Woodrow Wilson, Borah reported the measure back to the Senate with four modifying reservations which made its acceptance by the member nations of the World Court impossible. Coolidge, whose belief in the wisdom of American participation had been halfhearted at best, accepted

SMITH CAMPAIGNED HARD to defeat the opposition which attacked him for his "wetness" and his religion

THE SNIPER.

"LISTENING IN."

THESE CARTOONS OF THE 1928 ELECTION HIGHLIGHT THE MAIN ISSUES OF THE CAMPAIGN.

the President, taciturn as ever, would offer no clues until August 2, 1927—the fourth anniversary of his accession—when during an interlude at his "summer White House" in Rapid City, South Dakota, he suddenly called a press conference and handed to each reporter a slip of paper reading: "I do not wish to run for President in nineteen twenty-eight."

Speculation was rampant throughout the nation. Did Coolidge mean what he said? Did he really "choose" not to run? Some held that the statement was uttered in absolute sincerity, others thought that the President hoped for a deadlock in the national convention between the Hoover supporters and their opposition, which would cause the delegates to turn to him. Perhaps the alleged remark of Mrs. Coolidge— "Papa says there's going to be a depression"— had something to do with it.

To most observers, the message seemed ambiguous, but the anti-Coolidge factions of the party took it at its face value and began pushing other possible candidacies. By far the strongest pre-convention contender was Herbert Hoover, the Secretary of Commerce and wartime Food Administrator, who had first been considered as presidential timber at the 1920 convention. Most observers felt that Coolidge shared little

of the enthusiasm for Hoover; he had spoken slightingly of him on several occasions, and in 1927, when the President by a slip of the tongue referred to his Secretary of Commerce as "President" Hoover, he was so displeased with the resultant speculation that he put extensive restrictions on the right of reporters to quote his remarks.

The President's first cryptic announcement was not perceptibly clarified when, in December, he declared to Republican National Committee members at the White House: "My decision will be respected," and declined to amplify the remark. But the pro-Hoover factions considered it further encouragement for their activities. Meanwhile, Senator Robert M. La Follette, Jr., gave additional impetus to the anti-Coolidge factions by introducing an ingenious resolution, endorsing the tradition that no President should serve for more than two terms and complimenting Coolidge for conforming to the custom. Senator Fess of Ohio, a leader of the forces who still felt that Coolidge could be drafted, moved that the clause complimenting the President be deleted. In an ironic rejoinder, the insurgent Senator Norris of Nebraska replied:

"Here is a resolution to be passed by this

I do not choose to run for President in nineteen twenty eight

COOLIDGE'S FAMOUS NOTE which he wrote out for the newspaper reporters—"I do not choose to run . . ."

high legislative body in which we directly commend the President for a patriotic act that he did. . . . Then here come a few earnest, perhaps honest, perhaps ill-advised insurgents and they insist that we shall insult the President of the United States, that at least we shall not commend him for following in the footsteps of Washington."

The resolution finally passed with the reference to Coolidge deleted, but it tended to give a definite interpretation to the President's own cryptic pronouncements and encouraged other candidates to enter the field. While Hoover remained the strongest contender, Governor Lowden of Illinois, Senator Charles Curtis, the majority floor leader from Kansas, Senator Willis of Ohio, and James Watson of Indiana were mentioned as possible alternatives.

By the time the delegates assembled for the Republican convention in Kansas City in June, Hoover's nomination appeared to be a certainty. The platform, largely written by Senator Reed Smoot of Utah, pledged increased economy, tax reduction, and high tariffs, urged full enforcement of the Eighteenth Amendment, advocated international cooperation (but without American participation in the League of Nations), and in general took its stand on the accomplishments of the Coolidge administration. The only controversial plank was a renunciation of the McNary-Haugen Farm Bills which was unsuccessfully contested on the floor by spokesmen for the farm bloc.

As had been generally anticipated, Herbert Hoover won the nomination on the first ballot,

THE VOTES IN THE 1928 ELECTION

STATES	POPULAR VOTE				ELEC. VOTE	
	H. Hoover, Republican.	A. Smith, Democrat.	N. Thomas, Socialist.	Foster, Workers.	Hoover	Smith
Ala.	120,725	127,797	460	—	—	12
Ariz.	52,533	38,537	—	184	3	—
Ark.	77,751	119,196	429	317	—	9
Calif.	1,162,323	614,365	19,595	216	13	—
Colo.	253,872	133,131	3,472	675	6	—
Conn.	296,614	252,040	3,019	730	7	—
Del.	68,860	36,643	329	59	3	—
Fla.	144,168	101,764	4,036	3,704	6	—
Ga.	63,498	120,602	124	64	—	14
Idaho	99,848	53,074	1,308	—	4	—
Ill.	1,769,141	1,313,817	19,138	3,581	29	—
Ind.	848,290	562,691	3,871	321	15	—
Iowa	623,818	378,936	2,960	328	13	—
Kan.	513,672	193,003	6,205	320	10	—
Ky.	558,064	381,070	837	293	13	—
La.	51,160	164,655	—	—	—	10
Me.	179,923	81,179	1,068	—	6	—
Md.	301,479	223,626	1,701	636	8	—
Mass.	775,566	792,758	6,262	2,464	—	18
Mich.	965,396	396,762	3,516	2,881	15	—
Minn.	560,977	396,451	6,774	4,853	12	—
Miss.	27,153	124,539	—	—	—	10
Mo.	834,080	662,562	3,739	—	18	—
Mont.	113,300	78,578	1,667	563	4	—
Neb.	345,745	197,959	3,434	—	8	—
Nev.	18,327	14,090	—	—	3	—
N. H.	115,404	80,715	455	173	4	—
N. J.	926,050	616,517	4,897	1,257	14	—
N. M.	69,645	48,211	—	158	3	—
N. Y.	2,193,344	2,089,863	107,332	10,876	45	—
N. C.	348,992	287,078	—	—	12	—
N. D.	131,441	106,648	842	936	5	—
Ohio	1,627,546	864,210	8,683	2,836	24	—
Okla.	394,046	219,174	3,924	—	10	—
Ore.	205,341	109,223	2,720	1,094	5	—
Pa.	2,055,382	1,067,586	18,647	4,726	38	—
R. I.	117,522	118,973	—	283	—	5
S. C.	3,188	62,700	47	—	—	9
S. D.	157,603	102,660	443	232	5	—
Tenn.	195,388	167,343	631	111	12	—
Tex.	367,036	341,032	722	209	20	—
Utah	94,618	80,985	954	47	4	—
Vt.	90,404	44,440	—	—	4	—
Va.	164,609	140,146	250	173	12	—
Wash.	335,844	156,772	2,615	1,541	7	—
W. Va.	375,551	263,784	1,313	401	8	—
Wis.	544,205	450,259	18,213	1,528	13	—
Wyo.	52,748	29,299	788	—	3	—
	21,392,190	15,016,443	267,420	48,770	444	87

Reynolds, Socialist-Labor, 21,603; Varney, Prohibitionist, 20,106; Webb, Farm-Labor, 6,390. Total vote, 36,879,414.

and by an overwhelming majority. Senator Curtis of Kansas, who had the advantage of a strong farm following and a consistent record of party regularity, became his running mate.

The Democrats, meeting two weeks later in Houston, Texas, held a convention that was in marked contrast to their bitter and long-drawn-out session of four years earlier. The conflicts between South and North, wet and dry, urban and rural, and Klan and anti-Klan, were still present, but their effects had been nullified in September, 1927, by an important pronouncement from William Gibbs McAdoo, champion of the rural South and West. In a letter to the editor of the Chattanooga *News*, he had stated that, "in the interests of party unity," he would not be a candidate for the nomination. Thus it became certain that New York's Governor Alfred E. Smith would be the Democratic choice.

In contrast to the 1924 convention, the Democratic party platform was prepared and adopted with a minimum of discord. It charged that Republican rule had left America with "its industry depressed, its agriculture prostrate," and advocated farm-relief measures, tariff reform, and a "constructive" foreign policy (but with no mention of the League or the World Court). The plank dealing with Prohibition, which had been expected to stir up vigorous controversy, merely pledged the party to "an honest effort" to enforce the Eighteenth Amendment and castigated the Republicans' failure to do likewise.

For the third time in eight years, Franklin Delano Roosevelt placed the name of Governor Smith in nomination, this time concluding his speech with the now famous climax: "We offer one who has the will to win—who not only deserves success but commands it. Victory is his habit—the happy warrior, Alfred Smith." Nine other names were put in nomination—most notably those of Senator James A. Reed of Missouri, Representative Cordell Hull of Tennessee, Jesse Jones of Texas, and Senator Walter F. George of Georgia—but it was obvious that the New Yorker was the favorite. When, on the first ballot, he received only ten votes less than the necessary two-thirds majority, Ohio switched its vote in order to insure his nomination. For Vice President the delegates pro-

"THE WONDER BOY," as Coolidge referred to Herbert Hoover, conducted a campaign emphasizing prosperity.

ceeded to nominate—again on the first ballot—Senator Joseph T. Robinson of Arkansas, who, as a Southern Protestant with strong Prohibitionist sympathies, was considered a solid counterbalance for Smith. Then, as one observer wrote, "the Democratic donkey with a wet head and wagging a dry tail left Houston."

As in 1924, the Republicans' greatest asset was economic prosperity. This theme Herbert Hoover emphasized in his acceptance speech when he said: "We in America today are nearer to the final triumph over poverty than ever before in the history of the land. The poorhouse is vanishing from among us." This sentiment was echoed by businessmen like John Wanamaker, who called Hoover's election "the insurance policy of the nation," and by the popular Republican campaign slogan, "Let's keep what we've got: Prosperity didn't just happen."

For the first time since the passage of the Eighteenth Amendment, prohibition was a

"CRISIS IN WASHINGTON," a well-known cartoon by Gluyas Williams. "Mr. Coolidge refuses point blank to vacate the White House until his other rubber is found."

major issue. Hoover was flatly for full enforcement, describing it as "a great social and economic experiment"; Smith, despite the large number of drys in the Democratic party, came out equally flatly for modification of Prohibition laws. Still another major issue, though it was fought out for the most part behind the scenes, was the religious question raised by the

fact that Smith was a Catholic. Although appeals to bigotry were denounced by Hoover in a statement saying that they "give violence to every instinct I possess," there can be no doubt that many voters were made to feel that the election of Smith would mean that American policy would be dictated from the Vatican. In one state alone, it was reported, half a million dollars' worth of virulent propaganda directed against Smith was circulated.

Smith staged a vigorous campaign, stumping the country tirelessly and maintaining a constant barrage of fire against the Republicans. Hoover's campaign, though more active than the one conducted by Coolidge four years earlier, was relatively subdued. He ignored repeated challenges from his opponent to meet with him in public debate, and even managed to avoid mentioning Smith's name once during the entire campaign. In one other respect the campaign was notable: both sides courted the support of business interests to an extent never before practiced, and both sides received from them enormous amounts of money. Campaign expenditures for the Republicans amounted to nearly $9,500,000, while the Democrats spent more than $7,000,000. This was almost three times the amount that had been expended in any previous campaign.

Once again the election was a Republican landslide. Hoover carried forty states, including Smith's own state of New York and five states in the Solid South. His popular vote was 21,392,190 against Smith's 15,016,443, and in

PRESIDENT-ELECT HOOVER rides with President Coolidge to the Capitol for the inaugural ceremony.

THE HOOVER CABINET poses for the traditional group photograph on the lawn before the White House.

PRESIDENT COOLIDGE AND HIS SUCCESSOR, HERBERT HOOVER, ON INAUGURATION DAY, 1929.

the electoral college he won 444 votes to Smith's 87.

The remaining months of the Coolidge administration were no more eventful than the first three and a half years. In public, the President became more silent and dour than ever. His expression, as William Allen White remarked, was that of a person "looking down his nose to locate that evil smell which seemed forever to affront him." When the lame-duck session of Congress convened in December, he told them that "no Congress . . . on surveying the state of the nation, has met with a more pleasing prospect than that which appears at the present time." Although the nation had moved four years closer to the brink of the great depression, the administration thus ended with the same note on which it had begun.

FDR'S FIRST INAUGURAL ADDRESS

THE THIRTY-SEVENTH ELECTION—1932

FRANKLIN D. ROOSEVELT

"We have not yet reached the goal," said Herbert Hoover in accepting the Republican nomination in 1928, "but given a chance to go forward with the policies of the last eight years and we shall soon, with the help of God, be within sight of the day when poverty will be banished from the nation."

On the day he took office, the country was at the very pinnacle of prosperity. Business was booming; on the stock market shares were soaring; almost everyone—from industrialists to cabdrivers, from doctors to dishwashers—speculated, bought and sold shares, and made easy money. In a single month—January, 1933—more than a billion dollars' worth of new securities were absorbed by the eager public.

In his inaugural address Hoover made the confident prophecy that "in no nation are the fruits of accomplishment more secure." His optimism was supported by the chairman of the Democratic National Committee, millionaire John J. Raskob, who asserted: "If a man saves $15 a week, and invests in good common stocks, and allows the dividends and rights to accumulate, at the end of twenty years he will have at least $80,000, and an income from investment of around $400 a month. He will be rich. And because income can do that, I am firm in my belief that anyone not only can be rich, but ought to be rich."

Life was full of promise and the future looked rosy. The people lulled themselves into the belief that the upward trend would continue and that profits would be bigger and bigger. However, to the more thoughtful observers the picture looked far from promising. A more critical survey showed that prosperity was not built on solid rock and that the Republican oratorical fantasy of "two cars in every garage" and "two chickens in every pot" had little foundation in reality. The economic structure of the United States was poorly balanced, for prosperity was not equally shared by all classes. While speculators amassed fortunes, the income of wage earners remained more or less static. (During the five years before Hoover's election the index of speculative gains rose from 100 to 410, but wages advanced from 100 to a mere 112.) While industry and business reaped high profits, the purchasing power of the farm communities had dwindled by two thirds within the last decade. High

577

THE CANDIDATES

FRANKLIN D. ROOSEVELT (1882-1945). Governor of New York, was nominated by the Democrats. His promise of a "new deal" won him 472 electoral votes to 59 for Herbert Hoover.

JOHN NANCE GARNER (1868-19—) of Texas, Speaker of the House, became the Democratic vice-presidential candidate when Texas and California swung their support to Roosevelt.

HERBERT HOOVER (1874-19—) was renominated by the Republicans, although blame placed on him for the depression practically assured his defeat. He carried only six states.

CHARLES CURTIS (1860-1936) was again put on the Republican ticket as Hoover's running mate. The popular vote was 22,821,857 for the Democrats to 15,761,841 for the GOP.

NORMAN THOMAS (1884-19—), the choice of the Socialist party for a second time, had 2,000,000 votes in a preconvention poll, but in the election he received only 884,781.

WILLIAM Z. FOSTER (1881-19—) from New York, was Communist candidate. He had as running mate James Ford, a Negro labor leader, the first of his race to be chosen.

agricultural production kept farm prices low, causing great suffering to the people on the land. And while industrial production reached gigantic proportions, there were—even at the height of the boom—more than a million and a half workers without employment.

These economic danger signals—the unhealthy stock-market speculation, the overexpansion of capital goods, the inadequate purchasing power of the people, the depression in agriculture, the uncertainty of the foreign markets due to the chaotic postwar economic

THE VOTES IN THE 1932 ELECTION

STATES	POPULAR VOTE			ELEC. VOTE	
	F. D. Roosevelt. Democrat	Herbert Hoover. Republican	Norman Thomas. Socialist	Hoover-Curtis	Roosevelt-Garner
Alabama	207,910	34,675	2,030	—	11
Arizona	79,264	36,104	2,618	—	3
Arkansas	189,602	28,467	1,269	—	9
California	1,324,157	847,902	63,299	—	22
Colorado	250,877	189,617	13,591	—	6
Connecticut	281,632	288,420	20,480	8	—
Delaware	54,319	57,073	1,376	3	—
Florida	206,307	69,170	775	—	7
Georgia	234,118	19,863	461	—	12
Idaho	109,479	71,312	526	—	4
Illinois	1,882,304	1,432,756	67,258	—	29
Indiana	862,054	677,184	21,338	—	14
Iowa	598,019	414,433	20,467	—	11
Kansas	424,204	349,498	18,276	—	9
Kentucky	580,574	394,716	3,853	—	11
Louisiana	249,418	18,853		—	10
Maine	128,907	166,631	2,489	5	—
Maryland	314,314	184,184	10,489	—	8
Massachusetts	800,148	736,959	34,305	—	17
Michigan	871,700	739,894	39,205	—	19
Minnesota	600,806	363,959	25,476	—	11
Mississippi	140,168	5,180	686	—	9
Missouri	1,025,406	564,713	16,374	—	15
Montana	127,286	78,078	7,891	—	4
Nebraska	359,082	201,177	9,876	—	7
Nevada	28,756	12,674	—	—	3
New Hampshire	100,680	103,629	947	4	—
New Jersey	806,630	775,684	42,998	—	16
New Mexico	95,089	54,217	1,776	—	3
New York	2,534,959	1,937,963	177,397	—	47
North Carolina	497,566	208,344	5,591	—	13
North Dakota	178,350	71,772	3,521	—	4
Ohio	1,301,695	1,227,679	64,094	—	26
Oklahoma	516,468	188,165	—	—	11
Oregon	213,871	136,019	15,450	—	5
Pennsylvania	1,295,948	1,453,540	91,119	36	—
Rhode Island	146,604	115,266	3,138	—	4
South Carolina	102,347	1,978	82	—	8
South Dakota	183,515	99,212	1,551	—	4
Tennessee	259,817	126,806	1,786	—	11
Texas	760,348	97,959	4,450	—	23
Utah	116,750	84,795	4,087	—	4
Vermont	56,266	78,984	1,533	3	—
Virginia	203,979	89,637	2,382	—	11
Washington	353,260	208,645	17,080	—	8
W. Virginia	405,124	330,731	5,133	—	8
Wisconsin	707,410	347,741	53,379	—	12
Wyoming	54,370	39,583	2,829	—	3
	22,821,857	15,761,841	884,781	59	472

Reynolds, Socialist-Labor, 33,275; Foster, Communist, 102,991; Upshaw, Prohibitionist, 81,869; Harvey, Liberty, 53,425; Coxey, FarmLabor, 7,309. Total vote—39,816,522.

CONTRAST IN PERSONALITIES. The Roosevelt of 1932 created the impression of a happy and optimistic extrovert, while his opponent, President Hoover, appeared to many people as a dour and humorless introvert.

conditions in Europe—all these foreshadowed the impending disaster.

The crash came with great force. On October 24, 1929, when Hoover had been in office for only seven months, the prices of stocks began to sag. Three days later 12,894,650 shares were dumped on the panicky market, and within a few weeks securities lost forty billions of their value.

At first neither government nor people realized the seriousness of the situation. The bankers and the businessmen preached confidence, asserting that as soon as the selling hysteria subsided prosperous times would return. Hoover made encouraging statements. But events proved the prophets wrong. As purchasing power diminished and merchandise

A TRADITION-BREAKING flight. Roosevelt flew to Chicago to accept the nomination in person, dramatically proving to the nation that his physical disability would not hinder him in the performance of his presidential duties.

AT CHICAGO AIRPORT the Democratic candidate was met by Mayor Cermak (next to FDR). Cermak was killed the next year when an assassin tried to shoot Roosevelt.

piled up on the shelves of stores, factories had to curtail production. The legion of unemployed grew, and those who kept their jobs had to be content with reduced wages. In some department stores the salaries of clerks sank as low as $5 to $10 a week; domestic servants worked for $10 a month to have shelter and food. More often than not the pay of the workingman was hardly enough to meet his bills for food and rent, thereby curtailing all non-essential purchases. With more merchandise unsold, factories further restricted production, and more workers were on the street. The cycle of the depression drew wider and wider rings.

When after four months of tumbling prices and a steady decline in trade, employment, and business some seasonal gains were made, President Hoover hastily prophesied that "all evidences indicate that the worst effect of the

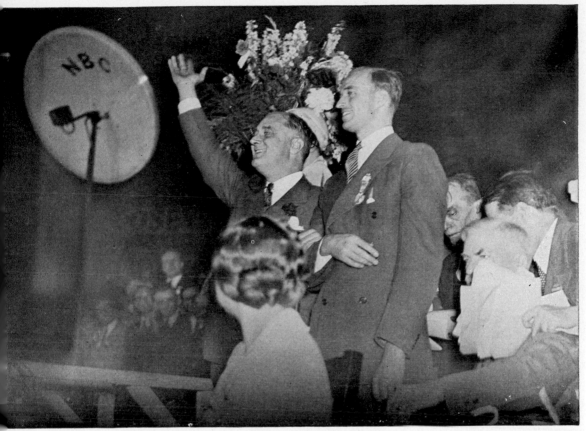

THE DEMOCRATIC CONVENTION cheered FDR enthusiastically when in his acceptance speech he promised aid not only to the forgotten man, but to the forgotten woman, and pledged "a new deal for the American people."

crash will have been passed within the next sixty days, with the amelioration of seasonal unemployment, the gaining strength of other forces, and the continued cooperation of the many agencies actively cooperating with the government to restore business and to relieve distress."

To the hard-hit millions the President's basic advice was to be brave and weather the storm. Hoover tried to impress upon the leaders of industry that further lay-offs of workers would only aggravate the crisis, and asked for their cooperation, but all the conferences between the President and the industrialists yielded nothing.

With the deepening of the depression, the cry for Federal aid to help the growing army of unemployed increased. Private charity was unable to cope with the relief problem any longer, nor had local and state governments

the necessary funds to combat the disaster. The breadlines grew in length; on the street corners of the Eastern cities unemployed men offered apples for sale; "Brother, can you spare a dime?" became the slogan of the day.

Although millions were idle and the crisis was at its height, Hoover still preached the doctrine of rugged individualism; the administration still clung to the *laissez-faire* idea of economics and to the traditional American philosophy that the Federal Government should not interfere with the business life of the country.

Not until late in Hoover's term were serious measures taken to cope efficiently and effectively with the depression. The Democratic Congress (the 1930 election had given the Democrats a majority in the House, while the Senate was evenly divided) passed the Reconstruction Finance Corporation Act and Hoover signed

THE HOOVER CAMPAIGN. The President made only ten major addresses, all in a similar vein. He defended the measures of his administration and asserted that the depression had been brought about by foreign causes.

it in January, 1932. The RFC was to lend money to railroads, banks, agricultural agencies, state and local governments to stimulate recovery.

Looking back at the Hoover administration, the four years seem to fall into five markedly different periods. The first phase lasted from inauguration day until the crash in October. During these months prosperity was on the upgrade and the President's popularity at its peak. The second phase extended from the crash until early 1930, when Hoover battled manfully against the disaster without realizing its gravity. The third phase lasted from March, 1930, until June, 1931, a period of despair. It was during this time that the President's attitude underwent a marked change. He now declared that the depression was part of the

international economic debacle and advised America to free itself "of world influences and make a large measure of independent recovery." During the fourth period—from June to October, 1931—the administration held that the German economic crisis had a retarding effect on American recovery, and the President, declaring a moratorium on war debts, bluntly admitted the seriousness of the crisis. From then on until the end of his term—the fifth period—Hoover faced the problems which confronted the nation more realistically.

During this last period some Republicans tried to persuade him not to seek renomination, but these efforts, like those of the Progressive Republicans who wanted to form a third party, were abortive. The Republican convention renominated the President on the first ballot

THE HOOVER SLOGAN, "We want to turn the corner to prosperity," appeared in the streets, but his prophecies, "The worst has passed," and "Prosperity is just around the corner," were used against him by the Democrats.

with 1,126½ votes. His only avowed rival, Dr. Joseph D. France, ex-Senator from Maryland, was taken bodily off the platform by the Hoover supporters when he attempted to withdraw his name and ask the delegates to give their support to ex-President Coolidge.

The 8,500-word platform of the Republicans had thirty-seven planks, but said nothing constructive about how to combat the depression. The nation's economic plight was disposed of in a few meaningless phrases. About prohibition the evasive proposal was made that Congress should submit to state conventions—not to the legislatures—a new amendment on the liquor traffic, and that these conventions should decide whether liquor should be manufactured and sold within the states' borders or not.

In contrast to the Republicans, the Democrats

THE ROOSEVELT SLOGAN, "Abolish bread lines," was written on banners advocating Roosevelt's election. The New York governor delivered twenty-seven major addresses throughout the country, outlining his optimistic program for the future and charming his audiences.

ROOSEVELT IN CALIFORNIA on the platform with his son James, William McAdoo, and the irrepressible Will Rogers, who told an audience of eighty thousand cheering spectators: "I pledge you, I pledge myself, a new deal."

"HELLO, YOU OLD POTATO" was reported to be Al Smith's greeting to FDR at the Democratic state convention. Thereafter Smith campaigned on Roosevelt's behalf.

were in high spirits as they assembled for their convention in Chicago. Victory was within their grasp at last. The years of the Republican administration—twelve long years—were nearing an end. With millions unemployed, with the country's economy on the brink of ruin, it was certain that the Republican administration would be replaced by a Democratic one.

The list of contenders for the nomination was a long one. Three former presidential candidates—James M. Cox, the standard-bearer of the party in 1920; John W. Davis, the candidate in 1924; and Alfred E. Smith, Hoover's opponent in 1928—vied for the high honor. The hats of two former vice-presidential candidates—Franklin D. Roosevelt, Cox's running mate in 1920, and Joseph T. Robinson, Al

HOOVER AT MADISON SQUARE GARDEN, winding up his campaign, repeated his belief that "grass would grow in the streets of one hundred cities" and "weeds overrun millions of farms" if Roosevelt won the election.

Smith's running mate in 1928—were in the ring. Among the other hopefuls were the former Secretary of War Newton D. Baker, Senators J. H. Lewis and James A. Reed, Speaker of the House John N. Garner, Governors and ex-Governors Albert F. Ritchie, Harry F. Byrd, Harry Moore, George White, and William H. Murray.

The favorites were Al Smith and Franklin D. Roosevelt. Of the two, Smith had the stronger support from the party regulars, though many Democrats complained that he was no longer the "Happy Warrior" of the brown derby and the cocked cigar, but that he had gone "high-hat, high-brow, and high-life." The obvious handicaps to his renomination were that he had suffered defeat in the previous elec-

tion and that he belonged to the Catholic Church.

The other favorite, Franklin D. Roosevelt, whom Smith had persuaded in 1928 to run for the governorship of New York, suffered no such disadvantages. Roosevelt's star was rising. His fame as an energetic, progressive, and liberal-minded governor was spreading, his vote-getting ability unsurpassed. (Two years before —in 1930—he had won re-election by a majority of 750,000 votes, carrying even the normally Republican upstate counties.) His bid for the nomination was skillfully managed by Louis McHenry Howe, a gnomelike, energetic little man, who had met him at Albany in 1911 and become his most devoted helper and admirer. Howe masterminded the highly successful pre-convention campaign, choosing able men to

585

TWO CHICKENS IN EVERY GARAGE.

THE DEPRESSION and President Hoover's optimistic predictions were a welcome target of the cartoonists.

assist him. Among them was James Farley, who recalls in his memoirs that "never in the history of politics was there anything like our letter-writing and long-distance telephone campaign." Every Democratic county chairman was approached and asked to send a report from his district. The candidate himself wrote thousands of letters, called men and women in key positions on the telephone, and sent them autographed photographs and phonograph records of his voice appealing for their support. If a county chairman's son were to marry, or his daughter to give birth to a child, he was sure to receive a congratulatory message from Roosevelt.

Not long before the Democratic convention was to meet, the friends of the New York governor conducted surveys. In one poll Jesse I. Straus asked the Democratic delegates and alternates to the convention whom they would prefer as candidate, and the majority answered Roosevelt. In other polls, bank presidents and directors of corporations were questioned about their choice and they, too, said Roosevelt. These polls had great influence on the convention, for they showed that of all candidates Roosevelt had the most popular support, thus paving the way to his nomination.

However, in pre-convention skirmishes the Roosevelt men suffered two notable setbacks. Their attempt to abrogate the century-old two-thirds rule, and their proposal to change the convention's order of proceedings, placing the nominations first and the discussion of the platform afterward, ended in defeat. (They feared that the fight over the platform would create such ill feeling between the factions that it would jeopardize their candidate's nomination.)

But after the convention opened, the strength of Roosevelt's adherents became apparent. His managers forced the convention to accept the pro-Roosevelt delegations from Louisiana and Minnesota, and they were successful in electing their man—Senator Walsh of Montana —for the permanent chairmanship.

The Democratic platform was a bold and forthright document. It promised unemployment relief, unemployment and old-age insurance under state laws, labor legislation, help for the farmer, conservation, development of power resources, regulation of securities exchanges, reciprocal trade agreements, and to top it all, a balanced budget and a sound currency. When the plank proposing the repeal of the Eighteenth Amendment was read, the delegates cheered for ten full minutes. A great debate followed this proposal. Minority reports advised the convention against out-and-out repeal. Senator Cordell Hull urged the party to submit the repeal amendment to the states and let them decide about the fate of prohibition, so that in the election the Democrats should not be branded as either dry or wet. In reality the question was not so much whether the Democratic party was for prohibition or repeal, but how wet it wished to appear to be. However, after the vote on the issue was taken, the wets carried it with 934¾ votes against 213¾ for the minority proposal, with many delegates abstaining.

It was three o'clock in the morning before the last of the Democratic orators ended his nominating speech. The weary delegates wished to adjourn, but the Roosevelt men, anxious to begin the voting, refused to support the motion. Thus the first ballot was taken at 4:25 A.M. Roosevelt led with 666¼ votes against Smith's 301¾. This was 103 votes less than the necessary two thirds. On the second ballot the

586

Roosevelt vote rose to 677¾, and on the next one he gained five more votes. His lines held during the night, but would they hold for another ballot? At nine o'clock in the morning, after the third ballot was taken, the convention adjourned.

During the next few hours the "President-makers" worked with great energy, bargaining for the necessary votes. Jim Farley conferred repeatedly with Sam Rayburn and Silliman Evans of Texas, promising the Vice-Presidency to the Texan, John N. Garner, if California and Texas would vote for Roosevelt. Howe called Roosevelt from Chicago, asking for his approval, and Roosevelt endorsed the deal. But the man who had the last word about it was the publisher William Randolph Hearst, who controlled the California delegation and had great influence over the Texas men. When after the adjournment in the morning it appeared that Roosevelt and Smith might block each other's nomination, and when Farley threatened to swing the Roosevelt vote to Newton D. Baker, an ardent internationalist and advocate of the League of Nations, Hearst was implored to give California's support to Roosevelt. The publisher, fearing the nomination of Baker, chose the lesser of two evils—or so he thought.

Thus when the convention reassembled, William McAdoo, the leader of the California delegation, mounted the rostrum and declared: "California came here to nominate a President of the United States. She did not come to deadlock the convention or to engage in another devastating contest like that of 1924. Therefore California casts forty-four votes for Franklin D. Roosevelt." The Smith supporters booed. At the Governor's Mansion in Albany, Roosevelt, who was listening to the radio, grinned broadly and exclaimed: "Good old McAdoo!" With California behind him, FDR's nomination was assured. At the end of the trial he had 945 votes against 190¼ for Smith. The "sage of Baltimore," H. L. Mencken, reported in his newspaper: "Here was a great convention . . . nominating the weakest candidate before it."

The following day the Democratic nominee took a plane to Chicago, dramatically showing that his physical disability (a year after the 1920 campaign he had been stricken by infantile paralysis) would not hinder him in performing

THE STRAIN IS BEGINNING TO TELL!

PROHIBITION was a major issue. The Republicans were half-hearted about repeal, the Democrats outspoken.

his duties. Addressing the convention, Roosevelt declared that he had "started out on the tasks that lie ahead by breaking the absurd tradition that the candidate should remain in professed ignorance of what has happened for weeks until he is formally notified of that many weeks later. You have nominated me and I know it, and I am here to thank you for the honor. Let it be symbolic that in so doing, I broke traditions. Let it be from now on the task of our party to break foolish traditions."

In his acceptance speech Roosevelt promised aid to the "forgotten man" (a term he had used repeatedly in previous speeches), to help him realize his hope for a return to the old standard of living in the United States. He endorsed the platform plank repealing prohibition, but he was willing—this as a political gesture toward the South—to protect the dry states in their wish to keep out intoxicating liquors and to prevent the return of the saloon. "I pledge you, I pledge myself," said the candidate, "to a new deal * for the American people. Let us all here

* Roosevelt took the phrase, "a new deal," from Mark Twain's Connecticut Yankee, who said that "when six men out of a thousand crack the whip over their fellows' backs, then what the other nine hundred ninety-four dupes need is a new deal."

587

assembled constitute ourselves prophets of a new order of competence and courage. This is more than a political campaign; it is a call to arms! Give me your help, not to win votes alone, but to win in this crusade to restore America to its own people."

With this the campaign began.

The early Republican strategy—according to a member of Hoover's Cabinet, as reported by Paul W. Anderson in *The Nation*—was developed around three main themes: the first, an attack on the vice-presidential candidate, Garner, as "unsound" and "radical," coupled with the surreptitious rumor that Roosevelt's health was so poor that the election of the Democratic ticket would mean the elevation of Garner to the Presidency within a year or two; the second, an attack on Roosevelt, underlining his adherence to radical theories, as his attitude on electric power and his allusion to "a new deal" and the "forgotten man" clearly showed; the third, a whispering campaign against Roosevelt for the consumption of his Catholic supporters, telling them that the anti-Catholic propaganda against Smith before the convention was the work of Roosevelt and his friends.

To counteract rumors about Roosevelt's failing health, James Farley told a radio audience: "In various parts of the country hateful stories are cropping up in regard to our candidate's physical and mental health. . . . The Governor recently insured his life for $500,000 with the Warm Springs Foundation as beneficiary. . . . His lameness, which is steadily getting better, has no more effect on his general condition than if he had a glass eye or was prematurely bald. . . . If he were a weakling in any respect he could not have gone through two gruelling campaigns for the governorship of New York. . . . Governor Roosevelt might be handicapped in a footrace, but in no other way need he fear comparison with his adversary."

The campaign strategy for Roosevelt was carefully mapped out. Howe, Farley, and Charlie Michelson used all the methods of modern propaganda. Their organization distributed sixty-three million pieces of campaign literature. Each of the 140,000 Democratic committeemen was bombarded with personal letters, telephone calls, and innumerable pamphlets from headquarters.

A CONFIDENT ROOSEVELT DROVE WITH A SOL

ER TO THE INAUGURATION. FDR TALKED ANIMATEDLY BUT HOOVER WAS MOROSE AND SILENT.

Roosevelt made an extended tour, giving twenty-seven major addresses and thirty-two shorter speeches, impressing his audiences with his radiant and magnetic personality. In the Western states he received an enthusiastic welcome. *Time* Magazine wrote: "If September crowds and applause meant November votes (which one rule says they do), the Pacific Coast was in his bag." At Sacramento the Democratic candidate praised the Progressive Republican, Hiram Johnson, and in Nebraska he told the Progressive Republican Senator, George W. Norris: "I go along with you because you follow in their footsteps—'radical' like Jefferson, 'demagog' like Jackson, 'idealist' like Lincoln, 'wild' like Theodore Roosevelt, 'theorist' like Wilson." And the Senator from Nebraska replied: "What this country needs is another Roosevelt in the White House."

Franklin D. Roosevelt made comprehensive proposals concerning the depression, discussing the recovery and reform measures which he would institute. "At Topeka," as he himself recalled in a campaign speech, "I outlined a complete national plan for the restoration of agriculture to its proper relationship to the nation. At Salt Lake City I outlined a definite program to give us a definite transportation policy, including the rehabilitation of the railroads of the nation. At Portland I set forth in definite terms a national policy for the conduct of utilities, and especially those engaged in manufacturing and distributing electric power. At Sioux City I proposed a tariff policy aimed to restore international trade and commerce not only with this nation but between all nations. At Boston I championed the principle that the national government has a positive duty to see that no citizen shall starve. At Columbus I proposed the protection of the investing public against the evils and the fraud perpetrated against them during the past ten years. At Pittsburgh I proposed an honest national budget." And of course he spoke about the repeal of prohibition, one of the major issues of this campaign. (There was such constant emphasis on repeal that Will Rogers caustically asked for a platform plank "to show the people where to get some bread with the beer.")

Compared to such activity, the Hoover campaign seemed placid and uninspired. The Presi-

dent made ten major addresses, all of similar tone. He defended his measures in broad terms, asserting that the depression was not the fault of the administration but was due to foreign causes, and "let no man say it could not have been worse." In many places he faced hostile crowds. People booed him in Detroit, Philadelphia, Salt Lake City. Reilly, the White House Secret Service man who accompanied Hoover in the campaign, recalled that men actually ran out into the streets to thumb their noses at the President as he passed. The sculptor Gutzon Borglum's remark that "If you put a rose in Hoover's hand it would wilt," was laughingly repeated.

The Democratic propagandists, under the leadership of Charles Michelson, turned their heavy guns against Hoover. Each of the President's mistakes was emphasized, enlarged, and harped upon; his unfortunate remarks and optimistic prophecies that "prosperity is just around the corner" and that "the worst has passed" were not allowed to be forgotten. His character was smeared, and the slanders against him were varied: one said that he was not an American but a British subject, another that he had made a fortune out of Belgian relief funds, a third that he was pro-German during the war and had been instrumental in the execution of Edith Cavell because she was about to expose him, a fourth that he had practiced crooked finance in Hong Kong, a fifth that he once employed Chinese coolies in South African mines.

Against such a barrage of abuse the Republicans seemed helpless. Their campaign orators ineffectually repeated that Hoover was a "great engineer" and a "great humanitarian," and assailed Roosevelt as "no real farmer, no true Democrat, no real friend of the industrialist, not a genuine Roosevelt and no true disciple of Jefferson in so far as religious tolerance is concerned." They branded the Democratic candidate a radical, a Socialist, and a Bolshevist. To these accusations Roosevelt replied: "My policy is as radical as American liberty; as radical as the Constitution of the United States." And he told an audience in Baltimore that Hoover's record was like that of the Four Horsemen—"Destruction, Delay, Despair and Deceit."

As the campaign reached its climax, the Re-

THE INAUGURATION OF THE THIRTY-SECOND PRESIDENT. Franklin D. Roosevelt takes the oath of office from Chief Justice Charles Evans Hughes with his hand on an old Dutch Bible belonging to the Roosevelt family.

publicans resorted to old-fashioned scare tactics. They intimidated workers, telling them that they would lose their jobs if Hoover was defeated; industrialists and bankers were warned that a Democratic administration would be fatal to their interests. Hoover himself told the country that "grass would grow in the streets of one hundred cities" and "weeds overrun millions of farms" if the Democrats should come to power.

Ex-President Coolidge spoke in Madison Square Garden for Hoover, saying that "The charge is made that the Republican party does not show any solicitude for the common run of people but is interested only in promoting the interests of a few favored individuals and corporations. . . . All this is a question of method. . . . We have advocated strengthening the position of the employer that he

might pay better wages to his employees." But the nation was not in a mood to listen to nice explanations. Radical steps were demanded to put the unemployed to work and bring back normal conditions. Neat evasions made little impression on the electorate.

In his final speech Hoover emphasized the difference between the Republican and Democratic positions. "The campaign is more than a contest between two men," he said. "It is a contest between two philosophies of government." The people had to choose between individualism and regimentation. "You cannot extend the mastery of government over the daily life of a people without somewhere making it master of people's souls and thought."

Election day was a grim day. Of the forty million men and women who went to the polls,

591

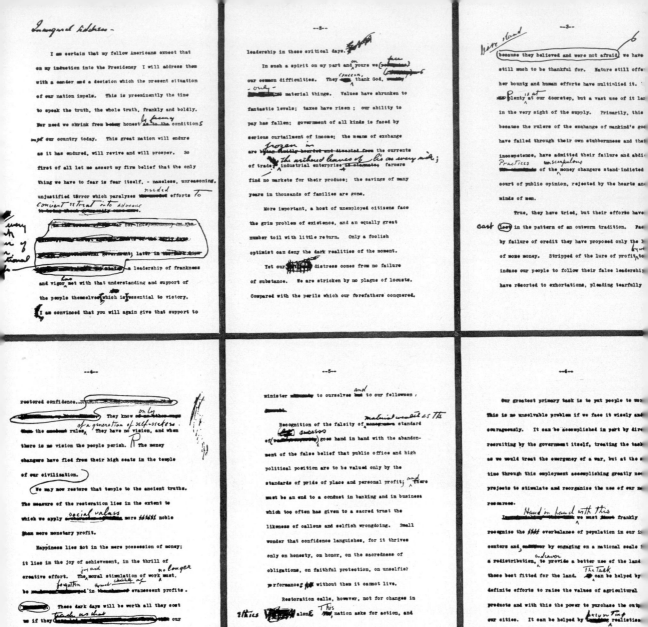

THE FINAL MANUSCRIPT OF FRANKLIN DELANO ROOSEVELT'S FIRST INAUGURAL ADDRESS S...

about one in three was without work and regular income. Discontent weighed heavily on their minds—discontent and gloom. The army of bonus marchers, who had been disbanded with tear gas and bayonets, were a vivid memory, as were the parades of hungry and jobless in the cities of the East and Midwest. *Time* Magazine wrote: "Doubtless the most potent factor in keeping the country steady and averting even the threat of an armed uprising has been the certainty—such as exists in no other large country—that November 8, 1932, would in due constitutional order bring a presidential and congressional election."

tragedy of the growing loss through foreclosure, of
small homes and our farms.   It can be helped by insistence
that federal, state and local governments act forthwith
on demand that their cost be drastically reduced.   It
can be helped by the unifying of relief activities which today
are often scattered, uneconomical and unequal *it can be helped*
There are many ways in which *but it can*
never be it can be helped than merely talking about it. We must
act quickly.

It can be helped by national planning
and supervision of all forms of transportation and of
communications and other utilities which have a definitely
public character.

Finally, in our progress toward a resumption of work
require two safeguards against a return of the evils of
old order: there must be a strict supervision of all
banking and credits and investments;   there must be an end

to speculation with other people's money,   and there must be
provision for an adequate but sound currency.

These are the lines of attack.   I shall presently
urge upon a new Congress in special session detailed measures
for their fulfilment, and I shall seek the immediate
assistance of the several states.

Through this *These* program of action we address ourselves
to putting our own national house in order *and making income balance outgo* Our international
trade relations though vastly important, are in point of
time and necessity secondary to the establishment of a sound
national economy.   I favor as a practical policy the putting
of first things first.   I shall spare no effort to restore
world trade by international economic readjustment, but the
emergency at home cannot wait on that accomplishment.

The basic thought that guides these specific
means of national recovery is not narrowly nationalistic.
It is the insistence, as a first considera-

tion, upon the interdependence of the various elements in and
parts of the United States -- a recognition of the old and
permanently important manifestation of the American spirit of
the pioneer.   It is the way to recovery.   It is the immediate
way.   It is the strongest assurance that the recovery will
endure.

In the field of world policy I would dedicate this nation
to the policy of the good neighbor -- the neighbor who resolutely
respects himself and because he does so, respects the rights of
others -- the neighbor who respects his obligations and
respects the sanctity of his agreements in and with a world of
neighbors.

If I read the temper of our people correctly we now realize
as we have never realised before our interdependence on each *let*
other;   that we cannot merely take but we must give as well; *if it stand*
that we are to go forward we must *move* as a trained and
loyal army willing to sacrifice for

the common discipline, *is* *no* because without such
no progress *can be made* *any* leadership *becomes*
are, I know, ready and willing to submit our
property to such discipline because it makes
leadership which aims at a larger good.
to offer them, pledging that the
losses will bind upon us all as a sacred obligation
of duty hitherto evoked only in time of armed

taken
pledge, I assume unhesitatingly the
ship of this great army of our people dedicated
aimed attack upon our common problems.

in this image and to this end is feasible under
government which we have inherited from our
Our constitution is so simple and practical
possible always to meet extraordinary needs by
emphasis and arrangement without loss of
form.   That is why our constitutional system

has proved itself the most superbly enduring political
mechanism the modern world has produced.   It has met every
stress of vast expansion of territory, of foreign wars, of
bitter internal strife, of world relations.

It is to be hoped that the normal balance of executive
and legislative authority may be wholly adequate to meet the
unprecedented task before us.   But it may be that an
unprecedented demand and need for undelayed action may call
for temporary departure from that normal balance of public
procedure.

recommend
I am prepared under my constitutional duty to
the measures that a stricken nation in the midst of a stricken
world may require.   These measures, or such other measures
as the Congress may build out of their experience and wisdom,
seek
I shall, within my constitutional authority, to bring
to speedy adoption.

12

But in the event that the Congress shall fail to take
one of these two courses, and in the event that the national
emergency is still critical, I shall not evade the clear
that
course of duty will then confront me.   I shall ask
the Congress for the one remaining instrument to meet the
crisis -- broad executive power to wage a war against the
emergency, as great as the power that would be given to me
if we were in fact invaded by a foreign foe.

For the trust reposed in me I will return the courage
and the devotion that befit the time.   I can do no less.

We face the arduous days that lie before us in the
warm courage of national unity; with the clear consciousness
of seeking old and precious moral values; with the clean
satisfaction that comes from the stern performance of duty
by old and young alike.   We aim at the assurance of a rounded
and permanent national life.

We do not distrust the future of essential democracy.
The people of the United States have not failed.   In their

HE MADE CORRECTIONS AND CHANGES UNTIL THE LAST MINUTE.

On election eve Herbert Hoover supposedly
said to his secretary: "I'll tell you what our
trouble is—we are opposed by six million unemployed, ten thousand bonus marchers, and
ten cent corn."

Beside the two major parties, a number of
smaller ones put up candidates. The Socialists

need they have registered a mandate that they want
direct vigorous action.   They have asked for discipline
and direction under leadership.   They have made me the *present*
instrument of their
wishes.   In the spirit of the gift I take it.

In this dedication of a nation we humbly ask the
blessing of God.   May he protect each and every one of
us.   May he guide me in the days to come.

again presented Norman Thomas, their perennial nominee; the Communists supported William Z. Foster, and for the second place nominated a Negro, James W. Ford of Alabama; the Prohibitionists rallied behind William D. Upshaw; the Farmer-Labor and Socialist-Labor parties behind Verne L. Reynolds.

The result was almost an exact reversal of the 1928 figures. Roosevelt won forty-two states; Hoover was only supported by six. FDR's victory indicated—in the opinion of that wise Republican, William Allen White—"a firm desire on the part of the American people to use government as an agency for human welfare."

Inauguration day opened with a twenty-minute service at the church across Lafayette Park from the White House, for Roosevelt felt that "a thought to God is the right way to start off my administration." A few hours before, Governor Lehman had declared a four-day bank holiday for New York and his statement was followed by a similar one from Governor Horner of Illinois. All security and commodity exchanges in New York and Chicago were closed when Roosevelt drove with Hoover to the Capitol. Hoover was in low spirits and sat morosely beside the President-elect. Trying desperately to make conversation, Roosevelt pointed to the girders of the unfinished Department of Commerce building as they passed by and exclaimed: "Lovely steel!" But Hoover remained aloof and silent.

Roosevelt took the oath from Chief Justice Charles Evans Hughes, his hand resting on the ancient Dutch Bible which had been in the Roosevelt family for three centuries. Then he began to speak. "This is preeminently the time to speak the truth, the whole truth, frankly and boldly." The hundred thousand shivering in the chilly Washington air and the millions at the radios listened intently. His voice, as John Dos Passos noted, "after a moment's hoarseness was confident and full, carefully tuned to the microphones; the patroon voice, the headmaster's admonishing voice, the bedside doctor's voice that spoke to each man and to all of us."

"This great nation will endure as it has endured, will revive and will prosper," continued Roosevelt, thrusting out his large chin defiantly. "So first of all, let me assert my firm belief that the only thing we have to fear is fear itself—nameless, unreasoning, unjustified terror which paralyzes needed efforts to convert retreat into advance." The masses listened in silence. "In such a spirit on my part and on yours we face our common difficulties. They concern, thank God, only material things. Values have shrunken to fantastic levels; taxes have risen; our ability to pay has fallen; government of all kinds is faced by serious curtailment of income; the means of exchange are frozen in the currents of trade; the withered leaves of industrial enterprise lie on every side; farmers find no markets for their produce; the savings of many years in thousands of families are gone. More important, a host of unemployed citizens face a grim problem of existence, and an equally great number toil with little return. Only a foolish optimist can deny the dark realities of the moment."

The vibrant voice went on: "The money changers have fled from their high seats in the temple of our civilization. We may now restore that temple to the ancient truths. The measure of the restoration lies in the extent to which we apply social values more noble than mere monetary profit."

Before the inaugural stand the solemn crowd blackened forty acres of park and pavement. "Happiness lies not in the mere possession of money," declared Roosevelt. "It lies in the joys of achievement, in the thrill of creative effort. The joy and moral stimulation of work no longer must be forgotten in the mad chase of evanescent profits. These dark days will be worth all they cost us if they teach us that our true destiny is not to be ministered unto but to minister to ourselves and to our fellow men."

The new President promised to accept the responsibility of leading the nation out of the crisis. "Restoration calls, however, not for changes in ethics alone. This nation asks for action, and action now. Our greatest primary task is to put people to work. I am prepared under my constitutional duty to recommend the measures that a stricken nation in the midst of a stricken world may require."

A new era in American political history had begun.

MARCH 4, 1933: "This is pre-eminently the time to speak the truth ... frankly and boldly. Nor need we shrink from honestly facing conditions in our country today.... So first of all let me assert my firm belief that the only thing we have to fear is fear itself.... In such a spirit on my part and on yours we face our common difficulties.... Values have shrunken to fantastic levels; taxes have risen; our ability to pay has fallen ... the farmers find no markets for their produce, the savings of many years in thousands of families are gone. More important, a host of unemployed citizens face the grim problem of existence.... Only a foolish optimist can deny the dark realities of the moment.... This nation asks for action and action now.... In our progress toward a resumption of work we require two safeguards against a return of the evils of the old order; there must be a strict supervision of all banking and credits and investment; there must be an end to speculation with other people's money, and there must be provisions for an adequate but sound currency.... I shall ask the Congress for the one remaining instrument to meet the crisis—broad executive power to wage a war against the emergency, as great as the power that would be given to me if we were in fact invaded by a foreign foe. For the trust reposed in me I will return the courage and the devotion that befit the time. I can do no less."

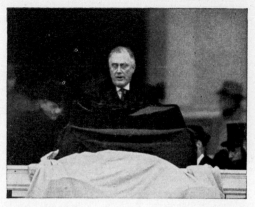

RAIN POURED DURING THE INAUGURAL

THE THIRTY-EIGHTH ELECTION—1936

FRANKLIN D. ROOSEVELT

Franklin D. Roosevelt broke sharply with the philosophy of past governments. No longer would the administration stand aside while millions were without work, suffering privation and despair. The new President believed that it was the responsibility of the Federal Government to help citizens who, through no fault of their own, were in dire straits. He held that it was for the State to take over the economic controls if private individuals failed. There could be no more "business as usual," no more "rugged individualism" when waves of destruction were washing at the foundations of the Republic.

Forty-eight hours after Roosevelt took office, Congress assembled for its memorable hundred-day session. The new administration demanded a far-reaching program of social and economic legislation, and the lawmakers complied. Within a short time a series of relief, recovery, and reform measures was enacted, attacking the depression on different fronts.

A host of Federal agencies sprang to life to relieve the distress of twelve to fifteen million unemployed whom Roosevelt had inherited from his predecessor. The Federal Emergency Relief Administration (FERA) under Harry Hopkins supplied the individual states and local communities with Federal funds to assist the unemployed, distributing over three billion dollars. The Civil Works Administration (CWA) undertook projects which could be completed within a short while to help the destitute during the coming winter months. Later on, the FERA gave way to the Works Progress Administration (WPA), also under Harry Hopkins, providing work for the jobless, stimulating business by increasing the amount of money in circulation ("priming the pump"), and last but not least, creating projects of enduring value. Another agency, the Public Works Administration (PWA) under Harold Ickes, mapped out long-range plans of public works, employing regular labor (not relief labor) and carrying out a diversified program of heavy construction projects which included waterworks, municipal power plants, hospitals, and school buildings.

To rehabilitate industry and better the conditions of the workers, the National Recovery Act (NRA) was instituted. Its basic program was to increase industrial production and em-

597

THE CANDIDATES

FRANKLIN D. ROOSEVELT (1882-1945), renominated unanimously by the Democrats, had the greatest plurality ever received in a national election and won all but 8 electoral votes.

JOHN NANCE GARNER (1868-19—) was selected again for the Vice-Presidency. When notified of his nomination, he renewed a pledge given four years before of fealty to Roosevelt.

ALFRED M. LANDON (1887-19—), Governor of Kansas was nominated by the Republicans. Acclaimed as a budget-balancer, he was badly beaten, winning Maine and Vermont.

W. FRANKLIN KNOX (1874-1944), publisher of a Chicago newspaper, chief rival of Landon for the nomination, became vice-presidential nominee when Vandenberg refused to run.

WILLIAM LEMKE (1878-1950) of North Dakota was the Union party choice. Their platform was designed to attract Townsendites, Coughlinites, Share-the-Wealthers.

NORMAN THOMAS (1884-19—) was again the presidential candidate of the Socialists. Their platform urged the voters "to defeat the growing forces of fascism and reaction."

ployment, to reduce ruthless methods of competition without encouraging monopolies, to secure higher wages for the workers (a minimum wage of forty cents an hour), better their working conditions, and reduce their working time (a thirty-six-hour week for industrial and a forty-hour week for clerical workers). It granted labor the right to organize and strike (Section 7A of the NRA said that "Employees shall have the right to organize and bargain collectively . . . and shall be free from the interference, restraint, or coercion of employ-

THE VOTES IN THE 1936 ELECTION

STATES	POPULAR VOTE				ELEC. VOTE	
	F. D. Roosevelt, Democrat.	Alf. Landon, Republican.	William Lemke, Union.	Norman Thomas, Socialist.	Landon and Knox.	Roosevelt and Garner.
Ala........	238,196	35,358	551	242	—	11
Ariz........	86,722	33,433	3,307	317	—	3
Ark........	146,765	32,039	4	446	—	9
Calif........	1,766,836	836,431	—	11,331	—	22
Colo........	295,021	181,267	9,962	1,593	—	6
Conn........	382,189	278,685	21,805	5,683	—	8
Del........	69,702	54,014	442	172	—	3
Fla........	249,117	78,248	—	—	—	7
Ga........	255,364	36,942	141	68	—	12
Idaho........	125,683	66,256	7,684	—	—	4
Ill........	2,282,999	1,570,393	89,439	7,530	—	29
Ind........	934,974	691,570	19,407	3,856	—	14
Iowa........	621,756	487,977	29,687	1,373	—	11
Kan........	464,520	397,727	—	2,766	—	9
Ky........	541,944	369,702	12,501	632	—	11
La........	292,894	36,791	—	—	—	10
Me........	126,333	168,823	7,581	783	5	—
Md........	389,612	231,435	—	1,629	—	8
Mass........	942,716	768,613	118,639	5,111	—	17
Mich........	1,016,794	699,733	75,795	8,208	—	19
Minn........	698,811	350,461	74,296	2,872	—	11
Miss........	157,318	4,443	—	329	—	9
Mo........	1,111,043	697,891	14,630	3,454	—	15
Mont........	159,690	63,598	5,549	1,066	—	4
Neb........	347,454	247,731	12,847	—	—	7
Nev........	31,925	11,923	—	—	—	3
N. H........	108,460	104,642	4,819	—	—	4
N. J........	1,083,850	720,322	—	3,931	—	16
N. M........	105,838	61,710	924	343	—	3
N. Y........	3,293,222	2,180,670	—	86,897	—	47
N. C........	616,141	223,283	—	21	—	13
N. D........	163,148	72,751	36,708	552	—	4
Ohio........	1,747,122	1,127,709	132,212	117	—	26
Okla........	501,069	245,122	—	2,221	—	11
Ore........	266,733	122,706	21,831	2,143	—	5
Pa........	2,353,788	1,690,300	67,467	14,375	—	36
R. I........	165,233	125,012	19,569	—	—	4
S. C........	113,791	1,646	—	—	—	8
S. D........	160,137	125,977	10,338	—	—	4
Tenn........	327,083	146,516	296	685	—	11
Tex........	734,485	103,874	3,281	1,075	—	23
Utah........	150,246	64,555	1,121	432	—	4
Vt........	62,124	81,023	—	—	3	—
Va........	234,980	98,336	233	313	—	11
Wash........	459,579	206,892	17,463	3,496	—	8
W. Va........	502,582	325,486	—	832	—	8
Wis........	802,984	380,828	60,297	10,626	—	12
Wyo........	62,624	38,739	1,653	200	—	3
	27,751,597	16,679,583	882,479	187,720	8	523

Browder, Com., 80,150; Colvin, Proh., 37,847; Aiken, Soc.-Lab., 12,7
The Roosevelt vote in N. Y. State includes 274,924 cast by
American Labor Party. Total vote, 45,646,817.

THE REPUBLICAN STANDARD-BEARER was Alfred Mossman Landon, affable Governor of Kansas. He was "a well guy," said the New Dealers, and they could afford to be complimentary for they had little to fear from him.

rs of labor or their agents"); it eliminated child and sweatshop labor, and provided funds for public works and emergency relief.

To uphold labor's right of collective bargaining, the National Labor Board was created, superseded by the National Labor Relations Board in June, 1934. The NLRB and its associated regional boards were given jurisdiction to settle labor disputes and mediate strikes.

After labor, the farmers suffered most under the depression. Postwar overproduction of farm products and shrinking markets drove prices down. At the beginning of Roosevelt's term two out of every five American farms were mortgaged. To relieve the farmers, the Agricultural Adjustment Act (AAA) introduced a crop-restriction program, paying subsidies to those who were willing to reduce the production of certain staple commodities. Under the AAA forty million acres were withdrawn from cultivation, cotton crops were re-

duced by four million bales, wheat reduction brought the farmers a hundred million dollars in benefit payments; tobacco production was cut by one third, corn by one fourth; six million pigs and hogs were purchased by the government and slaughtered.

The men whom the farm plan condemned to idleness were helped by the Resettlement Administration under Rexford Tugwell. Financial aid was given to some 635,000 farm families, farm mortgages were adjusted, camps for migratory workers built.

To assist those whose savings were gone, who were deeply in debt, and whose property was mortgaged, the government offered liberal credit facilities. The Federal Farm Credit Administration provided farmers with funds for new mortgages and loaned money at low interest rates, as did the Commodity Credit Corporation; the Home Owners' Loan Corporation refinanced mortgages on privately owned

599

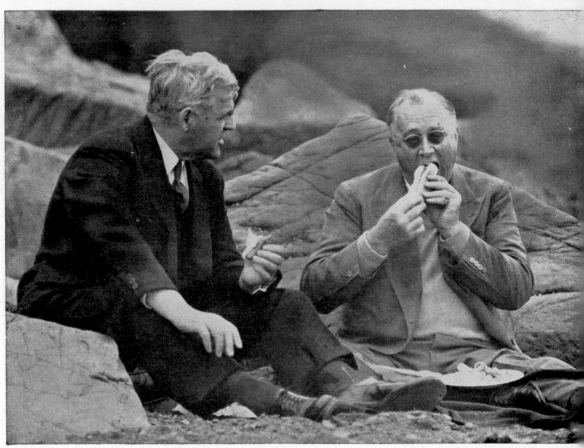

PICTURES LIKE THIS—OF FDR EATING HOT DOGS AT CAMPOBELLO—ENHANCED HIS POPULARITY

homes; the Federal Housing Administration insured existing mortgages, gave loans for the repairing of residential and business property, and encouraged the building of homes with government financing; the Reconstruction Finance Corporation—originally a Hoover agency—extended its loans to industrial enterprises.

To protect investors Congress passed measures on banking, finance, and revenue. The Glass-Steagall Banking Act restricted the use of bank credit for speculation, separated commercial and investment banking, and made provisions for the insurance of bank deposits. The Securities Exchange Act licensed stock exchanges, required registration of all securities, and fixed strict rules for marginal and speculative loans.

To stop the exploitation and destruction of the nation's natural resources, serious measures were undertaken. The Civilian Conservation Corps (CCC) carried out vital conservation work. Thousands of young men between seventeen and twenty-eight were taken away from the slums of the cities, where unemployment bred crime, to 26,000 camps in healthy rural surroundings. There they planted trees, fought forest fires, constructed erosion dams, guarded against plant and animal diseases, and improved drainage systems, their work adding more than seventeen million acres of new forest land to the nation's resources.

The reform legislation of the New Deal was wide in scope. To control floods, harness the Tennessee River, and supply cheap electric power to backward areas in seven Southern states, the Tennessee Valley Authority (TVA —one of the outstanding successes of the New Deal—was created. It was clearly a socialistic project, employing the methods of planned economy. To help young people between the

PICTURES LIKE THIS—OF FDR AND MRS. ROOSEVELT—ENDEARED HIM TO THE "COMMON MAN."

THE HAPPY REPUBLICANS—ALFRED M. LANDON WITH FRANK A. KNOX, HIS RUNNING MATE

ages of sixteen and twenty-five to secure occupational training and employment, the National Youth Administration came into being. The Social Security Act provided unemployment and old-age insurance, made benefit payments to the blind, dependent mothers and children, and appropriated money for public health work.

Because the New Deal measures were put into effect with such breathless speed, people spoke of the "Roosevelt Revolution." After twelve years of political stagnation and inertia, the activity of the new administration seemed revolutionary. Actually it was not. The Roosevelt reforms were long overdue. Democratic in spirit and progressive in nature, they were America's solution to the economic crisis which Russia, Germany, and Italy met in an entirely different way. They preserved the capitalist system by imposing regulations upon irresponsible capitalists. Furthermore, most of them had their roots in the American past. Regula-

tion of business and railroads began in the eighties, agricultural relief under Wilson, conservation under Theodore Roosevelt, supervision of securities exchanges under Harding and Coolidge, while social legislation had been previously enacted in many of the more progressive states.

We are still too close to the New Deal to be able to discuss it without emotion, but Professors Morison and Commager made this shrewd and succinct evaluation of the Roosevelt program: "Taken as a whole, the New Deal legislation contributed greatly to both recovery and reform, improved the status of the farmer and laborer, prepared the way for a more equitable distribution of wealth, brought business, banking, securities, utilities, and transportation under more effective regulation, and, most important of all, helped to salvage the natural resources of the nation. At the same time it interfered seriously with the freedom of busi-

602

THE DEMOCRATIC TICKET—ROOSEVELT AND GARNER AT THE CONVENTION IN PHILADELPHIA.

ness enterprise, inaugurated far-reaching controls over labor and farming, encouraged the growth of bureaucracy, created administrative confusion, impaired the integrity of the merit system, encouraged the fear of dictatorship and of class antagonism, greatly increased the national debt, and at some points conflicted with the Constitution."

That the philosophy and the measures of the New Deal were severely castigated by the opposition was not surprising. The President was attacked by both conservatives and progressives. The conservatives asserted that the New Deal would lead the nation down the path to communism, while the progressives held that the reforms were not far-reaching enough. The critics of the relief program charged that it was administered in a wasteful way, was much too costly, and departed from the traditional American system of free enterprise. Bankers and businessmen declared that the dole was a cheaper way of caring for the unemployed than work relief. Representatives of labor fought against the low wages under which work relief was carried out, fearing that industry would follow suit and stabilize these low wages.

Much of the criticism had validity. It was true that the administration of such a huge and novel social experiment did not always function smoothly. There were not enough experienced administrators; the fast-growing and poorly paid bureaucracy (241,000 new positions were added to 583,000 already existing) was sometimes ill-fitted for the tremendous task; there was squandering of money, waste, and incompetence. But whatever mistakes were made, the relief program put millions back to work, fostering their self-respect and maintaining their occupational skills. And the projects carried out had more often than not a lasting value, enriching the nation.

It was also true that the cost of the relief

and public works programs was tremendous. Under the New Deal the State, as Professor Hacker put it, had become "an enterpriser, buying and selling, lending and borrowing, building and managing; it used its great fiscal and financial powers to redistribute wealth and create income." It had taken over the function of private investors. This could only be accomplished by added expenditures and a greatly increased public debt. From July, 1933, to July, 1937, the national debt increased by approximately fourteen billion dollars: from roughly 22½ billions in 1933 to 36½ billions in 1937. But those who supported Roosevelt's policies agreed with Professor Schlesinger that the President "by extending Federal authority over the nation's economic life . . . hoped to prevent future abuses . . . by financial and industrial interests, to place the business order under firm public control, and to ensure the common folk a fuller, freer and securer existence."

Each individual New Deal measure aroused hostile voices. The subsidy program of the AAA was denounced because it created an "economy of scarcity." The NRA was attacked from all sides: by big business, which resented controls, opposed the labor provisions of the act, and cried "regimentation" (though until New Deal legislation checked the worst abuses, big business itself imposed regimentation through codes, cartels, price-fixing agreements, company-owned towns, and company unions); by small business, which feared the increased strength of monopolies; by liberals who were against the suspension of anti-trust laws; by labor, which felt that the codes were unsuccessful; and by the consumer, who resented the higher prices.

Eventually both these major New Deal laws —the NRA and the AAA—were held unconstitutional by the Supreme Court. The decision about the NRA proclaimed that "Congress can-

TWO WIDELY DISCUSSED CARTOONS DRAWN BY ARNO AND GALBRAITH FOR *THE NEW YORKER*.

The caption under this Peter Arno cartoon reads: "Come along, we're going to the Trans-Lux to hiss Roosevelt."

"And if Roosevelt is not re-elected, perhaps even a villa in Newport, my sweet," says the Galbraith caption.

not delegate legislative power to the President to exercise unfettered discretion to make whatever laws he thinks may be needed or advisable for the rehabilitation and expansion of trade and industry." And the farm program was overthrown because of its taxing provisions and because it was "the reserved right of the states," and not of Congress, to "regulate and control agricultural production." (However, the main provisions of both acts were later reenacted by Congress.)

With the New Deal battling its way over obstacles and criticism, the nation was well on the way to recovery when the time of the nominating conventions arrived.

Among the Republicans there were four chief contenders: Governor Alfred M. Landon of Kansas, Senator William E. Borah of Idaho, Senator Arthur H. Vandenberg of Michigan, and the publisher of the Chicago *Daily News*, Frank Knox. Before their convention assembled in Cleveland, there were suggestions of forming a coalition with some Democrats and giving the second place on the Republican ticket to a conservative anti-New Deal, anti-Roosevelt Democrat like Davey of Ohio, Ely of Massachusetts, or Al Smith of New York. However, nothing came of this plan.

Before the balloting began, Vandenberg, Knox, and other lesser candidates—save Senator Borah—had already withdrawn their names, leaving the nomination to Alfred Mossman Landon, who became the Republicans' choice on the first trial. The delegates sang:

"Landon, oh, Landon
Will lead to victory,
With the dear old Constitution
And it's good enough for me."

The Republican platform, beginning in the manner of the Declaration of Independence, proclaimed: "For three long years the New Deal administration has dishonored American traditions and flagrantly betrayed the pledges upon which the Democratic party sought and received public support." Then it enumerated the grievances: one was that the President had usurped the powers of Congress; another that the integrity and authority of the Supreme Court had been "flaunted"; a third that the "rights and liberties of American citizens" had

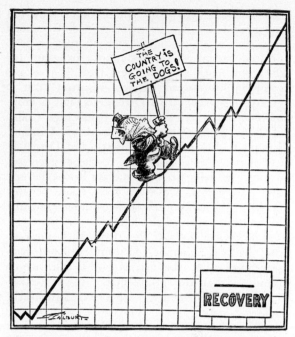

THE REASON why the Republicans had a hard time in the campaign—as Talburt of the Washington *News* saw it.

been violated; a fourth that a "regulated monopoly [had] displaced free enterprise," and so on.

On the positive side the Republicans promised to "maintain the American system of constitutional and local self-government," to preserve free enterprise, and to provide "encouragement instead of hindrance to legitimate business." With the New Deal domestic policies—relief, social security, the protection of the right of labor "to organize and bargain collectively through representatives of its own choosing without interference from any source," and the provision of ample farm credit "at rates as low as those enjoyed by other industries"—the platform had little quarrel. But it demanded an efficient civil service, a sound currency, and a balanced budget, and promised to "stop the folly of uncontrolled spending." And in the field of foreign policy it declared that "America shall not become a member of the League of Nations."

On the whole it was a dull convention, without excitement and enthusiasm, for the Republicans knew that they could not wrest the Presidency from Franklin D. Roosevelt.

When the Democrats met, no other name but the President's was even mentioned. Roosevelt was the only candidate and it was he who drafted the platform, outlining a program for the continuation of the New Deal. There was some opposition to his renomination from a group of conservative Democrats, but a communication which Al Smith, Bainbridge Colby of New Jersey, James A. Reed of Missouri, Joseph B. Ely of Massachusetts, and Daniel F. Cohalan of New York sent to the convention, urging the delegates to repudiate Roosevelt and the New Deal, was not even read. Senator Barkley, the temporary chairman, declared that he had not received the letter.

The proceedings of the Democratic convention will be remembered mainly for the decision abolishing the 104-year-old rule which required that the presidential and vice-presidential candidates must receive two thirds of the delegates' total vote. This rule, adopted on Andrew Jackson's insistence in 1832 in order to make Martin Van Buren's nomination for the Vice-Presidency a certainty, became a cornerstone of all Democratic conventions, and an obstacle to candidates who could not rally enough Southern support. It had prevented the nomination of Champ Clark in 1912, and now his son, Senator Bennett Clark, led the dramatic fight to overthrow it. Four years before, James Farley had made an unsuccessful attempt to kill the rule. Since then the abrogation of it had grown in importance. In 1940 Roosevelt was to retire—so it was thought—and Farley,

together with the outgoing President, hoped to present the name of the new candidate. With the two-thirds rule in effect, the South could offer effective opposition to their choice; without it, the candidate of the Roosevelt-Farley forces would have nothing to fear.

The Southern delegates fought tenaciously for the retention of the rule, and only after protracted arguments did they give up their opposition and accept a compromise proposal whereby in future Democratic conventions the states would not be represented according to their population, but according to the number of Democratic votes cast in elections.

The nominating speeches for Roosevelt lasted for a whole day and the better part of one night. Judge John E. Mack headed the list of fifty-seven orators who proposed the President's renomination. The New York *Times* reported that when Judge Mack finally "gave" the name of Roosevelt at the end of his long-winded speech, delegates "danced and pranced, whooped and hollered, marched and capered in a mighty effort to display their enthusiasm for their leader. For a full hour the parade milled round and round the hall, giving off all the noise that lungs and instruments could make, carrying placards with which each state tried to outdo the rest in promises of victory." Senators Connally and McAdoo "went prancing by the speakers' stand like trotting horses, with fixed grins on their faces," and the Massachusetts delegation seized James Roosevelt, the President's son, and bore him around the hall. A Mississippi banner carried the slogan, "Three hard years with Hoover," and under it marched an emaciated urchin in rags and tatters, followed by stout ladies carrying a banner which read, "If you can't guess—three good years with Roosevelt." A live donkey marching in the parade blocked the aisles, stopping stubbornly at the corners and refusing to move further. Delegates sang to the tune of "Marching Through Georgia":

"Herbie Hoover promised us two chickens in each pot;
Breadlines and depression were the only things we got.
I lost my job, my bank blew up, and I was on the spot,
That's why I'm voting for Roosevelt.

REPUBLICAN CAMPAIGN SYMBOL was the sunflower and the campaign slogan, "Life, Liberty and Landon."

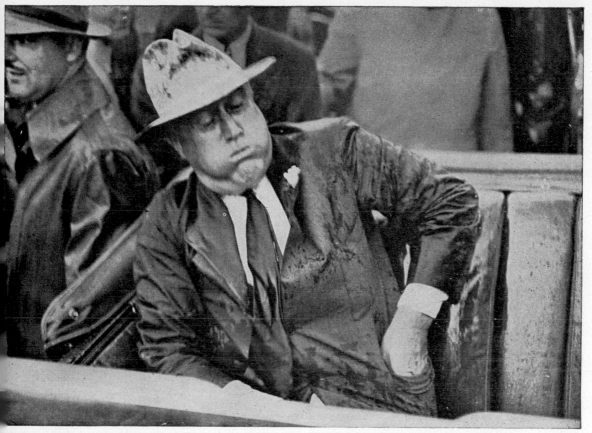

THE INDOMITABLE FDR PROVED HIS PHYSICAL HANDICAP WAS NO OBSTACLE TO HIS CAMPAIGN.

"Hooray, hooray, Herb Hoover's gone away,
Hooray, hooray, I hope he's gone to stay,
For now I'm back to work and get my three
    squares every day,
That's why I'm voting for Roosevelt.

They tell us Mr. Landon is a very clever gent,
He kids them out in Kansas though he never spends
    a cent.
But Willie Hearst and Standard Oil are coughing
    up his rent,
That's why I'm voting for Roosevelt."

The enthusiastic Democrats renominated Roosevelt by acclamation and endorsed John N. Garner again for the second place.

The President arrived in Philadelphia the same evening to accept the nomination. Under the starlit skies at Franklin Field, his voice, carried by loudspeakers, filled every corner of the arena. "There is a mysterious cycle in human events," he said. "To some generations much is given. Of other generations much is expected. This generation of Americans has a rendezvous with destiny.

"In this world of ours in other lands there are some people who, in times past, have lived and fought for freedom, and seem to have grown too weary to carry on the fight. They have sold their heritage of freedom for the illusion of a living. They have yielded their democracy."

The moon shone brightly over the field, filled with a hundred thousand people, while millions of Americans listened to the President's voice at their radios. "I believe in my heart that only our success can stir their ancient hope. They begin to know that here in America we are waging a great and successful war. It is not alone a war against want and destitution and economic demoralization. It is more than that; it is a war for the survival of democracy.

607

FRANKLIN D. ROOSEVELT WAS THE DARLING OF THE PRESS PHOTOGRAPHERS. HIS ANIMATED

We are fighting to save a great, a precious form of government for ourselves and for the world."

The President spoke eloquently of America, which had shaken off the power of royalists in politics, but he stated that "new kingdoms were built upon concentration of control over material things." The power to give or refuse jobs, the power to charge high or low prices, the power to permit or block new competing firms —these were the powers of "economic royalists."

Besides Roosevelt and Landon, a host of lesser candidates were in the field. The Union party named William Lemke, Representative from North Dakota, a sponsor of Federal legislation to shield mortgaged farms from foreclosure. Lemke was supported by Father Charles E. Coughlin, the leading spirit of the Native Union for Social Justice, and by Dr. Francis E.

Townsend, the advocate of Federal pensions for the aged. The Socialist party rallied behind Norman Thomas, the Communists behind Earl Browder, the Socialist-Labor party behind John W. Aiken, and the Prohibitionists behind David L. Colvin.

The orators of the smaller parties attacked the President as a conservative and denounced Landon as a reactionary. The Socialists exclaimed that "the New Deal, like the Old Deal, has utterly failed"; the Unionists asked the voters to "defeat the growing forces of fascism and reaction"; and the Communist rallying cry was "Defeat the forces of Wall Street."

In both the Republican and the Democratic ranks many prominent men crossed party lines. Alfred E. Smith "took a walk" from the Democratic convention and came out for the Republican nominee. He, together with Herbert

ESSIVE FACE MADE IT ALMOST IMPOSSIBLE TO TAKE AN UNINTERESTING PICTURE OF HIM.

Hoover, John W. Davis, William Randolph Hearst, and others, was a member of the Liberty League, an anti-New Deal organization which came into being in August, 1934, under an executive board of millionaires to oppose "the caprice of bureaucracy" and the "tyranny of autocratic power." Bainbridge Colby, Wilsons' Secretary of State, declared that the Roosevelt administration would nullify the Constitution, and charged that it was linked with men of communistic leanings. Former Senator Reed of Missouri called a conference of "Jeffersonian Democrats" to Detroit, which issued a declaration against the Roosevelt ticket without outspokenly endorsing Landon.

Among Republicans, Senator Norris divorced himself from his party and received his renomination as an independent. Senator La Follette endorsed Roosevelt, as did Senator Couzens of Michigan, while Senator Borah said nothing about supporting Landon.

Labor leaders, siding with John L. Lewis, promoted the formation of a body called Labor's Non-Partisan League, which campaigned for Roosevelt's re-election, though the AFL declared that it would "adhere to a non-partisan policy."

The Republicans presented Landon to the nation as a plain country boy, with a good heart and an honest purpose, who was to save the country from the anti-business and pro-radical Roosevelt. They hoped that under his leadership the New Deal would be abandoned and the nation would return to the *laissez-faire* philosophy of past governments. Their slogan was "Life, Liberty, and Landon," their emblem the sunflower—the state flower of Kansas. (At Tiffany's one could buy a nineteen-petal gold

609

A CHARACTERISTIC GESTURE, made during Roosevelt's Madison Square Garden speech—last of the 1936 campaign—in which he said that he welcomed the hatred of those who favored government by organized money.

JOHN L. LEWIS, the head of the United Mine Workers, gave Roosevelt both moral and financial support in 1936.

sunflower set with yellow diamonds for $815.) To the tune of "Oh, Susanna," they sang lustily:

"The alphabet we'll always have
but one thing sure is true,
With Landon in the New Deal's out
and that means P.D.Q.
Alf Landon learned a thing or two,
he knows the right solution,
And in the White House he will stay
within the Constitution."

Landon's colorless personality was no match for Roosevelt's. The "silent Coolidge from Kansas" was no spellbinder, but a quiet and pleasant person who thought that the President was a "very fine, charming gentleman." Yet as the campaign progressed, Landon's softness toward his adversary changed. Persuaded by his advisers, he reverted to the traditional method of slugging it out with his opponent, hurling charges of "willful waste" of the taxpayers' money and "strangling of free enterprise" against the Roosevelt administration. The relief and reform projects of the New Deal were heavily criticized and derided as mere "boondoggling" and "leaf-raking."

At the Democratic state convention in Syracuse, Roosevelt hit back against his opponent: "Let me warn you and let me warn the nation against the smooth evasion which says: 'Of course we believe in all these things; we believe in social security; we believe in work for the unemployed; we believe in all these things; but we do not like the way the present administration is doing them. Just turn them over to us. We will do all of them, we will do more of them, we will do them better; and most importantly of all, the doing of them will not cost anybody anything. . . .'

"You cannot," continued Roosevelt, "be an Old Guard Republican in the East and a New Deal Republican in the West. You cannot promise to repeal taxes before one audience and promise to spend more of the taxpayers' money before another audience. . . . Who is there in America who believes that we can run the risk of turning back our government to the old leadership which brought it to the brink of 1933?"

The President was cheered by huge audiences

THE PRESIDENT AND HIS MOTHER, Mrs. Sara D. Roosevelt, go to the polls at Hyde Park. Like her husband —a good Union Democrat—Mrs. Roosevelt took a great interest in politics, supporting the Democratic party. There was a close relationship between mother and son, but as Eleanor Roosevelt recalls, "if they were left together by themselves for very long they often disagreed. Those two were too much alike . . . to be left long alone."

wherever he spoke. He was at the height of his popularity. In Farley's opinion "he was more popular than the New Deal itself."

But while the people acclaimed Roosevelt, the majority of the newspapers assailed him. In this election he had the support of only 36 per cent of the nation's press. William Randolph Hearst, one of the leaders in the anti-Roosevelt crusade, asserted in a signed editorial that the President's "Communist entourage," consisting of Felix Frankfurter, Donald Richberg, Rexford Tugwell, Frances Perkins, and Henry Wallace, was sufficient proof of Roosevelt's radicalism. A Hearst jingle ran:

"The Red New Deal with a Soviet seal
Endorsed by a Moscow hand;
The strange result of an alien cult
In a liberty-loving land."

CONGRATULATIONS poured in after Roosevelt carried forty-six of the forty-eight states in a landslide.

The Chicago *Tribune* headlined: "Moscow Orders Reds in U.S. to Back Roosevelt," and asked for volunteers to help Landon's cause: "Be a volunteer in the great fight to save the nation!" A Roosevelt victory would mean "Moscow in the White House." This inspired Gail Borden to write in the Chicago *Times:*

"There was a young man from Topeka,
Whose campaign grew weaker and weaker,
Till the volunteers came
And made every old dame
A bellringer, singer or speaker."

Still, the New York *Times* came out for Roosevelt—the newspaper's "reasoned choice"—since Landon offered little but a second-hand New Deal, blighted by his party's traditional isolationism. On the other hand, the President, who was very perceptive of public opinion, would "provide insurance against radicalism of the sort which the United States has most to fear."

In the final weeks the presidential battle, as reported by *Time* Magazine, "had demonstrated to what depths of inanity, bad taste, and downright dishonesty American politics can descend. Normally intelligent men charged Roosevelt and Landon with fascism, communism, nazism—even with belief in bigamy. Leaders like Alfred E. Smith, Hugh Johnson, Harold Ickes, Father Coughlin, Herbert Hoover and Ogden Mills resorted to accusations that even politicians try to avoid."

The Republican National Committee, in a last-minute effort, made an all-out offensive against Roosevelt's Social Security Act. Circulars were distributed throughout the industrial sections warning the workers against the bill, which was to call for a 1 per cent deduction from wages and salaries. The leaflets omitted to mention that the money would be used to finance old-age pensions for workers and that employers must also put in 1 per cent, and they failed to say that employers alone would bear the cost of a complementary system of unemployment insurance. The chairman of the Republican National Committee, John Hamilton, declared in a radio address that the Social Security Act would require every worker to wear a number tag around his neck.

Roosevelt's anger was thoroughly roused. He devoted a great part of his final Madison Square Garden address to a defense of Social Security, pointing out that seventy-seven Republican members of the House voted for the act, and only eighteen against it, while in the Senate fifteen Republican Senators voted for Social Security and only five against it. In this speech Roosevelt declared: "Never before in all our history have these forces been so united against one candidate as they stand today. They are unanimous in their hate for me—and I welcome their hatred. I should like to have it said of my first administration that in it the forces of selfishness and of lust for power met their match. I should like to have it said of my second administration that in it these forces met their master."

Roosevelt's re-election was certain, though the *Literary Digest* poll predicted that Landon would be the winner with 370 electoral votes to Roosevelt's 161. The Gallup Poll made a better guess of 389 votes for Roosevelt and 141 for Landon.

Both polls were off the mark. Roosevelt won with 523 electoral votes from forty-six states while, as Farley correctly predicted, only Maine and Vermont with eight electoral votes were in Landon's column. The President's popular plurality was nearly five million larger than in 1932. In Congress the Democrats increased their number in the House to 333 seats against the Republicans' 103, and in the Senate to 75 seats against the Republicans' 17.

At the time Roosevelt took the oath—the inauguration was now held on January 20, the date having been changed by the Twentieth Amendment ratified February 6, 1933—the New York *Times* compared the country's situation with that of four years before. Comparative figures showed that on the stock markets an average of fifty stocks stood at 141.24 while in 1933 they stood at 50.5. The price of May wheat was now $1.30 and that of hogs $10, while four years before, May wheat was quoted at only 48⅞ cents a bushel and hogs at $4. Carloading in 1937 was 96.8 per cent of normal; in 1933 it was 52 per cent. Steel production in 1937 was 80 per cent, in 1933 only 16.9 per cent, and so forth. The nation, in the opinion of that newspaper, had made an amazing recovery under Roosevelt.

612

ANUARY 20, 1937: "Here is the challenge to our democracy. In this nation I see tens of millions of its citizens
.. who at this very moment are denied the greater part of . . . the necessities of life. I see millions of families trying
o live on incomes so meager that the pall of family disaster hangs over them day by day. I see millions whose daily
ives in city and on farm continue under conditions labeled indecent by a so-called polite society half a century ago.
. . I see millions lacking the means to buy the products of farm and factory and by their poverty denying work and
roductiveness to many other millions. I see one-third of a nation ill-housed, ill-clad, ill-nourished. It is not in
lespair that I paint you that picture. I paint it for you in hope—because the nation, seeing and understanding the
njustice in it, proposes to paint it out."

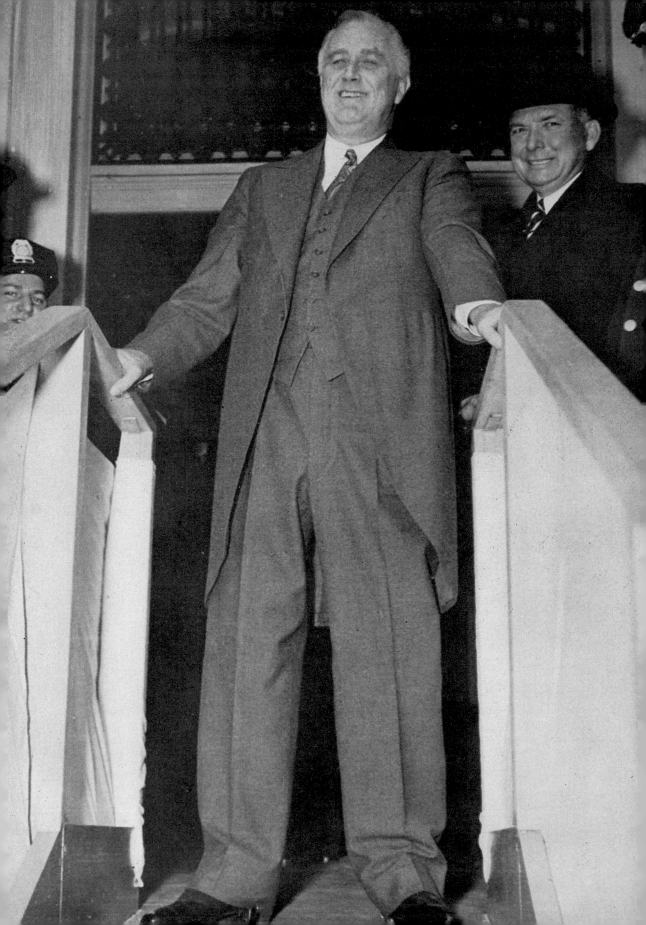

THE FIRST THIRD-TERM PRESIDENT

THE THIRTY-NINTH ELECTION—1940

FRANKLIN D. ROOSEVELT

Franklin D. Roosevelt entered his second term with the determination to continue his fight for social progress. To the new Congress he proposed measures to improve the economic status of the farmers and better the condition of the workers; he asked for legislation to aid the ill-housed, ill-clad and ill-nourished; he suggested the application of the TVA idea to the nation's six major regions, and demanded a thorough governmental reorganization.

The small Republican minority on Capitol Hill was ineffective in its opposition to the New Deal. Hence the grumbling adversaries of Roosevelt began to look wistfully toward the Supreme Court, where the "Nine Old Men" sat in their ivory tower, seemingly oblivious of the far-reaching social changes which the majority of the American people had endorsed in the elections of 1932, 1934, and 1936, and dreamed of the "good old days" of the "horse and buggy era."

During 1935 and 1936 the Supreme Court invalidated some of the key legislation of the New Deal. It rejected the NRA and the AAA, it overthrew the Railroad Retirement Plan, the Bituminous Coal Act, the protection of farm mortgages, the Municipal Bankruptcy Act. Sometimes the acts were thrown out on narrow technical grounds, or as one of the justices put it, through a "tortured construction of the Constitution."

Roosevelt was in a difficult position. In his opinion, "the language and the temper of the decisions indicated little hope for the future." If the Supreme Court should continue to cast doubts on "the ability of the elected Congress to protect us against catastrophe by meeting squarely our modern social and economic conditions," and to invalidate all the liberal legislation, his administration would accomplish little. If the Court should hand down decisions against the National Labor Relations Act or the Social Security Act, it would mean the end of the New Deal.

The President felt that the Court was out of step with the times. A phalanx of four conservative justices—McReynolds, Van Devanter, Sutherland, and Butler—blocked all reform proposals. So Roosevelt decided to do something about it. Taking the issue to the people, he pointed out that until his first term "practically every President of the United States had ap-

THE CANDIDATES

FRANKLIN D. ROOSEVELT
(1882-1945) was chosen by the Democratic party to run for a precedent-breaking third term. During the campaign he solemnly promised to keep the United States out of foreign wars. Roosevelt won the election with 449 electoral votes to Willkie's eighty-two.

HENRY AGARD WALLACE
(1883-19—), Secretary of Agriculture, was Roosevelt's choice for the vice-presidential office. After a bitter struggle, the Democratic convention half-heartedly accepted the champion of the "common man." He replaced conservative anti-New Dealer, John N. Garner.

WENDELL L. WILLKIE
(1892-1944), utilities executive and successful corporation lawyer, swept the Republican convention when it became evident that neither Dewey nor Taft had enough support to win the nomination. He assailed FDR in the campaign but endorsed most New Deal reforms.

CHARLES L. MC NARY
(1874-1944), minority leader of the Senate, was chosen by the Republicans for the Vice-Presidency. The direct antithesis of Wendell Willkie, McNary was an extreme isolationist and advocate of high tariffs, who drew his support chiefly from the conservative ranks.

pointed at least one member of the Supreme Court. President Taft appointed five members and named a Chief Justice; President Wilson three; President Harding four, including a Chief Justice; President Coolidge one; President Hoover three, including a Chief Justice." It was only he—Roosevelt—who during his entire first administration had no opportunity to make a single appointment. "Chance and the disinclination of the individuals to leave the Supreme Bench have now given us a Court in which five justices will be over seventy-five years of age before next June and one over seventy."

THE VOTES IN THE 1940 ELECTION

STATES	POPULAR VOTE		ELECTORAL VOTE	
	F. D. Roosevelt, Democrat.	W. Willkie, Republican.	Roosevelt and Wallace.	Willkie and McNary.
Alabama	250,726	42,184	11	—
Arizona	95,267	54,030	3	—
Arkansas	158,622	42,121	9	—
California	1,877,618	1,351,419	22	—
Colorado	265,554	279,576	—	6
Connecticut	417,621	361,819	8	—
Delaware	74,599	61,440	3	—
Florida	359,334	126,158	7	—
Georgia	265,194	23,934	12	—
Idaho	127,842	106,553	4	—
Illinois	2,149,934	2,047,240	29	—
Indiana	874,063	899,466	—	14
Iowa	578,800	632,370	—	11
Kansas	364,725	489,169	—	9
Kentucky	557,222	410,384	11	—
Louisiana	319,751	52,446	10	—
Maine	156,478	163,951	—	5
Maryland	384,546	269,534	8	—
Massachusetts	1,076,522	939,700	17	—
Michigan	1,032,991	1,039,917	—	19
Minnesota	644,196	596,274	11	—
Mississippi	168,267	2,814	9	—
Missouri	958,476	871,009	15	—
Montana	145,698	99,579	4	—
Nebraska	263,677	352,201	—	7
Nevada	31,945	21,229	3	—
New Hampshire	125,292	110,127	4	—
New Jersey	1,016,808	945,475	16	—
New Mexico	103,699	79,315	3	—
New York	3,251,918	3,027,478	47	—
North Carolina	609,015	213,633	13	—
North Dakota	124,036	154,590	—	4
Ohio	1,733,139	1,586,773	26	—
Oklahoma	474,313	348,872	11	—
Oregon	258,415	219,555	5	—
Pennsylvania	2,171,035	1,889,848	36	—
Rhode Island	182,182	138,653	4	—
South Carolina	95,470	1,727	8	—
South Dakota	131,362	177,065	—	4
Tennessee	351,601	169,153	11	—
Texas	840,151	199,152	23	—
Utah	154,277	93,151	4	—
Vermont	64,269	78,371	—	3
Virginia	235,961	109,363	11	—
Washington	462,145	322,123	8	—
West Virginia	495,662	372,414	8	—
Wisconsin	704,821	679,206	12	—
Wyoming	59,287	52,633	3	—
	27,243,466	22,304,755	449	82

Thomas, Socialist, 99,557; Browder, Communist, 46,251; Babson Prohibitionist, 57,812; Aiken, Socialist-Labor, 14,861; other, 48,610 Total vote, 49,815,312.

ROOSEVELT BELIEVED THAT HOPKINS could succeed him in the Presidency. Building him up for the job, FDR posed with him for news pictures and watched over his health. However, after Hitler overran the Lowlands and marched into France, and the English suffered serious reverses in the war, Roosevelt felt that he should remain in office and do his part to defeat fascism. So in the spring of 1940 he made up his mind to seek a third term.

Therefore he proposed a plan to infuse the Court with younger blood. If a judge over seventy years old and serving longer than ten years failed to retire, a new judge was to be appointed. The number of new appointees would be limited to six, so the maximum possible number would never be more than fifteen. Pleading for his plan, Roosevelt pointed out that it was not an unusual one; neither was it against the Constitution. The number of justices had been changed several times before in the administrations of John Adams, Thomas Jefferson, Andrew Jackson, Abraham Lincoln, and Ulysses Grant.

A tremendous outcry followed the proposal, for the political passions of the people were roused. During the next five months—from February, 1937, when Roosevelt first submitted his proposal, until June—in Congress and out, the plan was fervently debated. The President was accused of "packing" the Court and of trying to take control of it; he was assailed as a dictator who wanted to kill constitutional government in the United States and to destroy the independence of the judicial branch. The committee on the judiciary, to which the bill was referred, called Roosevelt's proposal "an invasion of judicial power such as has never before been attempted in this country."

Public opinion, fomented by constant agitation of the anti-Roosevelt groups, crystallized against the proposal; but a far greater influence in defeating the President's plan than all the arguments against it was the sudden change of

THE ROOSEVELT CHARM

HANDSHAKE WITH SENATOR GEORGE, a New Deal adversary whom FDR opposed in the 1938 primaries. But his efforts to "purge" his Southern opponents failed.

HANDSHAKE WITH DR. CARVER, noted Negro scientist, during Roosevelt's visit to Tuskegee Institute where George Washington Carver was a member of the faculty.

HANDSHAKE WITH JIM FARLEY in the summer of 1939, when the chairman of the Democratic National Committee hoped that he might become FDR's successor.

the Court's attitude, resulting in the reversal of its opinions in a number of cases. The Minimum Wage Law of the State of Washington was sustained, although previously a similar measure had been held unconstitutional in the State of New York. A revised Farm Mortgage Act, a new Railway Labor Act, provisions of the National Labor Relations Act, and the all-important Social Security legislation were sanctioned. "A switch in time saves nine," said the jokesters.

In the end Roosevelt had to shelve his Supreme Court plan, and his enemies declared that the President had suffered the greatest defeat of his career; but to an impartial observer Roosevelt's "defeat" looked more like a victory. True, he lost his battle, but he won what he was after. During the controversy the Supreme Court committed itself to the New Deal position.

This was not the only political upheaval of the second term. Others followed in its wake. In August, 1937—after government expenditures for relief and recovery were curtailed because of constant criticism from business and finance—a new business slump began and lasted for more than a year. The critics of the New Deal dubbed it the "Roosevelt Depression," but in the opinion of the neutral London *Economist* it was brought about, not so much by Roosevelt as by the American business classes, who "worked themselves into such a lather of hatred" against the administration that their fury "was choking the whole industrial and financial machine."

As unemployment increased and wages declined, the mood of the workers became threatening. A census in 1937 showed that eleven million people were without work and another 5½ million only partially employed. During this year more than five thousand strikes flared up. There was a serious struggle within the ranks of labor as well. The newly founded Committee for Industrial Organization (CIO) under the leadership of John L. Lewis proposed the unionization of industries as units, and not according to specific trades or skills, thus opposing the principles of the American Federation of Labor. The efforts of the CIO to organize the steel, automobile, and textile industries met with determined opposition. Sitdown strikes became a new feature of the American scene.

Yet the political picture was not all black. Bills for slum clearance and construction of low-cost housing were passed by Congress; a new Farm Security Administration, aiming to ease the plight of the farmers, was created. But the most outstanding New Deal measures which Congress introduced in 1938 were the new Agricultural Adjustment Act and the Fair Labor Standards Act.

The Agricultural Adjustment Act authorized the Secretary of Agriculture to determine the acreage to be planted in crops (if two thirds of the farmers involved agreed), and to establish marketing controls over the surplus crops. It instituted a "parity payments" system whereby producers of corn, wheat, cotton, tobacco, and rice were subsidized; it proposed soil conservation measures; it provided loans for surplus crops and plans for storage. The new AAA was an impressive success; within a year the cash income of the farmers more than doubled.

The Fair Labor Standards Act, which was hailed by Roosevelt as "the most far-reaching, far-sighted program for the benefit of workers ever adopted in this or any other country," provided for an ultimate maximum working week of forty hours, and a minimum wage of forty cents an hour for all workers producing goods for interstate commerce.

With these two major acts the domestic program of the New Deal was completed.

As the time of the congressional election of 1938 approached, Roosevelt prepared to take a stand against those Senators who were most recalcitrant toward the basic measures of the New Deal. He would not support the conservatives in his own party who persistently hampered his domestic program. He entered the Democratic primary campaign—not as President, but as the head of his party—endorsing the candidates who supported the New Deal, opposing those who were against it. He spoke in Kentucky on behalf of Senator Barkley, in Maryland on behalf of Davey John Lewis and against Senator Tydings, in Georgia for Lawrence Camp and against Senator George, in South Carolina for Governor Olin Johnston and against Senator "Cotton Ed" Smith, in New York against John O'Connor.

Roosevelt's interference in the Southern primaries met with strong criticism in and out of his party. He was compared to dictators who "purged" their enemies, though what he did was simply to appeal to the voters in a thoroughly democratic way, using the methods of persuasion rather than force. Great was the rejoicing in the anti-Roosevelt camp, however, when the President's efforts failed and Tydings, George, and "Cotton Ed" Smith were re-elected to the Senate.

As time went by and the election year of 1940 rolled around, all the domestic issues diminished in importance. The questions uppermost in the minds of the people were: Will America enter the war? Will it fight the Nazis? Will it help Britain?

For the anarchical conditions in Europe and the Far East the United States was not without blame. In the years after the First World War, a disillusioned America retreated into the seemingly secure shell of isolationism. With the most powerful country remaining outside the League of Nations, collective security became unworkable. Without an effective organization to block them, the aggressor countries overran their weaker neighbors.

In 1931 Japan invaded Manchuria and set up a puppet state. In 1935, under orders from Mussolini, Italian armies battled their way through Ethiopia. The year 1936 saw the beginning of the Spanish Civil War—that bloody rehearsal of the world conflagration—with one side supplied by Russian arms and the other strengthened by Nazi equipment. In 1937 Japan plunged the Far East into prolonged hostilities, battling the Chinese and subjugating much of their land. In 1939 Hitler overran Czechoslovakia; and in August of that year he signed a non-aggression pact with Russia—the prelude to the Second World War.

President Roosevelt realized that these moves were a grave menace to United States security. As early as October, 1937, he sounded a warning. "It seems to be unfortunately true that the epidemic of world lawlessness is spreading," he said in Chicago. "When an epidemic of physical disease starts to spread, the community approves and joins in a quarantine of the patients in order to protect the health of the community against the spread of the disease."

But Roosevelt's quarantine speech failed to rouse the country. The isolationists derided him as an alarmist. Senator Borah assured the nation as late as July, 1939, that according to his information there would not be a war in Europe. A month later the armies of the "master race" were on the march.

On September 21, 1939, Roosevelt called Congress into special session and asked for a revised Neutrality Act,* which would permit the U.S. to sell arms and other implements of war to such nations as were able to pay for them in cash and carry them away in foreign-registered ships—a proposal clearly benefiting Britain. The President also urged Congress to adopt a conscription law and not rely on raising an army on a voluntary basis.

These measures divided the American people into two opposing groups. The isolationists admonished the President to keep out of European affairs and not lead the nation into a war. The interventionists, though they too desired to avoid war, held that if Hitler and Mussolini were not checked, the U.S. would be their next victim, and that only by helping the democracies in Europe to defeat the totalitarian states could America avoid ultimate attack. William Allen White's Committee to Defend America by Aiding the Allies roused the conscience of the people to help Britain, while the America First Committee, its ranks swelled by Anglophobes, anti-Semites, conservatives and reactionaries of all sorts, preached pacifism and isolationism.

Against this political background and with the shadows of war lengthening over the United States, the nominating conventions met.

The Republican gains in the midterm election of 1938 raised the hopes of the GOP candidates who lined up for the contest. The favorite

* The first Neutrality Act to prevent American participation in any foreign war was passed in August, 1935, after the Italo-Ethiopian conflict. A year later the Act was strengthened by a clause which prohibited loans to the belligerents. In January, 1937, a further resolution forbade the export of munitions to either of the opposing forces in the Spanish Civil War. In May the earlier Neutrality Acts were again changed, giving the President larger discretionary powers. The great omission of the Neutrality Act was the failure to distinguish between aggressor and victim nations, thus inadvertently helping the former.

620

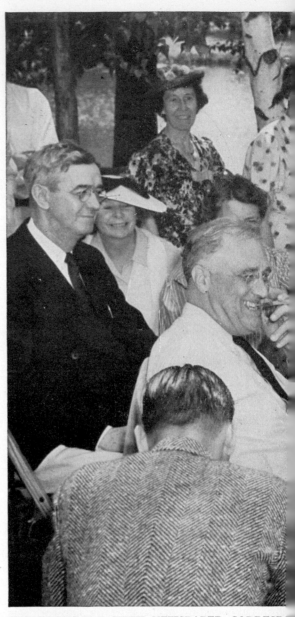

THE PRESIDENT WITH NEWSPAPER CORRESP(

Ever since Roosevelt took the oath a second time, news papermen had wanted to know whether he would rur for a third term. When early in 1937 Robert Post of the

among them was New York's energetic and ambitious gang-busting District Attorney. Thomas Edmund Dewey. His narrow defeat by Governor Herbert Lehman in the last gubernatorial election had proved him a vigorous campaigner and an efficient vote-getter Dewey's closest rival for the nomination wa:

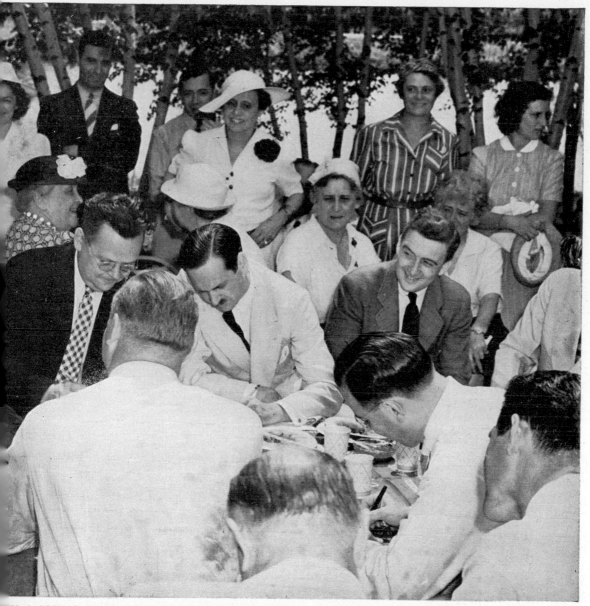

IN A JOVIAL MOOD AT A FOURTH OF JULY PRESS CONFERENCE ON THE LAWN AT HYDE PARK.

New York *Times* fired the question at the President, Roosevelt answered: "Bob Post should put on a dunce cap and stand in the corner." Two years later, in the sum-

mer of 1939 when the above press conference was held, FDR told Farley: "Of course I will not run for a third term." In 1940 the world crisis made him change his mind.

the Ohio Senator, Robert Alphonso Taft, a brilliant lawyer and one of the sons of the twenty-seventh President, while the third favorite was the Michigan Senator, Arthur H. Vandenberg.

Other names mentioned for the nomination were ex-President Hoover; the New York pub-

lisher, Frank Gannett; the energetic president of the Commonwealth and Southern utilities company, Wendell L. Willkie; Supreme Court Justices Harlan Stone and Owen Roberts; and Ohio's Governor John Bricker. And as usual many states offered their favorite sons. Pennsylvania upheld Governor Arthur H. James;

THE CHIEF REPUBLICAN CONTENDERS

THOMAS EDMUND DEWEY (born in 1902), the favorite candidate, went into the convention with 360 to 400 pledged votes. Dewey's career began when he prosecuted New York's gangsters, thus winning national fame. In 1938 he ran for Governor of New York and was narrowly defeated, but his vote-getting ability made him a strong contender for the Republican nomination.

ROBERT ALPHONSO TAFT (born in 1889), Senator from Ohio and son of President Taft, was another strong contender for the Republican nomination. Taft's conservative and often stubbornly erroneous stands on important issues earned him the enmity of the liberal wing, but he was backed by many Republicans who admired his forthright character and his capacity for hard work.

Rhode Island was behind Governor William H. Vanderbilt; Massachusetts named Joseph W. Martin; Oregon supported Senator Charles L. McNary; Iowa rallied behind Hanford Mac-Nider; New Hampshire presented Styles Bridges.

On the day the Republican convention assembled in Philadelphia—two days after France signed the armistice with Germany—Dewey was clearly in the lead with 350 to 400 delegates pledged to him, followed closely by Taft, who hoped to rally 300 votes on the first ballot. But during the months preceding the convention, the political outsider Wendell Willkie, a Wall Street lawyer and utilities executive, had gained

support. "Willkie for President" and "Win with Willkie" clubs mushroomed all over the country. Amateur politicians like Russell Davenport and Oren Root, Jr., conducted a well-organized campaign for Willkie, aided by the publicity director for the Committee of Utility Executives and other prominent advertising men. Henry Luce, with his magazines, was in this group, as were other newspaper publishers, and there were rumors that the House of Morgan had made large investments in the "spontaneous" campaign.

The last Gallup poll, taken shortly before the convention, gave Dewey 47 per cent and Willkie only 29 per cent support. But the New

ARTHUR HENDRICK VANDENBERG (born in 1884), Senator from Michigan, had a good chance to be nominated in case of a Dewey-Taft deadlock. Vandenberg was elected to the Senate in 1928, and was the only Republican Senator to keep his seat in the Democratic landslide of 1934. A staunch isolationist as late as 1939, he revised his opinions when the U.S. entered the war.

WENDELL LEWIS WILLKIE (born in 1892), Wall Street lawyer and utilities executive who voted Democratic as late as 1938, was a newcomer in the political arena. Backed by amateurs, idealists, newspaper publishers and some astute big businessmen, his star rose rapidly. He kept himself in the news by writing articles, speaking on the radio and giving numerous interviews.

York *Times* knew better. Its headlines read: "Willkie Is Called the Man to Beat" and "Willkie Chief Fear of Dewey Backers."

The Republicans adopted a platform which an eminent historian called "a masterpiece of equivocation, evasion, ambiguity and generalization," with a straddling foreign policy plank pledging the country to "Americanism, preparedness and peace," and promising the democratic victims of aggression "such aid as shall not be in violation of international law or inconsistent with the requirements of our own national defense." After the platform was adopted, the nominating speeches began, lasting for two full days. During this time the

managers of the candidates were in steady consultation with delegates, giving and exacting promises and making deals.

A day before the balloting started, two notable recruits joined the Willkie group: Representative Frank O. Horton of Wyoming, and keynoter of the convention Harold Stassen, thirty-three-year-old Governor of Minnesota, who now became Willkie's floor manager. They and the other Willkie men buttonholed delegates, asking for their support. Willkie himself campaigned actively. In a hotel corridor he approached Jim Watson, the old "standpatter" from Indiana, and this is how Watson recalled their conversation:

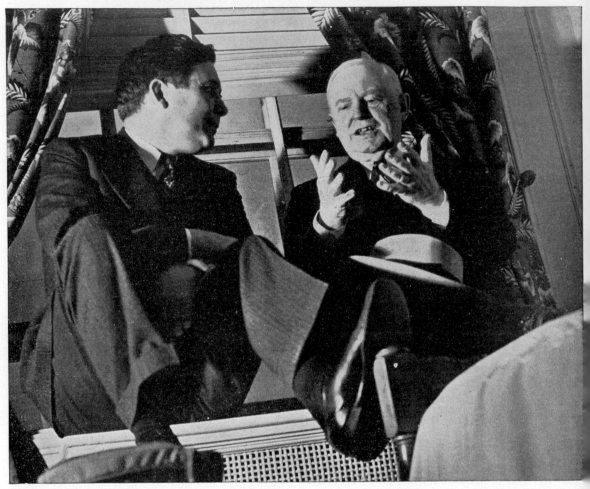

AT WILLKIE'S HEADQUARTERS, the night before his nomination, the Republican contender talks to William A. White, editor of the Emporia *Gazette*. It was chiefly because of White's efforts that Kansas voted for Willkie.

PLEADING FOR VOTES. Keynoter Harold E. Stassen, who became Willkie's floor manager at the convention, confers with Alf Landon, head of the Kansas delegation.

"Jim, couldn't you be for me?" asked Willkie.

"No, Wendell, you're just not my kind of Republican."

"I admit I used to be a Democrat."

"Used to be?" snapped Watson.

"You're a good Methodist," replied Willkie. "Don't you believe in conversion?"

"Yes, Wendell. If a fancy woman truly repented and wanted to join my church, I'd welcome her. I would greet her personally and lead her up the aisle to a front pew. But by the Eternal, I wouldn't ask her to lead the choir!"

Willkie had the last word: "Aw, Jim, you just go to hell!"

On the first ballot Dewey led with 360 votes against 189 for Taft, 105 for Willkie, and 7

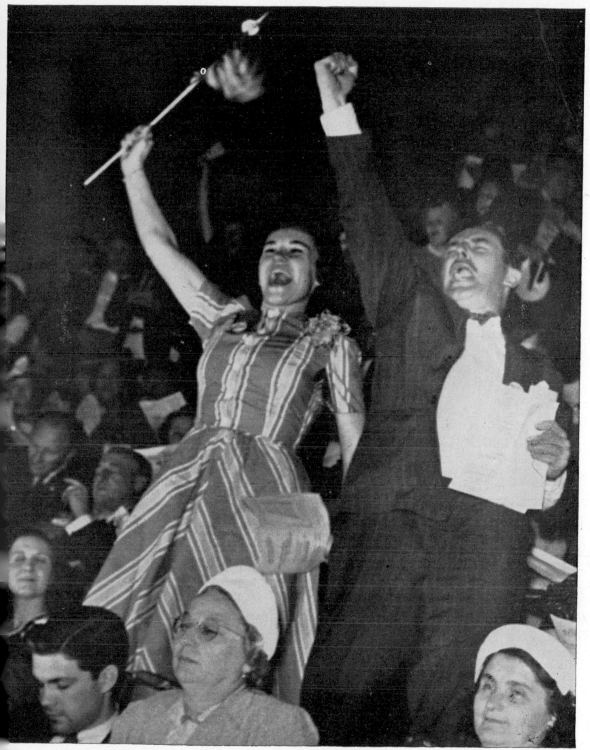

WO YOUNG PEOPLE IN THE GALLERY JOYFULLY ACCLAIM THE NOMINATION OF WILLKIE.

for Vandenberg. On the second trial it became apparent that the Dewey boom was over. His vote declined to 338, Taft's increased to 203, Willkie's to 171. On the next ballot Willkie overtook Taft. On this trial Dewey had 315 votes, Willkie 259, Taft 212. The fourth ballot saw Willkie in the lead with 306 votes against Dewey's 250 and Taft's 245.

While the voting proceeded, the galleries chanted "We want Willkie," and thousands of letters and telegrams urged the delegates to vote for Willkie.

On the fifth ballot Willkie's lead increased to 429 votes. (Persuaded by William Allen White, all the Kansas delegates voted for him on this trial.) Taft's strength grew to 377. (He now received Arkansas and most of the Iowa votes, the latter released to him by MacNider.) If Joseph N. Pew, who controlled the majority of the Pennsylvania delegates, had switched to Taft at this point, the Willkie boom could have been stopped. (Pennsylvania was split—51 of its delegates voted for Governor Edward Martin, while the other 21 supported Willkie.)

After this trial was over, Governor Bricker of Ohio reached for a floor microphone, trying to propose a recess as a last stratagem to stem the Willkie tide. But before his voice could be heard, the chairman announced: "There being no majority, the convention will proceed with the sixth ballot." The hall was tense with excitement. All eyes were on the Michigan and Pennsylvania delegates. Which way would they swing? Until Michigan was called, Willkie gained 29 votes from the other states against 12 for Taft. Then Michigan, released from Vandenberg, threw its strength into the Willkie column. The roar from the galleries raised the roof. During the roll call the divided Pennsylvania delegates held a final caucus outside the hall. When they returned to the floor, Willkie already had 400 votes—two shy of the nomination. Now—shortly after midnight on June 27—Pennsylvania finally swung solidly behind Willkie.

The galleries shouted, danced, trampled, and went wild with joy. "Nothing exactly like it ever happened before in American politics," reported *Newsweek*. "Willkie had never held public office or even sought it. Virtually a neophyte in politics, he had entered no primaries, made no deals, organized no campaign. . . . His backers were uninitiated volunteers, as strange to the ways of ward bosses and state chairmen as their hero."

But the astute political analyst, Thomas L. Stokes, wrote in retrospect that Willkie's nomination was the "culmination of a coup by a strange combination of big-business backers who had financed a short but very effective propaganda campaign on his behalf, beginning only a few months before the convention, and zealous 'amateurs' as they were called, consisting of people all over the country who were weary of the old-type politicians and political hacks and wanted a new face and new blood. The influence this combination brought to bear on the convention bowled over experienced and practical politicians who were on the verge of putting over Senator Robert A. Taft of Ohio, after the early front-runner, Thomas E. Dewey, had wilted."

For Willkie's running mate the convention named his exact opposite in political thinking, the isolationist Senator from Missouri, Charles McNary. The choice was made in the hope that while Willkie would appeal to the liberal Republicans and the anti-Roosevelt New Dealers, McNary would rally the isolationists, the high tariff adherents, and the conservative elements.

Wendell Willkie appeared before the convention, pledging "a crusading, aggressive, fighting campaign." His supporters sang to music from Walt Disney's *Snow White:*

"Heigh-ho, heigh-ho, its back to work we go, With Wendell Willkie leading us the jobs will grow;
Heigh-ho, heigh-ho, heigh-ho,
We've all been feeling low,
But Willkie's hand will save the land,
Heigh-ho, heigh-ho."

With Willkie as the chosen Republican nominee, the country was asking, as it had asked for a long time: Will Roosevelt run for a third term? There was no official pronouncement about it, though Washington was buzzing with rumors that Roosevelt had made up his mind. Looking through the evidence which has come to light since Roosevelt's death, it seems that before the beginning of the European war the President was against a third term. He told Farley so in the summer of 1939. To reporters

SEPH W. MARTIN, PERMANENT CHAIRMAN, PRESENTS THE CHOSEN REPUBLICAN CANDIDATE.

WHEN CHAIRMAN ALBEN BARKLEY mentione
Franklin Roosevelt's name in the Democratic conventio
the delegates demonstrated for twenty-two minute

WHEN MAYOR KELLY gave the signal from the floor
of the convention, the voice of Thomas McGarry, his
superintendent of sewers, boomed from the loudspeakers,
calling out at intervals: "We want Roosevelt . . . The
world needs Roosevelt . . . Everybody wants Roosevelt!"

who asked him about it, his answer was: "Pu
on a dunce cap and stand in the corner." La
in 1939, discussing a problem with Corde
Hull, he said: "That is something the nex
President will have to worry about, and th
will be you, Cordell." The Hopkins papers r
veal that Roosevelt was seriously thinking o
supporting Harry Hopkins as his successo
And when Farley asked Roosevelt whether l
should file his own name in the Massachuset
and New Hampshire primaries, Roosevel
answer was: "Go ahead, Jim. The water's fin
I haven't an objection in the world."

Roosevelt promised Farley that he wou
issue a statement early in 1940, declining to ru
But some time later he said to his Postmast
General: "I could not issue that statement.
would have destroyed my effectiveness as tl

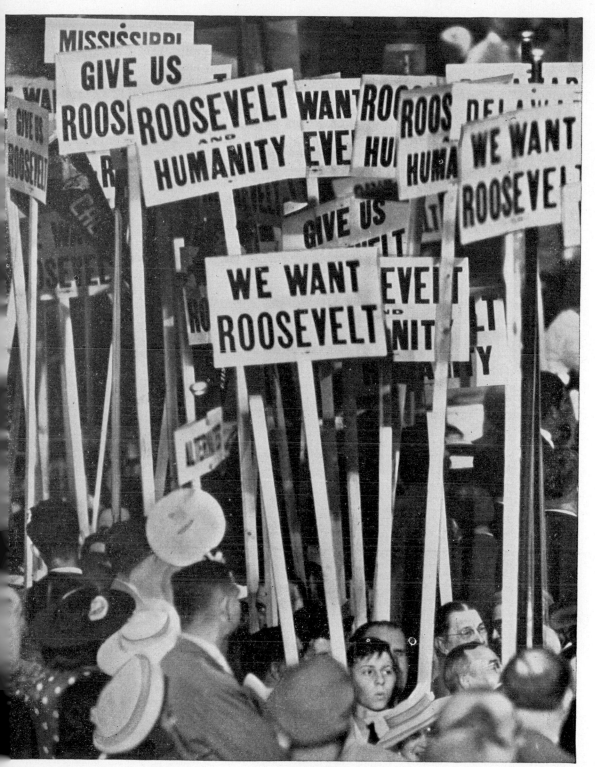

WHEN FDR'S NAME WAS PUT IN NOMINATION, THE DEMONSTRATION LASTED NEARLY AN HOUR.

leader of the nation in the efforts of this country to cope with the terrible catastrophe raging in Europe. To have issued such a statement would have nullified my position in the world and would have handicapped the efforts of this country to be of constructive service in the war crisis." The President also realized that to issue such a statement would have increased the difficulties in the Democratic ranks; a host of candidates, and their struggles against each other, would have brought the party to the brink of disaster.

It was the middle of May, after the Hitler hordes had overrun Holland, Belgium, and France, and after he was implored to remain at the helm of the nation and fight the fascist menace, when Roosevelt decided to run again. By then, even if he should have decided to retire, he could not have done so. There was no other candidate with whom the Democrats could have won. Neither Secretary of State

Cordell Hull, National Chairman James Farley Vice-President John N. Garner, Federal Security Administrator Paul McNutt, ex-Governor of Michigan Frank Murphy, Secretary of Agriculture Henry Wallace, Attorney General Robert Jackson, nor Justices Stanley Reed and William O. Douglas would have had the strength to defeat Willkie.

When the Democratic convention opened in Chicago on July 15, three fourths of the delegates were pledged to Roosevelt. Harry Hopkins, Roosevelt's unofficial representative, was in firm control of the situation. (From his bathroom in the Blackstone Hotel—the only place with privacy—he could talk on a private telephone line directly to the White House.) And when Senator Alben Barkley, in a fighting speech, first mentioned Roosevelt's name, Mayor Ed Kelly signaled to Thomas McGarry, his superintendent of sewers, and McGarry's voice, piped from a room beneath the audito-

THE FIGHT OVER THE VICE-PRESIDENCY

JAMES FARLEY, here talking to Senator Tydings, opposed Henry Wallace's candidacy for the Vice-Presidency. But Roosevelt insisted that it had to be Wallace.

HARRY HOPKINS, here talking to Clarence Cannon, worked for Wallace, persuading other candidates to withdraw. Under FDR's pressure, Wallace was accepted.

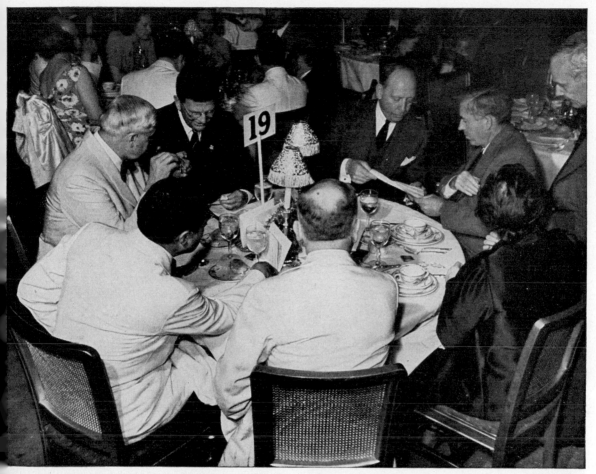

THE PARTY BOSSES SUPPORTED WALLACE. At a dinner given by Chicago's Mayor Kelly, the vice-presidential candidate had the most prominent party members at his table. From left to right, clockwise, are Mayor Kelly, Mayor Hague, Henry Wallace, Frances Perkins, Harold Ickes, Justice Robert Jackson and Jesse Jones.

rium, boomed from the loudspeakers: "We want Roosevelt. . . The world wants Roosevelt!" The "voice from the sewers," as it was dubbed later, continued to repeat the slogans for twenty-two minutes, after which the demonstration spent itself. Barkley concluded his speech with the long-awaited statement: "I and other close friends of the President have long known that he had not wished to be a candidate again. We knew, too, that in no way whatsoever has he exerted any influence in the selection of delegates, or upon the opinions of the delegates to this convention. The President has never had and has not today any desire or purpose to continue in the office of the President, to be a candidate for that office, or to be nomi-

LABOR LEADERS John L. Lewis and Philip Murray enjoy a joke with Henry A. Wallace, whose nomination for the Vice-Presidency was strongly backed by labor.

631

nated by the convention for that office. He wishes in all earnestness and sincerity to make it clear that all delegates to this convention are free to vote for any candidate. This is the message I bear to you from the President of the United States."

The organ played "Franklin D. Roosevelt Jones"; banner after banner was caught up and carried in the parade. The shouting and cheering increased and again, over the cries of the delegates, the thundering voice boomed at intervals: "The party wants Roosevelt. . . . New York wants Roosevelt. . . . Illinois wants Roosevelt. . . . The world needs Roosevelt. . . . Everybody wants Roosevelt!" The delegates tramped around the hall with banners and posters for fifty-three minutes.

The next day the platform was read by Senator Robert Wagner, pledging more help to "the land and the farmer," to "industry and worker," to "capital and the businessman." It

ROOSEVELT ADDRESSED the convention from Washington in the early hours of the morning. Accepting the nomination he said: "Today all private plans . . . have been repealed by an overriding public danger. In the face of that danger all those who can be of service to the republic have no choice but to offer themselves."

JAMES A. FARLEY, WHO WAS AGAINST A T

FOR ROOSEVELT, TELLS THE PRESS OF HIS RESIGNATION AS DEMOCRATIC NATIONAL CHAIRMAN.

promised an extension of the party's electric power program (providing cheaper electricity, with "vast economic benefits to thousands of homes and communities"), development of Western resources, war on unemployment, the extension of the social security system and health service, slum clearance and low-rent housing, consumer's protection against "unjustified price rises," an extension of the civil service, fair treatment of war veterans and their dependents, and "equal protection of the laws for every citizen, regardless of race, creed or color."

The platform-makers had a great debate over the party's foreign policy plank. The declaration, finally accepted by both the isolationist and interventionist factions, declared: "We will not participate in foreign wars, and we will not send our army, naval or air forces to fight in foreign lands outside of the Americas, except in case of attack. . . . In self-defense and in good conscience, the world's greatest democracy cannot afford heartlessly or in a spirit of appeasement to ignore the peace-loving and liberty-loving peoples wantonly attacked by ruthless aggressors. We pledge to extend to these peoples all the material aid at our command consistent with law and not inconsistent with the interests of our own national self-defense."

For the Democratic nomination the names of four candidates were presented. Those opposed to a third term for Roosevelt nominated James Farley, John N. Garner, and Millard Tydings. There was little excitement during the voting. Everyone knew that Roosevelt would win on the first ballot. He received 946 votes against Farley's 72, Garner's 61, and Tydings's nine. Cordell Hull, who was not an avowed candidate, had five votes.

Now came the great fight over the vice-presidential nomination. More than a dozen candidates vied for the office. When Roosevelt let it be known that he had chosen his Secretary of Agriculture, Henry A. Wallace, the delegates demurred at this "dictation" from the White House. Their main objection was that Henry Wallace had been a Republican as late as 1928. "For God's sake, just because the Republicans nominated an apostate Democrat for President, don't let us put one of those things over," said a delegate from Ohio.

634

WILLKIE RETURNS TO ELWOOD, INDIANA, W

DE HIS OFFICIAL ACCEPTANCE SPEECH ENDORSING MOST OF ROOSEVELT'S NEW DEAL POLICIES.

THE FIRST MAJOR ADDRESS. President Roosevelt opened his campaign for a precedent-breaking third term in Philadelphia on October 23. With great gusto he proclaimed: "I am an old campaigner and I love a good fight."

IN THE THIRD MAJOR SPEECH in Boston on October 30, the President declared: "I have said this before, but I shall say it again and again and again. Your boys are not going to be sent into foreign wars!"

Roosevelt told Farley some time before: "I think Henry is perfect. I like him. He's the kind of fellow I want around. He's honest. He thinks right. He's a digger." Farley argued with the President, telling him that Wallace was regarded as a mystic. Roosevelt snapped, "He is not a mystic. He is a philosopher. He's got ideas. He thinks right. He'll help the people think."

The President's attempt to force Wallace's nomination aroused such ill feeling that Barkley thought it wise to adjourn the afternoon session without letting the convention proceed with the nominating speeches. The recess gave Hopkins and the other Roosevelt men time to round up the necessary votes for Wallace.

While the quibbling and quarreling went on in Chicago, an angry and irritated Roosevelt

IN THE SECOND MAJOR SPEECH in New York on October 28, FDR answered Willkie's charges that America was "deficient in all items of defense—the airplanes, the guns, the tanks, and even the ability to make them."

IN HIS FOURTH SPEECH in Brooklyn on November 1, FDR took the offensive. "I am fighting against the revival of government by special privilege . . . vested in the hands of those who favor . . . foreign dictatorships."

THE LAST MAJOR SPEECH was delivered by Roosevelt in Cleveland, November 2. It was another fighting, vigorous appeal to the voters of the nation—one of the best and most rousing addresses of the entire campaign.

IMPERVIOUS TO HEAT

AWAITING HIS MASTER.

CHICAGO CONVENTION

FOUR CHARACTERISTIC CARTOONS OF THE 1940 PRESIDENTIAL CAMPAIGN DRAWN BY ROL

waited at the White House, "determined not to speak or address the convention unless and until the work of the convention has been completed," which meant until the Vice-President was nominated. He barked at Hopkins on the long-distance phone: "Well, damn it to hell, they will go for Wallace or I won't run, and you can jolly well tell them so." It was during these hours that Roosevelt prepared a speech refusing the nomination.

After the recess, the delegates gave vent to their feelings about the handpicked "Republican" vice-presidential candidate. "This is no rabbit convention," said a delegate from Missouri. "We want to carry Missouri in November, and we can't do it with a Republican. We want a Democrat for Vice-President to run with our Democratic President." Another man from Maryland asked for the nomination of Jesse Jones, who was a real Democrat—"and I think I know a Democrat when I see one."

To quell the ugly mood of the delegates, Mrs. Roosevelt flew to Chicago and made a gracious speech on Wallace's behalf. Farley, according to Mrs. Roosevelt's recollection, argued with the President on the phone against Wallace's nomination, but when he saw that Roosevelt was adamant, he gave in: "You're the boss. If you say so, I will do all I can to nominate Wallace. . . ." Farley worked fast. The nomination of the Secretary of Agriculture was supported by the party bosses of New York, New Jersey, Illinois, and Pennsylvania. Hopkins had conversations with the other candidates, reiterating Roosevelt's determination to have Wallace as his running mate, and one by one they withdrew their names. Only four of them remained to fight it out. Representative William Bankhead of Alabama had the strongest "anti-steamroller" support, but it was not strong enough to block Wallace, who received the prize on the first ballot.

After the nomination of Wallace was pushed

ALL CONNECTED UP.

THE FRUSTRATED SALESMAN

BY AND DANIEL FITZPATRICK, HIGHLIGHTING PERSONALITIES AND ISSUES OF THE CONTEST.

through, Roosevelt spoke to the convention in the early hours of the morning: "Today all private plans, all private lives have been repealed by an overriding public danger. In the face of that danger all those who can be of service to the republic have no choice but to offer themselves. . . ." The rebellious delegates were quiet now as they listened to their President. "Only the people themselves can draft a President. If such a draft should be made upon me, I will, with God's help, continue to serve with the best of my ability and with the fullness of my strength."

As to the practical consideration of a campaign, with war clouds hanging heavily over the United States, Roosevelt declared: "I shall not have the time nor the inclination to engage in purely political debate. But I shall never be loath to call the attention of the nation to deliberate or unwitting falsifications of fact."

Some weeks later—on August 17—Willkie made his official acceptance speech at Elwood,

his birthplace in Indiana which he had not visited for years. Elwood was selected so that the Republican candidate could shine in the role of a small-town boy, obscuring the fact that in reality he was a wealthy Wall Street lawyer and highly paid utilities executive.

In his speech Willkie supported Roosevelt's foreign policy (although he criticized the President for seeming to incite us to war), and agreed with most of the New Deal reforms. He endorsed "collective bargaining by representatives of labor's own free choice." He was for wages-and-hours legislation and Federal regulation of interstate utilities, securities markets, and banking. He favored Federal old-age pensions, unemployment insurance, rural electrification, benefit payments to farmers and agricultural cooperatives.

Willkie challenged Roosevelt to a series of joint debates and was keenly anticipating a slugging match with "the champ." But Harold Ickes, apparently speaking for the President,

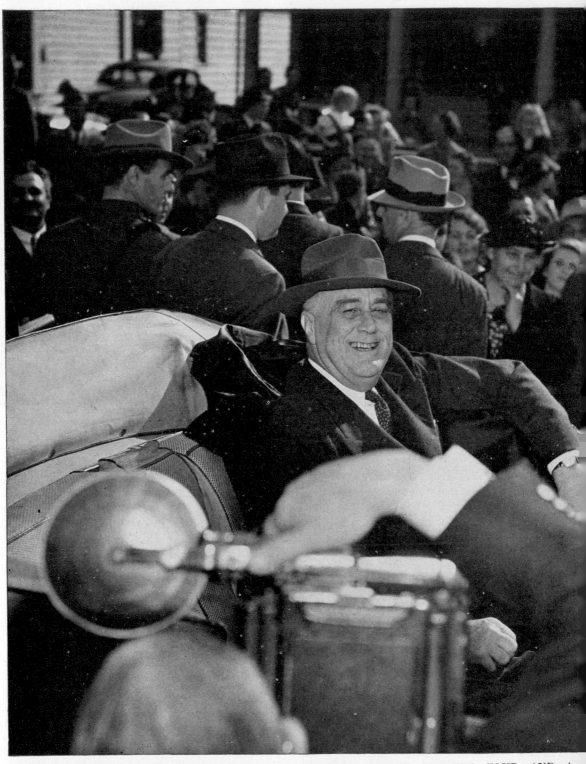

THE TRIUMPHANT ROOSEVELT CARRIED THIRTY-EIGHT STATES, WINNING FOUR AND A

stated that "the Battle of Britain could not be adjourned by Roosevelt in order to ride the circuit with Willkie."

The Republican candidate, whom Ickes christened "the simple, barefoot, Wall Street lawyer," running for office as a "rich man's Roosevelt," conducted a traditional campaign, traveling 30,000 miles in thirty-four states and making 550 speeches. His main charges against Roosevelt were that the President thought himself "indispensable," and that he wanted to perpetuate "one-man rule" by running for a third term. Willkie declared: "I deny that Franklin Roosevelt is the defender of democracy. . . . His influence has weakened rather than strengthened democracy throughout the world. . . . If, because of some fine speeches about humanity, you return this administration to office, you will be serving under an American totalitarian government before the long third term is finished."

But while Willkie barnstormed the country, beating Bryan's record of 1896, the President showed little interest in the campaign. Roosevelt planned to make not more than five major speeches during the two weeks preceding the election, and though hard pressed to change his mind, he refused to do so.

As the campaign reached its final weeks, Willkie, exasperated by Roosevelt's silence, lent his ear to the tactical politicians of his party, who persuaded him not to make understanding speeches about a bipartisan foreign policy and treat Roosevelt with gloved hands, but to campaign in the old-fashioned way and fight it out with "the third-term candidate." From then on Willkie used other tactics; now he told his listeners that if they voted for Roosevelt it would mean wooden crosses for their brothers and sons and sweethearts, and that if Roosevelt should become President again, America would soon be involved in a foreign war. He said that American boys were already on the transports to foreign shores, that "the floundering management of the New Deal" had "failed to build us a defense system," and that America was "deficient in all the essential items of defense—the airplanes, the guns, the tanks, and even the ability to make them."

Roosevelt, who began his campaign on October 23 at Philadelphia, replied to Willkie's charges five days later in New York's Madison Square Garden. In a fighting speech, he reminded the nation that it was not the administration but the Republican opposition in Congress which had tried to keep us unprepared and which had fought against an increased armed force and against aid to Britain. "Great Britain would never have received an ounce of help from us," said Roosevelt, "if the decision had been left to Martin, Barton and Fish." The President extolled the administration's aims of preparing the country but keeping out of war, and took credit for the Neutrality Law (of which he thoroughly disapproved).

It was a strange campaign, with Roosevelt upholding policies in which he did not believe and Willkie making "campaign oratory" which he later had to recant. Basically, Willkie and Roosevelt were not far apart in their policies. Willkie said: "There is no issue between the third-term candidate and myself on the questions of old-age pensions, unemployment insurance, collective bargaining, laws which guarantee minimum wages and prohibit men working more than so many hours per week, or the elimination of child labor and the retention of Federal relief. I am not alone *for* all these laws, but I advocate their improvement and reinforcement." In effect, Willkie was saying: "Let me do the job; I can do it better than Roosevelt."

Nor was there any disagreement between the two contestants regarding aid to Britain. Willkie said that he was "in favor of aiding Britain at some sacrifice to our own defense program. . . . Aid to Britain to the limits of prudence for our own safety." The Republican candidate was informed in advance that Roosevelt had decided to give England some fifty overage destroyers in exchange for a ninety-nine-year lease of sea and air bases in Western Atlantic islands, and Willkie, who approved the deal, promised not to make a campaign issue of it.

Roosevelt's third major speech was scheduled for Boston. The President was urged by Ed Flynn and the other party bosses to make a strong statement against the entry of America into the war, as reports had reached them that Willkie's reiteration of the "keeping-out-of-war" theme had increased his support. So

Roosevelt told his Boston audience: "I have said this before, but I shall say it again and again and again: 'Your boys are not going to be sent into foreign wars.'" Robert Sherwood, who claims responsibility for the statement, recalls that while the speech was being discussed on the train to Boston, Judge Rosenman suggested adding the phrase "except in case of attack," as stated in the Democratic platform. But this was discarded when Roosevelt said irritably: "Of course we'll fight if we're attacked. If somebody attacks us, then it isn't a foreign war, is it? Or do they want me to guarantee that our troops be sent into battle only in the event of another Civil War?"

In the same Boston speech Roosevelt referred to Joseph P. Kennedy as "my ambassador." Republican campaign orators took up the phrase, telling the nation that the use of the personal pronoun proved Roosevelt's dictatorial ambitions.

It was during his stay in Boston that the President was booed by students of the Massachusetts Institute of Technology, who chanted: "Poppa, I wanna be a captain," a reference to the commission which was given to Roosevelt's son Elliott—one of the personal issues of the campaign.

Roosevelt's fourth speech in Brooklyn showed him in fighting spirit. No longer was he on the defensive, a part which he never played well. He now launched an attack, accusing the Republicans of joining hands with the Communists, and pointing out that "there is something very ominous in this combination that has been forming within the Republican party between the extreme reactionary and the extreme radical elements of this country." Roosevelt said that "something evil is happening in this country when a full-page advertisement against the administration, paid for by Republican supporters, appears—where, of all places? In the *Daily Worker*, the newspaper of the Communist party." And he referred to the speech of a Republican judge in Philadelphia who said: "The President's only supporters are paupers, who earn less than $1,200 a year and aren't worth *that*, and the Roosevelt family." Roosevelt was quick to point out that half of the nation's population earned less than $1,200. "Paupers," said Roosevelt, "who are not worth

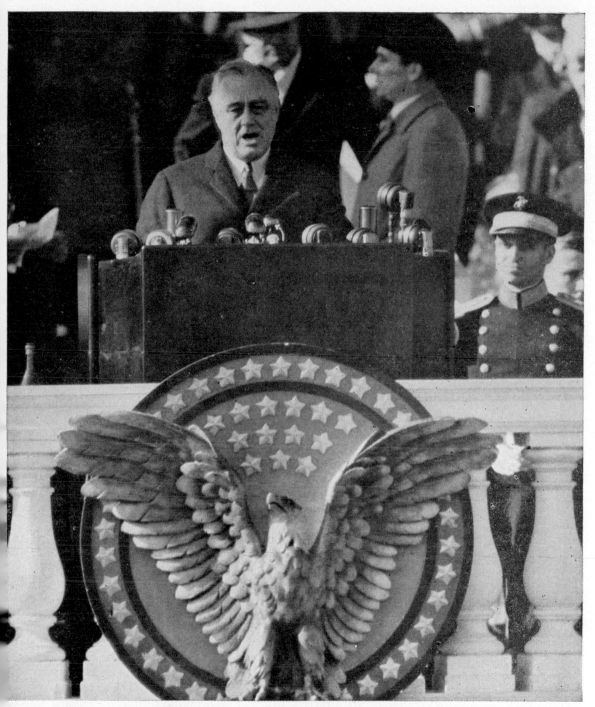

JANUARY 20, 1941: "Lives of nations are determined not by the count of years, but by the lifetime of the human spirit. The life of a man is three-score years and ten: a little more, a little less. The life of a nation is the fullness of the measure of its will to live. There are men who doubt this. There are men who believe that democracy, as a form of government and a frame of life, is limited or measured by a kind of mystical and artificial fate—that, for some unexplained reason, tyranny and slavery have become the surging wave of the future, and that freedom is an ebbing tide. But we Americans know that this is not true."

TANKS AND WAR EQUIPMENT WERE FEATURED PROMINENTLY IN THE 1940 INAUGURAL PARADE.

their salt—there speaks the true sentiment of the Republican leadership in this year of grace." Such remarks as this, he continued, were a "direct, vicious, unpatriotic appeal to class hatred and class contempt." And moving closer to the microphone, he said in a dramatic voice: "That, my friends, is just what I am fighting against with all my heart and soul. I am fighting for a free America—for a country in which all men and women have equal rights to liberty and justice. I am fighting against the revival of government by special privilege—government by lobbyists—government vested in the hands of those who favor and who would have us imitate the foreign dictatorships. And I will not stop fighting." The cheering which greeted these words echoed through the land.

Roosevelt's final campaign speech was delivered in Cleveland; it was another challenging appeal. But he spoke once more at

eleven o'clock on election eve, appealing to the voters to do their duty, and making the appeal memorable for the beautiful prayer which he recalled from his school days: "Bless our land with honorable industry, sound learning and pure manners. Save us from violence, discord and confusion, from pride and arrogance, and from every evil way. Defend our liberties, and fashion into one united people the multitudes brought hither out of many kindreds and tongues."

Besides Roosevelt and Willkie, there were the usual number of minor-party candidates contesting the election. The Socialists nominated Norman Thomas for the fourth time on a platform proposing collective ownership of the basic means of production, and their operation for use rather than profit as the way to conquer poverty and save democracy. The Socialists were firmly against the "collective

ROOSEVELT REVIEWS TROOPS IN A FUR-LINED COAT BORROWED FROM AMBASSADOR DAVIES.

suicide" of wars, and advocated neutral mediation in behalf of a negotiated peace. The Communists nominated Earl Browder who, following the Moscow line (the Nazi-Soviet pact was still in force), advocated: "Not a cent, not a gun, not a man for war preparations and imperialist war." The Prohibitionists rallied behind the statistician and market analyst, Roger Babson.

On election day every voter and his offspring were richly decorated with campaign buttons. Twenty-one million emblems were manufactured boosting the President, but thirty-three million were dedicated to Willkie. Besides the usual slogans there were buttons which said: "We don't want Eleanor either," and "Willkie for President—of Commonwealth and Southern." Others said: "No more fireside chats," or "Two good terms deserve another."

Labor leader John L. Lewis, made a bombastic radio speech for Willkie, declaring that if Roosevelt were re-elected he would resign as C.I.O. President. But when the votes were counted, it was Roosevelt again. The people of the country were not afraid that Roosevelt would become a dictator if they elected him for a third term; they had given little heed to ex-President Hoover's prediction that the defeat of the Republican candidate would mean socialism and totalitarianism in the United States; and they gave no credence to the newspapers, which declared that a Roosevelt victory would be the end of free elections. The people of America knew better. Roosevelt carried thirty-eight states with 449 electoral votes, receiving 27,243,-466 popular votes. Willkie, supported by ten states with 82 electoral votes, won 22,304,755 popular votes. The Republicans' effort to take the New Deal away from Roosevelt had failed. America had its first third-term President.

THE WHITE HOUSE INAUGURAL

THE FORTIETH ELECTION—1944

FRANKLIN D. ROOSEVELT

During Roosevelt's third term, domestic matters were relegated to the background by the all-important issue of preparing for the war and winning it quickly.

Two days after the Japanese attacked Pearl Harbor, the President recounted the past deeds of the Axis. "In 1931 Japan invaded Manchukuo without warning. In 1935 Italy invaded Ethiopia without warning. In 1938 Hitler occupied Austria without warning. In 1939 Hitler invaded Czechoslovakia without warning. Later in 1939 Hitler invaded Poland without warning. In 1940 Hitler invaded Norway, Denmark, the Netherlands, Belgium and Luxembourg without warning. In 1940 Italy attacked France and later Greece without warning. In 1941 the Axis powers attacked Jugoslavia and Greece and they dominated the Balkans without warning. In 1941 Hitler invaded Russia without warning. And now Japan has attacked Malaya and Thailand—and the United States—without warning." Roosevelt concluded: "We are now in this war. We are in it all the way. . . ."

The main task of the administration became the conduct of the war. After the nation entered the battle, political hostilities were temporarily forgotten; the people of America closed ranks and united behind the President. Roosevelt called for a vast armament program of 185,000 planes, 120,000 tanks, 55,000 anti-aircraft guns, eighteen million tons of shipping. Many of his adversaries held that such a goal could not be attained, but when American industry geared itself to a war economy, the goal was more than met.

The first part of 1942 brought defeats to the Allies. In the Far East, Singapore fell, the Burma Road was cut, Bataan was lost. Japanese troops landed in the Aleutians. Yet as the summer waned, American marines routed the Japanese in the historic Battle of Guadalcanal.

The next year, 1943, began auspiciously for the Allies. In January British troops took Tripoli; in February the German siege of Stalingrad was lifted; and three months later British and American troops freed Africa from the German invaders.

When 1944 came around, the tide of battle had turned. The final defeat of the Axis powers was only a matter of time. The Russians were pursuing the mighty German army back to their homeland; the siege of Leningrad was lifted;

FRANKLIN D. ROOSEVELT, AS
MILLIONS OF NEW YORKERS SAW HIM
DURING HIS TOUR OF THE CITY IN 1944

THE CANDIDATES

FRANKLIN D. ROOSEVELT (1882-1945) was the Democratic candidate for the fourth time. With the war nearing a victorious end, he worked strenuously to lay the foundations for a lasting peace. He was re-elected by 25,602,504 votes against 22,006,285 for Dewey. Five months later, Roosevelt died.

HARRY S. TRUMAN (1884-19—), Missouri Senator and chairman of the committee which investigated the national defense program, became the Democratic vice-presidential candidate after conservatives in the party insisted on ousting Henry Wallace because of his radical policies.

THOMAS E. DEWEY (1902-19—), Michigan born Governor of New York, was the Republican choice. He prophesied that the election would end "one-man government in America." Although Dewey won more votes than any previous Republican candidate, he failed to carry either New York or his home state.

JOHN W. BRICKER (1893-19—), Governor of Ohio and one of the most conservative members of the Republican party, was selected for Vice-President after he had withdrawn his name as a contender for first place. In the ensuing campaign, Bricker forcefully assailed the policies of Franklin D. Roosevelt.

the American Fifth Army liberated Rome. And on June 6, D-Day, the Allies struck at the coast of Normandy and breached the Atlantic Wall.

It was at the end of the same month that the Republican convention met in Chicago, with the nation more enthralled by the war news than by the proceedings of the nominating assembly. Walter Lippmann thought that the lack of popular interest was due to the fact "that the men who organized the convention and

THE VOTES IN THE 1944 ELECTION

STATES	POPULAR VOTE				ELEC. VOTE	
	F. D. Roosevelt, Democrat.	Thomas E. Dewey, Republican.	Norman Thomas, Socialist.	Claude E. Watson, Prohibitionist.	Roosevelt-Truman	Dewey-Bricker
Ala.	198,918	44,540	190	1,095	11	—
Ariz.	80,926	56,287	—	421	4	—
Ark.	148,965	63,551	440	—	9	—
Calif.	1,988,564	1,512,965	3,923	14,770	25	—
Colo.	234,331	268,731	1,977	—	—	6
Conn.	435,146	390,527	5,097	—	8	—
Del.	68,166	56,747	154	294	3	—
Fla.	339,377	143,215	—	—	8	—
Ga.	268,187	56,507	6	36	12	—
Idaho	107,399	100,137	282	503	4	—
Ill.	2,079,479	1,939,314	180	7,411	28	—
Ind.	781,403	875,891	2,223	12,574	—	13
Iowa	499,876	547,267	1,511	3,752	—	10
Kan.	287,458	442,096	1,613	2,609	—	8
Ky.	472,589	392,448	535	2,023	11	—
La.	281,564	67,750	—	—	10	—
Me.	140,631	155,434	—	—	—	5
Md.	315,490	292,949	—	—	8	—
Mass.	1,035,296	921,350	—	973	16	—
Mich.	1,106,899	1,084,423	4,598	6,503	19	—
Minn.	589,864	527,416	5,073	—	11	—
Miss.	158,515	3,742	—	—	9	—
Mo.	807,356	761,175	1,751	1,175	15	—
Mont.	112,556	93,163	1,296	340	4	—
Neb.	233,246	329,880	—	—	—	6
Nev.	29,623	24,611	—	—	3	—
N. H.	119,663	109,916	46	—	4	—
N. J.	987,874	961,335	3,358	4,255	16	—
N. M.	81,389	70,688	—	148	4	—
N. Y.	3,304,238†	2,987,647	10,553	—	47	—
N. C.	527,399	263,155	—	—	14	—
N. D.	100,144	118,535	943	549	—	4
Ohio	1,570,763	1,582,293	—	—	—	25
Okla.	401,549	319,424	—	1,663	10	—
Ore.	248,635	225,365	3,785	2,362	6	—
Pa.	1,940,479	1,835,054	11,721	5,750	35	—
R. I.	175,356	123,487	—	433	4	—
S. C.	90,601	4,547	—	365	8	—
S. D.	96,711	135,365	—	—	—	4
Tenn.	308,707	200,311	792	882	12	—
Tex.	821,605	191,425	593	1,013	23	—
Utah	150,088	97,891	340	—	4	—
Vt.	53,820	71,527	—	—	—	3
Va.	242,276	145,243	417	459	11	—
Wash.	486,777	361,689	3,824	2,396	8	—
W. Va.	392,774	322,819	—	—	8	—
Wis.	650,413	674,532	13,205	—	—	12
Wyo.	49,419	51,921	—	—	—	3
Total	25,602,504	22,006,285	80,426	74,754	432	99

†The Democratic figure in New York includes 496,405 American Labor and 329,235 Liberal votes.
Edward A. Teichert, Socialist-Labor, 45,335; Texas Regulars, 134,439; others, 32,520. Total vote, 47,976,263.

THE WAR MESSAGE: "Yesterday, December 7, 1941—a date which will live in infamy—the United States of America was suddenly and deliberately attacked by naval and air forces of the Empire of Japan. The United States was at peace with that nation, and at the solicitation of Japan, was still in conversation with its government and its Emperor looking toward the maintenance of peace in the Pacific. . . . Japan has . . . undertaken a surprise offensive extending throughout the Pacific area. The facts of yesterday speak for themselves. The people of the United States have already formed their opinions and well understand the implications to the very life and safety of our nation. As Commander-in-Chief of the Army and Navy, I have directed that all measures be taken for our defense. Always will we remember the character of the onslaught against us. . . . I ask that Congress declare that since the unprovoked and dastardly attack by Japan . . . a state of war has existed between the United States and the Japanese Empire."

THE COMMANDER IN CHIEF IN AN OPEN JEEP VISITS THE AMERICAN TROOPS IN AFRICA.

AUGUST 1941: The Atlantic Charter, an eight-point statement of peace aims, was drawn up by Roosevelt and Churchill aboard the English battleship, *Prince of Wales*.

JUNE 1942: Russian Foreign Minister Molotov cam Washington to confer with Roosevelt, asking for a ond front to relieve the hard-pressed Russian ar

are managing it and will write the platform are not the Republicans who could win the election. Even they themselves know it, as one can see from the drab defeatism which the journalists who reflect their views do not conceal."

After Thomas E. Dewey defeated Wendell Willkie in the Wisconsin primary, thus causing Willkie's withdrawal from the presidential race, it was obvious that the Republicans would turn to the forty-two-year-old Governor of New York. On the first ballot Dewey received all the votes of the delegates but one. The lone dissenter, Grant Ritter, a Wisconsin farmer, held out for General Douglas MacArthur, saying: "I'm a man, not a jelly fish." For the Vice-Presidency the convention chose Ohio's governor, the handsome John W. Bricker.

In his acceptance speech before the Republican convention, Dewey sounded the keynote of his forthcoming campaign. He charged that the Democratic administration had "grown old in office," and had become "tired and quarrelsome." It was "at war with Congress and at war with itself"; "wrangling, bungling and confusion" prevailed in the "vital matters of taxation, price control, rationing, labor relations, man power." The Republican candidate accused the New Deal of failing to solve the unemployment problem, which "was left to be solved by the war," and promised that "this election will bring an end to one-man government in America."

Neither the Democrats nor the nation as a whole were impressed by Dewey's charges. The general feeling in the Democratic ranks—and in the country—was that it would be inopportune to replace Roosevelt now that the war was in its final phase and the building of the peace required his political experience. For the Democratic party there was a very practical consideration as well—no one but Roosevelt could lead them to victory.

A week before the Democrats met, the President wrote to Robert E. Hannegan, the chairman of the party's national committee, stating that if the convention should renominate him, "I shall accept. If the people elect me, I will serve."

Thus on July 20—the very day that Tojo resigned as Premier of Japan and Hitler escaped death from a bomb explosion—President Roosevelt became the Democratic party's candidate for the fourth time, receiving 1,086 votes to 89 for Senator Byrd of Virginia and one for James A. Farley on the first ballot.

A rebellion by the Texas Democrats, who had threatened to vote against Roosevelt unless white supremacy were upheld and the two-thirds rule reinstituted, was easily quelled. But a great fight raged in the convention over the vice-presidential nomination. The renomination

1943: Roosevelt traveled to Casablanca for talks Prime Minister Churchill and the two stubbornly mistic French generals, de Gaulle and Giraud.

SEPTEMBER 1944: Roosevelt and a group of American military leaders met at Quebec with Churchill and members of his staff to plan the final strategy of the war.

THE REPUBLICAN CONVENTION, HELD SHORTLY AFTER D-DAY, CHOSE ON THE FIRST BALLOT

of Henry A. Wallace was opposed by the city bosses, the conservative element, and the Southern Bourbons. Wallace's advocacy of the "century of the common man," his radical stand on social issues, made him—in the opinion of these groups—a liability to the ticket.

A week before the convention, Roosevelt issued a lukewarm endorsement of his Vice-President. In a letter to Senator Jackson on July 14 he wrote: "I like him and I respect him and he is my personal friend. For these reasons I personally would vote for his renomination if I were a delegate to the convention."

But when the movement against Wallace gained momentum, the President wrote to the Democratic chairman on July 19: "You have written me about Harry Truman and Bill Douglas. I should, of course, be very glad to run with either of them and believe that either of them would bring real strength to the ticket." (Grace Tully, the President's secretary, recalls in her memoirs that in his letter Roosevelt originally placed Douglas's name first and Truman's second, but Hannegan persuaded him to reverse them.)

Besides Wallace, Douglas, and Truman, the President seemed to have encouraged James F. Byrnes as well to fight for the second place. However, when Philip Murray, President of the CIO, and Sidney Hillman, chairman of its Political Action Committee, declared that Byrnes was not acceptable to labor, the vice-presidential race narrowed down to two contenders: Wallace and Truman.

ACCEPTING THE NOMINATION, Dewey stated that the conduct of the war would be outside the campaign. "It is and must remain completely out of politics," he said.

Wallace, making a gallant fight before and during the convention, strongly backed by labor but violently opposed by the Southern anti-New Dealers, went into the convention with strong support. Arriving in Chicago, the Vice-President said: "I am in this fight to the finish." Two hundred university students serenaded him at his hotel, singing:

"You can talk about Senator Barkley,
You can talk about Senator Truman,
But the Democratic party has learned that
Wallace fought the battle for the common man,
Common man, common man,
Wallace fought the battle for the common man,
And he'll fight that battle again."

When the Vice-President appeared before the convention to second the nomination of Roosevelt, a tremendous demonstration greeted him, and the chant, "We want Wallace! We want Wallace!" reverberated from every corner of the stadium. Wallace made an impressive speech, going on record for his beliefs. "The future belongs to those," he said, "who go down the line unswervingly for the liberal principles of both political democracy and economic democracy, regardless of race, color or religion. . . . The Democratic party cannot long survive as a conservative party."

If the balloting for the vice-presidential nomination had begun then, Wallace could have walked away with the prize. But the chairman of the convention—sensing the Wallace sentiment—asked for adjournment, and though delegates and spectators shouted a resounding "No," the meeting dispersed.

During the night the city bosses worked assiduously to swing the delegates to Harry S. Truman, Senator from Missouri. Ed Kelly of Chicago, Ed Flynn of New York, Robert Hannegan, and Frank Walker argued and talked and insisted and begged for Truman's candidacy, which, according to Arthur Krock of the New York *Times*, was cleared with Sidney Hillman of the PAC. The "Clear-it-with-Sidney" charge, never substantiated, was denied by Roosevelt and those close to him, although some time later Truman confided to an interviewer that Hillman had told him during a breakfast that if labor could not have Wallace it would accept Truman.

When it appeared that not enough delegates would be in Truman's column on the first ballot, the bosses proposed favorite sons in order to block Wallace. Thus on the first trial Wallace led with 429½ votes. Truman trailed him with 319½, but the votes for the thirteen favorite sons amounted to 393½. Could a majority of these 393½ votes be brought into the Truman column? The bosses were confident that they could. Their tactics worked, and on the second ballot Harry Truman received the nomination.

Roosevelt made his acceptance speech over the radio from an undisclosed Western naval base—later identified as San Diego. Speaking from a private railroad car, he said: "The people of the United States will decide this fall whether they wish to turn over this 1944 job—this world-wide job—to inexperienced and immature hands, to those who opposed Lend-Lease and international cooperation against the forces of aggression and tyranny, until they could read the polls of popular sentiment; or whether they wish to leave it to those who saw the danger from abroad, who met it head on, and who now have seized the offensive and carried the war to its present stages of success; to those who, by international conferences and united actions, have begun to build that kind of common understanding and cooperative experience which will be so necessary in the world to come."

The President posed the question: "What is the job before us in 1944? First, to win the war, to win it fast, to win it overpoweringly. Second, to form world-wide international organizations and to arrange to use the armed forces of the sovereign nations of the world to make another war impossible within the foreseeable future. Third, to build an economy for our returning veterans and for all Americans which will provide employment and a decent standard of living."

Roosevelt declared that he would not campaign in the usual sense for the office. "In these days of tragic sorrow I do not consider it fitting. Besides in these days of global warfare, I shall not be able to find the time. I shall, however, feel free to report to the people the facts about matters of concern to them and especially to correct any misrepresentations."

"NEXT!" was the title of this Fitzpatrick cartoon in the St. Louis *Post-Dispatch* of July 5, 1944. The Democratic donkey with the characteristic Roosevelt cigarette holder waits for the nomination. But he did not have to wait very long. With most of the Democratic delegates already pledged to him, Roosevelt was renominated for a fourth term on the first ballot. In his acceptance speech he told the nation that "if the people command me to continue in this office and in this war, I have as little right to withdraw as the soldier has to leave his post in the line."

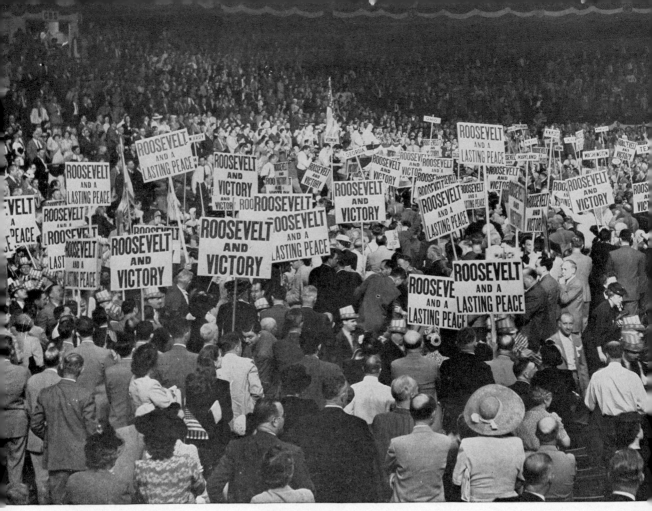

THE USUAL DEMONSTRATION OCCURRED WHEN FDR'S NAME WAS SUBMITTED TO THE CONVENTION.

Thus in the opening months of the presidential contest, Dewey did all the talking, speaking on specific subjects—in Louisville on foreign policy, in Seattle on labor, in San Francisco on government regulation, in Los Angeles on social security—to a seemingly apathetic and bored electorate.

Though the President kept himself aloof from speaking engagements, his Cabinet members did not. Harold Ickes, the Secretary of the Interior, was one of the most vitriolic campaigners, and his acid remarks were gleefully repeated. In one of his speeches he said: "Four years ago I observed that Mr. Dewey had thrown his diaper into the ring. At Los Angeles on Friday night, when he upbraided the New Deal for not being New Dealish enough, he threw the sponge after his diaper."

The campaign was without real political issues. Between the Republican and Democratic principles there was no great division. Dewey did not attack the social legislation of the New Deal. Most of it—such as labor's rights, collective bargaining, the SEC, unemployment insurance, the broadening of social security—he endorsed. The administration, he admitted, "did some good things" in its youth. And he did not criticize Roosevelt's conduct of the war, nor plan to change the military leadership if elected. He declared: "The military conduct of the war is outside this campaign. It is and must remain completely out of politics."

The issues on which Dewey dwelt were of a more personal nature. The Republican candidate repeated the charge that "tired old men" dominated the administration, without mentioning that the foremost military leaders of the nation were "tired old men" too. (Admiral

THE VICE-PRESIDENT, Henry A. Wallace, opposed for renomination by conservative Democrats and Southern Bourbons, told the convention in a seconding speech for Roosevelt: "The future belongs to those who go down the line . . . for political . . . and economic democracy."

PORTRAITS of fourteen Democratic Presidents adorned the hall. In 1801 Jefferson began forty unbroken years of Democratic rule, including John Q. Adams's term. But from the Civil War until World War II there were only four Democratic Presidents, though they served eight terms.

King was sixty-six, General MacArthur and General Marshall were sixty-four, Admiral Halsey was sixty-two, the same age as President Roosevelt.)

Republican newspapers assailed the President because of his Communist and radical support; Republican campaign orators proclaimed him a tool of Sidney Hillman and the PAC. Frequent mention was made of bickering and quarreling in the administration, and of the fact that if Roosevelt were to remain in office for another four years, every member of the Supreme Court would then have been appointed by him; thus he would dominate the highest judiciary. And there was the never-ending argument of his failing health, which had to be repudiated by Vice-Admiral Ross McIntire, Roosevelt's personal physician, who issued a statement that there was "nothing wrong organically with him at all. He's perfectly O.K. . . . The stories that he is in bad health are understandable enough around election time, but they are not true."

The Democrats were more worried about the President's disinterested attitude toward the campaign than about the Republican accusations. "He just doesn't seem to give a damn," said his aide, Pa Watson.

But late in September, Roosevelt made a speech at the Teamsters' Union dinner which injected life into the campaign. *Time* Magazine reported that "the old master still had it.

657

ACCEPTING THE NOMINATION from a railroad car at San Diego. "The people of the U.S. will decide this fall," Roosevelt said, "whether they wish to turn over this world-wide job to . . . those who opposed . . . international cooperation . . . or whether they wish to leave it to those who saw the danger from abroad and met it head on. . . ."

Franklin Roosevelt was at his best. He was like a veteran virtuoso playing a piece he has loved for years, who fingers his way through it with a delicate fire, a perfection of tuning and tone, and an assurance that no young player, no matter how gifted, can equal. The President was playing what he loves to play—politics."

Roosevelt began his speech with a mocking smile on his face: "Well, here we are together again—after four years—and what years they have been! I am actually four years older, which seems to annoy some people. In fact, millions of us are more than eleven years older than when we started in to clear up the mess that was dumped in our laps in 1933."

He then turned on those Republicans who "suddenly discover" every four years, just before election day, that they love labor, after having attacked labor "for three years and six months," and reminded the nation that the Republicans had opposed the National Labor Relations Act, the Wages and Hours Act, and the Social Security Act—statutes which they now upheld in their platform.

Roosevelt took some of the charges which the Republican campaign orators hurled against him and demolished them one by one. He did it quietly, with apparent good humor. But the highlight of the address, the passage which made the nation rock with laughter, was the

THE DEMOCRATIC VICE-PRESIDENTIAL CANDIDATE, Harry S. Truman, is escorted through the crowds to the platform after the party bosses had chosen to support the Missourian and labor had given him its blessing. On the first ballot Henry Wallace was in the lead, but the second trial resulted in Harry Truman's nomination.

one about his dog Fala. "These Republican leaders," said Roosevelt, "have not been content with attacks upon me, or my wife, or my sons—they now include my little dog, Fala. Unlike the members of my family, he resents this. Being a Scottie, as soon as he learned that the Republican fiction writers had concocted a story that I had left him behind on an Aleutian island and had sent a destroyer back to find him at a cost to the taxpayers of two or three or twenty million dollars, his Scotch soul was furious. He has not been the same dog since."

The Teamsters' Union speech—or as it became known, "that speech about Fala"—had the desired effect. Dewey, whom the sharp-tongued Walter Winchell characterized as "the little man on the wedding cake," lost his calm. A few days later, in Oklahoma City, he answered Roosevelt's jibes with a hard-hitting counter-attack. "He asked for it. Here it is!" cried Dewey, and in the manner of a prosecuting attorney he struck out at Roosevelt's so-called Communist sympathies, and cited statements of General Marshall, General Arnold, and Senator Truman that in 1940 the army of the United States was not prepared for war.

Roosevelt planned to make only five more major addresses, and despite all the clamor for a more extensive campaign, he stuck to his decision. His first address—after the Fala speech—

659

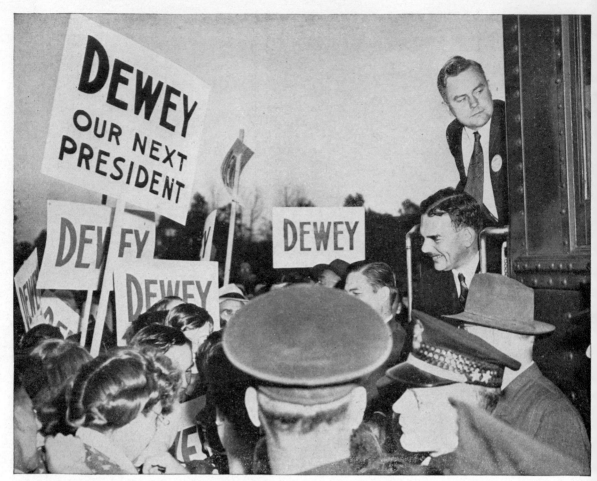

THE REPUBLICAN CANDIDATE at first conducted a high-level campaign, speaking on specific subjects. But after Roosevelt made his frolicsome Teamsters' Union speech, Dewey's anger was roused. Although he declared at Oklahoma City a few days later that "I shall not join my opponent in his descent to mud-slinging," Dewey charged that Roosevelt had left the country unprepared for war and accused the President of Communist sympathies.

CANDIDATE DEWEY and his wife traveled through the country, appealing to the people for November votes.

was scheduled for October 21 before the Foreign Policy Association in New York City. On that day the President toured the boroughs of the city. A bitter wind blew and the rain beat down mercilessly. Roosevelt drove fifty-one miles in an open car, proving to the millions who lined the pavement that he could still take it. Water rolled down his cheeks and dropped from his chin. His thinning hair was pasted flat and the raindrops trickled down the sleeve of his right arm as he raised it again and again to wave to the crowds. The newspapers printed photographs of the tour according to their political sympathies. In the pro-Roosevelt papers the President looked smiling and de-

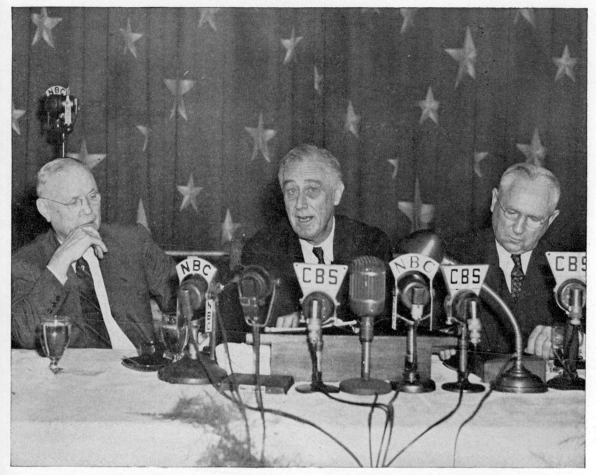

FDR'S FIRST CAMPAIGN SPEECH was given at a dinner of the Teamsters' Union where he sat between AFL President William Green and Teamster Boss Dan Tobin. His audience howled when he said that "these Republican leaders have not been content with attacks upon me . . . they now include Fala. . . . I am accustomed to hearing malicious falsehoods about myself. . . . But I think I have a right to object to libelous statements about my dog."

fiant; the opposition press showed pictures of a haggard, tired Executive.

His speech in the evening was a forceful attack on Republican shortsightedness about foreign issues. The President warned against the Republican isolationists, who still wielded great powers and who would come to the fore if Dewey should be elected. He recalled that the Republicans in Congress had opposed Selective Service in 1940, Lend-Lease in 1941, and the extension of Selective Service in August, 1941. "You see," said Roosevelt, "I'm quoting history to you. I'm going by the record, and I am giving you the whole story, and not a phrase here, and half a phrase

CANDIDATE ROOSEVELT spoke at a dinner given by the Foreign Policy Association at the Waldorf-Astoria.

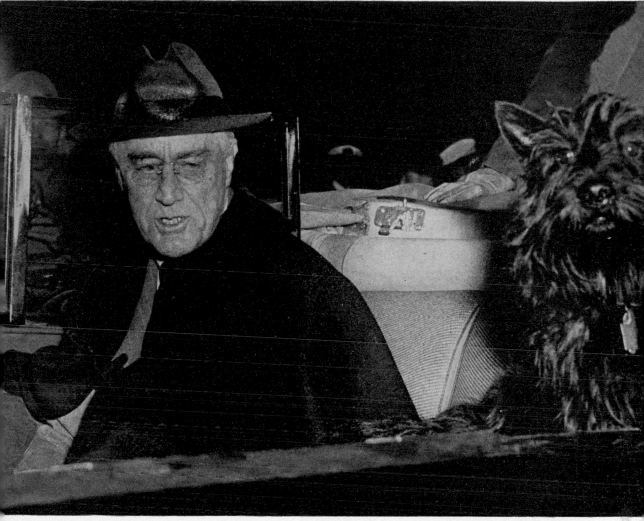

THE WEATHER WAS MOST UNKIND when Roosevelt, in his navy cape and famed hat which he wore in three previous campaigns, drove fifty-one miles through New York City in an open car, proving he could still stand such an ordeal. In Manhattan's garment district, confetti and torn telephone books swirled down from the windows (see opposite page) and the President was cheered by millions who lined the routes. "After the people have seen him," declared Robert Hannegan, Democratic chairman, "they can make up their own minds about his vigor and health."

there. . . ." The audience understood his allusion to Dewey's campaign speeches.

Speaking of the future, the President advocated completion of the United Nations organization before the end of the war. "The Council of the United Nations must have the power to act quickly and decisively to keep the peace by force if necessary. A policeman would not be an effective policeman if, when he saw a felon break into a house, he had to go to the Town Hall and call a town meeting to issue a warrant

before the felon could be arrested. It is clear that if the world organization is to have any reality at all, our representatives must be endowed in advance by the people themselves, by constitutional means through their representatives in the Congress, with authority to act."

It was around the time of the foreign policy speech that Roosevelt learned of Dewey's intention to use in the campaign the highly secret information that the United States had broken the Japanese code before the attack on Pearl

GOVERNOR DEWEY CONCEDES DEFEAT, CONGRATULATES ROOSEVELT ON HIS FOURTH VICTORY.

FOREMAN JOHN Q. VOTER GIVES THE VERDICT.

Harbor. Roosevelt remarked to Harry Hopkins: "My opponent must be pretty desperate if he is even thinking of using material like this, which would be bound to react against him." However, Dewey—after General Marshall implored him not to bring up the matter in his speeches—complied with the request.

Roosevelt's second campaign speech was given on Navy Day, October 27, in Philadelphia's Shibe Park. The news from the war theaters was exhilarating; a few days before General MacArthur had landed in the Philippines and the navy had the Japanese on the run. "I wonder whatever became of the suggestion," asked Roosevelt sarcastically, "that I had failed for political reasons to send enough forces or supplies to General MacArthur. Now, of course, I realize that . . . it is considered by

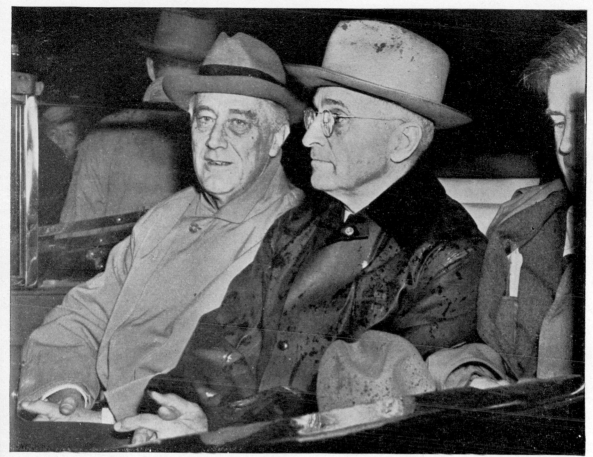

FDR AND HIS VICE-PRESIDENT RECEIVED A WARM WELCOME AS THEY RETURNED TO WASHINGTON.

some to be very impolite to mention that there's a war on. In that war I bear a responsibility that I can never shirk. . . . For the Constitution of the United States says—and I hope you'll pardon me if I quote it correctly—the Constitution says the President shall be Commander in Chief of the Army and Navy." He pointed out with pride that all the battleships, and all but two of the cruisers of Admiral Halsey's victorious Third Fleet, had been authorized during his administration, which should be an "answer to a Republican candidate who said that this administration had made 'absolutely no military preparation for the events that it now claims it foresaw.'"

A day later the President spoke in Chicago, addressing the largest political audience in the history of American presidential elections. One hundred thousand people filled the stadium to capacity, while another 150,000 waited outside, unable to get in. Roosevelt was tired and spoke from his car: "This is the strangest campaign I have ever seen," he said. "I have listened to various Republican orators . . . and what do they say? 'Those incompetent blunderers and bunglers in Washington have passed a lot of excellent laws about social security and labor and farm relief and soil conservation. . . . Those same quarrelsome, tired old men . . . have built the greatest military machine the world has ever known, which is fighting its way to victory,' and they say, 'If you elect us we promise not to change any of that. . . .' They also say, in effect, 'Those inefficient and worn-out crackpots have really begun to lay the foundation of a lasting world peace. If you elect us we

665

JANUARY 20, 1945: In bitter weather and without an overcoat, Roosevelt takes the oath for the fourth time on the portico of the White House. Delivering the second shortest inaugural address in our history—573 words—the President declared: "And so today in this year of war, 1945, we have learned lessons—at a fearful cost—and we shall profit by them. We have learned that we cannot live alone, at peace. . . . We have learned to be . . . members of the human community. We have learned the simple truth, as Emerson said, that 'the only way to have a friend is to be one.' We can gain no lasting peace if we approach it with suspicion and mistrust or with fear. We can gain it only if we proceed with the understanding and the confidence and courage which flow from conviction."

will not change any of that, either.' But they whisper, 'We'll do it in such a way that we won't lose the support even of Gerald Nye or Gerald Smith [or] the Chicago *Tribune*.' "

Roosevelt was in true campaigning form. "If anyone feels that my faith in our ability to provide sixty million peacetime jobs is fantastic, let him remember that some people said

the same thing about my demand in 1940 for 50,000 airplanes." He ended his speech with the promise: "We are not going to turn the clock back. We are going forward, my friends."

The last verbal battle between the candidates was fought in Boston. Dewey, in one of the worst efforts of his career, charged that "Mr. Roosevelt, to perpetuate himself in office for

667

ROOSEVELT, STEPHEN EARLY AND CHURCHILL AROUND THE CONFERENCE TABLE AT YALTA.

sixteen years, has put his party on the auction block—for sale to the highest bidder." And the highest bidders were Sidney Hillman's PAC and Earl Browder's Communists. The Republican candidate asserted that "the forces of communism" were capturing the Democratic party.

Roosevelt, speaking in the same city three days later, replied: "When any political candidate stands up and says solemnly that there is danger that the government of the United States—your government—could be sold out to the Communists, then I say that candidate reveals shocking lack of trust in America. He reveals a shocking lack of faith in democracy—in the spiritual strength of our people."

Speaking of the war, Roosevelt reminded his audience: "We got into this war because we were attacked by the Japanese—and because they and their Axis partners, Hitler's Germany and Mussolini's Italy, declared war on us. I am sure that any real American would have chosen, as this government did, to fight when our own soil was made the object of a sneak attack. As for myself, under the same circumstances, I would choose to do the same thing—again, and again, and again." It was the same phrase he had used four years before in his Boston speech, and the audience greeted it with tumultuous applause.

Dewey wound up his campaign in New York's Madison Square Garden, once more charging that Roosevelt's "own confused in-

669

THE FAREWELL SONG. As the funeral procession leaves Warm Springs, where Roosevelt died on April 12, 1945, Graham Jackson plays "Going Home." With tears running down his cheeks, Jackson's face mirrors the nation's grief.

CAPITOL SHADOWS THE FUNERAL CORTEGE.

competence" had prolonged the war, and that the President had "offered no program, nothing but smears and unspecified complaints, because the New Deal had nothing to offer."

With this the battle for the votes ended. According to Robert Sherwood, the President confided to Harry Hopkins that it was "the meanest campaign of his life. He said he thought they hit him below the belt several times and that it was done quite deliberately and very viciously. He was particularly resentful about the whispering campaign on his failing health which he believed was a highly organized affair."

Up to the last minute, the much-derided Political Action Committee of the CIO worked hard for Roosevelt's re-election. Two million

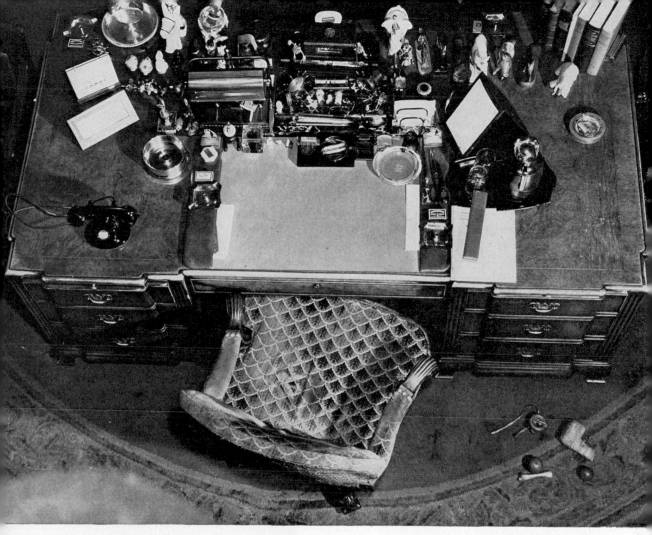

THE DESK HE LEFT BEHIND. Roosevelt liked to clutter the top of his White House desk with his favorite mementoes and bric-a-brac, sent to him by friends and admirers. Fala's toys are on the floor beside his chair.

CIO members rang doorbells and distributed literature rousing the people to get out and vote. It was a new and unique phenomenon in presidential elections, proving how decisive the political influence of the laboring classes could be. The Republicans met the challenge with posters which appeared on city walls, containing the veiled anti-Semitic appeal: "It's your country. Why let Sidney Hillman run it? Vote for Dewey and Bricker."

The pollsters predicted a very close election. Dr. Gallup gave the President 51.5 per cent of the votes, but left himself plenty of room to get back off the limb. Elmo Roper gave Roosevelt 53.6 per cent, a close guess, but said that the soldier vote, the vote of the migratory war workers, and the silent vote might be upsetting factors. *Time* Magazine said that the election seemed to be so close that the people might not know for possibly weeks after November 7 whether they had elected Tom Dewey or Franklin Roosevelt.

But a week later the same magazine reported: "It was Franklin Roosevelt in a walkover. His popular percentage was a shade lower than in 1940, his electoral college vote a smashing victory. Once the returns began pouring in there was no doubt." The popular vote was 25,602,504 for Roosevelt and 22,006,285 for Dewey. Roosevelt received 432 electoral votes to Dewey's 99.

The result meant that the American people were not afraid to elect a President four times, in a free election and by a secret ballot. It also

671

meant that the people desired to retain their commander in chief, who in the words of the New York *Times* "has a large first-hand knowledge of the problems that will arise in the making of the peace. Moreover, the great prestige and personal following among the plain peoples of the world which he has won with his war leadership, might easily prove in itself to be one of the most important cohesive forces binding together a new world organization in its first experimental years." It meant, too, that the country was definitely turning its back on isolationism and embracing the idea of international co-operation. And finally, it meant that it was not "time for a change."

The inaugural was simplicity itself. Of the $25,000 appropriated for the event, on Roosevelt's insistence only $2,000 were spent, for this was not a time for celebration, when American boys were dying in every corner of the globe. The President took the oath on the portico of the White House and not before the Capitol. About 7,800 invited guests, many of them wounded soldiers and sailors, listened to his short address, containing only 573 words.

The President said prophetically: "Today in this year of war 1945, we have learned lessons—at a fearful cost—and we shall profit by them. We have learned that we cannot live alone, at peace; that our own well-being is dependent upon the well-being of other nations far away. We have learned that we must live as men, and not as ostriches nor as dogs in the manger. We have learned to be citizens of the world, members of the human community. We have learned the simple truth, as Emerson said, that 'the only way to have a friend is to be one.'"

In February Roosevelt journeyed to the Crimea to confer with Stalin and Churchill. The end of the war was in sight, and the foundation of the peace had to be laid. On March 1 an exhausted Roosevelt appeared before Congress, apologizing for delivering his report on the Yalta conference sitting down. "I know that you will realize it makes it a lot easier for me in not having to carry about ten pounds of steel around on the bottom of my legs," he said, for the first time alluding publicly to his infirmity. He spoke at length, but his voice lacked the old fire and his precision of speech was gone. It was a different Roosevelt

AT EIGHT MINUTES PAST SEVEN O'CLOCK ON TH

who sat before Congress; he seemed tired and ill. Six weeks later he was dead.

On April 12, 1945, the heart of the nation stood still as the radio announced that the President had suddenly passed away at the Little White House in Warm Springs. "I am more sorry for the people of the world than I

...ING OF APRIL 12, HARRY S. TRUMAN TOOK THE OATH FROM CHIEF JUSTICE HARLAN F. STONE.

am for us," said Mrs. Roosevelt when told of her husband's death. On the evening of the same day, at eight minutes after seven o'clock, Vice-President Harry S. Truman took the oath in the green-walled Cabinet room of the White House from Chief Justice Harlan Fiske Stone.

The next morning, as he left for the Capitol to lunch with some of his former Senate colleagues, the new President confessed to newspaper reporters: "I feel as though the moon and all the stars and all the planets have fallen upon me. Please, boys, give me your prayers. I need them very much."

673

TRUMAN TAKES THE INAUGURAL OATH

THE FORTY-FIRST ELECTION—1948

HARRY S. TRUMAN

THE stunned nation closed ranks behind the new President. To inherit Roosevelt's mantle and to be faced with the enormous problems created by the war was a grave responsibility. Only a superman could have fitted Roosevelt's shoes, and Harry S. Truman was certainly no superman. He was modest and overawed by his job, and the people of the country sympathized with him. According to the Gallup Poll, 87 per cent of the voters backed him up three months after he took office.

Truman's career was the realization of the Great American Dream—the simple country boy who became President. Born on a farm near Lamar, Missouri, on May 8, 1884, he began his life as a farmer. During the First World War he served in France as captain with the 129th Field Artillery. When he returned from overseas, he became partner in a haberdashery store—Truman & Jacobson, Men's Outfitters—in Kansas City. Eventually the store went into bankruptcy and Truman turned to politics. He held a number of local offices—among them that of county commissioner, known in Missouri as "county judge." At that time the notorious Pendergast machine looked after the interests of deserving

Democrats in the state, and Truman was one of them.

His real rise in public life began in 1934, when he asked Pendergast for the job of Collector of Internal Revenue. He was told—so the story goes—that the post had been promised to someone else, but that he could run for the Senate. Truman allegedly accepted the offer and was elected Senator; six years later, when his term expired, he was re-elected for a second term. In the Senate, as chairman of the special committee to investigate first the national defense program, then war production, he did excellent work, winning widespread respect for his integrity.

Catapulted into the limelight, trusted by conservatives and laborites alike, he became the party's choice for the Vice-Presidency in 1944 when Southern Democrats and other conservative elements rebelled against Wallace's renomination. Little did the politicians think that in less than a year the unsuspecting Missouri Senator would be sitting in the Presidential chair and guiding the nation's affairs.

When Truman took the oath on April 12, 1945, the end of the war was in sight. The Allied armies were in Germany, and in the Pacific

HARRY S. TRUMAN (1884-19—),
THIRTY-THIRD PRESIDENT
OF THE UNITED STATES

HARRY S. TRUMAN
1884-19—) won the election after a hard-hitting campaign, to the surprise of pollsters and political experts who had predicted his certain defeat.

ALBEN W. BARKLEY
(1877-19—) of Kentucky became Truman's running mate. The Democratic candidates won 24,105,812 popular votes to 21,970,065 for the Republicans.

THOMAS E. DEWEY
(1902-19—) emphasized unity and was silent about specific issues, but the President cleverly stressed omissions of the "do-nothing" 80th Congress.

EARL WARREN
(1891-19—), Governor of California, was an asset as Dewey's vice-presidential candidate. He made proper speeches and showed himself with his large family.

HENRY A. WALLACE
(1888-19—) left the Democrats and campaigned as Progressive candidate, while Strom Thurmond, a Southern Democrat, rallied the Dixiecrats behind him.

GLEN H. TAYLOR
(1904-19—), Senator from Idaho, was Wallace's running mate. Republicans were sure Progressive and Southern defections would mean Dewey's victory.

American forces were preparing to invade Japan. This same month the United Nations Conference opened in San Francisco, with forty-six nations in attendance. Events moved fast. On April 28 Mussolini was killed at Lake Como, on April 30 the Russians hoisted their flag over the Reichstag in Berlin, and the next day the world learned with relief that Hitler was dead. A week later Germany surrendered.

On July 17 Truman crossed the ocean, meeting with Stalin and Churchill (who nine days later was overwhelmingly defeated by Labour in the General Election) for a final war conference at Potsdam. On August 6 United States fliers dropped the first atom bomb over Hiroshima; three days later a second bomb fell on Nagasaki. Japan asked for surrender, signed the terms, and the long war came to an end. A victorious America looked hopefully toward the peace.

Although the problems of reconversion were great, the people were eager to throw off wartime restrictions and return to peacetime conditions as rapidly as possible. Critical voices were heard to say that Truman was bungling the job. His changes in the Cabinet and his appointments to high government posts met with censure; sharp-tongued Harold Ickes coined the phrase that the new administration was a "government by crony." The President's handling of labor disputes seemed inept, and a flood of paralyzing strikes alarmed the country. "To err is Truman," cracked the wits, and the popularity polls showed that the President, who at first had had the support of seven-eighths of the voters, now was backed by only 30 per cent of the electorate. The midterm election of 1946 foreshadowed impending disaster. "Had enough?" screamed the posters. Then "Vote Republican." Housewives deplored the rationing muddle; end of the OPA was demanded; dissatisfaction with the administration's labor policy and its soft attitude toward the strikes mounted. On election day a less than average number of voters gave control of both Houses of Congress to the Republicans.

This defeat helped the President more than it hurt him, for it released him from his shackles. Until the midterm election he had tried to act as he thought Roosevelt might have acted, but now he could throw off the ghost of his predecessor. From now on he could be himself, he could show his real colors. He challenged John L. Lewis and showed the leader of the United Mine Workers that he would not bow to him. He appointed General George Marshall as Secretary of State to succeed Byrnes. The bipartisan foreign policy won him accolades; so did his plan for aid to Greece and Turkey. He won over many of the conservatives by his unbending attitude toward Wallace, who left the Cabinet in September, 1946 because of his disagreement with the "get-tough" policy toward Russia. The Marshall Plan, proposing United States aid on a large scale to restore the European economy, was widely acclaimed, and the majority of the people commended the President for his order to check on the loyalty of government employees.

While Truman seemed to be doing well in the eyes of the conservative middle class, he was violently criticized by the party's left wing, chiefly because of his foreign policy, and by the Southern Democrats because of his determined stand on the question of civil rights. A schism in the party ranks seemed inevitable.

At the beginning of 1948 the line-up of presidential candidates was complete. All of the old hats of 1944 were back in the ring. Among Democrats it was taken for granted that Truman would be their nominee. General Eisenhower, the President's only serious rival, had removed himself from the race. In a letter released in January he repeated his former refusal: "I am not available for and could not accept the nomination. . . . The necessary and wise subordination of the military to civil power will be best sustained when life-long professional soldiers abstain from seeking high political office."

Henry A. Wallace was certain to be the standard-bearer of the newly formed Progressive party, which advocated negotiations with Russia and settlement of the controversy by diplomatic means instead of a "cold war." The new party's first test—a by-election in the Bronx in which the Wallace-endorsed candidates overwhelmingly defeated the regular Democratic contender—threw a real scare into the Democratic high command. This initial show of strength indicated that Wallace might siphon off enough votes from the regular Democratic candidates to insure the election of a Republican President.

In the Republican ranks the favorites were

THE VOTES IN THE 1948 ELECTION

STATES	POPULAR VOTE				ELECTORAL VOTE		
	Harry S. Truman, Democrat	Thomas E. Dewey, Republican	Storm Thurmond, States' Right	Henry Wallace, Progressive	Truman ticket	Dewey ticket	Thurmond ticket
Ala......	—	40,930	171,443	1,522	—	—	11
Ariz.....	95,251	77,597	—	3,310	4	—	—
Ark......	149,659	50,959	40,068	751	9	—	—
Calif.....	1,913,134	1,895,269	1,228	190,381	25	—	—
Colo.....	267,288	239,714	—	6,115	6	—	—
Conn.....	423,297	437,754	—	13,713	—	8	—
Del......	67,813	69,588	—	1,050	—	3	—
Fla......	281,988	194,280	89,755	11,620	8	—	—
Ga......	254,646	76,691	85,055	1,636	12	—	—
Idaho....	107,370	101,514	—	4,972	4	—	—
Ill.......	1,994,715	1,961,103	—	—	28	—	—
Ind......	807,833	821,079	—	9,649	—	13	—
Iowa.....	522,380	494,018	—	12,125	10	—	—
Kan......	351,902	423,039	—	4,603	—	8	—
Ky.......	466,757	341,210	10,411	1,567	11	—	—
La.......	136,344	72,657	204,290	3,035	—	—	10
Me.......	111,916	150,234	—	1,884	—	5	—
Md......	286,521	294,814	2,476	9,983	—	8	—
Mass.....	1,151,788	909,370	—	38,157	16	—	—
Mich.....	1,003,448	1,038,595	—	46,515	—	19	—
Minn.....	692,966	483,617	—	27,866	11	—	—
Miss.....	19,384	5,043	167,538	225	—	—	9
Mo......	917,315	655,039	—	3,998	15	—	—
Mont.....	119,071	96,770	—	7,313	4	—	—
Neb......	224,165	264,774	—	—	—	6	—
Nev......	31,291	29,357	—	1,469	3	—	—
N. H....	107,995	121,299	7	1,970	—	4	—
N. J....	895,455	981,124	—	42,683	—	16	—
N. M....	105,464	80,303	—	1,037	4	—	—
N. Y.*..	2,780,204	2,841,163	—	509,559	—	47	—
N. C....	459,070	258,572	69,652	3,915	14	—	—
N. D....	95,812	115,139	374	8,391	—	4	—
Ohio.....	1,452,791	1,445,684	—	37,596	25	—	—
Okla.....	452,782	268,817	—	—	10	—	—
Ore......	243,147	260,904	—	14,978	—	6	—
Pa.......	1,752,426	1,902,197	—	55,161	—	35	—
R. I.....	188,736	135,787	—	2,619	4	—	—
S. C.....	34,423	5,386	102,607	154	—	—	8
S. D.....	117,653	129,651	—	2,801	—	4	—
Tenn.....	270,402	202,914	73,815	1,864	11	—	—
Tex......	750,700	282,240	106,909	3,764	23	—	—
Utah.....	149,151	124,402	—	2,679	4	—	—
Vt.......	45,557	75,926	—	1,279	—	3	—
Va......	200,786	172,070	43,393	2,047	11	—	—
Wash.....	476,165	386,315	—	31,692	8	—	—
W. Va...	429,188	316,251	—	3,311	8	—	—
Wis......	647,310	590,959	—	25,282	12	—	—
Wyo.....	52,354	47,947	—	931	3	—	—
Total.....	24,105,812	21,970,065	1,169,021	1,157,172	303	189	38

* The Truman vote includes 222,562 Liberal Party votes. Thomas, Socialist, 139,521; Watson, Prohibitionist, 103,343, Teichert, Socialist-Labor, 29,061; Dobbs, Soc. Workers, 13,613. Others, and blank votes, 148,971. Total vote, 48,836,579.

Governor Thomas E. Dewey and Senator Robert A. Taft, with Harold E. Stassen running a close third. Others mentioned were Senator Arthur Vandenberg (a good compromise choice if the leading candidates should deadlock each other), Ohio's Senator John Bricker, and California's Governor Earl Warren, while the Hearst papers campaigned vigorously for General Douglas MacArthur.

The Republican favorites fought hard in the primaries. In New Hampshire six delegates were chosen to vote for Dewey and two to support Stassen. In Wisconsin Harold Stassen challenged General MacArthur, whose managers confidently predicted that each of the state's twenty-seven delegates would go to the General. How mistaken they were! Stassen captured no less than nineteen Wisconsin delegates, leaving only eight for MacArthur, thus ending the General's aspirations. And in Nebraska Stassen won all but one of fifteen delegates. It was in the Ohio primary that the Stassen bandwagon was slowed down. Senator Taft captured in his home state forty-four delegates, while Stassen had only nine.

Then came the battle for Oregon. In any other election year the primary in that state would have caused little stir, but this time it was different. For both Dewey and Stassen the result in Oregon was of great importance. Dewey needed the victory to recoup his losses to Stassen in Wisconsin and Nebraska; Stassen needed it to make up for his poor showing in Ohio. After both candidates had campaigned intensively throughout the state, they met before the microphones at Portland to debate one of the major issues of the contest: "Should the Communist party be outlawed in the United States?" Stassen argued for it, Dewey against it.

The result of the primary gave the victory to Dewey, who carried Oregon with 111,657 votes to Stassen's 102,419. The meaning of the vote was best summed up by Arthur Krock, who wrote in the New York *Times:* "Governor Thomas E. Dewey's substantial victory in Oregon demonstrated that there is no continental demand among Republicans for Harold E. Stassen, just as earlier primaries established the same fact about Senator Robert A. Taft and Mr. Dewey himself." So the race among the Republicans was still wide open.

This was not true of the Democrats. They were resigned to the fact that Truman would be their candidate. And in the summer of 1948 there was only one opinion in the Democratic ranks—that the Republicans would walk away with the prize in November.

Only one man was confident that this would not happen—Harry S. Truman. He was busy planning a trip to take the issues before the people, discuss them vigorously, and turn the tide. In the first week of June he left Washington on a "nonpolitical" tour and headed for the West Coast, but twenty-four hours after his departure he was frankly appealing to the voters to re-elect him in November.

It soon became evident that wherever the President spoke, his earthy humor and friendly manner evoked a warm response from the people, who turned out in great numbers to listen to him. Truman spoke, as one reporter put it, "the language of Main Street, and Main Street understands it—even to the grammatical errors and slurred words which occasionally made purists on his special train writhe a bit. . . ." Here was a friendly man visiting among friendly people, who talked to them simply, in terms which everyone could understand.

The President's main theme was the Republican Congress—"the worst in my memory"—which was more interested "in the welfare of the better classes" than in ordinary men. "We need a Congress that believes in the welfare of the nation as a whole and not in the welfare of special interests," he said in Gary, Indiana, asserting that "when we get a new Congress, maybe we'll get one that will work in the interests of the common people and not in the interests of the men who have all the money."

"Lay it on, Harry!" the people cried, and Truman answered: "I'm going to, I'm going to. I'm pouring it on and I'm gonna keep pouring it on."

It was in Spokane that Truman said that the Republicans "are going down to Philadelphia in a few days and are going to tell you what a great Congress they have been. Well, if you believe that, you are bigger suckers than I think you are." And he bluntly told a labor audience: "I understand that you are not very happy over the labor act of 1948 as it is now in effect. But you know the reason for that is that in November, 1946, just one-third of the population voted. The people were not interested in what might happen to them. We have that law now, and I am the President and I have to enforce it. Your only remedy is November, 1948. And if you continue that law in effect, that is your fault and not mine, because I didn't want it."

As his trip wore on Truman's campaign strategy became clear: it was "the plain people's President against the privileged people's Congress."

Back in Washington the Republicans were

A FAMOUS PHOTOGRAPH. The obliging Vice-President, Harry S. Truman, poses at a National Press Club party with movie actress Lauren Bacall. This picture was widely reproduced in the newspapers, and before long the anti-Truman press was using it as proof of Truman's lack of dignity. From then on the Vice-President was more careful.

growing more and more irate. Finally Senator Taft spoke up. "Our gallivanting President is blackguarding Congress at every whistle-stop in the West," he said, and asked for immediate adjournment, because "there is little use in keeping Congress in session while President Truman is delivering an attack on the principles of representative government itself." Taft's "whistle-stop" remark was a boomerang. Their civic pride outraged, the small towns on Truman's route bristled with indignation.

There was no question that the President was a success in his role of crusader against Congress and that he enjoyed playing it. Sometimes he came out on the platform of his train in his pajamas. In Barstow, California, a woman called up to him that she thought he had a cold. Truman said he didn't. "But you sound like you have a cold," she persisted. "That's because I ride around in the wind with my mouth open," was the retort, to the joy of all who heard it. Truman spiced his speeches with local anecdotes, made compliments about the local scenery, asked his listeners whether they had been to church, and introduced his wife and daughter to the crowds. "Meet the boss," he would say, pointing to Mrs. Truman. And presenting his daughter, he won a laugh when he related how she had worked four years for a diploma from George Washington University, but on the same night that she got hers, he got one "for nothing."

"His contact with the people," wrote Thomas

AT POTSDAM, where grave decisions were made about the future of Germany, the President poses for a photograph with Marshal Stalin and Prime Minister Churchill.

THE SURRENDER OF JAPAN. The President announces to newspaper reporters on August 14, 1945, that the Japanese government has accepted America's sur-

ender terms without qualification. Mrs. Truman listens ▸ the announcement, sitting between Mrs. George S. choeneman and Judge Samuel Rosenman. On Rosen-

man's left is John W. Snyder, then War Mobilization director. Behind Truman sits Secretary of State James F. Byrnes, and behind Byrnes is Attorney General Clark.

THE SPLIT IN THE DEMOCRATIC PARTY

THE SOUTH REBELS. Senator Johnston's empty table at the Jackson Day dinner dramatizes the opposition of Southern Democrats to Truman's civil rights program.

THE PROGRESSIVES BOLT. Henry Wallace endorsed Leo Isaacson, who fought a by-election in the Bronx and won. His victory raised the hopes of the Progressives.

L. Stokes, who accompanied the President on the tour, "recreates again the amiable and friendly fellow who, as a haberdashery store proprietor and a local politician, enjoyed swapping yarns with his friends and exchanging wisecracks of the street-corner variety."

The reporter of the Washington *Evening Star* was less friendly. "The President, in this critical hour, is making a spectacle of himself in a political junket that would reflect discreditably on a ward heeler," wrote he.

During this time—while Truman was attempting to turn the tide in his favor in the West—Congress wrestled with an accumulation of unfinished business. The time of adjournment—June 19—was near and there was still no decision on civil rights legislation, oleomargarine tax repeal, long-range housing and farm legislation, Federal aid to education, and legislation to increase minimum wages from forty to seventy-

five cents an hour. Nothing had been done about the Mundt-Nixon Bill, the return of tidelands mineral rights to the states, the broadening of social security, and other measures. In the final weeks only a few bills were passed: one extended the terms of the Atomic Energy Commissioners for two years; another allowed displaced persons to enter the United States; a third came out for reciprocal trade agreements; a fourth for a stop-gap draft. All other measures were put off.

The inaction of Congress on many vital problems caused the Republican *Herald Tribune* to exclaim in despair: "For a Congress under Republican leadership to adjourn with such a record in a presidential year would be political suicide." In the opinion of the *Herald Tribune*, Congress should not adjourn but recess and return after the conventions "to finish the job and finish it well. Any other course would mean abdication."

THE CANDIDATE OF THE REPUBLICANS. Thomas E. Dewey fought tirelessly in the primaries, and exhibited an entirely different personality from the stiff, overstylized candidate of 1944. Joining in the spirit of local fun-making, he ate raw beef with Oregon cavemen and allowed himself to be kidnapped and hauled off to an initiation ceremony.

THE OREGON DEBATE

REPUBLICAN OPPONENTS in Oregon's primary were Dewey and Stassen. The result was important to both, for this was the last test of strength before the convention.

Nevertheless, Congress adjourned, and two days later the Republican nominating convention opened in Philadelphia. Governor Dwight H. Green of Illinois delivered the keynote address, seen and heard over hundreds of thousands of television sets throughout the country. He abused the New Deal and the Democratic party, which was "held together by bosses, boodle, buncombe and blarney," and praised the record of the Eightieth Congress, which had restored faith in representative government, had freed American economy from regimentation, balanced the budget, reduced Federal income taxes, and corrected chaotic conditions in labor relations.

The attractive Clare Boothe Luce, the woman keynoter, made a far more interesting appeal to her audience, spicing it with wisecracks and witticisms. Mrs. Luce said that President Truman was "a gone goose," whose "time is short and whose situation is hopeless," and whose three years in office were not "the pause that refreshes." She told the convention that "Democratic Presidents are always troubadours of trouble, crooners of catastrophe; they cannot win elections except in the climate of crisis. So

CLIMAX OF THE OREGON CAMPAIGN was a radio debate between Dewey and Stassen in Portland on the theme: "Shall the Communist party be outlawed?" In the election Oregon Republicans backed Dewey, who won the state's 12 delegates. The Stassen bandwagon, which had rolled so briskly in the previous primaries, came to an abrupt halt

A WIDELY PUBLICIZED PHOTOGRAPH shows the small audience which turned out to hear the President speak in Omaha at the outset of his Western tour in June. Though the empty hall was the result of an organizational slip on the part of the Democrats, the picture seemed to corroborate reports that Truman's tour created little interest.

the party, by its composition, has a vested interest in depression at home and war abroad."

Each of the Republican speakers underlined the Democratic party's association with Communists. Said Joseph W. Martin, Jr.: "The New Deal, over a period of fifteen years of experimenting with statism, had permitted hundreds of enemies of America to infiltrate into official positions. . . ." To this columnist Thomas Stokes retorted: "The Republican cry about Communists in government is, of course, myth. . . . But that does not matter. It's a good issue. It covers up so many omissions by Congress."

The platform emerged only after a heated controversy between the "internationalists," led by Senator Henry Cabot Lodge, Jr., chairman of the 104-member resolutions committee, and

THE ONE-MAN CRUSADE. Truman attacked the "do-nothing" Republican Eightieth Congress in most of his campaign speeches as "the worst Congress in history."

685

the "nationalists," under the leadership of Senator C. Wayland Brooks of Illinois. The chief disagreement between the two groups was over the foreign policy plank which, in its accepted version, asked for continuation of the European Recovery Program "within the prudent limits of our own economic welfare," but omitted any pledge to appropriate money for it. In other planks the platform supported the United Nations as "the world's best hope" for collective security, asked recognition of the new state of Israel "subject to the letter and spirit of the United Nations Charter," and advocated a foreign policy of "friendly firmness which welcomes cooperation but spurns appeasement."

The Republicans' domestic program contained a strong stand on civil rights, promised prompt action to correct "the recent cruelly high cost of living," and urged the maintenance of a strong military establishment. Furthermore, it advocated benefits to veterans, recommended the extension of social security, and proposed "equal pay for equal work, regardless of sex." On Federal aid to education—one of the bills Senator Taft had introduced in the Senate—the platform was noncommittal: "We favor equality of educational opportunity for all and the promotion of education and educational facilities," it said. On tidelands it declared that the party was in favor of "restoration to the states of their historic rights to the tide- and submerged lands, tributary waters, lakes, and streams." On communism it pledged "vigorous enforcement of existing laws against Communists and enactment of such new legislation as may be necessary to expose the treasonable activities of Communists and defeat their objective of establishing here a Godless dictatorship controlled from abroad." On labor it promised "continuing study to improve labor-management legislation in the light of experience and changing conditions."

If one scrutinized the platform closely however, it became apparent that most of its pledges were in direct contradiction to the Republican policies followed in the last Congress. The platform promised cooperation "on a basis of self-help and mutual aid, to assist other peace-loving nations to restore their economic independence," but in Congress members of the party had done their utmost to cut the European Recovery Program. The platform promised support to "the system of reciprocal trade," but in Congress the Republicans had fought the reciprocal trade agreements. The platform promised "Federal aid to the states for local slum clearance and low-rent housing programs," but in the House the Republicans had supplied a majority to defeat the Taft-Ellender Housing Bill. The platform solemnly upheld the "equality of all individuals in their right to life, liberty and the pursuit of happiness . . . never to be limited in any individual because of race, religion, color, or country of origin," but on Capitol Hill the Republicans had done very little about the pending bills abolishing the poll tax, making lynching a Federal crime, and removing segregation in the armed forces and discrimination in jobs. In their platform the Republicans favored "progressive development of the nation's water resources," but in Congress they had come out for restriction of the President's public power program.

The day before the balloting began, the Dewey machine stepped up its power and jolted the opposition with a telling blow. Senator Ed Martin of Pennsylvania announced the withdrawal of his own favorite-son candidacy and urged the Pennsylvania delegation to go to Governor Dewey on the first ballot. Supremely confident, Dewey's managers declared that their man would get "well over 400 votes on the first ballot," and that "it will be all over by the third ballot at the latest."

When the big day arrived, only seven names were proposed for the first place: Dewey, Taft, Stassen, Warren, Vandenberg, Senator Raymond Baldwin of Connecticut, and General MacArthur. "Cheering demonstrations greeted every name," reported the *Herald Tribune*, "but not all the enthusiasm for all the names could conceal the fact that the trading and dealing that has been going on in rooms that were smoke-filled or airy, has left scars that may be bared before the 15,000 spectators when the balloting begins."

Dewey was the acknowledged favorite and his bandwagon received several powerful pushes. After Senator Martin had brought forty-one of Pennsylvania's votes into the Dewey camp (the remaining Pennsylvanians clung to Vandenberg), Indiana's favorite son Charles Halleck dropped his own candidacy and released his

THE SYMBOL. A fifteen-foot balloon-rubber elephant, which collapsed and had to be reinflated, decorated the hotel where Dewey had his headquarters.

AN ANGEL in the streets outside Earl Warren's headquarters was hardly noticed as she distributed the address of an eating place to convention crowds.

DEMONSTRATORS parade at night with banners through the streets of Philadelphia in an effort to boost enthusiasm for their candidate, Harold E. Stassen.

RIVALRY is displayed in the lobby of the Benjamin Franklin Hotel, where a huge portrait of Senator Vandenberg is posted below a picture of Robert A. Taft.

state's twenty-nine votes to the New York governor.

Meanwhile the "Stop-Dewey" leaders—Taft, Stassen, and Governor Duff—met in conferences where they were joined by Governor Kim Sigler of Michigan on behalf of Senator Vandenberg. They desired, as Stassen expressed it, "to make this an open convention." Pennsylvania's Governor Duff, raging over Ed Martin's defection, fumed: "We are all agreed that this is the first time in American politics that European blitz tactics have been used to secure a nomination. Yes, and I mean Dewey by that. We have worked out a definite plan to guarantee the delegates the right of free expression."

The trouble with the anti-Dewey forces was that they could not agree on a candidate, for none of the anti-Dewey candidates was willing to make a place for another. "It'll be Tom or me," declared Taft. And because Stassen refused to accept second place on the ticket, the Taft-Stassen combination, curiously supported by Colonel Robert McCormick of the Chicago *Tribune*, came to nought.

On the first trial Dewey pocketed 434 votes to 224 for Taft, 157 for Stassen, 62 for Vandenberg, 59 for Warren, and 11 for MacArthur. (On this ballot Illinois voted for Dwight Green, New Jersey for Governor Driscoll, Connecticut for Raymond Baldwin.) On the second trial Dewey's vote increased to 515, only 33 votes short of the necessary majority. Taft had 274, Stassen 149, Vandenberg 62, and Warren 57 votes.

Governor Duff, still hoping to stop Dewey by a coalition, forced a recess. But when after a pause of two and a half hours the convention reassembled, each of the opposing candidates bowed out and Dewey became the unanimous choice of the convention.

That same evening the chosen Republican nominee—after a lengthy session in his hotel suite—endorsed Governor Earl Warren of California for the second place, and the next day the delegates ratified his choice.

Dewey won the nomination, "not because he had principles or even appeal, but because he had a machine," wrote columnist Max Lerner. "The machine was ruthless and well oiled, run by a group of slick and modern operators. It combined the age-old methods of power politics

with the newest strategies of blitz warfare and the precision tools of American industry and administration."

And *Time* Magazine, speaking of the Dewey-Warren combination, asserted: "Barring a political miracle, it was the kind of ticket that could not fail to sweep the Republican party back into power."

As the Republicans left the City of Brotherly Love, the Democrats moved in. Truman's opponents made a last-minute effort to stop the President's nomination. The anti-Truman forces embraced three main groups: the Americans for Democratic Action (ADA), the Southern dissidents, and some of the big city machines. They were divergent elements with no common political objective except opposition to Truman as the candidate of the party. The ADA, friendly to labor, supported the President's civil rights program, the conservative Southerners were firmly anti-labor, anti-New Deal, and violently against civil rights, and the city bosses were opportunists—they wanted to win the election, not lose it with Truman.

But if Truman were not the candidate, who would be? The ADA's suggestion to nominate Supreme Court Justice William O. Douglas was brusquely discarded by the Southerners, to whom the progressive Douglas seemed "just Wallace in black robes."

There was only one person who could "block Truman" and win the election for the Democrats—Dwight D. Eisenhower. In the nation the General was still leading in all public opinion polls. The movement to draft him as a Democratic candidate intensified (already the Georgia and Virginia delegations had pledged themselves to vote for him). On July 3 nineteen party leaders—among them James Roosevelt of California, Colonel Jacob Arvey of Illinois, Governor Strom Thurmond of South Carolina, Senator Lister Hill of Alabama, and the Mayor of New York, William O'Dwyer—wired to the 1592 chosen Democratic delegates and alternates, inviting them to a caucus in Philadelphia the Saturday before the opening of the convention, to "seek for the leader of our party the ablest and strongest man available." The telegram stated that "no man in these critical days can refuse the call to duty and leadership"—a hint to Eisenhower that he was ob-

FRIENDS BEFORE THE CAMERAS. The chief contenders for the Republican nomination—Stassen, Dewey and Taft—pose with Speaker of the House Martin at a welcoming party in Philadelphia before the convention. Smiles cover the resentment which they felt toward each other, and which was so obvious in the pre-convention campaign.

gated to accept the nomination if offered to him.

A day later—on July 4—New Jersey's Frank Hague spoke on behalf of his state's thirty-six delegates and declared that "the public will not let world leadership in either Truman or the Republican candidate. General Eisenhower led us to victory through the greatest war in history, and we want him back to complete the job."

But the movement for Eisenhower died down as fast as it had begun. On July 5 the General

(turn to page 692)

HERBERT HOOVER received an ovation when he mounted the platform to address the Republican convention. He warned the delegates that "if you produce nothing but improvised platitudes, you will give no hope."

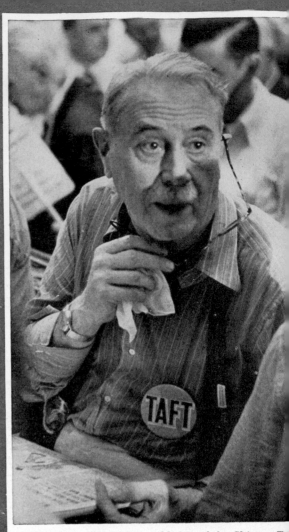

ROBERT McCORMICK, publisher of the Chicago *T une* and head of the Illinois delegation, was a stau supporter of Senator Robert A. Taft. On the first day the convention he came out for a Taft-Stassen tick

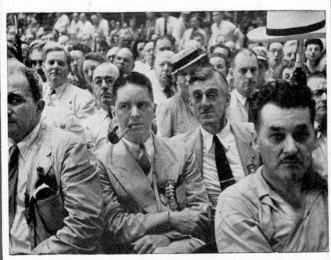

LISTENING TO THE NOMINATIONS, Senator Leverett Saltonstall of Massachusetts (in black tie) sits among the delegates. Seven contenders were mentioned: Dewey, Stassen, Taft, Vandenberg, Martin, Baldwin, MacArthur.

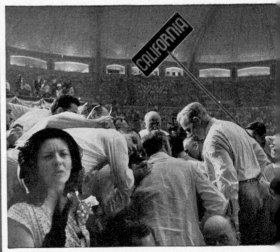

CALIFORNIA HOLDS a hurried caucus on the floo the convention hall, and decides to switch to favo Thomas Dewey after receiving word that Governor Warren has abandoned his candidacy for the first pl

LFRED LANDON, the 1936 Republican presidential
minee and chief of the Kansas delegation, listens with
eat concentration to the latest convention news, seem-
gly unruffled by Philadelphia's hot and humid weather.

CLARE BOOTHE LUCE, former Representative to Congress, was the woman keynoter of the convention. Here
she leads an enthusiastic floor demonstration for Connecticut's favorite son, Senator Raymond Baldwin.

CONNECTICUT CAUCUS discusses whether the en-
e delegation should continue to support their favorite
, Raymond Baldwin, or release the Dewey men so
y can vote for their candidate on the next ballot.

NEW ENGLAND DELEGATES listen intently to the
keynote address by Governor Dwight Green, in which he
charged that the Democratic administration "was held
together by bosses, boodle, buncombe and blarney."

blasted all hopes, saying that he "could not accept the nomination for any public office or participate in partisan political contests." On that day a New York *Times* survey revealed that Truman had the nomination in the bag, for 809 of the convention's delegates were already pledged to vote for him—a large enough number to assure his nomination on the first ballot.

Two days before the convention opened, the Associated Press reported: "It's all over now but the shouting, and even the shouting will be largely mechanical, organized and half-hearted next week when the Democrats nominate Mr. Truman."

The columnists of the land buried the Democratic party. Wrote Walter Lippmann: "The country may say to the Democrats as they relinquish the power they have held so long and the heavy responsibility they have borne through dangerous days: 'Hail and farewell. . . . We shall meet again.' " Said Drew Pearson: "Every seasoned Democratic leader is convinced Harry Truman will suffer a historic defeat." Wrote the New York *Times* from Philadelphia: "Arriving delegates found an atmosphere of gloom and despondency and encountered a spirit of defeatism among the party leaders already here that amounted to confession that President Truman seemed to have little chance of election."

There was a good deal of animated discussion among the delegates about who should be chosen for the second place. The President wanted Justice Douglas, but Douglas declined. His refusal put Senator Alben W. Barkley in the front of a large field of vice-presidential prospects. Said "Dear Alben": "I am willing. . . . But it will have to come quick; I don't want it passed around so long it is like a cold biscuit." And it came "quick." After Barkley had delivered his old-fashioned, sledge-hammer keynote address, there was no longer any doubt that he would be the convention choice for the Vice-Presidency.

But first the platform had to be drawn up. A fight over the civil rights plank assumed serious proportions. The Southerners, outnumbered three to one on the resolutions committee, were defeated on every issue. Their states'-rights plank went overboard and none of their other suggestions was accepted. The ADA group, led by Minneapolis Mayor Hubert Humphrey, demanded a definite declaration supporting legislation against the poll tax, lynching, and segregation in the armed forces, and for fair employment practices. Senator Scott Lucas, on behalf of the administration, opposed an outright declaration because he feared that it might wreck the party, and proposed a plank similar to that of 1944. When the South refused to accept a compromise, the issue came before the convention. In an unprecedented move, the delegates overruled the resolutions committee and by a vote of 651½ to 582½ wrote into the platform a declaration praising President Truman for his courageous civil rights stand and calling on Congress to carry it out. After a dramatic floor fight the entire Mississippi delegation and half of Alabama's—thirty-five delegates in all—walked out in a rage.

The convention tried to complete the nomination of President and Vice-President by 10:00 p.m. on Wednesday, the third day, when President Truman was to appear before the delegates to deliver his acceptance speech. However, it was well after midnight when, in a tense atmosphere and over loudly voiced protests from the South, the first roll call was completed and Harry S. Truman was named. Nine hundred forty-seven and a half votes were cast for him against 263 for Senator Richard Russell of Georgia—the hurriedly named presidential candidate of the Southern dissidents. For the Vice-Presidency the convention named Alben Barkley by acclamation.

It was two o'clock in the morning when the President, who had waited for hours outside the hall, made his entrance, opened a black notebook, and spoke to the convention. *Newsweek* reported: "Nothing short of a stroke of magic could infuse the remnants of the party with enthusiasm. But magic he had; in a speech bristling with marching words, Mr. Truman brought the convention to its highest peak of excitement."

"Senator Barkley and I will win this election, and make these Republicans like it, don't you forget that," cried Truman. "We'll do that because they're wrong and we're right." The ten thousand exhausted people in the hall awakened from their apathy, jumped to their feet and cheered. The word *win* electrified them. The President told them that the Democratic party had "been elected four times in succession and I'm convinced it will be elected a fifth time next November. The reason is that the people know the Democratic party is the people's party, and the Republican party is the party of special interests and it always has been and always will be. . . ."

He extolled the achievements of the Democratic administration. "Never in the world were the farmers . . . as prosperous . . . and if they don't do their duty by the Democratic party they're the most ungrateful people in the world. . . . And I'll say to labor just what I've said to the farmers. They are the most ungrateful people in the world if they pass the Democratic party by this year. . . ."

The President was in his element. He pointed out that the total national income "has increased from less than forty billion dollars in 1933 to two hundred and three billions in 1947, the greatest in all the history of the world."

He launched into a slashing attack on the Eightieth Congress and the Republican platform. "The Republican party favors the privileged few and not the common, everyday man. Ever since its inception, that party has been under the control of special privilege, and they concretely proved it in the Eightieth Congress. . . . They proved it by the things they failed to do. . . ."

He listed the sins of Congress. It had not extended price controls, thus prices had "gone all the way off the chart in adjusting themselves at the expense of the consumer and for the benefit of the people who hold the goods." It had not passed the Taft-Ellender-Wagner Housing Bill, which was "to clear the slums in the big cities, and to help erect low-rent housing." Instead of "moderate legislation to promote labor-management relations," it had passed the Taft-Hartley Act, which "disrupted the labor-management relationship and which will cause strife and bitterness to come if it's not repealed." It had done nothing about an increase in the minimum wage, nothing about more and better schools, nothing to improve the social security law, nothing about a much needed health plan, nothing about civil rights. But two

of the greatest failures of the Republican Eightieth Congress "are of major concern to every American family: the failure to do anything about high prices, and the failure to do anything about housing."

"They promised to do in that platform a lot of things I've been asking them to do and that they've refused to do when they had the power. The Republican platform urges extending and increasing social security benefits. Think of that—and yet when they had the opportunity, they took 750,000 people off our social security rolls. I wonder if they think they can fool the people with such poppycock as that."

The President spoke in anger, he spoke "too rapidly, too jerkily, too emotionally," wrote Max Lerner. "But he was caught up in what he was saying. It was a harangue . . . and it was what the polite people call 'demagogic.' But it carried conviction because it was the truth, and had been waiting to be said for a long time. It had no taste: the candidate used un-Dewey-like words like 'lousy,' and called the Republicans the 'enemy'. . . ." But somehow during the speech a rapport was built up between the speaker and an audience "which neither loved nor admired him. They sensed that this was the most militant presidential acceptance speech in either major party since Bryan. They liked the fact that he came out of his corner fighting." And they cheered him with enthusiasm.

The surprise of the speech came at the end: "My duty as President requires that I use every means within my power to get the laws the people need on matters of such importance and urgency," Truman said. Therefore, "On the twenty-sixth day of July, which out in Missouri they call Turnip Day, I'm going to call that Congress back and I'm going to ask them to pass laws halting rising prices and to meet the housing crisis which they say they're for in their platform. At the same time I shall ask them to act on other vitally needed measures such as aid to education, which they say they're for; a national health program, civil rights legislation, which they say they're for; an increase in the minimum wage, which I doubt very much they're for; funds for projects needed in our program to provide public power and cheap electricity . . . ; an adequate and decent law for displaced persons in place of the

(turn to page 696)

THE REPUBLICAN CANDIDATES

THE WINNER AND HIS WIFE. Governor and Mrs. Dewey, wearing wreaths of flowers around their necks, acknowledge the ovation of the cheering convention.

THE REPUBLICAN TICKET. The Warren and Dewey families pose for their convention photograph. Standing are the two Dewey sons and three Warren daughters.

THE VICE-PRESIDENTIAL candidate, Governor Earl Warren of California, and his wife wave thanks from the platform of convention hall to the applauding delegates.

THE REPUBLICAN CHOICE was New York's 46-year old Governor Thomas E. Dewey, the only candidate in the party's history to receive the nomination for a second

694

ne after having been defeated in a previous election.
is machine worked faultlessly in the convention. The
top-Dewey" movement failed because the opposition was unable to unite behind one man, and because neither Taft, Stassen, nor Vandenberg was strong enough to offer effective resistance to the Dewey managers' blitz tactics.

anti-Semitic, anti-Catholic law which this Eightieth Congress passed."

Thunderous applause greeted this announcement. "Now my friends," continued the President, "if there is any reality behind that Republican platform, we ought to get some action out of the short session of the Eightieth Congress. They could do this job in fifteen days if they wanted to do it. . . . What that worst Eightieth Congress does in its special session will be the test. The American people will decide on the record." A frenzied ovation ended the President's speech.

Next day the columnist Gerald W. Johnson wrote admiringly: "Nobody can deny that the Haberdasher has more guts than a fiddle-string factory. Who was the first politician with the nerve to black John L. Lewis' eye? Who punched the nose of Whitney, the railroad trainman . . . ? Battling Harry, the demon necktie salesman." And the columnist Thomas L. Stokes prophesied that the President, who had lifted the pall of defeatism, "will challenge the Republicans every step of the way between now and the November election." The New York *Times* declared: "The Democratic party came out of its Philadelphia convention mor-

ally stronger, if perhaps numerically weaker than it went in. It came out with fire in its eye, in place of the glazed look of a week ago."

But this momentary upsurge of renewed confidence could not heal the breach within the party ranks. The party was split into three factions. Gone were the Wallaceites, gone were the Southern dissidents. At Birmingham the resentful Southerners met in a boisterous, one-day convention and named Governor J. Thurmond of South Carolina as their presidential candidate, with Governor Fielding Wright of Mississippi as his running mate.

The platform of the Dixiecrats—a word coined by the Charlotte, North Carolina, *News* for the Southern Democrats who opposed Truman and civil rights for Negroes—proclaimed that the States' Righters "oppose and condemn the action of the Democratic convention in sponsoring a civil rights program calling for the elimination of segregation, social equality by Federal fiat, regulation of private employment practices, voting, and local law enforcement," because "such a program would be utterly destructive of the social, economic and political life of the Southern people, and of other localities in which there may be differences in race, creed, or national origin in appreciable numbers."

And Thurmond, their presidential candidate orated: "If the South should vote for Truman this year, then we might as well petition the government to give us colonial status. . . . We Southerners are going to cast our vote for candidates who are true believers of states' government. . . ."

The hope of the States' Righters was that no presidential candidate would receive the majority of electoral college votes required under the Constitution. Then the election would be thrown into the House of Representatives where the South would hold the balance of power and could swing the Presidency to someone who opposed Federal legislation on civil rights.

A few days later, after the Southern wing of the Democratic party had nominated its candidates, the Progressives met in a convention in Philadelphia, naming Henry A. Wallace for the Presidency and Senator Glen Taylor of Idaho for the second place. Thirty thousand people

THE BOOM FOR EISENHOWER continued regardless of the General's repeated refusals to run for high office.

"LOOK, SUPPOSE WE PUT IT TO HIM THIS WAY." A group of disconsolate Democratic politicians try to figure out how to persuade Harry Truman to bow out gracefully and leave the way open for another, stronger candidate.

listened at Shibe Park to Wallace's acceptance speech, in which he declared that unlike Truman and Dewey, who boasted that they had accepted their nominations without commitments, he committed himself to place human rights above property rights; to transfer power over big business from private to public hands "wherever necessary"; to negotiate peacefully with the Soviet government and strengthen the United Nations; to develop "progressive capitalism" and protect "truly independent enterprise" from monopoly; to fight restrictive labor legislation, expand health and education facilities, and provide "economic security" for elder citizens.

The multitude, made up mostly of young men and women, applauded vigorously. They had enthusiastically endorsed the platform, which repudiated the Marshall Plan, called for the destruction of the atomic stockpile, favored

Big Four control of the Ruhr, and asked for cessation of financial and military aid to Chiang Kai Shek.

Besides the two major candidates, and Thurmond and Wallace, a number of minor candidates were in the presidential race. The Socialists named Norman Thomas for the sixth time; the Socialist-Labor party selected Edward E. Teichert. Farrell Dobbs was the choice of the Socialist Workers, Gerald K. Smith of the Christian Nationalists, John C. Scott of the Greenbackers, Claude Watson of the Prohibitionists, and John Maxwell of the American Vegetarians.

Congress reconvened for its special session on Monday, July 25—Turnip Day in Missouri. It was hot in Washington; the mercury hovered near 90 degrees, with 88 per cent humidity, but the tempers on Capitol Hill were even higher. Republicans called the President's move "cheap

697

THE CONVENTION OPENS WITH PRAYER

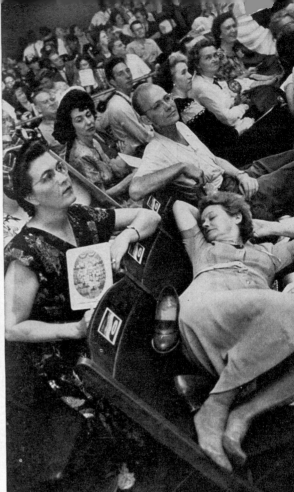

THE EXHAUSTED SPECTATOR

MRS. TRUMAN ON THE PLATFORM

SENATOR BARKLEY, THE KEYNOTER

politics and the handiwork of a desperate man," but it was acknowledged that Truman had "jolted Republicans generally" and had gotten in "the first good punch of the 1948 campaign."

The President addressed the joint session of Congress in person. He began by asking con-gressional action—"strong, positive action"—to check inflation and the rising cost of living, and he submitted an eight-point program which was "necessary to check rising prices and safe-guard our economy against the danger of de-pression."

THE ARDENT TRUMAN SUPPORTER

THE ANTI-TRUMAN DELEGATE

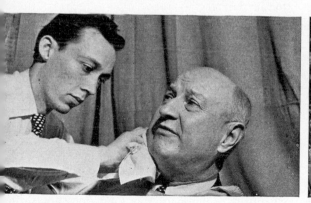

FARLEY GETS TELEVISION PAINT

ALABAMA'S DELEGATES PROTEST

Besides the anti-inflationary measures, the President asked for "housing at lower prices" and demanded legislation granting Federal aid to education. He pleaded for an increased national minimum wage and expansion of social security, for a "more equitable and realistic" pay bill for Federal employees, for civil rights legislation and a better "displaced persons" law, for a $65,000,000 loan for the construction of a permanent U.N. headquarters in New York City, for Senate ratification of the international wheat agreement, and for a restoration of

$56,000,000 for power and reclamation projects, including a TVA steam and generating plant.

But this was not all. The President emphasized a number of other problems which he thought should be dealt with. He asked for a comprehensive health insurance plan, a fair and sound labor-management relations law to replace the Taft-Hartley Act, a long-range farm program, a reciprocal trade agreements act, a universal training program, a national science foundation, strengthened anti-trust laws, and approval of the St. Lawrence Waterway treaty. Though—so Mr. Truman said—he realized that the limited time of the special session did not "readily permit action" on all the listed measures, "the next Congress should take them up immediately."

Senator Taft quickly pointed out that the President's recommendations were an "omnibus left-wing program," while a statement by Republican leaders branded the recall of Congress by the President "a political maneuver in the campaign for his own re-election." The Republicans held that "serious legislative problems cannot be satisfactorily handled in the midst of a political campaign," and that "in the President's program there is very little of an emergency nature"; therefore, the session should be completed as soon as possible.

The New York *Herald Tribune* warned: "Whatever the provocations, the Republican majority will not, we trust, allow itself to be driven into an attitude of intransigence. There are few of its members who can pretend that the record of the Eightieth Congress, hastily concluded as the convention drew near, is perfect or complete. There were measures upon which substantial agreement had already been reached, and for which the pressing need was— and still remains—indisputable. These should be passed as expeditiously as possible."

To such warnings the Eightieth Congress turned a deaf ear. Certain of victory in November, the Republican leadership had no intention of debating legislation now. Republican Senators allowed their Southern colleagues to filibuster the anti-poll tax bill, while the congressional banking committees prepared to kill every major part of President Truman's anti-inflation program. Two weeks after the special session started, Congress adjourned.

Thus the stage was set for the campaign, which began in earnest on Labor Day. President Truman fired the opening gun, addressing large meetings in and around Detroit. Harold Stassen spoke for Dewey in the same city, while Henry Wallace, who had been pelted with eggs and tomatoes in the South, returned to New York and spoke to an audience of fifty thousand people.

About that time—on September 9—pollster Elmo Roper announced that Dewey was leading Truman by the unbeatable margin of 44 per cent to 31 per cent—"an almost morbid resemblance to the Roosevelt-Landon figures as of about this time in 1936"—and therefore he would not issue any more polls, for in his opinion, no amount of electioneering would change a decisive number of votes. "Political campaigns," declared Mr. Roper, "are largely ritualistic. . . . All the evidence we have accumulated since 1936 tends to indicate that the man in the lead at the beginning of the campaign is the man who is the winner at the end of it. . . . The winner, it appears, clinches his victory early in the race and before he has uttered a word of campaign oratory. . . ." Roper informed his readers that his silence in the future should be construed "as an indication that Mr. Dewey is still so clearly ahead that we might just as well get ready to listen to his inauguration on January 20, 1949."

On September 17 President Truman left Washington for an extended campaign tour; Governor Dewey was to follow him in his special train two days later. Arthur Krock wrote in the New York *Times:* "If the public opinion pollsters are correct, and they were never more unanimous or certain of their findings, President Truman is launched on a speaking campaign to persuade a majority of the American voters to change their minds toward him before November 2. . . . If expert political managers are right in their general belief that a majority opinion of this kind does not shift after early September . . . then Mr. Truman has no chance to achieve the great objective of his gruelling journey."

But regardless of the pollsters, regardless of the hostile press, despite the fact that the Democratic party was broken into pieces and political control in key states was in the hands of Republicans, the President was convinced that he could turn the tide of public opinion in his favor. To Alben Barkley he promised: "I'm going to fight hard, I'm going to give them hell." *Them* meant the Republicans.

Truman's first major address was scheduled for Dexter, Iowa, where he told an enormous audience of rural folk that "there is every reason for the American farmer to expect a long period of good prices—if he continues to get a fair deal. His great danger is that he may be voted out of a fair deal and into a Republican deal."

He tore into "the Wall Street reactionaries," who "are not satisfied with being rich. They want to increase their power and their privileges, regardless of what happens to the other fellow. They are gluttons of privilege." The President seemed to enjoy the phrase, and within a few minutes he repeated it three times. He said that "these gluttons of privilege are now putting up fabulous sums of money to elect a Republican administration . . . that will listen to the gluttons of privilege first and to the people not at all," and he reminded his listeners that the American farmer and worker had been for the past hundred years the victims of boom-and-bust cycles, "with the accent on bust."

Truman continued: "You have already had a sample of what a Republican administration would mean to you. Two years ago, in the congressional elections, many Americans decided that they would not bother to vote. Others thought they would like to have a change, and they brought into power a Republican Congress —the notorious 'do-nothing' Republican Eightieth Congress." This Congress had "stuck a pitchfork in the farmer's back" and done its best to keep price supports from working. He reminded the farmers that it was the Republican big-business lobbyists, representing the speculative grain trade, who had persuaded Congress not to provide storage bins for the farmers. Concluding his address, the President said that if the farmers voted for him, they would be voting for themselves.

Two days later—on September 20—Governor Dewey made his first major address at Des Moines. "Tonight," he said, "we will enter upon a campaign to unite America. On January 20 we will enter upon a new era. We propose to install in Washington an administration which has faith in the American people, a warm understanding of their needs, and the confidence to meet them. . . ." He ignored the President's attack and spoke philosophically and on a lofty plane, avoiding specific issues.

Once Truman had begun his attack, he continued it relentlessly. At Salt Lake City he charged that the Republicans had helped special interests to "skim the cream from our natural resources," and that the power lobby in Washington, operating through the Congress, had "crudely and wickedly cheated" the people. "The Republican party has shown in the Congress of the last two years that the leopard does not change its spots. It is still the party of Harding-Coolidge boom and Hoover depression."

Again Dewey ignored the President's charges. The Republican candidate spoke at Denver calmly and sedately. His theme was conservation.

Though the President faced almost solid opposition from the polls and press, wherever he spoke, wherever his train stopped, large audiences were at hand to cheer him. *Time* Magazine reported: "Newsmen were nonplussed. They had spent most of their time on the train speculating on the extent of Mr. Truman's defeat in November. All across Republican Iowa large crowds turned out to see him. The crowds were friendly, a good deal of the cheering was enthusiastic." Possibly the phenomenon of Harry Truman's reception could be explained "by the U.S. citizen's sympathy for the underdog, by his admiration for spunkiness, or just plain curiosity."

All through Nevada and California Truman repeated his onslaughts against the Eightieth Congress. At Reno he called the Republican chairmen of the Senate and House committees "a bunch of mossbacks." In Los Angeles he suggested that the Progressives should vote for him and not for Wallace, as "a vote for the third party plays into the hands of the Republican forces of reaction whose aims are directly opposed to the aim of American liberalism." At Fresno he told a crowd that he had been a farmer in his youth and had joined the colors when war came. "I didn't claim any exemption

(turn to page 704)

on account of that farm, nor did I claim any exemption for being thirty-three years old. I went over and joined a battery of field artillery. . . . I am not bragging about that because that is just what I ought to have done. . . ." At Oakland he blamed the Eightieth Congress for the housing shortage. At San Diego he repeated his charge that "the Republicans are for the special interests." At El Paso he said that the Republicans would halt the Federal Government's cheap public power program and give the benefits and profits from Federally-built dams to the private utilities "so they can get rich at your expense." At Deming he declared that Congress had tried to "sabotage the West," and if it had not been for the Democrats, "you would have had your throats cut by this Congress."

By comparison, the Dewey speeches seemed pallid and lacking in conviction. At Phoenix, Arizona, the Republican candidate declared: "Ours is a magnificent land. Every part of it. Don't let anybody frighten you or try to stampede you into believing that America is finished. America's future—like yours in Arizona—is still

TRUMAN RECALLED CONGRESS to Washington for a special session to act upon legislation which, in the President's opinion, was vital to the nation's welfare.

ahead of us." But if the people of America had left matters to the government, "there would have been very little progress indeed," and "if it had been up to Washington to develop, let us say, our electrical industry, you can be pretty sure we'd still be using kerosene lamps." In Hollywood Dewey assailed communism, and at San Francisco he accused the administration of contributing to inflation by "dropping monkey wrenches" into the economic machinery and following "defeatist policies."

While the two chief contenders fought for votes in the West, Henry Wallace made a campaign tour of the Middle West. At St. Louis he blamed both the Democrats and Republicans for failing to make a really honest effort to pass Federal laws against racial discrimination and the "Jim Crow" system. In Chicago he declared that Russia was "no threat" to the United States, despite the fact that "our allies in war" were being "treated as enemies in peace."

The second week of the major campaign found Dewey touring Oregon and Washington while the President traveled through Texas. Again Truman took the offensive. In Dallas he said: "The Republican candidates are "trying to sing the American voters to sleep with a lullaby about unity in domestic affairs," but the Republicans "want the kind of unity that benefits the National Association of Manufacturers, the private power lobbies, the real-estate lobbies, and selfish interests." At Fort Worth his theme was that Congress had passed a rich man's tax bill and had taken "freedom away from labor"; at Oklahoma that the Republicans "have not hurt the Communist party one bit—they have helped it"; at Louisville that the NAM had used the Republican party as a tool for killing price control in 1946 in "a conspiracy against the American consumer." The President said that before price control ended, "profits after taxes of all corporations were running at the rate of twelve billion dollars a year," but in the spring of 1948 "they were running at the rate of 20½ billions—an increase of 70 per cent in corporation profits." And he posed the question: "Is the government of the United States going to run in the interest of the people as a whole, or in the interest of a small group of privileged big businessmen?"

Dewey repeated his one basic theme in all his

THE CANDIDATE OF THE DIXIECRATS, Governor Strom Thurmond of South Carolina, campaigned vigorously against the President's civil rights program. With the Southern defection on one hand and the Progressive break on the other, Truman's defeat seemed sure. In the election the Dixiecrats carried four states with 38 electoral votes.

speeches—that only a Republican President and a Republican Congress could provide the country with the unity it needed to insure peace in a troubled world. On the domestic side he promised a cut in government expenses, thus bringing inflation under control; he spoke for a reduction of the Federal debt, and for a revision of the tax laws to encourage production and savings; he endorsed the farm price subsidies of the government and came out for the strengthening of the soil conservation program and for an acceleration of the reclamation, irrigation, and hydro-electric projects. He promised to appoint a Westerner as Secretary of the Interior, and he emphasized his belief that people in the localities affected should have a voice in the planning and operation of the Columbia River and Missouri Valley projects.

In the opinion of columnist Thomas Stokes, Dewey's "soothing-syrup campaign" fitted perfectly the mood of the American people. "There is a feeling of uncertainty and insecurity abroad in our land," wrote Stokes. "The people want to be reassured. They want to believe in a fairy tale. They don't want to have to bother their heads about those problems that stare them in the face on the front pages of newspapers every day and about which President Truman talks—troubles in Berlin and Paris; continued high prices here at home and little bits of evidence all around of a boom before a bust; and that 'do-nothing Eightieth Congress' that the President raises up and shakes before them every day.

"Governor Dewey reassures them and flatters them where President Truman scares them and lectures them. Wherever the Republican candidate goes it is 'you good people' and 'your great country out here.' If you'll only have 'faith in yourselves' and 'faith in America' and be of 'stout purpose and a full heart' and 'move forward shoulder to shoulder,' then everything will be fine. For we know 'that every single individual is of priceless importance and that free men against whatever odds have an unbeatable quality,' and so forth and so on.

THE THIRD PARTY IN THE CAMPAIGN

PROGRESSIVE CANDIDATES Wallace and Taylor on the day the third party convention met in Philadelphia.

WILLING CONTRIBUTORS filled many baskets with campaign funds at the Progressive party's convention.

EGGS STRUCK Henry Wallace's car at Shreveport, Louisiana, as he left the local radio station after a speech.

"Day after day, on every hand, he passes out these pills that are bromides in the real sense of the word, that is, they calm jumpy nerves. The people reach eagerly for them and gulp them down.

"Labor troubles? International tensions and friction? Why just put competent and honest men in the government and give us 'unity' and 'unity of purpose' and all those things will vanish. There'll be prosperity in the land and peace with all mankind.

"The way he hammers away at the need of competent and honest men in government, you'd think there hadn't been no such in Washington in sixteen years. . . ."

And so the first round ended. Truman returned to Washington on October 2 with public opinion, according to press and radio, heavily against him. Fifty of the nation's political

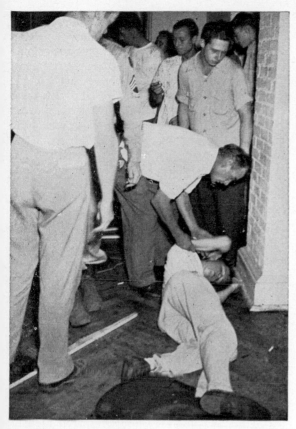

KNIFED AT DURHAM, North Carolina, was a young university student who carried an anti-Wallace poster.

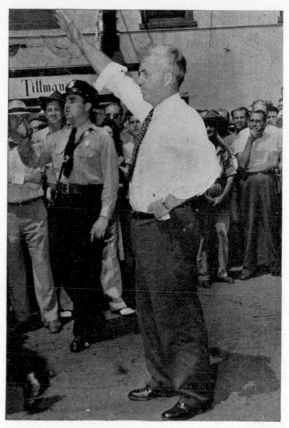

WALLACE ADDRESSED a hostile crowd at Burlington, North Carolina, despite a barrage of eggs and tomatoes.

writers predicted unanimously that Dewey would win. A betting commissioner in St. Louis called Dewey a 15 to 1 favorite. All the pollsters and commentators were certain he would be the next President. But Truman, more confident than ever, told a back-platform audience in Lexington, Kentucky, that "I am trying to do in politics what *Citation* has done in the horse races. I propose at the finish-line on November 2 to come out ahead because I think the people understand what the issues are in this campaign." And it seemed that his audience agreed with him.

After a few days respite, he was on the road again, campaigning almost without interruption until election day. In Philadelphia he attacked Dewey's "unity" theme. "We don't believe in the unity of slaves, or the unity of sheep being led to the slaughter," he said. "We don't believe

STUMPING FOR EQUAL RIGHTS at Greensboro. Wallace refused to speak wherever segregation was enforced.

in unity under the rule of big business—and we shall fight it to the end."

At Auburn, New York, Representative John Taber's home town, he advised the voters not to re-elect their Representative, because Taber had used "a butcher knife, saber, and meat-ax on every forward-looking appropriation in the public's interest that has come before Congress." In Buffalo he declared: "The leopard has not changed his spots; he has merely hired some public relations experts. And they have taught him to wear sheep's clothing and to purr sweet nothings about unity in a soothing voice. But it's the same old leopard."

Then Truman returned to Washington to straighten out the confusion which had arisen over his attempt to send Chief Justice Vinson to Moscow to consult with Marshal Stalin directly on the Berlin crisis. Secretary of State Marshall asked the President not to pursue his plan—not to start bilateral negotiations with the Soviet—but to leave the dealings about the Berlin blockade to the Security Council of the United Nations. Truman abandoned his idea of a "Vinson Mission," and Dewey capitalized on the President's "tragic blunder."

When Truman resumed his Middle Western campaign tour, according to the New York *Herald Tribune* he was "greeted by crowds that were large and enthusiastically in favor of seeing the President, whether or not they intend to vote for him." He repeated his domestic program: "I believe that we should increase the minimum wage from forty cents an hour to at least seventy-five cents an hour. I believe social security insurance should be extended to the large groups of people not now protected. I believe that the insurance benefits should be increased by approximately 50 per cent. I believe that we should expand our facilities for looking after the nation's health. I believe that the Federal Government should provide aid to the states in meeting the educational needs of our children. I believe the Congress should provide aid for slum clearance and low-rent housing. I believe we should do something, at once, about high prices."

On October 11 Dewey submitted a twelve-point workingman's program in Pittsburgh. He proposed "firm supports under wages" and a raise of the minimum wage; extension and over-hauling of the social security system; a more influential labor department; a more effective Federal Conciliation and Mediation Service; encouragement of "unions to grow in responsibility and strengthen the collective bargaining"; enforcing and strengthening of the anti-trust laws against business monopolies; provisions of houses "at reasonable cost for our people"; action against soaring prices; removal of the fear of "a boom and bust business cycle"; a solution of the problem of "race relations and of discrimination"; the strengthening of civil liberties, and "a world at peace."

Two days later President Truman called Dewey's speeches "mealy-mouthed" and accused him of having disrupted unity, which he now preached, on questions of foreign relations in his previous campaign during the war. The President denied that the main campaign issues were unity and efficiency. "Maybe the Wall Street Republicans are efficient. We remember that there never was such a gang of efficiency engineers in Washington as there was under Herbert Hoover. We remember Mr. Hoover was himself a great efficiency expert."

And ten days later the President offered a point-by-point rebuttal of Dewey's Pittsburgh speech in the same city. He compared Dewey to a doctor with a magic cure-all. "'You shouldn't think about issues,' says the doctor. 'What you need is my brand of soothing syrup —I call it *unity*.'" Truman said that Dewey had "opened his mouth and closed his eyes, and swallowed the terrible record of the Republican Eightieth Congress." And he declared that the whole Republican campaign could be summed up with two phrases: "Me, too. . . ." and "We're against it."

The Midwestern trip of the President turned out to be a great success. Democratic leaders reported a definite improvement in the chances of their own state tickets, and a remarkable upsurge of interest in Truman. Still, the belief was firmly embedded in the national mind—or so the newspapers reported—that he would be defeated in November.

As the campaign reached the final weeks, Truman and Dewey clashed for the first time on major issues—on the bi-partisan foreign policy, on labor-management relations, and social legislation. The foreign policy issue came

THE CAMPAIGN BEGINS IN EARNEST. CARTOON BY WALT KELLY IN THE NEW YORK *STAR*.

to the fore through the Vinson incident, which in Dewey's opinion made the United States "appear before the world as a fumbling giant." On labor-management relations Truman said that the Taft-Hartley law was "an instrument for union-busting by anti-labor employers," while Dewey held that "over the plaintive complaints of a helpless administration, the welfare of both labor and the whole of our people has been advanced. As a result, an overwhelming majority of our people approve . . . the law." (Growled John L. Lewis, the miners' chieftain: "That man hasn't even read the act.") On social legislation Dewey said that "the present minimum wage is far too low and it will be raised." Truman, who asked for an increase from forty to seventy-five cents an hour, said that the Republicans "favor a minimum wage—the smaller the minimum the better."

Still, in the opinion of the New York *Times*, "There have been few presidential campaigns in American history which have left the public as apathetic as that which will close two weeks from tomorrow night. This may be because most of the voters made up their minds long ago, or it may be because many of them simply don't care."

If one listened to the radio commentators, if one read the pollsters' predictions, if one followed the columnists, Dewey had already won the election. "Thomas E. Dewey's election as President is a foregone conclusion," said Leo Egan in the New York *Times*. Robert J. Donovan reported in the New York *Herald Tribune* that "Mr. Dewey is confident that the voters long ago made up their minds in favor of a change and that he has the election in the bag." Wrote Max Lerner in the New York *Star*: "It is three months to January 20, when Tom Dewey will in all probability move into the White House." And *Time* Magazine opined that "there was not much left to the presidential campaign except counting the votes. Harry Truman might get a good share of the popular vote, but few people outside of Harry Truman gave him an outside chance." Editorials throughout the country indulged in such witticisms as "The election must be held if for no other reason than to find out which national pollster comes the closest." The majority of the press was submerged in the mass hysteria of

wishful thinking. Critical evaluation of the facts was overlooked. Newspapermen took the predictions of the pollsters as the gospel truth. That Truman's audiences in the Middle West had consistently exceeded Dewey's, and that "at every village, town and city the crowds waited in startling numbers," were facts which received little attention.

By this time Wallace's strength had spent itself, and there was talk of the collapse of the Progressive movement. The steady propaganda in the press and radio, abusing the third party candidate as a tool of the Communists, was very effective. Furthermore, Wallace's indecision about supporting liberal Democratic candidates for Congress alienated many of his supporters.

In winding up their campaigns, Truman and Dewey mapped out almost identical itineraries, with Truman speaking one day ahead of Dewey at different cities. In Chicago the President declared that "the real danger comes mainly from powerful reactionary forces which are silently undermining our democratic institutions." These forces, working through the Republican party, want to "see inflation continue unchecked," to "concentrate great economic powers in their own hands," and to stir up "racial and religious prejudice against some of our fellow Americans."

Dewey stepped down from his lofty level and charged that the President was descending to a new low of "mudslinging" in spreading "fantastic fears" among the people "to promote antagonism and prejudice." The Republican candidate was a fighting candidate now. "We all know the sad record of the present administration. More than three years have passed since the end of the war and it has failed to win the peace. Millions upon millions of people have been delivered into Soviet slavery," said Dewey, "while our own administration has tried appeasement on one day and bluster the next. Our country desperately needs new and better leadership in the cause of peace and freedom."

The next encounter was at Cleveland, where Truman asserted that "we have the Republicans on the run. Of course, the Republicans don't admit that. They've got a poll that says they're going to win. . . ." These polls, the President said, were "like sleeping pills to lull voters into

THOMAS DEWEY conducted a lofty campaign, stressing the theme of unity and confining himself to generalities. He avoided any commitment to a specific program.

HARRY TRUMAN conducted an old-fashioned, slambang campaign, assailing the "do-nothing Republican Congress," and branding the GOP as the party of reaction.

sleeping on election day. You might call them sleeping polls."

Truman expanded on the theme. "These Republican polls are no accident. They are all part of a design to prevent a big vote on November 2 by convincing you that it makes no difference whether you vote or not. They want to do this because they know in their hearts that a big vote spells their defeat. They know that a big vote means a Democratic victory, because the Democratic party stands for the greatest good for the greatest number of the people."

Dewey, on the following day, told Clevelanders that "In the opening speech of this campaign at Des Moines, Iowa, I said this will be 'a campaign to unite America.'" Truman's campaign, however, was an attempt to split the nation.

The third round was in Boston, where Truman denounced as a "malicious falsehood" Re-

EARL WARREN, Dewey's running mate, made an impression wherever he spoke. Many felt he would have been a better presidential choice than the New Yorker.

publican charges that his administration had opened the door to Communists, and ridiculed Dewey's unity campaign. "In the old days Al Smith would have said: 'That's baloney.' Today the Happy Warrior would say: 'That's a lot of hooey.' And if that rhymes with anything it is not my fault. . . ."

But Dewey did not abandon his theme. He said: "Your next administration will unite our people behind a foreign policy that will strengthen the cause of freedom and bring peace to this world."

The final sparring took place in New York's Madison Square Garden, where Truman said sardonically that Dewey could follow him in the different cities, but he couldn't follow him in raising the minimum wage to at least seventy-five cents an hour, or in demanding laws for health insurance and medical care, or calling for a repeal of the Taft-Hartley Act, or for a law to control high prices. And he declared that whenever Dewey looked at the Democratic program he said "Me too," but his party's record said "Nothing doing." "And his party's record speaks louder than he does. . . ."

It was on this day that Bartley Crum, publisher of the New York *Star*, came down from the President's suite in the Hotel Biltmore and told journalists in the bar: "The old boy still thinks he's going to win. He's standing there under the shower telling everybody that he'll sweep the country." All the journalists laughed at the joke.

The next day Dewey wound up his campaign, pledging an administration devoted to promoting unity among the American people and furthering the cause of world peace. "We agreed that in this grave time we would conduct a campaign worthy of America. I am very happy that we can look back over the weeks of our campaigning and say: 'This has been good for our country!' I am proud that we can look ahead to our victory and say: 'America won!'" He ridiculed and scorned the type of campaign which Truman had conducted. "But," said Dewey, "our people have not been fooled or frightened. Halloween will be over tomorrow night, but next Tuesday the people of America are really going to bring this nightmare to an end."

By then Truman was on his way to his na-

tive Missouri, where at St. Louis he made his final speech. He told his listeners that he had "cracked the Republican East" and that "North, South and West are falling in line."

"Now I have an old-fashioned notion that a candidate for public office has a duty to tell the voters where he stands on the issues in a campaign. I have traveled 22,000 miles, made about 270 speeches, and taken a positive position on every issue. But the Republican candidate refuses to tell the American people where he stands on any issue. The campaign is ending and you still don't know. All you have got is platitudes and double talk. . . ."

He concluded: "The smart boys say we couldn't win. They tried to bluff us with a propaganda blitz, but we called their bluff, we told the people the truth. And the people are with us. The tide is rolling. All over the country I have seen it in the people's faces. The people are going to win this election."

With this the speechmaking came to an end. Said the Republican *Herald Tribune:* "Mr. Dewey's campaign has lacked fireworks because the advocacy of unity and the sober, efficient management of public concerns are not causes which lend themselves to oratorical pyrotechnics. The public reaction to the campaign has been calm, on the whole, because Mr. Dewey represents the viewpoint of the majority. Mr. Truman has won some vociferous support among labor unions by his opposition to the Taft-Hartley Act, but it is minority support. . . ."

The pollsters were still firm for a Dewey victory. On the day before the election, the Gallup Poll gave Dewey 49.5 per cent of the votes, Truman 44.5 per cent, Wallace 4 per cent, Thurmond 2 per cent. Elmo Roper gave Dewey 52.2 per cent, Truman 37.1 per cent, Thurmond 5.2 per cent, Wallace 4.3 per cent, and Thomas 0.6 per cent, declaring: "I stand by my prediction. Mr. Dewey is in." Mr. Roper went further. "This is the fourth national election which the polls have shown to be largely settled before the campaigns started," he wrote. "Apparently three years of performance are a more determining factor with voters than three months of campaign oratory."

On November 1 Bert Andrews wrote in the *Herald Tribune:* "All the signs indicate that

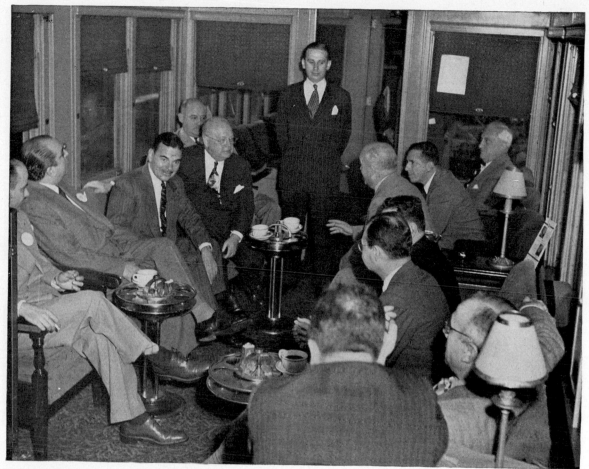

THE DEWEY TRAIN radiated confidence and efficiency. Schedules ran smoothly and the organization seemed faultless. The air was full of promise, for the experts said the election was in the bag. Meanwhile, certain that he would win, Dewey acted "like a man who has already been elected and is merely marking time, waiting to take office."

Thomas E. Dewey will be elected President on Tuesday over Harry S. Truman. The one big uncertainty is whether the Republicans will retain control of the Senate, which they now dominate by 51 to 45." *Life* Magazine printed Dewey's picture with the caption: "The next President of the United States." The *Kiplinger News Letter* declared: "Dewey will be in for eight years—until '57. . . ." The New York *Times* predicted, after examining the reports from forty-eight states, that the Dewey-Warren ticket would win with 345 electoral votes from twenty-nine states, against the Truman-Barkley ticket with eleven states and only 105 electoral votes. The Thurmond-Wright ticket would carry four Southern states—Alabama, Louisiana,

Mississippi and South Carolina—with a total of 38 electoral votes, while four states with 48 electoral votes were doubtful.

In the New York *Sun* George Van Slyke said that "The Republican sweep through the North will give the popular vote of at least thirty-two states to the Dewey-Warren ticket," while Hearst's New York *Journal-American* gave Dewey 337 electoral votes from twenty-seven states. In *Newsweek* Raymond Moley, Franklin D. Roosevelt's former braintruster, wrote that "as we view this campaign from a detached position, we all know that the trend is conservative." His colleague on the same magazine, Ernest K. Lindley, declared that "as a national organization the Democratic party is shattered."

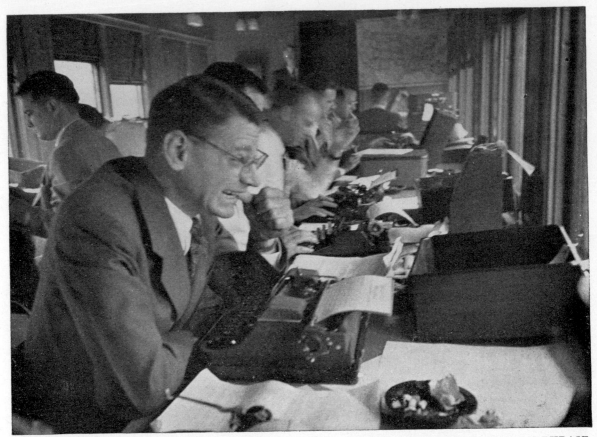

A NEWSPAPERMAN ON THE DEWEY CAMPAIGN TRAIN STRUGGLES WITH THE TURN OF A PHRASE.

BACK VIEW OF THE REPUBLICAN CANDIDATE

And Walter Lippmann warned that "the course of events cannot be halted for three months until Mr. Dewey has been inaugurated. There will be need for common sense, good will, co-operation." A *Herald Tribune* editorial stated on the eve of the election: "There can rarely have been a political campaign as strange as the one for the Presidency that ends today. As the polls have made manifest, the contest was over before it got under way. While the conventions were still fulminating, the country had made up its mind that it wanted a change in the White House. The campaign was a ratification meeting, never a debate."

When the first returns came in on election day, they revealed a surprising trend—there was no evidence of a Dewey landslide. "Wait for the rural regions," advised the radio commentators. Tensely the people waited—still no

A QUESTION IS POSED to President Truman after one of his earthy and good-natured back-platform speeches.

MISS AND MRS. TRUMAN were introduced by the President. "Meet the boss," he said, pointing to his wife.

Dewey landslide. As the evening wore on, Truman's lead became more marked. In the radio and television studios, the pollsters and commentators—redfaced—sweated as they tried to explain the phenomenon of Truman's strength.

After the first reports, Dewey's campaign manager told newspaper reporters: "This is definitely a Republican year. The people have made up their minds and have registered their decision in many of the states." The New York *Daily Mirror*, going to press early in the evening, stated: "First returns of the 50,000,000 all-time voting record throughout the nation yesterday indicated that Governor Thomas E. Dewey and the Republican ticket were headed for a popular vote margin and a possible electoral vote landslide." The Chicago *Tribune* headlined: "Dewey defeats Truman," reporting a sweeping victory of the Dewey-Warren

ticket by "an overwhelming majority of electoral votes."

At this time, Truman, who earlier in the evening had sneaked out of his hotel in Independence, was soundly asleep at Excelsior Springs, a little spa about thirty miles from the city.

Midnight passed—and still the returns showed that the President was leading. About two o'clock in the morning Fulton Lewis, Jr. told his radio listeners that it looked as if the election would be decided by the House of Representatives and that there anything might happen. The radio newscaster said that the House might even choose Marcantonio for President. Other commentators and radio speakers showed equal ignorance of the Constitution and the presidential election laws.

At five o'clock in the morning at his New

York hotel, Dewey told reporters that he was "still confident." But as the next day dawned, his chances dwindled to nothing. The seemingly impossible had happened; Mr. Truman had won the election. The newspapers of November 3, whose columns had been written and set the day before, made curious reading. "The first post-election question is how the government can get through the next ten weeks. Nowadays, unhappily, time's winged chariot has been equipped with jet propulsion. Events will not wait patiently until Thomas E. Dewey officially replaces Harry S. Truman," wrote the Alsop brothers in the New York *Herald Tribune*. On the same day one could read in Drew Pearson's column that he had "surveyed the close-knit group around Tom Dewey, who will take over the White House eighty-six days from now."

When the final result of the election became known the wrath of public and press was turned against the pollsters. And the poll-takers, who had "misled" them, offered only the meekest explanations. Said Dr. Gallup: "Truman captured many votes from Wallace. Also, a lot

HERBERT HOOVER guides the mechanical Dewey safely ashore through the sea of presidential politics.

of the undecided voters in the poll voted for Truman." Poll-taking, he said, was still "an infant science."

A science? Wilfred J. Funk, the editor of the old *Literary Digest*, which made the disastrously inaccurate poll in 1936, gleefully remarked: "I wonder if the word 'science' will continue to be used in connection with this type of public opinion poll."

Elmo Roper confessed: "On September 9 I predicted that Mr. Dewey would win by a wide margin and that it was all over but the shouting. Since then I have had plenty of chance to hedge on that prediction. I did not do so. I could not have been more wrong. The thing that bothers me most at this moment is that I don't know why I was wrong."

Archibald Crossley was even more bewildered. "The Crossley Poll showed that the Truman and the Dewey vote would be even if all adult citizens voted. . . . The result clearly showed what happens when one party gets out its vote and the other does not."

An irate correspondent of the Berkshire *Eve-*

SATIRIZING the attitude of the candidates toward the New Deal, Walt Kelly drew them sporting similar hats.

"FILL 'ER UP!"

N.A.M
INFLATION
GAS

WE
GUARANTEE
QUICK
REACTION

WHAT MAKES TOMMY RUN?

INFLATION GAS, supplied by the National Association of Manufacturers, is pumped into the Dewey machine.

ning Eagle, L. S. Briggs, summed up the feeling of the people toward the polls. He lamented:

"O section, cross-section and sample,
 O postcard and phone call and bell!
 O Crossley, Roper and Gallup!
 O George!
 O Elmo!
 O hell!"

Explanations were also forthcoming from the columnists. Wrote Marquis Childs: "We were wrong, all of us, completely and entirely, the commentators, the political editors, the politicians—except for Harry S. Truman. And no one believed him. The fatal flaw was reliance on the public opinion polls. No amount of rationalization ever can explain away this mistake by Gallup, Roper & Company. . . ." Said Walter Lippmann: "As one who did not foresee the result of the election, I can say . . . that I went wrong because I did not expect the Democrats to bring out their full vote." Arthur Krock's *mea culpa* in the New York *Times* went deeper: "We didn't concern ourselves, as we used to, with the facts. We ac-

cepted the polls, unconsciously. I used to go to Chicago and around the country, every election, to see for myself. This time, I was so sure, I made no personal investigation. . . . We have to go back to work on the old and classic lines— to the days when reporters dug in, without any preconception. . . ."

James Reston, the New York *Times*' outstanding political reporter, wrote a soul-searching letter to his editor. "Before we in the newspaper business spend all our time and energy analyzing Governor Dewey's failure in the election, maybe we ought to try to analyze our own failure. For that failure is almost as spectacular as the President's victory, and the quicker we admit it the better off we'll be. . . .

"In a way our failure was not unlike Mr. Dewey's: we overestimated the tangibles; we relied too much on techniques of reporting which are no longer foolproof; just as he was too isolated with other politicians, so we were

LITTLE INDIAN: "PALE FACE MACHINE IS BIG WIND. SAY NOTHING. WE WASTE TIME. GOOD BYE."

BIG INDIAN: "WE FOOL UM. HE WASTE TIME. WE CAN'T VOTE ANYWAY."

SYMBOLIZING Dewey's highly publicized efficiency, Kelly regularly drew him as an animated adding machine.

717

too isolated with other reporters; and we, too, were far too impressed by the tidy statistics of the polls. . . . In short, neither on the train nor in the capitals do we spend much time wandering around talking to the people. We tend to assume that somebody is doing the original reporting in that area, and if the assumptions of the political managers, or the other reporters, or the polls are wrong (as they were in this campaign), then our reports are wrong.

"The great intangible of this election was the political influence of the Roosevelt era on the thinking of the nation. It was less dramatic than the antics of Messrs. Wallace and Thurmond, but in the long run it was more important and we didn't give enough weight to it. Consequently we were wrong, not only on the election, but, what's worse, on the whole political direction of our time."

Time Magazine sounded a similar note: "The press was morally guilty on several counts. It was guilty of pride: it had assumed that it knew all the important facts—without sufficiently checking them. It was guilty of laziness and wishful thinking: it had failed to do its own doorbell-ringing and bush-beating, it had delegated its journalist's job to the pollsters. . . ."

What were the reasons for Mr. Truman's totally unexpected victory? Arthur Krock acknowledged that the President was "a master politician and analyst of the people of the United States." Walter Lippmann thought that it could be said "with much justice, and without detracting from Mr. Truman's remarkable personal performance, that of all Roosevelt's electoral triumphs, this one in 1948 is the most impressive." I. F. Stone believed that Truman had "waged the kind of campaign Mr. Roosevelt would have waged: for social reforms and peace. This was Mr. Wallace's achievement." And others found other explanations.

Most analysts agreed that Truman won the election because he received the farmer and labor vote. The strength of the President in the Midwest farm territory was surprising. He carried Ohio, Illinois, Wisconsin, and Iowa—states which were expected to be in the Republican column. The alleged reason why the Republican farmers voted for the Democrats was the fear that in the event of a Republican victory, the price support program would be abandoned.

Furthermore, labor, which according to the *New Republic* had "finally learned to organize politically as well as economically," and "millions of independent voters who remembered the lessons they learned under Hoover," voted against Dewey.

Other explanations of Truman's victory were "the bandwagon pressure of the public opinion polls, which encouraged many waverers to vote for the underdog, Truman, just to slow up the expected Dewey landslide, and caused many overconfident Republicans to stay away from the polls entirely"; the President's fighting campaign, which gained him votes and made the voters "revolt against the lofty Dewey platitudes"; the "strength of local Democratic tickets, which gave Harry Truman a boost in almost every key state"; the "pocketbook nerve," which made not only the farmers and workers but the housewives vote for Truman; and the voters' distrust of the Republican party, as mirrored in the Eightieth Congress, a distrust which Tom Dewey's promises of efficient government had never been able to erase. . . ."

Thomas Dewey, in his first announcement, blamed Republican overconfidence as "one of the outstanding factors." In his opinion, "two or three million Republicans stayed at home." (Yet in past elections it was always believed that a large vote favored the Democrats, while a small vote benefited the Republicans.)

Senator Robert A. Taft said: "The basic reason for the Truman victory lies in the great prosperity which exists today, especially in the rural sections, and the full employment. We Republicans grossly underestimated the difficulty of ousting an administration at the height of a boom. . . . It is almost impossible to put an administration out of office at the very peak of a boom."

Irving M. Ives, Senator from New York, said: "The defeat of the Republicans can be ascribed to . . . the inability of the Eightieth Congress to get together on a forward-looking, liberal program."

According to Senator Leverett Saltonstall, the principal reason for Dewey's defeat "came from overconfidence, from too great reliance on nationally known polls of public opinion. This led the Republicans to put on a campaign of generalities rather than interesting the people in

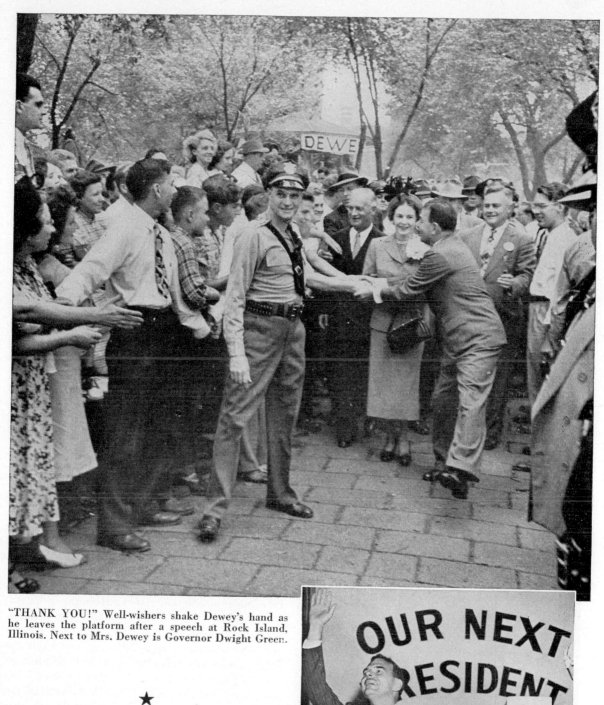

"THANK YOU!" Well-wishers shake Dewey's hand as he leaves the platform after a speech at Rock Island, Illinois. Next to Mrs. Dewey is Governor Dwight Green.

DEWEY WAS CERTAIN of victory and so were his managers. Signs on platforms mirrored this confidence.

HANDKISS BY TALLULAH. At the Liberal party rally in New York City, the actress Tallulah Bankhead greets the President. She campaigned for Truman and was one of the few people who thought that he would be re-elected.

MANY WERE THE GIFTS. At Brockton, Massachusetts, Harry Truman received two pairs of brand-new shoes.

what a Republican administration could and would do for them if elected. . . ."

But the progressive-minded Russell Davenport thought differently: "The theme of the last sixteen years (which must now become twenty years) has been—the Republican party versus the people. And the people have won. . . ." Davenport predicted that the Republican party, which had failed to win a presidential election since 1928, "will continue to fail until its members and especially its leaders turn toward the future and away from the past. It will fail until it takes full account of the changes in social and economic thinking which have evolved in the American mind during the last twenty years. It will fail until it realizes that the managerial revolution isn't broad enough to solve the complex problems which confront this nation, until it is convinced that both isolationism and *laissez-*

"DID I HEAR YOU RIGHT?" asks Truman of a reporter who posed an unwelcome question during the President's tour of Texas. His friendly horseplay appealed to crowds and newsmen alike on his swing around the country.

faire are anachronisms." A clever appraisal.

While Davenport pursued this line of reasoning, the conservative wing of the party insisted that the trouble was that Dewey had flirted too much with New Dealism instead of standing firm on ruggedly individualistic principles.

The unsuccessful Progressive candidates held that Truman had been elected because, as Glen Taylor put it, "He practically adopted the Progressive platform and began promising to carry it out." And Henry Wallace, in a letter to the New York *Herald Tribune*, explained: "It was the Progressive party alone that made peace an issue in the 1948 campaign. It was our insistence on a return to the Roosevelt one-world policy that forced the bi-partisans to slow down their cold-war program and at least make the gesture of negotiating with Russia. . . . It was the Progressive party which compelled a change in the whole character of the election campaign. It was our party which forced the Democrats to don the mantle of Roosevelt and to promise the American people a return to the New Deal. It was our party which destroyed the plans of reaction, and of the press through which reaction speaks, to deprive the voters of any choice between two programs."

The final figures of the election showed that Truman had polled 24,104,836 votes, carrying twenty-eight states; Dewey had 21,969,500 votes, carrying sixteen states. Wallace received only 1,157,172 votes, Norman Thomas 139,521, Thurmond 1,169,021. And in the Congressional election the Democrats had the majority in both Houses. The country sent 263 Democratic Representatives to the House against 171 Republicans; to the Senate 54 Democrats against 42 Republicans.

THE PRESIDENT VOTES AT INDEPENDENCE   GOVERNOR DEWEY VOTES IN NEW YORK CITY

Comparing the Democratic figures with those of the previous election, Truman won five states which in 1944 were carried by the Republicans: Colorado, Iowa, Ohio, Wisconsin, and Wyoming. But he lost nine states to Dewey: Connecticut, Delaware, Maryland, Michigan, New Hampshire, New Jersey, New York, Oregon and Pennsylvania. He also lost—because of the civil rights controversy—four states in the South to Governor Thurmond: South Carolina, Mississippi, Alabama and Louisiana.

However, he carried all thirteen of the country's biggest cities, and he carried the six large agricultural states: California, Iowa, Illinois, Texas, Minnesota, and Wisconsin. The Republican Corn Belt states—Ohio, Wisconsin and Iowa—probably because of the restrictive legislation of the Eightieth Congress, turned against the GOP. The wheat-producing states of the Great Plains—North Dakota, South Dakota, Nebraska and Kansas—remained in the Republican fold.

On January 5 Truman spoke to Congress and the nation for the first time as an elected President. It was his annual State of the Union message, and in it he outlined his Fair Deal program. He asked for legislation in the fields of social welfare, social security, education, medical care, economic controls, and civil rights. He asked for a balanced budget, partly through a tax increase of four billion a year, and requested broad authority to control inflation. Outstand-

ROWNELL WAS CONFIDENT OF DEWEY'S VICTORY   McGRATH WAS SURE IT WOULD BE TRUMAN

ing among eight anti-inflation points was one to
let the government build plants in such industries as steel, if private industry "fails to meet
our needs." He asked for low-rent public housing and a system of prepaid medical insurance.
He called for a repeal of the Taft-Hartley Act,
for an increase of the minimum wage to at least
seventy-five cents, and for the enactment of his
civil rights program. In the opinion of the New
York *Times*, "He pushed the New Deal beyond
the frontiers Franklin Roosevelt had staked out
sixteen years before."

A fortnight later Washington was ready for
the inauguration. The Republican Congress had
provided a few hundred thousand dollars to
make the ceremonies the "biggest damn inaugu-

ration in modern times." Curly Brooks was the
head of the committee in charge of the preparations, and money was spent freely to make the
celebrations in honor of a Republican President
—the first in sixteen years—really memorable.
The Democrats now utilized all the Republicans' bright ideas.

For the President inauguration day began
with a breakfast with his old buddies of World
War I—the members of Battery D of the 129th
Field Artillery. In a caustic speech he imitated
the voice and inflection of radio commentator
H. V. Kaltenborn reporting during election
night. "While the President is a million votes
ahead in the popular vote, when the county
vote comes in Mr. Truman will be defeated by

723

ABANDONED. Early on November 3, Republican head-quarters at New York's Hotel Roosevelt were deserted as the nation awoke to find the election still in doubt.

WHEN RETURNS INDICATED A TRUMAN VICTOR

GLOOM. The Republican candidate and his family listen to the disappointing election returns in the early hours of the morning in their hotel suite in New York City.

an overwhelming majority," he mimicked. Truman told his friends that after listening to the other radio commentators who declared the election would be thrown into the House, he went to bed and to sleep. Awakened at four o'clock, he "turned the darn thing on again." At that time Kaltenborn was saying that while the President had a two-million-vote lead, it was certainly necessary that the House decide the election, since Mr. Truman "hasn't an opportunity of being elected by a majority vote."

Meanwhile the streets of Washington were filled with a merry, celebrating crowd. Floats

...HE JUBILANT DEMOCRATS BEGAN TO CELEBRATE.

were driven to the assembling places, television technicians and movie operators made last-minute adjustments to their cameras, bands played, vendors offered badges, the city was ready for its biggest, showiest inaugural jamboree in the nation's history.

At noon the President drove to the Capitol, greeted with affectionate shouts. "Harry!", and "Hi, ya, Harry!" echoed after him all along Pennsylvania Avenue.

His inaugural speech was largely devoted to foreign issues. Truman said that the United States would give "unfaltering support" to the

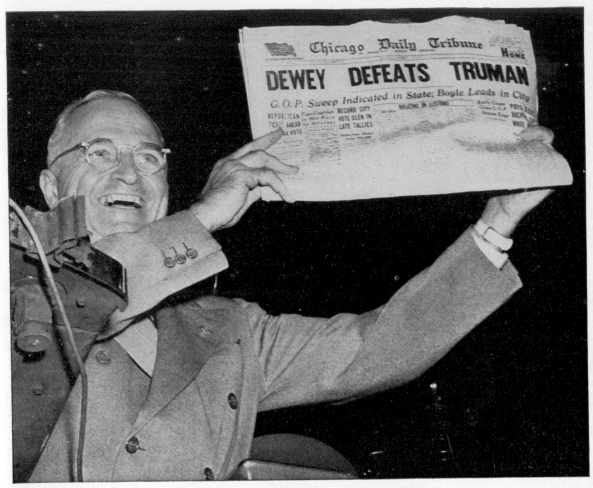

"THAT'S ONE FOR THE BOOKS," said Harry Truman, pointing to the Chicago *Tribune's* early edition of November 3, reporting that Dewey had won. While his train stopped at St. Louis, Truman happily posed for this picture.

United Nations, put its "full weight" behind the European Recovery Program, provide in the North Atlantic Security Pact "unmistakable proof" of the joint determination of the free countries to resist armed attack from any quarter, and embark on "a bold new program for making the benefits of our scientific and industrial progress available for the improvement and growth of underdeveloped areas" of the world. It was an unexciting address, unexcitingly delivered.

After the ceremonies at the Capitol, the inaugural parade began. Millions of Americans watched it on television sets. For the first time organized labor marched in it with its own floats. As Truman stood on the reviewing stand

acknowledging the ovations, the band played "I'm Just Wild About Harry," and the President danced a happy little jig in time to the music. It was his great day. Journalists reported that he did not acknowledge the greeting of Herman Talmadge of Georgia, others asserted that Talmadge was not snubbed. The parade went on for three long hours and the President seemed to enjoy every minute of it. His face beamed as he stood on the platform.

"Mr. Truman stands there," wrote the columnist Gerald W. Johnson in an inspiring piece, "not in his own right, but as representing you and me and Joe Dokes down the street, and Martha, his wife, and the kids playing baseball in a vacant lot. He represents a Negro and a

THE WINNERS RETURN TO WASHINGTON. Hundreds of thousands cheered Harry S. Truman and Alben Barkley as they returned in triumph to the capital. It was one of the most enthusiastic receptions in Washington's history.

Jew and an American-born Japanese. In reality, it is a Minnesota farmer taking the salute, a Georgia cracker, a Pittsburgh steelworker, a New York girl filing clerk, in whose honor the bombers darken the sky over Washington and fill the air with their thunder.

"This is more vividly apparent in the case of Mr. Truman than in that of most Presidents; for his election is due to the fact that the common man took matters into his own hands, regardless of the politicians, regardless of the great lords in business and journalism, regardless of the experts and wiseacres. He is conspicuously the common man's choice—and by the same token, the common man's responsibility. . . .

"The common man must make good, or incur

THE CAMPAIGN IS OVER and the work goes on as usual. President Truman walks to the Executive Offices.

"Look, No Hands!"

Look, No Victory

A PROPHECY WHICH CAME TRUE. The cartoon at the left by Dorman H. Smith appeared in many of the nation's newspapers on October 15, two weeks before the election; the cartoon at the right was published on November 8.

the scorn of his enemies and plunge his friends into despair. 'The last best hope' Jefferson called this government. There is no doubt about its

Kick Me!

ALL US POLITICAL EXPERTS

THE SUMMING UP. Cartoonist Talbert's apology for the wrong-guessers appeared in the Scripps-Howard papers.

being the last hope. If the democracy of America cannot master the existing crisis, it is idle to look for another; if we fail, tyranny must overwhelm the world.

"Mr. Truman's mistakes—and it goes without saying that he will make some—will be our mistakes, his failures will be our defeats. Such strength and wisdom as he has are the strength and wisdom of the common people of this country. . . .

"The ceremonial will be over by midnight and then the long pull will begin. The small man in drab clothes will leave the reviewing stand and take his place behind a desk; you and I will return to our normal occupations. But woe betide us if we forget the parade and what it means. We mean well; but how much of wisdom, how much of patience, how much of steady resolution we must display during the next four years is frightening to contemplate. We can well afford to turn away from the spectacle, murmuring an adaptation of the words of the crier of the Supreme Court: 'God save the United States and the nations of the world!' "

To which one can only say: "Amen."

LIST OF ILLUSTRATIONS

729

103. *The Library of Congress.*

104. ANDREW JACKSON. Painting by Ralph Earl. *The Library of Congress.*

    JOHN C. CALHOUN. Painting by Charles Bird King, 1826.

    JOHN QUINCY ADAMS. Painting by Stuart and Sully. *The Harvard Union*, Cambridge, Mass.

    RICHARD RUSH. From Willson, *American Ambassadors to France.*

105. *The Pennsylvania Historical Society.*

106-107. THE PEDLAR AND HIS PACK or THE DESPERATE EFFORT AN OVER-BALANCE. Unsigned cartoon. *The American Antiquarian Society.*

109. *The New York Historical Society.*

110. Painting by Ralph Earl.

112-113. Howard Pyle in *Harper's Weekly*, March 12, 1881.

114. Daguerreotype by Mathew B. Brady or one of his assistants, taken at "The Hermitage" on April 15, 1845. Jackson died on June 8, the same year.

115. A CABINETMAKER. Unsigned lithograph of 1831 by the firm of A. Imbert.

116. ANDREW JACKSON. Painting by Asher B. Durand, 1835.

    MARTIN VAN BUREN. Painting by Henry Inman, 1828. *The City Hall of New York.*

    HENRY CLAY. Painting by Theodore Morse. *The Metropolitan Museum of Art.*

    JOHN SERGEANT. Author's collection.

117. Published by H. Anstice, New York.

118. Photograph by Mathew B. Brady.

    THE RATS LEAVING A FALLING HOUSE. Lithograph by Edward W. Clay, published in Washington, 1831.

118-119. THE CELESTE-AL CABINET. Lithograph published by H. R. Robinson, New York.

120-121. A POLITICAL GAME OF BRAG or THE BEST HAND OUT OF FOUR. Lithograph published in 1831 by Pendleton, New York.

122-123. GENERAL JACKSON SLAYING THE MANY-HEADED MONSTER. Lithograph published in 1832 by H. R. Robinson, New York.

124-126. Campaign booklet of 1832.

127. Lithograph published in 1833 by Endicott & Swett.

128. Painting by Ralph Earl, 1835.

129. *The Library of Congress.*

130-131. THE GRAND NATIONAL CARAVAN MOVING EAST. Lithograph published in 1833 by Bland.

132. Painting by Henry Inman. *The City Hall of New York.*

133. *The Library of Congress.*

134. MARTIN VAN BUREN. *Brown Brothers*, New York.

    RICHARD M. JOHNSON. From L. C. Buttre, *The American Portrait Gallery.*

WILLIAM H. HARRISON. Engraving from a painting by E. D. Marchon.

    FRANCIS GRANGER. From Vanderhoff, *Historical Sketches of North New York.*

134-135. THE DOWNFALL OF MOTHER BANK. Lithograph published in 1833 by H. R. Robinson, New York.

136-137. SPECIE CLAWS. A Daumier lithograph, embellished and published by H. R. Robinson.

137. *Courtesy of the United States Senate.*

138. WHIG CANDIDATES FOR THE PRESIDENCY or TRYING ON THE WHIG. Lithograph published in 1837 by John Laurence, New York.

139. Lithograph by Napoleon Sarony, who later became a famous photographer. Published by H. R. Robinson, New York.

141. Top:
    Lithograph published in 1836 by H. R. Robinson.
    Bottom:
    Published by E. Jones, New York.

142. DRAWN FROM A SKETCH BY AN EYEWITNESS. Lithograph published in 1835 by Endicott, New York.

142-143. SET TO BETWEEN THE CHAMPION OLD TIP AND THE SWELL DUTCHMAN OF KINDERHOOK. Lithograph published in 1836 by H. R. Robinson, New York.

144. Painting by Hoyt.

145. The New York *Herald*, March 5, 1841.

146. WILLIAM HENRY HARRISON. *The Library of Congress.*

    JOHN TYLER. Photograph by Mathew B. Brady.

    MARTIN VAN BUREN. Author's collection.

    RICHARD M. JOHNSON. From L. C. Buttre, *The American Portrait Gallery.*

146-147. THE MODERN BALAAM AND HIS ASS. Published in 1837.

148-149. THE TIMES. Lithograph by Edward W. Clay, published in 1837 by H. R. Robinson, New York.

150-151. THE MEETING AT SARATOGA. "Like Boxers Thus Before the Fight, Their Hands in Friendship They Unite." Published in 1839 by H. R. Robinson.

151. Lithograph published by T. Sinclair, Philadelphia.

152-153. THE NORTH BEND FARMER AND HIS VISITORS. Published by H. R. Robinson, New York.

154. *The American Antiquarian Society.*

155. Lithograph published in 1840 by J. P. Giffing, New York. *The New York Historical Society.*

156. POLITICAL JUGGLERS LOSING THEIR BALANCE. Lithograph published by John Childs, New York.

157. Top:
    A HARD ROAD TO HOE! or THE WHITE HOUSE TURNPIKE MACADAMIZED BY THE NORTH BENDERS. Cartoon published by Huestis & Company, New York.
    Bottom:
    A contemporary engraving. Author's collection.

158. THE PEOPLE'S LINE—TAKE CARE OF THE LOCOMOTIVE. Cartoon sold at 105 Nassau Street, N. Y.

Page

158-159. THE ALMIGHTY LEVER. Drawn by Edward W. Clay and published by John Childs, New York.

160-161. THE DEATH OF HARRISON, APRIL 4, A.D., 1841. Lithograph published by N. Currier, New York.

163. Photograph by Mathew B. Brady.

164. Photograph by Brady, February 14, 1849.

165. The New York *Herald*, March 6, 1845.

166. JAMES K. POLK. Photograph by Mathew B. Brady.

GEORGE M. DALLAS. Photograph by Brady.

HENRY CLAY. Daguerreotype by Brady.

THEODORE FRELINGHUYSEN. *The Historical Society of Pennsylvania.*

JAMES G. BIRNEY. From "Letters to J. G. Birney." *The American Historical Association.*

JOHN TYLER. Photograph by Brady.

167. THE MOUNTAIN IN LABOR. Unsigned lithograph. *The Library of Congress.*

168-169. REQUESTING HIM TO RESIGN. Lithograph by H. Bucholzer, published by J. Baillie, New York.

170-171. POLITICAL COCK FIGHTERS. Published by J. Baillie.

171. POLK & CO. GOING UP SALT RIVER. Published by J. Baillie.

172. Top Left:

GROUND & LOFTY TUMBLING. Lithograph by H. Bucholzer, published by J. Baillie.

Top Right:

CLEANSING THE AUGEAN STABLE. Lithograph published by J. Baillie.

Bottom Left:

THE RACE COURSE. Lithograph published by J. Baillie.

Bottom Right:

POLK VERSUS WOOL or THE HARRY-CANE. Lithograph published by H. R. Robinson, New York.

173. Top Left:

"Not a drum was heard nor a funeral note
As his corpse to the ramparts we hurried—
Not a loco discharged his farewell shot
O'er the ditch where our hero we buried."
Lithograph published by J. Baillie, New York.

Top Right:

THE MAN WOT DRIVES THE CONSTITUTION. Lithograph published by John Childs, New York.

Bottom Left:

JAMES K. POLK GOING THROUGH PENNSYLVANIA FOR THE TARIFF. Lithograph published by H. R. Robinson, New York.

Bottom Right:

FLIGHT FOR THE CHAMPION'S BELT BETWEEN THE KINDERHOOK PET & THE GAME COCK OF THE WEST. Lithograph published by Willis & Probst, N. Y.

174. An anonymous lithograph of 1844.

175. ACT FOR THE BETTER MAINTAINING THE PURITY OF ELECTIONS. Lithograph by Edward W. Clay, published by Willis & Probst, New York.

Page

176. Top:

The Illustrated London News, November 24, 1844.
Bottom:
The New York Public Library.

177. THE RETURNS OF THE ELECTION. Lithograph published by John Childs, New York.

178. *The Metropolitan Museum of Art.*

179. Drawing by Tompkins H. Matteson, after a daguerreotype portrait.

180. ZACHARY TAYLOR. Daguerreotype by Brady, 1849.

MILLARD FILLMORE. Photograph by Brady.

LEWIS CASS. Photograph by Brady.

W. O. BUTLER. From Peterson, *Military Heroes of the War of 1812.*

MARTIN VAN BUREN. Photograph by Brady.

HENRY DEARBORN. From Stackpole, *History of New Hampshire*, Vol. III.

181. Lithographs published in 1848 by N. Currier, New York. *The New York Historical Society.*

182-183. THE ASSASSINATION OF THE SAGE OF ASHLAND. Lithograph published in 1848 by H. R. Robinson, New York.

184. AN AVAILABLE CANDIDATE, THE ONE QUALIFICATION OF A WHIG PRESIDENT. Published by Currier & Ives, New York.

185. Published in 1848 by Peter Smith, New York. *The American Antiquarian Society.*

186-187. THE MARRIAGE OF THE FREE-SOIL AND LIBERTY PARTIES. Published by Peter Smith, New York.

188-189. QUESTIONING A CANDIDATE. Published in 1848 by J. Baillie, New York.

189. Top:

THE CANDIDATE OF MANY PARTIES—A PHRENOLOGICAL EXAMINATION TO ASCERTAIN WHAT HIS POLITICAL PRINCIPLES ARE. Lithograph published in 1848 by H. R. Robinson, New York.

Center:

THE MODERN COLOSSUS, EIGHTH WONDER OF THE WORLD. Published by Peter Smith, New York.

Bottom:

THE BUFFALO HUNT. Lithograph published in 1848 by H. R. Robinson, New York.

190. Top:

Published by Horton & Company, New York
Bottom:
Published by Peter Smith, New York.

190-191. Published by Peter Smith.

192. THE DEMOCRATIC FUNERAL OF 1848. Published by Abel & Durang, Philadelphia.

193. Photograph by Brady.

194. Imperial photograph by Mathew B. Brady, made during Pierce's administration.

195. DEPARTURE OF PRESIDENT PIERCE FROM THE EAGLE HOTEL, CONCORD. A contemporary print.

732

Bottom Right:
STEPHEN FINDING "HIS MOTHER." Published in 1860 by Currier & Ives.

239. Top:
"UNCLE SAM" MAKING NEW ARRANGEMENTS. Published in 1860 by Currier & Ives.
Bottom Left:
THE RAIL CANDIDATE. Published by Currier & Ives.
Bottom Right:
THE NATIONAL GAME. THREE "OUTS" AND ONE RUN. ABRAHAM WINNING THE BALL. Published in 1860 by Currier & Ives.

240-241. PROGRESSIVE DEMOCRACY—PROSPECT OF A SMASH UP. Published in 1860 by Currier & Ives.

242. Top:
From Lorant, *Lincoln, His Life in Photographs.*
Bottom Left and Right:
Frank Leslie's Ill. News., November 17, 1860.

243. Top:
Harper's Weekly, October 13, 1860.
Bottom Left:
The Chicago Historical Society.
Bottom Right:
The Rail Splitter, Chicago.

244. *The Lincoln National Life Foundation,* Fort Wayne, Indiana.

245. Photograph by German taken on February 9, 1861, in Springfield, Illinois.

246. Photograph by Mathew B. Brady taken on February 23, 1861, in Washington.

247. From the Lincoln collection of the author.

249. *Frank Leslie's Ill. News.,* March 16, 1861.

250. *Harpers' Weekly,* March 16, 1861.

251. From the collection of the author.

253. *The Chicago Historical Society.*

254. Photograph by Mathew B. Brady, taken in Washington on February 9, 1864.

255. Photograph believed to be by Alexander Gardner.

256. Photographs from the author's collection.

257. Top:
POLITICIANS MEASURING LINCOLN'S SHOES. Published by H. H. Lloyd & Company, New York.
Bottom:
UNION AND LIBERTY, AND UNION AND SLAVERY. Published by M. W. Siebert, New York.

258-259. MAY THE BEST MAN WIN! *The New York Historical Society.*

260. Left:
Photograph by Mathew B. Brady taken in May, 1861, in Washington. In the collection of the author.
Right:
Photograph by Alexander Gardner taken on November 15, 1863, four days before the Gettysburg Address. In the collection of the author.

261. Left:
Photograph by Mathew B. Brady taken on February 9, 1864, in Washington. In the collection of the author.
Right:
Photograph by Alexander Gardner taken on April 9, 1865, in Washington. Six days later Lincoln died.

262. Top:
I KNEW HIM HORATIO; A FELLOW OF INFINITE JEST . . . WHERE BE YOUR GIBES NOW? by Howard Del. *The New York Historical Society.*
Bottom:
An anonymous cartoon of 1864.

263. Top:
THE TRUE ISSUE OR THAT'S WHAT'S THE MATTER. Published by Currier & Ives, New York.
Bottom:
ABRAHAM'S DREAM! Published by Currier & Ives.

264-265. *The National Archives.*

266. HOW FREE BALLOT IS PROTECTED. Drawing by J. E. Bakender.

267. *The Lincoln National Life Foundation.*

268. *Illinois State Historical Library,* Springfield, Ill.

269. Top:
The New York Public Library.
Bottom Left:
From the collection of the author.
Bottom Right:
Culver Service.

270. Top:
Brown Brothers.
Bottom:
The Lincoln National Life Foundation.

270-271. *Frank Leslie's Ill. News.,* Feb. 18, 1865.

272. Photograph by Alexander Gardner.

273-274. *The Library of Congress.*

275. Top:
Harper's Weekly, April 29, 1865.
Bottom:
Harper's Weekly, May 6, 1865.

276. Photograph by Mathew B. Brady.

277. *Frank Leslie's Ill. News.,* January 6, 1866.

278. Thomas Nast in *Harper's Weekly,* November 3, 1866.

279. Top:
Frank Leslie's Ill. News., April 20, 1867. .
Bottom:
Nast in *Harper's Weekly,* April 20, 1867.

280. Top:
Harper's Weekly, March 14, 1868.
Bottom Left:
Frank Leslie's Ill. News., April 4, 1868.
Bottom Right:
Harper's Weekly, April 18, 1868.

Page

281. Top:
Harper's Weekly, March 21, 1868.
Bottom Left:
Frank Leslie's Ill. News., March 21, 1868.
Bottom Right:
Harper's Weekly, March 21, 1868.

282. *Harper's Weekly*, March 28, 1868.

283. *Frank Leslie's Ill. News.*, June 6, 1868.

284. Top:
Harper's Weekly, May 30, 1868.
Bottom:
Harper's Weekly, March 21, 1868.

284-285. *Harper's Weekly*, March 21, 1868.

286. L. C. Handy, Washington, D.C.

287. *U.S. Army Signal Corps.*

288. From the collection of the author.
Top Right:
Frank Leslie's Ill. News., July 18, 1868.
Bottom Right:
Frank Leslie's Ill. News., July 25, 1868.

289. Top Left:
Frank Leslie's Ill. News., June 6, 1868.
Top Right:
Harper's Weekly, June 6, 1868.
Bottom:
Frank Leslie's Ill. News., June 13, 1868.

290. *Brown Brothers.*

291. Nast in *Harper's Weekly*, June 27, 1868.

293. Nast in *Harper's Weekly*, October 31, 1868.

294-295. Nast in *Harper's Weekly*, October 24, 1868.

297. Nast in *Harper's Weekly*, September 5, 1868.

298. Top:
Nast in *Harper's Weekly*, October 24, 1868.
Bottom:
Harper's Weekly, September 26, 1868.

299. Top:
Harper's Weekly, October 24, 1868.
Bottom:
Frank Leslie's Ill. News., November 21, 1868.

300. *Frank Leslie's Ill. News.*, November 30, 1867.

301. Left:
Frank Leslie's Ill. News., November 21, 1868.
Right:
Frank Leslie's Ill. News., February 27, 1869.

302. L. C. Handy, Washington, D.C.

303. *Frank Leslie's Ill. News.*, March 15, 1873.

304. From the collection of the author.
GREELEY and HENDRICKS from *Culver Service.*
Top Right:
Theodore R. Davis in *Harper's Weekly*, June 15, 1872.
Bottom Right:
Frank Leslie's Ill. News., July 20, 1872.

305. J. A. Wales in *Puck*, May 12, 1880.

Page

306. Top Left:
Frank Leslie's Ill. News., April 27, 1872.
Top Right:
Frank Leslie's Ill. News., August 17, 1872.
Bottom:
Frank Leslie's Ill. News., May 18, 1872.

307. Nast in *Harper's Weekly*, May 18, 1872.

308-309. *Frank Leslie's Ill. News.*, April 6, 1872.

309. *Frank Leslie's Ill. News.*, July 20, 1872.

310. *Frank Leslie's Ill. News.*, November 2, 1872.

310-311. *Frank Leslie's Ill. News.*, September 28, 1872.

312. Top:
Nast in *Harper's Weekly*, September 21, 1872.
Center:
Nast in *Harper's Weekly*, October 19, 1872.
Bottom:
Nast in *Harper's Weekly*, February 10, 1872.

312-313. Nast in *Harper's Weekly*, August 24, 1872.

315. Nast in *Harper's Weekly*, November 2, 1872.

316-317. Nast in *Harper's Weekly*, September 28, 1872.

318. *Frank Leslie's Ill. News.*, August 3, 1872.

319. Joseph Becker in *Frank Leslie's Ill. News.*, October 12, 1872.

321. Nast in *Harper's Weekly*, November 23, 1872.

322. Sarony, New York.

323. By Pranishikoff, after a Brady photograph in *Harper's Weekly*, March 24, 1877.

324. From the collection of the author.
WHEELER and COOPER from *Culver Service.*

325. *The Illustrated London News*, December 9, 1876.

326. Top:
Nast in *Harper's Weekly*, July 8, 1876.
Bottom:
Nast in *Harper's Weekly*, August 5, 1876.

327. Left:
Nast in *Harper's Weekly*, October 28, 1876.
Right:
A. B. Frost in *Harper's Weekly*, August 26, 1876.

328. Frost in *Harper's Weekly*, October 21, 1876.

329. *Frank Leslie's Ill. News.*, November 25, 1876.

330. Top:
Frank Leslie's Ill. News., March 10, 1877.
Bottom:
Frank Leslie's Ill. News., February 24, 1877.

330-331. Davis in *Harper's Weekly*, February 17, 1877.

333. Nast in *Harper's Weekly*, February 17, 1877.

334. Davis in *Harper's Weekly*, March 17, 1877.

335. Davis in *Harper's Weekly*, March 24, 1877.

336. C. S. Reinhart in *Harper's Weekly*, October 20, 1877.

337. Nast in *Harper's Weekly*, March 24, 1877.

338. From the collection of the author.

339. Frost in *Harper's Weekly*, March 19, 1881.

Bottom:
Reinhart in *Harper's Weekly*, August 22, 1896.

431. Top:
Lucius W. Hitchcock in *Harper's Weekly*, August 29, 1896.
Bottom:
J. S. Pughe in *Puck*, September 16, 1896.

432. *The Judge*, October 10, 1896.

433. Hitchcock in *Harper's Weekly*, October 31, 1896.

435. Pughe in *Puck*, April 29, 1896.

436. Top Left:
Rogers in *Harper's Weekly*, September 19, 1896
Top Right:
Rogers in *Harper's Weekly*, June 6, 1896.
Bottom Left:
Max Bachmann in *Leslie's Weekly*, September 3, 1896.
Bottom Right:
Bachmann in *Leslie's Weekly*, August 13, 1896.

437. Top Left:
Rogers in *Harper's Weekly*, August 29, 1896.
Top Right:
Rogers in *Harper's Weekly*, July 18, 1896.
Bottom Left:
Bachmann in *Leslie's Weekly*, September 10, 1896.
Bottom Right:
Bachmann in *Leslie's Weekly*, August 6, 1896.

439. *Underwood & Underwood.*

440. Top:
Opper in *Puck*, August 12, 1896.
Bottom:
G. V. Coffin in the Washington *Post*, August 15, 1896.

441. *Underwood & Underwood.*

442. Top:
Leslie's Weekly, October 8, 1896.
Bottom:
From Paxton Hibben, *William Jennings Bryan.*

444. Top:
B. West Clinedinst in *Leslie's Weekly*, March 11, 1897.
Bottom:
Photograph by J. C. Hemment.

444-445. de Thulstrup in *Harper's Weekly*, March 13, 1897.

446. *Brown Brothers.*

447. Rogers in *Harper's Weekly*, March 9, 1901.

448. From the collection of the author.

450. Top:
Dalrymple in *Puck*, April 18, 1900.
Bottom:
The Verdict, January 1, 1900.

451. *The Verdict*, March 13, 1899.

452. Top:
The Roosevelt Memorial Association, New York.
Center:
Brown Brothers

Bottom:
James Burton, New York.

453. Top:
James Burton, New York.
Bottom Left:
Hencke in *Leslie's Weekly*, July 7, 1900.
Bottom Right:
Leslie's Weekly, September 8, 1900.

454. Top:
Harper's Weekly, August 11, 1900.
Bottom:
Rogers in *Harper's Weekly*, August 4, 1900.

454-455. Pughe in *Puck*, September 5, 1900.

456. Top:
Keppler in *Puck*, September 19, 1900.
Bottom:
Hamilton in *The Judge*, September 15, 1900.

456-457. Pughe in *Puck*, July 11, 1900.

458. Top:
The Library of Congress.
Bottom:
Bush in the New York *World*, June 25, 1900.

458-459. *The Roosevelt Memorial Association.*

460. Top and Center:
R. L. Dunn, New York.
Bottom:
Peters in *Harper's Weekly*, November 14, 1896.

460-461. F. Cresson Schell in *Leslie's Weekly*, November 24, 1900.

462. *The Roosevelt Memorial Association.*

463. Top:
The Roosevelt Memorial Association.
Bottom:
Brown Brothers.

464. Top:
R. L. Dunn, New York.
Bottom:
Brown Brothers.

465. T. Dart Walker in *Leslie's Weekly*, September 21, 1901.

466. Top:
The Roosevelt Memorial Association.
Bottom:
Leslie's Weekly, September 9, 1901.

467. *The Roosevelt Memorial Association.*

468. *The Library of Congress.*

469. *Underwood & Underwood.*

470. *Brown Brothers.*

471. *Underwood & Underwood.*

472. From the collection of the author.
DAVIS from *Culver Service.*
Top Right:
Cook & Wagner.
Bottom Right:
George R. Lawrence Co., Chicago.

473. Top Left:
The New York *Herald.*
Top Right:
Underwood & Underwood.
Bottom Left:
Maybell in the Brooklyn *Daily Eagle,* July 11, 1904.
Bottom Right:
Photograph by Juley.

474. The New York *Herald.*

475. Homer Davenport in the New York *Evening Mail,* July 27, 1904.

476. Keppler in *Puck,* November 2, 1904.

477. *Brown Brothers.*

479. McCutcheon in the Chicago *Tribune,* November 10, 1904.

481. *The Library of Congress.*

482. Top:
Dalrymple in *The Judge,* December 3, 1904.
Bottom:
Pughe in *Puck,* March 1, 1905.

482-483. Keppler in *Puck,* March 1, 1905.

484. *Underwood & Underwood.*

485. *Brown Brothers.*

486. From the collection of the author.
DEBS, BRYAN, CHAFIN from *Culver Service.*

487. Bernard Partridge in *Punch,* June 17, 1905.

488. Top:
George R. Lawrence Co., Chicago.
Center and Bottom:
Photographs by H. D. Blauvelt.

488-489. Keppler in *Puck,* April 24, 1907.

490-491. E. W. Kemble in *Harper's Weekly,* September 5, 1908.

492. Top:
Underwood & Underwood.
Bottom Left:
Harper's Weekly, September 26, 1908.
Bottom Right:
Harper's Weekly, September 5, 1908.

493. Top:
Brown Brothers.
Bottom Left:
Harper's Weekly, September 5, 1908.
Bottom Right:
Harper's Weekly, August 29, 1908.

494. Top:
Rogers in *Harper's Weekly,* May 16, 1908.
Bottom:
Rogers in *Harper's Weekly,* February 1, 1908.

494-495. J. Campbell Cory in *Harper's Weekly,* August 22, 1908.

497. Partridge in *Punch,* November 11, 1908.

498. *The Roosevelt Memorial Association.*

499. Top:
Pictorial News.

Bottom:
The Duluth *News-Tribune.*

500. *Underwood & Underwood.*

501. *Brown Brothers.*

502. WILSON and MARSHALL from the author's collection.
ROOSEVELT and TAFT from *Brown Brothers.*
JOHNSON and SHERMAN from *Culver Service.*
Bottom Right:
Photograph by James F. Hughes.

503. Top:
Boardman Robinson in the New York *Tribune,* February 27, 1912.
Bottom:
Underwood & Underwood.

504. Top Left:
J. N. ("Ding") Darling in the New York *Globe,* January 9, 1912.
Top Right:
Robert Carter in the New York *World,* February 3, 1912.
Bottom Left:
C. R. Macauley in the New York *World,* January 18, 1912.
Bottom Right:
Ketten in the New York *World,* February 22, 1912.

505. Top Left:
H. T. Webster for *Associated Newspapers,* April 1, 1912.
Top Right:
Macauley in the New York *World,* June 7, 1912.
Bottom Left:
Macauley in the *World,* June 3, 1912.
Bottom Right:
Donahey in the Cleveland *Plain Dealer,* June 24, 1912.

506. Left:
Macauley in the New York *World,* March 10, 1912.
Right:
Macauley in the *World,* June 21, 1912.

507. Left:
Macauley in the *World,* June 14, 1912.
Right:
Macauley in the *World,* July 9, 1912.

508. Top:
Underwood & Underwood.
Bottom:
Macauley in the New York *World,* December 10, 1912.

509. Rollin Kirby in the New York *Sun,* May 16, 1912.

510. Left:
Kemble in *Harper's Weekly,* May 4, 1912.
Right:
Kemble in *Harper's Weekly,* March 23, 1912.

511. Left:
Kemble in *Harper's Weekly*, March 30, 1912.
Right:
Kemble in *Harper's Weekly*, June 1, 1912.

512. Top:
C. J. Budd in *Harper's Weekly*, August 3, 1912.
Bottom:
Kemble in *Harper's Weekly*, July 20, 1912.

512-513. The Philadelphia *North American*, April 12, 1912.

514. *Underwood & Underwood.*

515. Top:
Brown Brothers.
Bottom:
R. M. Brinkerhoff in *Harper's Weekly*, September 28, 1912.

516. Budd in *Harper's Weekly*, September 28, 1912.

517. *The Roosevelt Memorial Association.*

519. Kemble in *Harper's Weekly*, November 16, 1912.

520. Left:
International News Photos.
Right:
Brown Brothers.

521-522. *Brown Brothers.*

523. *The National Archives.*

524. From the collection of the author.

524-525. *Brown Brothers.*

527. *Harper's Weekly*, March 15, 1913.

528. *Culver Service.*

529. Top Left:
Kirby in the New York *World*, October 15, 1916.
Top Right:
Kirby in the *World*, October 5, 1916.
Bottom Left:
Kirby in the *World*, October 13, 1916.
Bottom Right:
Kirby in the *World*, October 11, 1916.

530. *Underwood & Underwood.*

531. *Look Magazine.*

532. Herbert Johnson in *The Saturday Evening Post*, August 26, 1916.

533. Left:
Johnson in *The Saturday Evening Post*, October 28, 1916.
Right:
Kirby in the New York *World*, November 14, 1916.

534. *Keystone Pictures Inc.*

535. *Brown Brothers.*

536. From the collection of the author.
COOLIDGE, CHRISTENSEN and ROOSEVELT from *Culver Service.*
Top Right:
Keystone.

Bottom Right:
F. T. Richards in *Life*, August 5, 1920.

537. Acme News Pictures.

538. *Keystone.*

539. Top:
The Independent, September 11, 1920.
Bottom:
Webster in *Life*, October 28, 1920.

540. Top:
Frost in *Life*, October 14, 1920.
Bottom:
Webster in *Life*, June 3, 1920.

541. *Life*, October 28, 1920.

542-543. *Life*, June 3, 1920.

544. *International News Photos.*

546. *Underwood & Underwood.*

547. *Keystone.*

548. Top:
Brown Brothers.
Bottom:
The Library of Congress.

549. *Brown Brothers.*

550. Bachrach from *Culver Service.*

551. *Brown Brothers.*

552. From the collection of the author.
BRYAN from *Culver Service.*

553. *United Press.*

554. *Acme.*

555. Left:
Brown Brothers.
Right:
Keystone.

556. Ellison Hoover in *Life*, March 6, 1924.

557. *Culver Service.*

558. Left:
Sykes in *Life*, April 24, 1924.
Right:
Sykes in *Life*, April 10, 1924.

559. Sykes in *Life*, October 2, 1924.

560. From the collection of the author.

561. Left:
Keystone
Right:
Keystone-Underwood.

562. *P. & A.*

563. *Brown Brothers.*

564. *Keystone-Underwood.*

565. *The National Archives.*

566-567. *Harris & Ewing.*

568. From the collection of the author.
CURTIS and ROBINSON from *Culver Service.*

568-569. *Keystone.*

569. *The Museum of the City of New York.*

Bottom:
George Skadding, *Life.*

694-695. H. G. Walker, *Life.*

696. Dorman H. Smith for *NEA,* April 15, 1948.

697. Herblock in the Washington *Post.*

698. Top:
Francis Miller, *Life.*
Bottom Left:
Acme.
Bottom Right:
Lisa Larsen, *Life.*

699. Francis Miller, *Life.*

702-703. Thomas D. McAvoy, *Life.*

704. Herblock in the Washington *Post.*

705. *International News Photos.*

706. Top Left:
Associated Press.
Top Right:
H. G. Walker, *Life.*
Bottom:
Acme.

707. Top Left:
Associated Press.
Top Right:
Frank Bruton
Bottom:
Acme.

709. Walt Kelly in the New York *Star,* July 26, 1948.

711. Top Left:
Francis Miller, *Life.*
Top Right:
Thomas D. McAvoy, *Life.*
Bottom:
Associated Press.

713. Ralph Morse, *Life.*

714. Top:
Ralph Morse, *Life.*
Bottom:
International News Photos.

715. Jim Whitmore, *Life.*

716. Top:
Walt Kelly in the New York *Star,* November 1, 1948.
Bottom:
Kelly in the New York *Star,* October 22, 1948.

717. Top:
Kelly in the New York *Star,* October 27, 1948.
Bottom:
Kelly in the New York *Star,* September 23, 1948.

719. Top:
Edward Clark, *Life.*
Bottom:
Acme.

720. Top:
Associated Press.
Bottom:
International News Photos.

721. *Acme.*

722. Left:
Eugene Smith, *Life.*
Right:
Thomas D. McAvoy, *Life.*

723. Left:
Sammy Schulman, *International News Photos.*
Right:
Cornell Capa, *Life.*

724. Top:
Ralph Morse, *Life.*
Bottom:
Thomas D. McAvoy, *Life.*

724-725. Cornell Capa, *Life.*

726. *Acme.*

727. Top:
A. E. Scott, *International News Photos.*
Bottom:
Harris & Ewing.

728. Top Left:
Dorman H. Smith for *NEA,* October 15, 1948.
Top Right:
Smith for *NEA,* November 8, 1948.
Bottom:
Talburt in the *Scripps-Howard Newspapers,* November 6, 1948.

SELECTED BIBLIOGRAPHY

I. ORIGINAL SOURCES

NEWSPAPERS

To name all the newspapers I have consulted would make much too long a list. Besides, it would serve little purpose. Every newspaper in the United States reports fully on the presidential campaign and election, the stories and reports growing in volume as the date of the election approaches. If one desires to see how this or that newspaper reported a campaign or the election, all that one has to do is to look up the issues preceding the month of November in election years.

Clarence S. Brigham's *History and Bibliography of American Newspapers* (2 vols., 1946) lists the titles of all the important early newspapers.

Frank Luther Mott's handy volume on *American Journalism* (1941) is an excellent guide, mentioning names of newspapers and giving an indication of their policies.

MANUSCRIPTS

The papers and correspondence of all Presidents and candidates for the Presidency have been consulted. The repository of their manuscripts and the titles of their published works may be found in the *Dictionary of American Biography* (22 vols., 1928–1944), edited by Allen Johnson and Dumas Malone.

DOCUMENTS

The state papers of the nineteenth century Presidents are collected in *A Compilation of the Messages and Papers of the Presidents* (20 vols., 1896–1899), edited by James Daniel Richardson.

The important papers of the Presidents of this century are all published and could be found in the respective President's printed works.

Presidential addresses, speeches, and other important documents are in Henry Steele Commager's *Documents of American History* (3d ed., 1949), in W. Macdonald's *Documentary Source Book of American History* (rev. ed., 1941), in Louis M. Hacker's *The Shaping of the American Tradition* (2 vols., 1947), and In the University of Chicago's *The People Shall Judge* (2 vols., 1949).

II. GENERAL HISTORIES

HILDRETH, Richard, *History of the United States* (6 vols., 1849–1852) deals with the country's history up to the year 1821, and is particularly useful for its contemporary newspaper sources.

ADAMS, Henry, *History of the United States During the Administration of Jefferson and Madison* (1889–1890), unsurpassed in style and contents.

CHANNING, Edward, *History of the United States* (6 vols., 1905–1925), covering the years till 1865.

McMASTER, John Bach, *History of the People of the United States from the Revolution to the Civil War* (8 vols., 1883–1913).

RHODES, James Ford, *History of the United States from the Compromise of 1850* (9 vols., 1891–1922). The first five volumes are excellent, the last four —from Hayes to McKinley and from McKinley to Theodore Roosevelt—are less so.

OBERHOLTZER, Ellis Paxson, *A History of the United States* (5 vols., 1917–1936) is a continuation of the Rhodes *History*, describing events from 1865 to 1901.

NEVINS, Allan, *Ordeal of the Union* (2 vols., 1947) and *The Emergence of Lincoln* (2 vols., 1950) are the first four volumes of what will become without doubt one of the most outstanding modern historical works. Professor Nevins begins his history in 1847 and so far has brought it down to 1861.

ANDREWS, E. Benjamin, *The History of the Last Quarter-Century in the United States, 1870–1895* (2 vols., 1896), a chatty work with many long-forgotten details.

SULLIVAN, Mark, *Our Times: The United States, 1900–1925* (6 vols., 1926–1937), a highly entertaining cultural and political history.

SCHLESINGER, A. M., and Fox, D. R., ed., *A History of American Life* (13 vols., 1929–1948), the most recent and most distinctive cooperative history.

JOHNSON, Allen, ed., *The Chronicles of America* (50 vols., 1918–1924), some admirable volumes.

HART, Albert Bushnell, ed., *The American Nation: A History* (28 vols., 1906–1918), covers the period from 1492 till 1917, written by different authors, but now out-of-date.

MORISON, Samuel Eliot and COMMAGER, Henry Steele, *The Growth of the American Republic* (2 vols., rev. ed. 1950), the most magnificent short history of the United States with an extensive, annotated bibliography.

III. CONVENTION LITERATURE

The *Official Proceedings* both of the Democratic and of the Republican National conventions are available in printed form. They may be found in libraries either under the heading *Proceedings*, or *Official Proceedings*, or *Democratic National Committee Proceedings* or *Republican National Committee Proceedings*.

The party platforms from 1789 to 1905 are printed in Thomas H. McKee's *The National Conventions and Platforms of All Political Parties* (6th ed., 1906) and in

K. H. Porter's *National Party Platforms* (1924). J. Tweedy's *History of the Republican National Conventions* (1910) is useful. Thais M. Plaisted's "Origins of National Nominating Committees and Platforms," an article in *Social Studies*, XXX (1939), 199-206, deals with the origins of modern party machinery.

The *New York Times* issued a special reprint of its front pages, carrying the convention reports from 1856 on to present days.

IV. STATISTICAL MATERIAL

The National Cyclopaedia of American Biography (1937) prints the electoral vote for President from March 4, 1789, to March 4, 1933.

Historical Statistics of the United States, 1789-1945 (1949) has all the vital figures.

The Presidential Counts (1877) is a complete official record of the proceedings of Congress at the counting of the electoral votes up to 1876.

Edgar E. Robinson's *The Presidential Vote, 1896-1932* (1934) tabulates the votes not only by states but by counties as well. Its supplement,

issued in 1940, prints the votes of the 1936 election.

Cortez A. Ewing's *Presidential Elections* (1940) is an interesting contemporary work, as is L. H. Bean's *Ballot Behavior: A Study of Presidential Elections* (1940).

Statistics on earlier elections are in *McPherson's Handbook* (from 1866 to 1894); in *Appleton's Cyclopedia* (from 1861 to 1903); on later elections, in the *American Yearbook* (from 1910 to present date) and in the *Information Please Almanac* (1951) and *World Almanac* (1951).

V. INAUGURATIONS

Usually there are a number of quickly assembled volumes on the Inaugural Exercises, printing the program and giving an illustrated story of the incumbent President.

Emil E. Hurja's *History of Presidential Inaugurations* (1933) is a small volume skimming over the surface of events.

Renzo D. Bowers's *The Inaugural Addresses of the*

Presidents (1929) prints all addresses from Washington to Hoover.

F. D. Roosevelt's inaugural addresses are in his *Public Papers and Addresses* (13 vols., 1938-1950).

I have written five articles on the inaugurations for *International News Service*. They were published in hundreds of newspapers in January 1949 under the title "Inaugurations of the past" by Stefan Lorant.

VI. ILLUSTRATIONS

I have made an extensive research for illustrations in contemporary periodicals. From the vast number of illustrated weeklies which I culled, I found most useful:

The Bee, New York, 1898
Collier's Weekly, New York, 1888 till the present
Every Saturday, Boston, 1866-1874
Gleason's and Ballou's Pictorial, Boston 1851-1859
Harper's Weekly, New York, 1857-1916
Judge, New York, 1881-1939
Leslie's Weekly, New York, 1855-1922
Life, (the humorous weekly) New York, 1883-1936
Life, New York, 1936 till the present
Look, Des Moines, 1937 till the present

Midweek Pictorial, New York, 1914-1937
The New Yorker, New York, 1925 till the present
The New York Times Magazine
Puck, New York, 1876-1918
The Verdict, 1898

For portraits of American statesmen I have consulted the Library of Congress's *A.L.A. Portrait Index*, edited by W. Coolidge and Nina E. Browne (1906).

Two works of great value are *The Pageant of America*, edited by Ralph H. Gabriel (15 vols., 1925-1929), an unsurpassed and scholarly pictorial story of the United States, and William Murrell, *A History of American Graphic Humor* (2 vols., 1933-1938), notable for its exquisite cartoons.

VII. CARTOONS AND CARTOONISTS

American Caricatures. Reproductions from Currier and Ives lithographs (1918).

BERRYMAN, F. S., "Cartoons of the Presidents" in D.A.R. Magazine, Vol. LXVII, 1933, 547-557.

CORY, J. C., *The Cartoonist's Art* (1912).
DAVENPORT, Homer, *Cartoons* (1898).
"DING" (J. N. Darling), *Aces and Kings* (1918).
DOWNEY, Fairfax, *Portrait of an Era* (1936).
DUNLAP, William, *History of the Arts of Design in America* (3 vols., 1917).
FIELDING, Mantle, *Engravers upon Copper and Steel* (1917).
FITZPATRICK, Daniel R., *Cartoons* (1947).
GROSS, Raymond, *T. R. in Cartoon* (1910).
HOPKINS, Livingston, *A Comic History of the United States* (1876).
JOHNSON, Herbert, *Cartoons* (1936).
KIRBY, Rollin, *Highlights, a cartoon History of the Twenties* (1931).
KEPPLER, Joseph, *Cartoons from Puck* (1893).
LINTON, W. J., *History of Wood Engraving in America* (1892).
MAURICE, Arthur B. and COOPER, Frederic T., *History of the 19th Century in Caricature* (1904).
McCUTCHEON, John T., *Cartoons* (1903).
——, *The Mysterious Stranger* (1901).
OPPER, F. B., *Willie and His Pop-pa* (1901).
——, *An Alphabet of Joyous Trusts* (1902).
PAINE, Albert B., *Thomas Nast—His Period and His Pictures* (1904).

PARTON, James, *Carciature and Other Comic Arts* (1877).
ROGERS, William A., *Hits at Politics: A Book of Cartoons* (1899).
——, *America Black and White Book* (1917).
——, *A World Worth While* (1922).
SHAW, Albert, *Abraham Lincoln: A Cartoon History* (2 vols., 1929).
——, *A Cartoon History of Roosevelt's Career* (1910). Cartoons of T. R.
SHERWOOD, John D., *Comic History of the United States* (1870).
SMITH, Dorman H., *101 Cartoons* (1936).
SMITH, Seba, *Letters of Major Jack Downing* (1857).
——, *My Thirty Years Out of the Senate* (1859).
STAUFFER, D. M., *American Engravers upon Copper and Steel* (2 vols., 1907).
WEISS, Harry B., *William Charles* (1932).
WEITENKAMPF, Frank, *American Graphic Art* (1924).
NEVINS, Allan, and WEITENKAMPF, Frank, *A Century of Political Cartoons* (1944).
YOUNG, Art, *Hades Up to Date* (1892).
——, *On My Way* (1928).
——, *The Best of Art Young* (1936).

VIII. BIOGRAPHIES OF THE PRESIDENTS

For every historian and student, the twenty-two volumes of the *DAB* (*Dictionary of American Biography*) with their many thousand biographies are of inestimable value.

The Biographical Directory of the American Congress, 1774–1949 (Government Printing Office, 1950), in one volume is a work of easy reference about everyone who served in Congress.

Of the 32 Presidents there are innumerable biographies. I name here only a few, the standard and most authoritative ones in order of their publications.

GEORGE WASHINGTON (1789–1897)

MARSHALL, John, *The Life of George Washington* (5 vols., 1804–1807).
IRVING, Washington, *Life of George Washington* (5 vols., 1855–1859).
LODGE, Henry Cabot, *George Washington* (2 vols., 1898).
FORD, P. L., *The True George Washington* (1896 and 1924).
HUGHES, Rupert, *George Washington* (3 vols., 1926–1930).
FITZPATRICK, John C., *Washington Himself* (1933).

All these works will probably be superseded when Douglas S. Freeman publishes the concluding volumes of his monumental biography on Washington, of which the first two appeared in 1948.

JOHN ADAMS (1797–1801)

MORSE, J. T., *John Adams* (1884).

ADAMS, James T., *The Adams Family* (1930).
CHINARD, Gilbert, *Honest John Adams* (1933).
BOWEN, Catherine Drinker, *John Adams and the American Revolution* (1950) is the most recent biography of Adams, dealing with his life till 1776. The volume has a rich and useful Bibliography.

THOMAS JEFFERSON (1801–1809)

RANDALL, H. S., *The Life of Thomas Jefferson* (3 vols., 1858).
MUZZEY, D. S., *Thomas Jefferson* (1918).
BOWERS, Claude G., *Jefferson and Hamilton* (1925).
CHINARD, Gilbert, *Thomas Jefferson, The Apostle of Americanism* (1929).
BOWERS, Claude G., *Jefferson in Power* (1936).
KOCH, Adrienne, *Jefferson and Madison* (1950).

The most recent biography, an exquisite work of high scholarship blended with superb writing is Dumas Malone, *Jefferson and His Time*, projected in four volumes, of which two appeared in 1948.

JAMES MADISON (1809–1817)

HUNT, Gaillard, *The Life of James Madison* (1902).
BRANT, Irving, *James Madison*, is the latest and most authoritative full-size biography in three volumes (1947–1950).

JAMES MONROE (1817–1825)

CRESSON, William Penn, *James Monroe* (1946) is a highly satisfactory, well-written and interesting biography. It was published after the author's untimely death.

746

JOHN QUINCY ADAMS (1825–1829)
Morse, John T., *John Quincy Adams* (1882).
Clark, B. C., *John Quincy Adams; Old Man Eloquent* (1932).

ANDREW JACKSON (1829–1837)
Parton, James, *Life of Andrew Jackson* (1860).
Bassett, J. S., *Life of Andrew Jackson* (1911).
Johnson, A. W., *Andrew Jackson* (1927).
James, Marquis, *The Life of Andrew Jackson* (1933–1937) is the modern definitive work on Jackson's life.
 Earlier works of the Jacksonian Period, like:
Macdonald, William, *Jacksonian Democracy* (1906).
Ogg, F. A., *The Reign of Andrew Jackson* (1919).
Bowers, Claude G., *The Party Battles of the Jackson Period* (1922).
Abernathy, Thomas P., *From Frontier to Plantation in Tennessee* (1932).
have paled in significance since Schlesinger, Arthur M., Jr., published *The Age of Jackson* in 1945.

MARTIN VAN BUREN (1837–1841).
Shepard, E. M., *Martin Van Buren* (1888).
Fitzpatrick, John C., ed. (1920), *The Autobiography of Martin Van Buren* in the Annual Report in the American History Association of the year 1918.
Lynch, D. T., *An Epoch and a Man: Martin Van Buren and His Times* (1929).
Holmes, Alexander, *The American Talleyrand* (1935).

WILLIAM HENRY HARRISON (1841).
Stoddard, W. O., *W. H. Harrison, John Tyler and James K. Polk* (1888).
Goebel, Dorothy B., *William Henry Harrison* (1926).
Cleaves, Freeman, *Old Tippecanoe: William H. Harrison and His Time* (1939).
Green, James A., *William Henry Harrison, His Life and Times* (1941).

JOHN TYLER (1841–1845).
Tyler, Lyon G., ed., *The Letters and Times of the Tylers* (3 vols., 1884–1896).
Chitwood, O. P., *John Tyler* (1939).

JAMES K. POLK (1845–1849).
Quaife, M. M., ed., *The Diary of James K. Polk* (4 vols., 1910).
Polk: The Diary of a President, was abridged from the above by Nevins, Allan (1929).
McCormac, E. I., *James K. Polk*, a political biography. (1922).

ZACHARY TAYLOR (1849–1850).
Hamilton, Holman, *Zachary Taylor, Soldier of the Republic* (1941).
McKinley, S. B., *Old Rough and Ready* (1946).
Dyer, Brainerd, *Zachary Taylor* (1947).

MILLARD FILLMORE (1850–1853).
Griffis, W. E., *Millard Fillmore* (1915).

FRANKLIN PIERCE (1853–1857).
Nichols, Roy F., *Franklin Pierce, Young Hickory of the Granite Hills* (1931).

JAMES BUCHANAN (1857–1861).
Curtis, G. Ticknor, *Life of James Buchanan* (2 vols., 1883).

ABRAHAM LINCOLN (1861–1865).
Nicolay, J. G., and Hay, John, *Abraham Lincoln: A History* (10 vols., 1890).
Sandburg, Carl, *Abraham Lincoln* (6 vols., 1926, 1939).
Beveridge, Albert J., *Abraham Lincoln, 1809–1858* (1928).
Randall, James G., *Lincoln, the President* (first 2 vols., 1945).

ANDREW JOHNSON (1865–1869).
Winston, R. W., *Andrew Johnson, Plebeian and Patriot* (1928).
Stryker, L. P., *Andrew Johnson* (1929).

ULYSSES S. GRANT (1869–1877).
Personal Memoirs of U. S. Grant (2 vols., 1885–1886).
Garland, Hamlin, *Ulysses S. Grant, His Life and Character* (1898 and 1920).
Woodward, W. E., *Meet General Grant* (1928).
Hesseltine, W. B., *Ulysses S. Grant* (1935).
Lloyd, Lewis, conceived a large-scale biography of the General. The first volume of it, and what an exquisite volume it was, *Captain Sam Grant*, appeared in 1950. The untimely death of the author leaves the work unfinished.

RUTHERFORD B. HAYES (1877–1881).
Williams, C. R., *The Life of Rutherford B. Hayes* (2 vols., 1914).
Eckenrode, H. J., *Rutherford B. Hayes, Statesman of Reunion* (1930).

JAMES A. GARFIELD (1881).
Smith, Theodore C., *Life and Letters of James Abram Garfield* (2 vols., 1925).
Caldwell, R. G., *James A. Garfield: Party Chieftain* (1931).

CHESTER A. ARTHUR (1881–1885).
Howe, G. F., *Chester A. Arthur; a quarter century of machine politics* (1934).

GROVER S. CLEVELAND (1885–1889, and 1893–1897).
McElroy, Robert M., *Grover Cleveland, the Man and the Statesman* (2 vols., 1923).

747

NEVINS, Allan, *Grover Cleveland: a Study in Courage* (1932).

BENJAMIN HARRISON (1889–1893).
WALLACE, Lew, *Life of General Ben Harrison* (1888).
VOLWILER, A. T., ed., *Correspondence Between Benjamin Harrison and James G. Blaine* (1940).

WILLIAM McKINLEY (1897–1901).
OLCOTT, C. S., *The Life of William McKinley* (2 vols., 1916).

THEODORE ROOSEVELT (1901–1909).
MORISON, Elting E., ed., *The Letters of Theodore Roosevelt*, projected in eight volumes, of which two appeared in 1951.
ROOSEVELT, Theodore, *Autobiography* (1913).
Selections from Correspondence of Theodore Roosevelt and Henry Cabot Lodge 1884–1918 (1925). There are other smaller volumes containing letters and correspondence of T.R. The Theodore Roosevelt Association issued a Roosevelt Cyclopedia containing everything of importance that T.R. uttered.
The official biography is Bishop, Joseph Bucklin, *Theodore Roosevelt and His Time* (2 vols., 1920), which was written during Roosevelt's lifetime. The best critical biography is by Pringle, H. F., *Theodore Roosevelt, A Biography* (1931), for which the author won the Pulitzer Prize.

WILLIAM HOWARD TAFT (1909–1913).
PRINGLE, Henry F., *The Life and Times of William Howard Taft* (1939).

WOODROW WILSON (1913–1921).
DODD, W. E., *Woodrow Wilson and His Work* (1920).
WHITE, W. A., *Woodrow Wilson: The Man, His Times and His Task* (1925).
BAKER, Roy S., *Woodrow Wilson, Life and Letters* (8 vols., 1927–1939).

WARREN G. HARDING (1921–1923).
CHAPPLE, Joseph M., *Warren G. Harding–the Man* (1920, 1924).
DAUGHERTY, Harry M., and DIXON, Thomas, *The Inside Story of the Harding Tragedy* (1932).
ADAMS, Samuel Hopkins, *Incredible Era: The Life and Times of Warren G. Harding* (1939).

CALVIN COOLIDGE (1923–1929).
The Autobiography of Calvin Coolidge (1929).
ROGERS, C., *The Legend of Calvin Coolidge* (1929).
WHITE, William Allen, *A Puritan in Babylon* (1938).
FUESS, Claude M., *Calvin Coolidge: The Man From Vermont* (1940).

HERBERT HOOVER (1929–1933).
REEVES, Earl, *This Man Hoover* (1928).
DEXTER, W. F., *Herbert Hoover and American Individualism* (1932).
JOSLIN, T. G., *Hoover Off the Record* (1934).
LYONS, Eugene, *Our Unknown Ex-President* (1948).
HINSHAW, David, *Herbert Hoover: American Quaker* (1950).

FRANKLIN D. ROOSEVELT (1933–1945).
Not enough time has gone by to evaluate FDR. There is no good biography of him yet. The best picture of him is in Sherwood, R. E., *Roosevelt and Hopkins* (1949), while Gunther, John, *Roosevelt in Retrospect* (1950) gives many anecdotes. A concise pictorial account of his life is Lorant, Stefan, *FDR– A Pictorial Biography* (1950).

HARRY S. TRUMAN (1945–).
COFFIN, T., *Missouri Compromise* (1947).
MARKEL, Lester, "After four years: Portrait of Harry Truman," *New York Time, Magazine*, April 10, 1949.
DANIELS, Jonathan, *The Man of Independence* (1950).
HERSEY, John, "Mr. President." A five part profile in *The New Yorker Magazine*, April 7–May 5, 1951.

IX. BIOGRAPHIES OF THE DEFEATED CANDIDATES

AARON BURR
PARTON, James, *The Life and Times of Aaron Burr* (1858).
WANDELL, S. H., and MINNEGERODE, Meade, *Aaron Burr* (1925).
SCHACHNER, Nathan, *Aaron Burr, a Biography* (1937).

DE WITT CLINTON
RENWICK, James, *Life of DeWitt Clinton* (1840).

RUFUS KING
The Life and Correspondence of Rufus King (6 vols., 1894–1900), ed. by his grandson, Charles R. King.

WILLIAM H. CRAWFORD
SHIPP, J. E. D., *Giant Days, or The Life and Times of William H. Crawford* (1909).

HENRY CLAY
SCHURZ, Carl, *Henry Clay* (2 vols., 1887).
CLAY, Thomas H. and OBERHOLTZER, E. P., *Henry Clay* (1910).
VAN DEUSEN, G. G., *The Life of Henry Clay* (1937).

LEWIS CASS
SMITH, W. L. G., *Fifty Years of Public Life–The Life and Times of Lewis Cass* (1856).
McLAUGHLIN, Andrew C., *Lewis Cass* (1899).

WINFIELD SCOTT

Scott, Winfield, *Memoirs of Lieutenant-General Scott, written by himself* (2 vols., 1864).

Wright, Marcus J., *Life and Services of General Winfield Scott* (1852).

Elliott, Charles W., *Winfield Scott, the Soldier and the Man* (1937).

JOHN C. FRÉMONT

———, *Memoirs of My Life* (1887).

Nevins, Allan, *Frémont, the West's Greatest Adventurer* (2 vols., 1928).

STEPHEN A. DOUGLAS

Johnson, Allen, *Stephen A. Douglas: A Study in American Politics* (1908).

Howland, Louis, *Stephen A. Douglas* (1920).

Milton, G. F., *The Eve of Conflict: Stephen A. Douglas and the Needless War* (1934).

GEORGE B. McCLELLAN

McClellan, G. B., *McClellan's Own Story* (1887).

Michie, P. S., *General McClellan* (1901).

Myers, William Starr, *A Study in Personalty, General George Brinton McClellan* (1934).

Macartney, Clarence E., *Little Mac* (1940).

Eckenrode, H. J., and Conrad, Bryan, *George B. McClellan* (1941).

HORATIO SEYMOUR

Croly, D. G., *Seymour and Blair* (1868).

Mitchell, Stewart, *Horatio Seymour of New York* (1938).

HORACE GREELEY

Isely, Yeter Allan, *Horace Greeley and the Republican Party, 1853–1861* (1947).

Hale, William Harlan, *Horace Greeley, Voice of the People* (1950).

SAMUEL J. TILDEN

Bigelow, John, *The Life of Samuel J. Tilden* (2 vols., 1895).

Flick, Alexander C., *Samuel J. Tilden, A Study in Political Sagacity* (1939).

WINFIELD SCOTT HANCOCK

Hancock, Almira Russell, *Reminiscences of Winfield Scott Hancock* (1887).

Junkin, D. X., and Norton, F. H., *Life of Winfield Scott Hancock* (1880).

Walker, Francis A., *General Hancock* (1895).

JAMES B. WEAVER

Allen, E. A., *Lives of Weaver and Fields, and Achievements of the People's Party* (1892).

Haynes, F. E., *James Baird Weaver* (1919).

JAMES G. BLAINE

Stanwood, E., *James Gillespie Blaine* (1905).

Muzzey, David S., *James G. Blaine* (1934).

WILLIAM JENNINGS BRYAN

Bryan, W. J., *The Memoirs of William Jennings Bryan* (1925). ed. by Mary Baird Bryan.

Werner, M. R., *Bryan* (1929).

Williams, Wayne C., *William Jennings Bryan* (1936).

ALTON B. PARKER

Brady, J. R., *The Lives and Public Services of Parker and Davis* (1904).

EUGENE DEBS

Karsner, David, *Debs: His Authorized Life and Letters* (1919).

———, *Talks with Debs in Terra Haute* (1922).

Coleman, McAlister, *Eugene V. Debs, a Man Unafraid* (1930).

Debs, Eugene V., Writings and speeches, Introduction by Arthur M. Schlesinger, Jr. (1948).

Ginger, Ray, *The Bending Cross; a biography of Eugene Victor Debs* (1949).

JAMES M. COX

Cox, J. M., *Journey Through My Years* (1946).

ROBERT LA FOLLETTE

La Follette, R. M., *La Follette's Autobiography* (1913).

ALFRED E. SMITH

Pringle, A. F., *Alfred E. Smith: A Critical Study* (1927).

Moses, Robert, "Al Smith, A Friend 'Looks at the Record.'" *New York Time, Magazine*, Jan. 21, 1945.

WENDELL WILLKIE

Willkie, W., *This is Wendell Willkie;* a collection of speeches and writings, with biographical notes by Stanley Walker.

THOMAS E. DEWEY

Walker, Stanley, *Dewey, an American of This Century* (1944).

X. GENERAL WORKS ON PRESIDENTIAL ELECTIONS

AGAR, Herbert, *The Price of Union* (1950), one of the outstanding political histories of the United States in one volume, with an excellent bibliography.

———, *The People's Choice* (1933), an excellent work on the Presidency.

BISHOP, J. B., *Presidential Nominations and Elections* (1916).

COOK, S. L., *Torchlight Parade* (1929).

McCLURE, A. K., *Our Presidents and How We Make Them* (1900).

MINNEGERODE, M., *Presidential Years 1787–1860* (1928).

SEITZ, D. C., *The "Also Runs"* (1928).

STANWOOD, E. M., *A History of the Presidency* (2 vols., 1884, many rev. ed. up to 1928); the standard work on presidential elections.

STONE, Irving, *They Also Run* (1943).

XI. HISTORIES OF THE PARTIES

ALLEN, E. A., *The Lives of Weaver and Fields, and Achievements of the People's Party* (1892).

BEARD, C. A., *The American Party Battle* (1928).

BINKLEY, W. E., *American Political Parties* (1943).

BOWERS, C. G., *Beveridge and the Progressive Era* (1932).

BRUCE, H. R., *American Parties and Politics; History and Role of Political Parties in the U. S.* (rev. ed. 1937).

BYRDSALL, F., *History of the Locofoco or Equal Rights Party* (1842).

CRANDALL, A. W., *The Early History of the Republican Party, 1854–1856* (1930).

CURTIS, Francis, *The Republican Party . . . 1854–1904* (1904).

DESMOND, J. J., *The Know-Nothing Party* (1905).

DE WITT, B., *The Progressive Movement* (1915).

GARVER, F. H., "Parties in Power in United States History," *Social Studies*, 1937, Vol. XXVIII, 344–347.

GORDY, J. P., *Political History of the United States With Special Reference to the Growth of Political Parties* (2 vols., 1903).

HAYNES, F. E., *Third Party Movements Since the Civil War* (1916).

HECHLER, K. W., *Insurgency: Personalities and Politics of the Taft Era* (1940).

HESSELTINE, W. B., *The Rise and Fall of Third Parties* (1948).

HICKS, J. D., *The Populist Crusade* (1931).

———, *The Populist Revolt* (1939).

———, "The Third Party Tradition in American Politics," *Mississippi Valley Historical Review*, 1933, Vol. XX, 3–28.

HILLQUIT, M., *The History of Socialism in the United States* (1910).

HOLCOMBE, A. N., *The Political Parties of Today* (1924).

KENT, F. R., *History of the Democratic Party* (1928).

KILROE, E. P., *The Story of Tammany* (1924).

KLEEBERG, G. S. P., *Formation of the Republican Party* (1911).

LAIDLER, H. W., *A History of Socialist Thought* (1927).

LYNCH, W. O., *Fifty Years of Party Warfare, 1789–1837* (1931).

McCARTHY, C., *The Antimasonic Party. A Study of Political Antimasonry in the United States, 1827–1840* (1903).

McVEY, F. L., *The Populist Movement* (1896).

MERRIAM, C. E., and GOSNELL, H. F., *The American Party System* (1940, rev. ed.).

MINOR, H., *The Story of the Democratic Party* (1928).

MITCHELL, W. C., *A History of the Greenbacks* (1903).

MYERS, Gustavus, *History of Tammany Hall* (1917).

MYERS, William, *The Republican Party, a History* (1928).

NOYES, J. H., *History of American Socialism* (1870).

ROBINSON, E. E., *The Evolution of American Political Parties* (1924).

ROCHESTER, Anna, *The Populist Movement in the United States* (1943).

ROSS, E. D., *The Liberal Republican Movement* (1919).

SAIT, E. M., *American Parties and Elections* (1939 rev. ed.).

THOMAS, Norman, *What Is Our Destiny?* (1944).

WERNER, M. R., *Tammany Hall* (1928).

WOODBURN, J. A., *Political Parties* (1924).

XII. ELECTIONS

Both the Democrats and the Republicans are publishing every four years a *National Committee Campaign Textbook*, which discusses the issues used in the campaign.

The New York Public Library has rich material on the various elections, bound together and pasted in scrapbooks.

1789 and 1792: GEORGE WASHINGTON

BOWEN, C. W., *The History of the Centennial Celebration of the Inauguration of George Washington as First President of the United States* (1892).

BOWERS, C. G., *Jefferson and Hamilton, the Struggle for Democracy* (1925).

GIBBS, George, *Memoirs of the Administration of Washington and John Adams* (6 vols., 1846).

HASSELN, Henry von, *The Work of the First Congress in 1789* (1946 unpublished M.A. thesis under James Hart at the University of Virginia).

MONAGHAN, F. and LOWENTHAL, M., *This Was New York* (1943).

1796: JOHN ADAMS

FAY, B., "Early Party Machinery in the United States; Pennsylvania in the Election of 1796," *Pennsylvania Magazine of History*, 1936, Vol. LX, 375–390.

1800 and 1804: THOMAS JEFFERSON

BAYARD, R. H., *Documents Relating to the Presidential Election in the Year 1801* (1831).

BEARD, C. A., *Economic Origins of Jeffersonian Democracy* (1915).

BOWERS, C. G., *Jefferson in Power; the Death Struggle of the Federalists* (1936).

HUNT, Gaillard, "Office Seeking During Jefferson's Administration," *American Historical Review*, January 1898, 270–291.

LERCHE, C. O., "Jefferson and the Election of 1800; A Case Study in the Political Smear," *William & Mary College Quarterly Historcal Magazine*, October 1948, 467–491.

PINCKNEY, Charles, "South Carolina in the Presidential Election of 1800," *American Historical Review*, 1898, Vol. IV, 111 129.

WARREN, Charles, "Why Jefferson Abandoned the Presidential Speech to Congress," *Massachusetts Historical Society*, 1924, Vol. LVII, 123–172.

1808: JAMES MADISON

MORISON, Samuel E., "The First National Nominating Convention, 1808," *American Historical Review*, 1912, Vol. XVII, 744–763.

1824: JOHN QUINCY ADAMS

BROWN, E. S., "The Presidential Election of 1824–1828," *Political Science Quarterly*, Vol. XL, 384–403.

HAY, Thomas R., "John C. Calhoun and the Presidential Campaign of 1824," *North Carolina Historical Review*, Oct. 1934 and Jan. 1935.

RAMMELKAMP, C. H., "The Campaign of 1824 in New York," *American Historical Association Annual Report for 1904*, 175–201.

1828 and 1832: ANDREW JACKSON

ABERNETHY, T. P., "The Political Geography of Southern Jacksonism," *East Tennessee Historical Society Publications*, 1931, No. 3, 35–41.

BASSETT, J. S., "Major Lewis on the Nomination of Andrew Jackson," *Proceedings of the American Antiquarian Society*, 1924, Vol. XXXIII, 12–33.

BEARD, William E., "Democracy's Two-Third Rule Rounds Out a Century," *Tennessee Historical Magazine*, 2nd ser., II, 87–95.

BIDDLE, Nicholas, *The Correspondence of Nicholas Biddle Dealing with National Affairs, 1807–1844*, edited by R. C. McGrane (1919).

BOWERS, C. G., *Party Battles of the Jackson Period* (1922).

ERIKSSON, E. M., "Official Newspaper Organs and the Presidential Elections of 1828–1836," *Tennessee Historical Magazine*, 1924–1925, Vol. VIII, 231–247, Vol. IX, 37–58, 115–130.

GAMMON, S. R., *The Presidential Campaign of 1832* (1922).

KELSAY, Isabel T., "The Presidential Campaign of 1828," *The East Tennessee Historical Society's Publication*, January 1933.

ROYALL, W. L., *Andrew Jackson and the Bank of the United States* (1880).

SCHLESINGER, A. F., *The Age of Jackson* (1945).

SMITH, C. H., "Propaganda Technique in the Jackson Campaign of 1828," *The East Tennessee Historical Society's Publication*, No. 6, 1934.

SMITH, Margaret B., *The First Forty Years of Washington Society*, edited by Gaillard Hunt (1906).

STENBERG, R. R., "Jackson, Buchanan, and the 'Corrupt Bargain' Calumny," *Pennsylvania Magazine of History and Biography*, Jan. 1934, 61–85.

WESTON, Florence, *The Presidential Election of 1828* (1938).

1836: MARTIN VAN BUREN

McGRANE, R. C., *The Panic of 1837* (1924).

1840: WILLIAM H. HARRISON and JOHN TYLER

CARROLL, E. M., *Origins of the Whig Party* (1925).

NORTON, A. B., *The Great Revolution of 1840* (1888).

1844: JAMES K. POLK

PERSINGER, C. E., "The Bargain of 1844," *Annual Reports of the American Historical Association*, 1911, Vol. I.

DE VOTO, Bernard, *The Year of Decision, 1846* (1943).

1852: FRANKLIN PIERCE

NICHOLS, R. F., *The Democratic Machine, 1850–1854* (1923).

SCHULTZ, H. S., *Nationalism and Sectionalism in South Carolina 1852–60* (1950).

1856: JAMES BUCHANAN

CRANDALL, A. W., *The Early History of the Republican Party, 1854–56* (1930).

NICHOLS, R. F., "Some Problems of the First Republican Presidential Campaign," *American Historical Review*, April 1923, Vol. XXVIII, 492–496.

———, *The Disruption of American Democracy* (1948).

MACARTNEY, C. E., "The First National Republican Convention," *Western Pennsylvania Historical Magazine*, 1937, Vol. XX, 83–100.

1860 and 1864: ABRAHAM LINCOLN and ANDREW JOHNSON

BARINGER, W. E., "Campaign Technique in Illinois, 1860," *Illinois State Historical Society Trans.*, 1932, 203–281.

BEALE, H. K., *The Critical Year: A Study of Andrew Johnson and Reconstruction* (1930).

BONHAM, M. L., Jr., "New York and the Election of 1860," *New York History*, 1934, XV, 124–143.

BOWERS, C. G., *The Tragic Era: The Revolution After Lincoln* (1929).

DEWITT, D. M., *The Impeachment and Trial of Andrew Johnson* (1903).

DU BOIS, W. E. B., *Blair Reconstruction* (1935).

DUDLEY, H. M., "The Election of 1864," *Mississippi Valley Historical Review*, 1932, Vol. XVIII, 500–518.

FITE, E. D., *The Presidential Campaign of 1860* (1911).

HALSTED, Murat, *Caucuses of 1860*. A History of the National Political Conventions (1860).

HAMILTON, P. J., *The Reconstruction Period* (1906).

HARBISON, W. A., "Zachariah Chandler's Part in the Reelection of Abraham Lincoln," *Mississippi Valley Historical Review*, 1935, Vol. XXII, 267–276.

KENDRICK, B. B., *The Journal of the Joint Committee of Fifteen on Reconstructon* (1914).

LUTHIN, R. H., *The First Lincoln Campaign* (1944).

McCARTHY, C. H., *Lincoln's Plan of Reconstruction* (1901).

MERRILL, L. T., "General Benjamin F. Butler in the Presidential Campaign of 1864," *Mississippi Valley Historical Review*, March 1947, 537–556.

MILLER, A. B., *Thaddeus Stevens* (1939).

MILTON, G. F., *The Age of Hate* (1930).

PROCTER, A. G., *Lincoln and the Convention of 1860* (1918).

SCHAFER, Joseph, "Who Elected Lincoln?" *American Historical Review*, Oct. 1941, Vol. XLVII, 51–63.

SMITH, D. V., "Salmon P. Chase and the Election of 1860," *Ohio Archaeological and Historical Quarterly*, 1930, Vol. XXXIX, 515–607.

WILLIAMS, W. C., *A Rail Splitter for President* (1951).

WILSON, C. R., "New Light on the Lincoln-Blair-Frémont 'Bargain' of 1864," *American Historical Review*, 1936, Vol. XLII, 71–78.

WOODBURN, J. A., *The Life of Thaddeus Stevens* (1913).

1868 and 1872: ULYSSES S. GRANT

COLEMAN, C. H., *The Election of 1868; The Democratic Effort to Regain Control* (1933).

COLES, Oscar, Seward or Grant in 1868? *New York History*, 1934, Vol. XV, 195–200.

NEVINS, Allan, *Hamilton Fish, the Inner History of the Grant Administration* (1937).

1876: RUTHERFORD B. HAYES

APPLETON, D. & Co., *The Presidential Counts: A Complete Official Record* (1877).

FIELD, D. D., *The Electoral Votes of 1876* (1877).

———, *The Vote That Made the President* (1877).

GIBSON, A. M., *A Political Crime* (1885).

GOODE, John, "The Electoral Commission of 1877," *American Law Review*, 1904, Vol. XXXVIII, 1–20, 161–180.

HAWORTH, P. L., *The Hayes–Tilden Disputed Presidential Election of 1876* (1927).

MARBLE, Manton, *A Secret Chapter of Political History* (1878).

NEW YORK TRIBUNE, *The Cipher Dispatches* (1879).

UNITED STATES: "Report of the Investigation of the Presidential Election of 1876," *House Miscellaneous Documents*, 45th Congress 3d Ses., No. 31.

———, *United States Electoral Commission of 1877* (Government Printing Office, 1877).

———, "United States Presidential Election of 1876," *U. S. Congress House Reports*, 45th Congress, 3d Ses., Vol. I, No. 140.

WOODWARD, C. V., *Reunion and Reaction: The Compromise of 1877 and the End of Reconstruction* (1951).

1884: GROVER CLEVELAND

FUNK, A. B., "The Republican National Convention of 1884," *Annals of Iowa*, 1940, 3d Series, Vol. XXII, 392–404.

PARKER, G. F., "How Grover Cleveland Was Nominated and Elected President," *Saturday Evening Post*, April 24, 1920.

THOMAS, H. C., *The Return of the Democratic Party to Power in 1884* (1919).

1888: BENJAMIN HARRISON

WILCOX, H. S., *The Trials of a Stump Speaker* (1906).

1892: GROVER CLEVELAND

KNOLES, G. H., *The Presidential Campaign and Election of 1892* (1942).

1896 and 1900: WILLIAM McKINLEY

BRYAN, W. J., *The First Battle: A Story of the Campaign of 1896* (1896).

———, *The Second Battle or The New Declaration of Independence, 1776–1900: An Account of the Struggle of 1900* (1900).

ELLIS, Elmer, "The Silver Republicans in the Election of 1896," *Mississippi Valley Historical Review*, 1932, Vol. XVIII, 519–534.

MALIN, J. C., "Notes on the Literature of Populism," *Kansas Historical Quarterly*, I, 160–164.

SILVEUS, Marian, "The Election of 1896 in Western Pennsylvania," *Western Pennsylvania Historical Magazine*, 1933, Vol. XVI, 99–124.

1904: THEODORE ROOSEVELT

DAVIS, O. K., *Released for Publication; Some Inside Political History of Theodore Roosevelt and His Times, 1898–1918* (2 vols., 1925).

SHAW, Albert, *A Cartoon History of Roosevelt's Career* (1910).

1908: WILLIAM H. TAFT

BOWERS, C. G., *Albert Beveridge and the Progressive Era* (1932).

BUTT, A. W., *Taft and Roosevelt, The Intimate Letters of Archie Butt, Military Aide* (1930).

1912 AND 1916: WOODROW WILSON

BRYAN, W. J., *Tale of Two Conventions* (1912).

DANIELS, J., *The Wilson Era* (2 vols., 1946).

ICKES, H., "Who Killed the Progressive Party?" *American Historical Review*, Jan. 1941, Vol. XLVI.

RING, Elizabeth "Progressive Movement of 1912 and Third Party Movement of 1924 in Maine," *University of Maine Studies, 1933, 2nd Series, No. 26.*

LYONS, M. F., *William F. McCombs, the President Maker* (1922).

McCOMBS, W. F., *Making Woodrow Wilson President* (1921).

MOWRY, George, *Theodore Roosevelt and the Progressive Movement* (1946).

PORRITT, Edward, "The Presidential Compagn," *Edinburg Review*, 1916, Vol. CCXXIII, 321-336.

ROSEWATER, V., *Back Stage in 1912* (1932).

1920: WARREN G. HARDING

COLCORD, Samuel, *The Great Deception* (1924).

COX, James M., *Journey Through My Years* (1946).

1928: HERBERT HOOVER

ALLEN, W. H., *Al Smith's Tammany Hall* (1928).

BOECKEL, R., *Editorial Research Reports: Presidential Politics* (2 vols., 1928).

CASEY, R., *Propaganda Technique in the Presidential Election of 1928* (unpubl., Madison, 1929).

LOVESTONE, Jay, *1928. The Presidential Election and the Workers* (1928).

MITCHELL, B., *Depression Decade, 1929-1941* (1947).

MYERS, W. G., and NEWTON, W. II., *The Hoover Administration* (1936).

OGBURN, W. F., and TALBOT, N. S., "A Measurement of the Factors in the Presidential Election of 1928," *Social Forces*, Dec. 1929, Vol. VIII, 175-183.

VIKING PRESS, *Oh Yeah?* (1931).

PEEL, R. V., and DONNELLY, T. C., *The 1928 Campaign—An Analysis* (1931).

SMITH, A. E., *Up To Now* (1929).

1932, 1936, 1940, 1944: FRANKLIN D. ROOSEVELT

ALLEN, F. L., *Since Yesterday* (1940).

ALSBERG, H. G., *America Fights the Depression; a Photographic Record of the CWA* (1934).

BEARD, C. A., and SMITH, G. H. E., *The Old Deal and the New* (1940).

BONE, H. A., *"Smear" Politics, an Analysis of 1940 Campaign Literature* (1941).

FARLEY, J. A., *Behind the Ballots* (1938).

——, *Jim Farley's Story* (1948).

HOOVER, Herbert, *Campaign Speeches of 1932* (1933).

JOHNSON, G. W., *Roosevelt: Dictator or Democrat?* (1941).

LAWRENCE, D., *Beyond the New Deal* (1934).

LASWELL, H. D., *Politics: Who Gets What, When, How* (1936).

LEONARD, J. N., *Three Years Down* (1939).

LINDLEY, E. K., *The Roosevelt Revolution: First Phase* (1933).

——, *Half Way With Roosevelt* (1936).

McINTIRE, R. T., *White House Physician* (1946).

MENCKEN, H. L., *Making a President* (1932).

MICHELSON, Charles, "Don't Let the Polls Fool You," *Readers Scope*, Oct. 1944.

MOLEY, Raymond, *After Seven Years* (1939).

ODEGARD, P. H., *Prologue to November, 1940* (1940).

OVERACKER, Louise, "Campaign Funds in the Presidential Election of 1936," *American Political Science Review*, June 1937, Vol. XXXI, 473-498.

PEEL, R. V., and DONNELLY, T. C., *The 1932 Campaign: An Analysis* (1935).

PERKINS, Frances, *The Roosevelt I Knew* (1946).

ROBINSON, E. E., *They Voted for Roosevelt* (1947).

ROOSEVELT, Eleanor, *This Is My Story* (1939).

RAUCH, Basil, *The History of the New Deal 1933-1938* (1944).

REILLY, M. F., as told to SLOCUM, W. J., *Reilly of the White House* (1947).

RODELL, F., *Democracy and the Third Term* (1940).

ROOSEVELT, Sara D., *My Boy Franklin* (1933).

SHERWOOD, R. E., *Roosevelt and Hopkins* (1948).

THORNTON, Willis, *The Third Term Issue* (1939).

WHARTON, D. (ed.), *The Roosevelt Omnibus* (1934).

1948: HARRY S. TRUMAN

ARNALL, Ellis G., "The Democrats Can Win." *Atlantic Monthly*, Oct. 1948.

ERNST, M. L., and LOTH, D., *The People Know Best* (1949).

MEIER, N. C. and SAUNDERS, H. W. (ed.), *Polls and Public Opinion* (1949).

ROGERS, Lindsey, *The Pollsters* (1949).

THOMAS, Norman, "Republican & Democrats are Stealing from My Socialist Platform," *Look*, August 17, 1948.

XIII. MEMOIRS AND REMINISCENCES

ALLEN, G. E., *Presidents Who Have Known Me* (1950).

AMES, Fisher, *The Works of Fisher Ames* (2 vols., 1854).

BARNES, T. W. (ed.), *Memoirs of Thurlow Weed* (1884).

BENTON, T. H., *Thirty Years' View* (2 vols., 1854-1856).

BLAINE, J. G., *Twenty Years in Congress, 1861-1881* (2 vols., 1884-1886).

BUTLER, N. M., *Across The Busy Years* (2 vols., 1939-1940).

CLARK, Champ, *My Quarter Century of American Politics* (2 vols., 1920).

CONKLING, A. R., *The Life and Letters of Roscoe Conkling* (1889).

COX, James M., *Journey Through My Years* (1946).

CROOK, W. H., *Memories of the White House: The Home Life of Our Presidents* (1911).

DAWES, Charles G., *A Journal of the McKinley Years* (1950).

DEPEW, C. M., *My Memories of Eighty Years* (1922).

DUNN, A. W., *How Presidents Are Made* (1920).

———, *From Harrison to Harding: A Personal Narrative* (1922).

FARLEY, J. A., *Behind the Ballots* (1938).

FORAKER, J. B., *Notes of a Busy Life* (2 vols., 1916).

GOMPERS, Samuel, *Seventy Years of Life and Labor* (2 vols., 1925).

GRANT, U. S., *Personal Memoirs of U. S. Grant* (2 vols., 1885–1886).

GREELEY, Horace, *Recollections of a Busy Life* (1868).

HOAR, G. F., *Autobiogaphy of Seventy Years* (2 vols., 1903).

HOOVER, I. H., *Forty-two Years in the White House* (1934).

HOUSTON, D. F., *Eight Years with Wilson's Cabinet* (2 vols., 1926).

HULL, Cordell, *Memoirs* (2 vols., 1948).

ICKES, H. L., *Autobiography of a Curmudgeon* (1943).

JULIAN, G. W., *Political Recollections* (1884).

KOHLSAAT, H. H., *From McKinley to Harding; Personal Recollections of Our Presidents* (1923).

LA FOLLETTE, R. M., *LaFollette's Autobiography* (1913).

McADOO, W. G., *Crowded Years* (1913).

MACLAY, E. S. ed., *The Journal of William Maclay* (1890).

McCLURE, A. K., *Recollections of Half a Century* (1902).

McCULLOCH, Hugh, *Men and Measures of Half a Century* (1888).

PLATT, T. C., *Autobiography* (1910).

PECK, H. T., *Twenty Years of the Republic, 1885–1905* (1906).

LANG, Louis J., ed., *The Autobiography of Thomas Collier Platt* (1910).

SCHURZ, Carl, *Reminiscences* (3 vols., 1907).

SHERMAN, John, *Recollections of Forty Years* (2 vols., 1895).

SMITH, I. R. T., with MORRIS, Joe A., *"Dear Mr. President"* (1949).

SPARKS, W. H., *Memories of Fifty Years* (1870).

STARLING, E. W., with SUGRUE, Thos., *Starling of the White House* (1946).

STEVENSON, A. E., *Something of Men I Have Known* (1909).

TAFT, Mrs. W. H., *Recollections of Full Years* (1914).

STODDARD, H. L., *As I Knew Them* (1927).

———, *It Costs to be President* (1938).

———, *Presidential Sweepstakes* (1948).

STONE, M. E., *Fifty Years a Journalist* (1922).

THOMPSON, C. W., *Presidents I've Known and Two Near Presidents* (1929).

TUMULTY, J. P., *Woodrow Wilson As I Know Him* (1921).

VILLARD, Henry, *Memoirs of Henry Villard* (2 vols., 1904).

WATTERSON, H., *Marse Henry: an Autobiography* (1919).

WEED, Thurlow, *Autobiography* (1883).

WELLES, G., *Diary of Gideon Wells* (3 vols., 1911).

WHITE, W. A., *The Autobiography of William Allen White* (1946).

WISE, H. A., *Seven Decades of the Union* (1872).

WISE, J. S., *Recollections of Thirteen Presidents* (1906).

XIV. ELECTORAL, PRESIDENTIAL, AND POLITICAL PROBLEMS

ADAMS, J. T., *Dictionary of American History* (5 vols., 1940).

ALLEN, F. L., *Only Yesterday. An Informal History of the Nineteenth-Twenties* (1931).

BEARD, C. A., *Economic Origins of Jeffersonain Democracy* (1915).

———, "Money in National Elections," *New Republic*, June 30, 1930.

BEARD, C., and M., *The Rise of American Civilization* (1927).

BEMAN, L. T., *The Abolishment of the Electoral College* (1926).

BEMIS, S. F., ed., *The American Secretaries of State and Their Diplomacy* (1927).

———, *Jay's Treaty* (1923).

———, *A Diplomatic History of the United States* (1936).

BINKLEY, W. E., *The Power of the President* (1937).

BOOTH, E. T., *Country Life in America As Lived by Ten Presidents* (1947).

BROOKS. R. C., *Political Parties and Electoral Problems* (1933).

BRYCE, James, *The American Commonwealth* (2 vols., 1889, rev. ed., 1921).

CARR, J. F., "Campaign Funds and Campaign Scandals," *Outlook*, Vol. 81, 1905.

CASEY, R. D., "Party Campaign Propaganda," *Annals of the American Academy of Political and Social Science*, vol. CLXXIX.

COLMAN, Edna M., *Seventy-five Years of White House Gossip* (1925).

COMMAGER, Henry S., *The American Mind* (1950).

——— "What Makes for Presidential Greatness," *New York Times Magazine*, July 22, 1945.

——— "Only Two Terms for a President?" *New York Times Magazine*, April 27, 1947.

——— "Yardstick for a Presidential Candidate," *New York Times Magazine*, Oct. 5, 1947.

CORWIN, E. S., *The President's Removal Power Under The Constitution* (1927).

———, *The President: Office and Powers* (1941).

CURTI, M., *The Growth of American Thought* (1943).

DOUGHERTY, J. H., *The Electoral System of the United States* (1906).

FIELD, O. P., "The Vice-Presidency of the United States," *American Law Review*, May–June, 1922, Vol. LVI, pp. 365–400.

FORD, H. J., *The Rise and Growth of American Politics* (1898).

GOEBEL, Dorothy G. and Julius, *Generals in the White House* (1945).

GOSNELL, H. F., *Machine Politics: Chicago Model* 1937).

HACKER, L., *Short History of the New Deal* (1934).

HART, James, *The Ordinance Making Powers of the President* (1925).

———, *The American Presidency in Action 1789* (1948).

HASBROUCK, P. D., "Caucus," *Encyclopedia of the Social Sciences*, Vol. III, Dec. 1930.

HATCH, L. C., and SHOUP, C. L., *A History of the Vice-Presidency of the United States* (rev. ed., 1934).

HENDRICK, B. J., *The Age of Big Business* (1921).

HERRING, E. P., *Presidential Leadership* (1940).

HIGH, S., *The Church in Politics* (1930).

HOCKETT, H. C., *Constitutional History of the United States* (1939).

HODDER, F. H., *The Genesis of the Kansas-Nebraska Act* (1913).

HOFSTADTER, R., *The American Political Tradition and the Men Who Made It* (1948).

HOLCOMBE, A. N., *The New Party Politics* (1933).

HURD, Charles, *The White House, a Biography* (1940).

JOHNSON, W., ed., *Selected Letters of William Allen White, 1899–1943* (1947).

JOSEPHSON, M., *The Politicos, 1865–1896* (1938).

———, *The President Makers* (1940).

———, *The Robber Barons* (1934).

KITSON, H. D., "Frequency of Republicans and Democrats among Eminent Americans," *Journal of Applied Psychology*, Sept. 1926, Vol. X, 341–345.

LASKI, H. J., *The American Presidency* (1940).

LEVIN, P. R., *Seven by Chance* (1948).

LOGAN, E. B., ed., *The American Political Scene* (1936).

LONG, J. C., *The Liberal Presidents* (1948).

LUETSCHER, G. D., *Early Political Machinery* (1903).

LAZARSFELD, P. F., *The People's Choice; How the Voter Makes Up His Mind in a Presidential Campaign* (1944).

McBAIN, H. L., *De Witt Clinton and the Origin of the Spoils System* (1907).

———, *Prohibition, Legal and Illegal* (1929).

MacIVER, R. M., *The Web of Government* (1947).

McLAUGHLIN, A. C., *A Constitutional History of the United States* (1935).

MERZ, C., *The Dry Decade* (1931).

MILTON, G. F., *The Use of Presidential Power, 1789–1943* (1944).

MINNEGERODE, M., *The Fabulous Forties, 1840–1850* (1924).

MOTT, F. L., *History of American Magazines, 1741–1850* (1930).

MUNRO, W. B., *The National Government of the United States* (1947).

NEVINS, Allan, ed., *American Press Opinion, Washington to Coolidge* (1928).

——— "Why They Win or Lose the Presidency," *New York Times Magazine*, Sept. 26, 1948.

ODEGARD, P. H., and HELMS, E. A., *American Politics; a study in political dynamics* (1938).

OGBURN, W. F., and JAFFE, A. J., "Business Conditions in Presidential Election Years," *American Political Science Review 1936* XXX, 269–275.

OSTROGORSKI, M. A., *Democracy and the Organization of Political Parties* (1902).

———, *Democracy and the Party System in the United States* (1926).

———, "The Rise and Fall of the Nominating Caucus," *American Historical Review*, Vol. V, 253.

OVERACKER, Louise, *The Presidential Primary* (1926).

———, *Money in Elections* (1932).

———, *Presidential Campaign Funds* (1946).

PARRINGTON, V. L., *Main Currents of American Thought* (3 vols. 1927, 1930).

POLLARD, J. E., *The Presidents and the Press* (1947).

POLLOCK, J. K., Jr., *Party Campaign Funds* (1920).

RAY, P. O., *The Repeal of the Missouri Compromise* (1909).

RESTON, James, "The Convention System," *New York Times Magazine*, July 11, 1948.

——— "The Qualities a President Needs," *New York Times Magazine*, Oct. 31, 1948.

SCHLESINGER, Arthur M., *Paths to the Present* (1949).

SCHULZ, G. J., *Election of the President of the United States by the House of Representatives*, issued as Senate Document 227, 68th Congress, 2nd Session (1925).

SINGLETON, E., *Story of the White House* (2 vols., 1907).

SMITH, A. J., *The Spirit of American Government* (1911).

SMITH, M., *A President Is Many Men* (1948).

STOKES, Thomas L., "What Goes On in That 'Smoke-Filled Room,'" *New York Times Magazine*, June 20, 1948.

TAFT, W. H., *The Presidency* (1916).

THACH, C. C., *The Creation of the Presidency, 1775–1789* (1922).

TURNER, F. J., *The United States, 1830–1850* (1935).

TYDINGS, M. L., *Before and After Prohibition* (1930).

VILLARD, O. G., *Prophets True and False* (1929).

WHITE, W. A., *Politics: The Citizen's Business* (1924).

YOUNG, K. H., and MIDDLETON L., *Heir Apparent* (1948). A study of the Vice-Presidents.

INDEX

H

Hacker, Louis M., quoted, 604
Hale, John P., 187, 205, 209
"Half-breeds," 339
Halleck, Charles, 686
Halpin, Maria, 383, 384
Halstead, Murat, 309; quoted, 248; eyewitness account of ballot which gave the nomination to Lincoln, 250
Hamilton, Alexander, 6, 14, 27f., 50; political deal with Jefferson, 28; conflict with Jefferson, 29ff.; proposal for national bank, 29; distrust of the people, 30; advocacy of Adams and Pinckney, 40; pamphlet denouncing Adams, 51
Hamilton, John, 612
Hancock, John, rejected as candidate for the Vice-Presidency, 14
Hancock, Winfield, 347; candidate for presidential nomination, 292; balloting for, 294ff.; subjected to political attacks, 358; quoted, 362
Hanna, Mark, 398, 429, 432ff., 440, 478; relations with Theodore Roosevelt, 473
Harding, Warren Gamaliel, 535ff., 543; nomination for the Presidency, 544; front-porch campaign, 546; election, 547; administration, 551ff.; death of, 555
Harper's Weekly, 382
Harrison, Benjamin, 393ff., 397, 398, 408; election, 405; ineffective administration of, 407f.; campaign of 1892, 415
Harrison, Pat, quoted, 557
Harrison, William Henry, 77, 83, 138, 142, 145ff.; presidential nomination, 153; campaign propaganda, 154ff.; election, 161; inauguration of, 162; death of, 165
Hartford, Conn., Federalist convention, 85
Hartford Resolutions, 86
Hartranft, John F., 327
Harvey, William H., *Coin's Financial School*, 426f.
Hawaii, annexation of, 450
Hawthorne, Nathaniel, 192
Hay, John, 443
Hayes, Rutherford Birchard, 323ff., 327; nomination for the Presidency, 328; election, 336; administration of, 339
Hayne, Robert Y., 123
Hearst, William Randolph, 491, 587, 609, 611
Hendricks, Thomas A., nomination for the Vice-Presidency, 329, 330; candidate for presidential nomi-

nation in 1868, 292; nomination for the Vice-Presidency, 380
Herndon, William H., 253
Hewitt, Abram, 332, 336
Hicks, John D., quoted, 355
Hill, David B., 405, 408, 438, 462
Hill, Isaac, quoted, 110
Hill, James J., 476
Hill, Lister, 688
Hillman, Sidney, 654
Hisgen, Thomas L., nomination for the Presidency, 498
Hoar, George F., quoted, 398
Hobart, Garret A., 454; nomination for the Vice-Presidency, 434
Home Owners' Loan Corporation, 599
"Hooray for Clay," campaign slogan of 1840, 177
Hoover, Herbert, 543, 551, 565ff., 571, 609, 621; nomination for the Presidency in 1928, 572; acceptance speech, 573; election, 574f.; administration, 577ff.; inaugural address, 577; quoted, 577; nomination for the Presidency in 1932, 582; campaign of 1932, 590
Hopkins, Harry, 597, 628, 630
Horner, Gov. of Illinois, 594
Horton, Frank O., 623
House, Edward Mandell, 543
Howard, John E., candidate for Vice-Presidency in 1816, 89
Howard, William A., 327
Howe, Louis McHenry, 585, 588
Huerta, Victoriano, 526
Hughes, Charles Evans, 486, 498, 513, 551, 552; nomination for the Presidency, 528; campaign blunders, 531; defeat, 533
Hull, Cordell, 573, 586, 628
Hunkers, 185f.

I

Ickes, Harold, 597, 656
Imperialism, main issue of campaign of 1900, 467
"Imperial Years," 485
Impressment of American sailors by Great Britain, 38
Income tax, imposition of, 428
Independent Chronicle, support of Jefferson in 1804, 64
Independent National party, convention, 331f.
Independent Republicans, 382
Indiana, votes challenged in 1816, 89
Indians, alliance with Great Britain, 77; alliance with the Spanish, 77
Ingersoll, Robert G., quoted, 327, 359

Internal improvements, controversies about, 91f.
International Conference on Limitation of Armaments, 551f.
Ives, Irving M., quoted, 718

J

Jackson, Andrew, 35, 85, 95, 103ff., 115ff.; proposed as candidate for Presidency in 1824, 98f.; accusations against Clay in 1824, 101; proposed as candidate for the Presidency in 1828, 103f.; political contest with John Quincy Adams, 106f.; accusations against, 108f.; election in 1828, 110; inauguration in 1828, 111; champion of Peggy Eaton, 119ff.; supporters of, 120; estrangement from Calhoun, 123ff.; advocate of Van Buren as Vice-President, 126; Presidential candidate in 1832, 128; opposition to Bank of the United States, 130ff.; election in 1832, 131; waning popularity, 133f.; Van Buren's escort to the White House, 142; acclamation after Van Buren's inauguration, 143
Jackson, Rachel, slanders against, 110, 111
James, Arthur H., 621
James, Ollie, quoted, 528
Jay, John, 50; negotiations with Great Britain, 38
Jefferson, Thomas, 27, 35, 39, 50f., 62; rejected as candidate for the Vice-Presidency, 13; political deal with Hamilton, 28; conflict with Hamilton, 29ff.; quoted, 43, 49; election in 1800, 56; administration of, 59; candidacy of 1804 opposed by New England states, 62f.; election in 1804, 64; efforts to keep the peace, 67f.; unpopularity in New England, 69; refusal to run for third term, 69; repeal of the Embargo Act, 72
Johnson, Andrew, nomination for the Vice-Presidency, 259; reconstruction policies, 270ff.; impeachment proceedings, 283ff.; denunciation by Republican party, 289f.; balloting for, 294ff.; absence from Grant's inauguration, 301
Johnson, Gerald W., quoted, 696, 726
Johnson, Hiram W., 531, 543, 556, 590
Johnson, Richard W., 136f.; election to Vice-Presidency in 1836, 142; contestant for 1844 nomina-

Waitt, William S., candidate for the Vice-Presidency, 187

Wallace, Henry A., 677; proposed for vice-presidential nomination in 1940, 634; nomination for the Vice-Presidency, 638; Roosevelt's estimate of, 636; contest for vice-presidential nomination in 1944, 653; nomination for the Presidency in 1948, 696; acceptance speech, 697; campaign tour, 704; newspaper propaganda against, 710; quoted, 721

Walsh, Thomas J., 555

Wanamaker, John, 573

Warren, Charles B., Senate's refusal to confirm his appointment, 565

Warren, Earl, 677, 686; nomination for the Presidency, 688

Washburne, Elihu B., 340, 344

Washington, George, chairman of Federal Convention, 3; election in 1789, 11ff.; journey to New York for first inauguration, 18; inauguration in 1789, 20; election of 1792, 25; consent to run for second term, 31; efforts to maintain place, 35; growing unpopularity, 38f.; Farewell Address, 39; abuse of, 40; appointment as commander in chief, 45f.

Washington, D.C., taken by the British, 84

Washington *Evening Star*, quoted, 682

Washington *Globe*, 170; as Jackson's mouthpiece, 124; distribution to Tennessee legislature by Jackson, 138

Watson, Claude, nomination for the Presidency, 697

Watson, Jim, 623f.

Watson, Thomas E., nomination for the Presidency in 1896, 438; nomination for the Presidency in 1908, 498

Watterson, Henry, 309, 332

Weaver, James B., 362, 415, 418, 421; nomination for the Presidency in 1880, 354; nomination for the Presidency in 1892, 412

Webster, Daniel, 138, 142, 183; quoted, 111; quoted, 123; opposition to Van Buren, 126; defeat, 142; debate with Calhoun, 197f.; supports the compromise, 202; failure to win presidential nomination, 204; death of, 209

Weed, Thurlow, 108, 153, 246; quotetd, 260

Wells, Gideon, quoted, 298

West, Judge, quoted, 375

West Florida, 77

Weyler, "Butcher," 448

Wheeler, Burton K., nomination for the Presidency, 561

Whig party, convention of 1844, 168; origin of, 133; convention of 1840, 151ff.; convention of 1848, 187f.; disintegration, 209

Whisky Rebellion, 38

White, Andrew D., quoted, 376

White, George, 585

White, Harry, 324

White, Horace, 309

White, Hugh L., 139

White, William Allen, 626; quoted, 594

White House, Ogle's description, 160

Whitman, Walt, 192

Whittier, John Greenleaf, 227

"Wide-Awake" companies, 224, 252

Willard, Frances E., 388

Willis, Frank B., 572

Willkie, Wendell L., 621, 622, 624f.; nomination for the Presidency, 626; acceptance speech, 639; campaign tour, 641; quoted, 641, 642; withdrawal from the 1944 presidential race, 651

Wilmot, David, opposition to slavery in new states, 191f.

Wilson, Henry, nomination for the Vice-Presidency, 314

Wilson, James, 4, 6

Wilson, Woodrow, 501ff., 523ff.; nomination for the Presidency in 1912, 518; election in 1912, 521; message to Congress, 523; administration from 1913–1917, 523; nomination for the Presidency in 1916, 527f.; criticism of his foreign policy, 532; election in 1916, 533; efforts to avoid war, 535; Fourteen Points, 538; popularity, 538; attendance at the Paris Conference, 539; political setbacks, 539; illness, 540ff.; fight to win ratification of treaty, 540

Wilson bill, 428

Winchell, Walter, quoted, 659

Windom, William, 340, 344

Wirt, William, 128, 131

Wolcott, Oliver, 50; quoted, 39

Wood, Leonard, 543, 544

Woodbury, Levi, 186

Woodrow Wilson Independent League, 530

Works Progress Administration (WPA), 597

World Court, 570

World War I, 526; armistice, 539

World War II, 647

Wright, Fielding, nomination for the Vice-Presidency, 696

Wright, Silas, 167, 172

Y

Yalta conference, 672

Yancey, William, 240f.

Postscript:

PROLOGUE TO 1952

The story of the Presidency changes with every day. Since this book went to press many have been the significant events pertaining the high office. In the main text I have ended with President Truman's inauguration in January, 1949. Now in this postscript, written in July, 1951—a year before the nominating conventions—I shall give a short chronological outline of the Presidential and political history of Mr. Truman's term, from January 20, 1949, till July 1, 1951.

NEW NATIONAL CHAIRMEN

In August, 1949, the Democrats chose William M. Boyle, a Kansas City lawyer, as their new National Chairman, while the Republicans selected Guy George Gabrielson of New Jersey.

In October the Eighty-first Congress—wisecrackers named it the "Eighty-Worst Congress"—adjourned. Its achievements were considerable, though not so revolutionary as the Democrats after their surprise victory in 1948 had predicted.

A long-range housing bill, featuring construction of low-rent public housing units and slum-clearance aids, was enacted; the statutory minimum wage of 40 cents an hour was increased to 75 cents; the reorganization of the Federal Government got under way.

On social security, an expanded coverage with increased benefits was approved by the House, but no action was taken in the Senate.

On farm legislation, after tossing aside the Brannan plan, a compromise price-support program was adopted, keeping the 90 per cent parity to replace the 60-90 sliding scale, and providing adequate government grain storage facilities.

However, the Democrat-dominated Congress had not acted on many of the basic Fair Deal proposals.

No repeal of the Taft-Hartley Labor Act was forthcoming; no action on the national health insurance plan, and very little progress on the President's Civil Rights proposal. The bill for Federal aid to education passed the Senate, but was pigeonholed in the House.

During the session an intensive propaganda campaign was waged by the Administration's opponents to check the President's social welfare program. Simple slogans were used to confuse the electorate. The "Fair Deal" was restyled the "Welfare State," the "Bureaucratic State," the "Handout State," and the President was accused of heading the country toward "Socialism" and instituting "Statism."

Housing, Federal aid to education, social security expansion, increase of the minimum wage, a Federal health insurance system—all these were lumped together under the slogan "Statism." The propagandists never specified what they meant by the term. To political observers the reason for this seemed obvious. Many of the "Statist" principles were endorsed by the Republican party platforms in 1944 and 1948, and by their Presidential candidates Wendell Willkie and Thomas E. Dewey; they were ratified by the majority of voters in no fewer than five presidential elections.

ELECTIONS IN 1949 AND THEIR AFTERMATH

In the 1949 elections the spotlight was turned on the Dulles-Lehman senatorial race in New York, as it was thought that the outcome of that contest would have a considerable effect on President Truman's welfare program. John Foster Dulles, the Dewey-backed Republican candidate, exclaimed, "I believe that the trend to statism needs to be stopped here and now," while his opponent, the democrat Herbert H. Lehman, came squarely out for the "Welfare State" concept of government. When the off-year election results were in, they showed that the Democratic tide was still running unabated. Lehman defeated Dulles; and once more the voters asserted themselves for the continuation of the New Deal. The Republican attack on the "Welfare State" had failed.

In most contests the liberal candidates won. Where the Democrats were victorious it was mainly against reactionary Republicanism. Where they lost—as in the Wene defeat by Alfred E.

Driscoll in New Jersey—it was a reactionary and machine Democrat who went down, and a liberal Republican supported by labor who won.

Progressive-minded Republicans were exasperated. To the New York *Herald Tribune* the son of Wendell Willkie wrote:

"Most of the American people are not concerned with an overwhelming fear of Socialism, Statism and the Welfare State. They are concerned with living. They think about the things which affect their own lives: their take-home pay, their rent, their grocery bill, the kind of a house in which they live, how to pay for a major operation and what is going to happen to them when they get old. Republican politicians, if they want to win, are going to have to start talking to the American people about the things in which they [the American people] are interested: that is, the problems of their own lives."

Therefore Philip Willkie suggested that the party should get "a more specific program and come more to grips with the minds of most Americans."

Dissatisfaction with the party leadership became widespread. Anne M. Armstrong, a member of the Young Women's Republican Club of New York, wrote in an open letter to the same newspaper:

"The time for revolution within the Republican party is long overdue. Young and active Republicans are tired of lost elections, tired of stodgy, ineffective leadership, tired of speaking and writing and doorbell pushing night after night in campaigns year after year that could have been won if the top leadership had had some of the imagination and courage necessary to win a modern election. . . .

"Before the Republican party can hope to win elections it must decide unequivocally for what principles it stands, and then it must fight for those principles with imagination and fervor."

These criticisms in the rank and file seemed to influence the party's National Chairman. Guy George Gabrielson announced that he would take a poll of 125,000 Republican workers to decide whether there should be a restatement of party principles and, if so, what the restatement should contain.

The answer to Gabrielson's questionnaire was an overwhelming demand for a policy on more progressive lines.

But when the Republican Strategy Committee met in December, it disregarded the discontent and turned sharply to the right, advocating an out-and-out fight with the Democratic party and no more "me-too-ism." The committee's chairman, Arthur E. Summerfield, announced "that the difference between the Roosevelt and Truman administrations is that with Roosevelt we were drifting toward socialism but with Truman there is no drift—it's a headlong rush." And he summed up the party's position: "It will be a fight between the Republican party and the Democratic party to prevent the socialization of this country."

A great segment in the Republican party were against such ideas. In editorials and in columns Republican newspapermen warned the party of its latest folly. They demanded that the Republicans in drawing their platform "say what they mean and mean what they say." They pointed out: "The trouble in recent years has been that they have said one thing and done another. While they had a me-too platform, there was nothing me-tooist about its actions." And they exclaimed that the party in Congress "not only failed to pass any of the social legislation it professed to favor, but it sought to repeal or weaken many New Deal measures." (Like housing legislation, minimum wage increase, Federal aid to education.)

Members of the liberal wing offered constructive suggestions. Senator Henry Cabot Lodge proposed a four-point program aimed at reducing the hostility between party and labor, finding a non-socialistic answer to the problem of medical insurance, treating the farm question from the point of food production and reducing waste and inefficiency in government. Others, like Senator Wayne Morse of Oregon had different, similarly forward-looking solutions.

The columnist Peter Edson asked 345 editors, "Do you feel that the Republican Party has a program that can compete politically with Mr. Truman's Fair Deal?" and 91 per cent of them—mostly Republicans—answered no.

THE PRESIDENT'S STATE OF THE UNION MESSAGE

On January 4, 1950, President Truman told Congress that the greatest military and economic dangers of the postwar era had begun to recede, and that this nation, if it followed wise policies, could lead the world to peace and unexampled prosperity in the half-century ahead.

The Chief Executive did not propose new and bold experiments, but renewed all his "Fair Deal" domestic legislative proposals, and called for continued bipartisan support of a foreign policy aimed at strengthening democracy throughout the world.

FIGHT OVER CIVIL RIGHTS

The first major battles in the second session of the Eighty-first Congress were fought on the issue of civil rights. Mr. Truman's Civil Rights program has figured in every session of Congress since 1947. Among the principal measures proposed have been: (1) outlawing of the poll taxes now levied by seven Southern states to bar most Negroes from voting; (2) Federal legislation against lynching; (3) creation of a Fair Employment Practices Commission to prevent racial and religious discrimination in employment.

In the House the passage of Civil Rights bills did not face great difficulties. But in the Senate the Southern Democrats were able to kill all Civil Rights measures.

Finally, in February, 1950, the House of Representatives—in a turbulent session—passed an FEPC bill—a watered-down substitute for the President's proposal.

SENATOR LODGE'S PROPOSAL TO CHANGE THE ELECTORAL SYSTEM

On February 1, 1950, the Senate approved a proposed Constitutional Amendment to revise the system of electing the President and Vice President by apportioning electoral votes in each state according to the state's popular vote.

Under the plan, sponsored by Senator Henry Cabot Lodge, electoral votes would be apportioned as before, one for each Congressman, but no actual electors would be chosen. Each state's electoral vote would be split, when counted, in proportion to its popular vote. To win, a candidate would have to have at least 40 per cent of the electoral vote. If no one reached that percentage, the Senate and House would jointly choose the President from the top two candidates.

The critics of the proposal pointed out that its enactment would favor the rise of splinter parties. Voices were heard against the introduction of the proportional representation principle into the election of the President and against the abolishment of the Electoral College.

Others—especially representatives from smaller states—favored the proposal because it would sharply reduce the influence of the great states like New York, Pennsylvania, California, and Ohio.

Though many Republicans welcomed Senator Lodge's suggestion as a means of restoring a real two-party system in the Solid South, Senator Taft feared that the party might lose more in the North than it could gain in the South.

The excitement about the Lodge-Gossett resolution was of short duration. It soon became manifest that Congress had no desire to act upon it.

THE REPUBLICANS' INTERIM PROGRAM

On February 6, 1950 the Republican National Committee issued a 2,500-word "statement of principles and objectives"—the interim platform for 1950, choosing "Liberty against Socialism" as their campaign slogan. The statement contained seven points.

Point 1 declared that "liberty cannot breathe the air of bankruptcy and live," and denounced many features of the Fair Deal, including deficit spending, high taxes, the Brannan plan, and the national health program.

Point 2 demanded immediate repeal of wartime excise taxes, asked for general tax reduction as rapidly as government spending could be curtailed.

Point 3 endorsed the Taft-Hartley Act with unspecified modifications.

Point 4 advocated the expansion of the social security system "with due regard to the tax burden" and on a "pay-as-you-go" basis.

Point 5 supported the principle of Civil Rights legislation and the protection of the right of minorities.

Point 6 demanded continued consideration for war veterans.

Point 7 attacked Communism and Communists in government service.

The principle of bipartisanship in foreign affairs was endorsed after members of the National Committee shouted down a proposal that the party junk it.

Republican reaction to the policy statement was great disappointment. The editorial writer of the New York *Herald Tribune* warned that it might "do more harm than good, being misrepresented by the opposition as the essence of Republicanism, and being mistakenly conceived by some party members as the whole answer to their needs. . . .

"The burden of the complaint is that this document not only fails to go beyond the 1948 platform, but that at crucial points it gives the impression of retreating from the position there established. Certainly the plank on civil rights, ending with the meek assertion that the party will 'continue to sponsor legislation to protect the rights of minorities,' seems a pale reflection of the earlier specific declaration against poll taxes, segregation in the armed forces and other evils. . . .

"The present platform fails to make sufficient appeal to the independent voter and to the younger elements of the party; and this failure has led to the underscoring of divisions within the party. The document thus seems to be in a fair way of falling short of both objectives."

And in the New York *Times* the astute political analyst Cabell Phillips remarked that the effort of the Republican party trying to put up a tent big enough for everybody to get under "was about as conspicuous a failure as the last two tries have been." In Mr. Phillips's opinion, the only people who can be supposed to be really content with the "Restatement of Principles and Objectives" were "that handful of powerful diehards in upper party councils who insisted on it in the first place. Thus, a device that was alleged by its sponsors to promise a new harmony within the party, an infusion of strength and clear-headedness for the election battles ahead, has had an almost opposite effect."

The declaration was a clear-cut victory for the Republican right wing. The New York *Times* said that "the conservatives were backed by the G.O.P.'s most important 'angels,' who refused to contribute funds unless the party went down the line against the Fair Deal."

Senator Lodge and other Republican Senators voiced their dissatisfaction. "The statement is a disappointment in several ways, notably in the field of civil rights, where no mention was made of a firm determination to enact legislation at this session and to break a filibuster if necessary," announced Lodge.

All over the country, independent Republican newspapers printed biting editorials against the latest mistake of the Republican bigwigs.

The Democrats, rejoicing over the uneasiness in the Republican ranks, quickly answered back.

At the Democrats' annual $100-a-plate Jefferson-Jackson Day dinner, President Truman charged that the Republican party insulted "the intelligence of the American people" when it decided to make socialism the 1950 campaign issue. It was "the same old moth-eaten scarecrow" that the Republicans have dragged out for each campaign since 1933, said the President. "It is perfectly safe to be against socialism," went on Truman, looking at the orchids, mink and dinner jackets of the 5,300 guests in the

hall, "but how in the world can the Republicans persuade people that all you Democrats . . . are socialists?"

"The Republicans," continued the President, building up to his punch line, "sit around waiting for us to make a proposal. Then they react with an outburst of scare words. They are like a cuttlefish that squirts out a cloud of black ink whenever its slumber is disturbed."

Cabell Phillips in the New York *Times* summarized the problems of the G.O.P. in this way:

"The Republican party at this rather critical stage of its life is a little like the man who knows he is sick but is afraid to go to the doctor and have his suspicions confirmed.

"The G.O.P. knows, for example, that if it is going to win any more elections it has got to develop a positive instead of a negative program with which to appeal to the voters.

"It knows, too, that the popular tide is running with the progressive viewpoint in most domestic matters, yet it feels itself irretrievably tied to the past.

"And it knows that isolationism is little more popular with the masses of the people today than it was during and immediately following the war; yet it finds itself inescapably identified with the most insistently isolationist voices in the country."

Furthermore: "The inability or disinclination of the party leadership to evolve and put forward a program of positive action is another source of deep disaffection within the G.O.P. The dominant powers within the party's councils have successfully resisted most efforts to advance positive alternatives for Fair Deal measures. The reason for this is twofold.

"On the one hand, there is strong pressure against 'me-tooism' by the wealthy and ultra-conservative wing. Any such concessions are viewed skeptically as yielding to the New Deal progressive influence, which they abhor. On the other, there is the strategical consideration that since a minority party cannot make national policy anyway—if they come up with a good idea, the majority will take it away from them—the greater political profit resides in opposing and criticizing. . . .

"While Democratic candidates will not, admittedly, have too much in the way of concrete accomplishments to crow about, their Republican opponents will have even less. And that is hardly conducive to overcoming the other fellow's head start in a race."

On April 21, 1950, the columnist Marquis Childs wrote in his column:

"The statement of Senator Robert A. Taft of Ohio that he backed McCarthy in the hope that if McCarthy missed one target he might hit another one was a shock to many Republicans who have gone along with the bipartisan foreign policy. Others felt that, regardless of the outcome of the McCarthy affair, the Taft statement would alienate independent voters who had believed in Taft's integrity even when they differed with his views.

"This reaction solidified the conviction in a large and important segment of the party that Taft must not be the party's nominee in 1952. Obviously, Eisenhower was the only man who could prevent Taft's nomination. And it seemed increasingly evident to many of these Republicans that the general was the only man who could defeat President Truman running for a third term.

"Here, plainly, a titanic struggle is foreshadowed. While the Taft forces now have a strong grip on the party machinery, a great deal will depend on the outcome of elections this fall."

THE PRESIDENT GOES WEST

In the beginning of May, President Truman left Washington, heading toward the West and delivering eight prepared addresses—the opening shots in the 1950 congressional campaign.

Republicans watched Mr. Truman's journey with increasing nervousness. Harold Stassen stated: "He will do a very, very clever and effective job of campaigning. . . . President Truman is the cleverest politician ever to occupy the White House. And he is also the worst President ever to occupy the White House."

DEMOCRATIC PRIMARIES

While there were nominating primaries and registration tests in other states in the spring of 1950 —Ohio, Indiana, and Oregon among them—the chief political interest centered on the Democratic polls in Florida and Alabama. In the first-named state, Senator Claude Pepper was soundly defeated for renomination by Representative George A. Smathers. In Alabama, Gessner T. McCorvey, a prominent Democratic politician, was voted out by the electorate.

G.O.P. Chairman Gabrielson took the Florida result as a major triumph for the Republicans, but more realistic-minded Republicans saw that while Senator Pepper, an out-and-out advocate of the "welfare state," had gone down in defeat, he was to be succeeded by a man who supported most of the President's domestic reforms.

REPUBLICAN PRIMARIES

Three states—California, Pennsylvania, and Oregon—voted progressively and against the Old Guard in the Republican primaries.

The most stunning victory was that of Governor James Duff in Pennsylvania, who captured his state's party control from eighty-seven-year-old former Senator Joseph R. Grundy, the powerful Republican leader for the last thirty years.

The other triumphs were accomplished by Senator Wayne Morse of Oregon, one of the most articulate critics of his own party, and by Governor Earl Warren in California, who walked off with 62 per cent of the state's total votes, defeating F. D. R.'s son James.

The Pennsylvania returns were a marked setback for Harold E. Stassen's Presidential aspirations. Stassen was in the corner of Jay Cooke, who was backed for Governor by the Grundy organization. This brought him the enmity of Governor Duff, who denounced Stassen as a "carpetbagger." As Duff will have complete control of the Pennsylvania votes in the 1952 nominating convention, Stassen could not very well count on any votes from his newly adopted state.

Thus the three most populous strongholds of the Republican party, which are also the three most populous states—New York, Pennsylvania, and California—were now in the camp opposed to the Old Guard. They have powerful influence in national conventions because of their delegate strength and in national elections because of their electoral vote. They have supporting strength of a progressive Republican character in the West and Northwest and in the East.

PROGRESSIVE REPUBLICANS AGAINST SENATOR MCCARTHY

On June 1, 1950, seven Republican Senators issued a "Declaration of Conscience" in which they repudiated the irresponsible tactics of Senator Joseph McCarthy of Wisconsin, who, fifteen weeks after he had made his charges of subversion in the State Department, still could not prove his allegations.

The seven Republican Senators who signed the document and who declared "We are Republi-

771

cans, but we are Americans first," were Margaret Chase Smith of Maine, Irving M. Ives of New York, Charles W. Tobey of New Hampshire, George D. Aiken of Vermont, Robert C. Hendrickson of New Jersey, Edward J. Thye of Minnesota, and Wayne L. Morse of Oregon—a liberal group engaged in a struggle for the control of the party with the conservative wing led by Senator Robert A. Taft.

On the Senate floor the declaration was read by Mrs. Smith, only woman member of the Upper House. She made a very effective speech, emphasizing "the mounting impatience and rebelliousness of many Republicans against the implacable conservatism that has become the party's symbol."

"The nation sorely needs a Republican," said Mrs. Smith. "But I don't want to see the Republican party ride to political victory on the four horsemen of calumny—fear, ignorance, bigotry and smear. . . . I am not proud of the reckless abandon in which unproved charges have been hurled from this side of the aisle."

The progressive bloc for whom Mrs. Smith spoke represented only a small number of Republicans. Out of forty-two Republican Senators, not more than ten can be listed as consistently holding the progressive view. Out of one hundred sixty-nine Republicans in the House of Representatives there are only twenty to thirty progressives at the most.

"What is it essentially that these members of Congress want from their party?" asked Cabell Phillips in the New York *Times?*

"The neatest answer would seem to be that they want it to become a party of constructive opposition as long as it is in the minority, and a party of dynamic conservatism when and if it gains the majority. What, above all, they do not want is that the Republican party shall deteriorate into angry, impotent obstructionism.

"Their party, as they see it, is too heavily influenced at the top by men whose political and economic thought patterns go back to Herbert Hoover, and beyond. . . .

"The constructive approach, in their view, is to accept the inevitability of political evolution and to move forward intelligently to meet it. . . .

"Where the Republican party has fallen down, they contend, is in having lost contact with the masses of the people. Its vision has focused upon a narrow segment of the country, that populated chiefly by business. It refuses to recognize that the

short-run interests of this narrow segment are often incompatible with the long-run interests of the people as a whole."

WAR BEGINS IN KOREA

Then all at once—with our entry into the Korean dispute—all domestic political issues were relegated to the background. On June 27 President Truman ordered American sea and air forces to go to the aid of South Korea. His prompt and courageous action to protect our national security and save the United Nations won him widespread support.

EISENHOWER BOOM

As the country prepared for the midterm election, the Eisenhower-for-President boom gained momentum. On October 22 Governor Dewey reiterated that he would not run in 1952, and when asked if he had any candidate in mind he replied that, if he should be reelected Governor and have influence with the New York delegation, "I would recommend to them that they support General Eisenhower for President if he would accept the draft."

Thomas L. Stokes in one of his penetrating columns said that the Republican "draft Eisenhower campaign" could be taken as a confession that the party lacks either a program or an available candidate with sufficient popular appeal and has to go beyond its professional ranks and pick an attractive person without a political record of any sort and rely on him, alone, to charm the voters. Issues would be submerged in a personality."

Then Stokes continued: "In times like these, it is a temptation for people to look for a savior or deliverer, and a military figure fits the mirage. But problems are not so easily solved. They are political problems that require political experience, with its give-and-take, its compromises, and its knowledge of people. It is no time for a military man in the White House."

THE CONGRESSIONAL ELECTION OF 1950

The midterm election campaign was strenuously fought by both the Democrats and the Republicans. Usually the party in power suffers the loss of seats in Congress in the midterm elections. This is explained by the fact that "the President himself does not head the ticket and is unable therefore to translate his influence into local contests. In such elections local issues are apt to predominate."

But besides local issues, of which there were a

772

plenty, the national and international ones played a great part. The Fair Deal, efficiency in government, what to do about the Communists in the United States, our Far Eastern policy, and who is "to blame" for Korea were debated with keen fervor.

Over forty-two million voters went to the polls —an all-time midterm vote record—and rendered a verdict on the nation's future course at home and in the world.

While the verdict was not exactly clear, the figures showed a nation-wide swing toward the Republican party. In domestic affairs the vote could be interpreted as indicating that people desired to check the social programs of the New and Fair Deals. In foreign affairs the question mark became bigger. The most outspoken critics of the President's foreign policies won clear-cut victories.

Although the Democrats suffered a setback they still had a fair majority in the House, 235 Representatives against the Republicans' 199; but in the Senate they had only 49 against the Republicans' 47 —a precarious majority, especially as many Southern Democrats were steadily voting with the Republicans.

In the New York *Times*'s political editor's opinion, the result of the election showed four leading losers:

"One was President Truman. Except for Senators Herbert H. Lehman of New York and William Benton of Connecticut, no administration partyliner survived the poll. . . .

"Another loser was the great federal Democratic machine, made up of big city organizations, and administration appointees in charge of the largest government payroll and bounty distribution in history, covering rural as well as urban areas. The machine lost the contests where it exerted heaviest pressure, and the midwest farm states which elected Mr. Truman in 1948 turned to the Republicans.

"A third loser was the Department of State. Wherever its conduct of foreign affairs was made an issue, save in the Lehman and Benton races, a vote of no confidence was registered, especially in Pennsylvania, Illinois, Ohio, Iowa, Utah and California.

"A fourth loser was the unified group of national labor leaders whose score was even less than the State Department's and whose rank and file in Cleveland and other cities deserted in large numbers to the proclaimed 'enemies' of labor."

The greatest victor in the election was undoubt-edly Senator Taft. His triumph in the Senatorial race over his Democratic opponent in Ohio was so overwhelming that it made him the most prominent contender for the 1952 Presidential nomination.

Governor Dewey's good showing in New York's gubernatorial contest gave him renewed strength. In 1952 he will assert a decisive control over the largest delegation to the Republican convention.

Governor Earl Warren's personal success in California enhanced his position as a Presidential possibility.

When reporters asked the President about the defeat of his party, Mr. Truman said that he could analyze every beating the Democrats suffered and could demonstrate that the losses were due to local conditions.

THE GREAT DEBATE

At the end of December—as the United Nations forces in Korea braced for a critical battle—the debate in the United States over the fundamentals of American foreign policy reached a new intensity.

The central question of the debate was whether America should continue the Truman-Acheson policy of resisting Communism, or whether we should withdraw our forces to clearly defensible positions and build the Western hemisphere into what ex-President Herbert Hoover in his countrywide broadcast on December 20 called "a Gibraltar" with island outposts—Britain in the Atlantic and Japan, Formosa, and the Philippines in the Pacific. The central issue of the debate was where our frontier should be.

Mr. Hoover thought we should concentrate on the Western hemisphere. But Mr. Truman believed that the frontier of the United States lies wherever we have friends who are willing to share the burdens of resisting aggression and we can bring our strength to bear directly or indirectly.

The anti-Administration forces denied this. Their argument was that Western Europe had not the will to resist Communism. To this the Democrats retorted that our allies would resist if they were assured of American economic and military aid.

The critics of the Administration hold that the Communists' man-power advantage both in Europe and in Asia was so great that the United States could not beat them. To this the Administration replied that the point in Western rearmament is not primarily to win a war but to prevent one from starting.

Neither Mr. Hoover nor President Truman had the entire support of his party. There were many Republicans who were against a withdrawal into a Western Gibraltar, and there were many Democrats who criticized the government for dangerously overextending our resources.

On January 15, 1951—when the debate was still at full blast—a Gallup poll survey showed that President Truman was favored by 41 per cent of the electorate, while Senator Taft's popularity had risen to 44 per cent. Ten days later, when a cross-section of the voters was asked whom they would like to have as President, only 28 per cent were for Mr. Truman, while 59 per cent came out in support of General Eisenhower.

In the New York Times, Anthony Leviero explained that the major causes of discontent affecting Mr. Truman's level of prestige were the large world and domestic issues. However, he added that "obviously some recent actions of the President have had their effect, too. His intemperate letter to Paul Hume, severe critic of Margaret Truman's singing; his denunciation of a Senate report on the Reconstruction Finance Corporation as asinine; his remark that the railroad union leaders were acting like Russians, and his dare to Congress to cut the budget—these are regarded by his adherents as secondary irritants that will soon pass."

THE TWENTY-SECOND AMENDMENT

On February 26, 1951, the Twenty-second Amendment was ratified. Its text, limiting the Presidents to two terms is as follows:

"No person shall be elected to the office of the President more than twice, and no person who has held the office of President, or acted as President, for more than two years of a term to which some other person was elected President shall be elected to the office of President more than once. But this Article shall not apply to any person holding the office of President when this Article was proposed by the Congress, and shall not prevent any person who may be holding the office of President, or acting as President, during the term within which this Article becomes operative from holding the office of President or acting as President during the remainder of such term."

THE MACARTHUR STORY

On April 11 President Truman, with the full approval of the Joint Chiefs of Staff, removed General MacArthur from his command. He did it crudely and without observing the diplomatic niceties. There was a tremendous outcry in the land. A MacArthur fever racked the country.

The Republicans in Congress looking for an effective campaign issue—rallied wholeheartedly behind the General. In a dramatic hearing twenty-six Senators heard the testimony of MacArthur, the Joint Chiefs of Staff, Secretary of State Dean Acheson, and other military and political figures. Over two million words filled the records; but, as soon as it came, the fever subsided. "The longer the hearings have gone on, the more ground the Administration has regained," wrote the New York Times. It became obvious that the MacArthur's policies, like bombing Manchurian bases, or the use of Chinese Nationalist troops in Korea embodied "great calculated risks," a risk that the Korean war would not be contained, but that it would develop into World War III.

As the inquiry dragged toward its end, the public viewed the issues with more calm than under the first spell of the General's dramatic appearance before Congress. The war news from Korea was excellent. General Ridgway had done a competent job, and on the first anniversary of the Korean War Jacob Malik, Russia's delegate to the United Nations, suggested a cease-fire parley, which—just as these lines are written—were accepted by the Chinese "volunteers" and North Korean Communists. The end of hostilities seemed within reach. A few more days, and the war would be over; communist aggression stopped, where it began—at the 38th Parallel. Those Republicans who believed that the MacArthur issue would ride them into power in 1952 became a sadly disappointed lot. In Tulsa, where the party counselors met to choose Chicago for the 1952 convention site, the three hundred Republican leaders were of one mind not to make an issue of MacArthur's dismissal in the coming campaign or to embrace his views on the war in Asia. And, when a reporter asked Arizona's committeeman, novelist Clarence Budington Kelland, whether the General could be chosen as Republican standard-bearer, Kelland answered: "To even think of MacArthur is utter nonsense."

LINE-UP OF THE REPUBLICAN CANDIDATES FOR 1952

Who will be the Republican candidates in 1952? Everybody agreed at the Republican conference in Tulsa that Robert A. Taft was the leading contender, though according to Time Magazine "many seemed to consider him less the man to nominate than the man to beat."

The Senator's supporters were confident that in the convention Taft would walk away with the nomination. They figured that unless a "Stop Taft" movement developed, the Senator would have enough votes to be chosen on the first ballot. As a nucleus, the Taft forces had 271 delegates from thirty-one states who had supported the Senator in 1948. He was so far out in front that the only man to stop him was General Dwight D. Eisenhower. But Eisenhower was back in the service, strengthening Europe's defenses. All the other potential candidates, such as Governor Earl Warren of California, Governor Thomas E. Dewey of New York, and Senator James H. Duff of Pennsylvania, were overshadowed by the strength of Taft. The Ohio Senator built up his power steadily and assiduously with Senator Kenneth S. Wherry of Nebraska as minority leader in the upper House of Congress. Taft was in complete control of the party machinery in the Senate. He had a majority of members of the Republican National Committee, and his influence was strong in the House.

But among Republicans there was widespread discontent with the Taft leadership. The Dewey-Duff-Warren axis, allied with progressive-minded Republicans like Senators Lodge, Morse, and Margaret Chase Smith, might make its influence felt in the convention. Together they represent a large segment of public opinion both in and out of the Republican party—and if they would unite and rally behind a strong candidate like General Eisenhower, they could stop Taft.

On the major political questions the Republicans are hopelessly split. On the foreign policy issue, which Mr. Taft desires to make the dominant one of the next campaign, there seems to be no compromise. They also have divided minds on "McCarthyism," the wild accusations of the Wisconsin Senator "in the belief that even if a lot of innocents are cut down in the process, some culprits are going to get caught too."

Underlying these conflicts is the fundamental antagonism and struggle for power between the Old Guard and the progressive faction.

WHO WOULD BE THE DEMOCRATIC CANDIDATE?

In April, 1951, President Truman, returning from a Florida vacation, told newspapermen that he already had made up his mind whether he would run next year, but he was in no hurry to announce his decision. To the newsmen it sounded as though the President would be running again. A month later at Denver, where the Democratic National Committee met to choose Chicago as the convention city, there did not seem to be any question as to who might be the candidate. The name of Truman was in the air; and the Democrats were quite contented with having him.

Here, as in Tulsa, the only other name mentioned was that of General Eisenhower. The New York *Times* wrote: "They would not mind having him . . . if Mr. Truman does not run. But they do not mention General Eisenhower with that sense of yearning of the Republicans who are looking so anxiously for a winner after more than seventeen years in the wilderness." At this early date, a year ahead of the convention, the delegates appeared to be giving no serious consideration to the possibility that General Eisenhower might become the candidate of the Republican party. The feeling among them appeared to be that, if the Administration could win in Korea, the party could win the election with whatever standard-bearer was chosen next July.

Thus today—July 1, 1951—it looks as if the next Presidential campaign would be a battle of the T's —Taft against Truman—assuming that General Eisenhower, on whose behalf a strong movement is under way, will not be drafted by the Republicans—nor jockeyed into position by President Truman as standard-bearer of the Democrats. But no one can predict a year ahead. In twelve months much can happen—and it usually does.

STEFAN LORANT

"Farview"
Lenox, Massachusetts
July 1, 1951

171 -